TEXT AND CONTEXT

TEXT AND CONTEXT

ESSAYS IN MODERN JEWISH HISTORY AND HISTORIOGRAPHY IN HONOR OF ISMAR SCHORSCH

edited by

Eli Lederhendler

Jack Wertheimer

ISBN: 0-87334-101-5

Printing and Binding by G & H Soho Inc.

TABLE OF CONTENTS

Table of Contents

Table of Contents

Ismar Schorsch
from the lens of George Kalinsky

FOREWORD

Theodore Roosevelt famously referred to the American presidency as a "bully pulpit"—by which he meant that those occupying the highest national office were uniquely blessed with a ready audience and an unrivalled opportunity to convey a message. If we might appropriate the phrase, by analogy, then the chancellorship of the Jewish Theological Seminary could be called both a "bully pulpit" and a "bully lecture hall": a position that magnifies the potential audience of a rabbi and vastly enlarges the classroom of the professional scholar.

Ismar Schorsch, whose achievements to date we—his friends, colleagues, and former students—salute in this volume, has occupied that enhanced dual position since 1986, when he succeeded Gerson D. Cohen as Seminary chancellor and president of the faculties. As a rabbi and an expert in the field of Jewish history, Ismar Schorsch had by that time established himself as a leading exponent of the scholarly and religious traditions of Western Jewry, in a direct line with his own immediate forebears; and as a professor in the American academy, he was actively involved in the post–World War II "naturalization" of university-level Jewish studies in the United States.

Those of us privileged to have known him over the years have been immeasurably enriched by our encounter with his reasoned and rigorous scholarship, his spirited commitment to Jewish learning and religious continuity, and his animated, exacting teaching. When he moved from the relative confines of the seminar room to that "bully pulpit," our "loss"—in relinquishing our hitherto privileged access to Ismar's knowledge and understanding of the Jewish past and present—was surely American Jewry's gain.

Many a public figure might venture a wistful backward glance at the loss of more cloistered pleasures; we feel assured that Ismar Schorsch himself will find in this volume a vindication of his ongoing work over the course of the past twenty years, as the contributors probe a broad array of issues and ideas which intersect with and build on his own academic and intellectual commitments. Indeed, we need not have had any qualms that the burdens of leadership would alter the substance and value of Ismar Schorsch's erudition, adversely affect his natural congenial modesty, or encroach on his personal bonds with friends, colleagues, and students. The present Festschrift is, therefore, a testament to those continuities in Ismar's influence over the years and that constancy of mutual affection, as expressed by some—and by no means all—of those whose lives and thoughts he has profoundly touched.

Born on November 3, 1935, in Hanover, in what was then Nazi-ruled Germany, Ismar Schorsch is the scion of a family steeped in Jewish service and learning. His mother, Fanny, was the daughter and granddaughter of Jewish educators (both served as directors of a Jewish boarding school in Esslingen), and as he has attested in a moving tribute to *Torat imekha*, the Torah of his mother, an important educational influence in his own development. His father Emil was ordained at the Breslau Jewish Theological Seminary (his ordination certificate is displayed with pride in Ismar's office at JTS). Along with his parents and sister, Ismar fled Germany in December 1938. He was raised in Pottstown, Pennsylvania, and southern New Jersey, where his father served as rabbi in several Jewish congregations, and was educated in local public schools and at Ursinus College, from which he was graduated in 1957. Dr. Schorsch then enrolled in rabbinical school at the Jewish Theological Seminary, in whose orbit he would remain with the exception of a stint as a U.S. military chaplain in Korea. He was ordained in 1962.

During his years at JTS, he began to do graduate work in Jewish history, completing a Master's degree at Columbia University in 1961. Already in these years, he evinced a strong interest in Jewish historiography and modern Jewish intellectual history. Indeed, his first published essay dealt with Nachman Krochmal's conception of Jewish history. (It appeared in *Judaism* magazine in 1961.) After returning from the military, he enrolled in Columbia's doctoral program, where he worked closely with Gerson D. Cohen and Salo W. Baron. Their influence would be formative: both historians had a broad conception of Jewish history and a profound mastery of the literature of the Jews. Baron was a staunch opponent of what he called "the lachrymose conception of Jewish history" and was fascinated with Jewish communal governance and religious history. Cohen was a careful reader of Jewish texts with a breathtaking command of cultural and intellectual history. These interests were reflected in Schorsch's first scholarly essay, on the rabbi and historian Moritz Guedemann. His essay opens with the words: "A preoccupation with intellectual history and medieval persecutions dominated the early efforts in the scientific study of the Jewish past in the nineteenth century."

Schorsch initially focused on political history by devoting his doctoral dissertation to Jewish responses to German antisemitism, arguing in this study and his later Leo Baeck Memorial Lecture against the notion, put forth by Hannah Arendt and others, that German Jews as a community had been politically obtuse and passive. He took the side of Baron in arguing against the lachrymose conception, which resulted in too great an emphasis on the Jews as objects, rather than subjects, of their own history.

After earning his doctorate in 1969, Schorsch initially taught at Columbia University and then joined the JTS faculty, along with Gerson Cohen, in 1970. At both institutions he served as a mentor to graduate students just as the field of Jewish Studies burgeoned in the 1970s. Over the course of his years at Columbia and JTS, he supervised numerous doctoral dissertations. (He supervised the doctoral dissertations of six contributors to this volume and played an influential role in shaping the work of several others.) He has also played a pivotal role in shaping the policies of the Leo Baeck Institute over the course of some thirty-five years, initially at its New York branch, and eventually presiding over the Institute's activities worldwide, thereby further influencing the development of the field of Jewish studies and of German Jewish history in particular.

Indeed, Schorsch has been a leading exponent in the postwar regeneration of German-Jewish scholarship. For much of the past thirty years, he has focused on Jewish intellectual history in Germany, especially revolving around the practitioners of *Wissenschaft des Judentums*. His first foray into this area was a volume of essays written by the great German-Jewish historian, Heinrich Graetz, which Schorsch translated and introduced. He then produced a series of trailblazing studies in Jewish historiography, intellectual and cultural history, the history of Jewish art, and the history of religious institutions, such as the modern rabbinate. His studies of these aspects of Jewish self-perception and self-representation, in which historians and scholars of the past performed an essential function as cultural agents in hotly contested rhetorical arenas, have in many respects anticipated the recent historiographical emphasis on "narrative," without falling into some of the more faddish, politicized pitfalls of contemporary narrative-studies.

By mapping the contributions of German Jewry's seminal scholarly figures and by portraying the communal steadfastness and creative capacity of German Jewry, he has eloquently and positively asserted that modern Jewry owes an abiding moral and intellectual debt to the German-Jewish heritage—in striking contrast to the famous disparagement of that heritage by Gershom Scholem, among others. Like his mentor Salo Baron, Schorsch has looked beyond historical catastrophe to mine the oft-hidden vitality of Judaism.

Schorsch's interests, however, have not remained parochial; indeed, they have embraced the entire Jewish world, including Sephardi influences on the modernizing myths of European Jewry, as well as the work of thinkers such as Solomon Schechter and Salo Baron in America, and Yechezkel Kaufmann in Israel. This perspective prompted him to assume an active leadership position at the Memorial Foundation for Jewish Culture, whose purview and academic mandate is pan-Jewish and worldwide.

Finally, Ismar Schorsch has consistently underscored his own belief in intellectual and religious continuity, exemplified by the Breslau tradition and its institutional reincarnation at JTS and in American Conservative Judaism. This clearly comes across in his studies of Zacharias Frankel, Heinrich Graetz, and Solomon Schechter; his valorization of the *Wissenschaft* project; his hewing toward the religious center (steering between "left-" and "right-" wing options) as the crucial axis of modern Judaism; and also—no less so—through his teaching by personal example that "context" (or history) alone is an insufficient guide to religious meaning for today's Jews.

The essays in this volume reflect the broad scope of Ismar Schorsch's wide-ranging interests. They fall under the rubrics of historiography, intellectual and cultural history, Central European Jewish life in the nineteenth and twentieth centuries, and modern Jewish societies in America and Israel. Each of these fields separately, and all of them combined, speak directly to Ismar's own preoccupations as a scholar and as a modern Jew. Eastern Europe as well as Germany, the Diaspora as well as Israel, the receding past as well as the present day, are ably represented by noted practitioners of modern Jewish history, each of whom—his friends, former students, colleagues, and admirers—seek in this manner to honor him on the occasion of his milestone seventieth year.

A word about our title is in order here: "Text in Context" is of course a playful reference to the name of Ismar Schorsch's third book, *From Text to Context: The Turn to History in Modern Judaism*. Schorsch was referring there to "text" as the original source and canonical foundation of Jewish culture, and to "context" as the historicized study of that culture, as this became a dominant cultural craft and philosophical outlook among modern Jewish scholars, superseding textual study and commentary.

For our part, when we speak of "text," we refer to that corpus of modern Jewish literature, scholarship, law, and art, which was produced by that "turn to history," and which we subject to scrutiny in the present volume; and we point to the background and historical ramifications of those texts as these have shaped the "context" of Jewish historiographical and intellectual endeavor.

Last but not least, we also wish, thereby, to echo Ismar Schorsch's intellectual journey, from text (the "tradition") to context (historiosophy), and back again, and thus to profile, in our title, the energies that have imbued his work and inspired us all.

The editors acknowledge with appreciation the diligence and support of several people who helped with the production of this volume. Peter T. Daniels has once again prepared the electronic manuscript of a complex book produced by the JTS Press. His copy editing and thoughtful queries have strengthened quite a few of the essays, and his advice has been of great help as this book moved through production. The staff at G&H Soho took great care with the design and printing of this volume. Special thanks to Jim Harris, Gerry Burstein and Kathie Kounouklos for their unfailing patience and responsiveness. Our thanks to Kevin Mill-ham for preparing the Index on a tight schedule, and also to George Kalinsky for permission to use his portrait of Ismar Schorsch, which graces the front matter. Finally, Elise Dowell of the JTS Communications Department graciously extended her help to solve a few knotty problems.

Eli Lederhendler   Jack Wertheimer
Jerusalem   New York

CONTRIBUTORS

Gershon Bacon holds the Klein Chair for the History of the Rabbinate in Europe in the Modern Period at Bar-Ilan University. He is one of the editors of the forthcoming *Yivo Encyclopedia of Jews in Eastern Europe*. Among his recent publications are *The Politics of Tradition: Agudat Yisrael in Poland 1916–1939* (English version, 1996; revised Hebrew version, 2005), "The New Jewish Politics and the Rabbinate in Poland: New Directions in the Interwar Period" (2004), and "Partial Success, Great Achievements: On Jewish Autonomy in Interwar Poland" (2004).

Naomi W. Cohen, now professor emerita, taught American Jewish history at the City University of New York and the Jewish Theological Seminary. Her two most recent books are *Jacob H. Schiff: A Study in American Jewish Leadership* (1999) and *The Americanization of Zionism, 1897–1948* (2003).

Richard I. Cohen holds the Paulette and Claude Kelman Chair in French Jewry Studies at the Hebrew University of Jerusalem and serves as the Academic Head of Revivim: Honors Program for the Training of Teachers of Jewish Studies in Israeli Secondary Schools. Among his recent publications are *Le Juif errant: Un témoin de temps* (Paris, 2001; edited with Laurence Sigal) and "Urban Visibility and Biblical Visions: Jewish Culture in Western and Central Europe in the Modern Age," in *Cultures of the Jews: A New History*, ed. David Biale (New York: Schocken, 2002), 731–96.

David Ellenson is President and I. H. and Anna Grancell Professor of Jewish Religious Thought at Hebrew Union College—Jewish Institute of Religion. His latest publication is *After Emancipation: Jewish Religious Responses to Modernity* (2004). He and Daniel Gordis are currently completing a book-length study on Orthodox responsa on conversion and intermarriage in the modern period.

Immanuel Etkes is a Professor of Modern Jewish History at the Hebrew University of Jerusalem. His particular fields of specialization are the religious movements in East European Jewry in the eighteenth and nineteenth centuries, and the history of modern Jewish education. Among his books are: *Rabbi Israel Salanter and the Mussar Movement* (1993), *The Gaon of Vilna: The Man and His Image* (2002), and *The Besht: Magician, Mystic and Leader* (2005).

David E. Fishman is Professor of Jewish History at JTS, and director of Project Judaica, a program in Jewish studies in Moscow sponsored by JTS and Russian State University for the Humanities. His most recent publications are *The Rise of Modern Yiddish Culture* (University of Pittsburgh Press, 2005), and *Jewish Documentary Sources in the Trophy Collections of the Special Archive of the USSR: A Guide.* (in Russian) (Russian State University for the Humanities Press, 2005).

Shmuel Glick is the Director of the Schocken Institute for Jewish Studies in Jerusalem and Associate Professor of Rabbinic Literature and Jewish Education at the Schechter Institute. Among his many publications are *Education in Light of Israeli Law and Halachic Literature* (Jerusalem, 1999/2000) and a revised edition of Simcha Assaf's *Meqorot le-toldot ha-Hinukh be-Yisra'el*. He is presently preparing the Jedu-Database on the History of Jewish Education.

Harvey E. Goldberg is the Sarah Allen Shaine Professor in Sociology and Anthropology at the Hebrew University of Jerusalem. His books include *Jewish Life in Muslim Libya* (University of Chicago Press, 1990), and *Jewish Passages: Cycles of Jewish Life* (University of California Press, 2003).

Paula E. Hyman is the Lucy Moses Professor of Modern Jewish History at Yale University. She has published widely on modern Jewish history, focusing particularly on French Jewry and on the experience and representation of women. Ismar Schorsch, with whom she studied in the graduate program at Columbia University, was, and remains, an important mentor and model.

Marion A. Kaplan is Skirball Professor of Modern Jewish History at NYU. Her recent publications include *Jewish Daily Life in Germany* (contributing editor, Oxford University Press, 2005), *Juedische Welten* (Wallstein, 2005), *Between Dignity and Despair: Jewish Life in Nazi Germany* (Oxford University Press, 1998), and *The Making of the Jewish Middle* Class (Oxford University Press, 1991).

Dr. Mark W. Kiel is rabbi of Congregation B'nai Israel in Emerson, New Jersey. Among his recent publications are "Nokhum Oyslender's Principles of Jewish Realism" (in Yiddish), *Yivo bleter*, and "Sefer Ha'agadah: Creating A Classic Anthology" in *The Anthology in Jewish Literature*, ed. David Stern. He served as coeditor of *The Jews of Czestochowa: Coexistence, Holocaust, Memory*.

Contributors

Eli Lederhendler is the Stephen S. Wise Professor of American Jewish History and Institutions at the Avraham Harman Institute of Contemporary Jewry of the Hebrew University, Jerusalem. He received his doctorate from the Jewish Theological Seminary under the supervision of Prof. Ismar Schorsch. Among his recent publications are *New York Jews and the Decline of Urban Ethnicity, 1950–1970*, and two edited volumes: *The Six-Day War and World Jewry* and *Who Owns Judaism? Public Religion and Private Faith in America and Israel.* He has also co-edited, with Jonathan D. Sarna, a volume of essays, *America and Zion: Essays and Papers in Memory of Moshe Davis.*

Robert Liberles is David Berg and Family Professor of European History at Ben Gurion University in Beersheva. Most recently, he contributed the section on the early modern period to the volume *Jewish Daily Life in Germany*, ed. Marion Kaplan (Oxford University Press, 2005).

Ivan G. Marcus is the Frederick P. Rose Professor of Jewish History, Professor of History and of Religious Studies, and Chair of the Program of Judaic Studies at Yale University. His most recent book is *The Jewish Life Cycle: Rites of Passage from Biblical to Modern Times* (University of Washington Press, 2004).

Michael A. Meyer is the Adolph S. Ochs Professor of Jewish History at Hebrew Union College—Jewish Institute of Religion, Cincinnati, and the International President of the Leo Baeck Institute. He is the editor of the four-volume *German-Jewish History in Modern Times* and recently published *Judaism within Modernity: Essays on Jewish History and Religion.*

Moshe Rosman teaches Jewish history at Bar Ilan University in Israel. His research is currently focused on Jewish cultural history and the history of Jewish women in Poland in the early modern period. His book *How Jewish is Jewish History?* is in advanced stages of preparation.

Marsha L. Rozenblit is the Harvey M. Meyerhoff Professor of Jewish History at the University of Maryland, College Park. She is the author of *Reconstructing A National Identity: The Jews of Hapsburg Austria during World War I* (Oxford University Press, 2001) and *The Jews of Vienna, 1867–1914: Assimilation and Identity* (SUNY Press, 1984). She has recently co-edited (with Pieter M. Judson) *Constructing Nationalities in East Central Europe* (Berghahn Press, 2005).

Shuly Rubin Schwartz is the Irving Lehrman Research Associate Professor of American Jewish History and Dean of the Albert A. List College of Jewish Studies at JTS. Dr. Schwartz has just completed a book entitled *The Rabbi's Wife: The Rebbetzin in American Jewish Life* (NYU Press, 2005).

Contributors

Michael F. Stanislawski is the Nathan J. Miller Professor of Jewish History at Columbia University and the Associate Director of the Institute for Israel and Jewish Studies. His books include *Zionism and the Fin-de-Siècle* and *Autobiographical Jews.*

Shulamit Volkov, Professor of Modern History and incumbent of the Konrad Adenauer Chair for Comparative European History at Tel-Aviv University, Israel. Among her recent publications: *Antisemitismus als kultureller Code,* 2nd ed. (Munich: Beck, 2000), and *Das jüdische Projekt der Moderne* (Munich: Beck, 2001). In Hebrew: *The Magic Circle: Germans, Jews and Antisemites* (Tel Aviv, 2002).

Jack Wertheimer is Provost and the Joseph and Martha Mendelson Professor of American Jewish History at JTS. He has recently edited volumes of newly commissioned essays on the nature of Jewish religious leadership; the intersection of families, communities, and Jewish education in contemporary America; and images of Jewish community in the U.S.

INTRODUCTION

Ismar Schorsch, the Historian

A Critical Appreciation

MICHAEL A. MEYER

Beginning in 1961, when he was still a student, and continuing down to the present, Ismar Schorsch has published about fifty scholarly books, articles, and reviews, in addition to many popular writings, lectures, and addresses. During the early years of his career, scholarship and teaching dominated his professional activity, gradually giving way to the ever more pressing tasks of administrative office at the Jewish Theological Seminary as well as intellectual and spiritual leadership of the Conservative movement. A full appreciation of his career and significance would require a discussion of both realms of his activity. That, however, is not my intention here. Instead, I will concentrate on the scholarly publications that have flowed from Ismar Schorsch's pen, seeking to probe their scope and significance, not in chronological order, but rather according to dominant themes.

I have entitled this essay a "critical appreciation" as I believe an uncritical treatment would pay less homage to his accomplishments as a scholar. Taking his work truly seriously requires evaluation as well as praise. It is, after all, Ismar Schorsch, whose seventieth birthday this volume celebrates, who has impressed upon all of us that what sets modern Jewish scholarship apart from its traditional antecedents is its critical temper. In this spirit, and admittedly from my own perspective, I shall seek to discern the contours of Ismar Schorsch's scholarly work and to assess his achievements.

In his scholarly writings, Ismar Schorsch has addressed three major themes: the reaction of Jews to antisemitism in Germany; various aspects of *Wissenschaft des Judentums*, with particular emphasis on historiography; and the development of the Jewish religion, especially with regard to the modern rabbinate. From time to time he has also undertaken forays into other areas of research, extending his grasp with regard to period or subject matter. I shall begin with the areas of fullest concentration and then give at least brief attention to one of those that bears witness to the breadth of Schorsch's scholarly scope.

It is not possible for a historian of modern Jewry to avoid the subject of antisemitism, and Schorsch has not done so. Relatively early in his career, in 1974, he published a survey of recent literature on German antisemitism. Without rejecting the view of one of his mentors, Fritz Stern, that *völkisch* ideology played a decisive role in sustaining antisemitic attitudes, Schorsch departs from Stern in focusing rather on the state. It was the vacillating role of the state in both emancipating but also discriminating, he suggests, that kept alive the sense of Jewish otherness. Likewise thereafter, when Schorsch dealt with antisemitism, he tended to stress the political dimension rather than the ideological one, not so much the image of the Jews as the way in which they were actually treated.

However, in contrast to the thought of Uriel Tal, whose *Christians and Jews in Germany* (Hebrew edition, 1970) was an early influence on him, antisemitism itself is not a major theme in Schorsch's work. His interest has lain consistently in the Jews themselves, in their role as subjects rather than objects. Moreover, it is not the history of ideas that Schorsch sees as crucial, but rather the history of institutions.[1] Hence in choosing to write his doctoral dissertation at Columbia University on German-Jewish history during the Second Reich, Schorsch decided to concentrate on how Jews reacted to the new wave of antisemitism that assaulted them not long after the final achievement of emancipation rather than to analyze in detail the origins and motivation for that attack. The award-winning book that emerged in 1972, *Jewish Reactions to German Anti-Semitism*, continues to be of value a generation after its appearance. Unlike two overlapping books that followed it, by Jehuda Reinharz and Sanford Ragins,[2] Schorsch gave little attention to the Zionist response. His interest lay in the organizations that were established specifically for the purpose of defending the Jews against their antisemitic antagonists, especially the *Centralverein deutscher Staatsbürger jüdischen Glaubens* (Central Association of German Citizens of the Jewish Faith), by far the largest German-Jewish membership organization and the most representative of contemporary German Jewry.

In its own time, Zionists stigmatized the *Centralverein* as deficient in Jewish consciousness; and frequently scholars as well have accepted that judgment, sometimes reaching their determination simply by reference to the association's name. It is the burden of Schorsch's book to refute that view. Using such archival materials as were available at the time (the *Centralverein*'s own archives were only discovered in Moscow in 1991) as well as printed sources, Schorsch was able to substitute for the caricature the image of a group of Jews who not only fought to protect themselves and their coreligionists from antisemitic accusations, but also, in the face of attrition from Jewish identification, increasingly developed an "internal mission" to diminish apostasy, heighten Jewish self-respect, and secure Jewish survival. Here is the most succinct formulation of Schorsch's central thesis with regard to the *Centralverein*:

> The history of the Centralverein before the First World War reveals a progressive assertion of Jewish consciousness. At first limited to a defiant determination to challenge every instance of

scorn and harassment, the assertion of Jewish consciousness steadily assumed more positive forms as the Centralverein took up the battle to stem the rising tide of defections from Judaism. As a direct consequence of this new role, the Centralverein, during the final decade before Sarajevo, groped cautiously for a more inclusive definition of post-emancipation Judaism.[3]

Although Schorsch's new understanding of the *Centralverein* as moving in the direction of positive Jewish content is on the whole persuasive, it is possible to argue, as Reinharz did in his review of the volume, that the *Centralverein* sometimes defended traditions and institutions that it did not itself believe in.[4] Certainly, most of its members were not in any significant sense practicing religious Jews. Moreover, when one considers the efforts of earlier champions of Jewish dignity, like Gabriel Riesser, or the reaction of many German Jews to the Damascus Blood Libel of 1840, the *Centralverein*'s assertiveness seems less novel. To view the larger picture, it would be necessary also to place Schorsch's analysis of the defense organizations into a more detailed comparative context with the reactions of Zionists and Orthodox Jews during the same period. However, there can be little question that Schorsch has proven his point against deriding judgments by Hannah Arendt, among others. His conclusion is persuasive: "To characterize this record of the Centralverein as mild, naive, or submissive, is simply to ignore the evidence."

As political naïveté was not characteristic of the *Centralverein*, it was likewise not typical of German Jewry as a whole or, for that matter, of modern Jews elsewhere in Central and Western Europe. In a Leo Baeck Memorial Lecture that he delivered two years after the appearance of the book, Schorsch argued vigorously against the Zionist assertion that Diaspora Jewry had been powerless before 1948. A decade before David Biale engaged the topic even more broadly,[5] Schorsch pointed out that although medieval and modern Jews did not possess sovereignty, their group cohesiveness and their economic value were sufficient to support effective political strategies. Moreover, modern Jews in the West, beginning with Moses Mendelssohn, were fully conscious of the relationship between the nature of political institutions and Jewish status. In revolutionary fashion, Schorsch argues that the emancipationists, in seeking the replacement of discriminatory institutions, represented a greater departure from medieval models of adaptation than did the Zionist movement, which tended to work within existing political structures. The thesis is striking and thought-provoking. It is certainly deserving of further reflection, perhaps even as the subject of a symposium. Like the book that preceded it, the lecture is a further scholarly endeavor to forfend against historical interpretations driven by ideology.

Since Schorsch has regarded the political judgment of Diaspora Jews as essential to their survival, he has rightly been concerned about the impact that the Holocaust's centrality in Jewish consciousness has had upon it. Awareness of the Holocaust, he notes, has tempted Jews to divide their historical and contemporary worlds between Jewish victims and antisemitic oppressors, thereby covering up and distorting a much more complex reality. The centrality of the Holocaust, moreover, has tended to reinforce what the historian Salo Baron, one of Schorsch's teachers, famously called the lachrymose view of Jewish history—a view that Schorsch has argued against repeatedly, notably as it manifested itself in the writings of Simon Bernfeld and Yitzhak Baer.[6]

On at least one further occasion, Schorsch set out to defend the German Jews against their detractors. When the Leo Baeck Institute held a conference in 1985 dealing with German Jewry during the Nazi years, Schorsch's brief presentation sought to show that even as the German Jews did not lack political judgment, neither did they lack broadly influential cultural institutions.[7] Before the Nazi period, German Jewry had created a "dynamic religious subculture," represented for example by Jewish book clubs and literary associations. Contrary to the common view, it was not on the edge of exhaustion when the National Socialists took over. Admitting that assimilation had indeed ravaged many, Schorsch argued here that the readers of the popular *Bücherei des Schocken Verlags*, the eighty-three small books issued by the Schocken Publishing House from 1933 to 1938, were indicative of a second, not insignificant sector of German Jewry that had not fully lost its connection with Jewish culture. Later writings, especially by Michael Brenner on the Weimar period,[8] have richly documented the existence of such countertrends to the process of Germanization.

Jewish historiography has been one of Ismar Schorsch's dominant scholarly interests since the start of his academic career. While he was still a rabbinical student at the Jewish Theological Seminary, he devoted his first scientific article to "The Philosophy of History of Nachman Krochmal."[9] Following Simon Rawidowicz, Schorsch rejected the then prevalent view that regarded Krochmal as a Hegelian, arguing for the presence of an immanent notion of progress in Krochmal's *Moreh nevukhe ha-zeman*, rather than a dialectical one.[10] As Schorsch sees him, Krochmal is better understood in terms of inner Jewish history than of confrontation with the prevailing philosophies of his day—a position that I find wholly persuasive.[11] Schorsch is able to demonstrate Krochmal's importance as a profound philosopher of Jewish history, though his work did not appear until 1851, when others, especially, Isaac Marcus Jost, Abraham Geiger, and Heinrich Graetz, had begun not only to reflect on Jewish history but to begin writing it.

A few years later, during his period as a graduate student at Columbia, Schorsch published the first of about a dozen articles for the *Leo Baeck Institute Year Book*, which soon became the principal venue for his scholarly work. Perhaps originating as a paper for his mentor Gerson Cohen, this first essay was Schorsch's initial critical analysis of the work of a Jewish historian.[12] His subject, Moritz Güdemann, was a rabbinical graduate of the Conservative Breslau seminary, who had written a major three-volume work on the history of education and culture in medieval French, German, and Italian Jewry. His focus on social history and connections between the Jewish world and its non-Jewish environment mark Güdemann as a pioneer. Schorsch's thoroughly researched and penetrating article on Güdemann evidences great appreciation for Güdemann's accomplishment but also calls attention to his deficiencies: the almost total neglect of economics, the tendency toward apologetics, and the failure to recognize the diversity within medieval Judaism. His discussion points toward what would become a major theme of his work: critically analyzing the work of modern Jewish historians.

In 1975, Schorsch issued a collection of theoretical writings by the most prominent Jewish historian of the nineteenth century, Heinrich Graetz.[13] In addition to making the selection and translating them from the German, Schorsch also supplied a lengthy introduction, which was less of an entry into the sources contained in the volume than a highly original interpretation of Graetz and his work as a whole. Briefly stated, Schorsch here argued that the key to understanding Graetz's philosophy of Jewish history lies in the nexus between his early anti-Reform bias and the scholarly positions he later adopted. No less than the Reformer he detested so thoroughly, Abraham Geiger, Graetz wrote under the influence of ideology. Like Krochmal, he cannot be understood by reference to external influences, but only within the Jewish context of his time; and for Schorsch, that means Graetz's battle against what he regarded as the destructive tendencies of the Reform movement. Appropriately, Schorsch entitles his introductory essay, "Ideology and History in the Age of Emancipation."

Schorsch perceptively realizes that in nineteenth-century Germany, Jewish history assumed an unprecedented importance. It became a new source of religious authority. As Schorsch put it here: "In the wake of emancipation, with the repudiation of Jewish law and the historicization of philosophy, history assumed the role of both. It became the functional equivalent of halakhah and philosophy in the medieval world." Given these stakes, it is understandable that the competing conceptions of history would be of far more than academic interest. They were both reflective and determinative of contemporary Jewish life.

Schorsch therefore does not limit himself to a discussion of Graetz's approach to Jewish history but sets it into the perspective of competing views, especially those of Isaac Marcus Jost and Abraham Geiger. While Schorsch is appreciative of Jost's daring biblical criticism, he is critical, as was Graetz, of this pioneer Jewish historian's unmitigated assault on rabbinism, which Schorsch attributes to the influence of the French *philosophes*. Similarly, what Schorsch calls "the Reform theory of Jewish history," represented by Geiger, is seen to be deficient for its historicization and hence removal of authority from elements in Jewish tradition lacking relevance for the present. Like Graetz and like Zacharias Frankel, Schorsch himself defines such a quest for relevance as "excessive." The Breslau school, of which Graetz was a part, was determined to right the balance. Schorsch tries to associate Leopold Zunz with this outlook as well, though Zunz was a severe critic of the Breslau Seminary and of the contemporary rabbinate in general.

At this point in his essay, Schorsch sums up the context for the following discussion of Graetz himself in a rather rhetorical passage:

> The emerging conservative bloc had sensed that *Wissenschaft* was an instrument that could be employed to preserve traditional Judaism as well as to revamp it, to resist the price of emancipation as well as to pay it. The Reform monopoly of *Wissenschaft* had been broken. A handful of historians had

begun to formulate an alternative program based on a different reading of Jewish history. In the mid-1840s the young Heinrich Graetz threw his lot with this conservative bloc in resounding fashion.[14]

This passage, which betrays a certain emplotment, strikes me as problematic in two respects. First, it suggests far too sharp a distinction between the two groups. Zunz also had used Jewish scholarship for purposes of religious reform and political emancipation, and Frankel likewise saw a positive connection between them. Even the conservatives did not want to preserve "traditional" Judaism if that meant a non-modernized variety. Nor was there hitherto a Reform monopoly on *Wissenschaft* unless Zunz be counted among the Reformers. Second, and more significant because the theme occurs elsewhere in Schorsch's work, is the assumption that religious reform was largely, if not solely, motivated by political considerations: a price measured out in the coin of tradition in return for political progress toward emancipation. Such an assumption leaves out of consideration the likely possibility that reforms were motivated by religious no less than political considerations, that they were made no less out of personal conviction than out of subservience to government demands. In fact, contemporary sources richly attest to the fact that even radical reformers vowed they would not give up sincerely held religious principles for the sake of political gain.

Yet Schorsch is indisputably correct when he speaks of Heinrich Graetz's "unfailing antipathy toward the Reform movement." Graetz was a man of strong opinions, and he had contempt both for Abraham Geiger as a person and for what he believed to be the thrust of Geiger's work. Clearly Graetz's approach to Jewish history differed from Geiger's, though not I believe because Geiger's overriding motive was to sweep away the authority of large sectors of the past. Schorsch calls Graetz's approach a "national definition of Judaism." Although it was not fully national, in the sense of a

Simon Dubnow, it certainly implied a broader view than that of Geiger, for whom Jewish history was largely the history of a religious idea rather than of a people. Moreover, as Schorsch correctly points out, Graetz possessed an unparalleled ability to evoke identification with his subject and to make a diverse and divided history seem to coalesce. His was a partisan history, its pages filled with heroes and villains.

It is to Schorsch's credit that, for all of his intent to set Graetz sharply apart from the religious reformers, he does not pass over the fact that in the course of time Graetz's own views more and more resembled theirs. Even as he continued to deride the Reform movement, Graetz began to advocate the idea of a Jewish mission among the nations and wrote teleologically of a world history that points toward a "messianic kingdom of peace, brotherhood, and the pure knowledge of God."[15] More remarkably, in some of the writings Schorsch included in his volume, Graetz expresses his belief that ritual is primarily intended for the masses who require it. Gradually, he turns into no less of a rationalist than Abraham Geiger. Few would guess that Graetz wrote these lines: "Of course, Judaism contains an elaborate ritual besides these ideal principles [monotheism], which unfortunately, owing to the tragic course of history, has developed into a fungoid growth which overlies the ideals."[16] Even the laws of kashruth, which every professor in Breslau was obliged to observe, for the elder Graetz become subject to historicization as reactions to Egyptian practices.

In short, Graetz remains an enigma. In denouncing the Reform movement was he struggling with his own inner demon that saw the light of day only late in his life, after Abraham Geiger's and Zacharias Frankel's death? How could he justify idealizing the renegade Spinoza and the apostate Heinrich Heine while traducing reformers who sought Jewish survival? Yet his recognition of the significance of Jewish history for Jewish identity and survival are beyond question, as is his unparalleled ability to draw

fellow Jews to an identification with their past, both its martyr-
dom and its creativity. Schorsch's conclusion about Graetz is right
on target: he was "the greatest Jewish preacher of the nineteenth
century."

In 1977, Ismar Schorsch began to publish in the *Leo Baeck Institute
Year Book* a series of studies dealing with different aspects of *Wissenschaft des Judentums*, which were meant, Schorsch informs us,
"to test my ideas and pave the way to mature and synthetic work."
That work was to be "a social and intellectual history of the Wissenschaft movement."[17] Regrettably for the Jewish academic
world, Schorsch's responsibilities as Chancellor of the Jewish
Theological Seminary prevented him from reaching that goal.
Fortunately, however, in 1994 these studies, along with others,
were combined within the single volume *From Text to Context*,
making it easier to survey them together. Although they remain
unintegrated, the breadth as well as the depth of Schorsch's contribution to this subject are clearly apparent.[18]
    Among the protagonists of Jewish *Wissenschaft*, Schorsch has
had a consistent predilection for its founder and central figure,
Leopold Zunz, whose writing Schorsch admires for its "rigorous
method, immense learning and fierce honesty" and whom he
even refers to as "one of the great servants of Providence."[19] As in
his introduction to the Graetz volume, Schorsch is considerably
more critical of Isaac Marcus Jost, the first major Jewish historian
of modern times. Although he is willing to recognize that "Jost's
achievement transcended his faults and earned him at least passing
recognition," Schorsch sharply distinguishes him from Zunz. The
former, he believes, was a radical *Maskil*, whose early work "fluc-
tuates between animosity and ambivalence," whereas Zunz identified himself with the objects of his research.[20] Schorsch sees Jost
as essentially negative in his approach to the Jewish past, eager to

criticize rabbinism and to follow the prevailing prejudice in favor of Sephardic Jewry. By rejecting so much of Jewish history in his *Geschichte der Israeliten,*[21] Jost left little with which to identify and so, Schorsch argues, he in fact legitimized a program of "total assimilation." Jost wrote in the tradition of the eighteenth-century radical Voltaire, whereas Zunz is better understood (as is Abraham Geiger, I would add) as a pupil of Herder, the romantic philosopher who described the historian's task as *Einfühlung*, being able to sense historical truth from within.

Schorsch's differentiation between these two pioneers of *Wissenschaft* is fundamentally valid, though I would not have drawn it as sharply. One has to remember that the young Zunz, like Jost, was a severe critic of rabbinism, at least in its contemporary manifestations, and that it was he, not Jost, who at one point considered apostasy. Schorsch correctly describes Jost's later work as revealing a different face, as presenting "a balanced, incisive and sanguine panorama [of contemporary Jewish history] with a profound sense for the whole."[22] I believe that both men underwent a shift to greater identification with their subject matter, though Schorsch is certainly right that they represented different types in personality and scholarship and that to differentiate them is to shed light on the parameters of early *Wissenschaft des Judentums.*

Schorsch's other articles on this subject deal with the phenomenon in broader terms, seeking to delineate its character and novelty. Here Schorsch makes a very large contribution to our understanding of its principal elements. A crucial point of departure, he points out, is the introduction of the concept of time, a dynamic factor, into the perception of Judaism; a second is the insistence on freedom of inquiry; a third the readiness to subject the claims of tradition to standards of truth that lie outside of it; and finally the shift from the exegetical to the conceptual. Thus *Wissen* (simply knowing) is transformed into *Wissenschaft* (a critical, historically oriented search for truth). The historically trained eye of the scholar begins to tear apart the chain of tradition, questioning whether early rabbis correctly understood the biblical text or later rabbis their predecessors. That, however, leaves the attendant synthetic task of creating a new continuity through historical narrative. As Schorsch has perceptively noted, the historians—with an elitist élan—set out to displace the rabbis as arbiters and shapers of Jewish tradition; and to some extent they did. Their achievements are the more remarkable as they were attained outside the university, by men who made their living as rabbis in large and small communities and as teachers in Jewish schools.

Although the practitioners of *Wissenschaft des Judentums* subscribed to the academic ethos, seeking truth for its own sake, few of them refused to use it for other purposes as well. Zunz strongly believed that gentile respect for Judaism would occur only once Jewish scholars had proven they could deal critically with their own tradition. He and others also believed that such recognition was, in turn, requisite for the achievement of full emancipation. A third instrumental motivation for critical scholarly study was to find justification for religious reform. If Judaism could be shown to have developed in the past, then future development could be rooted in Judaism itself and not appear as grafted on from the outside. Schorsch examined this relationship in detail in an article entitled "Scholarship in the Service of Reform." Once again the young Jost makes an appearance in this essay, again as a critic of rabbinism, seeking to destroy its influence. And the young Zunz is again Schorsch's foil, like Jost seeking emancipation and reform but, in his historical study of the sermon, for example, engaged in creating continuity rather than demolishing it. Zunz, and Michael Creizenach after him, did not indict rabbinism as such but saw only its contemporary manifestations as a degeneration. Classical rabbinism might be restored to being a creative force in contemporary Jewish life.

As Schorsch very persuasively argues, Abraham Geiger, who was in the first rank as scholar as well as religious reformer, was engaged in both tasks: in demolition and in reconstruction. In the first instance, he dismantled rabbinic Judaism by discrediting its exegetical system. He did this, Schorsch notes perceptively, by demoting ancient texts from sources of truth to states of consciousness. But, especially in his later work, Geiger shifted from "a trope of degeneration to a trope of development." The result, Schorsch notes, "was of momentous import, for it yielded a patrimony for reform drawn from the ranks of normative Judaism."[23] Rabbinic exegesis became for the mature Geiger "an instrument of liberation that mediated the tension between continuity and development."[24] Midrash, Geiger realized, is an agent of change within rabbinic tradition. Schorsch also devotes attention to other reformers in this broadly ranging study: to Levi Herzfeld, Samuel Holdheim, the Galician Joshua Heschel Schorr, and the Hungarian Leopold Loew—though surprisingly not to Zacharias Frankel. This essay, with its abundant insights and its helpful reference to parallel activity among Christian scholars, is, I believe, one of Schorsch's finest.

To my mind, however, the very best—and I think the most influential—of all of Schorsch's writings is his article entitled "Emancipation and the Crisis of Religious Authority: The Emergence of the Modern Rabbinate." Schorsch himself may have been cognizant of its importance when he decided to place it first in his collection of essays. The traditional rabbi, well versed in Jewish law, functioned as teacher of Talmud and arbiter of the Halakhah. His preserves were the academy and the *Bet Din.* For the most part, he remained ignorant of secular studies, regarding them not only as a waste of precious time but as dangerous to faith. The modern rabbi, by contrast, acts principally in the synagogue, where he (or today she) delivers edifying sermons, and in such places as he is able to give strength to the sick and comfort mourners. His learning must now be not only in Jewish law, but in secular studies, the latter represented by a higher degree from a university.

In his article, Schorsch for the first time describes the dimensions of this fundamental transformation and provides statistical evidence for its spread. He traces the proliferation of the doctoral degree and the changing expectations of Jewish communities with regard to rabbinical qualifications. That transformation was fraught with controversy as traditionalist rabbis like Solomon Tiktin held out against the new rabbinical role. But the new situation of German Jewry in particular, with its exposure to the universities and the parallel of a university-trained Christian ministry, made change irresistible. As Schorsch points out, the transformation of the rabbinate was not a matter of one stream against another, but rather a movement that affected German-Jewish religious leadership across the spectrum from Neo-Orthodox to Reform. The breakthrough came when Abraham Geiger, who made the most radical use of critical textual studies, was supported by numerous colleagues as a legitimate candidate for the rabbinical position in Breslau.

Another significant aspect of Schorsch's article concerns the struggle for power between this new rabbinate and the laity. With the beginnings of Jewish political and social integration in Germany, a strong anticlericalism arose among some Jewish community leaders who questioned the necessity and viability of the rabbinate under the new conditions. Even Zunz was no friend of broad rabbinical authority. A flashpoint for this conflict came when Zacharias Frankel was courted for the rabbinate of Berlin but insisted on rabbinical supremacy. Another was the formation of radical lay groups in Frankfurt am Main and other cities that threatened to catapult the Reform movement from its historical foundations. Schorsch insightfully notes that the German rabbinical conferences of the 1840s must be seen, at least in part, as a "counterattack" by rabbis, open only to less rupturing changes, to recapture rabbinical authority. This was the more crucial in Prussia which, unlike some of the other German states, refused to give rabbis the same governmentally sanctioned authority that was extended to Christian clergy. As Schorsch points out, that made the doctorate even more important as a kind of "surrogate for state certification."

Linking this article with his work on *Wissenschaft des Judentums*, Schorsch shows here too how the shift from *Wissen* to *Wissenschaft* was crucial, in this case because the university-trained rabbinate owed its status in large measure to its high level of secular education. This set the German rabbinate sharply apart from its counterparts not only in the East, where the old model remained largely intact, but also from rabbis in France who, like their Christian counterparts, did not receive a higher secular education. Schorsch concludes that the bridge between the old and the new rabbinate in Germany was not the material studied and certainly not the approach to the texts, but rather the ideal of a learned rabbinate as such. Learning in the broadest sense continued to be the source of rabbinical authority on into the modern period as, we may safely conclude, Schorsch wishes that it remain even in the present.

Schorsch has been relatively less interested in ritual reform than in the broader transformations affecting the nature of Jewish scholarship and the rabbinate.[25] However, one article focuses on a general trend in German Jewry that had ramifications for various aspects of Jewish life, including religious practice:[26] the inclination to seek models for modern Judaism within the Sephardic heritage and thereby to provide reforms with an internal paradigm. The turn to Sephardic Jewry by the *Maskilim* and the early religious reformers has been well known. The value of Schorsch's article on the subject is that for the first time it discusses the phenomenon in all its breadth, specifically in liturgy, synagogue architecture, literature, and scholarship. Moreover, he has been able to trace criticism of the Ashkenazic tradition and admiration for Sephardic Jewry back beyond what had been thought to be their beginnings in the late eighteenth century and has also revealed their continuation throughout much of the nineteenth. Although Schorsch might have called more attention here to countertendencies in all of the areas he discusses—for example, in Zunz's writings and in the popular ghetto stories—his article demonstrates just how widespread and variegated was the fascination of what he calls "the myth of Sephardic supremacy."

Given Schorsch's position within the Conservative movement, it is not surprising that he should have devoted articles to the two central figures in its development: Zacharias Frankel, its progenitor in Europe, and Solomon Schechter, the scholar who established it firmly in the United States. Schorsch understands Frankel as a moderate reformer, who was willing to make whatever desirable changes in Jewish practice were not opposed to Halakhah. More important for Schorsch, however, is Frankel's turn to history, using *Wissenschaft des Judentums* especially to restore respect for the ancient rabbinic elite. Schorsch correctly notes that Frankel's biographical essays "are not specimens of critical scholarship but rather of heroic history." By humanizing and modernizing the ancient rabbis, Frankel was able to diminish their discontinuity with the present. My own interpretation of Frankel would lay more stress on the importance he gave to personal faith rather than arguing, as Schorsch does, that the "ultimate source of commitment in Frankel's conception of Judaism" was Jewish history itself and that in his eyes antiquity had in large measure become "a surrogate for divinity."[27] Perhaps it is Schorsch's own commitment both to history and to faith that has helped to shape his understanding of Frankel.

Schorsch's article on Solomon Schechter[28] is filled with admiration for the man whom Schorsch calls "the greatest Jewish scholar of his age." It traces his life and views his scholarly work with deep appreciation. The parallels between subject and author lie not only in their common devotion to Jewish history, but also in their shared appreciation of Leopold Zunz, their combination of religious conservatism with political liberalism, and most obviously in the willingness of each to step from scholarship into a position of religious leadership. The article on Schechter, which is the most recent of Schorsch's historical writings, is both indicative of Schorsch's remarkable ability to still find time for scholarly research and his desire to explore the Seminary's and perhaps his own religious roots.

Although Schorsch's scholarly work has been centered on the intellectual history of modern German Jewry, he has made occasional forays into other realms. He has analyzed and interpreted portions of the liturgy,[29] published an erudite and innovative article on the seventeenth-century Dutch rabbi Menasseh ben Israel,[30] and was able to draw upon a largely unpublished group of some 280 opinions with regard to the acceptability of Jews in academic positions in Prussia in order to shed light on the intellectual elite's attitudes toward allowing Jews to produce and purvey *Wissenschaft*.[31] However, Schorsch's most interesting scholarly departure from his usual field of concentration is his highly valuable article on the nineteenth-century German-Jewish painter Moritz Oppenheim.[32] It is not Schorsch's purpose here to analyze Oppenheim's art, but rather to hold it up as a mirror that reflects German Jewry's attitudes to their religious tradition. Oppenheim achieved extraordinary popularity, Schorsch argues, because he accurately represented the German Jews' "collective state of mind": their religious nostalgia as well as their hopes for a complete emancipation, their "piety and patriotism." Oppenheim's paintings also contained a veiled polemic: contra Kant, Judaism was not an ossified legal system but the expression of a deeply felt, family-centered religiosity. Schorsch has expressed the broader implication of this art memorably: "For Oppenheim, and I dare say for many Jews of the modern era, Judaism was neither creedal nor behavioral but emotional—a sense of place, an organizing principle of reality acquired in childhood and anchored in filial piety." His article is evidence of Schorsch's ability to contribute significantly to one of the principal frontiers of Jewish historiography: the utilization of art and object for the elucidation of social and religious history.

With Ismar Schorsch's assumption of his duties as Chancellor of the Jewish Theological Seminary and spiritual leader of Conservative Jewry, his work as a historian had to make room for the tremendous burden of his new tasks. Schorsch himself recognized that beneath the shift of effort lay a deeper transformation. In 1989 he wrote: "After three years as Chancellor, my public and private lives have been reversed. The quest for historical truth is confined to what is left of my private life, while the struggle for religious meaning is of the very essence of my public role."[33] Yet it is clear in retrospect that his years of active toil within the vineyard of historical study produced a rich harvest and that his private hours continue to add to it. Perhaps one can pay Schorsch no higher tribute than to apply to him the accolade he accorded to Nachman Krochmal and Leopold Zunz: he has written of the past "with empathy as well as integrity."[34]

Notes

1. "Identity or Integration—Which?" (review of Hebrew edition of *Christians and Jews in the Second Reich (1870–1914)*, by Uriel Tal), *Judaism* 19 (1970): 373–77.
2. Jehuda Reinharz, *Fatherland or Promised Land: The Dilemma of the German Jew, 1893–1914* (Ann Arbor: University of Michigan Press, 1975); Sanford Ragins, *Jewish Responses to Anti-Semitism in Germany, 1870–1914* (Cincinnati: Hebrew Union College Press, 1980).
3. *Jewish Reactions to German Anti-Semitism, 1870–1914* (New York: Colum-

bia University Press; Philadelphia: Jewish Publication Society, 1972), 117.

4. The Reinharz review appeared in *Jewish Social Studies* 35 (1973): 297–99.

5. David Biale, *Power and Powerlessness in Jewish History* (New York: Schocken, 1986).

6. See "The Holocaust and Jewish Survival," *Midstream*, January 1981, 38–42; "The Lachrymose Conception of Jewish History," in Schorsch's volume of essays, *From Text to Context: The Turn to History in Modern Judaism* (Hanover, N.H.: University Press of New England, 1994), 376–88. For ease of consultation all citations from essays that were later included in this volume will refer to it, where the original venues of publication are also listed.

7. *From Text to Context*, 360–67.

8. Michael Brenner, *The Renaissance of Jewish Culture in Weimar Germany* (New Haven: Yale University Press, 1996).

9. It appeared in *Judaism* 10 (1961): 237–45.

10. מורה נבוכי הזמן, ed. Leopold Zunz (Leopoli: Schnayder, 1851).

11. Schorsch would return to the subject of Krochmal more than a decade later when he was able to utilize and publish twenty-nine unpublished letters pertaining to Leopold Zunz's edition of Krochmal's *Moreh* in his "The Production of a Classic: Zunz as Krochmal's Editor," *Leo Baeck Institute Year Book* (*LBIYB*) 31 (1986): 281–91.

12. "Moritz Güdemann: Rabbi, Historian and Apologist," *LBIYB* 11 (1966): 42–66.

13. Heinrich Graetz, *The Structure of Jewish History and Other Essays*, translated, edited, and introduced by Ismar Schorsch (New York: JTS, 1975).

14. In Graetz, *Structure*, 31.

15. Graetz, *Structure*, 170.

16. Ibid., 287.

17. *From Text to Context*, xi, 233 note.

18. Schorsch was also among the first, if not the first, to discard the misleading translation of *Wissenschaft des Judentums* as "science of Judaism." His choice for a substitute was "the academic study of Judaism."

19. *From Text to Context*, 245, 343.

20. Ibid., 236.

21. I. M. Jost, *Geschichte der Israeliten seit der Zeit der Maccabäer bis auf unsere Tage*, 10 vols. (Berlin: Schlesinger, 1820–47).

22. *From Text to Context*, 242.

23. Ibid., 317.

24. Ibid., 318.

25. An exception was prompted by Schorsch's discovery in the Zunz Archive of a manuscript that he argues was written by Moritz Steinschneider. It presents basic ideas with regard to the liturgical reform that was being considered by the Berlin Jewish community at the time when it was about to open its new non-orthodox synagogue on the Oranienburger Strasse in 1866. The document shows the great bibliographer, usually considered to have been removed from the Jewish life of his time, as having distinct ideas on practical liturgical issues. Schorsch analyzes the document and publishes it in the original German and in his English translation. See Ismar Schorsch, "Moritz Steinschneider on Liturgical Reform," *Hebrew Union College Annual* 53 (1982): 241–64.
26. "The Myth of Sephardic Supremacy," in *From Text to Context*, 71–92.
27. *From Text to Context*, 263.
28. "Schechter's Seminary," *Conservative Judaism* 55 (2003): 3–23.
29. For example, "A Meditation on Maoz Zur," *Judaism* 37 (1988): 459–64.
30. "From Messianism to Realpolitik: Menasseh ben Israel and the Readmission of the Jews to England," *Proceedings of the American Academy for Jewish Research* 45 (1978): 187–208.
31. *From Text to Context*, 51–70.
32. It was included in *From Text to Context*, 93–117, but regrettably without illustrations. See the original publication, "Art as Social History: Moritz Oppenheim and the German Jewish Vision of Emancipation," in the catalogue of the Israel Museum's Oppenheim exhibition, *Moritz Oppenheim: The First Jewish Painter* (Jerusalem, 1983): 31–61.
33. "The Limits of History," *The Rabbinical Assembly Proceedings* (New York: The Rabbinical Assembly, 1989), 108–9.
34. "Production of a Classic," 291.

HISTORIOGRAPHY

STEEPED IN THE PAST

Heinrich Graetz's Views
of the Jewish Future

ROBERT LIBERLES

By the middle of the nineteenth century, a diverse group was emerging in Germany who stood opposed to the initially strong but now hesitant initiative of Jewish reformers. Jewish leaders who once conceived of a possible dialogue with the Reform movement now assumed an active and forceful position of opposition. Following a real-life association with Abraham Geiger during his brief studies at the University of Bonn, Samson Raphael Hirsch had conducted a fictional exchange with Reform in his *Nineteen Letters of Ben Uziel*. But Hirsch's "dialogue" more resembled a pontifical monologue, and his relationship with Geiger, already strained by their actual correspondence, did not survive. In addition, the loose lines dividing the reformers from the traditionalists in the early 1830s became more clearly delineated with the bitter polemics that followed and intensified in the 1840s.[1]

Zacharias Frankel also seemed to seek cooperative ties with the reformers when he arrived at the 1845 rabbinical conference held in Frankfurt-am-Main. But Frankel's rather hasty and demonstrative withdrawal from the conference after a split on the role of Hebrew in synagogue services, followed by his public condemnation of the conference's decisions that exaggerated their radical nature, leads to the suspicion that he had planned the entire maneuver to position himself for leadership of the traditionalist opposition to Reform in Germany. Shortly thereafter, Frankel announced his own plans for a conference of traditionalists and quickly discovered that the more Orthodox rabbis had no desire to participate in a conference of any kind, nor were they willing to accept Frankel as their spokesman.[2]

A few years later, Frankel went on to become the founding director of the newly established Jewish Theological Seminary in Breslau. In organizing his faculty, he called upon Heinrich Graetz, who was just beginning to make his mark as a pioneering scholar of Jewish history. Raised in the traditional milieu of Posen, Graetz had long opposed what he saw as the radical tendencies of Reform. When Hirsch's *Nineteen Letters* appeared, Graetz was enthusiastic about the emergence of a religious leader with a clear vision of a future direction for Judaism, a vision that combined the need to evolve with a strong commitment to traditional life and practices. But three years of actually living with the Hirsch family and immersing himself in Hirsch's world took their toll, and Graetz eventually left, disillusioned with Hirsch's strict adherence to Orthodox practices and his lack of leadership momentum—an assessment that Hirsch disproved when, after following his own tortured path, he became rabbi of the new, independent Orthodox congregation in Frankfurt and was established as the outstanding leader of German Orthodox Judaism.

The next few years were difficult ones for Graetz, who had no obvious way to support himself. He lacked the talents and the will to become a rabbi, and academic positions were nonexistent. Frankel's invitation to Graetz to teach Jewish history at the Breslau seminary initiated a significant partnership that contributed to the institution and to the education of generations of students, while allowing Graetz to pursue more fully his personal dream of historical scholarship.[3]

During the 1850s, the group of cultural and ideological critics of Reform grew in strength. Personalities as diverse as Hirsch, Zacharias Frankel, and Graetz all issued scathing critiques of the

Reform program for German-Jewish life. The early socialist and proto-Zionist thinker Moses Hess followed suit a few years later in his *Rome and Jerusalem,* published in 1862,[4] with his own scathing critique of Reform Judaism. Graetz's ideas uniquely bridged these various positions—Neo-Orthodox, Historical, and nationalist—as the twists and turns of his career led him from his initial relationship with Hirsch to his sustained association with Frankel, and finally to the close friendship he established with Moses Hess.

As a young man, Graetz started to establish his public reputation in 1844 with a series of anonymous articles that appeared in the weekly *Der Orient* attacking Geiger and the Reform camp in Breslau, where Graetz lived at the time.[5] The next year, he completed his doctoral dissertation on Gnosticism and Judaism.[6] As Ismar Schorsch has demonstrated, Graetz's writings were influenced throughout his scholarly career by his opposition to Reform Judaism and the scholarship written in its support. "Long before Graetz was to make his mark as a scholar he had developed a profound abhorrence for the Reform movement, fed by an envious dislike for the man who embodied and led it [Geiger]."[7]

As Schorsch put it, "On a symbolic level Graetz's doctoral dissertation mirrored the dilemma of his age." In that work, Graetz depicted as his hero

> the lowly born, uneducated Akiba [who] dramatically surmounted his origins to provide Judaism with the ideological vitality to turn back the challenge [of Gnostic dualism]. ... The religious turmoil of the present replayed the script of an earlier struggle, with Graetz defending traditional Judaism with novelty and daring against the [archetypical heterodox figure] Elisha ben Abuya of his day.[8]

Graetz remained vehemently opposed to Reform, referring to it in 1869 as "the christianization of Judaism";[9] but his critique of German Reform as such in these early years eventually gave way as time passed to an increasingly negative assessment of German Jewry at large. With the outbreak of his controversy with Treitschke in 1880, he became embittered and increasingly isolated from the German Jewish community.

The controversy between Graetz and Prussia's prominent historian Heinrich von Treitschke continues to fascinate Jewish historians not only as one of the notorious highlights of the antisemitic movement of the late 1870s and early 1880s, but also as a clash between two nationalist historians goring each other over disputed turf.[10] In his 1881 essay "A Word about Our Jewry,"[11] Treitschke cited Graetz to demonstrate how the leading historian of the Jews referred to Germans, Germany, and Christianity with deep hostility, even though a decade had already passed since German Jews had received emancipation. In his original attack, Treitschke focused on specific passages in Graetz's *Geschichte* that described Luther, Goethe, and Fichte in a negative light. In fact, though, Graetz vented his resentment against Germany and German nationalism throughout the entire last volume of his work, sharply condemning the unyielding hostility of the Germans toward the Jews and adversely comparing Germany with its more civil neighbors: France, Holland, and Italy. Graetz attacked with all the literary skill at his command, both in his rhetorical style and in his exceptionally gifted power of synthesis. In one passage that was watered down in subsequent editions, Graetz wrote of the unfortunate condition of Alsatian Jews at the time of Moses Mendelssohn, which prompted Christian Dohm's treatises on their behalf:

> The German population of this region ... as Germans in general, adamantly maintained their hostility toward the Jews far more than the French, the Dutch, the English, and the Italians, nations of culture, who had already abandoned this hostility almost entirely.[12]

In an effective contrast of Jewish patriotic efforts on behalf of Germany and the venom and violence that they received at the hands of their German neighbors, Graetz described the sacrifices Jews made to support the war against Napoleon:

> Large numbers of Jews, especially in Prussia, animated by burning love of country, had joined the volunteers, had rejoiced to be accepted in the ranks, and wipe away with their blood on the battlefield the stain of cowardice, so often imputed to them by the opponents to their emancipation. Jewish young men paid for the freedom accorded them on paper with their lives. Jewish physicians and surgeons sacrificed themselves in the camps and hospitals in their devoted attendance on the wounded and the plague-stricken. Jewish women and girls spared no efforts to bring help and comfort to the wounded.[13]

But the successful end of the fighting did not bring the expected rewards of acknowledgment of the Jews' service to their country. "Nevertheless, the seemingly forgotten Jew-hatred was rekindled in the hearts of the Germans, extended even further, and robbed the Jews of the reward which the hard-won victories had promised to bring them." This reversal of the Jewish situation resulted when extreme German nationalism emerged in the post-Napoleonic stage and set out to remove Jewish rights that had been obtained under French rule. "Christian Teutomania was the armed specter which for many decades robbed the German Jews of rest, honor, and joy in life." Eventually, the Jew-hatred in Germany resulted in the Hep-Hep riots of 1819. Graetz pointedly contrasted this situation with the far more benevolent behavior of non-Jews in Denmark, which "shamed German narrow-mindedness," and with France itself, where Napoleon's former restrictions on the Jews were now lifted.[14]

Graetz greatly admired Moses Mendelssohn and indeed crowned Mendelssohn as the herald of a new age of Jewish history. But he hardly followed Mendelssohn's restrained response to Lavater's famous conversion challenge when Mendelssohn chose to avoid any public confrontation that might implicate his fellow Jews or endanger their lives and welfare. Graetz did not demonstrate similar restraint. One can respect him for his candid truthfulness in depicting the hostility or disdain with which nineteenth-century Germans continued to treat the Jews in their midst, but one can also question his tactlessness, perhaps even his lack of communal responsibility, when he chose to speak out so militantly against German culture and nationalism. Did he not consider the possible repercussions for his community? Graetz was indeed fully aware of his pugnacious style in composing the controversial eleventh volume of his *History*. He wrote to Moses Hess that he relished the opportunity to express his wrath:

> But the Germans! No, what a narrow-minded and arrogant people! I have while working on volume 11 concerning the beginning of this century ... become reacquainted with them from different sides, and I am looking forward with pleasure to castigating them and their authorities Schleiermacher, Fichte, and the entire beastly romantic school.[15]

In the *History*, he described Fichte as follows: "Fichte may be regarded as the father and apostle of national German hatred of the Jews, of a kind unknown before, or rather never before so clearly manifested."[16]

Later editions removed some of the material most offensive to Germans, and Graetz himself apologized in the second edition for his overly critical stance toward Germany, explaining that he had written the volume in 1868, prior to the establishment of the Second Reich and its emancipation of the Jews.[17] It was a lame response, since parts of Germany like Frankfurt and Hamburg had already passed emancipation legislation in the early 1860s, and emancipation was clearly on the horizon in Prussia as well.

Despite his considerable misgivings about German society's treatment of its Jews, and despite his sometimes scathing criticism of contemporary Jewish life, Graetz expressed in his *History* and elsewhere a rather positive prognosis for the future of Jewish life. He emphasized that world Jewry now demonstrated a strong sense of renewed vitality and self-confidence. In a carefully selected comparison with Rome, in which Graetz envisioned Romans waking after centuries of slumber in which they still recall their former greatness, Graetz went on to assert that while no such revival had taken place in Rome,

> a nation actually did arise from the darkness of the tomb, the only example chronicled in the annals of man. This resuscitated people, the Jewish race, endeavored at its resurrection to collect its thoughts and memories, and recall a vision of its glorious past; feeling itself to be at once old and young, rich in memories and lacking in experience.[18]

Matters had not yet advanced far enough for Jews to openly assert themselves, he admitted, but a new self-esteem permeated Jewish life that included a thirst for increased knowledge about what it meant to be a Jew. Insightfully, Graetz maintained that the long struggle for equality had given the Jews a growing self-reliance, a better appreciation of who they were, and an enhanced political maturity. Their new self-respect resulted primarily from the endeavors of the Science of Judaism (*Judenwissenschaft*), which had focused its research on the long history of the Jews, on the basic teachings of Judaism, and on the unique and enduring strength of the Jewish nation.

In Graetz's view, the heroes of this renewed cultural vitality were primarily scholars, men deeply immersed in Hebrew and classical Jewish sources. Graetz was generous with his praise of those who had preceded him and many still active in Jewish scholarship. Among these, the rabbi of Prague and *Wissenschaft* scholar Solomon Rapaport received special note. Graetz even offered some praise of Isaac Jost, whose earlier comprehensive history of the Jews might have precluded the need for another such endeavor so soon. But his critique of Jost illustrates what Graetz sought to accomplish in his own version of Jewish history:

> [Jost] gave to Jewish history, undeniably heroic, a dry, Philistine character, despoiling it of the brightness with which it was endowed even in the eyes of unprejudiced Christian observers. He tore to shreds the heroic drama of thousands of years.[19]

He also praised the political activist and parliamentarian Gabriel Riesser for his determination in pursuing the cause of Jewish equality, although he was critical of Riesser's indifference to religious practice and took him to task for not reacting forcefully enough to the Damascus crisis of 1840.[20] But despite the many directions that Graetz indicated as showing signs of renewed Jewish strength, he·did not include Zionism; nor, curiously, did he mention the literary activity on behalf of Zionism of his close friend Moses Hess.

By the time Graetz completed his *History*, an endeavor that had taken him close to twenty years, he was extremely conscious of tumultuous changes taking place around him in Jewish life and culture. For Graetz, these were developments of sweeping historical significance. Twice before in their history the Jewish people had appeared to be lost, plagued with a sense of physical and spiritual decay, and on both occasions a fundamental revival had taken place. Now again decay was giving way to a resurgence of the Jewish spirit, characterized by growing religious fervor, an increasing sense of solidarity, and the development of a keen historical consciousness that included a revival of the Hebrew language itself. Negative trends continued to threaten Jews, and the final words of his *History* referred explicitly to renewed antisemitism that was also growing in strength. Graetz did not elaborate in the *History* on the antisemitic movement, as he also ignored altogether Jewish nationalist aspirations. For his thinking on these subjects, we have to turn to his essays, especially those written after he had completed the *History.*

⚛️

In his essays written from the 1860s to the late 1880s, Graetz emphasizes the rejuvenation taking place among the Jewish people, and he indicates very clearly his far more positive assessment of the Jews of England and France, in contrast with his own German Jewish community. Already in "The Rejuvenation of the Jewish Race," published in 1864, Graetz had written: "The Jewish people is heading before our very eyes toward a process of rejuvenation which previously was scarcely imagined." A small kernel of devoted Jews, he noted, had led the return to the Holy Land at the time of Cyrus and in so doing initiated a new age of national glory.[21] This essay was written just after the publication of Hess's *Rome and Jerusalem*, but there was no hint here that Graetz intended to call for a parallel movement of return to Palestine.

In "The Correspondence of an English Lady," written and published in 1883–84, and therefore under the influence of the controversy with Treitschke specifically and of the antisemitic movement in general, Graetz describes the widespread ills of Europe, with an unusual emphasis on physical ailments. Europe had been reduced to no more than a sick society, he argues, as exemplified by the presence of widely transmitted sexual diseases. As a result, according to Graetz, many children were born deformed, so that European society was clearly degenerating. Moreover, German Jews seemed to be infected by these diseases as well, and were themselves close to the grave. Such, however, was not the case with the Jews of England, France, and Italy, he asserts. In the last chapter of these essays, Graetz offers a qualified endorsement of the new efforts on behalf of Zionism, but in essence, he still leaves the issue hanging without any significant discussion of Zionism and what it could offer the Jewish people.[22]

As noted at the outset, Graetz was a key figure in the group of social and cultural critics of German Jewry that emerged in the mid nineteenth century. Some of these critics—such as Frankel, Graetz, and Hess—collaborated in their efforts. Others were extremely hostile toward the rest, such as S. R. Hirsch. All of these men saw that the issues of the day affected the totality of Jewish life, culture, and politics. Their common opposition to Reform Judaism was not limited to the religious sphere, although Hirsch defined his opposition in such terms. As Jewish historians, we are fascinated by Graetz and his career for many reasons, but the notion of the historian as active participant in the historical process is of course a source of special interest for us. Here was one of "us" having a significant impact on the burning issues of his times—and indeed, what times they were! It was through Graetz's activity that one of the earliest Zionist essays was published. It was Graetz who taught Jewish history to countless traditional rabbis, and it was Graetz who through his writings conveyed an identification with Jewish history to generations of Jews not only in Germany, but also throughout Europe, and eventually to scattered English-speaking communities in America and elsewhere. Graetz the writer had enormous impact, as testified by the reluctant but unavoidable praise heaped on him by Gershom Scholem, surely one of his most scathing latter-day critics. It was Graetz's *History*, according to Scholem, that played a major role in his teenage search for a Jewish identity.[23] Finally, we are fascinated by Graetz as the target and respondent in his bitter controversy with Treitschke. Here we have a Jewish historian on trial, so to speak, for his candor about Germany's attitudes and treatment of its Jews, and here were two historians, each framing his respective narrative in order to inflame the nationalist aspirations of two different groups, one living within the sphere of the other.

Historians have not always proven politically astute. I once argued that Salo Baron's generally sound political judgment was compromised during the Nazi years by his lifetime commitment to disengage the lachrymose hegemony over Jewish history and Jewish historians. How intriguing to now pose a similar question regarding the historian most often identified with the lachrymose conception! Did Graetz serve his cause well by antagonizing the society in which German Jews lived? Certainly, he caused considerable discomfort to German Jews themselves, and he himself clearly suffered from his subsequent isolation. In the years after the Treitschke controversy, Graetz felt strongly embittered toward the German Jewish community that had not only failed to come to his defense, but had placed him into semi-quarantine.[24]

His almost total silence on the emerging Zionist movement would seem to have resulted one way or another from a political paralysis caused by the controversy and its aftermath. Not only did Zionist aspirations correspond with much of his own thinking, but Graetz had from very early on cast his lot with the new ideology when he arranged for the publication of *Rome and Jerusalem*, followed by letters and essays he wrote after his own trip to the land of Israel in 1872. And yet when approached by the leadership of the new Hibbat Zion movement in Russia to join its board, Graetz endorsed their efforts but explained in a letter to the head of Hibbat Zion, Leon Pinsker, his inability to become publicly involved. Graetz felt that he had already spent his political capital among German Jews, and he was even more doubtful that German Jewry would respond to the Zionist call. Here he clearly revealed the toll he had paid in the controversy with Treitschke:

> I hasten to answer you in order to avoid any misunderstanding.
> I have in no way become an opponent of the society. I take a
> strong interest in its advancement and will use my strengths to

further its cause. But my name should not used in this connection, for my name instead of being useful could prove a rallying point for rabid antisemites and for dejudaized Jews. Our Russian coreligionists are more strongly devoted [literally: feel warmer] for the matter and cannot always restrain their language. This could, however, damage the cause in cool Germany.

The committee should in general not count on the support of German Jews, for there is little interest there. Greater support will be found in France and England. As I am informed by Simmel, you will find sufficient support among Russian Jews and do not need bother looking for help in Germany, for the German Jews are deeply immersed in Byzantium and are full of fear that Jupiter, that is Bismarck, will react against them.

I reiterate once again, that my own sympathy for the society is nevertheless not weakened.[25]

If Graetz was optimistic that a Jewish revival had begun in his own day, he was far less than sanguine that German Jews would offer a significant contribution to that revival. Even before the Treitschke controversy, Graetz had sharply criticized the compromises made by Reform Jews.[26] Later, especially given his disappointment in the lack of vocal support given to him, Graetz consistently poured scorn on German Jews. In his view, Germany itself had demanded too much from its Jews in exchange for emancipation and in so doing had robbed them of their spirit. Graetz looked elsewhere for the strengths that would carry out the rebirth of Jews and Judaism. Indeed, Graetz began to speak in quite positive terms about Russian Jews. In contrast with his earlier hostile attitude toward Polish Jews, in discussing his own nineteenth century, Graetz was quite complimentary about the Jewish revival taking place in Russia and Galicia.[27]

Circumstances also caused Graetz to speak highly of English Jewry and its potential to lead a modern Jewish renaissance. A historian looking back has to share with Graetz a combination of pride, pain, and irony when reading his address to the opening of the Anglo-Jewish exhibition in 1887. Honored on the occasion of his seventieth birthday and by the invitation to address the exhibition, Graetz spoke enthusiastically to his British audience about what they had attained in the past and might still accomplish in the future:

> A century ago Israel stood with downcast eyes and bowed back all over the earth, despised like an outcast. And today? This brilliant assembly, the elite of Judaism, that has established a Jewish Historical Exhibition ... this assembly speaks more clearly and efficaciously of our marvelous metamorphosis, of our rise and phenomenal position, than any picture in words, however dramatic it might be.
>
> The heart is rejoiced at such an exhibition. ... For a Jewish visitor from the Continent, it is especially surprising and praiseworthy to see such an exhibition. From the continent, I say, *for there such a thing would be an impossibility.* The importance and influence of this exhibition consist in large measure in the sentiment which it expresses. For, after all, of what importance are these relics and records ...? If I interpret your motives correctly, you desired rather to give evidence of your true Jewish convictions. You wished to display the inner connection of your past and your present.[28]

Toward the end of his talk, Graetz explained quite clearly the reason for these differences between English Jews and those on the Continent:

> You dwell in a land blessed by God where the Holy Scriptures, the study of our lives, our alpha and omega, are highly honored, and the study of our glorious antiquity greatly encouraged. You live with your Christian fellow-citizens in full accord, so that they fully recognize that your love for your fatherland need not exclude love for the land of your fathers.

He summarized the differences by explaining that what was important was the way English Jews had been granted emancipation freely as a consequence of public opinion, not with doubts and compromises as had been the case in Germany and Austria. "Nor had you on this account to give up a jot of your religious convictions, as the French Sanhedrin had to do at the demand of the Corsican despot." Finally, Graetz urged his audience to act on the mandate of world Jewish leadership that had been placed on them and to establish an academy for Jewish research. Again, he clearly alluded to the freedom and ability of English Jews to act where others could not.

Graetz's global and historical perspective of Jewish problems and prospects extended far beyond that of any contemporary among German Jewry's leaders. Like Graetz, Moses Hess looked elsewhere for support to elevate the Jewish situation. Hess was convinced that the Jewish national cause would find support from his adopted France, but he had little to say about other Jewish communities. Altogether different in his perspective was Graetz's early mentor, Samson Raphael Hirsch, who struck a chord quite similar to what one might have expected from his Reform adversaries. For Hirsch, Judaism was a religion based on Torah, while his nationalist allegiances belonged exclusively to Germany. Not only was he opposed to early Zionist endeavors that emerged in his last days, but he also refused to cooperate with the Alliance Israélite Universelle founded in 1860 and based in Paris.[29] In light of these contrasts, the scene of Graetz addressing English Jewry near the end of his life is truly worth pondering, as it provides an image of a nineteenth-century global Jew, steeped in the Jewish past, and still optimistic about the Jewish future. England's Moses Montefiore (1784–1885) is the only other contemporary to come to mind who was endowed with a similar broad Jewish outlook, prior to the rise of Zionism.

As noted, one shares with Graetz a sense of pride, pain, and irony in reading his address to Anglo-Jewry. He must have been very proud to be thus honored by British Jews on this occasion, but it undoubtedly reminded him of the pain of rejection by his own community, a pain referred to frequently in his address with the recurring observation that "this could only be accomplished here, certainly not there." The irony is my own addition to these complex feelings: By turning to that community which seemed the least accomplished of all European communities in the realm of Jewish culture, while rejecting out-of-hand the German Jewish community that seemed to have achieved so much in Jewish thought and activity, Graetz underscored his belief that the life and thought of German Jewry was not authentic and free, but a product of oppression and coercion. Other communities both to the West and to the East could do more for world Jewry and do it better.

The scholar and leader whom we honor in this Festschrift has spent almost his entire career actively engaging the question of scholarship and community. He did so at first with his series of panoramic examinations of the nineteenth-century *Wissenschaft* scholars and their relation to the political and religious issues of their day. How fitting that Ismar Schorsch's second book was devoted to Heinrich Graetz. Schorsch has insisted throughout his scholarly career that Jewish religious and scholarly leaders were thoroughly immersed in communal struggles, encapsulating his approach in a now classic essay "On the History of the Political Judgment of the Jew."[30] He himself then donned the mantle of communal leadership, a role he has filled with dignity and courage. Like Graetz and Baron, he has taught generations through his writings, through his many students, and in recent decades through his active communal teaching, in which he has adumbrated the roles of religion and scholarship in the formulation of a Jewish future. For this, we are in his debt.

Notes

1. For the change in atmosphere around the middle of the nineteenth century, see Robert Liberles, *Religious Conflict in Social Context: The Resurgence
of Orthodox Judaism in Frankfurt am Main* (Westport, Conn.: Greenwood,
1985), esp. chaps. 2 and 3, and "The So-Called Quiet Years of German
Jewry (1849–1869), A Reconsideration," *Leo Baeck Institute Year Book* 41
(1996): 65–74.

2. Less has been written on Frankel than on other major Jewish religious
leaders of the nineteenth century, but see the very useful volume by Rivka
Horwitz, זכריה פרנקל וראשית היהדות הפוזיטיבית היסטורית (Zacharias Frankel
and the beginnings of positive-historical Judaism) (Jerusalem: Mercaz
Shazar, 1984).

3. On Graetz, an old biography appears in the English edition of the *History*:
Philip Bloch, "Memoir of Heinrich Graetz," in Graetz, *History of the Jews*
(Philadelphia: Jewish Publication Society, 1898), 6:3–86; cf. Graetz, דרכי
ההיסטוריה היהודית (The structure of Jewish history) (Jerusalem: Bialik,
1969), with introductory essays by Shmuel Ettinger and Reuven Michael;
Ismar Schorsch's introductory essay, "Ideology and History in the Age of
Emancipation," in Graetz, *The Structure of Jewish History and Other Essays*,
ed. Ismar Schorsch (New York: JTS, 1975); and most recently, Reuven
Michael, היינריך גרץ: ההיסטוריון של העם היהודי (Heinrich Graetz, the historian
of the Jewish people) (Jerusalem: Mosad Bialik, 2003).

4. Moses Hess, *Rome and Jerusalem*, trans. Meyer Waxman (New York: Bloch,
1943).

5. Bloch, "Graetz," 28.

6. Hirsch Grätz, *Gnosticismus und Judentum* (Krotoschin: Monasch, 1846).

7. Schorsch, "Ideology and History," 34–35.

8. Ibid., 36–37.

9. Ibid., 31.

10. There is considerable literature on this controversy, but see especially the
comprehensive and creative essays by Michael Meyer, "The Great Debate
on Antisemitism: Jewish Reaction to New Hostility in Germany, 1879–
1881," *Leo Baeck Institute Year Book* 11 (1966): 137–70, and "Heinrich
Graetz and Heinrich von Treitschke: A Comparison of Their Historical
Images of the Modern Jew," in his *Judaism within Modernity* (Detroit:
Wayne State University Press, 2001), 64–75.

11. Heinrich von Treitschke, *A Word about Our Jewry*, trans. Helen Lederer
(Cincinnati: Hebrew Union College, [1958]).

12. Cited in Michael, *Graetz, Historian*, 121.
13. Graetz, *History*, 5:511–12.
14. Ibid., 5:516, 519.
15. Heinrich Graetz, *Tagebuch und Briefe*, ed. Reuven Michael, Schriftenreihe wissenschaftlicher Abhandlungen des Leo Baeck Institute (Tübingen: Mohr, 1977), 287, letter of March 31, 1868.
16. Graetz, *History*, 5:462.
17. Michael, *Graetz, Historian*, 123.
18. Graetz, *History*, 5:589–90.
19. Ibid., 5:595.
20. Ibid., 5:598–600.
21. "Rejuvenation of the Jewish Race," in *Structure*, 143.
22. "The Correspondence of an English Lady," in *Structure*, 191–258.
23. Gershom Scholem, *From Berlin to Jerusalem* (New York: Schocken, 1980), 37–38.
24. Ismar Schorsch, *Jewish Reactions to German Anti-Semitism* (New York: Columbia University Press, 1972), 43–46.
25. Graetz, *Tagebuch und Briefe*, 404, letter of February 7, 1885.
26. Michael, *Graetz, Historian*, 123–24.
27. On the important role of Galician scholars in the Jewish revival, see especially *History*, 5:607–20. For one explanation on why Graetz did not write more about Russian efforts, see Michael, *Graetz, Historian*, 155.
28. "Historical Parallels," in *Structure*, 263–64; emphasis added.
29. On Hirsch's attitude toward the Alliance, see the discussion in *Rabbiner Esriel Hildesheimer Briefe*, ed. Mordechai Eliav (Jerusalem: Rubin Mass, 1965), 155–56 n. 91.
30. Ismar Schorsch, "On the History of the Political Judgment of the Jew," *Leo Baeck Memorial Lecture* 20 (New York: Leo Baeck Institute, 1976).

POLISH–JEWISH RELATIONS IN MODERN TIMES

The Search for a Metaphor and a Historical Framework

GERSHON BACON

I. Poles and Jews: A Special Relationship

In the midst of writing a synthetic history of Polish Jewry in modern times, I find myself time and again forced to deal with the complex issue of Polish–Jewish relations. Nor is the present author alone in this struggle, for in a number of books on more limited topics that have appeared over the past two decades, we find the authors struggling with this very issue, with no one successful resolution. The special and complex relations of Poles to Jews, of Jews to Poles, the debate over the place of Jews in Polish society all began from the very inception of modern Polish nationhood. The metaphors employed by politicians, publicists, and historians alike reflect both descriptive and prescriptive tendencies in politics and historiography. In this short review, my goal is to survey the various attempts at characterizing this relationship, to analyze the elements of that relationship that render it so special and sensitive, and, finally, to offer what I see as the most

This is an expanded and revised version of a lecture originally delivered at the Center for Advanced Judaic Studies at the University of Pennsylvania, January 2003. My thanks to the staff at the Center for their assistance, and to my colleagues in the research group on "East European Jewry" for their comments and suggestions.

useful model for dealing with Polish-Jewish history. I find this topic especially fitting for a volume in honor of our esteemed teacher, Prof. Ismar Schorsch. Whether in class discussion or in private deliberations, Schorsch always impressed on his students the obligation to consider the wider implications of whatever limited topic they were examining. Only in the wider historical framework did the facts and documents attain their historical significance and fit into the larger historical narrative.

For generations, there has been a feeling that there is something special about the Polish Jewish situation, with each historian trying to find those elements that make it so special, as for example in the case of Raphael Mahler: "The Jewish community of Poland and Lithuania accounted for approximately a half of all European Jewry. It stood out from amongst all the Diaspora settlements because of its closeness to the land it lived in, the wide degree of autonomy that its institutions enjoyed, and the unique attributes of its national culture."[1] In this concise formulation, Mahler touches on many of the points that would be raised by numerous historians and publicists before and after him, the most important of which was the perceived closeness between Jews and Poland. Some would find this closeness positive, others curious, and still others destructive, but no one would ignore it. There was something special in the Polish–Jewish relationship, but the question was how to explain that relationship; and the ongoing, often bitter debate was over how that relationship should proceed either when Poland found itself under foreign rule or when Polish independence would be restored.

In premodern Poland, there were those who saw this relationship as stemming even from primordial times, as mentioned by Michael Steinlauf:

> By the mid-18th century, when there were about 750,000 Jews living in the Commonwealth, one quarter of all the Jews in the world lived in Polish shtetlekh. Jews had become a fixture of

the Polish landscape, as familiar an element of the natural order as the peasant village or the landowner's manor. Indeed, one popular szlachta conception identified this tripartite division of the social world with the races descended from the sons of Noah: the peasant as Ham, the landowner as Japhet, the Jew as Shem.[2]

And as a part of this special relationship we must consider those characteristics of Polish Jewry that survived as a heritage of the pre-partitions period into the modern era, most succinctly formulated by Gershon Hundert: "Wherever they went Polish Jews carried with them something which characterized them at home too: a very particular attachment to their people and a uniquely positive view of their identity as Jews."[3]

Of course, our search for an appropriate metaphor for the Polish–Jewish relationship cannot be isolated from the more general problem of the characterization of Poland, the Polish nation, and the Polish State, which is also in flux but with some newer approaches being offered in the last few years. Norman Davies makes the salient point that one of the problems of dealing with Polish history in general is that in the Polish tradition the "Word" has precedence over the "Fact":

> ... where more attention is paid to what people would have liked to happen than to what actually occurred. In Polish eyes, the refusal to accept the political situation as the reality has formed an essential spur to national consciousness; but it has tended to cloud the vision of the past. At the same time, one cannot deny that idealism is itself real enough. In the revolutionary era, as in the nineteenth century, there were many Poles who were not content to dream. They worked and fought and bled for their ideals in the most real and practical way. The problem is whether they should be brought to the center of the historical stage, or left in the wings. Does it not matter that their sacrifices brought no tangible result?[4]

In historical narrative as well, after the shattering experience of partitions and the loss of independence, too often the idea has also prevailed over fact, and the debate over who is a Pole, what is Poland, and what is Polish history has been reflected in the story told, which is more prescriptive than descriptive. In at least one telling passage, Davies himself falls into this trap, giving a very one-sided characterization of what exactly is Polish history and the Polish nation:

> The fact is: the modern Polish nation is the end product of modern Polish Nationalism. Its growth has proceeded erratically for nearly two centuries, and its ultimate success was far from certain for most of recent history. The exact date at which it assumed a preponderant role in the affairs of the Polish lands is a matter for dispute. Some historians see the decisive moment in 1864. ... Others would delay it to the Rebirth of the Polish state in 1918. The most rigorous observers would argue that the national process could not be regarded as complete until a homogeneous Polish population, uniformly conscious of their national identity, took undivided control of their own national territory. That point was not reached until 1945.[5]

Such a view of modern Polish history leaves little room for Jews or other minorities in the larger picture. In recent decades, however, there have appeared other trends in general Polish historiography that reflect the multinational, multiethnic, and multireligious reality of the Polish Commonwealth and the interwar Second Republic, while at the same time cataloging those ideologies that aspired to an ethnically Polish state where the diversity on the ground was rejected outright. The similar titles of the books by Andrzej Kamiński on the old Commonwealth[6] and Jerzy Tomaszewski on the interwar Second Republic[7] express this newer approach. In the past, those historians or politicians who were advocates of a single nation-state, "did not want, nor could they try to accept, cultural heterogeneity along the line that had existed in Poland from the dawn of its history."[8]

The search for a suitable term for the Jews' place in Poland goes back to the debates about the reform of the Polish state in the second half of the eighteenth century, especially to the pamphlet literature surrounding the Four-Year Sejm (1788–92). Typical in this regard are the words of Mateusz Butrymowicz in his pamphlet published in 1789:

> Jews in Poland until now had had no status, that is, they were not nobles, nor burghers, nor peasants. This was an error of the nation's constitution, this was a defect of our laws, in a word, this was an evil. ... Granting the Jews a status and from eternal wanderers making them into citizens of this country, in which they have been until now as guests (*gości*), this is a duty of the first order. In my view the urban class is most suitable for them.[9]

Here we have one classic metaphor for the position of the Jews in Poland, which is very much part of the prescriptive–descriptive axis mentioned above. The search for an appropriate term reflects the search both to describe reality and to remake that reality. Butrymowicz himself maintained that Jews "are so ill suffered in all circles that between a Jew and us there seems to be an unbridgeable division."[10] In his view, the Jews were *in* Poland, but certainly not *of* Poland, and the host–guest relationship would change only with the absorption of the Jews into the burgher class, a goal that would prove illusory both then and subsequently. Another noted Polish reformer of the partitions era, Stanisław Staszic, also saw the Jews as a ubiquitous feature of the Polish landscape but regarded them as most unwelcome guests, describing them as "a plague who impoverish the villages and stink up the cities."[11]

Finally, the debates of the partitions era left as a legacy another metaphor for the Jewish presence in Poland, a metaphor that would prove extremely long-lasting: the Jews in Poland constituted a "state within a state" (*państwo w państwie*). As in revolutionary France, reformers in Poland regarded any survival of an autonomous Jewish community in a modern bureaucratic state as an anachronism. As time passed, the term became ever more ideologically and politically charged, symbolizing the alien nature of the large Jewish minority in Poland. In the eyes of their political adversaries, the Jews desired an intolerable continuation of their prepartition status into modern times. Even if the Jews would modernize and polonize, their enemies found reasons to state that the Jewish threat to Poland continued unabated, or even intensified.[12]

Both in the eyes of contemporaries and in many of the retrospective accounts by historians and others, the problem of Polish–Jewish relations in modern times represented a change from the premodern era, usually a change for the worse. The place of the Jews in the prepartition Polish Commonwealth was generally secure, though the Jews could be and were subject to extortionate taxes, occasional violence, and the caprice of kings, royal officials and noble landowners.[13] Beyond the practical day-to-day issues of economic or physical security, the Jews saw themselves as part of the fabric of Polish society, despite the obvious differences of language, culture, and religious faith. They were, in Gershon Hundert's phrase, both insular and integrated. They identified with the land of their birth, home to Jews for centuries, to the point that, in another felicitous formulation of Gershon Hundert, it was possible to talk of "Jews and other Poles":

> Among Jews in the Polish Commonwealth, there developed an undeniable Polish self-identification. The Jews' universe was larger than their local places of residence. ... There was also a sense of permanence and rootedness about the Polish Jewish

community itself; its members did not see themselves as mere sojourners. .... The perception of the Polish Jewish community as a permanent part of Polish society was shared by non-Jews in the commonwealth. Legislation ... forbade not only the establishment of new places of worship by non-Catholics but also the recruitment of foreign teachers and preachers. Public worship, sermons, and even singing at private services were prohibited. From all these laws, Jews were specifically and explicitly exempt. Jews were different; they were an integral part of the Polish social landscape.[14]

Being part of the fabric of Polish society did not mean, of course, that Jews were beloved or had no enemies. The set of social values adopted by the ruling Polish nobility had a rigid set of rules on which the system was based. This included definitions applied to the inferior ranks of society, in which the peasant was a boor (*cham*), the Christian burgher a petty bourgeois (*łyk*), and the Jew a scab (*parch*). Adapting the analysis of Aleksander Hertz of Polish society as a caste system, Rosa Lehmann notes that designating the Jew as a "scab" defined the place of the Jewish caste, fixing its position in the entire structure of society. Such a judgment may not have been flattering, but it was not necessarily a sign of hostility.[15]

For a significant sector of Polish Jewry, the relationships between Poles and Jews that had developed in the landed estates and private towns of the nobles continued in the smaller towns into the nineteenth and even the twentieth century, despite changes in the status of peasants and noble landlords. What had changed most significantly, however, was the attitude in Polish society to that relationship, which since the end of the eighteenth century had come under scrutiny as part of a wider rethinking of the fundamentals of Polish national existence. What had been an assumed fact of life, perhaps even a part of nature no less than the fields, forests, and the stars in the heavens for traditional Polish society, now was regarded as an issue for public debate and a social problem to be solved.

Assembling even a partial list of attempts to typify the Polish–Jewish relationship in modern times results in a long list of terms coined by politicians, literary figures, anthropologists, and, of course, historians. Common to almost all of them is the perception of the closeness of Poles and Jews, this despite the wide cultural and linguistic gap between them. Thus the noted Polish author Stefan Żeromski spoke of Polish Jews as "native foreigners," the historian Jacob Shatzky called them "different but kindred," and the anthropologist Jack Kugelmass termed them "native aliens."[16] In his discussion of the issue, Kugelmass cites the work of his predecessors on the Polish–Jewish relationship or on other such relationships of long standing between host societies and minorities in their midst, recalling, among others, the formulation of Max Weinreich that the Jews' condition was one of "distinctiveness but not separateness" (*bazunderkayt ober nit opgezunderkayt*) or "being distinguished but not being detached" (*oysgetaylkayt ober nit opgetaylkayt*). To characterize the relationship between Jews and Polish nobles, he also cites Pierre van den Berghe, to typify a relationship that, although based on caste structure and subordination, still contained what van den Berghe called in other contexts "distant intimacy."[17] This paradoxical relationship typified the everyday lives of Jews and Polish peasants into the twentieth century:

> Polish shtetls were usually made up of two poor, traditionalist, and fairly incongruous subcultures: Orthodox Jews and premodern peasants. Morally and spiritually, the two societies remained resolutely separate, by choice on both sides. Yet they lived in close physical proximity, and, willy-nilly, familiarity. In the shtetl, pluralism was experienced not as an ideology but as ordinary life. Jews trading horses in a small market town, speaking in haphazard Polish—that was the shtetl. Poles gradually

picking up a few words of Yiddish and bits of Jewish lore—that was also the shtetl. Jewish bands playing at Polish weddings and local aristocrats getting financial advice and loans from their Jewish stewards—all that went into the making of the distinctive, mulchy mix that was shtetl culture. This was where prejudices and bonds were most palpably enacted—where a Polish peasant might develop a genuine affection for his Jewish neighbor despite negative stereotypes and, conversely, where an act of unfairness or betrayal could be most wounding because it came from a familiar.[18]

The political and economic developments of the nineteenth century added further layers of meaning to the complex relationship between the two peoples. The hopes for forging a new, closer tie out of the common struggle for independence in the revolts against Russian and Austrian rule proved illusory and turned out to be, in the title of the important study by Magdalena Opalski and Israel Bartal, a "failed brotherhood."[19] Nevertheless, the cooperation of Poles and Jews in the insurrections would continue to serve as a symbol of what might have been, and it would often be cited by Jews to show their devotion to the Polish national cause.[20]

The massive industrial buildup of the cities of Congress Poland, particularly Warsaw and Łódź, and the growth of other major Polish cities in Galicia, created an entirely new arena for the interaction of Poles and Jews. While on the one hand this opened the way for the development of a growing class of polonized Jews who played major roles in the development of Polish industry and commerce, it ironically engendered a separation of Poles from the large mass of Jews in the crowded neighborhoods of the cities. Writing about interwar Warsaw, the Jewish journalist Bernard Singer made the same point:

The Jewish quarter in Warsaw occupied one-fifth of the city. It had 250,000 people, and thus one-third of the population. There were no drawbridges or guards on its borders; the ghetto had been abolished long before, but nevertheless there still existed an invisible wall that separated the quarter from the rest of the city. Many Polish children spoke about it with fear, and their elders often treated it with contempt.[21]

Of primary importance, for Jews in both the shtetls and the large cities, was not the presence or absence of physical proximity, but the rise of newer political parties and ideologies that questioned the very existence of Jews in Poland altogether. This was the period, in the words of the title of another recent volume, when nationalism learned to hate, and the Jews were one of the main targets of that hatred.[22] In Kugelmass's view, this was one of the ironic results of the modernization of the Polish lands:

> The most striking difference between the social integration of Jews in Poland in the modern and the premodern period is that in the latter, Jews had, in a sense, the run of the land, whereas, in the former, Jews were treated as marginal, alien; as an entirely redundant and dispensable element.[23]

This is far from the only instance where modernization and the modern bureaucratic national state have been a mixed blessing as far as Jews' status was concerned.

In the case of Poland, at least one historian, citing the analysis of Arthur Hertzberg on revolutionary France, saw in the beginnings of the Polish bourgeois democratic tradition the seeds of the organized political antisemitism of the late nineteenth and early twentieth centuries.[24]

The experiences of the interwar period and the Holocaust (on the latter, see below) further intensified the troubled yet special relationship between Poles and Jews. This is epitomized in the titles of a series of recent publications on the period, most notably *Together and Apart in Brzezany: Poles, Jews and Ukrainians, 1919– 1945*, by Shimon Redlich,[25] and *Symbiosis and Ambivalence: Poles and Jews in a Small Galician Town*, by Rosa Lehmann.[26] Lehmann notes the togetherness-apartness through the geographical boundaries still in the minds of her informants decades after there were no longer any Jews in the town: "The division between a Jewish center and a Polish periphery is clearly expressed by the common notion that *the Jews lived in town, whereas 'the people' (read: the Poles) lived on the outskirts*" [emphasis added].[27] My own short study of Jewish education in interwar Poland pointed out the paradoxical concurrent trends of Jewish national awakening along with acculturation to the Polish environment.[28] Finally, there is the book with seemingly the simplest title of all, but which has aroused much debate in Poland itself and around the world, and whose starting point is once again the everyday intimacy and distance between Poles and Jews in the small towns of Poland. I refer, of course, to Jan T. Gross's small book *Neighbors: The Destruction of the Jewish Community in Jedwabne, Poland.*[29] For our present discussion, it is worthwhile to call attention to the original Polish title of the work, *Sąsiedzi: historia zagłady żydowskiego miasteczka,*[30] that is, *Neighbors: The History of the Extermination of a Jewish Small Town*, which resonates even more strongly than the English title, in that it touches on the core issue of "territory" and identity. Were the hundreds of small towns scattered throughout Poland "Jewish" enclaves in "Poland," separate entities in some manner, or were they also part of the larger entity called Poland and part of its history and tradition? A similar, perhaps unconscious, struggle with questions of ultimate identity echoes from the title of Eva Hoffman's study of the small town of Brańsk entitled *Shtetl: The Life and Death of a Small Town and the World of Polish Jews*[31] (the subtitle of the British edition was the less charged *Shtetl: the History of a Small Town and an Extinguished World*).[32]

II. Poles and Jews: What Was So Special?

As we have seen so far, the search for the elusive term to typify Polish–Jewish relations has gone on for over two centuries. The sensitivity of the issue seems, if anything, to have intensified with the passing of time and continues unabated even after the virtual disappearance of the Jewish community in Poland (though it has, in recent years, undergone a small revival). Only the tortuous relations between Jews and Germans, and between Jews and Germany, approaches the complexity of the ties between Jews and Poles. In the region of Eastern Europe, however, there seems to be no relationship so complex or so troubled. With the obvious exception of the Holocaust period, the relations between Jews and Lithuanians, between Jews and Latvians, or between Jews and Estonians do not seem as burdened as those between Jews and Poles. The two relationships which come the nearest to that between Poles and Jews in a complex dance of closeness, occasional flirtation, along with mutual recrimination and ongoing grudges over wrongs perceived, are those between Jews and Russians and between Jews and Ukrainians. In the former case, however, we are dealing with a relationship, as alluded to in the title of the recent book by Aleksander Solzhenitsyn, of "two centuries together."[33] In a formulation reminiscent of some of our terms for Polish–Jewish relations over the centuries, Richard Pipes entitled his review of Solzhenitsyn's work "Alone Together."[34] The intensive relations between Jews and ethnic Russians are of much more recent vintage and date essentially only to the period after the Bolshevik Revolution, when for the first time large numbers of Jews left the multiethnic former Pale of Settlement, where ethnic Russians were a small minority, and moved to the Russian Republic, especially to the two main cities of Moscow and Leningrad.[35] Regarding Jewish–Ukrainian relations, issues for debate and sensitivity hark back to the seventeenth century and the Chmielnicki revolt and carry through to the pogroms of the late nineteenth and early twentieth centuries, occasional talk of cooperation between the two peoples (including only partially realized plans for significant Jewish national autonomous rights in a short-lived Ukrainian state after World War I), massive slaughter of Jews during the 1919–21 Russian civil war, and issues of Ukrainian collaboration with the Nazis during the Holocaust. Yet to this day, the dialogue/debate between Jews and Ukrainians does not approach the level of discussion of the dialogue, in whatever form, between Jews and Poles. Part of the reason, certainly, is that no independent Ukrainian state existed until very recently. Before that time, the historical narrative of the relations between the two peoples has been, in the subtitle of a book from the 1980s, "Two Solitudes,"[36] and any new historical narrative is only in the formative stages.

Thus the Polish–Jewish relationship stands out as an especially sensitive one. What makes the relationship so special? The major reasons have already been alluded to in the course of our discussion, but now I would like to set them out in a more orderly fashion. My claim is that four leading factors are involved, which for the sake of our analysis here I will designate by the following terms: beginnings, end, numbers, and disappointments.

Beginnings

The fabled "thousand years of Polish Jewry," even if it may fall shy of that round number by a century or so, still attests to the long-standing connection of Jews with Poland. That long period, coupled with the legends of the beginnings of Jewish settlement there, whether historically accurate or not, had a profound influence on Jewish self-perception. The long era of Polish Jewish history witnessed a variety of attitudes on the part of the various sectors of Polish Christian society to the Jews in their midst, with oftentimes significant differences between ideologies and everyday reality. The overall impression, though, was that Jews were basically secure in Poland, enjoying a status that they had in no other country in Christian Europe, to the point that Poland was called in numerous contemporaneous sources *paradisus judaeorum*, paradise of the Jews.[37] This legacy had its effects into the modern era, when a perceived worsening of Jewish status occurred and the old station of the Jews in premodern Poland lasted as a symbol of what had been, but also what should be in the present and the future, as far as many Jews were concerned.

END

Any discussion of Polish–Jewish relations must, at one point or another, touch on the painful topic of the extermination of some three million Polish Jews, 90 percent of the prewar Jewish population, acts of extermination perpetrated by the Germans, but on Polish soil. The recent controversy over the events in Jedwabne and a few other towns in eastern Poland, where local Poles killed their Jewish neighbors with little or no help from the Germans, brought to the public's consciousness those cases where Poles were not just unwilling (or willing) bystanders in the murder of Jews, but also to some degree participants and beneficiaries of the removal of Jews from the map of Poland. For historians, the Holocaust presents a direct challenge to writing any history of modern Polish Jewry. Are we able to deal with Polish–Jewish relations over the last two centuries without engaging in "backshadowing," seeing the twisted path to Auschwitz and Treblinka in every dark alley of Polish–Jewish tension in "normal," pre-Holocaust times? The recent book by Redlich demonstrates that it can be done. While giving ample coverage to interethnic strife and violence in his hometown during those years and with no trace of irony, Redlich entitles his chapter on the interwar years "the good years."[38] Without ignoring or downplaying the connections between the events of World War II and previous eras, we have the obligation to understand those periods on their own terms.

The Jedwabne debate,[39] like the previous public controversy in Poland engendered more than a decade earlier by Jan Błoński's article "The Poor Poles look at the Ghetto,"[40] opened old wounds and may have untold effects on the overall historical narrative. The ultimate question raised in both documents from the time and later historical narratives is whether the Jewish and Polish stories, no less than the differing fates of the two communities under Nazi rule, were really one story or not. In a novel published before the Jedwabne controversy began, but which contains a Jedwabne-like story at its core, Charles T. Powers puts a speech on this issue in the mouth of the local priest addressing his flock:

> For too many of us, what happened to those people was not a sorrow. It was a horror, but not a sorrow. Do you see that there is a difference? The horror was not traceable to us. We were not to blame for it, and so, in a way, we could accept it. ... What we are really saying is these ten percent were something else to us—among us but not of us. We say, Yes, three million of them died on our soil, but then another three million of ours died, too, in the same horror. And so we have not a likeness, but a distinction. Our own, and them. Ours are Poles. They are Jews. ... Their loss is canceled out by our own loss, as we canceled out their footprints, boarded over the marks of their devotion (to a God that gave rise to our own), leaving their burned temple unmarked by even a single stone. ... We left their graves untended, forgotten, while looking after those of "our own." We walk the streets they helped make, enter buildings where they once conducted their business, under roofs where their families once slept in peace.[41]

Two peoples lived in such close proximity, but there seemed to be an unbridgeable gap between them that the Holocaust left as an unanswered dilemma:

We needed some way to comprehend why we bought from them and sold to them, why they could read and Poles couldn't, why they could do business and Poles tilled the fields. Maybe in the cities, where there were no fields, it was different. Maybe they had a different way to explain why Catholic Poles were Poles (and not just Catholics), while Jewish Poles were always just Jews. The Poles and the Not-Poles. Now it was the Poles and the Not-Here, the Poles and the Vanished.[42]

While I speak here of the end of Polish Jewish history with the Holocaust, we should be careful here not to consider Polish Jewish history to be a closed book after 1945. New chapters were added to the troubled relationship of Poles and Jews, with new opportunities and new disappointments. With the opening of archives and the increased distance from the events of the postwar period, there is much room for reconsideration of later periods as well. This includes the immediate postwar years and the hopes for a reconstituted Polish Jewry, but also the later decades of Communist rule, including the painful chapter of the "anti-Zionist" purges of 1968.

NUMBERS

The demographic weight of Polish Jewry from the eighteenth century onward looms large both in the context of world Jewry and within Polish society. In no other country did Jews reach the proportion of the population that they did in Poland. On several occasions, Gershon Hundert has made the point that the historical experience of this, the largest Jewish community, must be taken into account when we speak of the modernization process of Jewry.[43] But it was not just their absolute numbers in Poland, but their demographic distribution in the country that had a direct effect on Jews' self-perception in the hundreds of small and mid-sized towns where a majority or close to it of the inhabitants were

Jews. Many of the Polish town dwellers, though residing in the town, actually made their livelihood from agricultural pursuits located outside the towns. For Polish Jews, talk of the "Jewish street" reflected a daily reality where Jews would live and work in a space inhabited mostly by other Jews, and such talk contributed to a self-perception of Jews that was not one of being a minority.[44] This perception would continue into the twentieth century, as exemplified by the memoirs of the noted Yiddish socialist essayist Hayyim Zhitlovsky. Speaking of his younger years in the Belorussian region, he wrote of the Jews' "rule":

> I spent my childhood years in purely Jewish surroundings. Had I not known that, in theory, we Jews lived in Diaspora, and had I been asked to formulate my life's experiences as they appeared at first glance, I would then have had a right to say that I live in a Jewish country—so little was the exile felt in our region of Belorussia in the fifteen years between 1865 and the end of the 1870s. ... Such a purely Jewish life, where the Russian elements played not a shred of a role, one could without exaggeration—proclaim the illusion that it was not we who lived in exile among the "Russians," but perhaps the exact opposite: that the "Russians," to the extent we had dealings with them, lived in exile among us, in our own Jewish land.[45]

Zhitlovsky notes further on that his family's Gentile serving girl was fully "assimilated" to the "ruling people" to the point that she spoke a fine idiomatic Yiddish. With the exception of the maid's linguistic skills (which in earlier eras seem to have been much rarer), and taking into account the ideological nationalist bent of his remarks, Zhitlovsky's characterization of his hometown could well have fit the self-perception of the Jews in hundreds of towns of Poland from the eighteenth century until well into the twentieth. This "Jewish land" may have been an imagined community, but it helped forge the consciousness of generations of Jews until the Holocaust put an end to the Jewish towns and quarters of Poland.

DISAPPOINTMENTS

In the past two centuries, both Jews and Poles have expressed disappointment with the current state of their relationship. Each side articulated a vision of Poland that did not match that of the other. Jews harked back to the old Polish Commonwealth and the relatively good status they enjoyed in late medieval and early modern times. The one-time "paradise for Jews," in which Jews had been an integral part, had been replaced by a vision of Poland in which Jews would have no place. At the end of the nineteenth century, Jews felt that the old Polish heritage of tolerance had been replaced, with the rise of political parties of the right, by an ideology of exclusivist nationalism. Many Poles expressed their exasperation with a group that had lived in Poland for so long yet had not acculturated. Echoing the old charge of Jews forming a state within a state, in 1889 Klemens Junosza (Szaniawski) articulated a feeling of frustration, although he was resigned to make the best of the situation:

> Thus we do not have the slightest possibility of parting with the Jews. The tempests of history drove them here, and the lack of foresight of our legislators created of them a nation in a nation and safeguarded their separateness until the present day. ... And since we cannot part from them, we must live alongside them and exert every effort to make that life as bearable as possible for both parties.[46]

In the tense years of the interwar period, even some Jews felt uncomfortable about this state of affairs. Thus in a fictionalized memoir, Isaac Bashevis Singer puts these words in the mouth of his lover Sheba Leah:

The situation of the Jews here is desperate. The Poles have had quite enough of us and I can see their side of it. We've lived here for eight hundred years and have remained strangers. Their God is not our God, their history is not our history. Most of us can't even speak a proper Polish. One time I watched a huge Zionist demonstration with blue and white flags and Stars of David and the whole falderal. They stopped the trolleys and shouted slogans in Hebrew or Yiddish. The Gentiles stood around staring as if at a freak show.[47]

Both groups engaged in denial of one sort or another: the Jews, unwilling to acknowledge the strong nationalist feelings of a people that had recovered its independence in a strongly nationalist era and offering an alternative vision of a multiethnic Poland where minorities could play an important role; the Poles, unwilling to acknowledge the multiethnic and multinational nature on the ground of the reborn Polish state, in which more than a third of the population were from minorities.

With all the disappointments and ambivalent feelings, with the heavy burden of the horrific events of the twentieth century, there still remains the perception that Jews and Poles had a special closeness, still unbroken. In a trip to Poland to discover her family's Polish roots, the Australian journalist Diane Armstrong recounts a dialogue with Jacek, her Polish guide:

At the end of a heavy day, at a Silesian restaurant, Jacek and I toss back several glasses of vodka the Polish way—without stopping for breath. Soon he's regaling us with tales of Polish gallantry and patriotism and quoting ballads about spilt blood and scarlet poppies. Now that I've downed three glasses of vodka, I feel relaxed enough to acknowledge that he's as obsessed with Polish heroism as I am with Jewish persecution. "You might feel angry about the past," he says suddenly, "but you're still closely linked to Poland. You can't deny that there's a bond. It's like a family feud: you feel anger because you also feel love."[48]

III. Poles and Jews:
Toward a Historical Framework

How best to portray this ambivalent, oftentimes tortuous relationship? We need a historical framework that expresses the special place of Jews within Poland: their centrality to many economic, social, and even some cultural processes in the development of modern Poland. In this context, I find myself returning time and time again to some sort of fabric metaphor, where Jews are part of the warp and woof of Polish society, where the separate threads are woven in and around each other, where different hues are preserved when one looks up close. The historian/observer, however, standing at a distance, contemplates a wider reality in which Jews were an integral part of Poland. In putting together the historical narrative of Polish Jewry, drawing back has an additional advantage, in that it enables us to look at an entire complex of relationships – Jews as part of Poland, as part of European Jewry, as part of modern Jewry as a whole. This combined model appears to be the best framework for telling the story of Polish Jewry, placing that large community in the larger context of modern Jewry, as well as portraying them as part of the fabric of Polish society.

Placing Polish Jewry within a general European context would seem to be self-evident, but until very recent times the models of emancipation revolved around the experience of Central and West European Jewish communities. To do justice to the topic of emancipation itself, it behooves us to take into account the experience of this largest of Jewish communities in Europe. David Sorkin has done just that in his article entitled "Port Jews and the Three Regions of Emancipation."[49] Seeing Polish Jewry in this larger context sometimes entails a search for analogous rather than identical processes undergone by that community. Gershon Hundert has suggested just such a perspective in his examination of the modernization of Polish Jews. Looking for the causes of the breakdown of communal authority in Poland, he found it in a form slightly different from what we encounter in Central Europe, reflecting the different nature of Poland itself:

> Magnate authority, then, contributed significantly to the disintegration of the Jewish corporation and therefore to the freeing of the Jewish individual in a way that is somewhat analogous to what happened to the Jews in the Absolutist states of Central Europe.[50]

In general, the writing of modern Jewish history has benefited from the breaking down of the strong east–west dichotomy in the narrative, as evidenced, among others, by the work of Jonathan Frankel and Eli Lederhendler.[51] Seen thus, the experience of Polish Jewry is just one more example of the "modernization project of Jewry," to use Shulamit Volkov's felicitous adaptation of a phrase coined by Jurgen Habermas. Volkov herself has demonstrated that with all the genuine local differences in each country of Europe, the questions asked by Jews confronting modernity were essentially the same questions, and many of their answers were the same as well.[52]

Where do Poland and Polish Jewry fit on the continuum of those phenomena that together we call the emancipation process of the Jews—as compared to, for example, the Jews of France? In both Poland and France, we are witness to a small, if influential, group of modernizing Jews; where the small number of wealthy Jewish merchants of Warsaw and a few intellectuals who took part in the public polemics surrounding the Four-Year Sejm parallel the relatively small number of Jews in Paris, the Sefardim of the south of France, and the few Maskilim in Alsace. There existed a small modernist minority in both countries, who would have symbolic value way beyond their numbers, whether it be those Jews who joined the Revolutionary Guard in Paris or the fighters in the unit of Berek Joselewicz who participated in the defense of Warsaw in the Kościuszko uprising. Looking at the processes in both countries reminds us that the parallels work in both directions. In France, as in Poland, there existed a large traditional element, and the modernization process of Jewry took long decades.[53] At the end of the eighteenth century and the beginning of the nineteenth, complaints about the harmful effects of Jewish moneylenders and peddlers in Alsace reached tones no less cataclysmic than the public debate on Jewish innkeepers in Poland in those same years.

Of course, the essential difference remained: in France, despite reservations about the Jews, whether out of a desire for consistency or out of opposition to leaving any remainders of the former corporate state, legal emancipation was granted to the Jews. Even if that status was temporarily undermined by Napoleonic decrees, with the restoration of the monarchy Jews continued to enjoy equal rights. In Poland, on the other hand, the leaders of society were unwilling to deal with basic structural problems of the state, and those reforms that were proposed were partial at best. Furthermore, in Poland there lacked, in Gershon Hundert's phrase, a "beckoning bourgeoisie" that existed in other countries.[54] Through the interwar period, the Polish middle class would, like the pre-Partition burgher class, regard the Jews as enemies and competitors rather than potential allies in the struggle against entrenched interests. The Jewish question was but one of many unanswered questions at the time of the demise of the Polish State, if one of the most intractable. Legal emancipation, when granted in the nineteenth century, would not change the problematic status of Jews in Poland.

This brings us to the second part of the framework, that is, the special nature of Poland, Polish Jewry, and the Polish–Jewish relationship in modern times. The "Jewish question" in Poland was born simultaneously with the demise of the Polish State, to the point that it cannot be separated from the "Polish question" in both senses of the phrase—the ongoing striving for the restoration of Polish statehood, and the simultaneous debate over the very definition of Polish nationhood. The Jews were viewed as part of the problem of remaking Poland, whether the burgeoning cities or the rural villages and former noble estates. For the contending forces in the Polish political arena, the Jews could be either part of the problem, the eternal scapegoats for the misdeeds of others or for faults in the system; or, occasionally, part of a proposed solution. Whatever the case, Jews were simply too numerous to ignore, and their importance in the country's overall economy made them impossible to overlook in any plans to reshape modern Poland. That same demographic weight had implications for the larger picture of world Jewry, since changes of even a few percentage points in the economic, cultural, or social structure of Polish Jewry translated in absolute terms to tens or even hundreds of thousands, the size of entire communities in other lands.

One could argue that in objective terms the Jews' place was much more central in Poland than in Germany, hence the urgency and the vehemence of the arguments surrounding the "Jewish question." On this score we note that Jews formed part of the warp and woof of life in the new Poland no less than in the old. The expression of this fact could come in high culture, high finance, in petty commerce, or in folk culture. Part of the landscape in the old Poland, Jews by conscious identification at various levels of intensity cast their lot with the newly emerging Poland. In the organism of the Polish village, Jews played the role of connective tissue, not only through commerce between village and town, but also as the bearers of news of the outside world.[55] The itinerant Jewish book peddler always had a few Polish books in his stock, and the Jewish musicians, so much a fixture of the rural landscape, preserved and transmitted the heritage of Polish folk music.[57] In the mid nineteenth century, the Polish book trade in general was completely in the hands of Jews.[57]

For Polish peasants, the Jews were part of the background of their lives, no less than the phenomena of nature. As one analysis put it:

If a nineteenth-century peasant were ever asked if Jews should assimilate or emigrate, he would have been surprised and unable to respond. For him they were part of the unchangeable landscape as God had first created it. A demand to change the existing order would have seemed revolutionary to him. The Jews with their side-curls and kaftans were part of life as created by God, testimony to the Passion of Christ, something threatening and strange, but necessary and unalterable.[58]

More modern secularized approaches to the future of Poland took all these elements of the former seemingly divine order of the universe, including the troublesome Jewish minority, and opened them up to renewed scrutiny, with recommendations for drastic solutions.

In portraying modern Polish Jewry, we must also emphasize those elements of the Polish Jewish community that made its path to modernity special. We have already mentioned the importance of numbers and how this affected both the Jews' self-perception and the way that others regarded them. An additional factor that must be taken into account is the Hasidic movement, which encompassed much of both rural and urban Polish Jewry. In Hasidic areas, there was greater success in delaying the entry of modern education and modern societal notions. Hasidic leaders and the Hasidic community provided a solidarity that reached beyond the boundaries of a single community. In that sense it was a modern, voluntary community that gave direction to perplexed individuals confronting modernity.[59] For historians of Polish Jewry and modern Jewry as a whole, it is worthwhile remembering that one of the possible options for the Jew facing modernity was rejection or resistance.

The large size of Polish Jewry and the territorial vastness of Poland makes the task of adequately portraying that community all the more difficult for another reason. When we speak of the Polish–Jewish relationship, in reality we refer to a complex series of relationships between "the Jews" and the various classes and estates of Poland, relationships that changed over time. Beyond that, we must take into account the often-significant local and regional variations on this theme: the thousands of relationships forged between individual Poles and "their" Jew or Jews. In those relationships, Jews and Poles influenced each other in myriad ways. Moshe Rosman has recently urged a rethinking of the very concept of "influence" when speaking of the cultural relations between Jews and their neighbors, at least as far as premodern times are concerned:

> Jews are a multi-colored strand within the European cultural polysystem. Perhaps the metaphor for Jewish–Gentile cultural interaction should not be that of two magnetic fields coming into contact with each other and influencing or distorting each other; but rather a metaphor of recombinant DNA that originates from a widely available repertoire of building blocks, but achieves a unique character by virtue of the combining process. Put differently, it is a kind of intertextuality that defines Jewish culture, not the degree of purity of the origins of the "texts" themselves. Authenticity is dependent not on pedigree but on practice.[60]

Rosman bids us to distance ourselves from former simplistic models of influence and the influenced. In modern times, if we extend his metaphor, we encounter the additional complication of attempts at "genetic manipulation," both on the part of Poles and on the part of the Jews themselves.

As in other countries, so in Poland, not everything in life was dictated by political or ideological considerations. The situation in reality could be better or worse as far as Jews were concerned. The pressures of everyday needs could overcome ideological scruples if exigencies were great enough. We should also remember that relations between Jews and Poles could and did stem from "normal" human needs and animosities between neighbors without ethnic or religious labels attached.

In numerous forms and variations, the "Jewish question" has existed in Poland throughout the last two centuries. The basic question remained: Could the Jews become part of the Polish nation? To a large extent the question remains open to this day, when Polish Jewry is but a small remnant of the millions who lived in that country on the eve of World War II. The discussion that began as Poland struggled for its survival and failed continues today in the post-Communist period, when the Jewish issue can still, for better or worse, call up the rhetoric of the recent, more distant, and centuries-old past. New voices, however, sought a more "normal" view of the Jewish presence in Poland and, through it, another view of Poland itself. Michael Steinlauf quotes in this context a declaration by an independent Polish group from the 1980s, commemorating the fortieth anniversary of the sealing of the ghettos:

> Let us look at Polish Jews. And not only to honor their martyrdom, but because, though Jews themselves are no longer among us, the subject of Jews constitutes a problem for us. The problem is the very language with which we speak of them— that very THEY. But they were a part of US, of our society (regardless of their degree of integration into that society). We say that they lived on our lands. But those lands were also their lands. They lived, quite simply, at home [żyli po prostu u siebie].

As a new historical narrative takes shape in Poland, as Polish historians increase their interest and participation in writing the history of Polish Jewry, there is a need for a historical framework of the type that we have outlined here. As we have seen, the Polish–Jewish relationship was beyond all else a unique mix of intimacy and alienation on an everyday basis that defies simple definition or characterization. Polish Jews adjusted to Poland at their own pace and in their own way, not always (in fact, most of the time definitely not) in accord with the expectations of surrounding Polish society. Their story is an integral part of the Polish story, and part of the story of European and modern Jewry as a whole. Only in this complex of contexts can the story be adequately told. We must bring out the ideals and ideologies enunciated by the participants in this relationship, the ways one group viewed the other, as well as the situation on the ground. The challenge to historians is to carry out this task of synthesis.

Notes

1. Raphael Mahler, *A History of Modern Jewry, 1780–1815* (London: Vallentine Mitchell, 1971), 279.
2. Michael Steinlauf, *Bondage to the Dead: Poland and the Memory of the Holocaust* (Syracuse: Syracuse University Press, 1997), 5.
3. Gershon Hundert, "Some Basic Characteristics of the Jewish Experience in Poland," *Polin* 1 (1986): 33.
4. Norman Davies, *God's Playground: A History of Poland* (Oxford: Oxford University Press, 1981), 1:532.
5. Ibid., 2:13–14.
6. Andrzej Sulima Kamiński, *Historia rzeczpospolita wielu narodów 1505–1795* (Lublin: Instytut Europy Środkowo Wschodniej, 2000).
7. Jerzy Tomaszewski, *Rzeczpospolita wielu narodów* (Warsaw: Czytelnik, 1985).
8. Alina Cała, The Question of the Assimilation of Jews in the Polish Kingdom (1864–1897): An Interpretive Essay," *Polin* 1 (1986): 147.
9. Artur Eisenbach, Jerzy Michalski, Emanuel Rostworowski, and Janusz Woliński, eds., *Materiały do Dziejów Sejmu Czteroletniego* (Wrocław: Ossolineum-PAN, 1969), 6:86.
10. Ibid., 6:83, cited in Jacob Goldberg, "Poles and Jews in the 17th and 18th Centuries: Rejection or Acceptance?" *Jahrbücher für Geschichte Osteuropas* 2, no. 2 (1974): 280.
11. Harold Segel, *Stranger in Our Midst: Images of the Jew in Polish Literature* (Ithaca: Cornell University Press, 1996), 38–39.

12. On the debate surrounding notions of autonomy in the interwar period, see Jolanta Żyndul, *Państwo w Państwie? Autonomia narodowo-kulturalna w Europie Środkowowschodniej w XX wieku* (Warsaw: Wydawnictwo "DiG", 2000).

13. See Moshe (Murray) Rosman, "Jewish Perceptions of Insecurity and Powerlessness in 16th–18th Century Poland," *Polin* 1 (1986): 19–27.

14. Gershon Hundert, *The Jews in a Polish Private Town: The Case of Opatów in the Eighteenth Century* (Baltimore: The Johns Hopkins University Press, 1992), 36–37.

15. Rosa Lehmann, *Symbiosis and Ambivalence: Poles and Jews in a Small Galician Town* (New York: Berghahn Books, 2001), 13.

16. Żeromski and Shatzky cited in Alexander Hertz, *The Jews in Polish Culture* (Evanston: Northwestern University Press, 1988), 6, 31; Jack Kugelmass, "Native Aliens: The Jews of Poland as a Middleman Minority" (Ph.D. diss., New School for Social Research, 1980).

17. Kugelmass, "Native Aliens," 71, 74, 193.

18. Eva Hoffman, *Shtetl: the History of a Small Town and an Extinguished World* (London: Vintage, 1997), 12–13.

19. Magdalena Opalski and Israel Bartal, *Poles and Jews: A Failed Brotherhood* (Hanover, N.H.: Brandeis University Press, 1992).

20. See Gershon Bacon, "Messianists, Pragmatists and Patriots: Orthodox Jews and the Modern Polish State (Some Preliminary Observations)," in *Netiot le-David: Jubilee Volume for David Weiss Halivni*, ed. Yaakov Elman, Ephraim Halivni, and Zvi Arieh Steinfeld (Jerusalem: Orhot, 2004), 15–30.

21. Bernard Singer, *Moje Nalewki* (Warsaw: Czytelnik, 1959), 7, cited in Stephen Corrsin, "Political and Social Change in Warsaw from the January 1863 Insurrection to the First World War: Polish Politics and the Jewish Question" (Ph.D. diss., University of Michigan, 1981), 117.

22. See Brian Porter, *When Nationalism Began to Hate: Imagining Modern Politics in Nineteenth-Century Poland* (New York: Oxford University Press, 2000), 37–42, 227–32.

23. Kugelmass, "Native Aliens," 61.

24. Daniel Stone, "Jews and the Urban Question in Late Eighteenth Century Poland," *Slavic Review* 50 (1991): 540–41.

25. Bloomington: Indiana University Press, 2002.

26. New York: Berghahn Books, 2001.

27. Ibid., 45.

28. Gershon Bacon, "National Revival, Ongoing Acculturation: Jewish Education in Interwar Poland," *Simon-Dubnow-Institute Yearbook* 1 (2002): 71–92.

29. Princeton: Princeton University Press, 2001.
30. Sejny: Fundacja Pogranicze, 2000.
31. Boston: Houghton Mifflin, 1997.
32. See n. 18 above.
33. Aleksandr Solzhenitsyn, *Dvesti let vmeste (1795–1995)* (Moscow: Ruskii Put', 2001). Selection in English published under the title "Two Hundred Years Together" in *Common Knowledge* 9 (2003): 204–27. See also John Klier's review, "No Prize for History," *History Today*, November 2002, 60–61.
34. *The New Republic Online*, November 21, 2002, https://ssl.tnr.com/p/doc-sub.mhtml?i=20021125&s=pipes112502.
35. I thank Prof. David Fishman for this insight.
36. *Jewish Ukrainian Relations: Two Solitudes*, ed. Howard Aster and Peter J. Potichnyj (Oakville, Ont.: Mosaic Press, 1983).
37. See Gershon Hundert, "Poland: Paradisus Judaeorum," *Journal of Jewish Studies* 48, no. 2 (1997): 335–48.
38. Redlich, *Together and Apart in Brzezany*, 34–70.
39. On that debate, see the important collection of materials assembled in *The Neighbors Respond: the Controversy over the Jedwabne Massacre in Poland*, ed. Antony Polonsky and Joanna B. Michlic (Princeton: Princeton University Press, 2004).
40. "The Poor Poles look at the Ghetto," published originally in *Tygodnik Powszechny* and in English translation in *Polin* 2 (1987): 321–26. See also the illuminating discussion by Antony Polonsky, "Polish–Jewish Relations and the Holocaust," *Polin* 4 (1989): 226–42.
41. Charles T. Powers, *In the Memory of the Forest* (New York: Scribner's, 1997), 372.
42. Ibid., 312.
43. Gershon Hundert, *Jews in Poland-Lithuania in the Eighteenth Century: A Genealogy of Modernity* (Berkeley and Los Angeles: University of California Press, 2004), 1.
44. Hundert, "Poland: Paradisus Judaeorum," 338–39.
45. Hayyim Zhitlovsky, געקליבענע ווערק (Selected works), ed. Yudl Mark (New York: CYCO, 1955), 321–22. Cited in slightly different form by Jeffrey Shandler, "Imagining Yiddishland: Language, Place and Memory," *History and Memory: Studies in Representations of the Past*, 15 (Spring/Summer 2003), 129.
46. *Our Jews in Towns and Villages* (1889), cited in Segel, *Stranger in Our Midst*, 187.

47. Isaac Bashevis Singer, *Love and Exile: The Early Years; A Memoir* (New York: Farrar, Straus and Giroux, 1984), 125.

48. Diane Armstrong, *Mosaic: A Chronicle of Five Generations* (New York: Random House, 1998), 519–20.

49. *Jewish Culture and History* 4 (Winter 2001): 31–46.

50. Hundert, "Some Basic Characteristics," 32.

51. Jonathan Frankel, "Assimilation and Jews in Nineteenth-Century Europe: Towards a New Historiography?" in *Assimilation and Community: the Jews in Nineteenth-Century Europe*, ed. Jonathan Frankel and Steven J. Zipperstein (Cambridge: Cambridge University Press, 1992), 1–37; Eli Lederhendler, "Modernity without Emancipation or Assimilation? The Case of Russian Jewry," ibid., 324–43.

52. Shulamit Volkov, מפעל המודרניות של יהודי אירופה: פיצול ואחידות (The modernity project of European Jewry: Division and uniformity), in הערכה מחדש הציונות והחזרה להיסטוריה: (Zionism and the return to history: A reappraisal), ed. S. N. Eisenstadt and Moshe Lissak (Jerusalem: Yad Yitzhak Ben-Zvi, 1999), 285–86.

53. See Jay R. Berkovitz, "The French Revolution and the Jews: Assessing the Cultural Impact," *AJS Review* 20, no. 1 (1995): 25–86.

54. Hundert, *Jews in Poland-Lithuania*, 239.

55. Beatrice Baskerville, *The Polish Jew: His Social and Economic Value* (New York: Macmillan, 1906), 72.

56. Hertz, *Jews in Polish Culture*, 230.

57. אנציקלופדיה של גלויות, (Encyclopedia of the Diaspora), ed. Hayyim Barlas, Arieh Tartakower, and Dov Sadan (Jerusalem, 1973), vol. 12 [3rd vol. on Warsaw], cols. 46–47.

58. Cała, "Question of the Assimilation," 148.

59. Hundert, *Jews in Poland-Lithuania*, 210.

60. Moshe Rosman, "A Prolegomenon to the Study of Jewish Cultural History," *Jewish Studies Internet Journal* 1 (2002): 118–19, http://www.biu.ac.il/JS/JSIJ/1-2002/Rosman.doc.

61. Steinlauf, *Bondage to the Dead*, 98–99.

INTERPRETIVE CONTEST

Art Critics and Jewish Historians

PAULA E. HYMAN

Jewish historians have only recently turned to the visual arts as potential sources for understanding the modern Jewish experience. To be sure, Jewish museums, an outgrowth of individual collections and communal efforts, have existed for about a century, displaying both ritual objects and the works of Jewish artists. The Jewish involvement with art, however, did not engage the attention of historians, or scholars of art, despite the prominence in the modern period of Jews as art patrons, consumers, and merchandisers. As Kalman Bland has argued in his recent definitive study, the concept of Jewish aniconism, the claim that there was no Jewish art, was a distinctly modern construction, but the challenges to that claim that were mounted throughout the nineteenth and twentieth centuries, perhaps in voices that were too muted, did not have much of a response.[1] By the last quarter of the twentieth century, historians no longer shared the popular misconception that Jews shied away from art, but visual culture was at best a marginal "text."

Historians and art historians, trained as they were in different disciplines, did not intrude very often on each other's turf. The key exception was, and continues to be, Richard Cohen, Professor of Jewish History at the Hebrew University, a student of art history and a collaborator in the design of exhibitions and their catalogs at the Jewish Museum in New York.[2] Cohen edited an important symposium, "Art and Its Uses," for volume 6 of *Studies in Contemporary Jewry*, which appeared in 1990. He then produced a pioneering volume entitled *Jewish Icons: Art and Society in Modern Europe*. That splendid and ambitious book investigated the representation of Jews in art as well as the development of Jews as artists, patrons, and collectors over the course of four centuries, from the sixteenth through the early twentieth, all from the perspective of a social and cultural historian of European Jewry.[3] He was animated by the question of what the involvement of Jews with the visual arts revealed about their status and self-understanding in the societies in which they lived. And he stated a premise that has animated the work of historians and art historians who consider visual imagery a critical aspect of Jewish as well as general culture: "Visual material, or its appropriation, has been overly compartmentalized and totally separated from research into Jewish society."[4]

In the decade and a half that has passed, historians and art historians alike have become fascinated with exploring the linkages between art and the Jewish experience, but they have done so in very different fashion. Indeed, historians and art historians display little appreciation for each other's work. Art historians view the efforts of historians in the domain of visual culture as hopelessly naïve and unconcerned with artists' technique and subterranean messages. Jewish historians find some of their colleagues in the field of art history to be guilty of over-interpretation, finding signs of Jewishness, or of antisemitism, wherever they look.

Some years before Cohen's work appeared, in the early 1980s, Ismar Schorsch had turned his attention to a nineteenth-century German-Jewish artist named Moritz Oppenheim, whose oeuvre was being displayed at the Israel Museum. Schorsch had already established his reputation as a historian of the *Wissenschaft des Judentums* movement, the attempt by German-Jewish intellectuals of the nineteenth century to use the tools of secular Western scholarship, and especially historiography and philology, to understand the religious culture of the Jews and to make it intelligible, and meaningful, for their contemporaries. He had also explored the complex consciousness and the self-defense strategies of the leadership of German Jewry in the four decades preceding World War I.[5]

In "Art as Social History: Moritz Oppenheim and the German Jewish Vision of Emancipation," which appeared in the 1983 catalog of the Israel Museum, Schorsch addressed a cultural phenomenon, the popularity among German Jews in the mid and late nineteenth century of Oppenheim's paintings, just as *Wissenschaft* scholarship reached its peak with the publication of the work of the historian Heinrich Graetz.[6] Oppenheim was most famous for his scenes of Jewish family life: he both presented traditional Jewish observance in a favorable, and somewhat nostalgic, light; and visually depicted, also with sympathy, some of the changes that acculturation had introduced among German Jews. Those genre pictures were reproduced for popular consumption in portfolio and book form, in several editions extending into the twentieth century.

Schorsch's article demonstrated his recognition that texts take many forms, and that visual texts were a valuable resource for all who sought to understand how Jews responded to new conditions and presented themselves both to themselves and to a broader public. The article complemented his other pioneering studies of acculturated German Jews; once again, those Jews who were often dismissed as lacking in Jewish pride and consciousness because they were defined as "assimilated" manifested an interest and pride in their Jewish identity. As a historian, Schorsch was interested primarily in the reception of Oppenheim's paintings by German Jews, rather than in the technique of Oppenheim the artist. He contextualized the art, analyzing it far more for what it revealed of German-Jewish society than for its style. Art served as another mode to explore Jewish consciousness, especially the complex attitude of Jews to their origins and the traditional practices many had abandoned.

It is not surprising, given their radically different disciplinary training, that historians and art historians, both of whom address the nature and meanings of the visual representation of Jews in general and Jewish culture and the role of Jewishness in a Jewish artist's oeuvre, approach their topics differently. What is of interest is that, despite their disparate perspectives and the mutual disdain they often express for each other's work, they are dependent on each other to answer the questions they pose.

Art historians turn to the writings of Jewish historians to understand the social and cultural background of Jewish artists, to explore the experience of Jews at different times and in different places in the modern world, and to learn about antisemitism. Historians provide the social and cultural data for understanding the societies in which Jewish artists lived. From their citations, it is clear that art historians are aware of the developments in Jewish historical literature of the modern period and in approaches to the study of modern Jewish identities. Their own work seems to display a parallel move to the "New Historicism" that has emerged in literary criticism in the last few years. That is, they are far more attuned to the importance of the social and ethnic elements in an artist's identity and their impact on his work than was the case in earlier decades. But adopting the "New Historicism" does not mean becoming a historian. Art historians make use of historical scholarship for their own ends, just as historians who interpret visual texts use them for goals quite different from those of their art historian colleagues.

Jewish historians, influenced by cultural studies, have been willing to accept new sources as relevant for the writing of history. Fiction, memoirs, television, and film, as well as material artifacts and artistic productions, are all now seen as potential keys for understanding both individual and collective consciousness. Historians recognize that cultural representations and self-representations are critical for reconstructing the texture of a period and for addressing questions of identity. Art historians' interpretations have been important in teaching historians what to look for in visual texts. But written documents still take pride of place in historical analysis. Moreover, the discourse of literary and art criticism, with its emphasis on subjectivity and postmodernist theory, has been resisted by all but the youngest generation of historians. Moreover, even scholars who define themselves as cultural historians rarely include the analysis of visual art in the collective volumes they edit.[7]

The disciplinary boundaries are evident in any examination of the texts collected together that display the collaboration of historians and art historians. Richard Cohen, quite accurately, called the 1990 symposium on Jewish art that he organized for *Studies in Contemporary Jewry* "the first serious attempt of any Jewish historical journal to address the visual sphere and reflect on its implications for the study of Jewish history."[8] Although four historians and four art historians participated in the collection of articles, there was little dialogue among them. The scholars retained the disciplinary perspective in which they were trained and did not use the opportunity of the symposium to question the boundaries of their respective fields. Historians tended to raise social and historical issues for consideration, while art historians were concerned with questions of style. Michael Berkowitz, for example, a social and cultural historian, focused on popular culture that often escaped the investigation of art historians, in this case primarily the myriad visually adorned postcards produced by the Zionist movement to win adherents to its cause.[9] As an art historian, Milly Heyd interrogated the work and the biography of the Zionist artist Reuven Rubin to identify the sources of his primitivist style. Although she pointed largely to artistic influences, she also demonstrated how the particular form of primitivism he chose met the needs of an artist creating in a new nationalistic society.[10]

The implications of the *Studies in Contemporary Jewry* symposium far exceeded the findings of the eight articles themselves. Their publication signaled that there were at least a few historians and art historians who recognized that it was valuable to publish their work together, even if there were no obvious conversations among their articles. Although few of the contributions to the journal were truly multidisciplinary, they demonstrated an overlap in concerns. Both historians and art historians sought to explore the connection between the Jewishness of an artist and his cultural production; both were concerned with how Jewishness was displayed culturally and received by different audiences.

Cohen's symposium was important in self-consciously bringing together historians and specialists in art, but museum exhibitions were central in asserting the need for providing a historical context for art and artifacts when they were on display. Beginning in the 1980s, the Jewish Museum in New York took the lead in mounting exhibitions in which history and art walked hand in hand, or perhaps side by side. Its 1987–88 exhibit, The Dreyfus Affair: Art, Truth, and Justice, included four historians among the eight interpreters of the display in the catalog.[11] The exhibit itself provided much textual background on the history of the Affair. Similarly, a major exhibit on Jewish culture in Central Europe from the seventeenth to the early nineteenth century, From the Court Jews to the Rothschilds, 1600–1800, placed its cultural artifacts within the historical context of the emergence of a wealthy elite of Jewish merchant financiers who were involved in the transfer of luxury goods and in serving the princes of their time. Historians provided the socioeconomic and cultural background for the exhibit in its printed catalog.[12] Both of those exhibitions foregrounded a historical phenomenon or event; but even exhibitions that were less ostensibly historical, such as the 1989–90 Gardens and Ghettos: The Art of Jewish Life in Italy, were multidisciplinary in their approach to the ritual objects on display.[13] Museums seemed increasingly to recognize that art and ritual objects had to be historicized. Although historically focused exhibits by no means displaced those that focused on aesthetic concerns, the Jewish Museum also designed a series of exhibits that depended on the dialogue of historians and art historians: the

1999 *Berlin Metropolis: Jews and the New Culture, 1890–1918*, for example, successfully drew on art historians, specialists in literature, and historians to illuminate a particular moment in which Jews played a prominent role in the creation of an urban and urbane high culture.[14]

Despite the new endorsement by historians of the importance of visual texts for their understanding of Jewish consciousness and culture, art historians and specialists in literature seem to have been more open to incorporating aspects of social history into their interpretation of artistic production than historians were in introducing discussions of Jews and visual culture into analyses of the construction of modern Jewish identities. Art historians have initiated the multidisciplinary, and comparative, explorations of Jewish visual representation and self-representation, such as the 1995 volume *The Jew in the Text: Modernity and the Construction of Identity.*[15] Despite its historical interest, the volume includes no historians. Its contributors, though, demonstrated the existence of a wide range of specialists in literature, popular visual culture, cultural criticism, and psychology for whom postmodernist theory and criticism are central. Presumably the editors of the volume assumed that all historians—except cultural historians—would shy away from theory, as indeed many did in 1995.

Art historians have also been willing to exploit their interpretive license. Thus, starting from the premise that representations construct and do not merely reflect meaning, Irit Rogoff pointed out that this approach allows the art historian to analyze paintings' political implications that are not, in her words, "directly self-evident in the iconography of the work."[16] In her study of the German-Jewish artist Max Liebermann, Rogoff explored the tensions of his triple identification as Prussian, Jewish, and bourgeois as they played themselves out in the public sphere. Indeed, she asserted that when combined with his position as a wealthy bourgeois, his Jewishness led to his self-perception as both insider and outsider. And, as insider/outsider he was able to find a powerful voice for social criticism. Nicholas Mirzoeff's study of Camille Pissarro similarly, though in more overtly postmodernist language, asserts that Pissarro's experience as a Sephardi Jew from the Caribbean island of St. Thomas shaped his painting there and in France.[17] As a Jew in the Caribbean he was Other, outside the class of white plantation owners and sympathetic to native blacks; as a Caribbean Jew in a European Diaspora he confronted a double Otherness. Mirzoeff suggests that although Pissarro never included overtly Jewish subjects in his paintings, the connotations of Jewishness were apparent in his depictions of the situations of blacks in the Caribbean and in his late stylistic development, which Mirzoeff reads as a response to the rampant French anti-semitism that he felt even in the company of artists. Referring to one early painting of two black women in conversation that he interprets as requiring an ethical decision on the part of viewers as to the meaning of what they are seeing, Mirzoeff notes, "It is this focus on the necessity of ethics that gives a consistently Jewish dimension to Pissarro's work."[18]

In the past decade and a half, then, art historians have begun to explore the implications of Jewishness in the creativity of some Jewish artists. Catherine Soussloff injected another dimension to the general theme. Building on the importance of the subjectivity of cultural producers, including scholars, she raised the issue of the prominence of Jews for much of the past century in the creation of the modern discipline of art history itself in the United States and in the English-speaking world more broadly. In "Introducing Jewish Identity to Art History," the essay that serves as the introduction to *Jewish Identity in Modern Art History*,[19] a volume of articles she organized and published in 1999, she argues that despite the considerable influence of Jews in the field of art history, "We find in the discipline a critical situation in which significant topics in the history of art that related to Jewishness have been elided or are absent."[20] The reluctance of scholars of art history to explore the impact of Jewishness, she continues, means that a key piece in

the creation of art historical discourse is missing from consideration. Soussloff emphasizes that "historiographic resistance adheres
to the topic of Jewish identity more than to other aspects of visual
studies."[21] Soussloff's call to investigate the linkage between biography and cultural product or interpretive stance seems to have
resonated with art historians, who have continued to explore these
issues, as she has acknowledged in a subsequent article. It is less
compelling for Jewish historians, however, because the latter
require substantially more, and more direct, evidence of the connection between biographical data and cultural creativity or social
activity. Jewish historians take note of the social role of Jews as
critics and patrons of art, and they value the research of their colleagues in art history who contribute to their knowledge of the
dimensions of this aspect of the modern Jewish experience; they
welcome such articles in *Jewish Identity in Modern Art History* as
Robin Reisenfeld's on the role of German-Jewish émigrés in the
popularization of German expressionist art in America, in which
she suggests that their act of collecting and preserving such art was
a way to identify with, and disseminate, a form of German culture
that was despised by the Nazis.[22]

Aside from Cohen's reading of the work of Jewish artists in
Jewish Icons, only one Jewish historian, Ezra Mendelsohn, who
collaborated closely with Cohen on the "Art and its Uses" symposium, has attempted to link the Jewishness of a particular artist
with his artistic creation. Drawing on his considerable skills as a
historian, he has written the biography of a modern Jewish artist,
Maurycy Gottlieb, a young Galician Jew who died in 1879 when
he was only twenty-three. Mendelsohn interpreted Gottlieb's
artistic project as, in the words of his title, *Painting a People*.[23] In
Mendelsohn's view, Gottlieb saw as his mission the depiction of
the spiritual life of the Jews in a period of social and cultural transition. Although he valued acculturation to Polish life and sought
the reconciliation of Poles and Jews, he still portrayed Jews as
somewhat foreign, accepting and valuing their difference. Men-

delsohn attributes his popularity among Poles as well as Jews to their contrasting readings of his work: for Poles he was a memorialist of a Jewish past that he recognized had been superseded; to Jews he was proof of the cultural creativity sparked by the promise of political emancipation and enlightened education. Mendelsohn thus uses Gottlieb's artistic creations as evidence of the complex identity of young Jews who had broken with traditional Judaism and yet were unwilling to repudiate it, and of the conflicting views of Poles and Jews regarding the place of Jews within Polish society. In exploring the Jewish as well as Polish reception of Gottlieb's paintings, and in bringing a particular sensitivity to place and social context to his interpretation of one Jewish artist, Mendelsohn displayed the historian's social and cultural sensibility to Jewish art and the Jewish artist that characterized Schorsch's discussion of Oppenheim.

The working definition of Jewish art that Cohen first presented in the introduction to his symposium, that "Jewish art is art which reflects the Jewish experience,"[24] is one with which Jewish historians feel comfortable. Art historians, in contrast, have been prepared to expand "the Jewish experience" to include psychological and cultural attributes that may be connected to Jewishness or not. They closely examine the visual texts of Jewish artists and the depiction of Jewish subjects to draw far-reaching conclusions about the Jewishness of Jewish artists and the cultural representations of Jews. That is, they have interpreted "reflecting the Jewish experience" so flexibly that they feel empowered to derive some aspect of the Jewish experience from visual texts even if it is not explicitly depicted. Some art historians have been far bolder than historians in foregrounding antisemitic elements in the visual representation of Jews, particularly in modern portraits.

That boldness was displayed in *The Jew in the Text*. Its editors, Linda Nochlin and Tamar Garb, along with their multidisciplinary group of contributors, saw as their mission the exploration of the ways in which Jews were perceived and represented in modern culture, and the theorization of the construction of identity to the Jewish case. By looking at the Jew who emerges from texts, both literary and visual, the volume demonstrated the power of images to create a cultural reality. The contributors paid close attention to the issue of gender, showing how the construction of the seductive Jewess, "la belle juive," simultaneously denied a voice to Jewish women as they were and also diminished the masculinity of Jewish men. Sander Gilman's article, "Salome, Syphilis, Sarah Bernhardt, and the 'Modern Jewess,' "[25] linked the seductive Jewess, embodied in the actress Sarah Bernhardt's most famous role, Salome, with disease. Also examining Sarah Bernhardt as the representative Jewish female at the fin de siècle, Carol Ockman focused on the visual images of her that proliferated. Although resisting the notion that Jewishness is ever perceptible, Ockman asserted that in the nineteenth century Jewishness was always known and commented on. Indeed, in the case of Bernhardt and her predecessor Rachel (Félix), both of French birth, the association of actress and prostitute simply contributed to the disparagement of Jewish women as oversexed and unrespectable and also ironically to their being considered unwomanly or even mannish. Ockman resolved these contradictory images of Bernhardt by noting they "were informed, at least in part, by the subtext of womanhood gone awry, either in the sexual arena through promiscuity or in the creative one through mannishness."[26] Bernhardt's visual image also displayed antisemitic elements--capitalist rapaciousness, orientalism, and racialized facial characteristics, that is, a prominent nose. Both Gilman and Ockman illuminated the gendered nature of nineteenth century antisemitism, especially its fear of women's power, and demonstrated its dissemination through caricature.

The visual stereotyping of Jews has long been noted. Eduard Fuchs's *Die Juden in der Karikatur*, a massive collection, was published as early as 1921.[27] But art historians have recently taken a new look at the development of caricatured Jewishness in the modern period. Here interest in the Dreyfus Affair, and the use by both sides of the struggle of mechanical reproductions of posters and lithographs, led to the revisiting of the forms of antisemitic imagery, which was energized and popularized during the cause célèbre. The Jewish Museum's 1987 exhibit on art and the Dreyfus Affair dramatically displayed the visceral appeal of antisemitic visual images and influenced the reassessment of the significance of antisemitism during the Affair.[28]

Art historians have not always succeeded, however, in determining the meaning of antisemitic stereotypes. In her article on Toulouse-Lautrec's 1890s illustrations of Jewish subjects for two writers who were, or later became, supporters of Dreyfus during the Affair, Gale Murray points out that stereotypical elements in the illustrations strike contemporary viewers as "implicitly or overtly anti-Semitic."[29] However, Murray must mobilize nonvisual historical data, about Lautrec and the two authors whose work he was illustrating, Victor Joze and Georges Clemenceau, before coming to the conclusion that antisemitism was endemic to French society and culture in the 1890s and that it was hard to distinguish between the true believers and those who simply indulged in popular stereotypes. Those like Clemenceau who ascribed negative characteristics to Jews could, at the same time, support the Dreyfusard position and recognize the danger of political antisemitism. As for Lautrec, the verdict regarding the level of his antipathy to Jews is still out.

If Murray cannot fully interpret the blatant antisemitic stereotypes of French artistic representations of Jews, other art historians are discovering antisemitism in portraits that appear neutral or ambiguous. They are looking closely at artistic representations of Jews that are not blatantly antisemitic to alert the untrained eye of the audience to the negative messages that may be encoded in ostensibly sympathetic portraits. Here the expertise of the art historian is mobilized to destabilize our assumptions about how portraits convey meaning and to alert us to the ambivalence of the image of the Jew even in ostensibly neutral representation.

The outstanding example of such work is Kathleen Adler's examination of John Singer Sargent's fin-de-siècle portraits of the Wertheimer family, a prosperous and acculturated middle-class British family of German origin, whose paterfamilias was an art dealer.[30] Sargent painted twelve portraits of Asher Wertheimer, his wife, and various of his ten children between 1898 and 1908. The multiple commissions and the Wertheimers' personal responses and friendship with the artist indicate familial satisfaction with the paintings. Moreover, Sargent had many Jews among his clients and claimed to "prefer painting Jewish women because they had 'more life and movement' than English women."[31] Yet by comparing these portraits with non-ethnic British subjects whom Sargent painted, Adler discerns in them elements of caricature, stereotyping, and orientalism.

Adler finds that Sargent's portraits of Asher Wertheimer and of his daughters Ena, Betty, and Almina display antisemitic tropes. Asher Wertheimer's physical characteristics—"hooded eyes, large nose, and above all fleshy lips"—identify him as a Jew while the cigar that he smokes "indicates not only wealth but also vulgarity and sexuality." Moreover, in Adler's reading, his sideward gaze suggests the furtiveness that non-Jewish Europeans attributed to Jewish behavior.[32] Ena and Betty, painted together and separately, violated the conventions of demure daughters of respectable wealthy families. Their revealing dresses suggested that they were sexually bold, and, Adler concludes, Sargent depicted them as embodying "the fantasy of the sexual Jewess." A portrait of Ena in male military dress challenges sexual boundaries and "explodes the conventional expectations of society portraiture." Finally, the youngest daughter, Almina, is painted in Oriental costume, pointing to the foreignness of Jewish women and playing with the stereotype of the exotic and beautiful Jewess.[33]

Adler's readings of the portraits compel us to see them in the context of popular stereotypes of Jews within European culture at the time and of the conventions of Orientalism. However, her readings may represent a late twentieth-century imposition of antisemitism on the portraits that was invisible not only to the sitters and the painter but also to most contemporary critics. To be sure, contemporaries were well aware that these sitters were Jews, and some observers made clear their distaste for Jews. However, not only did the Wertheimers take pleasure in the paintings, but commentators at the time noted that Sargent preferred Jews to aristocratic sitters. Moreover, the *London Times* critic described Sargent's Ena as a "dashing young lady in fancy costume" and the double portrait of the sisters as "instinct with life."[34] The young women apparently chose what costume they would wear, and one, Hylda, decided, against convention, to be painted in two portraits wearing her eyeglasses.

Similarly, in her consideration of Ingres's 1848 portrait of the Baronne Betty de Rothschild, Carol Ockman compares her portrait with those he painted of Christian aristocratic women and concludes that the shape of the eyebrows, her crossed knees, and her pose, leaning forward, serve as visual indicators of the subject's ethnicity (or better yet, race).[35] Ockman concludes that the contemporary remarks about the portrait by a visitor to Ingres's studio who mentioned the Baronne's "two large eyebrows à l'orientale" along with her liveliness "conjure up the world of the harem rather than that of the well-bred Western home." The commentator's "orientalist vocabulary" indicates that he viewed the portrait as a representation of "the quintessential Jewish woman," "a distinctly different type" than Ingres's other female sitters.[36]

Adler and Ockman are both aware that the signs of difference attributed to Jews, and especially Jewish women, are not unambiguously antisemitic. Adler notes that "Sargent's knowledge of and affection for the ... [Wertheimers] works [*sic*] to counter the stereotype, and his sitters ... appear to have delighted in the opportunity to strike exaggerated poses and wear fancy dress."[37]

Ockman acknowledges that portraits of the Baronne, even Ingres's, present her as "the model upper class wife prescribed by the clichés of respectability."[38] Yet both insist that the portraits contribute to the stereotyping of Jews, particularly Jewish women, as Other.

Adler's and Ockman's articles demonstrate a perspective characteristic of both art history and literary criticism. Perhaps because they have far more freedom in interpreting their texts than do historians, art historians and literary critics are likely to present arguments that historians would reject as highly speculative and unsupported by evidence. Although Adler and Ockman assert a controversial reading of the portraits they have studied, they are careful to qualify their boldest assertions. Their interpretations are plausible, if not fully convincing.

That is not the case with Mason Klein, the curator of the 2004 Jewish Museum exhibition on the Italian Jewish painter Amedeo Modigliani, who was part of the Montmartre art scene in Paris. Although there is no concern in his paintings with explicitly Jewish subjects, Klein sees Modigliani's Jewishness as the central feature not only of his identity but also of his art. Klein states in his introductory essay in the exhibit catalog that Modigliani's "art and portraiture originate (in part) in the religious, in his Sephardic understanding of the indelibility of his Jewishness, regardless of acculturation."[39] In fact, he delineates a specific form of Jewish identity that Modigliani expressed—that of an Italian Sephardic Jew who grew up in Livorno under the influence of the Sephardic Jewish humanism of Rabbi Eli Benamozegh. Most important, Klein asserts that "Modigliani's reemergence as a Jew is a medium that helps provide him with a formidable conceptual means of expressing new relations between the visible and the invisible. ... It also clarifies the increased attenuation of his abstract style" during and after World War I. He concludes his assessment of Modigliani the painter with the avowal that his "idealism is born of his Livornese heritage and based on a cultural pluralism and religious humanism eloquently espoused among nineteenth-century intellectual circles of Sephardic Livornese.[40] It is intriguing to consider that the particular Jewish culture of Modigliani provides the key for interpreting his paintings, and Klein's claims necessitate an intense look at his art as well as at the work of other Jewish artists. Historians, however, who have long wrestled with the meanings of Jewishness in the modern period, as overt markers of Jewishness have disappeared and as the participation of Jews in a defined religious and educational culture has eroded, need a clearer definition of the different manifestations of modern Jewishness and a precise delineation of how they are reflected in cultural products. It is difficult to contend with an argument whose evidence is amorphous.

In my reading of the interpretation of the representation of Jews and Jewishness in modern art, the most compelling analysis consists of the work of Catherine Soussloff. As already mentioned, in her book, *Jewish Identity in Modern Art History*, she noted the dominant role of Jewish critics in the shaping of the discipline of art history in the twentieth century and pointed to the reticence of practitioners in the field to analyze that role and its significance. She brought together a diverse group of articles that illustrated her themes, analyzing the discipline of art history and its theoretical perspectives, exploring classic art critics like Meyer Schapiro and Aby Warburg, and interpreting Jewishness in the work of artists as diverse as Maurycy Gottlieb and Judy Chicago.

Soussloff demonstrates in her analysis of Oskar Kokoschka's 1909 double portrait of Hans Tietze and Erica Tietze-Conrat, husband and wife and both Viennese art historians of Jewish origin who subsequently had to flee from the Nazis, that the art historian's sensitivity to subjectivity—in this case the subjectivity of the sitters portrayed—has much to offer when combined with social and cultural context. While acknowledging the lack of visual markers of Jewishness in portraits of assimilated European Jews and of Jews in colonial America, she is quick to assert the importance of the place of display of the portrait and the audience who viewed it. When displayed in a home setting, portraits of Jews expressed the Jewishness of their sitters as a normal aspect of who they were. The denial of overt signs of Jewishness becomes apparent when portraits are decontextualized, either by removal from their domestic environment or through analysis only in the context of genre, and pertinent information about the sitters' background is left unstated. Such happened to the Tietze–Tietze-Conrat double portrait when the Tietzes had to sell it to a museum to sustain themselves as refugees in America, and it was viewed simply as a fine example of the early Kokoschka. Yet, as Kokoschka himself wrote of his pre–World War I portraits, painted when his work was perceived as particularly controversial, "Most of my sitters were Jews. They felt less secure than the rest of the Viennese Establishment, and were consequently more open to the new. ... Their own historical experience had taught them to be more perceptive in their political and artistic judgments."[41] Soussloff concludes, contrary to the conventional history of por-traiture, that the sitter in a portrait is "a subject incapable of com-plete representation." The viewer, therefore, bears the responsibility of being attentive and contributing, through his or her own interpretation, to the sitter's subjectivity.[42] The back-ground information that historians provide thus becomes crucial to the viewer's gaze.

Jewish historians, however, are consulted far too rarely in the recent literature on the construction of identities in the modern world. The various scholars interested in theorizing the construc-tion of modern identities have produced volumes such as the mul-tidisciplinary comparative study entitled *Diaspora and Visual Culture: Representing Africans and Jews.*[43] Despite the fact that his-torians have much to say about the different forms of Jewish diasporic experience, their perspectives are absent.

The interpretive strategies of Jewish historians and art histori-ans are likely to remain distinct. If Jewish historians approach Jewish art from the perspective of the title of Schorsch's collection of essays, "from text to context," with the understanding of the social and historical context as the goal of the enterprise, art historians, with some exceptions, choose the interpretive strategy of "from context to text," with the understanding of the visual text itself as the focus of the project. What has changed in the past two decades is that historians and art historians, along with scholars of literature, are far more aware of each others' work; they recognize their mutual dependence on the insights that are generated outside their own discipline. The social, cultural, and historical data provided by the historian are vital to the meaning of the visual text, and the art historian's way of looking uncovers signs that historians need to understand if they are concerned with Jews' identities and their representations.

Notes

1. Kalman P. Bland, *The Artless Jew: Medieval and Modern Affirmations of the Visual* (Princeton: Princeton University Press, 2000), 1–12.
2. See, for example, *From Court Jews to the Rothschilds: Art, Patronage, and Power, 1600–1800*, ed. Richard I. Cohen and Vivian Mann (New York: The Jewish Museum, 1996).
3. *Studies in Contemporary Jewry*, ed. Ezra Mendelsohn, vol. 6, *Art and its Uses: The Visual Image and Modern Jewish Society*, ed. Richard I Cohen (New York: Oxford University Press, 1990); Richard I. Cohen, *Jewish Icons: Art and Society in Modern Europe* (Berkeley and Los Angeles: University of California Press, 1998).
4. Cohen, *Jewish Icons*, 9.
5. See, in particular, Ismar Schorsch, *Jewish Reactions to German Anti-Semitism, 1870–1914* (New York: Columbia University Press, 1972), and the lengthy introduction to his edited volume of the essays of Heinrich Graetz, *The Structure of Jewish History and Other Essays* (New York: JTS, 1976).
6. See the catalog of the exhibit, *Moritz Oppenheim: The First Jewish Painter* (Jerusalem: Israel Museum, 1983). The essay was reprinted in Ismar Schorsch, *From Text to Context: The Turn to History in Modern Judaism*

(Hanover, N.H.: University Press of New England for Brandeis University Press, 1994), 93–117.

7. Both *Modernity, Culture and 'the Jew'*, ed. Bryan Cheyette and Laura Marcus (Stanford: Stanford University Press, 1998), and *Insider/Outsider: American Jews and Multiculturalism*, ed. David Biale, Michael Galchinsky, and Susannah Heschel (Berkeley and Los Angeles: University of California Press, 1998), two multidisciplinary books that reflect new perspectives on Jewish culture and the relations of Jews to multiculturalism, ignore the visual dimension of Jewish culture and the representation of Jews in the visual arts. In the magisterial *Cultures of the Jews*, ed. David Biale (New York: Schocken, 2002), Richard I. Cohen, whose influence is discussed below, did integrate visual elements, including synagogue architecture, into his chapter on modern Jewish culture. See his "Urban Visibility and Biblical Visions: Jewish Culture in Western and Central Eurorpe in the Modern Age," 731–96.

8. Richard I. Cohen, "An Introductory Essay: Viewing the Past," in Cohen, *Art and Its Uses*, 8.

9. Michael Berkowitz, "Art in Zionist Popular Culture and Jewish National Self-Consciousness, 1897–1914," ibid., 9–42.

10. Milly Heyd, "The Uses of Primitivism: Reuven Rubin in Palestine," ibid., 43–70.

11. *The Dreyfus Affair: Art, Truth, and Justice*, ed. Norman Kleeblatt (Berkeley and Los Angeles: University of California Press,1987).

12. Cohen and Mann, *From Court Jews to the Rothschilds*.

13. *Gardens and Ghettos: The Art of Jewish Life in Italy*, ed. Vivian B. Mann (Berkeley and Los Angeles: University of California Press, 1989).

14. In addition to *Berlin Metropolis: Jews and the New Culture, 1890–1918*, ed. Emily Bilski (Berkeley and Los Angeles: University of California Press, 1999), the Jewish Museum has sponsored these recent historically based catalogues: *Russian Jewish Artists in a Century of Change, 1890–1990*, ed. Susan Tumarkin Goodman (Munich: Prestel, 1995); Daniel J. Schroeter et al., *Morocco: Jews and Art in a Muslim Land*, ed. Vivian B. Mann (London: Merrell, in association with the Jewish Museum, 2000); *The Emergence of Jewish Artists in Nineteenth-Century Europe*, ed. Susan T. Goodman (London: Merrell, in association with the Jewish Museum, 2001); *Entertaining America: Jews, Movies, and Broadcasting*, ed. J. Hoberman and Jeffrey Shandler (Princeton: Princeton University Press; New York: The Jewish Museum, 2003).

15. Ed. Linda Nochlin and Tamar Garb (London: Thames and Hudson, 1995).

16. Irit Rogoff, "Max Liebermann and the Painting of the Public Sphere," in Cohen, *Art and its Uses*, 91–110, at p. 91.

17. Nicholas Mirzoeff, "Pissarro's Passage: The Sensation of Caribbean Jewishness in Diaspora," in *Diaspora and Visual Culture: Representing Africans and Jews*, ed. Nicholas Mirzoeff (London: Routledge, 2000), 57–75.

18. Ibid., 63.

19. Ed. Catherine M. Soussloff (Berkeley and Los Angeles: University of California Press, 1999), 1–13.

20. Ibid., 2.

21. Ibid., 7.

22. Robin Reisenfeld, "Collecting and Collective Memory: German Expressionist Art and Modern Jewish Identity," in Soussloff, *Jewish Identity*, 114–34.

23. Ezra Mendelsohn, *Painting a People: Maurycy Gottlieb and Jewish Art* (Hanover, N.H.: University Press of New England for Brandeis University Press, 2002).

24. Cohen, "Introductory Essay," 6, citing *The Seminar on Jewish Art: January–September 1984: Proceedings*, ed. Vivian Mann and Gordon Tucker (New York, Jewish Theological Seminary and The Jewish Museum, 1985), 10.

25. In Nochlin and Garb, *Jew in the Text*, 97–120.

26. Carol Ockman, "When Is a Jewish Star Just a Star? Interpreting Images of Sarah Bernhardt," in Nochlin and Garb, *Jew in the Text*, 121–39.

27. Eduard Fuchs, *Die Juden in der Karikatur: Ein Beitrag zur Kulturgeschichte* (Munich: A. Langen, 1921).

28. Kleeblatt, *The Dreyfus Affair*. See also Paula E. Hyman, "The Visual and the Historical," *Journal of Modern History* 41 (1989): 88–109 and Richard I. Cohen, "The Visual Dreyfus Affair—A New Text? On the Dreyfus Affair Exhibition at The Jewish Museum, New York," in Cohen, Art *and its Uses*, 71–90.

29. Gale B. Murray, "Toulouse-Lautrec's Illustrations for Victor Joze and Georges Clemenceau and their Relationship to French Anti-Semitism of the 1890's," in Nochlin and Garb, *Jew in the Text*, 57–82.

30. Kathleen Adler, "John Singer Sargent's Portraits of the Wertheimer Family, in Nochlin and Garb, *Jew in the Text*, 83–96. The article was reprinted in *John Singer Sargent: Portraits of the Wertheimer Family*, ed. Norman Kleeblatt (New York: The Jewish Museum, 1999).

31. Ibid., 87.

32. Ibid., 89.

33. Ibid. 91, 92.

34. Ibid.
35. Carol Ockman, "Two Large Eyebrows à l'Orientale: Ethnic Stereotyping in Ingres's *Baronne de Rothschild*," *Art History* 14 (1991): 521–39.
36. Ibid., 523.
37. Adler, "Sargent's Portraits," 94.
38. Ockman, "Two Large Eyebrows," 525.
39. Mason Klein, "Modigliani against the Grain, " in *Modigliani: Beyond the Myth* (New York: The Jewish Museum; New Haven: Yale University Press, 2004), 1-23, at p. 1.
40. Ibid., 22, 23.
41. Catherine M. Soussloff, "Portraiture and Assimilation in Vienna: The Case of Hans Tietze and Erica Tietze-Conrat," in *Diasporas and Exiles: Varieties of Jewish Identity*, ed. Harvey Wettstein (Berkeley and Los Angeles: University of California Press, 2002), 113–49, at 126-27.
42. Ibid., 144–45.
43. Mirzoeff, *Diaspora and Visual Culture*.

Defining the Postmodern Period in Jewish History

MOSHE ROSMAN

I. Definitions of Jewish Modernity

When is Modern?

In Professor Schorsch's graduate history seminars at the Jewish Theological Seminary of America in the 1970s (in which I was a student), a recurrent theme of discussion was historical periodization, especially the question of the beginning of the modern period of Jewish history. This was also true at the Hebrew University's Jewish History department, and I daresay wherever Jewish history was taught, in those years. A standard exercise or examination question, then, was to summarize and critique the various periodization schemes or dates for the starting point of Jewish modernity that had been proposed from Isaac Marcus Jost through Shmuel Ettinger.

By highlighting this subject, Schorsch and other teachers aimed to demonstrate that periodization, in addition to its function of defining conventional starting points and caesuras for historical narratives, is a coarse form of historical interpretation. In picking a certain date or event as indicative of the beginning or end of a historical period, each scholar telegraphed what to his[1] mind was the most significant feature, theme, or process of that period. Periodization is an attempt to capture in shorthand the "essential nature" of a historical era. For example, Heinrich Graetz

My thanks go to David Biale, Kimmy Caplan, Elliott Horowitz, David Resnick, Shmuel Feiner and Shira Wolosky who read drafts of this essay and made many valuable bibliographic, stylistic and substantive suggestions.

believed in the primacy of ideas in history and that the primary idea animating Jewish modernity was Enlightenment. He also possessed a "penchant for reducing historical trends and intellectual currents to personalities." Thus he dated the Jewish modern period from the late eighteenth century rise of the figure who symbolized Jewish Enlightenment and who, to Graetz's mind, did the most to shape the essence of Jewish modernity, Moses Mendelssohn.[2] Simon Dubnov thought that the key transformation of the Jews in their attempts to modernize and live in the modern world was political integration into their countries of residence and accompanying loss of communal autonomy. He therefore dated Jewish modernity from the French Revolution and specifically from the granting of citizenship to the Jews, that is, political emancipation.[3]

Another lesson that discussions and exercises on periodization imparted was the elusiveness of the "noble dream" of objectivity. It seemed that one could discover in scholars' definitions of periods—and especially of the modern period in which they themselves lived—their constructions of their own historical experience and their own general metahistories.[4] The Zionist Ben-Zion Dinur consciously attempted to create a usable historical past for what was in his day the new Israeli society and polity, and he was active in building many important Israeli institutions. He believed that the entire thrust of Jewish modernity was to bring the modern Jewish state into existence. For him, then, the rise of an apparently organized, protonationalist movement with Eretz Israel as its objective (the migration of hundreds of people to Eretz Israel with Judah Hasid in 1700) marked the starting point of Jewish modernity.[5] Salo W. Baron was an immigrant to America and one of the founders of university-style Jewish studies in the United States. He placed the start of Jewish modernity in the seventeenth century when, by his lights, the migratory, demographic, socioeconomic, cultural, and technological trends that eventuated in American society—and led to the formation of

American Jewry—had their genesis.[6] Examples such as these suggest that there are certainly no objective criteria for determining the boundaries of periods. All is interpretation based on personal convictions that can be argued but never proven.

While never completely abandoned, by the end of the 1970s the consideration of periodization greatly declined in intensity. The students had learned their lessons well. As they became teachers, they saw limited value in investing much time in an irresolvable debate, especially as the interpretive nature and necessary subjectivity of historiography were rapidly becoming commonplace notions.[7]

They also learned that history is made up of particulars that do not necessarily form a pattern. As Eli Lederhendler, another of Schorsch's students, has observed, "The trim lines of a unified history are undermined by the 'heaviness' and sheer volume of discrete data."[8]

With the fashioning of "postmodern consciousness," there also came a retreat from the attempt to essentialize. Internalizing our teachers' criticisms of the classic historians, my generation of historians has exhibited profound skepticism toward grand schemes and broad generalizations. As Lederhendler wrote in comparing the approach of Dubnov (and Dinur, Scholem, Graetz, Kaufmann, and Baron) with that of contemporary scholars,

> History on a grand scale is a model we no longer *choose*. To write a comprehensive history requires the selection of a red thread of continuity, an organizing principle or theme. It means going back to the notion of an "essence" of the Jewish experience that can be distilled from the whole. It means imposing a superstructure based on that essence, choosing a defining characteristic of each successive "stage" of development. It is, in fact, a teleological model that departs only slightly from traditional, Judaic theological models, and goes back to the old Hegelian triad. ... Most of us today have far less trust in abso-

lutes, in overarching schemes, in eternal essences. When we try to do justice to the multiplicity and uneven nature of the Jewish experience, we unavoidably take a different path from that of the great masters.[9]

Consequently, Jewish historical writing by my peers has tended to take the form of narrowly focused studies analyzing individual subjects,[10] rather than sweeping surveys that attempt to make sense of the big picture. Having ourselves unmasked the unhistorical foundations of the grand structures conceived of by the greatest lights of our profession, as well as having been humbled by the amount of information that is there for the processing, we are chary to venture pronouncements on subjects outside of our immediate specialty, to risk reduction and oversimplification by widening our scope, to pretend to an understanding that explains more than those details we have thoroughly mastered. We willingly submit to the tyranny of specialization, trusting it might protect us from the types of critiques which we ourselves were so effectively taught to formulate. (Of course, given the easily demonstrated connection of any historical interpretation—no matter how constricted the scope—to some metahistory, this is no more than a vain hope.)[11]

MEYER ENDS THE DISCUSSION

In my opinion, a major facilitator of the decline of the preoccupation with periodization was an article written in 1975 by Michael A. Meyer, "Where Does the Modern Period of Jewish History Begin?"[12] Meyer summarized the theories of the beginning of Jewish modernity as proposed by Jost, Zunz, Krochmal, Graetz, Dubnov, Scholem, Ettinger, and Baron (mentioning in passing Martin Philippson, Raphael Mahler, Azriel Shohet, Jacob Toury, and Jacob Katz). He then explicated the problems with the entire endeavor.

First came the fact that periodization was rooted in metahistory (although that word had not yet gained currency): "All-embracing schemes of periodization, nearly everyone now acknowledges, rest more on stipulation than on inference." Such stipulation was based on "religious and ideological motivations" and "shifting conceptions of Jewish existence" (329–30).* Scholars' differing metahistories ("from Marxist economic determinism to an idealism which largely ignores the relevance of societal change," 335) also create the impossibility of agreeing on the causes or components of Jewish modernity.

Even if a consensus could be reached that, say, "economic, political and cultural integration be taken together as representative of Jewish modernity, the question as to when they became constitutive must still be settled" (335). What is to be made of apparently "modern" characteristics that appeared in earlier periods (such as the cultural integration of medieval Spain or Renaissance Italy)? How does one dispose of "pre-modern artifacts" (e.g. traditional religious beliefs) that persist into the modern period?

Finally, who counts as representative of "the Jews"? If Sephardim in Western Europe exhibited "modern" characteristics but Ashkenazim didn't, had Jewish modernity begun? If the upper and lower classes were "integrated" but the middle class was "traditional," was the Jewish people modern? If Diaspora Jews are living as heirs to the Enlightenment and Israelis to modern nationalist ideology, are both in the same period of history? (335–38).

Asking, "Is there any value in setting a definite terminus for the beginning of modern Jewish history?" Meyer came to the pessimistic conclusion that "There is not. ... Any endeavor to mark a borderline which will be meaningful for all Jewries and

---

* Henceforth, page references to Meyer's article are enclosed in parentheses in the text.

embrace the origin or rise to normative status of all—or even most—of the characteristics of Jewish life as it presently exists seems to me bound to fail." Meyer's solution was to skip the debate over the beginning of Jewish modernity and concentrate instead on "the process of modernization," that is, to trace the economic, social, and intellectual transformations of Jews, community by community, class by class, region by region (336).

Meyer's article took much of the tension out of the debate over Jewish historical periodization. It seemed that after Meyer there was little interesting or novel to say on the subject. Rather than have the periodization question surface again and again, continually rehearsing the same—and, post-Meyer, stale—arguments, one could assign Meyer's article to students, discuss it, summarize its conclusion, and move on.

Meyer did point out that "one must begin somewhere." There had to be a conventional date for beginning courses in modern Jewish history and writing surveys of the subject. Meyer suggested the seventeenth century because "according to nearly all views today, many of the elements that became constitutive of later Jewish life first made their appearance to any degree" then (336–37). This might be termed the lowest common denominator approach to periodization. In the seventeenth century one could point to at least adumbrations of "modern" political, cultural, social, economic, intellectual, geographic, and demographic trends. Each of these developments had been nominated at some point as indicators of Jewish modernity. It was the seventeenth century, then, that could serve, even if imperfectly, as the point of origin of the greatest number of processes defining the modern period in Jewish history.

Intriguingly, despite his insistence on the futility of searching for a single starting date that marks the onset of Jewish modernity, Meyer contended that there is a need to formulate a description of modernization which "could meaningfully be used to characterize a basic process which has led to both of the forms of Jewish existence today: that of the Diaspora and that of the State. The conceptual unity of Jewish history would thus be preserved even down to the present" (338). Here, it would seem, Meyer implied his own metahistory: one that postulates the unity of Jewish history both vertically through the past and horizontally today, with Israel and the Diaspora being two closely related components in a shared world Jewish experience.

After Meyer, treatments of Jewish historical periodization—especially in comparison with such elaborate schemes as those of Krochmal, Dubnov, Dinur, and Baer[13]—have been mostly unoriginal and even perfunctory. They either adopt one of the standard dates[14] or the lowest common denominator approach,[15] or they try to finesse the problem of periodization.[16] Perhaps taking up Meyer's challenge to "focus on the process of modernization," there have been new interpretations of the nature and varieties of Jewish "modernity" or Jewish "modernization";[17] but no new periodization scheme, with one signal exception.

ISRAEL'S NEW PERIODIZATION

In 1985, Jonathan Israel published *European Jewry in the Age of Mercantilism, 1550–1750.* He noted the need to draw "a firm dividing-line between the medieval and early modern epochs" because beginning around 1570 "a freer, more flexible [European] society and cultural system" allowed for the "reintegration" of the Jews into the mainstream of European culture, society, and economy, with Jews being freed from many traditional restrictions; so they in turn "exerted, especially in the period 1650–1713, the most profound and pervasive impact on the west." Had Israel merely moved the starting date of Jewish modernity forward to the late sixteenth century? No, because he also maintained that the reintegration beginning at that time did not evolve smoothly into the Jewish emancipation and assimilation/acculturation of the nineteenth century. Israel asserted that for the Jews, the eighteenth century was "an era of stagnation, decay, and impoverishment, both economic and cultural." There was no continuity between the integration process before 1700 and that after 1789. In addition, the earlier process was marked by the Jews' retention of "a large measure of social and cultural cohesion ... a recognizably national character. ... The emancipation of the seventeenth century ushered the Jews into the western world as a tightly cohesive group." Later emancipation required the Jews to become "uprooted individuals stripped of their former political and social autonomy and culture."[18]

Israel, in effect, reperiodized Jewish history in three ways. He defined a new period of (European) Jewish history,[19] the early modern period, ca. 1550–1750. A time when Jews were "emancipated" and "integrated" but still traditionally Jewish, both individually and collectively, this era was distinct from both the "Middle Ages" and the "modern period." Next, Israel felicitously synchronized Jewish historiography with general European historiography, which had been treating the early modern period as a discrete era for decades. Finally, Israel proffered a new date for the Jewish modern period, beginning it from the decline of Jewish economic success (something none of the standard treatments had suggested) and the dissolution of traditional Jewish religious and communal life from around the mid eighteenth century.[20]

While Israel did attract some criticism,[21] his singling out of an early modern Jewish period parallel to the general European one has gained a large measure of acceptance.[22] Still, like his predecessors, Israel defined his period on the basis of an "essential" characteristic: integration-cum-tradition. The integration he highlighted, however, was political and economic—not cultural or social—in nature, and he did not offer a very profound analysis of Jewish tradition at the time beyond its political, institutional, and obvious religious aspects. Moreover, as Meyer (and others since) had pointed out, much of what has been associated with Jewish "modernity" (e.g. population growth, migration westward, geographic expansion, weakening of traditional institutions, cultural and social integration) did begin in the seventeenth century and—pace Israel—continued through the eighteenth and after. Israel's period definition, appealing as many have found it, still does not account for all variables, sharing at least part of the weakness of other attempts to impose period divisions on history.

Meyer wanted the historical description of Jewish modernization to lead to an understanding of what led to the formation of "Jewish life as it presently exists."[23] This might be accomplished, as Meyer came close to saying, by formulating a constellational definition. That is, rather than emphasize a single process (and the date on which it began) that epitomizes Jewish modernity, we might posit that all of the thoughtful suggestions have merit and highlight a constellation of processes that were important in forming modern Jewry: demographic growth and geographic spread, nationalism, political and legal emancipation and Western-style citizenship, cultural and social integration (traditionally termed acculturation/assimilation), economic integration, enlightenment and secularization, the decline of religion as a force for governing people's lives, the breakdown of traditional sources of authority and traditional institutions, the reorganization of the Jewish community on a voluntary basis, and modern Jew-hatred and antisemitism. Moreover, these processes were not necessarily present simultaneously, and modernization in a given community might occur even in the absence of some of them. We may not be able to pinpoint a date that marks the beginning of Jewish modernity, but we can enumerate the constellation of processes that composed its content. Where and when we find them in operation, we know we are observing people of modernity.

If this is so, it is my contention that by now this constellation has broken down; thirty years after Meyer's review, it no longer delineates the modernization processes that constitute "Jewish life as it presently exists." Nearly all the processes the constellation contained have either come to final realization, disappeared,

reversed, or transformed to the point where they are unrecogniz-
able. In addition, some new processes and issues have appeared
that were not germane to the modern period. It follows that the
modern period of Jewish history is over. We are now in a new
period that began in the wake of the Shoah and the establishment
of Israel. Influenced by the Zeitgeist, we call it the "postmodern
period of Jewish history."[24]

II. Jewish Postmodernity
Differentiated from Modernity

Let us consider the conventional constituents of the constellation
of criteria of Jewish modernity and how their status has changed
in the postmodern period.

DEMOGRAPHIC GROWTH

Between 1700 and 1939, the world Jewish population grew from
approximately 1.1 million to 16.5 million people.[25] Like the cities
in which they were located, Jewish communities grew in size
exponentially. For example, around 1600 Constantinople
included the largest Jewish community in the world by far, numbering between 30,000 and 40,000 Jews.[26] In 1764, the largest
Jewish community in all of Poland was in the town of Brody and
its outskirts, with somewhat more than 7,000 Jews.[27] In contrast,
by the time of the period between the world wars, "provincial"
Jewish communities like that in Pinsk numbered in the tens of
thousands,[28] while in Warsaw, London, Budapest, and Vienna
there were hundreds of thousands of Jews, and in New York
nearly two million.[29]

Since the Shoah, however—and bracketing off the catastrophic demographic loss of those years[30]—the world Jewish
population, outside of Israel, has been almost consistently shrink-

ing. In 1950 it was 10,170,000; in 1980, 9,557,000; in 1996, 8,457,000. Even counting Israel, the number of Jews in the world grew only modestly, from 11,373,000 to 13,025,000 in the last half of the twentieth century. This trend of modest increase, due primarily to Israeli population growth while most other communities decreased, is expected to continue through at least the first quarter of the twenty-first century.[31]

The modern period was a time of Jewish population growth. The postmodern period seems to be a time of population stability and even decline.[32]

GEOGRAPHIC SPREAD

From the seventeenth century through the early twentieth century, the Jewish presence in the world was spreading. Beginning with a core of Jewish settlement in Europe, North Africa, and western Asia, new Jewish communities were established (or discovered) in the Americas and the Carribean, sub-Saharan Africa, South and Southeast Asia, Australia, and Oceania. The number of Jewish communities in both new and old regions of Jewish settlement multiplied and most of them grew in size, although many remained small in absolute numbers.

Since the Shoah and the establishment of Israel, the number of Jewish communities in the world has contracted sharply. Those in Ethiopia and in Muslim lands in Africa and Asia have virtually disappeared. In Western countries, Jews have rapidly abandoned rural and provincial locales for large metropolitan areas (by the end of the twentieth century, almost 60 percent of world Jewry was concentrated in only ten metropolitan areas worldwide; and only one of those—Paris—was outside the USA or Israel), thus significantly reducing the number of viable Jewish communities in outlying areas. In Central and Eastern Europe and the former Soviet Union, most of the communities destroyed during the Shoah were never reestablished, and emigration and aging demography have doomed many of those that remained.

In short, as compared with 1939, there are many fewer places in the world today where significant numbers of Jews can be found. The Diaspora has been reduced in number of people, in number of communities, and in number of major groups of communities. Today we can speak of at most three major centers of Jewish life: North America, Israel, and Europe (with the last getting progressively smaller). Moreover, demographers predict that, sometime during the first quarter of the twenty-first century, a plurality, and perhaps even a majority, of the Jewish people will be in Israel, where already the majority of Jewish children in the world are born and reside.[33]

If the modern period was typified by "Diversities of Diaspora,"[34] it seems that the postmodern period is characterized by a process of redistribution of the Jewish population among two or perhaps three large centers and scattered small nuclei. This may ultimately lead to competition between the centers, with each attempting to establish primacy; to a nearly complete rupture of relations among them; or to a new version of homeland and diaspora.

POLITICAL AND LEGAL EMANCIPATION
AND WESTERN-STYLE CITIZENSHIP

The overwhelming majority of Jews today live in lands governed by democratic regimes and are full-fledged citizens of their countries. There is no legal discrimination or official political disability.

This last sentence is an amazing statement in light of the history of the modern era, when Jews suffered notorious discrimination and persecution and expended tremendous energy fighting for legal and political equality. Most historians treated the quest for full political emancipation as one of the main themes of Jewish modernity. In the postmodern period, this appears no longer to be an issue. In no place where they live in appreciable numbers are

Jews in danger of being relegated to an inferior legal status or of being deprived officially of political rights. Jewish political equality is politically correct.

The fundamental political problem for Jews in the postmodern era seems to be to what extent their politics should be "Jewish." That is, should Jews participate in the political process qua Jews, as an identified collective interest group, and work for or against certain issues in areas such as educational policy, Middle Eastern policy, welfare policy, economic policy, etc., based on perceived Jewish interests; or should Jews regard their Jewishness as politically neutral and behave politically in accord with other facets of their personal identity and status?[35]

Related to this is the question of Jewish political liberalism. In the premodern period, Jews tended to be politically conservative, preferring the status quo (which included time-tested arrangements enabling them to live) to revolutionary regimes that might bring with them new obstacles to Jewish survival. This changed, however, with the liberal revolutions of 1848, which demonstrated that it was liberal and even radical ideology put into practice that could bring the Jews equality and opportunity.[36] Thus the long identification of modern Jewry with liberalism apparently began with the events of 1848.

Here, too, there are signs that in the postmodern period, Jewish political behavior has changed. The association of Jews and Jewish organizations with the rise of neoconservativism in the United States and with various conservative political movements elsewhere, as well as the tenure of conservative governments in Israel, all imply that liberalism as a peculiarly Jewish tendency ran its course in the modern period, but that postmodern Jewish political proclivities are becoming more pluralistic.

NATIONALISM

Zionist and other Jewish national movements arose in the modern period advocating nationalism as the solution to "the Jewish Problem," that is, the modus vivendi by which Jews could survive and flourish under the conditions of modernity. Connected to general nineteenth-century notions of nationalism, Jewish nationalist ideology was dedicated to the propositions that the world was organized according to nation-states, that the Jews are a nation, and that the only way the Jews will be able to live in the modern world is by organizing as a political nation which, some believed, needed to be based on a self-governing, territorial, Jewish-majority state. According to the Zionist version, there should be a Jewish state in the Land of Israel that would be as Jewish as England is English, France is French, and Poland is Polish.

In the postmodern period, the status of nationalism has become ambiguous. Smaller and smaller collections of people have claimed national rights and in recent years such countries as Slovenia and Estonia have been (re)created with populations under two million. European nationalism and European-style nationalism elsewhere is not dying. To the contrary, it has undergone radicalization, with terrorism becoming the tactic of choice for small minority nationalities who seek to break off from larger political entities and gain independence in their own sovereign territory. Such terrorism has to some extent kept their nationalist claims on the world political agenda.[37]

However, England and France and all of the other major long-established ethnic states are becoming less and less English or French or whatever they have traditionally been, with large and growing immigrant populations of people whose ethnicity is much different from the founding majority. The modern Western state is becoming ever more pluralistic, with a multiplicity of religions, racial groups, and ethnic identities, along with their multiple histories, rituals, social customs, institutions, and cultures.[38]

The establishment, expansion, and continuing articulation of the European Union is potentiating this process. The homogenizing tendencies of the EU are one strong indicator that it is the American model that keeps gaining momentum; that is, the essence of the postmodern state is shared political commitments and not ethnic identity.

Israel, the culminating expression of modern Jewish nationalism, has been forced to turn its attention to a raft of challenges to its declared objective to be a "Jewish state." Its growing Arab and other non-Jewish populations, originating mainly in the former Soviet Union, demand that Israel become a "state of all of its inhabitants." Even without official concessions in this regard, the immigration of tens of thousands of church-going Christians, for example, surely has an effect on the tenor of Israeli culture.[39]

For postmodern Jews, the problem of nationalism is no longer whether the Jews are analogous to other nations and therefore deserve political sovereignty of one type or another. The new issue is how nationalist the Jewish sovereign state can be, given its demographic, social, and cultural composition. Can a modern democratic state maintain a dominant ethnic identity? Is a Jewish state a viable concept in a multicultural world?

Furthermore, has Israel "solved" the Jewish problem? While Israel has indeed gained the Jews a place at the table of world politics and thus guaranteed that Jews will have a say in how their own fate is determined, Israel has been since its inception a focus for controversy. It is certainly not a "normal" country, if by normality is meant routine acceptance on the world stage, peaceful existence, and lack of involvement in major political and military conflicts. Being the lightning rod for so much animosity, has Israel improved Jewish status in the world or has it further problematized it? Is world Jewry drawn into unnecessary confrontations and existential complications by virtue of its association with Israel?

Another issue for Jewish nationalism has been the growing realization on the part of Jews during the postmodern period of the competition between Jewish and Arab, specifically Palestinian, nationalism. For most of the history of Jewish nationalism in the modern period, Arab or Palestinan nationalism was not a main focus of most Jewish nationalists. As Walter Laqueur contended in a chapter entitled "The Unseen Question":

> A minority of Zionists and Palestinian Jews were aware from the beginning of the crucial importance of relations with the Arabs. Some of them thought that the national aspirations of the two peoples could be reconciled, while the pessimists early on reached the conclusion that conflict was basic and unavoidable. The majority of Zionists were less concerned with the Arab question. Only gradually did they face it. ... It seemed almost insignificant in view of the need to save European Jewry.[40]

In the postmodern period, and especially after the consequences of the Six Day War, "the Arab Question" has moved to the center of Israeli and Jewish concern. More and more Jews have been willing to concede the existence and even the legitimacy of Palestinian nationalism, the ramifications of which are that Jewish nationalism must limit itself. The debate over this position, and the actions taken by both its proponents and opponents, have become one of the central loci of postmodern organized Jewish discourse and activities.

ECONOMIC INTEGRATION

During the modern period, Jews struggled to penetrate all sectors of the modern economy. Their objectives were to be fully economically integrated and prosperous wherever they lived. Like political and legal emancipation, this has been largely achieved.

Postmodern Jews can potentially occupy virtually any economic niche they set their sights on, and there is no longer official discrimination against Jewish economic endeavors. There are poor Jews, particularly among the elderly, in the former Soviet Union and in certain sectors of the Israeli population, but from the collective perspective Jews worldwide have achieved a high degree of economic success. The postmodern goal is not so much the attainment of economic success as the maintaining of it.[41]

VOLUNTARY COMMUNITY

A commonly cited hallmark of Jewish modernity was the decline of the Jewish community organized as a medieval-style corporation that wielded coercive power over its members. In premodern times, rabbinic-led courts enjoyed the backing of the Gentile authorities and could impose sanctions to enforce their decisions. Taxes and laws imposed by the communal leadership were mandatory for all Jews. The only alternative for someone who did not want to accept Jewish communal authority was to convert and join the Christian or Muslim community. During the modern period, the Jewish community became a voluntary organization whose members freely chose to join it and support it materially and morally.[42]

In the postmodern period, the voluntary nature of the Jewish community has been taken for granted. However, what was taken for granted almost universally by Jews throughout the modern period—that Jews need an organized community to provide essential services such as political and economic defense, religious and educational services, and welfare functions—is no longer automatically understood. The question for postmodern Jewry is not the basis of authority for the Jewish community, but how to convince Jews that a Jewish community is worth preserving and supporting. It is the very existence, and not the nature, of the Jewish community that is at issue.[43]

CULTURAL AND SOCIAL INTEGRATION

During the modern period, the integration of Jews into majority society and culture was considered to be a central process and one that presented both challenges and dilemmas. Such integration was usually represented by historians as negative ("assimilation") because the absorbing Gentiles expected a concomitant effacement of signs of Jewish identity as the price of acceptance.[44] Hence the dilemma: integration into the majority, or loyalty to Jewishness?

More recent scholars spoke of good integration ("acculturation"), which entailed adapting aspects of non-Jewish culture and even "judaizing" them in an effort to ensure Jewish survival—and sometimes actually to reinforce Jewish identity—in a non-Jewish context.[45] This approach too, however, recognized the threat that integration posed and the need to carefully control it if Jewish identity was to survive.

In the postmodern period, the nature of the integration process has changed significantly. The majority in most places where Jews live, outside Israel, now espouses a commitment to social inclusiveness, cultural pluralism, and sometimes even multiculturalism.[46] Jewishness (if not always Jews—see below) has undergone a new positive evaluation. Conversion to Judaism is no longer a rarity. In most formal social situations, Jewish identity is not something to be apologetic about and is frequently something to be celebrated and proud of.

In practical terms, postmodern Jews, both inside and outside Israel, rarely need to choose between identities; they, like many other minorities, can assume the markers of multiple identity. For example, one can work at a high-salaried job, shop in the best stores, drive the flashiest car, be the most loyal fan of professional sports teams, play the most popular music, vacation at trendy resorts, and have Gentile friends, and still, if one chooses, strictly observe the Sabbath and kashruth, pray regularly, dress "Jewishly," send children to a Jewish school, have Jewish friends, be active in Jewish organizations, promote Jewish political positions, contribute to Jewish philanthropies, and marry a Jewish spouse. If they desire, Israelis can be loyal to their country and their Jewish identity and still feel themselves to be culturally full-fledged members of the "Western World."[47]

Furthermore, even what was once considered the penultimate form of assimilation, exogamous or "mixed" marriage (the ultimate was conversion), has become so common (surpassing the 50 percent mark)[48] that Jewish institutions, including many religious ones, seek methods of keeping the Jewish partner actively identified as Jewish, as well as ways of involving mixed couples and families in their activities. This legitimizes what in the modern period was usually viewed by endogamous Jews as betrayal; but, more portentously, it offers the previously unavailable option of a syncretistic identity.[49]

Postmodern integration, then, is not a zero-sum game. It need not be a dilemma or a threat. Even when it results in exogamous marriage, it can be compatible with some configurations of Jewish identity. The problem is no longer the perceived demands of Gentile society for Jewish "cultural conversion," but rather the lack of desire of Jews themselves to maintain a Jewish identity, even when it is not an obstacle to full participation in the general society and culture.

ENLIGHTENMENT, SECULARIZATION, AND BREAKDOWN
OF TRADITION

The modern period was witness to a progressive weakening of traditional forms and institutions accompanied by ever more intensive secularization. By the late 1940s, with European Jewry virtually destroyed, Orthodoxy in general was in retreat, Hasidism seemed to be in its death throes, liberal versions of Judaism ruled the Jewish street in the Diaspora, and secularism was triumphant in

Israel. This appeared to be the telos of some two hundred years of Enlightenment, rationalist inroads, secular critiques, and religious reform. The prima facie winners of the modern Kulturkampf between those who believed Jewishness to be dependent on religious tradition and those who championed a secular basis for Jewish identity were the secularists.[50] Even those who maintained a commitment to tradition tried to make it more rational, reflective of modern values and responsive to modern sensibilities.[51]

How surprising, then, seemed the postmodern recrudescence of fundamentalism and mysticism (mirroring more or less simultaneous trends in other religious cultures). As the period has progressed, Orthodoxy has turned triumphalist, Hasidism has been thoroughly reconstituted, and tens of thousands of people from secular backgrounds have decided to become *ba'alei teshuvah*, devoting themselves to various versions of Orthodox belief and practice.[52] In Israel there is still but minimal separation of synagogue and state, and traditional sources of authority such as rabbis and mystics sometimes pose a threat to the authority of the Knesset, the courts, and the government bureaucracy.

Secular culture is far from undermined, but the often successful challenge to it from religion and tradition is something that was not foreseen in the modern period and would have seemed out of place then. The balance of forces in the Kulturkampf appears to have shifted and the anticipated modernist demise of tradition has not been realized.[53]

CONTINUITIES

Some features of the modern period have continued on into the postmodern. One example is Jew-hatred or antisemitism. This did not begin in the modern period, but there was a modern version. In ancient times, Jew-hatred was based on Jews' purported arrogance, xenophobia, superstition, and unwarranted political privileges. In the medieval world, anti-Jewish animus was primarily a function of the Jews' religious alienation. In the modern period, Jew-hatred was secularized and dubbed antisemitism. It targeted Jews as possessing traits, even racial ones, which resulted in their behaving in ways that undermined civilization in the service of their own nefarious interests.

While traces of both medieval- and modern-style antisemitism continue, particularly in some Muslim countries, there has also appeared a postmodern version of Jew-hatred, one that eschews the racism of the modern period but insists that Jews in their efforts to advance their questionable political agenda violate the human rights of others and the interests of their countries of residence. It complains, for example, about inordinate and detrimental "Jewish influence" over politics and policy-making in the United States. It raises the specter of dual loyalty of Diaspora Jews and identifies all Jews with the policies and actions of Israel, which are often equated in motivation, cruelty of execution, scale, objectives, and results with those of Nazi Germany. It considers Israel and Jews to be aligned with the reactionary and oppressive forces in the world and to bear great, and even primary, responsibility for many serious problems, such as terrorism, racism, the negative effects of globalization, and clashes of Muslim individuals, groups, and states with people and states in the West. If only Israel and/or the Jews would go away, these evils would be greatly ameliorated.[54]

Another example of a modern trend that continues into postmodernity is the process of altering the gender structure of Jewish society and culture (again, with obvious parallels to what has occurred in other contemporary cultures and societies). Although not usually noted by conventional portrayals, the Jewish modern period was characterized by the continual, if very slow, transformation of Jewish women's role from cultural bystanders to that of participants; and from social facilitators of the activities of their menfolk to performers who engaged in the most socially valued activities themselves.[55]

Beginning in the sixteenth century, a Yiddish literature was created that counted women as well as men in its audience. It included translations and reworkings of the Bible based on rabbinic interpretation; manuals that instructed women in the observance of the commandments especially incumbent on them; morality anthologies and behavior manuals incorporating admonitions illustrated by didactic anecdotes; and pious story anthologies. There also appeared prayer collections containing *tekhines*, petitionary prayers, intended for women. Throughout the modern period, women took a progressively more active role in synagogue life, beginning with sixteenth-century halachic rulings that made it easier for women to attend synagogue services and the seventeenth-century spread of women's sections (*'ezrat nashim*) that were architecturally integral to the synagogue building; the eighteenth-century increase in women's *tekhines* to be said during the synagogue service; the nineteenth-century abolition of gender-segregated seating in some Reform congregations (adopted in the twentieth century by the Conservative movement and even by some Orthodox synagogues); the institution of confirmation and, later, bat mitzvah rituals for girls; and the admission of women to synagogue governing bodies.

This process of increasing women's Jewish cultural and social capital has continued at a much more rapid pace in the postmodern period, with some significant additions: it has become more consciously aimed at blurring gender distinctions in the name of equality; it has revolutionized Jewish education; it has been embraced, albeit hesitatingly, by certain Orthodox elements. Emblematic of the change that has occurred is that women rabbis, who were barely even a curiosity in the modern period, are now commonplace (even beginning to appear among the Orthodox).

NEW ISSUES

The postmodern period has also brought with it some new questions, challenges, and processes. Some examples follow.

Israel–Diaspora Relations

From the Muslim conquest until the establishment of Israel (or, at
the earliest, the founding of the new Zionist *yishuv* in the first half
of the twentieth century), the question of relations between Eretz
Israel and the Diaspora did not loom very large from a practical
point of view. In theory, if not always in practice, Diaspora Jews
saw it as their duty to support economically (and, in the case of
important Ottoman communities like Alexandria and Istanbul,
sometimes politically) whatever Jews were in the Holy Land; a
small number of them aspired to move there; and a still smaller
number actually did.

Political Zionism, and especially the establishment of Israel,
changed the relationship profoundly. Israel resolves to be the center of world Jewish life, to represent the Jewish People and to lay
claim to the loyalty of Jews everywhere. As the postmodern
period has progressed, many Diaspora Jews have enthusiastically
seconded these aims, and more than 2.5 million of them have
moved to Israel and become Israeli.[56] Many, however, have not
seen the relevance of Israel to their lives and have not allotted it a
significant role in their actions. A sizeable number have regarded
Israel's ambitions toward them as pretentious or worse. They
resent being associated with its policies and actions and view Israel
as an albatross rather than a source of inspiration and pride. In and
around these three positions there are many nuances, and it seems
clear that one of the great themes of postmodern Jewish history
has been and will continue to be the dialectic between the State of
Israel and Israeli Jews, on the one hand, and Diaspora Jewries as
organized entities and Diaspora Jews as individuals, on the
other.[57]

The Economics of Jewish Identity

Through the modern period, a large majority of Jews in the world probably maintained a standard of living that was not too distant in either direction from some theoretical poverty line. This was virtually irrelevant to their Jewish identity, except to the extent that in some areas, such as Eastern Europe, poverty and Jewishness were highly correlated, and the former often seemed, subjectively at least, to be an intrinsic aspect of the latter. There certainly was no bar to poor people feeling identified as Jews.

In the postmodern period, as noted above, the majority of Jews live far above the poverty line. Yet, outside Israel, maintaining ties to the institutions of the organized Jewish community, providing one's children with the experiences considered basic to a sophisticated Jewish identity, and just being part of the general Jewish ecosphere impose a significant financial burden. It is interesting that a prime tenet of Jewish fundraising has become the equation of the need to preserve Jewish "continuity" with the need to raise money.

In practice, synagogue and Jewish club memberships, "normal" charitable contributions, school and camp tuitions, trips to Israel, financial requirements of Jewish organizations, kosher food, and housing in most Jewish neighborhoods all represent a hefty slice of family income that must often come at the expense of some of the essentials of middle class life. If there a lifestyle dilemma for postmodern Jews that has replaced "Can we be Jewish and culturally integrated?" it is "Can we afford to be Jewish?"[58]

The New Hebraism

I have already alluded to the fact that, notwithstanding the persistence of antisemitism, in the postmodern world Judaism and Jewishness have enjoyed a new positive re-evaluation and acceptance. This goes beyond mere tolerance. Jews are "establishment." Jews are high government officials and leaders of political parties, captains of industry, presidents of universities. Culturally, in a world premised on the ideals of pluralism or multiculturalism, virtually every major university has a Jewish Studies program (most of them financed by Jewish donors), where many non-Jewish scholars also specialize in Jewish Studies; Hanukkah recently began to be publicly marked by kindling a *ḥanukkiyah* at the White House in the presence of the President of the United States, and there are US Hanukkah postage stamps; the Holocaust is a subject on many school curricula; Jewish museums and monuments are architecturally and culturally prominent in many of the world's great cities; Jewish community leaders are routinely consulted by politicians on appropriate issues; and one can even order kosher meals at Disney World.

Older Jews, with a consciousness formed by the modern period, rub their eyes. Is this more than condescending philosemitism or Holocaust guilt? Can it last? How does it relate to the "new" antisemitism? When dealing with Gentiles do we dare take "yes" for an answer?

Postmodern Jews, more sanguine, are willing to believe. This time there really seems to be a neutral society where all meet equally, where one's Jewishness is purely a personal matter, where minority status is irrelevant.[59] More than that, they know that Jewish culture can both benefit and benefit *from* the general culture. They have convincing arguments that such cardinal elements of postmodern sensibility as egalitarianism, ecology, pluralism, tolerance, self-determination, and even feminism and multiculturalism have roots in Jewish tradition, and they welcome the chance to explore these together with non-Jews, reciprocally learning no less from the heritages of others. The development of a new relationship with Gentile society and culture has been and will be a major factor in shaping Jewish existence in the postmodern period.

Who is a Jew?

In the sophisticated demographic research work that has been done on the world Jewish population since the latter part of the twentieth century, the data are usually based on the "core Jewish population," defined by an "operative definition": "all those who, when asked, identify themselves as Jews. ... This is a comprehensive approach that reflects both subjective feelings and community norms and bonds."[60]

The alternative to an operative definition of who is a Jew would be a "normative definition" derived from the halachic maxim that a Jew is someone whose mother is Jewish or who has formally converted to Judaism. In the postmodern period, such a definition would obviously include significantly fewer people than the operative definition resting on self-identification.[61] This is because the operative definition recognizes as Jews not only formal converts, but also those who "have decided to join the Jewish group informally." It also accepts the common usage in the former Soviet Union and Eastern Europe and the controversial (from a normative point of view) decision by the Reform movement whereby those with a Jewish father (but a non-Jewish mother) are counted as Jews. In addition it includes many Israelis who profess to Jewishness although they are not halachically qualified.

It is very probable (although it needs to be proven) that in the modern period the gap between the two approaches was much smaller. The reason for this is that the possible permutations of a person's relationship to Jewishness then were more limited. It was relatively rare for a person who was not halachically Jewish to want to claim that status (probably the opposite was much more frequent). In the postmodern period, with the breakdown of traditional nuclear and extended family structures, the dramatic increase in the percentage of mixed Jewish–Gentile marriage, the Israeli Law of Return enabling many types of "nonnormative Jews" to become part of Israel, and the positive reevaluation of Jewishness on the part of the majority culture, there are more ways, often not coextensive with halacha, for an individual to see herself or himself as associated with Jewishness than in the past.[62]

The result is that "the Jewish People" in the postmodern period is really a somewhat different entity from what it was in the modern period (which raises the issue of the comparability of the numbers of Jews in the two periods). Its genealogy, the historical heritage of its members, their collective consciousness and collective objectives, their family relationships, the kinds of ties they seek and maintain with each other, their conceptions of what it means to be a Jew, their modes of Jewish identification—all are much more variegated than they were even as recently as 1950. This, combined with the changing political and economic configuration of the general world context and the expiration or transformation of most of the primary issues that preoccupied the Jews during modernity, suggests that in the postmodern period Jewish history will be as different from the modern as the modern was from the Middle Ages and antiquity.

III. An Unphilosophical Postmodernity

When in contemporary discourse we say that ours is a postmodern age, we are usually utilizing the term in a heedless, unrigorous manner. It is much the same as the application of Freudian terminology to everyday events by people who have never read Freud. In this paper I have used the term "postmodern" not in a philosophical way[63] but to code a new set of circumstances that mark the period in which they became operative as substantially different from the preceding time. What I have argued here is that, at least in terms of Jewish history, the "postmodernity"—in the literal sense of succeeding modernity—of the current era is demonstrable.

Does my schema share the weakness of all "grand structures"? To be sure. By proposing this periodization am I revealing my own metahistory? Doubtless. Nevertheless, I offer this construction in the hope that it will be part of a process of reconsideration of how we configure, organize, and present the Jewish past, as well as how we conceive of the Jewish present. If we are not modern Jews, what does that say about modernity? What does that say about us?

Notes

1. In those days no scheme suggested by a female scholar was analyzed.
2. Heinrich Graetz, *The Structure of Jewish History*, trans., ed. and introduced by Ismar Schorsch (New York: JTS, 1975), 37, 41, 119–24.
3. Simon Dubnov, "The Sociological View of Jewish History," in *Nationalism and History*, ed. Koppel S. Pinson (Philadelphia: Jewish Publication Society, 1958), 336–53. For analysis of Dubnov's historiographic theory and its ramifications and applications, see Jonathan Frankel, "Assimilation and the Jews in Nineteenth Century Europe: Towards a New Historiography?" in *Assimilation and Community: The Jews in Nineteenth Century Europe*, ed. Jonathan Frankel and Steven J. Zipperstein (Cambridge: Cambridge University Press, 1992), 1–37.
4. The periodization discussions also gave the participants the opportunity to articulate and critique their own metahistories and interpretations of the meaning of the period in which they were living.
5. Ben-Zion Dinur, *Israel and the Diaspora* (Philadelphia: Jewish Publication Society, 1969), 90–95; cf. Meir Benayahu, ה״חברה קדושה״ של רבי יהודה חסיד ועלייתה לארץ ישראל (The 'Holy Brotherhood' of Rabbi Judah Hasid and their settlement in Jerusalem), *Sefunot* 3–4 (1960): 137–82, which undermined Dinur's argument.
6. Salo W. Baron, *A Social and Religious History of the Jews*, vol. 9 (New York: Columbia University Press, 1965).
7. Peter Novick, *That Noble Dream: The "Objectivity Question" and the American Historical Profession* (Cambridge: Cambridge University Press, 1988), 522–629.
8. Eli Lederhendler, *Jewish Responses to Modernity: New Voices in America and Eastern Europe* (New York: NYU Press, 1994), 194.
9. Ibid., 193–94. See similarly Frankel, "Assimilation and the Jews," 15–16.

10. My own two monographs, *The Lords' Jews* (Cambridge: Harvard University Press, 1990) and *Founder of Hasidism* (Berkeley and Los Angeles: University of California Press, 1996), are examples of this. It remains to be seen whether Jonathan Sarna's *American Judaism* (New Haven: Yale University Press, 2004), chronicling 350 years of Jewish religious life in America, is an exception or the harbinger of a new trend as those trained in the 1970s enter the sixth and seventh decades of life.

11. Robert F. Berkhofer, "The Challenge of Poetics to (Normal) Historical Practice," *Poetics Today* 9 (1988): 435–52.

12. *Judaism* 24 (1975): 329–38.

13. Dubnov, "Sociological View"; Dinur, *Israel and the Diaspora*; see also N. Krochmal, כתבי רבי נחמן קרוכמל (The writings of R. Naḥman Krochmal), ed. S. Rawidowicz (Berlin: Yanus, 1924), 112; Yitzḥak F. Baer, מחקרים ומסות בתולדות עם ישראל (Studies in the history of the Jewish people), 2 vols. (Jerusalem: Israel Historical Society, 1985), esp. 1:19–46, 2:9–59.

14. Some recent examples: In the spirit of Dubnov (although limiting their periodization to European Jewry), David Vital, *A People Apart: The Jews in Europe, 1789–1939* (Oxford: Oxford University Press, 1999), 3 (cf. vii), declares, "All turned, therefore, in the final analysis, on the matter of emancipation"; and similarly, Francis Malino and David Sorkin (eds.), *Profiles in Diversity: Jews in a Changing Europe* (Detroit: Wayne State University Press, 1998), 1, state, "Emancipation, the granting of equal civil and political rights, came both to epitomize this period and to define its history." Apparently giving Graetz his due too, Hilary L. Rubinstein, Dan Cohn-Sherbok, Abraham J. Edelheit and William D. Rubinstein, *The Jews in the Modern World: A History since 1750* (London: Arnold, 2002), chap. 2, consider "Enlightenment and Emancipation" to constitute "the roots of modernity." Lloyd P. Gartner, *History of the Jews in Modern Times* (Oxford: Oxford University Press, 2001), 25, adopts his teacher Baron's 1650 date.

15. E.g., Paul Mendes-Flohr and Jehuda Reinharz, *The Jew in the Modern World: A Documentary History*, 2nd ed. (Oxford: Oxford University Press, 1995), 4: "What is, however, manifest in all of these conceptions [of Jewish modernity], despite their often extreme variation, is the conviction that the last two hundred years or so have witnessed a radical transformation of Jewish life." In practice, the earliest documents in the collection, pointing to the first steps in the transformation process, date from the mid seventeenth century.

16. A recent important survey of Jewish history, *Cultures of the Jews: A New History*, ed. David Biale (New York: Schocken, 2002), does not offer a

theoretical explanation for the periodization chosen: "Mediterranean Origins" (biblical times through the formative period of Islam), "Diversities of Diaspora" (the "Golden Age" of Islam through the eighteenth century), and "Modern Encounters" (nineteenth and twentieth centuries). To me this implies a recognition that there can be no better reasons than convention and convenience for dividing up historical time.

17. E.g., Jay R. Berkovitz, *Rites and Passages: The Beginnings of Modern Jewish Culture, 1650–1860* (Philadelphia: University of Pennsylvania Press, 2004); Lois C. Dubin, *The Port Jews of Trieste: Absolutist Politics and Enlightenment Culture* (Stanford: Stanford University Press, 1999); Todd M. Endelman, *The Jews of Georgian England, 1714–1830: Tradition and Change in a Liberal Society* (Ann Arbor: University of Michigan Press, 1999); Shmuel Feiner, *The Jewish Enlightenment* (Philadelphia: University of Pennsylvania Press, 2003); Gershon D. Hundert, *Jews in Poland-Lithuania in the Eighteenth Century: A Genealogy of Modernity* (Berkeley and Los Angeles: University of California Press, 2004); Paula E. Hyman, *The Emancipation of the Jews of Alsace: Acculturation and Tradition in the Nineteenth Century* (New Haven: Yale University Press, 1991); Yosef Kaplan, *An Alternative Path to Modernity: The Sephardi Diaspora in Western Europe* (Leiden: Brill, 2000); Steven J. Zipperstein, *The Jews of Odessa: A Cultural History, 1794–1881* (Stanford: Stanford University Press, 1986).

18. Jonathan I. Israel, *European Jewry in the Age of Mercantilism, 1550–1750* (Oxford: Oxford University Press, 1985), 1–3, 252–53. Israel further articulates his argument for the discrete identity of this period in *Diasporas within a Diaspora: Jews, Crypto-Jews and the World Maritime Empires (1540–1740)* (Leiden: Brill, 2002).

19. Israel, *European Jewry,* succeeded in integrating the history of Jews in Western and Eastern Europe and the Ottoman Balkans, primarily by demonstrating the economic and family links among them. He also mentioned ties with Jews in Turkey itself and the Levant, but he did not quite produce a comprehensive portrait of world Jewry at the time.

20. Ibid,, 253–58.

21. David Ruderman, "Israel's European Jewry in the Age of Mercantilism," *Jewish Quarterly Review* 78 (1987): 154–59; Hillel Levine, יהודים ויהדות בעידן המרקנטיליזם (Jews and Judaism in the age of mercantilism), *Zion* 53 (1988): 65–71.

22. For example, in August 2004 the Mellon Foundation sponsored a workshop at Wesleyan University on early modern Jewish history entitled "Early Modern Jewries." Such institutionalization bespeaks the belief of

scholars that the idea of an early modern period has utility for teaching and research.

23. Meyer, "Where Does the Modern Period," 336. Cf. idem, *The Origins of the Modern Jew: Jewish Identity and European Culture in Germany, 1749–1824* (Detroit: Wayne State University Press, 1967), esp. 8–10, 181–82.

24. Actually, Dinur, *Israel and the Diaspora*, was the first to assert that the modern period had ended and that a new period has begun. Believing the essence of the modern period in Jewish history to be the struggle for relief from the vicissitudes of minority status and for the reestablishment of Jewish political nationhood, he saw the creation of Israel as the climax of Jewish modernity and what followed as the onset of a new era. I adopt a similar date not because of some teleology, but because I think that all of the changes I describe below either began or became manifest in the period that commenced in the late 1940s. However, I fully realize that, as with Meyer's choice of a starting date for the modern period described previously, this is a no more than a convention based on the "lowest common denominator approach" whose main utility is to provide a convenient platform for focusing attention on the transformations that occurred. By speaking of periods of Jewish history, I by no means mean to imply that Jews are not subject to the conditions and processes that affected the people among whom they lived. As is perhaps most easily seen in the case of demography (see next note), in every period Jews are participants in the general social, cultural, economic, religious, etc., environment. However, due to their particular history and circumstances, the effect of general conditions and processes on the Jews may be different from their effect on others. Jewish history is often distinctive. For some stimulating suggestions as to the possible relationships between Jewish and general history, see Elliott Horowitz, review of *The Autobiography of a Seventeenth-Century Venetian Rabbi: Leon Modena's Life of Judah*, ed. and trans. Mark R. Cohen, *Jewish Quarterly Review* 81 (1991): 460–61.

25. Sergio DellaPergola, *World Jewry beyond 2000: The Demographic Prospects* (Yarnton: Oxford Centre for Hebrew and Jewish Studies, 1999), 13 (This booklet is a felicitous summary of results of the fundamental demographic research DellaPergola has been conducting for over thirty years. For the specialized studies behind the statements cited here, please consult his notes.) This was a period of general population growth in most of the regions of the world where Jews lived, and Jewish demography is intimately linked to the general processes at work. At the same time, however, Jewish demography featured distinguishing characteristics; see ibid., 7–8,

13–14, 25–28, 38–43, 50–51.

26. Baron, *Social and Religious History*, vol. 18 (1983), 200; Jacob Barnai, היהודים באימפריה העותמאנית (The Jews in the Ottoman Empire), in תולדות היהודים בארצות האסלם (History of the Jews in Islamic lands), ed. Shmuel Ettinger (Jerusalem: Zalman Shazar Center, 1981), 81.

27. Shaul Stampfer, "The 1764 Census of Polish Jewry," *Bar-Ilan* 24–25 (1989), 91, gives the raw data number, 7,357. According to the adjustment criteria for this census proposed by Raphael Mahler, תולדות היהודים בפולין (History of the Jews in Poland) (Merhavia, Eretz Israel: Sifriat Poalim, 1946), 231–33, the real number may have approached 9,000.

28. Azriel Shohat, פינסק (Pinsk) (Tel Aviv: Association of Pinsk-Karlin Jews in Israel, 1977), 1/ב:205.

29. אטלס כרטא לתולדות עם ישראל בזמן החדש (Carta's atlas of the Jewish people in modern times), ed. Evyatar Friesel (Jerusalem: Carta, 1983), 15 fig. 8.

30. For interesting speculation on what might have occurred to the world Jewish population had six million Jews not been murdered in 1939–45, see DellaPergola, *World Jewry beyond 2000*, 14–16.

31. Ibid., 16–18, 66–70. There were non-Israeli Jewish communities that grew during this period, notably in the United States. While there is no agreement over how many Jews there were in the United States at any given time, the maximum possible growth between 1950 and 2000 (i.e. using the lowest 1950 estimate and the highest 2000 estimate) could have been from 4.5 million to 6.15 million, i.e., 1.65 million or about 37% (Sarna, *American Judaism*, 375; cf. DellaPergola, *World Jewry beyond 2000*, 21, 24, 69). This number is less than half of the 85 percent increase in the overall American population (1950: 152,300,000; 2000: 282,400,000; increase: 130,100,000) and pales next to Israeli growth of 3.4 million (1. 2 million to 4.6 million, 280%) during the same period. It should be remembered that the numbers reported by DellaPergola represent the "core Jewish population," i.e., those people who self-identify as Jews. This probably inflates the number of Jews as compared to pre-Holocaust figures; see ibid., 9–12, and "Who is a Jew?" page 120 below.

32. Cf. David Vital, *The Future of the Jews* (Cambridge: Cambridge University Press, 1990); Bernard Wasserstein, *Vanishing Diaspora: The Jews in Europe since 1945* (Cambridge: Cambridge University Press, 1996); Alan M. Dershowitz, *The Vanishing American Jew: In Search of Jewish Identity for the Next Century* (Boston: Little, Brown, 1997); Zvi Gitelman, "The Decline of the Diaspora Jewish Nation: Boundaries, Content and Jewish Identity," *Jewish Social Studies* 4, no. 2 (1998), 112–32.

33. DellaPergola, *World Jewry beyond 2000*, 28–29, 48–53, 66–72.
34. See n. 16.
35. This was an issue during the process of the formation of modern Jewish political consciousness in the nineteenth century as well (see Eli Lederhendler, *The Road to Modern Jewish Politics* [Oxford: Oxford University Press, 1989], and Ezra Mendelsohn, *On Modern Jewish Politics* [New York: Oxford University Press, 1993]). Then, however, it was subsumed under the larger question of how the Jews might best attain political equality. Currently, the larger question is moot.
36. Salo W. Baron, "The Impact of the Revolution of 1848 on Jewish Emancipation," *Jewish Social Studies* 11 (1949): 195–248.
37. For analysis of the connection between modern nationalist struggles and war and terrorism, see Martin Van Creveld, *The Transformation of War* (New York: Free Press, 1991).
38. See, for example, Charis Waddy, *Shaping a New Europe: The Muslim Factor* (London: Grosvenor, 1991); *The New Islamic Presence in Western Europe*, ed. Tomas Gerholm and Y. G. Lithman (London: Mansell, 1988); Danielle Joly, *Britannia's Crescent* (Aldershot: Avebury, 1995); *Muslims in Europe: Social Change in Western Europe*, ed. Bernard Lewis and Dominique Schnapper (London: Pinter, 1994).
39. Asher Cohen, מדמוקרטיה הסדרית לדמוקרטיה משברית (From arranged democracy to crisis democracy: The struggle over collective identity in Israel), *Politika* 3 (1999): 9–30; idem, התבוללות ישראלית (Israeli assimilation: On changes in identity definition and the boundaries of the Jewish collective), *Gesher* 145 (2002): 17–27; Adriana Kemp, "Christian Zionists in the Holy Land: Evangelical Churches, Labor Migrants and the Jewish State," *Identities* 10 (2003): 295–318.
40. Walter Laqueur, *A History of Zionism* (New York: Schocken, 1972), 268–69.
41. DellaPergola, *World Jewry beyond 2000*, 25–30, 38–40.
42. Salo W. Baron, "Aspects of the Jewish Communal Crisis in 1848," *Jewish Social Studies* 14 (1952): 199–244; Arthur A. Goren, *New York Jews and the Quest for Community: The Kehillah Experiment, 1908–1922* (New York: Columbia University Press, 1970); I. Robinson, "The Foundation Documents of the Jewish Community Council of Montreal," *Jewish Political Studies Review* 8 (1996): 69–86. As David Biale has pointed out to me, one might argue that Israel represents a new incarnation of the coercive Jewish community, because as a state where the ruling elite is Jewish it is an instance of Jews ruling Jews by sanction of law as in premodern times.

43. More than half of Diaspora Jews do not affiliate with the organized Jewish community: DellaPergola, *World Jewry beyond 2000*, 55–56; Chaim I. Waxman, *Jewish Baby Boomers: A Communal Perspective* (Albany: SUNY Press, 2001), 66, 92–93, 123–24, 127, 154–59, 161.

44. Frankel, "Assimilation and the Jews," 5–15.

45. Ibid., 21–27, and see many of the other essays in Frankel and Zipperstein, *Assimilation and Community*.

46. For discussion of the difference between cultural pluralism and multiculturalism as frameworks for the organization of culture in society, see *Insider/Outsider: American Jews and Multiculturalism*, ed. David Biale, Michael Galchinsky, and Susannah Heschel (Berkeley and Los Angeles: University of California Press, 1998), 3–4, 29–32, 57–59, and passim.

47. Cf. Stephen Sharot, "Judaism and Jewish Ethnicity: Changing Interrelationships and Differentiations in the Diaspora and Israel," in *Jewish Survival*, ed. Ernest Krausz and Gitta Tulea (New Brunswick, N.J.: Transaction, 1998), 87–105; Arnold Eisen, "The Problem Is Still Very Much With Us," in "The Problem of Judaism in America," special supplement, *Conservative Judaism* 56 (2004): 21–24; Diana Pinto, *A New Jewish Identity for Post-1989 Europe*, JPR Policy Paper 1 (London: Jewish Policy Research, 1996).

48. DellaPergola, *World Jewry beyond 2000*, 45–48.

49. The ramifications of this for the Jewish future can be viewed in different ways; see Egon Mayer, *Love and Tradition: Marriage Between Jews and Christians* (New York: Plenum, 1985); Avis Miller, Janet Marder, and Steven Bayme, *Approaches to Intermarriage: Areas of Consensus* (New York: American Jewish Committee, 1993); Bruce A. Phillips, *Re-examining Intermarriage: Trends, Textures, Strategies, Report of a New Study* (New York: American Jewish Committee, 1997); Sylvia Barack Fishman, *Double or Nothing: Jewish Families and Mixed Marriage* (Waltham, Mass.: Brandeis University Press, 2004); *New Jewish Identities: Contemporary Europe and Beyond*, ed. Zvi Gitelman et al. (Budapest: Central European University Press, 2003); Pinto, *New Jewish Identity*.

50. See, for example, Julian Levinson, "Transmitting *Yiddishkeit*: Irving Howe and Jewish-American Culture," *Jewish Culture and History* 2, no. 2 (1999): 42–65.

51. Cf. Shmuel Feiner, *The Jewish Enlightenment* (Philadelphia: University of Pennsylvania Press, 2003), 13, who has observed that the Kulturkampf between modernists and fundamentalists did indeed start in the eighteenth century and has continued till today.

52. Demographers seem to dismiss the significance of these developments because they account for only a relatively small proportion of all Jews and the overall trend is still a net flow away from religious lifestyle (DellaPergola, *World Jewry beyond 2000*, 57, 75; Waxman, *Jewish Baby Boomers*, 58). However, given demographic predictions, it is logical to assume that the demographic weight of the traditionalists will progressively increase.

53. M. H. Danzger, *Returning to Tradition: The Contemporary Revival of Orthodox Judaism* (New Haven: Yale University Press, 1989); Lynn Davidman, *Tradition in a Rootless World: Women Turn to Orthodox Judaism* (Berkeley and Los Angeles: University of California Press, 1991). Waxman, *Jewish Baby Boomers*, 129, cites the common view that renascent fundamentalism is but a confirmation of the ascendancy of secularism. As fundamentalism gains strength and momentum, this may prove to be, at best, a description of early stages of the process.

54. A. Finkielkraut, "In the Name of the Other: Reflections on the Coming Antisemitism," *Azure* 18 (autumn 2004): 21–33; *A New Antisemitism: Debating Judeophobia in 21st Century Britain*, ed. Paul Iganski and Barry Kosmin (London: Profile, 2003); Abraham Foxman, *Never Again? The Threat of the New Antisemitism* (San Francisco: HarperCollins, 2003).

55. Moshe Rosman, "The History of Jewish Women in Early Modern Poland: An Assessment," *Polin* 18 (2005): 25–56.

56. DellaPergola, *World Jewry beyond 2000*, 32–35.

57. Arnold M. Eisen, *Galut: Modern Jewish Reflection on Homelessness and Homecoming* (Bloomington: Indiana University Press, 1986), 117–80; idem, "The Problem," 24–25; *Contemporary Jewries: Convergence and Divergence*, ed. Eliezer Ben-Rafael, Yosef Gorny, and Yaacov Ro'i (Leiden: Brill, 2003); David Mittelberg, *The Israel Connection and American Jews* (Westport, Conn: Praeger, 1999); O. Seliktar, *Divided We Stand: Jews, Israel and the Peace Process* (Westport, Conn: Praeger, 2002); Barry Kosmin, Antony Lerman, and Jacqueline Goldberg, *The Attachment of British Jews to Israel* (London: Institute for Jewish Policy Research, 1997); David Cesarani, "The Dynamics of Diaspora: The Transformation of British Jewish Identity," *Jewish Culture and History* 4, no. 1 (2001): 62; David Weinberg, "Between America and Israel: The Quest for a Distinct European Jewish Identity in the Post-War Era," *Jewish Culture and History* 5, no. 1 (2002): 91–120; Y. M. Bodemann, *In der Wogen der Erinnerung: jüdische Existenz in Deutschland* (Munich: Deutscher Taschenbuch, 2002), 164–84; Gabriel Sheffer, "From Israeli Hegemony to Diaspora Full Autonomy: The Current State of Diaspora Ethno-National Diasporism and the Alternatives Facing World

Jewry," in *Jewish Centers and Peripheries: Europe between America and Israel Fifty Years after World War II*, ed. S. I. Troen (New Brunswick, N.J.: Transaction, 1999), 41–64; idem, "A Nation and Its Diaspora: A Re-Examination of Israeli – Jewish Diaspora Relations," *Diaspora* 11 (2002): 331–58; Pinto, *New Jewish Identity*.

58. Aryeh Meir and Lisa Hostein, *The High Cost of Jewish Living* (New York: American Jewish Committee, 1992).

59. This in contrast to developments in late eighteenth-century Germany, which Jacob Katz, *Out of the Ghetto: The Social Background of Jewish Emancipation, 1770–1870* (New York: Schocken, 1978), 42–56, termed a "semi-neutral society."

60. DellaPergola, *World Jewry beyond 2000*, 9–11, 25. There is also something called the "enlarged Jewish population" that includes the core Jewish population, plus Jews by birth or parentage who do not currently identify as Jews, plus non-Jewish household members living with Jews (p. 10).

61. Ibid., 45.

62. Many religious leaders, especially Orthodox ones, are fighting hard to retain the primacy of the normative definition. However, the sheer numbers of "non-Jews" seeking to be identified as Jews, especially in Israel, and the problems implied by the Jewish demographic decline delineated above, are powerful forces opposing their efforts. It seems, given the postmodern impracticality of imposing the policy of the biblical Ezra (Ezra 10:11), they eventually may have to choose between the policy of Zerubbabel (Ezra 2:59) and outright schism.

63. For philosophical musings on the meaning of "postmodern," see Andreas Huyssen, *After the Great Divide* (Bloomington: Indiana University Press, 1986); Steven Best and Douglas Kellner, *Postmodern Theory: Critical Interrogations* (New York: Guilford, 1991); Jean-Francois Lyotard, *The Postmodern Condition* (Minneapolis: University of Minnesota Press, 1984); Jürgen Habermas, *Lectures on the Philosophical Discourse of Modernity* (Cambridge: MIT Press, 1987); Adi Ophir, פוסטמודרניזם: עמדה פילוסופית (Postmodernism: A philosophical position), in חינוך בעדן השיח הפוסטמודרניסטי (Education in the postmodern era), ed. I. Gur-Ze'ev (Jerusalem: Magnes, 1997), 148–60.

Intellectual and Cultural History

On Prayer in Yiddish

New Sources and Perspectives

DAVID E. FISHMAN

In nineteenth-century German Jewry, prayer in the vernacular was a highly charged and controversial issue that divided the adherents of Reform Judaism from Orthodoxy and the Positive-Historical school. Prayer in German was one of the primary innovations of the Hamburg Israelite Temple, established in 1818, and this practice was severely and repeatedly attacked in the pamphlet of rabbinic letters, *Ve'eleh divrei haberit* (And these are the words of the Covenant) (1819), which denounced the Hamburg Temple. Some twenty-six years later, the issue resurfaced at the Frankfurt assembly of rabbis (1845), in a heated confrontation between Zacharias Frankel, Abraham Geiger, and others, on whether Hebrew should be the primary language of prayer or play a minor, residual role in the service. The resolution passed at the conference in support of Geiger's position (that German predominate in the service) led Frankel to dissociate himself from the conference.[1]

In the rather intense polemics surrounding the issue, some of the traditionalist participants argued that prayer in Hebrew had been the universal practice among Jews since antiquity. But was this indeed the case? Leaving aside the language of Jewish prayer in antiquity, in medieval Persia, Sepharad, and Italy, one may ask: Did medieval and early modern Ashkenazic Jews in Central and Eastern Europe ever pray in their vernacular, that is, in Yiddish? This question relates not to the body of *tkhines*, voluntary and supplementary devotional prayers recited by women, but to the obligatory, statutory liturgy. Did individuals or groups ever recite the *Shema'* or the *'Amidah* in Yiddish? And if so, was the practice found only among women, or also among men?

Two major scholars of Yiddish studies were divided on this question. Max Weinreich responded in the affirmative in his *History of the Yiddish Language*. Basing himself mainly on the existence of old Yiddish-language prayerbooks, written or printed without any Hebrew text, which date back to the late fifteenth century, he concluded:

> We can assume that these exclusively Yiddish texts were not only tools for study. Some congregants probably prayed from them. And perhaps not only in private. It is certainly possible that while the congregation prayed in Hebrew, some of those present prayed in Yiddish.[2]

Weinreich added that while "there is no absolute certainty that the Yiddish texts were used for real prayer ... there is an internal persuasiveness to the facts, when viewed together."[3]

In direct contrast, Chone Shmeruk stated quite categorically in his *Yiddish Literature: Chapters in Its History* that Jews never prayed in the synagogue in Yiddish.

> The canonization of the prayerbook did not allow for the inclusion of texts in the vernacular during synagogue prayers. ... The Yiddish translations of the prayers were intended to assist the understanding of the Hebrew texts, which alone were obligatory. It is highly doubtful that it was ever the custom to recite these translations during public congregational prayer.[4]

Shmeruk conceded that "from time to time, there were those who urged that prayers be conducted in Yiddish,"[5] but he apparently held that such calls were voiced by a few idiosyncratic individuals and did not reflect a broader social trend.

This difference of opinion between Weinreich and Shmeruk reflects in miniature their differing views on the role of Yiddish in traditional Ashkenazic Jewry. Whereas Weinreich strove to demonstrate that Yiddish gradually occupied more and more "new territories" (by which he meant literary and cultural roles), and eventually attained a status of "co-sanctity" alongside Hebrew, Shmeruk stressed the limited possibilities for Yiddish in traditional Jewish culture, where Hebrew predominated. Yiddish could only occupy the "open 'blanks' which were left behind for it."[6] The question of prayer in Yiddish was a touchstone for their conflicting conceptions of the flexibility or hierarchical rigidity of the bilingual system of Ashkenazic Jewish culture. For this reason, Weinreich dealt at length with the "aspiration to introduce prayer in Yiddish," whereas Shmeruk dismissed the phenomenon briefly and categorically.[7]

In this study, I would like to reopen the consideration of this question, examining it from both a methodological and an empirical perspective.

I. Methodology: What Constitutes Evidence

The existence of Yiddish prayerbooks without accompanying Hebrew texts, both in manuscript and in print, constitutes the raw material for the thesis that some Jews once prayed in Yiddish. The best known examples of such prayerbooks are the Yiddish manuscript *maḥzor* for the festivals composed by Menachem Oldendorf in Mestre (near Venice) in 1504, and Yosef bar Yakar's Yiddish *siddur*, published in Ichenhausen (Bavaria) in 1544, to which many more can be added.[8] It would have been technically possible to use these manuscripts and books for synagogue prayer, because the first words of every prayer were given in Hebrew, usually in larger script, followed by the full text of the prayer in Yiddish: "*Ma ṭovu ohalekha ya'aqov: vi gor gut zayn dayne getselt yankev,*" and so on. Thus, a congregant using the Yiddish prayerbook could follow the cantor's Hebrew chanting with relative ease. On the other hand, the Yiddish text was considerably longer than the Hebrew original (because of Hebrew's compactness), and it might have been difficult for the congregant praying in Yiddish to keep up with the cantor and others around him.

But one cannot draw hard conclusions from technical possibility alone. There is no explicit evidence that Menachem Olendorf, Yosef Bar Yakar, and their like intended that their works be used for the actual recitation of the prayers. Quite the contrary; the extant introductions to Yiddish prayerbooks suggest that such texts were intended for private reading and study, in preparation for prayer in Hebrew. When Yosef bar Yakar exclaimed, "I consider those who pray in Hebrew without understanding a word to be fools; I'd like to know what kind of intention they can have," his point was to urge people to study the prayers in Yiddish translation and familiarize themselves with their contents, so that they would have sincere intention when they prayed in Hebrew.

Indeed, Bar Yakar's introduction began with a tribute to the Hebrew language, in which he declared that it was the most beautiful language in the universe for prayer.[9] This auxiliary, preparatory objective was stated most clearly in the introduction to the first printed Yiddish *maḥzor* without Hebrew (Prague, 1600): "Any Jewish woman who has read through this *maḥzor* once or twice may consider herself a learned lady."[10] The volume was intended for reading, not for praying.

Thus, the mere existence of a literature of Yiddish prayerbooks does not warrant the conclusion that they were used for actual prayer.

The second type of evidence offered in support of the "prayer in Yiddish" hypothesis is the exhortative statements in favor of praying in Yiddish that may be found in a number of moralistic and other works. Israel Zinberg assembled such statements from *Sefer ḥasidim*, *Lev ṭov*, the writings of Yehiel Mikhael Epstein, and

Aaron b. Shmuel's *Liblikhe tfileh* in a classic article entitled "The Struggle for Yiddish in Old Yiddish Literature."[11] When one "views together" these appeals with the extant prayerbooks, one may conclude that there was a self-conscious social movement for prayer in Yiddish, in which rank-and-file Jews participated. If one finds both exhortations and books to implement them, then one can safely assume that a part of the community adopted the practice that was being urged—prayer in Yiddish.

These exhortations await a new, critical, dispassionate, and contextual analysis. The writings of the late-seventeenth-century moralist R. Yehiel Mikhael Epstein exemplify the need for such texts to be read with great care. Shlomo Noble, basing himself on Zinberg's work, extracted a number of quotations from Epstein's writings to demonstrate that the latter strongly urged Jews to pray in Yiddish. However, Noble's contentions were promptly refuted by Hayim Liberman, who read the same quotations in the broader context of Epstein's works and reached an opposite conclusion: Epstein held that the statutory prayers composed by the Men of the Great Assembly *must* be recited in Hebrew and buttressed this position with kabbalistic and other arguments. It was only regarding liturgical poems by the medieval *paytanim*, and other supplementary texts, that Epstein argued for recitation in Yiddish, if one did not understand the Hebrew. According to many halachic authorities, the liturgical poems could be omitted altogether from one's prayers, and Epstein also suggested that if one didn't understand their meaning, one could skip them.[12]

But even were one to conclude that all the statements by Epstein and others actually urged their readers to recite the statutory prayers in Yiddish, this phenomenon should be seen in its proper proportions. One must not conflate statements from disparate countries and centuries to create the impression of a social movement. In reality, we are dealing with a few short sentences from the thirteenth century (*Sefer ḥasidim*); two statements from Poland—one from the sixteenth and one from the early seventeenth century (*Lev tov* and Isaac Sulkes's *Sefer shir ha-shirim*); one work from late-seventeenth-century Germany (Epstein), and another from the eighteenth century (Aaron B. Shmuel). That is a far cry from a documented trend or movement. If a social movement had developed in favor of prayer in Yiddish, one would also expect to find statements by its opponents, but there are no polemical writings *against* prayer in Yiddish. The computerized database of responsa literature at Bar Ilan University does not record a single responsum dealing with this issue in the sixteenth, seventeenth, or eighteenth centuries—the period when this movement purportedly existed.

In the absence of further historical evidence, these authors should be considered lone, idiosyncratic voices. The extent to which they had a following or impact remains unclear. It is methodologically unsound to rely on exhortations or appeals as descriptions of fact. If a preacher such as R. Ephraim of Lunschitz, for example, urged the community of Posen in his sermons to increase its charity-giving, we would not be able to conclude from that alone that Jewish philanthropy in Posen increased in the early seventeenth century. First of all, the sermon may have been no more than an exhortation by a preacher and moralist, and the statement does not indicate that R. Ephraim himself took any follow-up action. Even if R. Ephraim did follow up with action to mobilize philanthropy, there is no way to know whether the community responded. To conclude that funds for charity increased is yet another logical jump. The latter could only be determined using descriptive sources.

The same considerations apply to prayer in Yiddish. Without descriptive sources attesting to the fact, the hypothesis remains uncertain. And the scholars who dealt with the subject did not present any such sources.

II. Sources from Medieval France and Germany

I would like to present and analyze three rabbinic sources from the twelfth and thirteenth centuries that confirm explicitly that women prayed at the time in the vernacular (Hebrew: *bela'az*). It should be noted that students of the history of Yiddish language, literature, and folklore in pre-modern times have made very little use of rabbinic literature, particularly of talmudic commentaries and codes, which are a treasure-trove for Jewish social history. Jacob Katz and Haym Soloveitchik have shown that entire dimensions of Jewish life (economy, communal relations, religious ritual and theology) can be reconstructed and illuminated based on such sources.[13] Much information can likewise be gleaned regarding the social functions and status of Yiddish, if one knows how to navigate talmudic literature and read it historically.

Before turning to the medieval rabbinic sources, it is best to summarize the talmudic passage that deals with the issue of language of prayer, since all subsequent rabbinic authorities refer back to it. Mishnah *Sotah* 32b states in straightforward fashion: "The following are said in any language ... the reading of the *Shema'* and the *'Amidah*." But in the Gemara that follows, we learn that both parts of this statement are subject to dispute.

Regarding the *Shema'*, the Gemara eventually rules according to the view of the Sages, that "*Shema'—bekhol lashon she-ata shomea',*" "'Hear o Israel' [may be said] in any language that you understand," and rejects the opposing opinion of R. Judah the Prince (*Sotah* 32b, *Berakhot* 13a).

Regarding the *'Amidah*, the Gemara's ultimate ruling is not as categorical as the original mishnaic statement and constitutes a compromise between two conflicting approaches. The Sages maintain their principle, that any language is acceptable in prayer, and say of the *'Amidah*: "It is [a plea for] mercy—one prays however one needs to." But R. Judah objects that "One should never ask for one's needs in Aramaic" and quotes an earlier statement by the Tana R. Yohanan: "Whoever asks for his needs in Aramaic is not heard by the ministering angels, because the ministering angels do not recognize the Aramaic language." The Gemara reaches a compromise in the conflict between the Sages and R. Yohanan by ruling, "This [view is followed]—in private, and that [view is followed]—in public." Rashi explains the ruling as follows: Private prayers must not be said in Aramaic, because an individual praying alone is in need of the assistance of the ministering angels to bring his prayers before the Almighty, and the angels do not recognize Aramaic. But public prayers recited by a *minyan* may be said in any language, including Aramaic, because a *minyan* does not need the intermediacy of the angels for their prayers. The Divine presence rests in their midst, and God accepts their prayers directly (*Sotah* 33a; this ruling is cited by Alfasi to *Berakhot* 9a).

Now let us turn to the medieval sources. In each case, we will introduce the author of the quotation and offer a translation–interpretation of his words.

JUDAH BAR YAKAR (D. BETWEEN 1201 AND 1218)

R. Judah bar Yakar was born in Provence, studied in France with the tosafists, later returned to Provence, and eventually settled in Spain. His greatest claim to fame is the fact that he was Nahmanides' teacher. Despite his ultimate migration to Spain, R. Judah is considered to be a product and representative of the French tradition in rabbinic culture. The customs he cites are French ones ("And we say it thus ... in the entire land of France"), and the vernacular words he uses (*bela'az*) are old Judeo-French.[14] R. Judah composed a commentary to the above-mentioned talmudic passage that has survived in several places, an indication that it was considered important and influential.[15]

R. Judah bar Yakar begins with the proposition that R. Yohanan's objection was not only to praying in Aramaic, but to prayer in any language other than Hebrew.

We many interpret [this passage to mean] that the ministering angels do not recognize any language on earth other than Hebrew, which is the language of the angels. We should read it as follows: "Rav said, one should not ask for his needs in Aramaic," by which he meant *even* in Aramaic, which is close to Hebrew.[16]

This interpretation expands the ruling of the Gemara to mean that a person should recite his private prayers (without a minyan) *only* in Hebrew—a conclusion which creates discomfort for R. Judah because it leads to a direct conflict between talmudic law and the practice of his own generation.

According to this interpretation, the [prayers of the] women are not heard when they pray in the vernacular without a congregation, because the angels do not bring before God [prayers said in] any language other than Hebrew, which they understand. But with a congregation, the women may pray in any language.[17]

R. Judah felt compelled to justify the contemporary popular practice of women praying in the vernacular and to reconcile it with the law. He did so by offering the following novel basis for leniency:

But if they [= the women] pray with tears and cry out because of an injustice, then they are in no need for the angels to bring their prayers before God. For the [Lord's] gates of tears and injustice are not sealed. And this is also the case if they pray with great fervor due to distress; they will be heard even though the angels do not recognize their language.[18]

R. Judah's lenient ruling alludes to the talmudic dictum that "Since the day the Temple was destroyed, the gates of prayer have

been sealed. ... But the gates of tears have not been sealed." To
which Rav Hisda added, "All gates are sealed, except for the gates
of injustice" (*Berakhot* 32b, *Bava Meṣiah* 59a). R. Judah drew on
these dicta to argue that the fervor and intensity of women's
prayer in the vernacular enables them to circumvent the angels
and be heard by God directly.

This source allows us to conclude that in late twelfth-century
France, women recited the statutory prayers, both in private and
in the synagogue, in the vernacular (*bela'az*). The context of R.
Judah's remarks, as a commentary on the talmudic passage in
Sotah, leaves no room for doubt that the discussion is of statutory
prayer and not of voluntary devotional prayers. He also offers a
vivid description of the style of women's prayer in the vernacular:
with tears, with cries against God's injustice toward them, and
with great fervor due to their distress. This characterization is
strikingly similar to the tearful, plaintive style in which Yiddish
tkhines were recited, according to depictions in nineteenth-century Yiddish literature. R. Judah bar Yakar could not accept the
idea that such moving, heartfelt prayers were said in vain and
would not be received by God because of the language in which
they were recited. He therefore reconciled the existing practice
with the talmudic view of R. Yohanan.

R. JONAH OF GERONA (D. 1263)

Nothing is known concerning R. Jonah's birth and childhood.
He studied in the academy of the Sages of Evreux, the most
important French rabbinic academy in the thirteenth century, and
later moved to Spain, where he composed his famous moralistic
treatise *Sha'arei teshuvah*. Contemporary historians attribute great
importance to R. Jonah's role in transmitting the teachings of the
French tosafists and German pietists (*Ḥasidei ashkenaz*) to Spain.[19]

R. Jonah addressed the issue of language of prayer in his commentary to Alfasi's compendium on tractate *Berakhot*, a commen-

tary which was compiled by his disciples during his lifetime. Writing in a period several decades after R. Judah bar Yakar, R. Jonah confirmed the latter's testimony that women prayed in the vernacular:

> We conclude that prayer in private should be said only in Hebrew. And this raises a question concerning the custom found throughout the world that women pray in other languages. Since they are obligated to pray, they should pray in no other language but Hebrew.[20]

R. Jonah noted that the practice was found in many countries— not only in France, as one might conclude from R. Judah bar Yakar's testimony. This might suggest that the custom of women's vernacular prayer originated in twelfth-century France and spread from there to other countries. In any case, the comment is important in our context, because it is the first known intimation that in Germanic lands women prayed in old Yiddish. R. Jonah cited an explanation reconciling the custom with talmudic law.

> The rabbis of France, of blessed memory, wish to provide a basis for the custom, and say: When an individual recites the same prayers in private that the congregation recites in public, these are considered public prayers. An individual may therefore say them in a different language. And as for the statement by R. Judah 'one should never ask for one's needs in Aramaic'—this refers to private devotions, such as praying for a sick person, or for some sorrow which one has at home, etc.[21]

Thus, according to R. Jonah, women's prayer in the vernacular attracted the attention not only of R. Judah bar Yakar, but of "the rabbis of France" at large. They felt compelled to justify the custom by interpreting the talmudic text so that the two did not conflict with each other. This was in keeping with the general tendency of the French tosafists to justify and sanctify existing customs, even if it required creative or contrived interpretations of the talmudic passages with which they conflicted.[22]

The explanation offered by the French rabbis was entirely different from the one given by R. Judah bar Yakar —further evidence that the rabbis struggled to find solutions on the matter. It was not the women's tears that purified and legitimized their prayers in a foreign (non-Hebrew) tongue, but the fact that the prayers recited were statutory prayers, which were also said communally in the synagogue. When the Talmud admonished against asking for one's needs in other languages, it was referring to private devotions for the health and well-being of one's family and friends, not to the recitation of the statutory prayers.

It is important to note that this explanation gave with one hand but took away with the other. It justified saying the *'Amidah* in other languages, but it would have prohibited the recitation of *tkhines* in Yiddish or other vernaculars. This restrictive corollary would not have troubled the French rabbis if women did not yet recite *tkhines* in the early thirteenth century.

R. Asher b. Yehiel (b. ca. 1250, d. 1327)

R. Asher was born in Germany, where he was a foremost disciple of R. Meir of Rothenberg. After the latter's arrest in 1286, R. Asher was recognized as the rabbinic leader of German Jewry. He left Ashkenaz in 1303 and settled in Spain, where he lived until the end of his life. It is widely accepted that R. Asher wrote his talmudic commentary while still living in Germany, and he is therefore considered to be one of the foremost Ashkenazic authorities.[23]

R. Asher begins his commentary on this talmudic passage by citing R. Jonah's remarks, with its explanation that statutory prayers are considered public prayers (even if recited in private) and may be said in any language. But instead of endorsing it, he adds:

It seems to me that this is not a difficult problem. For it was specifically in this language [Aramaic] that R. Judah said that one should not ask for one's needs. ... This language is repulsive in their [the angels'] eyes, to listen to it.[24]

One may deduce from R. Asher's comment that he was likewise familiar with the custom of women praying in other languages, which in his native Ashkenazic context meant praying in Yiddish. But he offered yet another, a third, explanation to reconcile the custom with talmudic law: R. Judah's admonition was only against prayer in Aramaic, and there was no analogy between Aramaic and other languages.

It is worth considering why R. Asher was not satisfied with the explanation offered by his predecessors, the French tosafists, for whom he usually had great reverence. There must have been a practical difference between his explanation and theirs. As we noted above, the explanation of the French rabbis would have prohibited the recitation of private devotions such as the *tkhines* in any language other than Hebrew. R. Asher's explanation permitted recitation of private devotional prayers in Yiddish, by restricting the entire talmudic prohibition of prayer in the vernacular to Aramaic. R. Asher's son, R. Jacob b. Asher, in his code *Arba'ah ṭurim*, stated this difference explicitly. Under the laws of prayer, R. Jacob cited the view of the French rabbis, that the *'Amidah* could be recited—even in private—in any language, but that individual devotional prayers must be said in Hebrew. He contrasted this with the view of his father, R. Asher: "My father wrote that even an individual asking for his needs may do so in any language other than Aramaic."[25]

Based on this difference of opinion between the French rabbis and R. Asher, I believe one can draw the conclusion that women's Yiddish *tkhines* existed by the late thirteenth century. R. Asher, like his French predecessors, wanted to justify existing custom, but he realized that for his time and place, the French rabbis' explanation was not sufficient. A new interpretation was needed to make halachic space for the practice of reciting Yiddish *tkhines*.

CONCLUSIONS

Several scholars have called attention to the statements in *Sefer hasidim* (mid 13th-c. Ashkenaz) endorsing prayer in the vernacular if one does not know Hebrew.

> It is better for a person to pray and recite the *Shema'* and the blessings in a language he understands, than to pray in Hebrew and not understand.
> If the [person's] heart does not know what is coming forth from his mouth, of what use is it to him? It is therefore better that he pray in the language he understands.[26]

As we argued above, such admonitions in a moralistic treatise cannot be taken as reflections of social reality, and this is all the more so in the case of *Sefer hasidim*, whose authors' relationship to mainstream Jewish society is itself subject to dispute.[27] But when the statements from *Sefer hasidim* are taken together with the descriptive testimonies regarding prayer in the vernacular given by R. Judah bar Yakar, R. Jonah of Gerona, and R. Asher b. Yehiel, it becomes convincingly clear that there was real ferment in this area in France and Germany during the late twelfth and thirteenth centuries. Women recited the *'Amidah* in Judeo-French and in old Yiddish both at home and in the synagogue.[28]

There is no evidence to suggest that men prayed in the vernacular. On the contrary, R. Judah bar Yakar's comments suggest that women's prayer differed from that of men both in language and in style. Only women prayed as a matter of course with tears and vocal outcries.

The work of one of the authorities we reviewed, R. Asher b. Yehiel, testifies to the fact that personal devotional prayer in the vernacular emerged slightly later than statutory prayer in the vernacular—in the thirteenth century. This leads to the conclusion that the phenomenon of Yiddish *tkhines* is much older than previously assumed, and that it was part of a larger burgeoning of vernacular prayer among women in Franco-German Jewry.

III. Later Sources

Did the practice of women's prayer in Yiddish persist in later centuries? The evidence is sparse, because the issue of prayer in the vernacular, which drew the attention of the French tosafists and R. Asher, disappears from the pages of later talmudic commentaries. Later authorities do not even bother to add "and we rely on the French rabbis in this matter," which would confirm continuity of Yiddish prayer; or to state the opposite, "and this is not practiced today." Most of the testimonies I have found indicate a shift in women's prayer from Yiddish to Hebrew.

ECHOES FROM ITALY

The most fascinating text of all emanates from a remote corner—from an unknown rabbinic author in sixteenth-century Italy, Shelomo Sha'ar Arye (Portaleone). The author's name indicates that he was of Italian-Jewish origin, but his place of residence and social milieu remain unclear. One should recall that sixteenth-century Italian Jewry was a mixture of Ashkenazic, Sephardic, Italian, and other subcommunities, and a considerable concentration of Yiddish-speaking Ashkenazic Jews resided in the northern part of the country. But whether Portaleone hailed from the north, or there were other reasons for his taking an interest in the question of vernacular prayer, is unknown.[29]

After citing R. Jonah of Gerona's explanation for women saying the 'Amidah in the vernacular, Portaleone writes in his notes to Alfasi's compendium:

It is possible to explain [the women's practice] by remarking that necessity is the basis for its own rules—because most women do not memorize [the prayers] in Hebrew, as do the men. In the time of the ancients, when the printing press did not yet exist, women used to be taught to memorize the prayers in the vernacular, for it was easier to learn them [that way]. And this continued a certain amount of time after the innovation of printing, according to the previous custom. But in our time, the matter has been corrected by the easily printed prayerbooks. Thus, also among the women, the vast majority pray from prayerbooks in Hebrew. But it seems to me that the earlier custom was a proper and good custom, because in that way they knew what they were saying. This is not the case when they pray in Hebrew; nearly all of them chirp without knowing what they are chirping.[30]

Portaleone reports that the custom of women's prayer in the vernacular has declined, and only remnants of it exist in his time, the sixteenth century. He connects the old custom with the practice of reciting the prayers by rote, before the advent of print and the proliferation of printed prayerbooks. Modern scholars of Jewish prayer confirm Portaleone's remark regarding memorized recitation of the prayers in the Middle Ages, noting that manuscripts of the liturgy were great rarities and that only the cantor and select individuals read their prayers from a written text.[31] Portaleone adds that it was very difficult for women, who did not understand Hebrew, to memorize the liturgy in an unknown language. They therefore memorized their prayers in the vernacular and recited them in it. Only after the advent of print, and the dissemination of printed prayerbooks, did memorization become superfluous. From then on, men and women alike could read the prayers in Hebrew.

Portaleone's testimony is plausible, but is any of it corroborated by sources from medieval Ashkenaz? I believe so. The full text of one of the statements in *Sefer ḥasidim* cited above reads as follows:

If someone approaches you who does not understand Hebrew, and is God-fearing, and wants to have intention [during prayer]; or if a woman approaches you, tell them to *learn* the prayers in the language they understand, for prayer must be with understanding of the heart. If the heart does not know what is coming forth from the mouth, of what use is it to him? It is therefore better that he pray in the language he understands.[32] [emphasis added]

Why does the source advise people to *learn* the prayers in their own spoken everyday language? Anyone knowing the Hebrew alphabet could simply pick up the text of the prayers and *read* them in the vernacular without difficulty! But in thirteenth-century Ashkenaz, prayers were not simply read, but were memorized. Therefore *Sefer ḥasidim* advised women and unlearned men to learn, that is, study and review, the prayers in the vernacular, until they were able to recite them by heart.

There is another text indicating that Portaleone's testimony applies not only to Italy, but to Ashkenaz as well. R. Eleazar of Worms, a leader of the German-Jewish pietists and author of *Sefer ha-roqeaḥ* (mid 13th c.), authored a lament for his martyred wife, Dolca, which includes several stanzas describing her manner of prayer. Several of the phrases in those stanzas might be read as indicating that Dolca prayed and even authored prayers in Yiddish ("she chanted hymns and prayers, and recited supplications"), but their formulation is ultimately ambiguous. In the middle of those stanzas, one somewhat unusual phrase stands out: "In all the lands, she taught the women and sang hymns."[33] Why does the poem speak of Dolca as a teacher in the midst of stanzas describing her praying and singing? With the help of Portaleone's testimony, we can now understand that this is not a digression or an aside from the main theme: Dolca taught women the prayers—teaching them to chant them by heart in the vernacular, that is, in Yiddish.

Thus Portaleone's testimony does not stand alone. There is

corroborating evidence that it accurately portrays the state of women's prayer before the advent of print. The evidence from the thirteenth century is ample and diverse, while the fourteenth and fifteenth centuries are shrouded in mystery, because there are no explicit testimonies. But if one accepts Portaleone's account, the shift among women from vernacular prayer to Hebrew prayer took place in the late fifteenth to early sixteenth century, with the widespread dissemination of printed Hebrew prayerbooks. If so, Ashkenazic women still prayed in Yiddish in the fifteenth century and Weinreich may have been partially correct: The fifteenth-century manuscripts of the *siddur* and *maḥzor* in Yiddish may very well have been used as textbooks for women to memorize their prayers.

MIXED EVIDENCE

Several later sources lead to the conclusion that the practice of statutory prayer in Yiddish disappeared in most places. What follows are three rabbinic testimonies which confirm this as fact:

(a) R. Hayyim b. Bezalel, late sixteenth–century rabbi, and brother of the famed Maharal of Prague, writes:

> And it is our custom that also the women, children, and igno-rant [men] pray in Hebrew. Even though they do not under-stand Hebrew, the soul rejoices in using the holy tongue. ... And although they do not understand, they can at least direct their hearts to their Father in heaven. And although it is virtu-ally certain that they will make mistakes many times [while reciting the prayers], nonetheless, since their intention is beloved [before God], 'the kindness of God will surround them' [Ps. 32:10]. For the letters of the word חסד *ḥesed* [kind-ness] precede the letters of the word טעה *ṭa'ah* [erred].[34]

(b) R. Judah Leyb b. Shimon, rabbi of Frankfurt in the late seventeenth century, offered identical testimony in his commentary to R. Menahem Azariah of Fano's kabbalistic treatise, '*Asarah ma'amarot*. R. Menahem Azariah, a well known Italian-Jewish scholar, wrote that God took more pleasure in prayers recited in a foreign tongue, but with intention and a broken heart, than in prayers recited without intention in Hebrew.

Concurring with this view, R. Judah of Frankfurt lamented:

> And this is not the practice. For women, children, men, and those like them all pray in Hebrew, and chirp without knowing what they are chirping. They believe that moving their lips in Hebrew is an act which is favorable and desirable in God's eyes.[35]

R. Judah wrote these words with evident dissatisfaction. But his description was unqualified; women, children, and men all prayed in Hebrew. In order to correct the situation of people not understanding their own prayers, R. Judah proposed that women and unlettered men hire tutors to teach them the meaning of the Hebrew liturgy. He did not mention, let alone endorse, the past Ashkenazic custom of women praying in the vernacular.[36]

(c) One hundred years later, in the late eighteenth century, R. Ephraim Zalman Margoliot of Brody, Galicia—an important rabbinic authority and author—offered the same picture (with a slight variation). He noted that women recited the '*Amidah* in Hebrew and perused a translation during the cantor's repetition of the prayer. He advised unlettered men to do the same.

> If one does not want to take the trouble of studying the meaning of the words, he can certainly pray with the congregation in Hebrew, and nothing prevents him from reading the prayer again afterwards in the vernacular [*bela'az*]. *This is the custom of the women, who pray with the congregation, and then read again to themselves the printed translation in the vernacular.*[37] [emphasis added]

However, if in Galician Brody women were saying the '*Amidah* in Hebrew, this was apparently not the case in the towns of Byelorussia. R. Shneur Zalman of Liady, the founder of Habad Hasidism and a contemporary of Margoliot's, indicated in his halachic code, *Shulḥan 'arukh harav,* that women were reciting the statutory prayers in Yiddish.

In the relevant passage, R. Shneur Zalman departed from the terse language of R. Joseph Karo's *Shulḥan 'arukh* (16th c.) to review the explanations by R. Jonah of Gerona and R. Asher b. Yehiel justifying women's recitation of statutory prayers and private devotions in the vernacular. R. Shneur Zalman drew the following conclusion:

> All of this is in order to judge favorably the women, who are obligated in prayer, [and to explain] why they pray in the vernacular [*bela'az*], rather than study the prayers in Hebrew along with an explanation of the words.[38]

R. Shneur Zalman was writing as a practical codifier of halacha, not as a historian or anthologist of rabbinic commentaries. For him, women's vernacular prayer was a living custom. So far, this is the sole testimony I have found from the eighteenth century indicating that women recited the formal liturgy in Yiddish. It suggests that there were regional variations in practice in this area. Further testimonies need to be collected to complement the emerging picture.

IV. Conclusions

Based on the material assembled above, the use of Yiddish in prayer varied according to gender, period, and region. Prayer in Yiddish can neither be affirmed nor denied in a broad sweeping generalization.

We have found several sources indicating that women recited the statutory liturgy, including the *'Amidah*, both at home and in the synagogue, in Yiddish in the thirteenth century. This practice was apparently connected with their need to pray from memory, in the absence of widespread manuscript texts of the prayerbook. Vernacular prayer declined once printed Hebrew prayerbooks became widely available, in the early sixteenth century. Most, but not all, testimonies thereafter indicate that women prayed in Hebrew. Printed Yiddish *siddurim* and *maḥzorim* were used as textbooks to study the meaning of the prayers.

Notes

1. See the most recent treatment of these controversies in Michael Meyer, *Response to Modernity: A History of the Reform Movement in Judaism* (New York: Oxford University Press, 1988), 53–61, 136–38. Earlier discussions include Jakob Petuchowski, *Prayerbook Reform in Europe: The Liturgy of Liberal and Reform Judaism* (New York: World Union for Progressive Judaism, 1968), and Moshe Samet, הלכה ורפורמה: ההלכה מול תביעות המציאות בראשית העידן המודרני (Halacha and Reform: The Halacha confronts the demands of reality at the beginning of modern times) (Ph.D. diss., Hebrew University, 1967), part 3.
2. Max Weinreich, געשיכטע פֿון דער ייִדישער שפּראך (History of the Yiddish language) (New York: YIVO, 1973), 1:264.
3. Ibid., 3:272.
4. Shmeruk, ספרות יידיש: פרקים לתולדותיה (Yiddish literature: Chapters in its history) (Tel Aviv: Institute for Poetics and Semiotics of Tel Aviv University, 1978), 42 (and similarly on p. 11).
5. Ibid., 42 n. 7.
6. Weinreich, *History*, vol. I, chaps. 3 and 4, esp. 258, 262–63, 281–82; Shmeruk, *Yiddish Literature,* chap. 1, p. 11.
7. See Weinreich, *History*, 1:265–70.
8. For bibliography, selections, and analysis, see Max Grünbaum, *Jüdisch-deutsche Chrestomathie* (Leipzig: Brockhaus, 1882), 289–328; M. Steinschneider, "Deutsche Gebetbücher," *Hebraeische Bibliographie* 12 (1887): 125–29; Elazar Shulman, שפת יהודית־אשכנזית וספרותה (Judeo-German lan-

guage and literature) (Riga: A. Levin, 1913), 55–75; Weinreich, *History*, 3:271–72; Ch. Shmeruk and A. Romer-Segal, שרידים מסידור תפילה בתרגום בגניזת קהיר (?) ידיש מן המאה הט״ו (Fragments of a prayerbook in Yiddish translation from the 15th (?) century in the Cairo Geniza), *Tarbiz* 50 (1981): 456–62.

9. Cited by Weinreich, *History*, 3:272, the full introduction to his Yiddish *siddur* is reprinted in A. M. Habermann, המדפיס חיים שחור, בנו יצחק, וחתנו יוסף בר יקר (The printer Hayim Shakhor, his son Yitzhak, and his son-in-law Yosef Bar Yakar), *Qiryat Sefer* 31 (1956): 496–97.

10. מחזור של שלש רגלים וארבע פרשיות (*Maḥzor* for the festivals and special sabbaths) (Prague, 1600). Further evidence is provided by the testimony of R. Shabbetai Sheftl Horowitz (late 16th c.). He criticized those "who pray, and don't understand what their lips bring forth," and as a result, he decided during his tenure as rabbi of Frankfurt to establish groups for Jews to study the meaning of the prayers. He suggested that Jews sit down and master the translation of the prayers, or hire a tutor, if they were unable to do so independently. See his ווי העמודים (The corners of the pillars) (Frankfurt, 1717), chap. 10, p. 19.

11. דער קאמף פאר ידיש אין דער אלט־יידישער ליטעראטור (The struggle for Yiddish in Old Yiddish literature), *Filologishe shriftn fun Yivo* (Vilna) 2 (1928): 69–106; abbreviated English version in *Never Say Die: A Thousand Years of Yiddish in Jewish Life and Letters*, ed. Joshua A. Fishman (The Hague: Mouton, 1981), 161–70. See also Zinberg's געשיכטע פון דער ליטעראטור ביי יידן (History of Yiddish literature) (New York: Shklarsky, 1943), 6:185, 279–282; *History of Jewish Literature*, trans. Bernard Martin (New York: Ktav, 1975), 7:219–20.

12. Shlomo Noble, ר׳ יחיאל־מיכל עפשטיין: א דערציער און קעמפער פאר ידיש אין זיבעצנטן יארהונדערט (Rabbi Jehiel Mikhl Epstein: An educator and fighter for Yiddish in the seventeenth century) *Yivo bleter* 35 (1951): 121–38; Hayim Liberman, באמערקונגען צו ש. נאבלס ארטיקל (Comments on Sh. Noble's article) and Noble's retort in *Yivo bleter* 36 (1952): 305–21; in English, "Discussion regarding Rabbi Jehiel Mikhl Epstein," *Yivo Annual* 7 (1952): 296–304. Liberman's article was reprinted in his אהל רח״ל (R. Hayim Liberman's tent) (New York: 770 East Parkway, 1980), 2:201–30.

13. See, for instance, Katz's studies collected in הלכה וקבלה (Halacha and kabbalah) (Jerusalem: Magnes, 1984) and Soloveitchik's article "Can Halakhic Texts Talk History?" *AJS Review* 3 (1978): 153–96.

14. Chaim Dov Chavel, רבינו משה בן נחמן (Nachmanides) (Jerusalem: Mosad Harav Kook, 1967), 38-44; introduction by Shmuel Yerushalmi to R.

Judah bar Yakar's פירוש התפילות והברכות (Commentary on the prayers and blessings) (Jerusalem, 1968), 1–2.

15. The commentary is found in (a) לקט ראשונים (A compendium from the Rishonim), in תוספות איוורא – תוספות הרא״ש (*Tosafot* Evreux – *Tosafot* R. Asher) (Jerusalem, 1969), 105–7; (b) R. Avraham b. David, שאלות ותשובות תמים דעים (Responsa *Temim De'im*), no. 184; (c) Judah bar Yakar, *Commentary on the prayers*, 19–22. All citations are from (a).

16. Ibid., p. 106.

17. Ibid., p. 107.

18. Ibid.

19. Israel Ta-Shma, חסידות אשכנז בספרד: רבינו יונה, האיש ופעלו (German pietism in Spain: R. Jonah, the man and his activity), in גלות אחר גולה (ספר היובל לכבוד פרופסור חיים ביינארט) (Exile after Dispersion [Professor Chaim Beinart Festschrift]), ed. Aharon Mirski, Avraham Grosman, and Yosef Kaplan (Jerusalem: Ben-Zvi Institute, 1988), 165–94.

20. R. Jonah's commentary on Alfasi to *Berakhot* 9a.

21. Ibid. 9a–b.

22. See Jacob Katz, מעריב בזמנו ושלא בזמנו: דוגמא לזיקה בין הלכה מנהג וחברה (Ma'ariv at its time, and not at its time: An example of the relationship between halacha, custom, and society), in *Halacha and kabbalah*, 175–200; Haym Soloveitchik, "Religious Law and Change: The Medieval Ashkenazic Example," *AJS Review* 12 (1987): 205–22.

23. A. Freiman, " R. Ascher ben Jechiel," *Jahrbuch der Jüdisch-Literarischen Gesellschaft* 12 (1918): 237–317, 13 (1919): 142–254.

24. R. Asher on *Berakhot* 13a.

25. ארבעה טורים, Orah ḥayyim, end of no. 101.

26. ספר חסידים (Sefer ḥasidim), ed. Reuven Margoliot (Jerusalem, 1970), nos. 785 and 588 (in the Freimann-Vistinetzky edition [Jerusalem, 1969], nos. 1590 and 11).

27. The social position of *Hasidei Ashkenaz* (the German-Jewish pietists of the 12th and 13th centuries) is a difficult issue that has preoccupied scholars. Some argue that they were a separatist sect, which was marginal to the mainstream Jewish community, while others contend that their leaders were the recognized leaders of German Jewry. The number of members or followers of Hasidei Ashkenaz is likewise subject to dispute. See Haym Soloveitchik, "Three Themes in the Sefer Hasidim," *AJS Review*, vol. 1 (1976), pp. 311–358; Ivan G. Marcus, *Piety and Society: The Jewish Pietists in Medieval Germany* (Leiden: Brill, 1981).

28. R. Judah bar Yakar's and R. Jonah of Gerona's statements that women

prayed in the vernacular do not distinguish between their practice at home and in the synagogue. If there had been any such difference, the sources would have referred to it.

29. On Ashkenazic Jewry in Northern Italy, see M. A. Shulvass, חיי היהודים באיטליה בתקופת הרינסנס (Jewish life in Italy during the Renaissance) (New York: Histadruth Ivrith of America, 1955); on old Yiddish literature in Northern Italy, see Shmeruk, *Yiddish literature*, 72–79.

30. Cited in S. D. Luzzatto, "Bibliothèque de feu Joseph Almazi," *Hebraeische Bibliographie* 6 (1863): 54, and compared against the manuscript, British Library Add.27,176, a microfilm copy of which is in the library of the Jewish Theological Seminary of America.

31. Ismar Elbogen, התפילה בישראל בהתפתחותה ההיסטורית (The historical development of the Jewish liturgy) (Tel Aviv, 1972), 279.

32. *Sefer ḥasidim*, ed. Margoliot, no. 588; ed. Freimann-Vistinetzky, no. 11.

33. The full stanza reads: "She chanted hymns and prayers and recited supplications; the daily confession, the Sabbath '*nishmat*', and the High Holiday '*vekhol ma'aminim*'; she pleasantly uttered the sacrificial order and the Ten Commandments; in all the lands, she taught the women and sang hymns; she arranged the morning and evening prayers; she set out early for the synagogue, and left it late." Cited from Israel Kamelhar, רבינו אלעזר מגרמייזא הרוקח (Rabbi Eleazar of Worms, the Rokeach) (Raijsze, Poland, 1930), 18; see Ivan G. Marcus, "Mothers, Martyrs, and Moneylenders: Some Jewish Women in Medieval Europe," *Conservative Judaism* 38, no. 3 (spring 1986): 34–35.

34. Hayyim b. Bezalel, ספר החיים, ספר סליחה ומחילה (The Book of Life, the Book of Forgiveness and Pardon), chap. 9 (in the 1857 Lemberg edition, p. 29b). *Sefer haḥayim* was first published in 1593.

35. R. Menahem Azariah of Fano, ספר אמרות טהורות עם פירוש יד יהודה (Imrot ṭehorot, with the Yad Yehudah commentary) (Frankfurt, 1698), מאמר אם כל חי (Maxim concerning the mother of all living things), n. 31.

36. "And one whose heart is not with Him should hire a teacher who will teach him what he is praying, so that his prayers will be pure before Him." R. Judah's suggestion is identical to the practice introduced by one of his predecessors in the Frankfurt rabbinate, R. Shabbetai Sheftl Horowitz; see n. 10 above.

37. See Margoliot's commentary "Yad Ephraim" to the *Shulḥan Arukh*, Orah ḥayyim, 101:4.

38. שולחן ערוך הרב (The Rabbi's Shulḥan 'arukh), Orah ḥayyim, 101:5.

THE EARLY HASIDIC "COURT"

IMMANUEL ETKES

Whether or not one agrees that the Baal Shem Tov ("Besht") was the founder of Hasidism—a question that has recently been the subject of historiographical debate—it is evident that in his lifetime there was as yet no Hasidic movement.[1] As a socioreligious phenomenon and a force in Jewish life, Hasidism did not arise until after the death of the Besht in 1760, that is to say, during the 1760s and 1770s. Two decisive expressions of this development were the organized efforts made by some of the Besht's disciples and associates to disseminate the Hasidic way of worshiping God and the establishment of the Hasidic leader's "court" as a site of pilgrimage.

In the present article, I wish to discuss the role played by the Hasidic court in the expansion of Hasidism. I will focus on two such courts: the one centered on Rabbi Dov Ber the Maggid of Mezirech (Miedzyrzecz) and the one established by one of his disciples, Rabbi Chaim Chaikel of Amdur. The court of the Maggid of Mezirech, which was active from the mid 1760s until the Maggid's death in 1772, was, as far as we know, the first Hasidic court. The court of Rabbi Chaim Chaikel of Amdur was established in 1773, soon after the Maggid's death, and it was active until Rabbi Chaim Chaikel died in 1787. The chronological continuity between the two courts, and the fact that we are dealing with a master and his disciple, invite a comparative examination, which can teach us about the patterns that characterized the Hasidic court at its origins.

The term "court" refers to the physical enclosure in which the Hasidic leader dwelled; however, the term "court" also relates to the ceremonies practiced there, which gave content and meaning to the pilgrim's sojourn there. These ceremonies were intended, among other things, to regulate contact between the leader and the Hasidim who sought proximity to him by staying at his court. In the early stages of the consolidation and expansion of the Hasidic movement, a visit to the court served as a primary means for attracting new adherents to the ways of Hasidism and integrating them in the circle of those faithful to the Hasidic leader.

I. In the Court of the Maggid of Mezirech

As noted, Rabbi Dov Ber established the first known Hasidic court in the mid 1760s. This court was documented in the autobiography of Solomon Maimon.[2] His testimony is unique, insofar as memoir writing was rare, if not unheard of, among Polish Jews of the eighteenth century. Only Maimon's later incarnation as an Enlightenment philosopher in Berlin explains his decision to write his memoirs and publish them.[3] Indeed, the cultural and spiritual changes that Maimon had undergone between the time when he spent a few days at the court of the Maggid of Mezirech in the 1760s and the writing of his memoir in the early 1790s explain not only the very act of writing the book but also its character and tone.

Central to Maimon's autobiography is the story of a lad, blessed with talent and hungry for knowledge, who was regarded as an *'iluy* but did not find satisfaction within "the four ells of the halacha." After considerable efforts, hopeless in his opinion, to study kabbalah and to adopt the ways of Hasidism, he began to make his way persistently and determinedly to the Enlightenment.[4] While describing his life, Maimon paints a picture of Polish Jewish society in which he grew up and was educated, and from which he extricated himself in order to obtain knowledge in Western Europe. Naturally Maimon, who wrote his book for German readers, evaluated and judged traditional Jewish life according to the standards of the Enlightenment. It is not surprising, therefore, that he described certain aspects of the life of the Jews as faulty and even grotesque, and Hasidism certainly did not emerge unscathed from Maimon's judgment. However, the critical tendency that characterizes his book does not detract from its value as a historical source, for the tendentious slant is transparent and fairly easy to set aside. Furthermore, Maimon's description of his Hasidic adventure reveals the attraction that Hasidism held for him—at least during the short period when he was involved in it.[5]

The questions that underlie our examination of Maimon's memoirs are: How and why did he come to visit the court of the Maggid of Mezirech? What lasting impressions did he later recollect of his visit and his meeting with the Maggid? What can be learned from Maimon's personal story about the early stage in the expansion and consolidation of the Hasidic movement?

Let us begin with Maimon's account of how he was first exposed to Hasidism and why he decided to visit the Maggid's court:

> I could not form any accurate idea of the new sect, and did not know what to think of it, till I met with a young man, who had already been initiated into the society, and had enjoyed the good fortune of conversing with its superiors. This man happened to be traveling through the place of my abode, and I seized the opportunity of asking for some information about the internal constitution of the society, the mode of admission, and so forth. The stranger was still in the lowest grade of membership, and consequently knew nothing about the internal constitution of the society. He was therefore unable to give me any information about the subject; but, as far as the mode of admission was concerned, he assured me that that was the simplest thing in the world. Any man, who felt a desire of perfection, but did not know how to satisfy it, or wished to remove the hindrances to its satisfaction, had nothing to do but apply to the superiors of the society, and *eo ipso* he became a member.

He did not even require, as you must do on applying to a medical doctor, to say anything to these superiors about his moral weakness, his previous life, and matters of that sort, inasmuch as nothing was unknown to the superiors, they could see into the human heart, and discern everything that is concealed in its secret recesses, they could foretell the future, and bring near at hand things that are remote. Their sermons and moral teachings were not, as these things commonly are, thought over and arranged in an orderly manner beforehand. This method is only proper to the man, who regards himself as a being existing and working for himself apart from God. But the superiors of this sect hold that their teachings are divine and therefore infallible, only when they are the result of self-annihilation before God, that is, when they are suggested to them *ex tempore*, by the exigence of circumstances, without their contributing anything themselves.

As I was quite captivated by this description I begged the stranger to communicate to me some of these divine teachings. He clapped his hand on his brow as if he were waiting for inspiration from the Holy Ghost, and turned to me with a solemn mien and his· arms half-bared, which he brought into action somewhat like Corporal Trim, when he was reading the sermon. Then he began as follows:—

" 'Sing unto God a new song; His praise is in the congregation of saints [Hasidim]' (Psalm 159:1). Our superiors explain this verse in the following way. The attributes of God as the most perfect being must surpass by far the attributes of every finite being; and consequently His praise, as the expression of His attributes, must likewise surpass the praise of any such being. Till the present time the praise of God consisted in ascribing to Him supernatural operations, such as the discovery of what is concealed, the foreseeing of the future, and the production of effects immediately by His mere will. Now, however, the saints, that is, the superiors, are able to perform such supernatural actions themselves. Accordingly in this respect God has no longer pre-eminence over them; and it is therefore necessary to find some new praise, which is proper to God alone."

Quite charmed with this ingenious method of interpreting the Holy Scriptures, I begged the stranger for some more expositions of the same kind. He proceeded therefore in his inspired manner:—" 'When the minstrel played, the spirit of God came upon him' (2 Kings 3:15). This is explained in the following way. As long as a man is self-active, he is incapable of receiving the influence of the Holy Ghost; for this purpose he must hold himself like an instrument in a purely passive state. The meaning of the passage is therefore this: When the minstrel (המנגן, the servant of God), becomes like his instrument (כנגן), then the spirit of God comes upon him."

"Now," said the stranger again, "hear the interpretation of the passage from the Mishnah, where it is said, 'The honor of thy neighbor shall be as dear to thee as thine own.' Our teachers explain this in the following way. It is certain that no man will find pleasure in doing honor to himself: this would be altogether ridiculous. But it would be just as ridiculous to make too much of the marks of honor received from another, as these confer on us no more intrinsic worth than we have already. This passage therefore means merely, that the honor of thy neighbor (the honor which thy neighbor shows to thee) must be of as little value in thine eyes, as thine own (the honor which thou showest to thyself)."[6]

Maimon's text implies that he had heard about the new sect even before he met the young Hasid. However, he apparently had heard of it only indirectly and his conceptions of it were vague. Now, for the first time, he met someone who was a Hasid himself and could tell him about it from personal experience. Although Maimon describes the young man as a recent adherent of the movement and a frank speaker, it is difficult to avoid the suspicion that the young man was a propagandist on behalf of the cause, one of those emissaries sent out by the Maggid of Mezirech for that purpose. It is possible, however, that Maimon was correct, and that the young man had recently been exposed to Hasidism and was burning to speak about it to others. That ardor need not surprise us, for people who have experienced a conversion commonly seek to share with others the new truth to which they have subscribed. If indeed that was the case, then what emerges from the narrative is highly instructive: even a young and inexperienced Hasid, who met Maimon by chance, was able to arouse a high degree of curiosity and enthusiasm in him by means of his stories.

What elements in the Hasid's discourse fascinated and inspired Maimon? The first answer that occurs to one is the exceptional qualities of the Hasidic leaders. Indeed, in the light of what the young Hasid told Maimon, a new type of religious leadership had appeared, one that deviated from everything previously known in Judaism. First, although this was not said explicitly, it is clear from Maimon's report that these leaders were said to be willing to offer personal guidance to those who sought perfection. In that sense, they were different from the well-known *maggidim* and *mokhihim* (preachers) who sought to arouse their listeners to repentance and spiritual elevation, but whose exhortations remained in the realm of public instruction. Not only were the Hasidic leaders apparently willing and able to provide guidance to individuals who sought perfection, but their instruction depended on their wondrous ability to gaze into the hearts of those who addressed them and to lay bare their private secrets. Moreover, they preached while in a state of "holy inspiration."

Beyond the benefit that might accrue from the spiritual guidance of such leaders, Maimon was also likely to have been attracted by the very possibility of having direct contact with such wonderworkers. Such is the implication of his description of the young Hasid, "who had already been initiated into the society, and had enjoyed the good fortune of conversing with its superiors." Similarly, Maimon tells us later on that, upon his arrival in Mezirech, he went to the Maggid's house in hopes of being "introduced to him at once." Indeed, it is likely that even before Hasidism began to establish itself widely, rumors circulated regarding the presence of holy men endowed with remarkable virtues. The innovation constituted by the Hasidic court lay in the availability of this holy man, his willingness to confer with those who came to him to address their spiritual improvement.

Maimon's recollection of Hasidic homilies, as related to him in the name of the Hasidic leaders, was another component of the Hasid's story that made a deep impression on him and influenced his decision to go to Mezirech. As Maimon states explicitly, "I could not help being astonished at the exquisite refinement of these thoughts, and charmed with the ingenious exegesis, by which they were supported."[7] We find that Maimon was impressed both by the content of the discourses and by the interpretive sophistication they embodied. As for their content, the first homily attributed powers to the Hasidic leaders that hitherto had been the sole purview of the divine, and this was conspicuously daring. The second, referring to the passivity of the servant of the Lord as a precondition for the inspiration of the holy spirit, reflects a prominent trend in the school of the Maggid of Mezirech.[8] The innovation inherent in that idea, when seen in the context of the activism that characterized traditional expressions of worship, apparently attracted Maimon. The third homily proposes a sophisticated stratagem for overcoming pride, which apparently impressed him as well. It should be pointed out that scholars have located the written versions of the sermons that Maimon recalled from memory, thus corroborating his testimony.[9]

Thus, we find that Maimon heard tell of the exceptional virtues of the Hasidic leaders and the words of wisdom ascribed to them, and these stories impelled him to visit Mezirech himself. Before discussing his encounter with the court at Mezirech, however, we should take note of another conclusion that arises from Maimon's testimony. As noted, Maimon asked the Hasid to tell him about the internal arrangements of the society of Hasidim and how it was possible to be initiated into it. Most probably, the background of that question was Maimon's acquaintance with the arrangements of the *ḥevrot* (societies) that were common among the Jews of Poland at that time, and which operated within the framework of the traditional community. These were typically societies of artisans, or groups intended to serve a specific charitable purpose (such as arranging burials or raising money for poor brides), and there were also societies whose purpose was Torah study. Despite the differences in their goals and the character of their memberships, these societies shared a common characteristic: the formal nature of their organization. This was expressed in regulations imposing obligations on all members and enumerating procedures for acceptance. In that context, we can readily understand why Maimon asked about the rules governing acceptance in the Hasidic society. However, the young Hasid's answer was reassuring: "Any man who felt a desire of perfection ... had nothing to do but apply to the superiors of the society, and *eo ipso* he became a member."[10] The openness of the Hasidic court was evidently a factor in encouraging those who wished to visit it.

In his autobiography, Maimon relates the following about his visit to Mezirech:

> At last I arrived at M———, and after having rested from my journey I went to the house of the superior under the idea that I could be introduced to him at once. I was told, however, that he could not speak to me at the time, but that I was invited to his table on Sabbath along with the other strangers who had come to visit him; that I should then have the happiness of seeing the saintly man face to face, and of hearing the sublimest teachings out of his own mouth; that although this was a public audience, yet, on account of the individual references which I should find made to myself, I might regard it as a special interview.
>
> Accordingly on Sabbath I went to this solemn meal, and

found there a large number of respectable men who had met there from various quarters. At length the great man appeared in his awe-inspiring form, clothed in white satin. Even his shoes and snuffbox were white, this being among the Cabbalists the color of grace. He gave to every newcomer his salaam, that is, his greeting. We sat down to table and during the meal a solemn silence reigned. After the meal was over, the superior struck up a solemn inspiriting melody, held his hand for some time upon his brow, and then began to call out, "Z—— of H——, M—— of R——," and so on. Every newcomer was thus called by his own name and the name of his residence, which excited no little astonishment. Each recited, as he was called, some verse of the Holy Scriptures. Thereupon the superior began to deliver a sermon for which the verses recited served as a text, so that although they were disconnected verses taken from different parts of the Holy Scriptures they were combined with as much skill as if they had formed a single whole. What was still more extraordinary, every one of the newcomers believed that he discovered, in that part of the sermon which was founded on his verse, something that had special reference to the facts of his own spiritual life. At this we were of course greatly astonished.[11]

Maimon thus expected to meet the Maggid immediately upon his arrival in Mezirech, but he had to restrain his anticipation and suit himself to the procedures of the court. These consisted of social rituals intended to arrange and regulate contact between the Maggid and the guests who wished to approach him. Underlying these rituals were two opposite motives: creation of distance between the visitors and the Zaddik, on the one hand, and creation of the experience of personal contact between every one of the visitors and the Zaddik, on the other. The combination of these two tendencies probably enhanced the fascination of a visit to the court.

A typical example of the distancing technique was the Maggid's late entry into the dining hall, while the many visitors were awaiting his arrival. One may infer, without reading too much into the text, that the Maggid's late entry was intentional. It may also be supposed that, while awaiting the Maggid's entry, those assembled related stories to each other about his wonders. In any event, the anticipation of meeting an exceptional and extraordinary figure was immediately confirmed upon his arrival: "At length the great man appeared in his awe-inspiring form." Although the wearing of white garments on Sabbath and holidays was a kabbalistic custom adopted by the early Hasidim, the Maggid's white garments were conceived, in retrospect, as an outward expression of his personal merit.

Three elements of the Maggid's sermon fascinated Maimon, as they also impressed the other participants at the meal: the Maggid's homiletic creativeness, whereby he managed to fit together a harmonious sermon out of various and sundry verses; the personal message that everyone present found in the Maggid's words; and the fact that the personal message depended on the Maggid's ability to penetrate the depths of the listeners' souls with his gaze.

Thus, it is clear that there was substantial agreement between what Maimon had been told about the powers of the Hasidic leaders and what he himself was privileged to see and hear in the Maggid's court. The expectations that motivated him to go to Mezirech were therefore fulfilled, at least at this stage.

Further examination of Maimon's story shows that the meal and the sermon that was central to it, events that so impressed Maimon, were not at all ingenuous. Indeed, they were a carefully crafted ritual intended to impress visitors and to attract them to the new path. In the course of these proceedings, the Maggid's attention was given mainly to those whom Maimon called "newcomers." These were men who had come for the first time to spend Sabbath in the Maggid's court, and naturally they were candidates for recruitment. Upon his entry into the room where the meal was served, the Maggid greeted every newcomer. At the beginning of his sermon, he called each one by name and invited him to recite a verse. The climax of the sermon was, as noted, the personal message that everyone imagined he was finding in the Maggid's words. Thus, although this was a public event in which many people participated, the Maggid tried to give every one of the newcomers an experience with personal significance.

Confirmation and corroboration of what we have so far seen can be found in the following passage, where Maimon explains why he decided to cut himself off from the Hasidim and Hasidism:

> It was not long, however, before I began to qualify the high opinion I had formed of this superior and the whole society. I observed that their ingenious exegesis was at bottom false, and, in addition to that, was limited strictly to their own extravagant principles, such as the doctrine of self-annihilation. When a man had once learned these, there was nothing new for him to hear. The so-called miracles could be very naturally explained. By means of correspondence and spies and a certain knowledge of men, by physiognomy and skillful questions, the superiors were able to elicit indirectly the secrets of the heart, so that they succeeded with these simple men in obtaining the reputation of being inspired prophets.[12]

Thus we find that the innovative and original character of the ideas that he heard from the Maggid, as well as the Maggid's seemingly superhuman ability to perceive that which was hidden in the hearts of his listeners, aroused initial amazement and admiration for the Maggid and a desire to belong to the group of Hasidim connected to him. When these charms faded, the Hasidic episode in Maimon's life came to an end.

What were the ideas that Maimon heard in the Maggid's sermon? On this, all we seem to hear is a brief hint: "Such as the doctrine of self-annihilation." Nevertheless, Maimon provided further detailed information about the content of the ideas to which he was exposed while in Mezirech, albeit indirectly. The chapter of his memoirs that Maimon devotes to Hasidism is divided in two. The second part, from which we have quoted so far, describes his personal encounter with Hasidism. In the first part of the chapter, Maimon offers a general characterization of the Hasidim and of Hasidism. Although he claims to present Hasidism in general, this description is also probably based on his own experience in Mezirech.

In seeking to explain the essence of Hasidism and its innovations, Maimon compared the new Hasidism to the older version.[13] He characterizes the old Hasidism as a method that strives for closeness to God by means of severe asceticism. In contrast, he describes the new Hasidism in the following way:

On the other hand, those who sought to enlighten the people required, as an indispensable condition of true virtue, a cheerful state of mind disposed to every form of active exertion; and they not only allowed, but even recommended, a moderate enjoyment of all kinds of pleasure as necessary for the attainment of this cheerful disposition. Their worship consisted in a voluntary elevation above the body, that is, in an abstraction of the thoughts from all created things, even from the individual self, and in union with God. By this means a kind of self-denial arose among them, which led them to ascribe, not to themselves, but to God alone, all the actions undertaken in this state. Their worship therefore consisted in a sort of speculative adoration, for which they held no special time or formula to be necessary, but they left each one to determine it according to the degree of his knowledge. Still they chose for it most commonly the hours set apart for the public worship of God. In their public worship they endeavored mainly to attain that elevation above the body, and as they gave out, the body became in this state wholly devoid of feeling.

Such abstraction, however, was a very difficult matter; and accordingly, whenever they came out of this state by new suggestions taking possession of their minds, they labored, by all sorts of *mechanical operations*, such as movements and cries, to bring themselves back into the state once more, and to keep themselves in it without interruption during the whole time of worship. It was amusing to observe how they often interrupted their prayers by all sorts of extraordinary tones and comical gestures, which were meant as threats and reproaches against their adversary, the Evil Spirit, who tried to disturb their devotions; and how by this means they wore themselves out to such an extent, that, on finishing their prayers, they commonly fell down in complete exhaustion.[14]

What considerations lead us to the supposition that this passage reflects the experiences Maimon himself had during his visit to the Maggid's court? First, we should consider the fact that the ideas mentioned in this passage are indeed consistent with what is known to us about the Maggid's teachings. Second, when Maimon left Poland on his way to Europe in 1777, Hasidic books had not yet been printed. Although at that stage copies of Hasidic texts were circulating in manuscript, it is very doubtful whether such manuscripts had reached Maimon's hands, for in his memoirs he does not mention any close contact with Hasidim or Hasidism after leaving the Maggid's court. If these considerations are valid, then it is possible to conclude that the sermons that Maimon heard and the scenes that he witnessed in the Maggid's court included instruction for attaining mystical union with God through the methods known to us, later on, from the writings of the Maggid and his disciples.[15]

As noted, at a certain stage, the charm exerted on Maimon by the Hasidim and Hasidism faded, and his Hasidic adventure came to an end. However, Maimon's testimony sheds light on the experience of many others who came to Hasidism along a similar route but, unlike our memoirist, clung to it for a long time.

II. The Court of Rabbi Chaim Chaikel of Amdur

Let us now turn our attention to the court of Rabbi Chaim Chaikel of Amdur. He had been exposed to Hasidic teachings while at Karlin, apparently under the influence of Rabbi Aharon the Great, a disciple of the Maggid. From Karlin, Rabbi Chaim Chaikel headed for Mezirech and himself became a disciple of the Maggid. After the Maggid's death in 1772, Rabbi Chaim Chaikel began to maintain his own court in Amdur, and we may assume that by 1780 it had achieved some renown, since it is mentioned in a writ of excommunication issued by the rabbi of the district of Horodna in 1781. Rabbi Chaim Chaikel maintained his court in Amdur until his death in 1787.[16] Thus, this Hasidic court was active during the two decades of the Hasidic movement's consolidation and expansion.

The main contemporary source that sheds light on Rabbi Chaim Chaikel's court is a pamphlet entitled *Shever posh'im* (Smashing of criminals), a pamphlet that contains a vehement polemic against Hasidism, attributed to Rabbi David of Makov.[17] The passages describing Rabbi Chaim Chaikel's court were apparently written in 1787 and seem to refer to the 1770s and 1780s. The identity of the writer is not clear. It has been assumed that Rabbi David of Makov himself was the "eyewitness" described in the book, but neither the text itself nor external sources support this assumption. It is certainly possible that the author of the testimony was an acquaintance of Rabbi David of Makov's and that for obvious reasons he refrained from mentioning his name. In any case, the testimony is very valuable, for although it repeatedly expresses hostility toward Hasidism and its adherents, it is evidently based on close acquaintance with the phenomenon that it describes. This impression derives from the detailed and realistic character of the descriptions of the court. The testimony's authenticity is also evident in that it demonstrates a keen understanding of the attractive power of the Hasidic court.[18]

Let us begin with a passage dealing with the recruitment of new Hasidim for Rabbi Chaim Chaikel's court in Amdur. The author introduces it with a homily found in *Sefer toledot Ya'aqov Yosef*, which refers to the possibility in the present day of observing all 613 commandments, a well-known theological problem in Judaism that is resolved by the following proposition:

> That a person embodies in his powers and qualities all the stories of the Torah such as the Exodus from Egypt and the like and all 613 commandments and all the [mystical] worlds of *'asilut* (nobility) and *yeṣirah* (creation) and *'asiya* (action) and all that is in them, even the *merkavah* (divine chariot) and the like. Thereby, a person can keep all 613 commandments even in the present day, as explained in the aforementioned polluted book [*Sefer toledot Ya'aqov Yosef*, fol. 64]. In the Torah portion *Ve'atah teṣaveh* [and you shall command] we find the following verse: "They shall bring thee pure olive oil" [Ex. 27:20]. As one of the 613 commandments, Maimonides listed the lighting of lamps in the Temple. And this is a problem: how could this commandment be void in the present, for is not the Torah eternal? And he said that *ṣav* [commandment] comes from the term *ṣavta* [together, in Aramaic] and companionship, and this is how "and you shall command" should be understood: You shall share togetherness with people and bring them to repentence, and then, "they shall bring thee pure olive oil," that is to say, they will bring down great abundance for you and public merit, which are the lamps.[19]

The author of the testimony relates to this notion positively but complains about the harmful use of it by Hasidic propagandists:

> And in truth this is a virtuous and good lesson and there are those among them who indeed expound further on this matter. However, thereby they seek to capture souls among the lesser sons of Israel, with emissaries that they send to all the Jewish

cities to incite and to seduce as is their custom, saying to them: Look, we have a new way, which the ancients did not imagine. And moreover, you can cleave to your Maker by means of all the 613 commandments, of which until now you and your fathers only kept a portion. Furthermore, when you go with me to the rabbi in the community of Amdur and the like you will hear from his mouth such and more in this [spirit].[20]

The picture that emerges from this passage regarding Hasidic propaganda techniques is essentially similar to what we found in Maimon's memoir, although the text also enriches that picture and sharpens it. While Maimon tells us that his acquaintance with Hasidism followed a chance meeting with a young Hasid, this testimony speaks of emissaries who initiated such encounters to "incite and seduce" young men to come and visit the Hasidic court. This phenomenon was already decried bitterly in anti-Hasidic writings that were sent from Vilna in 1772,[21] so we know that propagating the sect by means of missionaries was carried on during the 1770s and 1780s, if not later. The common feature in Maimon's story and the testimony in *Shever posh'im* is the manner of enticement: Hasidism offered a new and promising way to those seeking perfection in the worship of God. Maimon became aware of that possibility under the influence of the homilies that he heard from the young Hasid. For his part, the author of *Shever posh'im* refers to a novel interpretation in *Sefer toledot Ya'aqov Yosef* which purports to enable a Jew to observe all 613 commandments "in the present"—that is, even under the limits of exilic conditions. Although not stated explicitly, the proximity in the text of this sermon to the description of the sect's recruitment efforts implies that the emissaries of the court in Amdur used such homilies as instruments of propaganda. We find that in both cases this type of Hasidic discourse served as a kind of bait to attract visitors to the Hasidic court.

The Hasidic argument cited by the author of *Shever posh'im* is interesting: the new way proposed by Hasidism, which leads to perfection in worship of God, had not been available to earlier generations. Naturally such a claim, which conveys a sense of revolutionary consciousness, was interpreted by the traditional elite as defiance toward religious authority. It is hardly surprising, therefore, that it provoked an opponent of Hasidism such as the author of *Shever posh'im*. However, by the same token, it could furnish inspiration to restless young men who were exposed to Hasidic propaganda.

Another technique ascribed by the author of Shever posh'im to Hasidic emissaries is described in the following paragraph:

> It is known that they are clever in their harmful ways ... and the chief of the inciters seduces the multitude by saying to every man who is trapped in their corruption: "Go to our rabbi Chaikel, penetrate deeply to his chamber, and confess all your sins before him that you ever committed up to this day, and he will give you a correction and will make a *pidyon* (redemption) for you, and your transgression will be removed and your sin atoned. And if you do not confess and wish to hide something from him, he will tell you, since he knows thoughts." And the fools who are caught in their evil net believe them, because he appoints two witnesses.[22]

Thus, we find that Rabbi Chaim Chaikel's emissaries encouraged the visitors to his court to meet with him alone. This personal encounter was meant to offer the aspiring Hasid spiritual instruction and moral correction. We also learn that the person seeking correction was expected to confess his sins and that Rabbi Chaim Chaikel performed an act of *pidyon* (redemption) for him. Maimon's story and the testimony here both share the knowledge that the Hasidic leaders were reputed to possess clairvoyant powers. We find that such ability, which was attributed to the Maggid, was similarly attributed to other Hasidic leaders as well. One may infer that the Maggid served as a model in this matter for his disciples, who stood at the head of Hasidic communities.[23] At any rate, the author of the testimony before us admits that belief in the power of Rabbi Chaim as "knowing thoughts" was indeed common among those who visited his court. He attributes the acceptance of this belief to the influence of "witnesses." Later on we find that the witnesses were none other than Rabbi Chaim Chaikel's emissaries, who traveled from city to city and enticed young men to visit the court.[24] Thus, as in Maimon's memoir, the testimony before us also shows that the enticement to visit the courts of the Hasidic leaders was based on stories about their wondrous powers.

A similar picture emerges from the following passage as well:

> He said such things to his disciples at the Third [concluding] Meal of the Sabbath, and they say that the deepest secrets come from his mouth, and also that he divides them severally, into the ear of each one, according to his [particular] concern. The truth indeed is that the ear of each one is more barren and more obtuse for hearing than that of his companion: indeed many of them do not prepare at all what to say before his disciples at the Third Meal on the Sabbath. They only sit and put their hands on their heads and faces and wink with their eyes and roll with their finger for a moment. And he says that thereby his thoughts cling to heaven until the spirit descends upon him. And he says to one of his disciples, who sits before him [waiting] to hear his words, that he should ask him [to interpret] whatever verse falls into his head, and the second one asks another verse, and so does the third, and he begins to say words of Torah to them according to their manner and aforementioned subject.[25]

As noted, the experience that impressed Maimon most of all during his visit to the Maggid's court in Mezirech was the sermon that he heard during the meal. Here, in the testimony before us, the sermon given by Rabbi Chaim Chaikel to the visitors to his court during the Third Meal on Sabbath is also described as a central event. As in Maimon's version, Rabbi Chaim Chaikel's sermons are given spontaneously, as it were, inspired by the holy spirit. The inspired aspect of the sermon is expressed in the preacher's body language. Moreover, as in Maimon's story, every one of those listening to Rabbi Chaim Chaikel's words finds a message in them that relates to him personally. The similarity in the way the Hasidic leader encourages the involvement of his listeners is also conspicuous: he asks each of them to ask a question about some verse, most likely from the weekly Torah portion. In his sermon, Rabbi Chaim Chaikel relates to all of the verses and the questions asked about them.

The similarity between Maimon's memoir and the passage in *Shever posh'im* not only supports the reliability of these two sources but also leads us to a further conclusion: the patterns that were consolidated in the court of the Maggid of Mezirech were adopted by several of his disciples when they in turn became leaders of Hasidic groups of their own. In other words, over time, the primary and original patterns of behavior in the Hasidic court were established and became characteristic of it.

As noted, the moral remedy proposed by Rabbi Chaim Chaikel to those who addressed him was connected to the concept of *pidyon*. The question arises: what was the nature of this *pidyon* and what was its meaning in the present context? Here we should note another passage that sheds light on the practice of *pidyon* in the court of Rabbi Chaim Chaikel:

> The assistant, who is the inciter in his city, and is called Ra' [i.e., "wicked," rather than the usual honorific "Reb"] Isaac Manshes, remarks to one or another of the *Bnei Heikhalot*[26] who are there: is it not true that your soul is ill and you require a *pidyon* [redemption] of the soul? Therefore give a gold coin or

more for *pidyon* of the soul to our rabbi and your transgression will be removed and your sin will be atoned. And in that way the Rabbi makes a very decent living without working at all.[27]

We find that the *pidyon* that Rabbi Chaim Chaikel performed involved monetary payment, and that this money was used for the livelihood of Rabbi Chaim Chaikel himself.

The issue of the sources of *pidyon* and its place in Hasidism has been examined at length in the instructive article of Haviva Pedaya, "On the Development of the Social-Religious-Economic Model in Hasidism: Pidyon, Society, and Pilgrimage."[28] Pedaya traces the institution of *pidyon* in its earliest forms until it was absorbed into the Hasidic court. It is first mentioned in texts anchored in the Lurianic Kabbalah as a magical-kabbalistic ceremony intended to cure a sick person. The concept of *pidyon* refers, among other things, to the gift of money by means of which the patient was supposed to be cured of his illness. Usually this was 160 coins, which were to be divided into two parts: 129 coins were for charity, and the remaining 31 coins were given to the man who performed the *pidyon*. Pedaya locates a later stage in the development of the custom in the literature of *segulot* (magic spells) that was published at the beginning of the eighteenth century. She points out the connection of that literature to *ba'alei shem* who were active in Poland at that time and deduces that the performance of *pidyon* ceremonies was a common practice among these *ba'alei shem*.

Her article cites the findings of Abraham Rubinstein, who noted the innovation that Hasidism introduced in the character of *pidyon*. His main point is: "Beshtian Hasidism made *pidyon* into a routine practice accompanying the visit to the Zaddik. This practice had three stages: the Hasid gave a monetary present to the Zaddik, the Zaddik made use of the *pidyon* according to a certain formula, the Zaddik gave a blessing to the Hasid."[29] Following Rubinstein, Pedaya sought to discover what was new in Hasidism regarding the character of the *pidyon*. She concludes that the main innovation lay in the use of the money for secular purposes, to finance the expenses of the Hasidic court. This evolution in the purpose of the *pidyon* money did not, in her opinion, take place all at once; rather, it was a prolonged and gradual process. On the basis of detailed analysis of the testimony in *Shever posh'im*, Pedaya shows that in the court of Rabbi Chaim Chaikel of Amdur, the *pidyon* money was used to maintain the court. However, at that stage they still justified this use of the money with the argument that those sojourning at the court, who benefited from the money, were essentially poor people.[30]

In the light of Pedaya's findings, and in view of the testimony about Rabbi Chaim Chaikel in *Shever posh'im*, we find that *pidyon* was no longer a magical-kabbalistic ceremony used to heal physical ailments, but rather it became an act of moral purification. The kabbalistic formulas were no longer what cleansed a person of his iniquities, nor was it the money donated to the Zaddik. Confession, always an important component in repentance, and of course the "correction"—the spiritual instruction given by the Zaddik—had become the decisive factors.[31] Indeed, the term *pidyon* was emptied of its original meaning and limited to the monetary donation that the Hasid gave to the Zaddik. This monetary gift was a prerequisite for the meeting with the Zaddik and one could view it as a kind of fee. However, use of the term *pidyon*, with all its kabbalistic connotations, gave the monetary donation religious justification and a virtuous air.

As noted, in Rabbi Chaim Chaikel of Amdur's court, the *pidyon* funds were used to support those staying at the court. That phenomenon is described in detail in *Shever posh'im*. Here is the essence of that description:

> It is true that out of the money that he gets from the men of ability for *pidyon*s he distributes [sums] and supports poor people as well, who are dwelling there with him, for it is their

way that a person comes to mingle with them for a year or half
a year or at least a quarter of a year, and the longer one stays,
the more praiseworthy that is. Sometimes even if he wants to
depart fairly soon, [they prevail] against his will by saying to
him: you can't correct anything if you are a hasty man; and if
he does not listen to them in that either and wishes to go
home, they resort to threats.

Here the witness tells about a certain Hasid, who wanted to
return to his home early, against the opinion of Rabbi Chaim
Chaikel, and the latter threatened him that calamity would befall
him on the way. The witness explains the pressure that Rabbi
Chaim Chaikel and his people exerted on the visitors staying in
the court in the following way:

> The reason is that they make a living from the men of ability
> among them, because usually they only incite young Jewish
> men, who have not yet reached twenty years of age, and when
> an inciter comes to him and entices him, he says: you, take
> some of the gold coins and save money in your hand and go to
> the place, to the land that I will show you, and you will use the
> money as you wish and you will eat there, because perish the
> mention of fasts and deprivations, and you will be only happy
> and of good cheer, and sadness is forbidden there. And you will
> also have some [money] for the *pidyons*.[32]

It appears that the institution of *yoshvim* (dwellers), that is, Hasidim who dwelled in the Zaddik's court for a considerable time,
was rather well consolidated in the court of Rabbi Chaim Chaikel
of Amdur. As noted, Maimon spoke of "newcomers" to the court
of the Maggid of Mezirech. Such a visit might last a few days, in
the course of which the visitor would be expected to become
acquainted with Hasidic customs and with the ideas and ethos
practiced in the court. The desired result of such a visit was the

visitor's conversion to the path of Hasidism. Dwelling in the court, in contrast, was a more advanced stage in the process of integrating into Hasidic circles. The *yoshvim* were people who had already been initiated, and their decision to dwell in the court for an extended period expressed their desire to delve deeper into the group's ways and to acquire greater enlightenment.

Though we have no clear testimony about this, it is not impossible that the practice of long sojourns at the court began to take hold as early as the time of the Maggid of Mezirech. However, the present testimony gives the impression that the phenomenon of the *yoshvim* had taken on an established character at the court of his disciple, Rabbi Chaim Chaikel of Amdur. This was expressed, among other ways, in the division of the *yoshvim* into two subgroups: the men of ability and the poor. The first group included wealthy men who subsidized the sojourn of the others with their *pidyons*. Thus, we have a social and financial system of a progressive nature. The men of means supported those without means. The adversarial, *mitnaged* witness who describes this reality cannot but accuse the managers of the court of cynical exploitation of the men of means. He claims, inter alia, that when the wealthier visitors ran out of funds they were sent back home. Nevertheless, he is constrained to admit that their money served a worthy purpose.

We have found that Rabbi Chaim Chaikel's assistants encouraged young men who wanted to become Hasidim to stay in the court for an extended period, lasting anywhere from a quarter of a year to a year. We have also found that in the atmosphere reigning in the court, social pressure was applied to prevent *yoshvim* from leaving too soon. For our purposes, the claim that, in their desire to solicit young men to remain in the court, Rabbi Chaim Chaikel's assistants offered them a kind of monetary "bribe," is an important one. Indeed, it is likely that the possibility of living close to the Zaddik for a long period, without financial worries, encouraged young men without means to join the *yoshvim*.

Another enticement offered by Rabbi Chaim Chaikel's court to the young men it sought to attract was the style of life that required joy and condemned asceticism. It appears that the condemnation of sadness and the view that it was proper to serve the Lord in joy led to the adoption of new and daring standards regarding what was forbidden and permitted. Not surprisingly, the author of *Shever posh'im* saw fit to include testimony in his pamphlet about an incident that illustrated this phenomenon: In the course of the leader's repetition during Sabbath morning prayers, one of the worshippers was seen lying on the floor, while his comrades beat him. When the witness wondered about the meaning of this strange behavior, in the midst of solemn prayer, the men doing the beating answered that they felt they were not praying with sufficient joy. That feeling became more severe when the prayer leader recited the phrase, "Moses was joyous in the allotment of his portion." Now, after they had beaten their friend, they felt that "grief and sighing had fled and now there is gladness and rejoicing."[33]

The image of a man lying on the floor in the middle of the prayer leader's recitation, while a group of worshippers gathered around him and beat him, is difficult to credit. The critical reader might dismiss this story as the hostile invention of a zealous opponent of Hasidism. However, Solomon Maimon describes a similar episode in his memoirs, and here are his words:

We met once at the hour of prayer in the house of the superior. One of the company arrived somewhat late. When the others asked him the reason, he replied that he had been detained by his wife having been that evening confined with [giving birth to] a daughter. As soon as they heard this, they began to congratulate him in a somewhat uproarious fashion. The superior thereupon came out of his study and asked the cause of the noise. He was told that we were congratulating our friend, because his wife had brought a girl into the world. "A girl!" he answered with the greatest indignation, "he ought to be whipped." The poor fellow protested. He could not comprehend why he should be made to suffer for his wife having brought a girl into the world. But this was of no avail: he was seized, thrown down on the floor, and whipped unmercifully. All except the victim fell into an hilarious mood over the affair, upon which the superior called them to prayer in the following words, "Now, brethren, *serve the Lord with gladness!*"[34]

It is easy to distinguish between the story of the beating presented in *Shever posh'im* and the one that Maimon describes. However, these differences are insignificant. For our purposes, the similarities between the two events are more important: a pattern of behavior that traditional society regarded as deviant, and which was certainly out of place in a Beit Midrash (house of study), suddenly received legitimate status. In both cases, the beating was seen as a suitable means for arousing the hearts of those present to joy in performing a commandment. Here we have an unmistakable instance of a change in values. Even if we assume that such incidents were rare, they nevertheless reflect a certain state of mind that was also expressed in other ways. Indeed, Maimon emphasizes that the story of the beating is merely an example of the sect's "cynical spirit and the excess of merriment," and that this phenomenon was one of the factors that led him to leave the Maggid's court. Nevertheless, it is likely that these manifestations of the new Hasidic ethos, which aroused repugnance in Maimon, and which was described in dark colors by the opponents of Hasidism, attracted many young people and bound them to the Hasidic court.

Another characteristic of Rabbi Chaim Chaikel's court, which also attracted young men, was Hasidic prayer. Here is how the author of *Shever posh'im* relates to that phenomenon:

It is known regarding their inciters, who incite and seduce

young Jewish men to go away with them, which is truly a matter of stealing souls from the people of Israel, that when the inciter is with him on the road, he seduces him and says to him: in your whole life, you have never enjoyed prayer because you have been praying in a whisper without song and without prolonging it, which is not the case with our rabbi. ... He has a very pleasant voice, and he knows tunes, and so do all the worshippers there. Some sing songs, and some intone melodies, and these and those sing melodiously [a phrase referring to the text of a well-known hymn from the High Holiday service]. Our Rabbi Chaika, his palate is sweet, and he is full of grace, he pounds with both hands and strikes palm against palm toward them. Some sing melodies, and some sing sweetly, and these and those triumph with their voice and attract a person's heart, so that even if it is stone, it dissolves. ... And in truth, that gullible man, who comes there and hears the melodies and their pleasant voices—for most of them have pleasant voices and they know how to sing and with their great sweetness—will adhere to them with great love and follow them like a bull to the slaughter.[35]

Here we have an explicit admission of the attractive power of Hasidic prayer. Whereas the polemical writings that were issued from Vilna in 1772 emphasized the ecstatic manifestations of Hasidic prayer—the sharp movements of the body and the raising of the voice, manifestations that were regarded by the opponents of Hasidism as shameful and blameworthy—the testimony before us reveals the musical qualities of this prayer and acknowledges its aesthetic power.

III. Summary and Conclusions

In conclusion, we find that there was considerable continuity between the patterns formed in the Maggid of Mezirech's court and those that characterized the court of Rabbi Chaim Chaikel of Amdur. This continuity shows that the Maggid's court served as a kind of archetype that influenced the courts founded by his disciples.[36]

Both the Maggid and his disciple, Rabbi Chaim Chaikel, viewed a visit to the court as a prime opportunity to attract new men to the ways of Hasidism. Hence it is understandable why Hasidic propaganda concentrated on the effort to convince potential adherents to visit the Zaddik's court. These efforts at persuasion were made both by delegated emissaries and by recent recruits who wanted to share their experiences with others.

The main effort to recruit new adherents to Hasidic circles concentrated on young men with scholarly backgrounds.[37] The primary mode of propaganda was the telling of stories about the exceptional powers of the Hasidic leaders. A similar purpose was served by the homilies transmitted in their names. According to the stories, the Hasidic leaders appeared to be endowed with a divine spirit and the ability to gaze into the souls of those who addressed them. The Hasidic homilies show that Hasidism was teaching a new and promising path to those who sought perfection in the worship of God.

The visit to the Hasidic court was meant to cause a spiritual revolution in the souls of the visitors. Participation in the rituals held at the court and exposure to experiences connected to the new Hasidic ethos, the experience of direct encounters with the marvelous figure of the Zaddik and with the spiritual message he gave to each individual—all of these were meant to induce the visitors to join the new movement.

In conclusion, one of the important keys for understanding the spread of Hasidism during the decades following the death of the Besht was the combination of novel and attractive ways of worshipping God with a new type of religious leadership. The connection between these two components of the Hasidic message is quite clear: the Hasidic Zaddik was the one who embodied the new way of worshiping God, he was the one who endowed it with authority, and he was the one able and committed to transmit it to others. All of these elements received powerful and focused expression in the Hasidic court.

Notes

1. The view that the Besht was not the founder of Hasidism is presented in Moshe Rosman, *Founder of Hasidism: A Quest for the Historical Ba'al Shem Tov* (Berkeley and Los Angeles: University of California Press, 1996). A different position on this matter can be found in my *The Besht: Magician, Mystic, and Leader* (Waltham, Mass.: Brandeis University Press, 2004). I agree with Rosman that the Besht did not found a movement, nor did he intend to do so, but I nevertheless maintain that the Besht made a critical contribution to setting in motion the process that led to the growth of Hasidism as a movement.
2. *Solomon Maimons Lebensgeschichte* (Berlin, 1792–93). The citations here are taken from the English translation, *Solomon Maimon: An Autobiography,*. trans. J. Clark Murray (Urbana: University of Illinois Press, 2001).
3. See Shmuel Werses, זְרָמִים וְצוּרוֹת בְּסִפְרוּת הַהַשְׂכָּלָה (Trends and forms in Haskalah literature) (Jerusalem: Magnes/Hebrew University, 1990), 249–60.
4. On Maimon's life see P. Lachover, חַיֵּי שְׁלֹמֹה מַיְימוּן (Solomon Maimon and the book of his history), introduction to the Hebrew translation of *Solomon Maimons Lebensgeschichte* (Tel Aviv: Ligvulam Press/Bialik Institute, 1953), 9–50.
5. On the issue of Maimon's reliability, see Adam Teller, "The Reliability of Salomon Maimon's Autobiography as a Historical Source," *Gal-Ed* 14 (1995): 13–22. Teller concentrates on what Maimon wrote about the phenomenon of Jews in the business of leasing concessions from the Polish nobility. He concludes that Maimon's memoirs are as reliable as an autobiography can be. The inaccuracies appear when Maimon tries to generalize at large from what he knew in the village of his birth.
6. *Maimon: Autobiography*, 165–67.
7. Ibid., 167.
8. See Joseph Weiss, "*Via Passiva* in Early Hasidism," in *Studies In Eastern European Jewish Mysticism* (Oxford: Oxford University Press, 1985), 69–94.

See also Rivka Schatz-Uffenheimer, הַחֲסִידוּת בְּמִסְטִיקָה (The quietistic element in eighteenth-century Hasidic thought) (Jerusalem: Magnes/Hebrew University,1968), 21–31.

9. Joseph Weiss located the literary sources of the first two sermons; see עַל דְרַשָׁה שֶׁל הַמַּגִּיד מִמֶּזְרִיטְשׁ (On a sermon of the Maggid of Mezirech), *Zion* 12 (1947): 97; עַל תּוֹרָה חֲסִידִית אַחַת (On a Hasidic "Torah"), *Zion* 20 (1956): 107–8. Recently David Assaf discovered the literary source of the third sermon. This finding is included in an unpublished article.

10. *Maimon: Autobiography*, 164.

11. Ibid., 167–69.

12. Ibid., 169.

13. On the old kind of Hasidim and Hasidism, see my *The Besht*, chapter 5.

14. *Maimon: Autobiography*, 160–62.

15. See n. 8.

16. For biographical details about Rabbi Chaim Chaikel, see Wolf Rabinowitsch, *Lithuanian Hasidism, from the Beginning to the Present* (Hebrew) (Jerusalem: Bialik Institute, 1961), 92-96.

17. The pamphlet שֶׁבֶר פּוֹשְׁעִים was republished by Mordecai Wilensky in the second volume of his (1772-1815) חֲסִידִים וּמִתְנַגְדִים (Hasidim and Mitnagdim: A study of the controversy between them, 1772–1815) (Jerusalem: Bialik Institute, 1970). In the introduction to this volume, Wilensky presents a detailed discussion of the identity of the author and suggests various arguments against the position of scholars who attributed it to authors other than David of Makov. Wilensky's main arguments refer to the positions taken by Abraham Rubinstein on this matter. I do not intend to enter into this controversy here. My decision to adopt Wilensky's position in the following discussion is meant merely to facilitate matters for the reader. See the remarks of Haviva Pedaya in *Zaddik and Devotees: Historical and Sociological Aspects of Hasidism* (Hebrew), ed. David Assaf (Jerusalem: Zalman Shazar Center, 2001), 372 n. 103.

18. On this matter see the instructive remarks of Haviva Pedaya, ibid., 373–74. Pedaya assumes that the witness was a Mitnaged who disguised himself as a Hasid and spent an extended time at the court.

19. Wilensky, *Hasidim and Mitnagdim*, 2:160.

20. Ibid.

21. Ibid., 1:59, 38, 63.

22. Ibid., 161–62.

23. The ability to bare the secrets of the souls of his Hasidim was also ascribed to Rabbi Menachem Mendel of Vitebsk. See the letter of the emissary

Rabbi Shlomo Zalman in אִגְרוֹת חֲסִדִים מֵאֶרֶץ יִשְׂרָאֵל (Hasidic letters from Eretz-Israel), ed. Ya'acov Barnai (Jerusalem: Yad Izhak Ben-Zvi, 1980), 160–61, letter 38.

24. For the biographical details of these emissaries, including their names, see Wilensky, *Hasidim and Mitnagdim*, 2:162.

25. Ibid., 2:165.

26. This term as used here is a double entendre, referring both to those who joined the Hasidic court (*Bnei heikhalot*) and also to the affluent men among the visitors (*Bnei hayekholet*). See ibid., 2:171 n. 318.

27. Ibid., 171.

28. See n. 17.

29. Abraham Rubinstein, "Commentaries on a Document about the Collection of Testimony against Hasidism" (Hebrew), *Tarbiẓ* 32 (1973):93–94, cited by Pedaya, "Social-Religious-Economic Model," 367.

30. Ibid., 378.

31. Cf. Ada Rapoport-Albert, "Confession in the Circle of R. Nahman of Braslav," *Bulletin of the Institute of Jewish Studies* 1 (1973–75): 65–96.

32. Wilensky, *Hasidim and Mitnagdim*, 2:172–73.

33. Ibid., 163.

34. *Maimon: Autobiography*, 169–70.

35. Wilensky, *Hasidim and Mitnagdim*, 2:173.

36. One may learn that the disciples of the Maggid regarded their master's patterns of leadership as a model worthy of imitation from the polemical letters of Rabbi Abraham of Kalisk against Rabbi Shneur Zalman of Lyadi. See, for example, D. Z. Hilman, אִגְרוֹת בַּעַל הַתַּנְיָא וּבְנֵי דוֹרוֹ (The letters of the author of the Tanya and his contemporaries) (Jerusalem: Masorah, 1953), 105–7, letter no. 58.

37. On the great preponderance of young men in early Hasidism, see Gershon David Hundert, *Jews in Poland-Lithuania in the Eighteenth Century* (Berkeley and Los Angeles: University of California Press, 2004), 179–81. On the scholarly background of those who adhered to Hasidism at this stage, see Immanuel Etkes, רֵאשִׁיתָהּ שֶׁל הַתְּנוּעָה הַחֲסִידִית (The beginning of the Hasidic movement) (Tel Aviv: Ministry of the Defense Press, 1998), 59–67.

THE REGENERATION EVEN
OF THE JEWS?

Henri Grégoire and his Essai

IVAN G. MARCUS

In the intimacy of the first year of the Institute for Advanced
Study of the Humanities, now the Graduate School of JTS,
Mark Cohen and I had the good fortune to take private seminars in modern Jewish history with a very enthusiastic, recently
minted modern Jewish historian, Ismar Schorsch. As I recall, we
sat around his desk in the tiny office of a new assistant professor of
Jewish history, unable even to close the door, and studied together
several lengthy primary texts from the time of Samuel Usque, in
the sixteenth century, through aspects of the Jewish emancipation
in England, France, and, of course, Germany in the seventeenth,
eighteenth, and nineteenth centuries, respectively.

Although I planned to work on an earlier period, the modern
seminar left an indelible impression. Ismar demonstrated how to
probe a text and how one can influence another, this well before
the literary critics spoke about "intertextuality." Close readings of
some of the key documents of modern European Jewish history
opened up worlds of nuance and proved that modern Jewish studies did not mean "journalism," a jibe that many of us heard at the
time.

We had the good fortune of sitting with a rising star whose
light has helped guide my path, and that of so many others, ever
since. This study about one of the more enigmatic seminal texts of
modern Jewish history began as a seminar paper in those early

years. I have gone back and tried to see if I understand now what
I wrote then. Along the way, I have reread Grégoire's *Essai* and
many new secondary sources, made significant and minor adjust-
ments, and updated the literature produced by two new generations of scholars. I discovered that Grégoire's reputation has
grown in stature in recent decades in tandem with the career of
our honoree, and that both are exemplars, though in different
times, places, and cultures, of movements of "religious enlightenment."

In late eighteenth-century France, many learned societies sponsored essay contests as a way of airing controversial issues in public. These competitions played a role in creating what was being
called "public opinion," something we take for granted today in
free societies. Newspapers, pamphlets, and books all played their
part in promoting different points of view that men, sometimes
women, discussed in clubs, salons, academies, societies, cafés, and
coffee houses, as well as in the street. Careers sometimes were
launched by such contests. Among the best known of these is that
of Jean-Jacques Rousseau, who entered a prize essay competition
on the question: "Has the revival of the arts and sciences done
more to corrupt or purify morals?" Rousseau tells us that when he
visited Diderot, editor of the massive *Encyclopédie*, the *philosophe*
encouraged the young man to defend his maverick opinion that
the revival of arts and sciences led not to enlightenment but to the
corruption of morals. Rousseau won the competition and found
himself famous overnight.[1]

It was just such a prize competition that Henri Grégoire
entered in 1785. Sponsored by the Society of Arts and Sciences in
Metz, the competition was about the issue of how Jews might fit
into the larger Christian society. Although Grégoire had apparently already written the core of his essay in an earlier Strasbourg

competition in 1779, that essay has not survived. The present discussion is about the one that did.[2]

Until recently, Henri Grégoire's advocacy of Jewish emancipation in France was an enigma. Born in the small town of Veho, in rural Lorraine, on December 4, 1750, Grégoire grew up in parochial surroundings. His parents were modest artisans whom he chose to remember especially for their piety and virtue. Educated first by Jesuits at Nancy, he later studied philosophy and theology at the university there and at a seminary in Metz. He was ordained a priest (*abbé*) in 1775, and by 1782 he became parish priest (*curé*) in Embermênil. Grégoire, then, was a member of the lower clergy of Lorraine, a group known for its anti-Jewish sentiments, shaped by the presence of Jewish moneylenders holding economic power over poor Christian farmers. Moreover, his parish was under the ecclesiastical jurisdiction of a bitter antisemite, de la Fare, Bishop of Nancy. In light of this background, one might have predicted the essay to come out forcefully against any possibility of Jews ever becoming French citizens.[3]

And yet, Grégoire not only wrote a long essay to explain the reasons Jews should be granted citizenship, but he also proposed measures that Jews could undertake to merit it. It was Grégoire who moved to have the delegation of eastern French Jewry seated at the bar of the National Assembly on October 14, 1789, and it was Grégoire, again, who offered his *Motion en faveur des juifs* during the Assembly debate on Jewish emancipation, even though he was not at the forefront of the subsequent debate itself.[4]

Various explanations have been advanced to account for his activities on behalf of the Jews, each trying to find a single key to Grégoire's motives. In an essay commemorating the centennial of Grégoire's death, Paul Grunebaum-Ballin hesitatingly offered two suggestions. Perhaps Grégoire's interest in the Jews' cause and their history was the result of his devotion to the compassionate ethics of the Gospels? Or was it based on his friendly relations with educated Jews such as Beer-Bing in Metz? Puzzled by the problem, Grunebaum-Ballin pointed to other essays written at that time on the Jews, and he concluded that "the idea was in the air." But he was dissatisfied with all of his explanations; the enigma remained.[5]

Others who studied Grégoire's political and religious thought advanced the view that his defense of Jews, Negroes, mulattos, Irish Catholics, and Greek Orthodox was grounded in his religious ethics and political liberalism. Dale Johnson argued that there is a fundamental unity in Grégoire's political and religious ideas that led him to defend the rights of all oppressed minorities. On the Jewish questions, however, Johnson thought that Grégoire's political liberalism was compromised by conversionist motives: "Concern for conversion was never far behind his desire for Jews to obtain their natural rights."[6]

In 1962, Grunebaum-Ballin offered a new twist in the pro-conversion interpretation behind's Grégoire's support for Jewish emancipation. Arthur Hertzberg adopted it and concluded: "There can be no doubt that much of [Grégoire's] fervor for the emancipation of the Jews derived from a religious semi-underground that was at least a century old in France. It had proposed kinder treatment of the Jews as a preamble to their conversion." According to this view, Grégoire shared certain millenarian ideas of eighteenth-century Jansenists, a Calvinist-like group of Catholics that believed in predestination and in personal austerity. Grégoire was helping the Jews not so much to convert them in the present as to help create the necessary conditions for a divine act that would make the Jews' conversion the beginning of the end of days.[7]

Grégoire's essay on the Jews supports the interpretation that he hoped that Jewish emancipation would ultimately result in their conversion. But viewing Grégoire's support for Jewish emancipation simply as a means to a conversionist end blurs the complexity of his nuanced religious and enlightened political identities during the years prior to and especially during the

French Revolution. Against the background of most of the essay, the passage about Jewish conversion appears as a contradiction to Grégoire's liberalism rather than as an application of it.

Looking at Grégoire in relation only to the Jews and then using an either/or paradigm to explain how he viewed them does not explain his essay. Grégoire was both a dedicated Catholic priest of a certain persuasion who never renounced his vows, even during the Terror, and an enlightened revolutionary. He tried to craft a middle position between two worldviews that were in conflict in eighteenth-century France. One was the supernatural traditionalism of Roman Catholicism; the other was the emerging anticlerical political liberalism of the *philosophes* in the French Enlightenment. As well known as these positions are, they were not the only ones at the time, and Grégoire was not alone in facing the dilemma of not wanting to choose between them. Although his ecclesiastical affiliation made his situation more dangerous than that of many others, he remained part of "the religious Enlightenment."[8]

As a liberal Catholic, Grégoire constantly found himself engaged in polemics on two fronts. Conservatives in the Church decried his defiance of the Pope's condemnation of the Revolution. Anticlerical republicans always suspected he was loyal to the Church rather than to the state. To the former he had to prove that legitimate popular government would not lead to irreligion; to the latter, that the Catholic faith was compatible with civic virtue. In his writings and public career he sometimes emphasized one persona, and at other times, the other.[9]

To negotiate between his political and religious loyalties, Grégoire separated citizenship and Catholic faith into distinct spheres. He argued that only dogmas were eternal; social and political behavior was the province of humans, not God; of the state, not the Church. Moreover, he thought Christianity's social ethic agreed with the *philosophes'* concept of civic virtue, the good of all in society, and he affirmed his orthodox commitment to the revealed truths of Catholic dogma as a purely private matter between himself and a distant God. Grégoire's distinction was grounded in Jansenist ideas that argued that the divine sphere was so utterly different from humanity that it was withdrawn from the social sphere, thereby opening up a realm where human beings could create their own society and nation.[10] The possibility of nationalism, of men willing to create a state and a society according to norms that they devised, emerged in late eighteenth-century France, at least in part, because of changes in religious ideas. The change in theology that created the possibility of a secular society has been called the religious origin of the French Revolution.[11]

Grégoire's distinction between private dogmas and social ethics had implications for his proposed image of a regenerated French Jew in the future. The key to understanding Grégoire and the Jews is this two-part strategy, to paraphrase a later East European Jewish thinker and poet about living in European culture while retaining a Jewish identity, of being at the same time a devout Catholic "at home" and a *philosophe* "in public."[12]

Grégoire's religious enlightened belief that a Catholic priest could become a good citizen was audacious enough, but he went further by arguing that even a Jew could. When it came to writing his essay on the regeneration of the Jews, he applied the intellectual tools that he had forged for understanding himself as an enlightened priest. The essay contest improbably launched this local parish priest into a career at the center of the French Revolution. He was now ready to create a nation that included the Jews whom he knew so well from his youth in rural Lorraine.

One way Grégoire was able to negotiate between the two moral poles of Catholicism and Enlightenment was by helping to assign new political and moral meanings to the old religious term "regeneration." The idea derived from contexts that referred in the seventeenth and early eighteenth centuries to the rebirth that occurred after baptism or to the life after death. It also had a medical association of bringing back the near dead from a serious illness. By the late eighteenth century, the term was taking on new social and political meanings, in large measure thanks to Grégoire.

For Grégoire, the concept referred not to God's acts during baptism or the afterlife of the soul, but to human beings actively creating a new society and a new nation. To reshape parochial people into French citizens required a cultural transformation or "regeneration," breathing new life into the nearly dead. Although the term was grounded in religious contexts of personal salvation, Grégoire gave it a new social and political meaning while never quite divorcing it from its religious overtones. Like Grégoire, the term remained ambivalent. It criticized the very people it sought to transform into something new.[13]

His advocacy of Jewish regeneration in particular needs to be considered in light of his advocacy of French regeneration in general. He did not apply this term only to the Jews. In fact, it became a central metaphor to evoke how he thought the nation should be forged. For example, he wrote vigorously against would-be Frenchmen using their local languages (*patois*) instead of French. This included Alsatian Christians who spoke German as well as Alsatian Jews who spoke Yiddish.[14]

Grégoire's advocacy of Jewish emancipation of a certain kind disagreed with many who either accused the Jews of being unchangeable or who thought the logic of equality meant that Jews should simply receive citizenship like everyone else. In contrast to both camps, Grégoire proposed the conditional emancipation of the Jews, just as he thought that all who would become French needed to improve their character, language, and habits and become new people: French citizens.[15]

In this regard, the Jews were like other potential Frenchmen only more so. All needed to be changed into French-speaking, sociable Frenchmen; the Jews certainly did since they had picked up more antisocial habits in their millennial history than others. Grégoire's first opportunity to take a public stand as a liberal

Catholic came in 1785 when the Royal Society of Arts and Sciences in Metz proposed an essay contest on the topic "Is it possible to make the Jews more useful and happier in France?" Here was a platform from which he could argue for the viability of his intellectual position of religious enlightenment.

The title that Grégoire gave his essay on the Jews betrays the image he had of them as a degraded people and of himself as a moral as well as political reformer. He called it *Essai sur la régénération physique, morale, et politique des juifs* (Essay on the physical, moral, and political regeneration of the Jews). Grégoire made a fundamental assumption about French Jewish emancipation. Granting the Jews their civic liberty would make sense only if they agreed to become worthy of citizenship by undergoing a process of collective character transformation. He referred to this process sometimes as a regeneration, at other times, as a moral revolution.

Before proposing a program for accomplishing this change, he first had to prove that Jewish change was possible. Consequently, the first argument in the *Essai* sets out to refute the claim that the Jews were hateful, avaricious, usurious, and so on by nature and thus could never change. In designing his case that the Jews could be reformed, Grégoire set aside theology as inappropriate for social analysis. Instead, he applied to the Jewish question certain Enlightenment assumptions about how social change can occur. For example, the *Essai* takes for granted features of Enlightenment historiography that Ernst Cassirer discussed in connection with Montesquieu's *Spirit of the Laws*:

> Montesquieu ... is a genuine thinker of the Enlightenment in that he expects from the advancement of knowledge a new moral order and a new orientation of the political and social history of man. And this is what brings him to the philosophy of history. From a knowledge of the general principles and moving forces of history he looks for the possibility of their

effective control in the future. Man is not simply subject to the necessity of nature; he can and should shape his own destiny as a free agent, and bring about his destined and proper future. But the mere wish remains powerless as long as it is not guided by sure insight. Such insight ... requires the most painstaking observation of empirical and historical details.[16]

If we substitute "Jew" for "man," Cassirer provides a theoretical analysis of Grégoire's philosophy of social change that underlies his *Essai*. Grégoire, too, has a definite view about a "new moral order," and he also makes a historical analysis the basis for achieving it. Only by understanding Jewish history properly, he argues, can one hope to change it. When we know "the general principles and moving forces of [Jewish] history," we can change them. The idea that the future of a social group can be changed only if one analyzes the moving forces in their collective history is the rationale for Grégoire's *Essai*.

In his presentation of the dominant forces in Jewish history, Grégoire stresses the discontinuity between the biblical era and the Jew in the diaspora (*dispersion*) since the time of Vespasian. One need only think of the Israelites in Palestine to find clear evidence that Jewish nature had not been constantly perverse and socially backward. In Palestine the Jews lived in a theocracy characterized by their full participation in all aspects of public life (178).* This early society had egalitarian features that Grégoire admired: "Their jubilee year made them approach a pristine equality which social institutions incessantly oppose" (26).

To prove that Jews can become farmers, Grégoire reminds the reader of this earlier period: "Perhaps there has never been a people so occupied with agriculture as the Israelites in Palestine"

---

* Henceforth, page references to the *Essai* (repr. 1968) are enclosed in parentheses in the text.

(115). For the same reason, the Jews' potential for industry need not be doubted: "Their stay in Palestine proves the possibility by the actual fact" (100). The biblical period demonstrates, then, that the Jews are not economically limited by nature; the explanation for their present disabilities must lie elsewhere.

It was the exile after Vespasian that changed the Jewish people for the worse in two basic ways. Previously they had rebelled against observing their religion. In the exile, they adhered to their exclusivist cult out of hatred for other religious groups. Moreover, they developed an avariciousness that has marked their national genius until the present time (29). The Jews acquired the traits of hatred for others and of avarice during Roman imperial and medieval European experiences, respectively.

During the Jewish exile while Rome still existed in the West, hatred developed between Jew and non-Jew. It became the dominant social force that led pagan and Christian mobs to accuse Jews of all sorts of crimes and to persecute them for committing them. Since most of the accusations had no historical merit, some other reason must underlie their invention.[17] Grégoire offers an explanation for mob hatred of the Jews based on his social psychology of religious groups.

> It is concerning religion that one pardons least of all those who think differently from oneself. If any single religion can offend the egotism of those who are not its practitioners, that is surely the Jewish religion. The Divine Author designed it this way in order to place a barrier between the people and the corruption of the idolatrous nations which surrounded it. Judaism provides for an exclusivist cult, and although it imposes the duty of universal love, its exclusivism seems to promote the view that other men are considered hateful pagans. (24–25)

Jewish monotheism challenged pagan religion, and the devotees of the latter revolted against "a dogma which undermined the basis of paganism." The pagans were not simply displeased with Jewish exclusiveness; they made the mistake of mocking the Jews for their peculiar practices such as circumcision. It was a short step to go from ridicule to scorn, and this is how the hateful Jewish response originated. Gentile derision prompted them to hate their accusers, and the cycle of mutual recrimination began (25).

Although the exclusiveness of Judaism appears to be the original source of the pagan response, Grégoire does not fault early Judaism for this. He stresses that the divine author planned it this way to protect the purity of monotheism from pagan contamination. In this part of the *Essai*, he is interested in blaming the non-Jewish response. Pagan scorn of the Jews began the pattern of anti-Jewish hatred that then made the Jews into hateful fanatics.

When Christianity appeared, the forces of mutual hatred continued. Grégoire blames the Christian masses for ignoring the teachings of their Founder to forgive his executioners, the Jews. The Christians assumed that the Jews hated them but lacked the power to persecute them. As a result, Christians assumed that the Jews perpetrated various symbolic acts of contempt toward them. These alleged crimes then served to justify Christian massacres of the Jews (25–26).

Even though popular hatred led to various outrages against the Jews during the Roman Empire, enlightened emperors generally held back the full force of anti-Jewish hostility while granting the Jews complete civic rights within the Empire:

> In the first four or five centuries of the Christian era, the exiled Jews ... practiced all the arts and trades; filled all civic functions. Scattered among the nations, all went to pray separately in different temples. ... Here is a fact, a point of departure from which to judge if they can be incorporated into general society. All objections fall when experience [i.e. history] speaks. (124–25)

Thus not only the sojourn in Palestine but also the exile during the Roman Empire offer evidence that the Jews had sometimes been fit for citizenship. Although popular anti-Jewish hatred had harmful psychological effects on the Jews, it had few political or economic consequences. This changed when Rome came to an end.

The second era of Jewish exile, the barbarian Middle Ages, is marked by the new force of political tyranny:

> The weakness of the Roman Empire, crushed under its own weight, had undermined the laws; and popular hatred, which laws do not extinguish, was no longer checked by force. It renewed its outrages, and these were then sanctioned by legislators. If ever a people ... merit the name barbarian ... it is the Visigoths. (4)

In Grégoire's outline of Western history, the barbarian invasions begin the dark Middle Ages for diaspora Jewry in Europe. Popular hatred, now unchecked by law, drove the Jews more and more to cling to their religious prejudices and practices. In addition, official political persecution restricted them economically and politically. The force of political tyranny created the Jewish spirit of avarice: "But if the Jews ... have no idol besides money, no leprosy besides usury, ... the governments should accuse themselves of driving them to this extreme by depriving them of all other means of subsistence" (84).

Politically, tyrants violated their basic human rights. "What a difference there is between the right of Louis XVI and that of Dagobert I ... who gave them the choice of baptism or death, a cruel decree which deprives a man of his liberty over something [his religious beliefs] with which politics has no right to interfere" (126). It was tyranny to expel them in order to take their property or to release Christian debtors from repaying their Jewish creditors (10).

In his analysis of Jewish history in the diaspora, Grégoire isolated two moving forces. Popular hatred and political tyranny, not any alleged Jewish nature, are responsible for creating the misanthropic, greedy Jew of the *ancien régime*. Since these forces have been discovered, it is possible to work toward reversing them and effect a moral regeneration of the Jews. It is not a coincidence that the positive forces that Grégoire wants to employ are love and political liberty, the two components of his enlightened Catholicism.

In the *Essai*, Grégoire reveals his defense of liberal Catholicism in an even more direct way. He consistently defends the clergy as the most compassionate group in medieval society. By stressing this point, Grégoire disagreed not only with enlightened anticlerical writers who opposed Jewish improvement, but also with men who shared a similar view of Jewish history and who supported Jewish emancipation, such as John Toland and Christian Wilhelm Dohm, who criticized the medieval Church.[18]

When Grégoire describes the Jews' fate in the Middle Ages, he notes that "the clergy rarely persecuted them" (5–6). During the Crusades, "St. Bernard preached against the cruelty of the crusaders, and not satisfied with writing moving letters, he traveled through Germany and successfully protected the Jews with the influence which his reputation, learning, and virtues conferred on him." Against Toland's attack on the clergy, Grégoire applied the principle of not generalizing from a few cases, an argument Toland had used to defend the Jews (5–6).[19]

The problem, Grégoire concludes, is that people often accuse the clergy of being intolerant but do not understand what toleration means in its various senses. Elsewhere in the *Essai*, he gave his interpretation:

> Often cited as intolerant, the clergy is the group which best practices the opposite virtue, if we understand tolerance to mean that enlightened reason which preaches steadfast adher-

ence to revealed truths and that constant goodness which
desires that all Christians join together to devote themselves to
the good of all men. ... Charity is the cry of the Gospels, and
when I see persecuting Christians, I am tempted to think they
did not read it. (127)

A Catholic can be tolerant because one's orthodoxy is a private
matter dictated by "enlightened reason." In society, however, the
Gospel commands the Catholic to work for "the good of all
men." Grégoire's definition of toleration expresses his separation
of Catholicism into revealed dogmas and social ethics.

As Cassirer suggested, history served as the basis of a theory of
social change in the Enlightenment, and Grégoire's account of
Jewish history is based on the social theory of enlightened historiography. Still, his methodology reflects the ambivalence that
marks him as an enlightened priest. Critical historical reasoning
and theological assumptions exist side by side.

One of the new features of eighteenth-century historiography
is the growing acceptance of historical criticism that replaces traditional authority.[20] The most dramatic instance of this shift is a new
approach to the Bible. Whereas before Spinoza sacred history was
understood by reference to the revealed authority of the Bible,
Spinoza proclaimed that the Bible itself (and the history in it) was
explicable by reference to the investigator's historical method. The
former source of authority had itself now become the datum to be
explained by the new authority of critical reason.[21]

Like Bayle and other Enlightenment historians, Grégoire
exhibits a critical spirit that he applies to understanding Jewish
history. He refers to sources in his notes and weighs competing
claims and arguments. Thus, despite his pro-Jewish bias, the evidence he had prompts him to accept some of the medieval accusations about some of the Jews: "If we cannot absolve you [the
Jews] of all of them [crimes], it will become clear that most of
them were an invention" (16).

Grégoire pays special attention to the accusation that the Jews in the Middle Ages poisoned Christian water sources. Here, the criterion for his discussion is critical reason: "To commit a crime one must have motives and a hope of success. What success could Jews expect in poisoning ... wells which continually renew themselves where they themselves drew water?" (21). Before offering his own explanation for this accusation, Grégoire launches into a sarcastic diatribe on medieval superstition and ignorance worthy of an anticlerical *philosophe*:

> To understand this [accusation of Jewish water poisoning], imagine yourselves living in those centuries of the Middle Ages, "brilliant" centuries when "learned men" had the secret of explaining everything. A pestilence appears everywhere, like the plague of 1348 which wiped out a third of Europe. Those profound thinkers at the time want to know and tell others the cause of the plague. They refrain from consulting nature when they have ready at hand a bunch of treatises "about everything knowable." They could, if necessary, ... invoke magic ... but they prefer to attribute the devastation of the plague to poison. Then it is decided that the Jews are the cause of the plague with which God wishes to punish the world. Besides, [the Jews] have a language unknown to the mob. Does one speak Hebrew unless it is to concoct schemes? (22)

The accusation, then, is the product of medieval superstition and prejudice, and reason refutes it. In reality, Grégoire concludes, the Jews' debtors invented the calumny to rid themselves of their creditors. Such accusations fit the "history of tigers, not that of men" (23–24). The Jews are human, and we must assume they act like human beings, that is, rationally; one cannot expect them to poison themselves!

Although Grégoire's analysis of the well-poisoning canard is based on Enlightenment assumptions, the *Essai* also reflects

Catholic theology about the Jews. At times, there appears to be no surface inconsistency between his appeal to political liberalism and the "enlightened truth" of his Catholic faith. For example, he thinks that the state ought to punish all sacrilege as political acts of sedition that "profane something revered by some of their fellow citizens." There is no political difference between what the Catholics did to the Moslems in Granada or to the Jews' synagogue in Worms, on the one hand, and when "enraged Jews violated the sacred host of the image of the Savior," on the other (19). But then he adds about the latter that Christians who are enlightened by the light of truth should consider each sacrilege of Christian objects especially contemptible. For an anti-Catholic act, religious and political considerations are involved.

At other times, the *Essai* suggests the tension between Grégoire's liberal and theological perspectives. For example, the epigraph to the *Essai* reads: "You let them devour us like sheep; You disperse us among the nations" (Ps. 44:12) (p. i). The verse epitomizes Jewish suffering in the exile, and Grégoire designed his *Essai* in part to blame that suffering on Christian persecution, not on the Jews' own nature. But would not this Catholic priest be aware of the biblical parallels to the verse in the Vulgate? They explain Jewish suffering from a theological perspective. For example, Leviticus 26:33 echoes the same idea as the verse in Psalms, but the context makes it clear that this suffering is viewed as future divine punishment for the Jews' rebellion: "But if ... you disobey Me and remain hostile to Me ... I will scatter you among the nations" (Lev. 26:27, 33). Christian theology had developed this explanation of Jewish suffering and defined the Jews' sin as "blindness" to the new dispensation and as deicide.

A Christian reading of the epigraph finds support in the *Essai*, when Grégoire refers to Jewish suffering immediately after the destruction of the Temple. The Jews had to pay for the privilege of visiting the Temple site on the anniversary of its destruction: "The Jews bought the right to shed tears at the places where they had bought and shed the blood of Jesus Christ" (2). Elsewhere he remarks that when a Jew opens "his Talmud, he finds there the advice of killing the best man who existed in the world" (68).

He also alludes to the traditional idea that the Jews do not understand the true meaning of their sacred writings. What is the Jew? He is:

> Bearer of the first archives of the world, prophecies which he does not understand. He goes Bible in hand to prove the predictions of this book and to bear witness to the truth of a religion he hates. ... The blood of Jesus Christ has fallen on the Jews as they wished. Since that bloody act at Calvary, they display themselves to the whole world where they go seeking a messiah even in Cromwell. (15)

It appears at first that Grégoire is professing two contradictory explanations of the cause of Jewish suffering: the enlightened view that Christians persecuted them irrationally, and the theological interpretation that it was because of the Jews' deicide. But Grégoire was able to advocate both perspectives because he applied to the history of the Jews his dichotomy between the divine and social orders. The theological dogma about Jewish deicide could have no social implications in society. He makes this position clear in a rhetorical question near the end of the *Essai*: "O nations, for eighteen centuries you ruin the remnant of Israel. Divine vengeance displays hardships toward them, but have you been commissioned to be the agents?" (193).

Grégoire's exposition of Jewish history laid the ground for his concrete proposals for Jewish reform. Theologically, the Catholic priest could believe that God was punishing the Jews for their sins, but the Catholic citizen must grant the Jew the same rights as Christians enjoyed. They were both human beings and had the same natural rights. By placing the blame for Jewish social defects on Christian persecution, not Jewish nature, Grégoire had isolated a historical force that could be changed. The substitution of political liberty for persecution would check the negative Jewish responses of exclusivist hostility as well as avarice.

But Grégoire did not think that liberal legislation alone would undo centuries of damage to the Jewish character. The Jew would be the same; he merely would not get worse. Portuguese Jews in France had letters of naturalization since the sixteenth century but "they are not yet French, and the work of their transformation has only just begun" (136).

The Jews could become more useful and happier only by a moral regeneration of their character. Political rights would not be enough:

> Let us make the Jews citizens. Regenerated physically as well as morally. ... Their hearts, directed toward virtue, their hands, hardened in labor, will bring benefits to the larger society. ... They themselves will achieve that degree of happiness that this low world allows, ... for virtue and happiness are synonymous. ... By this revolution we will gain friends and the state will gain an increase in industry and wealth. (141)

Grégoire expressed the idea of reform in moral terms. He wanted the Jew to conform to a definite ideal of a good citizen, and he justified the state's imposing temporary restrictions on their freedom because he thought that they did not yet deserve equal treatment with Christian citizens. But to what standard did he hold up the Jews and find them wanting? Was it the members of the Christian French nation? If we focus only on his *Essai* on the Jews, we might be misled to think that Grégoire thought that Christian Frenchmen were already reformed and that only the Jews needed to change. But in reality, Grégoire did not think that the ideal citizen existed among Christians any more than it did among Jews. His larger scheme as an enlightened religious revolutionary was to refashion all who would become part of a French nation, Jew and Christian alike, into a new kind of socially responsible kind of French nation. All had to be regenerated, not just the Jews.

Still, the Jews were different: they needed more work. He wanted to deprive the Jew of certain civil liberties as temporary measures to protect the rest of society until the Jews were completely reformed. Grégoire agreed with Rousseau in advocating "sentiments of sociability, without which it is impossible to be either a good citizen or a loyal subject."[22] The idea of *sociabilité* was all-important in the late eighteenth century, and Grégoire's program for Jewish assimilation is an expression of it.[23] But unlike Rousseau, Grégoire thought that Catholicism's social ethics were compatible with promoting the values of civic virtue that the anti-clerical secularists advocated: "Consider that religion, known better every day, supports the rights of humanity by moving the heart and that the Christians of today are not those of the twelfth century" (148).[24] Religion's social ethics complemented reason: the former moved the heart; the latter, the mind. Both agreed on a vision of a free, enlightened, and homogeneous social man.

When Grégoire looked at the Jews and measured them against the ideal of *sociabilité* he found them wanting. He even argued that to grant the Jews political equality without trying to change their character would be dangerous to the French society he was trying to fashion.[25] Despite recent enlightened legislation in France and Austria, the Jew was still the antisocial, avaricious creature that medieval persecution had created. With a few notable exceptions, like Moses Mendelssohn, Jewry uniformly possessed dangerous character traits. This homogeneity, however, was based not on a perverse Jewish nature, but on history.

To tolerate the Jews as they were would pose a physical, moral, and economic threat to France. The physical danger lay in Jewish overpopulation that threatened to inundate the country. While most people assume, Grégoire pointed out, that "a large population is a source of wealth to the state, ... let us see if the

Jewish population is not an exception to this rule" (59). The Jews were physically weak, degenerated, but at the same time prolific. Their high growth rate was a danger because the Jews are "a nation which consumes without producing and will never make up for what it eats by its retail trade" and they are "parasites" (61–62).

The solution for an enlightened society lies not in adopting inhumane laws limiting the number of their marriages, nor in expelling them. Every man has the natural right to live where he was born. Nevertheless, unless something positive is done to reform them, while granting them civic rights, they will endanger the nation.

A second dangerous feature of the Jews is their ignorant, antisocial moral character. Withdrawn from society in the Middle Ages, they became addicted to the talmudic tales which their rabbis taught them. Many of the Jews' prejudices, so inculcated, are blatantly anti-Christian, hence antisocial. These prejudices, moreover, are also no reason for killing the Jews.

Most offensive of all, the Jews are possessed by an avariciousness that would be disastrous for France if permitted to continue. The Jews are destroying the French peasant class that Grégoire loved so much from his childhood background in Lorraine:

> What will become of this good farmer ruined by the Jews? His mind is degraded by poverty; he is only a step away from becoming a scoundrel. Led astray by despair, he will soon cross over that thin line. If his wife has not died of grief, she will soon have to become his helper, and the poorly raised children will provide a future generation of corrupt citizens. (78–79)

Such an antisocial Jew had to be changed in conformity with the ideals of *sociabilité* and civic virtue. It would have to be a gradual process because the Jew had been conditioned by centuries of persecution. Certain features like avariciousness "perhaps will only disappear completely in a century; but except for that we like to think two generations will suffice for their reform because everything works together to bring it about" (190). By "everything" Grégoire meant the cooperation of all elements in French society: government, artisans, farmers, and most of all the Jews.

Grégoire thought that Jews' moral character should change economically, politically, socially, religiously, and even physically through intermarriage, physical labor, and a healthier diet that included not removing blood from the meat they consumed. Until a complete reform especially of the first area occurred, Grégoire proposed that the state enact temporary restrictive measures to protect society.[26] First of all, Jewish usury must end. Grégoire proposed laws that would require Jews to sell only for cash; all future credit transactions would be prohibited to Jews in retail trade. Bills outstanding against Christians should be registered with the government to prevent Jews from fabricating and antedating new ones. He further suggested that Jews should not be allowed to work at occupations that offered opportunities for extortion such as tax or customs agents (146).

Grégoire stressed that such measures did not conflict with the principle of civic liberty because they are for the good of society and for the Jews' own good as well. This paternalism dominates all of his proposals. A true child of the Enlightenment, he always knew what would be good for the Jews and the nation, and that was to make everyone conform to the ideal of civic virtue. He pointed out that, once Jewish character had changed, such restrictions would no longer be needed. But this would take time: "One does not change a nation's character the way one changes a military uniform" (98).

In addition to limiting the Jews' direct dealings with money, Grégoire proposed that new economic avenues should be opened to the Jew. Underlying these plans is the goal of Jewish assimilation. Only the anticipation of serious difficulties prompted him to compromise on this point. For example, he hoped that the Jews would enter the artisan class but he stopped short of requiring them to be accepted into the artisan guilds. "No, let us not offend [Christian] prejudices so as to combat them more effectively." Instead, he thought Jewish craftsmen could be organized separately, and their competition with Christian guilds would improve products and prices to everyone's satisfaction. Granting the Jews strict equality was less important to him than avoiding Christian resentment. In this way civic harmony would best be served.

He also assumed that Jews would be able to acquire artisan skills because only a little money is needed for the necessary training and "soon we will see enthusiastic and prudent individuals ... provide free workshops for them." Necessity could encourage Jewish interest in the crafts:

> The Jews of certain locations could be required to live only in houses they themselves have built and to wear only clothing they have manufactured, ... Their products should be distributed and praised. Thus, necessity ... will develop the abilities in the Israelites whose docile genius predisposes them for anything: honor and love for profit will give them more incentive. (114–15)

Grégoire also thought that the Jews should enter agricultural work. This occupation would help improve their moral character because "the first of the arts [agriculture] is still the first in [promoting] virtue" (117). The Jews' physical weakness will not prevent them from becoming farmers, because they should be permitted to hire Christian workmen until the Jews recover their physical vigor. By mixing freely with their Christian laborers, the Jews will acquire a sound moral character. The result of such a program will be the acquisition by France of the benefits of a new source of labor.

The new Jew should also participate in civic affairs, though once again under certain temporary limitations: "Such exclusions are based only on [the Jews'] hatred for Christianity and their moral depravity. … When our observation will not longer be true, transported with joy, we will hasten to remove them" (164). Jews could, however, become attorneys and should be freed from taking the Catholic Oath. In addition, they should be eligible for election in all provincial assemblies. Finally, there was no reason why Jews should not be admitted to *lycées* and academies if they had the academic qualifications.

Social mixing would encourage assimilation even more effectively than economic or civic integration. The Jews should not be allowed to live together in separate areas from Christians. Such isolation only provides a target for Christian vilification of the Jews. Religion and reason encourage the belief that Christians are becoming more tolerant of Jewish neighbors (148). The state should not leave this redistribution of Jewish settlement up to the Jews but should establish quotas in each neighborhood, and when the quota is filled, the other Jews will have to live elsewhere. The new Jewish Frenchman would become a good citizen whether he liked it or not.

What price would the Jew have to pay as far as Judaism was concerned? Grégoire's previous proposals were designed to encourage the Jew's assimilation into French society where he could be schooled in civic virtue. To what extent did he see Judaism as an obstacle to achieving this goal?

Apart from Christian state persecution, Grégoire thought that rabbinic Judaism was the greatest obstacle to reforming the Jews. He assumed that the Jewish character had become uniformly antisocial largely because of the all-pervasive influence of rabbinic Judaism that he thought was uniformly observed. Persecution during the Jews' dispersion, Grégoire had argued, caused the Jews to cling ever closer to their religion. Thus, Grégoire thought of Judaism as an intermediate cause in creating a uniformly benighted antisocial group.

Grégoire's assumption that Judaism was a contributory factor to Jewish character defects explains why he differed from John Toland's conclusions about Jewish acculturation, although he held mostly the same premises. In his essay *Reasons for Naturalizing the Jews in Great Britain and Ireland,* Toland had argued that the Jewish concentration in commerce was not a natural defect but was a product of their education and environment. If environment, and not nature, is responsible for various traits in Jewish character, it follows that

> They have no common or peculiar inclination distinguishing 'em from others; but visibly partake of the Nature of those nations among which they live, and where they were bred. The ordinary sentiments and manners of the Portuguese or Italian Jews differ not from those of other Portuguese or Italians.[27]

Toland had explained the reason for the high concentration of Jews as "Brokers" of trade: "they are driven to this way of Livelihood by mere Necessity; from being excluded everywhere in Europe."[28] Grégoire also invokes the principle of environment as responsible for man's character in general, but he does not conclude that Jewish character resembles the various nations among which they live (109). The cause of their uniformity is their religion:

> The Rabbinists, successors of the Pharisees, constitute the majority of the nation, and at Leghorn as at Metz, at Hamburg as at Bordeaux, you find among them a conformity of dogmas, rites, and moral habits because no religion has created such uniformity of conduct as the Mosaic religion. ... His genius has been impeded to no avail; one cannot change it, and perhaps there is more similarity between the Jews of Ethiopia and those of England than between the inhabitants of Picardy and those of Provence. (28–29)

In two ways, then, Grégoire admitted that the Jews had changed in the diaspora. Persecution restricted their avenues of economic pursuits and they turned to usury; this gave the Jewish character the taint of avarice. And the exile had a second effect: it made them obstinately loyal to their religious way of life, and this resulted in a uniform pattern of moral depravity. Thus while Grégoire and Toland would agree that persecution led to the same economic results, they differ on the impact of the Jewish religion on Jewish character formation. Toland stressed the acculturation of Jewish attitudes to the host society; Grégoire thought that Judaism had uniformly affected the Jews in the diaspora to their detriment. Persecution caused them to be loyal to Judaism, and the religion itself created their negative moral character.

To regenerate the Jew, then, it would be necessary not only to open new avenues for Jewish economic pursuits such as agriculture and crafts, but also to reform Judaism. But is the Jewish religion entirely bad? How then account for the fact that under Rome, the Jews were full citizens, active in all governmental and economic activities while living under talmudic legislation? Grégoire's ideas for the reform of Judaism are based on the enlightened distinction that he made within Catholicism between dogma and public morality. He invoked this distinction to express and defend his own religious enlightenment in liberal Catholicism. In a similar fashion, Grégoire hoped to create a religious French Jew, at least temporarily, in his own image as an enlightened French Catholic.

Rousseau had argued that Catholicism was that type of religion that "gives men two legislative orders, two rulers, two homelands, puts them under two contradictory obligations, and prevents their being at the same time both churchman and citizen. Such is ... Catholic Christianity."[29] Grégoire thus faced the anticlerical attack, similar to the accusation made about the Jews, that the Church represented a "state within a state" (110).

Grégoire answered these accusations by restricting the functions of Church and state to dogmatic and social jurisdictions respectively. If any ecclesiastical law had been promulgated against the best interests of society, it could be abrogated. A case in point is Grégoire's argument permitting Catholics to marry Jews. The prohibition in canon law is not a dogma but a regulation necessitated by a temporary social problem: the Church feared that Jews would seduce Christians and encourage their apostasy. Since this danger is no longer a problem, the prohibition can be abolished.

Grégoire applied the same distinction between dogma and social order to Judaism. The Jewish religion as practiced is incompatible with civil virtue because ignorance and misery in the exile have misguided the Jews into thinking of these additions as having dogmatic authority. It is necessary to distinguish between dogmas and changeable public rituals. What, then, are the dogmas of Judaism? From certain "educated Jews, with whom he has spoken often" he had learned that their basic dogmas are three: "the unity of God, the immortality of the soul, and future rewards and punishments" (101).

Unlike dogmas, social regulations can be changed when their rationale no longer applies. Grégoire had stated this principle in regard to Judaism in his discussion about pagan animosity to primitive Judaism. The Divine Author gave the Hebrews an exclusive cult to protect them from paganism. Once the threat disappeared, however, such laws were no longer binding. Most of rabbinic Judaism falls under the category of temporary laws. Since the dietary rules of clean and unclean animals were designed to separate the Hebrews from pagans, they could now be disregarded. He thought the army would provide an occasion for eliminating the peculiar features of the Jews' diet. Intermarriage, too, had been prohibited to Jews because of the dangers of paganism. Soon the strange practices with the Sabbath could be ended, and so on.

Grégoire expected that Jews would give up public rituals, and history proves that they always dropped or modified ritual laws when difficult or impossible to execute. Sometimes they have been dropped even without constraint: witness Jewish art collecting, then, especially in Italy (101). Ignorance and prejudice have mistakenly raised these temporary rules to the level of dogmatic or ethical precepts. As additional features of religious reform, he proposed limiting the power of the rabbis by supervising their education. He also demanded of Judaism what he advocated for the Church: the use of French in the liturgy.

The most drastic implication of Grégoire's definition of Judaism, however, was that Jewish autonomy would have to end:

> Let us distinguish in Mosaic law between that which pertains essentially to conducting the cult and that which is only the object of civil and criminal law. ... Let us grant to the Jews complete liberty in the first matter, in everything that does not affect the goods of liberty and honor of a citizen. But as concerning all the rest, let him submit to the laws of the nation. (155)

In later years, Grégoire thought his hopes for Jewish regeneration in France were disappointed. His rationalism and convictions misled him into thinking that everyone else could see things his way. Man is not entirely rational, and Grégoire grew bitter in later years when the Jews resisted complete assimilation as he had outlined it. In his *Essai* he had written that man is born good and can become better, but in his *Mémoires*, written in 1808 and published posthumously, he had second thoughts about the Jews: "I think it was Jean-Jacques who said: 'Man is good; men are wicked.' He might have been right, but one has to live with men, not abstract Man." In a note he added: "It is wrong to say 'Man is good,' because original sin corrupted him, and I should rectify this error in my work on the Jews."[30]

One cause for despair was the resistance on the part of the Jews to complete assimilation. Shortly after the Jewish emancipation was enacted into law, Berr Isaac Berr, the wealthy leader of French Jewry who argued for Jewish emancipation at the National Assembly, reacted to the Jews' newly won freedom. Although grateful for emancipation and aware of an obligation to change, he drew the line sooner than Grégoire would have liked: "Let us form communities, such as we had in Lorraine." Voluntary communities would replace the older corporations, and they would protect Jews from complete assimilation. Children should be "thoroughly initiated in the principles and spirit of our religion" before sending them to share the advantages of national education in the public schools. Even worse, from Grégoire's point of view, Berr counseled the Jews to take advantage of their rights slowly: "Let us avoid *grasping* at our rights. ... Let it be sufficient for us, at present, to have acquired the invaluable right of [attending] all assemblies of French citizens; but let us not attend them until we have acquired knowledge sufficient to make ourselves useful members."[31]

Although Grégoire was disappointed that some of his proposals did not have immediate results, the ideas in his *Essai* had important consequences for Jewish Emancipation elsewhere in Europe. Some Jews did accept his idea that they would have to pay a price for their political rights by reforming themselves either before or after they were made citizens. Perhaps it was naïve of Grégoire to expect Alsatian Jews to give up their particularism when Alsatian Christians resisted.[32] The most significant sign of an acceptance of Grégoire's offer of conditional emancipation was in the area of religious reform. By applying to Judaism Grégoire's enlightened Catholic distinction between eternal dogmas and changeable rituals, Jewish Reformers had a rationale for crafting Jewish religious reforms in Germany.

Notes

1. Maurice Cranston, introduction to *The Social Contract*, by Jean-Jacques Rousseau, trans. Maurice Cranston (Baltimore: Penguin, 1968), 15.
2. Henri Grégoire, *Essai sur la régénération physique, morale, et politique des Juifs* (Metz and Paris, 1789), repr. in *La Revolution française et l'émancipation des Juifs* (Paris: Editions d'Histoire Sociale, [1968]), part 3, which I have used throughout. For an early English translation, see *An Essay on the Physical, Moral, and Political reformation of the Jews ... by the Abbé Grégoire* (London, n.d.). Translations are my own. In anticipation of the bicentennial of the French Revolution, two other editions appeared with new introductions: Henri Grégoire, *Essai*, with a preface by Rita Hermon-Belot (Paris: Flammarion, 1988), and *Essai*, ed. Robert Badinter (Paris: Stock, 1988).

   For the way the contest was run, the two versions of Grégoire's Metz essay, and the significance of the final, published one, see Alyssa Goldstein Sepinwall, "Strategic Friendships: Jewish Intellectuals, the Abbé Grégoire, and the French Revolution," in *Renewing the Past: Reconfiguring Jewish Culture*, ed. Ross Brann and Adam Sutcliffe (Philadelphia: University of Pennsylvania Press, 2004), 189–212.
3. On Grégoire's life and career, see Ruth Necheles, *The Abbé Grégoire 1787–1831* (Westport, Conn.: Greenwood, 1971); Arthur Hertzberg, *The French Enlightenment and the Jews* (New York: Columbia University Press, 1968), 297–98, 264–65, 335–38; Paula Hyman, *The Jews of Modern France* (Berkeley and Los Angeles: University of California Press, 1998), 20–21; Jay R. Berkovitz, *The Shaping of Jewish Identity in Nineteenth-Century France* (Detroit: Wayne State University Press, 1989), 30–38; Rita Hermon-Belot, *L'Abbé Grégoire, la politique et la verité* (Paris: du Seuil, 2000); *The Abbé Grégoire and His World*, ed. Jeremy D. Popkin and Richard H. Popkin (Dordrecht: Kluwer, 2000); Ronald Schechter, *Obstinate Hebrews: Representations of Jews in France, 1715–1815* (Berkeley and Los Angeles: University of California Press, 2003), 90–94; and Alyssa Goldstein Sepinwall, "Regenerating France, Regenerating the World: the Abbé Grégoire and the French Revolution, 1750–1831" (Ph.D. diss., Stanford University, 1998), published in revised form as *The Abbé Grégoire and the French Revolution: The Making of Modern Universalism* (Berkeley and Los Angeles: University of California Press, 2005). My thanks to Professor Sepinwall for sending me a prepublication copy of her revised chapter on Grégoire and the Jews, in which she also discusses the penultimate version of Grégoire's essay that she recently discovered.

4. The motion was published in Paris in 1789 and more recently in *L'abbé Grégoire évêque des lumières*, ed. Frank Paul Bowman (Paris: Editions France-Empire, 1988), 21–43.
5. Paul Grunebaum-Ballin, *L'Abbé Grégoire et les Juifs* (Paris: Imprimerie française, 1931), 5.
6. Dale Arthur Johnson, "The Political and Religious Thought of Henri Grégoire" (Ph.D. diss., Union Theological Seminary, 1966), 160.
7. Paul Grunebaum-Ballin, "Grégoire convertisseur? ou la croyance au 'retour d'Israel,'" *Revue des études juives* 121 (1962): 383–98; Hertzberg, *French Enlightenment*, 9. This is also the view in Necheles, *Abbé Grégoire*, 10–15; Rita Hermon-Belot, "L'Abbé Grégoire et la conversion des juifs," in *Les juifs et la Révolution française: Histoire et mentalités*, ed. Mireille Hadas-Lebel and Evelyne Oliel-Grausz (Louvain: Peeters, 1992), 21–27. See also Catherine-Laurence Maire, *Les convulsionnaires de Saint Médard* (Paris: Gallimard, 1985), and *De la cause de Dieu à la cause de la nation: Le jansénisme au XVIIIᵉ siècle* (Paris: Gallimard, 1998).
8. On the two worldviews, see Robert R. Palmer, *Catholics and Unbelievers in Eighteenth-Century France* (Princeton: Princeton University Press, 1939); and on "religious enlightenment" in France, see Dale K. Van Kley, *The Religious Origins of the French Revolution: From Calvin to the Civil Constitution, 1560–1791* (New Haven: Yale University Press, 1996) and David A. Bell, *The Cult of the Nation in France: Inventing Nationalism, 1680–1800* (Cambridge: Harvard University Press, 2001). My thanks to my colleague John Merriman for calling David Bell's important book to my attention.
    David Sorkin analyzed a different seminal figure, Moses Mendelssohn, and compared religious emancipations within Germany of Jews, Protestants, and Catholics (see *Moses Mendelssohn and the Religious Enlightenment* [Berkeley and Los Angeles: University of California Press, 1996] and *The Berlin Haskalah and German Religious Thought: Orphans of Knowledge* [London: Vallentine Mitchell, 2000]. It would be of interest to compare the religious Enlightenment of Grégoire and Mendelssohn, whom Grégoire admired, to understand the Janus-like writings and behavior of both. At times, each wrote as committed traditional Jew or Catholic; at others, they advocated ideas of the Enlightenment even when they conflicted with some of the representatives of the religious culture to which each belonged. See Sepinwall, "Strategic Friendships," 191, who suggestively compares Grégoire to "Maskilim."
9. Johnson, "Political and Religious Thought," 43–44.
10. Bell, *Cult of the Nation*, 22–49.

11. See Marcel Gauchet, *The Disenchantment of the World: A Political History of Religion*, trans. Oscar Burge (Princeton: Princeton University Press, 1997); Van Kley, *Religious Origins*; and Bell, *Cult of the Nation*, esp. 185–94.

12. See Judah Leib Gordon, "Awake, my People!" trans. in Michael Stanislawski, *For Whom Do I Toil? Judah Leib Gordon and the Crisis of Russian Jewry* (Oxford: Oxford University Press, 1988), 49–51. Stanislawski points out that Gordon's line "Be a man in the streets and a Jew at home" has been misunderstood as advocating the separation of church and state, religion and nationality, a view that is actually close to Grégoire's position about Catholicism and politics.

13. For the history of the term, and Grégoire's role in redefining it, see Mona Ozouf, "Regeneration," in *A Critical Dictionary of the French Revolution*, ed. François Furet and Mona Ozouf (Cambridge: Harvard University Press, 1989), 781–91; Sepinwall, "Regenerating France," 83–86 and *Abbé Grégoire*, chapter 3; and Bell, *Cult of the Nation*, 42–43, 74–76.

14. See David A. Bell, "Lingua Populi, Lingua Dei: Language, Religion, and the Origins of French Revolutionary Nationalism," *American Historical Review* 100 (1995): 1403–37, and Bell, *Cult of the Nation*, 169–97.

15. See Sepinwall, *Abbé Grégoire*, chapter 3.

16. Ernst Cassirer, *The Philosophy of the Enlightenment*, trans. Fritz C. A. Koelln and James P. Pettegrove (Princeton: Princeton University Press, 1951), 214–15.

17. Grégoire dismisses most but not all of the medieval accusations against the Jews as fabrications. See *Essai*, chapter 3, 17–24.

18. John Toland, *Reasons for Naturalizing the Jews in Great Britain and Ireland* (London: J. Roberts, 1714; repr., Jerusalem: Hebrew University, Department of Jewish History, 1963), original pp. 26, 28, 31, 33, 36; Christian Wilhelm Dohm, *Concerning the Amelioration of the Civic Status of the Jews*, trans. Helen Lederer (Cincinnati: Hebrew Union College – Jewish Institute of Religion, 1957), 25, 32.

19. Toland, *Reasons for Naturalizing the Jews*, 20.

20. Cassirer, *Philosophy of the Enlightenment*, 205–9.

21. Ibid., 186.

22. Rousseau, *Social Contract*, 186.

23. See especially Daniel Gordon, *Citizens without Sovereignty: Equality and Sociability in French Thought, 1670–1789* (Princeton: Princeton University Press, 1994), 43–85, and Bell, *Cult of the Nation*, 147.

24. Compare Rousseau, *Social Contract*, 181.

25. Grégoire, *Essai*, chapters 10 and 11.

26. On the physical recommendations, see Sepinwall, *Abbé Grégoire*, chap. 3, and Grégoire, *Essai*, chap. 7.

27. Toland, *Reasons for Naturalizing the Jews*, 19.

28. Ibid., 14–15.

29. Rousseau, *Social Contract*, 181.

30. [Henri Grégoire], *Mémoires de l'abbé Grégoire*, ed. H. Carnot, 2 vols. (Paris: J. Yonet, 1840); ed. J. M. Leniaud with a preface by J. N. Jeanneney (Paris: Editions de Santé, 1989), 110.

31. Paul Mendes-Flohr and Jehuda Reinharz, *The Jew in the Modern World: A Documentary History*, 2nd ed. (New York: Oxford University Press, 1995), 118–20, and Berr Isaac Berr, "Lettre d'un Citoyen" (Nancy, 1791), in M. Diogenes Tama, *Transactions of the Parisian Sanhedrin*, trans. F. D. Kirwan (London, 1807), 11–29.

32. Berr, "Lettre d'un Citoyen," and compare Frances Malino, "Attitudes toward Communal Autonomy in Prerevolutionary France," in *Essays in Modern Jewish History: A Tribute to Ben Halpern*, ed. Frances Malino and Phyllis Cohen-Albert (Rutherford, N.J.: Fairleigh Dickinson University Press, 1982), 95–117; Sepinwall, "Strategic Friendships," on attitudes of contemporary Jews toward the Revolution; David A. Bell, "Nation Building and Cultural Particularism in Eighteenth-Century France: the Case of Alsace," *Eighteenth-Century Studies* 21 (1988): 472–90, on the resistance of Alsatian Christians to conforming to the French national ideal; and Paula E. Hyman, *The Emancipation of the Jews of Alsace: Acculturation and Tradition in the Nineteenth Century* (New Haven: Yale University Press, 1991).

Samuel Hirszenberg's Imagination

An Artist's Interpretation
of the Jewish Dilemma at the Fin de Siècle

RICHARD I. COHEN

It is a truism that the reputation of artists seesaws over time. Artists of Jewish origin face a more complex historical reception. Depending on cultural and political circumstances during and after their lifetimes, they may be enshrined in a pantheon of national heroes, even as others seek to situate their art within the confines of Jewish creativity or identity, attributing significance to their Jewish origin even when their art shows little if any connection to a Jewish source or particular Jewish influence.

Art historians employ a wide range of arguments, sometimes contradictory in nature, to co-opt such works to the domain of "Jewish influence," intimating an ideological subtext of a conscious or subconscious nature. This strategy inevitably tends to oversimplify an inherently complex issue, for the artists themselves, who experimented with changing styles and were attracted to different ideological and political tendencies over the course of their lives, cannot easily be fit into one single construct. Nineteenth- and twentieth-century artists of Jewish origin, from both

Ms. Dorota Sniezek of the Musée d'art et d'histoire du Judaïsme in Paris, with whom I am planning a larger study on Hirszenberg, has been extremely helpful and insightful since our first discussions of his work. My sincere thanks to Ms. Tali Brener of the Hebrew University for her assistance with various aspects of this paper.

Western and Eastern Europe, or the Americas, were part of a rapidly changing social, geographic, and political context, which often challenged and reoriented their sense of belonging and attachment. To avoid essentialism on the one hand, or omission on the other, critics and historians need to assess the inevitable complexity of artists of Jewish origin, whose unique minority experience and individualism may or may not have found expression in their diverse subject matter.

These remarks are pertinent, certainly, to the reception of Camille Pissarro, Simeon Solomon, Maurycy Gottlieb, Mark Antokol'skii, Isidor Kaufmann, Amedeo Modigliani, and Max Liebermann, to name but a few of the more celebrated figures, each of whom openly confronted their Jewish identity and whose work was in turn the source of conflicting appraisals. Such was also the case with Moritz Oppenheim (1800–1882), whose creativity has received serious scholarly attention in the last generation, highlighted by Ismar Schorsch's pathbreaking essay, "Art as Social History: Moritz Oppenheim and The German Jewish Vision of Emancipation." The paper out of which that essay emerged was first delivered in 1982 at an international conference on the city of Danzig at Harvard University, under the auspices of the Center for Judaic Studies headed by the late Professor Isadore Twersky. It was my first encounter with Ismar Schorsch and, for me, a most memorable one. Though he was already a recognized and distinguished historian, and I a very junior one, there was no sense of hierarchy or formality in our conversation. Other encounters were to follow in different settings. The Oppenheim lecture first appeared in the Israel Museum's exhibition catalogue *Moritz Oppenheim, The First Jewish Painter* (Jerusalem, 1983), curated and edited by the late Elisheva Cohen. I was pleased to have served as the intermediary for and Hebrew translator of the essay. It later appeared in the volume on Danzig, and was reprinted in *From Text to Context: The Turn to History in Modern Judaism* (1994). Its impact is evident from the numerous references

to it in all works treating Oppenheim and in discussions on the
interrelationship between art and Jewish history.[1] Oppenheim's
Scenes from Traditional Jewish Family Life might otherwise have continued to be considered a naive expression of "poetry and earnest-
ness, piety and tenderness, sobriety and conscientiousness ... the
human and the pathos of that old-time Jewish life";[2] but following Schorsch's illuminating cultural-historical essay, the nature of
the discussion was deepened and Oppenheim's work was opened
to a wider range of perspectives, culminating in an impressive retrospective exhibition in Frankfurt in 1999–2000.[3] In the spirit of
our original dialogue, I wish to devote the following pages to the
oeuvre of Samuel Hirszenberg (1865–1908), an artist whose work
also engaged Ismar Schorsch's attention,[4] and whose art was
informed by a profound sense of engagement with the dilemmas
faced by Polish Jewry at the fin de siècle—offering an interesting
parallel to Oppenheim's relationship to German Jewry.

In 1865, a year before Oppenheim turned his efforts almost exclusively to the creation of his famous series, Samuel Hirszenberg was
born in Łódź, Congress Poland, an industrial city that was on the
verge of a major demographic boom. Łódź numbered 50,000 residents in the census of 1877, whereas twenty years later the city
had increased more than sixfold, reaching a total population of
315,209, 31 percent of whom were Jews (98,677). Known for its
thriving textile industry, Łódź attracted a large number of landless
peasants and a small number of disenfranchised nobility, as well as
an influx of Lithuanian Jews from western Russia, and Germans,
who joined the largest center of German nationals in Congress
Poland. Yiddish continued to be the mother tongue of over 93
percent of Łódź Jews, though Russian, Polish, and German began
to be spoken by a small percentage of them.[5] Basically a working
class population, the vast majority of Jews were artisans who

labored in small shops in traditional crafts such as tailoring and carpentry. Like many others in the city, Hirszenberg's father, a weaver, struggled to support his large family (the tenth child was born in the mid 1890s), as factories were rapidly replacing the employment of artisans. Often Jewish laborers, like Hirszenberg's father, would earn a meager 4 rubles a week, guaranteeing a very difficult existence for a large family.[6]

An enterprising Jewish bourgeoisie was also present in the city. Some Jews owned factories and were involved in purchasing raw material. The most successful of these, Izrael Kalman Poznański, was also to figure in Hirszenberg's career. Poznański's family moved to Łódź in 1834 when the town was still in its earliest stage of growth. Gradually he amassed much wealth and purchased land to build a factory and a housing estate for its workers. By the 1870s and 1880s he owned the city's largest palace and was considered the "King of Cotton," master of the largest textile plant in Łódź, where he employed some six thousand workers, only a few dozen of whom were Jewish. Poznański served on various Jewish cultural and welfare committees, was president of the Liberal synagogue in Łódź, and he, and his son Ignaczy, served on the city's municipal council. An example of enterprising and successful Jewish industrialists who acculturated to Polish life and figured prominently in both worlds, the Poznańskis' star faded dramatically during World War I when Łódź and its textile industry suffered tremendous losses.[7]

The industrialization in Łódź that skyrocketed the Poznański family to great wealth and prominence at the end of the nineteenth century was partially responsible for the Hirszenbergs' difficult economic situation. In response to their declining economic situation, pressure was put on Samuel, the eldest son, to assist his father and apprentice as a weaver. Unlike the family of his compatriot Maurycy Gottlieb, who strongly encouraged his artistic talents,[8] Hirszenberg's parents frowned on and discouraged his artistic interests. At the age of 11, against his own inclinations,

Hirszenberg began to learn his father's trade. However, his faltering health brought him into contact with Dr. Maksymiljan Cohn, who had a special interest in art and began to cultivate Hirszenberg's talent. It was Cohn who succeeded in releasing Hirszenberg from the tutelage of his parents and supported his move, at the age of 15, to Warsaw to study art.[9] Since the Polish uprising in 1863, Warsaw had been growing annually by the thousands through internal migration and offered a much more dynamic setting, culturally and ideologically, than his home town. Still, Hirszenberg's stay in Warsaw proved short-lived and unpleasant, as he lacked sufficient means, encountered little warm hospitality, and failed to find a niche for himself. His unfortunate experience in this first move from home was characteristic of many aspiring artists as they attempted to integrate into artistic academic institutions. Hirszenberg returned to Łódź but was not deterred from his original goal; he opted to return to Cracow to study in its school of fine arts, following the lead of many Polish artists before him, including Gottlieb. Under the directorship of Poland's leading national artist of the day, Jan Mateko, the school had become a major training ground for leading Polish artists of the generation; Hirszenberg remained there for two years, studying with several Polish artists—Feliks Szynalewski, Izydor Jabłoński, and Władysław Łuszczkiewicz. There too he subsisted on a meager subsidy doled out by supporters in Łódź, but there were other compensations: he was taken by the city's beauty, its rich architectural and historical tradition, and its attractive Jewish sites, so dramatically different from his native Łódź. Following the constitution that granted Galician residents legal equality, Cracow emerged as a budding center of Polish culture and nationalism and offered a predominantly liberal atmosphere. Its vibrant Jewish community of some thirty thousand—almost a third of the city's population—consisted of a dominant Orthodox community with a high percentage of Hasidim (Belz, Bobov, and other Hasidic groups), but also included a growing number of acculturated Jews who were engaged in both local and Jewish affairs. The city and its mélange of traditions remained a source of desire for the young artist, who would eventually return to it two decades later at a very difficult moment in his life. Cracow and Warsaw were the settings of his early artistic education, but few works from these years have survived, preventing an adequate appraisal of his development before he moved on to Munich.[10]

In 1885, Hirszenberg followed the route of many Polish artists (e.g. Jan Mateko, Józef Chełmoński, Alexander Gierymski, and Gottlieb) to Munich, one of Europe's leading art centers of the day. Its Academy of Art, then headed by Alexander Wagner, a distinguished artist of historical themes, would provide Hirszenberg's advanced artistic education for four years (1885–89). Though Hirszenberg continued, as before, to struggle for his existence and suffered periods of illness, hunger, and outright despair, he became deeply attached to the city and returned there on several occasions in the next two decades. In Munich he came of age, and he began exhibiting works in each of the cities where he had trained. Themes that were to remain central to his oeuvre appeared in several paintings from the years 1887–88, prior to his departure for a further period of study in Paris at the Académie Philippe Colarossi. Two of these works reflect Hirszenberg's need to contend with the Orthodox Jewish milieu he knew from his childhood and from his student days in Warsaw and Cracow.

Dated 1887, Hirszenberg's study of a group of five Jews "burning the midnight oil" as they pore over the Talmud is a typical genre scene employed by various artists of Jewish origin in the nineteenth and twentieth centuries. Their portraits of men studiously engaged with an open text expressed a mix of fascination and repulsion, sometimes tinged with a melancholy and tragic view of the subject. Polish artists, who depicted Jews in many different situations, were less attracted to this genre scene, though several artists (e. g. Antoni Piotrowski and Tadeusz Rybkowksi) painted Jewish students with characteristic interest and perception.[11]

Figure 1. Samuel Hirszenberg (1865–1908), *Yeshiva*, 1887. Oil on canvas, 137 × 212 cm.

National Museum, Cracow, IIa-798.

Hirszenberg's treatment of the *Yeshiva* (fig. 1) brings together the figures in the corner of a small room, seated around a table near a window with a curtain.[12] The morning light already penetrates the room. The students seem to be exhausted from the night's study; one has given in to his fatigue and has fallen asleep at the table, while his colleagues, though still awake, seem far from absorbed in study. The elderly man, probably their teacher, leans on his hand, which rests on the open Talmud, musing distantly as he seems to lose contact with the lesson and his students. The painting offers a poignant comment on the world of Jewish learning: it captures the energy and stamina needed to preserve the rigor of study but it portrays, as well, the lapse of involvement, enthusiasm, and hope. In this sense, the painting veers from the typical genre imagery as it lacks the more sentimental and entertaining elements characteristic of that genre.[13] Hirszenberg's realism already was asserting itself.

In tandem with this work Hirszenberg embarked on the first of his historical paintings, *Uriel da Costa and Spinoza* (fig. 2), whose whereabouts is unknown. Perhaps inspired by the historical paintings of his mentor Wagner and/or by Gottlieb's interest in Da Costa, Hirszenberg added his own commentary to the cultural engagement with these celebrated seventeenth-century ex-Marranos. Both figures went against the grain of traditional Jewish society, battled basic Jewish belief systems, and collided with the oligarchy of Amsterdam's rabbis. Da Costa (1585–1640) was excommunicated on several occasions, in Amsterdam, Venice, and Hamburg; and Spinoza similarly was excommunicated in the year 1656 by the Mahamad in Amsterdam, for espousing what were considered heretical beliefs. The former committed suicide in 1640, seemingly unable to overcome the sense of humiliation following the degrading ritual he was forced to undergo to annul his excommunication.[14] Both Spinoza and Da Costa were figures of recurrent interest, especially in the nineteenth and twentieth centuries, among playwrights, authors, composers, and artists of non-Jewish and Jewish origin.[15] Karl Gutzkow (1811–1878), a recognized leader of the Young Germans,[16] contributed significantly to the interest in Da Costa through his 1834 historical drama, *Der Sadduzäer von Amsterdam*—a work translated into Polish and several other languages (including Hebrew and Yiddish)[17]—and especially through its theatrical rendition. Gutzkow hailed the battle Da Costa fought against fundamentalist Christianity and Judaism, critically depicting rabbinic authority and wealthy Jews but praising the beauty of Jewish women. In Gutzkow's novella, Da Costa the rationalist is pitted against religious obscurantism, but rather than terminate his life due to his humiliation by the rabbis, he commits suicide because the woman he adored, Judith Vanderstraten, has left him for another man. Gutzkow added another element to the mythic version of Da Costa's life: He ended the drama with Spinoza's presence at Da Costa's funeral, thus magnifying the mythic relationship between the two and

Figure 2. Samuel Hirszenberg, *Uriel da Costa and Spinoza* 1887/8. Oil on canvas.

Whereabouts unknown.

forging a lineage of rational opposition to an unswerving rabbinical authority. Gutzkow's treatment of Da Costa sparked a response by the German-Jewish author Berthold Auerbach, in the latter's *Spinoza* (1837). Motivated in part by a desire to glorify Spinoza as a "secular redeemer" and project him as the personification of universalism, Auerbach's Spinoza also rejected the critique of Jewish life embedded in Gutzkow's account. Both works encouraged others to inquire into the biographies and philosophical approaches of both Da Costa and Spinoza.[18]

Echoing Gutzkow's dramatic association of the two Sephardic figures, Hirszenberg directly linked Uriel Da Costa with Spinoza. In his work, Da Costa is seen seated, crouched over the young Spinoza, a dreamy-eyed boy with golden hair, aged 8 or 9, dressed in colorful and fancy clothing, as he gazes penetratingly into the distance in an intense, almost haunted fashion.[19] Depicted with drawn cheekbones, Da Costa is bearded and wears a large black skullcap, intimating that notwithstanding his ideas he lived within the fold of traditional Judaism. The open book on the table, a reminder of a lesson on natural science that Da Costa was giving Spinoza, is clearly not on Da Costa's mind. His compelling look, dark hair, and dress contrast sharply with the bright-haired Spinoza and his comportment, intimating the hope invested in the child, who eyes the flowers and book from the corner of his eye. Similar to the physical setting in *Yeshiva*, the spartan room is bare, save the books strewn over the tables and on a nearby shelf. Hirszenberg places the figures to the right of the canvas, squeezed into the edge of the painting to such an extent that of Da Costa's body only his head, the source of his intellectual and spiritual quest, can be seen clearly. Together with the attention and centrality Hirszenberg gives the heavy and well-worn books, the spiritual encounter between Da Costa and Spinoza is intensified, granting further meaning to the former's intellectual legacy to Spinoza. In the spirit of historical works of art, Hirszenberg was not concerned with historical accuracy. In fact, Spinoza was only 8 years old when Da Costa ended his life in 1640, and no historical evidence attests to a meeting between the two. In adopting the theme of a spiritual linkage between them, Hirszenberg intimated that Spinoza was Da Costa's disciple, thus creating a genealogy of Jewish freethinkers, and affirmed their symbolic significance to Jewish culture. It would appear that he was expressing his support for their struggle against the rabbis, much in the way that Gutzkow had invoked their connection to disparage traditional Judaism.[20]

These paintings were shown in major exhibitions in Paris (1889) and Berlin (1891) and attracted a certain amount of positive acclaim; *Yeshiva* was even the recipient of a silver medal at the Paris International Exposition. Both works seem to have engendered a certain interest among Polish Jews, who apparently hung reproductions in their homes.[21] But Hirszenberg's work also drew a certain amount of criticism, most notably from the distinguished Russian critic Vladimir V. Stasov, who rebuked Hirszenberg and other Polish artists for having fallen too deeply under the sway of the Munich academy and forgoing their own native traditions. Indeed, the Russian critic constantly berated artists of various national and ethnic backgrounds for their preference for international art forms. Yet this criticism was not justified in this case, for it was not substantially true of Hirszenberg, whether at this point in his career or in later years. The artist's involvement and engagement in Jewish themes was an abiding part of his agenda: his landscapes, portraits, decorative compositions, and other universal concerns never took precedence over those themes.[22] Hirszenberg, like other artists of Jewish origin, vied for the public showing of his "Jewish" works, no less than he did for his general works, implying that he saw no reason to desist from such themes or hide them from the eyes of general audiences.[23]

Following his stay in Paris (ca. 1889–91), where he studied and participated in several international exhibitions and created inter alia his *Esther and Haman* (whereabouts unknown),[24] Hirszenberg returned to Łódź, via Munich, to his needy family. His parents' financial situation had deteriorated further and necessitated his assistance. Moreover, it appears that the Hirszenberg family, like many East European Jewish families of the period, was in a state of complete disarray. The toll exacted by the needs of a very large family with little income was significant. Several of his siblings had followed Samuel's lead and began to study art. They, too, left the city that was undergoing economic difficulties and could not assist their parents.[25] Before settling back in Łódź,

Hirszenberg apparently sold many of his sketches, drawings, and paintings to provide immediate relief for his siblings, without leaving a trace of evidence as to their owners and whereabouts.

Prior to his return, he created the first version of his dramatic depiction of a Jewish cemetery, now in the Musée d'art et d'histoire du Judaïsme[26] (fig. 3). It would open a new direction in Hirszenberg's work, one in which he evocatively addressed the various realms of the Jewish experience at the fin de siècle. Created in Munich, the large canvas (200 × 297cm), depicts a section of the historic Jewish cemetery in Cracow, and shows three women in rather theatrical positions bewailing their personal fate. The concentration here on women, in a nontraditional manner, may represent the intensification of the tragedy facing Jewish families in a time of transition. Hirszenberg was not relating to a specific event in the experience of Polish Jewry but to the sense of dislocation that affected many among them in those years—not the least among them, the artist and his family. His return to Łódź and to the increasingly difficult family situation weighed heavily on him, and in the painting he expressively evoked the pain of these individual women, merging their personal sadness with the memories of former generations. It was this link with the past and associations with the predicament of contemporary Jews that drew much sympathy at the turn of the century, especially among individuals associated with Jewish nationalist tendencies.[27] Yet Hirszenberg's political or ideological leanings were not clearly enunciated at this stage of his career, though his identification with the plight of the Jews was apparent and underscored some of his major undertakings in the years that followed.[28]

He returned to Łódź in 1893, resolved to help his family survive and endure their economic plight. *The Sabbath Rest* (1894)[29] (fig. 4) seems to represent his re-encounter with the family he came to assist. A somber atmosphere dominates the mood of the large canvas (151 × 212 cm). Though one can assume that Hirszenberg was acquainted with Oppenheim's famous painting

Figure 3. Samuel Hirszenberg, *The Jewish Cemetery*, 1892. Oil on canvas, 200 × 297 cm.

Musée d'art et d'histoire du Judaïsme, Paris.
Acquired through a gift from Claude Kelman.

on this theme, there is no trace of the warmth and exuberance that it evoked. The candlesticks on the table are the only indication that it is the Sabbath; a plate holding some nuts and fruit is also on the table. Those present, probably representing three generations of a family, are all self-engrossed in pensive moods. They seem to be deep in thought, either due to what is being read to them by the young man in the center of the canvas, or by the outside world—intimated by the images of the large factories seen through the window—impinging on them. Standing next to the window, looking melancholy, the young woman, maybe one of Hirszenberg's sisters, forms a link between the view from the window and the internal space. She conveys a foreboding presence. Even the young child leaning on his grandfather lends little cheer to the scene. Family photographs on the otherwise bare

Figure 4.   Samuel Hirszenberg, *The Sabbath Rest*, 1894. Oil on canvas, 151 × 208 cm.

Ben Uri Gallery, The London Jewish Museum of Art.
Purchased with the assistance of Mosheh Oved, 1923.

walls add a further heaviness to the atmosphere, as does the elderly woman in bed, to whom none of the figures turn their gaze. Hirszenberg's family scene leaves little room for optimism or faith in these people's ability to face modern adversities. *The Sabbath Rest* did, however, bring the artist some distinction: it was shown at the Secession exhibition in Munich in 1896 and was awarded first prize by The Society of the Friends of the Arts of Warsaw and Cracow in that year.

During the ensuing years, working in his studio in Łódź, Hirszenberg suffered continued health problems and produced no major works, but his trips to Italy and Munich produced a variety of landscapes. Though no written text attests to it, the artist was apparently engaged during these years in constant reflection on the fate of the Jews. His *The Last Jew* (1897, fig. 5), depicting an

Figure 5.   Samuel Hirszenberg, *The Last Jew*, 1897.
Oil on canvas, 160 × 130 cm.
Courtesy of Museum of Art, Ein Harod, Israel.

Orthodox Jew sitting alone at a table in front of a candle, draped in a *tallit* and deep in contemplation, would seem to be part of these musings.[30] Reminiscent of the sensitive portrayals by Isidor Kaufmann (1853–1921) of the Orthodox world, Hirszenberg's lone figure holds a book that fails to command his attention. He is also oblivious to the shadow, in the form of a figure, on the wall to his side. This work was not typical of Hirszenberg, as he was not involved in the nostalgic attempt to recapture the atmosphere of the traditional world, common among Jewish artists of the nineteenth century. It had no sequel in his known work.

Figure 6.   Samuel Hirszenberg, *The Wandering Jew*, 1899. Oil on canvas, 343 × 293 cm.

The Israel Museum, Jerusalem, B04.1484.

What was to follow was his classic *Wandering Jew* (1899, fig. 6), which seems to evince his preoccupation with various encounters with antisemitism and his perennial feeling of Jewish vulnerability.[31] As few works by Hirszenberg carry dates from 1893 to 1899, and no substantial biographical information is presently available, the internal background to this haunting painting remains unclear. Though various sources acknowledge that the *Wandering Jew* was a four-year project, one cannot assume that other than *The Last Jew* he produced no other works of note. Hirszenberg's *Wandering Jew* starkly brought together the tradition of Polish realism in art and a Jewish portrayal of an endless struggle with Christianity.

Seen in the center of two long aisles of crosses more than twice his height is a Jew wearing a loincloth. Gazing dazedly *en face*, he is trying to emerge from the valley of death—to escape the fate of other Jews, whose dead bodies are strewn on the ground, naked. The *Wandering Jew*, a Christ-like figure, has avoided the fate of Jesus on the cross, but the fate of his people has been perilous. He raises one hand while the other covers his forehead, avoiding the sharp light that shines on him. His penetrating gaze, with the look of a madman, reveals to the onlooker what moments of terror and destruction he has seen, how he has wandered through the wreckage of Jewish history and miraculously escaped, but only physically. He leaves the dark, eerie field as a solitary figure, with no possessions and without a clear sense of the road that lies ahead.[32]

The art historian Avraham Ronen has suggested that Hirszenberg, who visited Munich on several occasions, most probably visited the Neue Pinakothek where Wilhelm von Kaulbach's *The Destruction of Jerusalem by the Emperor Titus* (1841–46, fig. 7) was dramatically exhibited. Kaulbach's presentation of the burning of Jerusalem and the expulsion of the Jew from the city by demons, as seen in the bottom left side of the huge painting, must have shaken Hirszenberg and "directly inspired" his work. Ronen has argued that Hirszenberg rejected Kaulbach's interpretation by turning the "legendary offender of Christ ... into a victim and a Martyr of Christian Persecution."[33] This may indeed have been one of the important iconographic sources for Hirszenberg, though the artist was also probably aware of Gustave Doré's well-known series (1856) when he turned his hand to the image of the Wandering Jew.[34] Interestingly, in describing the *Wandering Jew,* Dinah Hirszenberg, the artist's wife, presented the legendary figure in terms that recall Doré's work more closely than Kaulbach's. She vividly depicts the figure as one who can be seen walking through time, civilizations, and religions oblivious to what surrounds him, driven by his inner goal to survive and by the desire to reach the Promised Land eventually.[35]

Whatever may have been its iconographic inspiration, the painting powerfully confronts previous Christian interpretations of the legend of the Wandering Jew and places the onus for Jewish wandering, suffering, and sacrifice on Christianity. In attributing the cause for Jewish victimization to a clear source, Hirszenberg, unlike Gottlieb, showed no ambivalence about the meaning of the figure of Ahasuerus. In this sense, Hirszenberg asserted a more traditional interpretation of the lachrymose approach to Jewish history, one that found definite resonance among Jews in Eastern Europe, as exemplified by Leon Pinsker's classic work *Autoemanzipation* (1882).

Exhibited first in Cracow and then in Warsaw, the painting was sent to the international exhibition in Paris in 1900, where it was awarded a bronze medal. Hirszenberg's painting became a Zionist icon in the first generation of the movement,[36] thus fulfilling the same cultural-political function, *mutatis mutandis*, which Ludwig I of Bavaria apparently had in mind for *The Destruction of Jerusalem* at the Neue Pinakothek. Martin Buber, who strove to integrate the visual arts into the Zionist movement, singled out Hirszenberg's "moving Ahasuerus" among his other "superb realistic moods of modern Jewish life" in his survey of Jewish artists at

Figure 7. Wilhelm von Kaulbach (1804–1874), *The Destruction of Jerusalem by the Emperor Titus*, 1841–46. Oil on canvas, 585 × 705 cm.
Neue Pinakhotek, Munich, WAF 403.

the Fifth Zionist Congress in 1901.[37] He also planned to include Hirszenberg in a second volume of his essays on Jewish artists, but this never materialized. Boris Schatz, founder of the Bezalel Art Institute in Jerusalem (1906), conceived as a museum with an accompanying school for arts and crafts, accorded Hirszenberg's painting similar pride of place. Driven by a nationalist agenda and in search of Jewish artists who "would prove to the world that there is such a thing as Jewish art," who would provide "an example for [other] Jewish artists, and prompt them to create in the Jewish spirit,"[38] Schatz hung the *Wandering Jew* in a central location in Bezalel for almost a generation. Stasov would have been pleased with this effort to place art with Jewish content on center stage. Schatz, indeed, granted the painting a unique place in the interpretation of the Jewish past, as it coincided with his own efforts to attribute a significant role in the Jewish national renaissance to an awareness of the tragedies of Jewish history. Hirszenberg's social realism fit Schatz's vision and may have contributed to the latter's decision to invite the artist to join the Bezalel school in 1907.

The *Wandering Jew*, in all of its forthright nature, did not end Hirszenberg's exploration of the Jewish dilemma. In the following years, while continuing to suffer from a variety of ailments, including neurasthenia, Hirszenberg tried in vain to find comfort in Italy and Munich, painted a series of landscapes, and worked on a commission for the Poznański *palais* in Łódź that was completed in 1903. These allegorical works that gave pride of place to the wealth and power of the patron Izrael Kalman Poznański did not constitute a break in Hirszenberg's concerns, however.[39] During these same years the lonely and downtrodden Jewish figures he encountered continued to attract his attention. The elderly traditional Jew leaning on his cane and with his back to the wall, his head facing the ground, seemed to encapsulate the various titles attributed to this painting: e. g. *The Needy Jew, The Jewish Beggar*. This painting also resonated within Jewish circles that empathized with this figure but rejected its meaning for their lives.[40]

In this penetrating search to reach the essence of the Jewish spirit, Hirszenberg, like Jewish artists before and after him, and in the spirit of the reevaluation of Christ among Jewish scholars and writers, turned his imagination to the image of Jesus. He, too, struggled with Christ's meaning for Jews and Judaism, and he, too, took to reading Graetz's *History of the Jews* during this period of his life.[41]

At least two of his Christ-images are known, and both concentrate on his head, seen in profile. In one image, Christ appears

Figure 8. Samuel Hirszenberg, *Christ*, ca. 1904. Pastel on carton,
47 × 33 cm.

Courtesy of the Museum of Art, Ein Harod.

as an Orthodox Jew, with beard and skullcap, and in another
work in pastel (1904, fig. 8), he appears with a small goatee and
long coiffed hair, without a skull cap.[42] In both images the facial
expression is intense. In the former he appears sad and downcast;
in the latter, though not shorn of sadness, Christ appears with a
more visionary gaze. What significance can be attributed to these
two almost completely opposing images? Hirszenberg was married to a Catholic convert to Judaism, who writes harshly in her
memoir of Hirszenberg of Christianity's treatment of Jews over
time. Her critical tone seems to reflect both her voice and that of
her late husband. Clearly, she did not inhibit him from negatively
portraying Christianity in the *Wandering Jew*; in fact, in her
description of the painting, she poetically gave voice to its historical implications. If the dating of these depictions of Christ is cor-

rect, ca. 1902–4, their relationship to the *Wandering Jew* and to his dramatic depiction of Jewish exile (*Exile*, 1904) is significant, as he is contemplating fundamental issues of the Jewish fate, past and present. Hirszenberg appears to be trying to comprehend how the visionary leader, once an Orthodox Jew, could have left behind such a trail of sadness for his former brothers. Unlike Gottlieb, who constructed his Jesus as a bridge between Judaism and Christianity, Hirszenberg offered a more questioning approach to Christ and his legacy.

During the period in which he was apparently working on the Christ images, Hirszenberg threw himself passionately into one of his most celebrated works, *Exile*, commonly entitled *Golus* (1904, fig. 9). Created in Łódź in 1904, the painting depicted Jews of all ages and social positions, men, women, and children—a cross section of East European Jewry at the dawn of the twentieth century—making their way through the freezing snow to an undetermined destination. They represent individual worlds and contrasting ideologies, but their fate as Jews has made them a collective mass. Leading the trek is an elderly Jew with a long white beard, bent over, his hands folded into his chest in an effort to stay warm. Nearby another elderly man leans on his walking stick, arousing associations with the *Wandering Jew*. He is amidst a throng of individuals, most of whom seem to be engaged in deep thought, as if they were carrying all of history with them along with their personal burdens. Time did not allow them to take any but the most essential and sacred belongings. An elderly man carries a sack with documents and a prayer shawl, another a *sefer torah* wrapped in a *tallit*, and a young girl holds a tea kettle. The huge canvas (1.5 × 2.5 m), whose present whereabouts is unknown, is one of the few works Hirszenberg produced that enables us to see how it was created. *Ost und West*, the German-Jewish journal that accorded Hirszenberg's works constant attention in its first years of publication, gave pride of place to this dramatic depiction of Jewish suffering, elaborately illustrating the journal in 1904 with

Figure 9. Samuel Hirszenberg, *Exile*, 1904. Oil on canvas.
Whereabouts unknown.

details of the painting (even prior to its completion) and Hirszenberg's preliminary sketches in chalk and charcoal. The sketches show how the artist worked intently on the facial expressions of the wanderers, their downcast eyes, particular head coverings, posture, and their position amidst the group.

Exile may have been related to one or another iconographical source, such as Honoré Daumier's *The Fugitives*, or *The Weary* (1897) by the Polish artist of Jewish origin Jules Adler, or the contemporary works of the Russian Wanderers (e.g. Valentin Serov, Ilya Répin, and Isaac Levitan). Yet the historical context determined its contours. Jews were on the move. Following the infamous Kishinev pogrom on April 6, 1903, a very extensive wave of emigration from Eastern Europe ensued. Living in a city with a large Jewish population, and sensitive to the Jewish plight, Hirszenberg could not have been oblivious to the outpouring of emotions that agitated his fellow Jews.

Was *Exile* a flashback to an expulsion of Jews he had apparently witnessed in his youth in Cracow, a memory retrieved by the news from Kishinev? Or was it simply a response to the larger, unfolding historical crisis of East European Jewry? As social realism was at the heart of the artist's language, it would seem that the general malaise occasioned by recent events led to his *cri de cœur*. This interpretation would accord with his wife's memoir, which does not relate to any specific event as the catalyst but portrays vividly the ambience of the painting and emphasizes its intention to capture the essence of the Jews' fate through history. Dinah Hirszenberg noted: the Jews in the painting "entertain no hatred toward those who so condemned them, without appeal, to their wandering—and they do not blaspheme this God, strong and jealous, who appears to have abandoned them, after having made them, by the voice of the prophets, many unfulfilled promises. ... It is the complement to the Wandering Jew."[43]

Exile was completed in 1904 and exhibited at the Salon des sociétés des artistes français in Paris in 1905. Hirszenberg may have been prompted to seek major public exposure for this work, with all its harsh implications vis-à-vis the Gentile world, to better highlight the plight of the Jews. But it was within Jewish, and especially Zionist, circles that the painting was granted its most iconic reception. Exhibited in several venues in Poland, it was later shown at two pioneering exhibitions of Jewish art and artists (at the Whitechapel art gallery in London, 1906, and at the Galerie für alte und neue Kunst, Berlin, 1907). Berthold Feiwel (1875–1937), the Moravian Zionist and editor of the *Jüdischer Almanach*, hailed *Exile*'s social message, regarding it as the foremost painting of the exhibition, for it alone succeeded in synthesizing the Jewish experience of the age. It was recognized by Jewish commentators as "the truth"—the fulfillment of the inner emotions, state of being, and profound tragedy of the Jews. Along with studies and details of the painting, *Ost und West* published a long and spirited description, celebrating Hirszenberg's ability to plumb the depths of suffering amongst Russian Jewry, the age-old experience of the Diaspora, and the trauma of constant wandering.[44]

Exile became a household item in both the West and East. Early in the century, in a period when publishers marketed cards illustrated with images from Jewish artists, *Exile* was featured on postcards with Yiddish, German, and Russian captions. Various contemporary accounts, and several written long after Hirszenberg's death, attested to the authors' having seen reproductions of the work in many Jewish homes, even in Tel Aviv in the early 1950s. One commentator, writing in 1929, considered this widespread phenomenon as a form of sacred memorial, analogous to Jewish symbols of mourning for the destruction of the Temple.[45]

Yet the power of the painting also evoked negative responses. Some German Jews who saw the painting in 1906 were taken aback by its overtly Jewish nature. For his part, Yosef Ḥayyim Brenner, the modern Hebrew writer, expressed in an early story (*Actions*, 1905), his unswerving revulsion for the Diaspora as epitomized in *Exile*. Brenner concluded the story by describing how its protagonist, a manual laborer from Palestine, tore to shreds a reproduction of the painting that hung in his room as an act of rage against the Jewish life he encountered in London. The worker cried out: "We are gypsies, gypsies, and not sons of the Galut, damned gypsies."[46]

Exile came on the eve of even more cataclysmic events for East European Jewry. The Russian Revolution of 1905 was to have a dramatic impact on Jewish life, politics, and culture. At the outset, Jewish workers were in high spirits, and in Łódź, a city with a large percentage of Jews, they mobilized quickly and joined hands with non-Jewish workers. On June 5, 1905 a joint demonstration was broken up by police gunfire, resulting in the killing of several workers. The following day some fifty thousand workers took to the streets to take part in the funeral procession. Severe fighting in various areas of the city, including the Jewish quarter, ensued. Of hundreds of people killed in the fighting, over three hundred were Jews.[47] The Hirszenbergs were apparently still in Łódź during those revolutionary days. Dinah Hirszenberg recalled the traumatic atmosphere of those days, the fear that the civil turmoil would turn against the Jews, notwithstanding initially encouraging signs of social solidarity in the streets. The events may have been a factor in the Hirszenbergs' decision to leave Łódź for Habsburg Cracow, a city that was not affected by the Russian insurrectionary movement, and where the artist had maintained a circle of close friends that included Jewish artists, critics, doctors, and others since his days there as an art student. Cracow, moreover, was a burgeoning center of the arts and literature during this period, boasting the presence of celebrated Polish artists (e.g. Julian Fałat, Leon Wyczółkowski, and Stanislas Wyspiański).

The Hirszenbergs took leave of Łódź with the artist's elderly and ailing parents. Cracow offered the artist companionship, conviviality, and friendly concern, but his own deteriorating health impeded his strength and ability to work. Only a few paintings date from the years in Cracow, 1905–7, and some of these have been lost, their whereabouts unknown. Portraits of his wife, his friend and doctor, Dr. Anszela Schudmaka, and several landscapes and floral scenes are extant in various collections, but Hirszenberg also continued to be attentive to the opposing ideological trends among East European Jews. Two works address these themes in the stark realism that had become the artist's trademark: *The Black Banner* and *Spinoza*.

The Black Banner (fig. 10) conveys a sense of upheaval. The viewer again confronts Jews on the move, crowded together. But unlike *Exile*, this is a homogeneous group of Orthodox Jewish men, dressed in dark colors in a funeral procession. The trying moment is accentuated by a foreboding sky and the startled and unsettled looks on many of the mourners' faces. They follow a

Figure 10. Samuel Hirszenberg, *The Black Banner*, 1905. Oil on canvas, 30 × 81 cm.

Courtesy of The Jewish Museum, New York.
Gift of the Estate of Rose Mintz, JM 63-67.

coffin draped in black and many outstretched, desperate hands try to touch it or the open book attached to the coffin.

The focus on troubled Orthodox male Jews alone has led to a variety of interpretations of the painting. Various Polish writers attribute its inspiration to the funeral of the Zaddik of Halberstamm from Zanz, without actually identifying which particular Zaddik of this extensive dynasty was the supposed subject, and on what date the event depicted might have taken place. In point of fact, no Zaddik of the dynasty passed away in 1905, and it was completely unlike Hirszenberg to depict an actual historical event directly.[48]

Others have alluded to a possible counter-reference to the Russian-based Black Hundreds, who were involved in antisemitic activity in 1905, and to the group's newspaper *The Russian Banner* (*Russkoe Znamia*), which began to appear in late November 1905(!). Behind this hypothesis lay the notion that Hirszenberg referred cynically to the Black Hundred banners, "and suggests that the coffin bears the body of one of their victims."[49] Aside from the problematic chronological assumption, the contention seems hard to accept, as one cannot then explain the atmosphere of the mourners, nor their desire to tangibly reach the coffin and the book.

On the other hand, Dinah Hirszenberg's comments on the painting dissociated it from any particular historical event, treating the "black banner" metaphorically as a signifier of "powerlessness, nostalgia, sadness, and mourning."[50] It appears to me that her reading was closer to the essence of the work than those of later commentators.

To my mind, the painting is neither a direct reference to the revolutionary events of 1905, nor again to a particular funeral, but relates rather to Hirszenberg's general brooding on the dark future of Judaism, as represented by the Orthodox Jews engaged in a funeral procession. Their world is in jeopardy; the Holy Book, lying on the coffin, whose guidance they followed, did not provide them with an adequate key to the dilemmas of the age. Light shines on only one young boy in the middle of the painting; unlike the others he appears undisturbed and engrossed in his own thoughts. Was this Hirszenberg's vision of the future? Certainly it did not find expression in the lives of the aged and frightened.

From this perspective and within a wider understanding of Hirszenberg's oeuvre, *The Black Banner* points toward the last major work the artist was to create in Cracow, *Spinoza* (fig. 11). He began working on *Spinoza* in 1906, had the Polish-Jewish artist Leopold Gottlieb model for him as Spinoza, and intended to travel to Holland to prepare sketches for the painting; but it appears that his bad health, and/or the death of both of his parents during that year, prevented him from undertaking the journey.[51]

What brought Hirszenberg back to Spinoza after two decades? The Polish-Jewish artist offers his undeniable identification with the philosopher, who walks calmly and confidently, absorbed deeply in his reading, oblivious to the commotion he has created around him. A group of Jews huddle together and gesticulate their animosity toward Spinoza, displaying their fear of being contaminated by the ideals he represents—freedom of thought,

Figure 11.   Samuel Hirszenberg, *Spinoza*, 1907. Oil on canvas.
Art Gallery, Kursk.

individualism, and enlightenment. The features of the Orthodox faithful are stereotypical and unattractive, arousing disdain, similar to some of the figures in *The Black Banner*. One of them is seen stooping down to lift a stone to throw at Spinoza. Hirszenberg's composition places Spinoza in the foreground of the painting, intimating that his presence has caused the Orthodox world to respond to him and engage him. Indeed, one younger traditional Jew, apparently of Spinoza's age, is set apart from the others by a small space that compositionally is partially covered by Spinoza's figure. Spinoza has seemingly created a certain rift between the Orthodox elders and this younger man. Not identifying with those who revile the philosopher, the lone figure shows some trepidation but no clear defiance of Spinoza. He is a figure in limbo, ambivalent, not certain with whom to associate. Hirszenberg has placed in high relief the choices Jewry faced at this time.

In returning to Spinoza after almost twenty years, Hirszenberg brought to the forefront what was intimated in *Uriel da Costa and*

Spinoza (fig. 2). Hirszenberg, who lived a secular life and spoke (and wrote) Polish, Yiddish, and French, threw in his lot with Spinoza, intimating that wherever such noble figures appear they wreak havoc, frightening some and unnerving others. But this is the path that must be taken—Spinoza is seen as a possible savior who would open new vistas, raise the flag of anticlericalism, and champion liberated thought. In contrast, the Orthodox Jews, as in many of Hirszenberg's paintings, seem incapable of rising out of their inner world to shape a new future and confront Jewry's modern predicament.

That modern world would appear to include, and possibly prioritize, Zionism, even though the artist was not known among his friends as an ideologue or as a political activist.[52] Hirszenberg's choice of Spinoza paralleled the views of Martin Buber, who regarded the philosopher as personifying the ultimate break with the passive world of the "talmudic Jew." For Buber, Spinoza was able "to step from the ghetto into the cosmos actively and peacefully and to take hold of the Infinite as no one else before him. ... The new Jew, the Jew of the Emancipation era strolls in the paths of Spinoza, without genius but with a daemonic daring. He was no longer passive, but acting freely; he no longer acted according to the Law, but according to his own thought and feeling."[53]

Indeed, Buber, and other contemporary Zionists, attributed to Spinoza support for the restoration of the Jewish state and thus claimed him as one of their precursors, along with such messianic figures as Shabbatai Zvi. Activism, belief in a new ideal, and freedom from the constraints of the past and traditional ways were characteristics that both Hirszenberg and Buber (and Theodor Herzl, for that matter) saw in the visionary Spinoza. They thus co-opted him to a prestigious place in the Zionist pantheon. Zionism was not the only Jewish movement to claim Spinoza for its cause, but none of the others, covering a wide gamut of twentieth-century Jewish secularist movements, gave him the visual presence that Hirszenberg accorded him.

In October 1907, the Hirszenbergs left Cracow for Jerusalem, where Samuel was to assume a teaching position at the Bezalel Art School. During the eleven months that he resided in the city his artistic language and concerns changed remarkably, leaving behind the cultural and ideological struggles that had shaped his art for over two decades. His imagination wandered in new directions and his art followed suit—images of the Temple Mount from many different vantage points, showing his fascination with the Mediterranean light; landscape and floral scenes; portraits of Jews and Arabs—these replaced the embattled life Hirszenberg had depicted earlier.[54] Dinah Hirszenberg's memoir records the transformation the artist sensed during these months, how he was swept up in his new surroundings, his treks up the Mount of Olives, his immersion in the smells, sounds, and sunlight of Jerusalem.

Hirszenberg's health, however, caught up with him and on September 14, 1908, he passed away after several weeks of suffering from high fever and dysentery. Hirszenberg's personal life had taken an extraordinary turn during these last months, but his legacy lies in his piercing attempts to interpret the predicament of the Jews at the turn of the century.

Notes

1. *Danzig, Between East and West: Aspects of Modern Jewish History*, ed. Isadore Twersky (Cambridge: Harvard University Press, 1985).
2. *The Jewish Year Illustrated by Pictures of Old-Time Jewish Family Life Customs and Observances from the Paintings by Moritz Oppenheim* (Philadelphia: Levy-type, 1895), n.p.
3. *Moritz Daniel Oppenheim: Die Entdeckung des jüdischen Selbstbewusstseins in der Kunst/Jewish Identity in 19th Century Art*, ed. Georg Heuberger and Anton Merk (Cologne: Wienand, 1999).
4. Ismar Schorsch, *From Text to Context: The Turn to History in Modern Judaism* (Hanover, N.H.: Brandeis University Press, 1994), 378–79.

5. Joshua D. Zimmerman, *Poles, Jews, and the Politics of Nationality: The Bund and the Polish Socialist Party in Late Tsarist Russia, 1892–1914* (Madison: University of Wisconsin Press, 2004), 10–18; Paweł Samuś, "The Jewish Community in the Political Life of Łódź in the Years 1865–1914," in *Studies from Polin: From Shtetl to Socialism,* ed. Antony Polonsky (London: Littman Library, 1993), 103–19.

6. Daniel Blatman, הבונד: מיטוס המהפכה ועבודת היומיום (The Bund: The myth of revolution and daily activity), in קיום ושבר: יהודת פולין לדורותיהם (The broken chain: Polish Jewry through the ages), vol. 2: חברה, תרבות, לאומיות (Society, culture, nationalism), ed. Israel Bartal and Israel Gutman (Jerusalem: Zalman Shazar Center, 2001), 494–96.

7. A. Z. Aescoli, קהלת לודז: תולדות עיר ואם בישראל (The Łódź community) (Jerusalem: Sifriat Kav Lekav, 1948); the Poznańskis built an impressive palace at the turn of the century that since 1975 has housed Łódź's city museum. See http://www.poznanskipalace.muzeum-lodz.pl.

8. Ezra Mendelsohn, *Painting a People: Maurycy Gottlieb and Jewish Art* (Hanover, N.H.: Brandeis University Press, 2002), 26–27; anon., "Samuel Hirszenberg," *Ost und West,* 8 (1908): 623–24; Józef Sandel, יידישע מאָטיוון אין דער פּױלישער קונסט (Jewish motifs in Polish art) (Warsaw: Farlag Yidish Bukh,1954), 151–52.

9. Probably the earliest source for this biographical information is his wife's brief memoir in French (44 handwritten pages) from May 1, 1909 (DH, *Memoir*) (Warsaw: Muzeum Żydowski Instytut Historyczny). My thanks to Ms. Renata Piątkowska of the Museum for providing me a photocopy of this document, and to Ms. Dorota Sniezek of the Musée d'art et d'histoire du Judaïsme, Paris, for her assistance. Dinah Hirszenberg was a French Catholic poet who married Hirszenberg in 1896 in Munich and converted to Judaism. Hirszenberg made several portraits of his wife. See e.g. *Ost und West* 4 (1904): 686, 8 (1908): 77–78.

10. A small oil on canvas, *Houses by the River* (1884), was sold at the Gordon Gallery in 1999. My thanks to Esta Kilstein of Sotheby's Tel Aviv for supplying me with this information.

11. *Żydzi w Polsce: Obraz i słowo* (Jews in Poland: Paintings and text), ed. Marek Rostworowski (Warsaw: Interpress, 1993); Marek Rostworowski et al., *Żydzi-Polscy Czerwiec-Sierpień 1989* (Polish Jews: June to August 1989) (Cracow: Muzeum Narodowe w Krakowie, 1989); Halina Nelken, *Images of a Lost World: Jewish Motifs in Polish Painting 1770–1945* (Oxford: Institute for Polish-Jewish Studies, 1991).

12. See a charcoal and pencil study for the *Yeshiva* in Sotheby's *Judaica* cata-

logue (Tel Aviv, 1991), lot 131; *Yeshiva* (137 × 212 cm) is presently in the National Museum of Cracow.

13. See Gabriel P. Weisberg, *Redefining Genre: French and American Painting, 1850–1900* (Seattle: University of Washington Press; Washington, D.C.: The Trust for Museum Exhibitions, 1995); "Jewish Naturalist Painters: Understanding and Competing in the Mainstream," in *The Emergence of Jewish Artists in Nineteenth-Century Europe*, ed. Susan Tumarkin Goodman (New York: Merrell, 2001), 145–46.

14. For a brief summary of Da Costa's entanglement with the rabbinic authorities in Amsterdam, see Miriam Bodian, *Hebrews of the Portuguese Nation: Conversos and Community in Early Modern Amsterdam* (Bloomington: Indiana University Press, 1997), 119–21.

15. Ernst Altkirch, *Spinoza im Porträt* (Jena: Eugen Diederichs, 1913).

16. On Gutzkow's attitude toward Jews and Judaism, see Paul Lawrence Rose, *Revolutionary Antisemitism in Germany from Kant to Wagner* (Princeton, N.J.: Princeton University Press, 1990), 185–210.

17. On Yohanan Twersky's Hebrew rendition of the book see Ruth Shenfeld, אמשטרדם של אוריאל אקוסטה (Amsterdam of Uriel Acosta), in מחקרים על תולדות יהדות הולנד (Studies on the history of Dutch Jewry), vol. 4, ed. Jozeph Michman (Jerusalem: Institute for Research on Dutch Jewry, 1984), 285–93. The play version, *Uriel Acosta* (1846), mitigated the anti-Jewish animus of the novella. *Uriel Acosta* was performed on Hebrew and Yiddish stages on several occasions, including a special performance by the Łódź Hebrew Theater Society for the participants in the Zionist Conference in Vienna in 1913.

18. I follow here Jonathan S. Skolnik's illuminating interpretation of Auerbach's work ("Writing Jewish History between Gutzkow and Goethe: Auerbach's *Spinoza* and the Birth of Modern Jewish Historical Fiction," *Prooftexts* 19 (1999): 101–25; "Kaddish for Spinoza: Memory and Modernity in Celan and Heine," *New German Critique* 77 (1999): 169–86; see also Rose, *Revolutionary Antisemitism*, 227).

19. According to DH, *Memoir*, 11, the painting was sold for a very small sum ("for a piece of bread") to a private individual in the late 1880s or early 1890s.

20. Sections of the above discussion are based on my article "Challenging Rabbinic Hegemony. Visual Representation of Modern Heroes," in *Jewish Religious Leadership: Image and Reality*, ed. Jack Wertheimer (New York: JTS, 2004), 773–813.

21. S. Gottlieb, "Samuel Hirszenberg. Wspomnienie" (S. Hirszenberg, a

memoir), *Wschód* 39 (1908): 2–3. My thanks to Ms. Dorota Sniezek of the Musée d'art et d'histoire du Judaïsme, Paris, for her translation of this article and others to be referred to in the following pages, and for fruitful discussions of Hirszenberg's work.

22. No comprehensive list of Hirszenberg's works is available. I have traced more than a hundred works in various media, though the whereabouts of many of them are unknown. See Jerzy Malinowski, *Malarstwo i rzeźba Żydów Polskich w XIX i XX wieku* (Polish Jewish painting and sculpture in the 19th and 20th centuries) (Warsaw: Wydawnictwo Naukowe PWN, 2000), 77–85.

23. Weisberg, "Jewish Naturalist Painters," 144.

24. The work is commonly cited during his lifetime and shortly thereafter but we have yet to uncover its whereabouts or see a reproduction.

25. My thanks to Ofra Bruno-Hirszenberg of Jerusalem, the artist's niece, for supplying me with biographical material on the family.

26. It entered their collection in 1992. See Laurence Sigal-Klagsbald, "Samuel Hirszenberg, du realisme social dans l'art juif," *Revue des études juives* 153 (1994): 415–27.

27. Hirszenberg created another version of the painting (ca. 1900), presently in Ein Harod Museum, that showed strong impressionist influences. The original version was published in *Ost und West* 2 (1902): 685–86; *Jüdischer Almanach 5663* (Berlin: Jüdischer Verlag, 1902), 233.

28. DH, *Memoir*, constantly stressed this element of Hirszenberg's outlook. One need not rely fully on her reflections to determine Hirszenberg's inner turmoil, but her dramatic description is worthy of consideration: "The artist heard in the silence of his studio this horrible misery not to have a place to rest one's head, this cry of the exiled, this sobbing impotence" (16).

29. The painting, like many others, carries different names. Malinowski, *Malarstwo*, 77, entitled it *News from Argentina*; in Ruth. [unidentified pseudonym], "Samuel Hirszenberg. Eine Biographische Skizze," *Ost und West* 2 (1902): 683, it is entitled *Sabbatnachmittag*, so too when reproduced ibid., 697–98; and again in Theodor Zlocisti, "Sabbatnachmittag," ibid. 4 (1904): 664–65. Ruth., "Samuel Hirszenberg," mentions that the brochure being read was entitled "A Letter from Argentina." However, I was unable to decipher any text on the brochure when I examined the painting in London in February 2005. My thanks to the staff of the Ben Uri Art Society, London, for enabling me to view the painting. It has been in their possession since 1923, when it was purchased with the assistance of Moshe

Oved. Apparently a small oil study for this painting exists in the Museum of Fine Arts in Łódź that I have yet to see.

30. Ein Harod Museum, Israel. Unfortunately, I am not certain whether this was the title that Hirszenberg gave the painting or whether it was so entitled by a donor of the painting or a museum curator.

31. DH, *Memoir*, stresses Hirszenberg's constant concern with the Jewish plight and his confrontations with antisemitism. Again, it may well be that her memoir exaggerates these feelings, but the text shows that she was not simply imagining them. On the basis of his paintings and her testimony one cannot dismiss his inner struggle with the non-Jewish world completely.

32. Based on Richard I. Cohen, *Jewish Icons. Art and Society in Modern Europe* (University of California Press: Berkeley, Los Angeles, and London, 1998), p. 226.

33. Avraham Ronen, "Kaulbach's Wandering Jew: An Anti-Jewish Allegory and Two Jewish Responses," *Assaph* 3 (1998): 253. Kaulbach's painting is on permanent exhibit at the Neue Pinakothek.

34. See *Le Juif errant: Un témoin de temps*, ed. Laurence Sigal-Klagsbald and Richard I. Cohen (Paris: Adam Biro and Musée d'art et d'histoire du Judaïsme, 2001), 202–3.

35. DH, *Memoir*, 22–24.

36. Aside from the wide exposure the painting received among Jewish circles in Warsaw, Cracow, Lemberg, Łódź, and elsewhere, it was printed in *Ost und West* 2 (1902): 661–62, and later appeared as a poster and postcard in the series published by Kunstverlag Phönix, Berlin. See Marek Arnstein, "Obrazy Hirszenberga. (Salon Krywulta)" (The paintings by Hirszenberg), *Izraelita* 4 (January 11, 1902): 40–41; Emil Breiter, "S. Hirschenberg (artysta malarz). Proba charakterystyki: Z cyklu malarze-Żydzi w Krakowie" (S. Hirszenberg (artist). Test of character: On the circle of Jewish artists in Cracow), *Izraelita* (May 4, 1906): 199–201.

37. Martin Buber, "Referat über jüdische Kunst," *Die Welt* 6, no. 4 (January 24, 1902): 6. Translation from *The First Buber: Youthful Zionist Writings of Martin Buber*, ed. and trans. Gilya G. Schmidt (Syracuse, N.Y.: Syracuse University Press, 1999), 58.

38. Boris Schatz to Harry Friedenwald, September 15, 1930, Central Zionist Archives, Jerusalem, L42/6.

39. Some of the images appeared in *Ost und West* 4 (1904): 674–80; see also http://www.poznanskipalace.muzeum-lodz.pl.

40. Ruth., "Samuel Hirszenberg," 679, 677–78; repr. in *Jüdische Almanach*

5663, 237.

41. See the enlightening discussion in Mendelsohn, *Painting a People*, 129–38. How Hirszenberg's reading of Graetz influenced him is difficult to discern, but his painting of Isaac Abarbanel is apparently one such example— unfortunately lost, and no visual record of it is extant. Graetz's loaded portrayal of Jewish–Christian relations may have been a source for Hirszenberg. See "Hirszenberg – jakim byl" (Hirszenberg as he was), *Chwila* 2531 (April 4, 1926): 7.

42. The image of Christ as a Jew appeared in *Ost und West* 4 (1904): 663; the whereabouts of this work is unknown. His *Head of Jesus* in the Ein Harod Museum has been dated 1904.

43. DH, *Memoir*, 28.

44. See Cohen, *Jewish Icons*, 230–31; E. K. Borck, "Sie Wandern … (Unter dem Eindruck des neusten Gemäldes von Hirszenberg 'Golus'," *Ost und West* 4 *(*1904): 553–60.

45. For the response in Eastern Europe, see David G. Roskies, *Against the Apocalypse: Responses to Catastrophe in Modern Jewish Culture* (Cambridge: Harvard University Press, 1984), 279 and literature there. S. Ernst, הצייר הלאומי ש. הירשנברג (למלאות עשרים שנה למותו) (The Jewish national artist S. Hirszenberg, marking twenty years since his death) *Galim* 15 (1929): 2. For a similar response, see Zvi Scharfstein, שמואל הירשנברג: ספור תולדותיו ויצירתו (Samuel Hirszenberg: The story of his life and his work) (New York: Shilo, 1929), 14–15; Gideon Ofrat, שבחי גלות (In praise of exile) (Jerusalem: Carta, 2000), 206–8. Ofrat placed the painting on the cover of his book and writes of its profound hold on him; also idem, על הארץ. האמנות הארצישראלית: פרקי־אבות (On the ground: Early Eretz-Israeli art) (Jerusalem: Omanut Israel, 1993), 1:213–26.

46. As quoted in Avner Holtzman, תמורות במעמדה של האמנות הפלסטית במחשבת הספרות העברית (תרכ״ב־תרפ״ג) (Changes in the status of the plastic arts in Hebrew literary thought (1862–1923)), *Tarbiz* 43 (1994): 578; מלאכת מחשבת: תחיית האומה. הספרות העברית לנוכח האמנות הפלסטית (Aesthetics and national revival: Hebrew literature against the visual arts) (Tel Aviv: Zmorah-Bitan, 1999), 71; see also Cohen, *Jewish Icons*, 233; Ofrat, *On the Ground*, 215–16.

47. Jonathan Frankel, *Prophecy and Politics: Socialism, Nationalism, and the Russian Jews, 1862–1917* (Cambridge: Cambridge University Press, 1981), 134–48.

48. E.g. Jozef Liebeskind, "Ze wspomnień o pobycie Samuela Hirszenberga w Krakowie" (A recollection relating to S. Hirszenberg's stay in Cracow),

Nowy Dziennik 129 (May 12, 1933): 9. My thanks to David Assaf of Tel-Aviv University for his assistance on this point.

49. The first to raise this interpretation was Norman Kleeblatt, in Norman Kleeblatt and Vivian B. Mann, *Treasures of the Jewish Museum* (New York: Universe, 1986), 166; cf. Hans Rogger, *Jewish Policies and Right-Wing Politics in Imperial Russia* (Berkeley and Los Angeles: University of California Press, 1986), 198–205.

50. DH, *Memoir*, 32.

51. Dr. Emil Breiter, who was one of Hirszenberg's close friends in Cracow, followed his work closely. See Breiter, "S. Hirschenberg," 200; see his fine description of the finished painting, "Młody Spinoza: S. Hirszenberga" (Young Spinoza), *Izraelita* (March 29, 1907), 149–50. For Gottlieb's role as model, see also Liebeskind, "Recollection," 9.

52. Dr. Seweryn Gottlieb lived in the same house with Hirszenberg in Cracow from 1905 to 1907. His testimony corroborates remarks by others. See S. Gottlieb, "Samuel Hirszenberg. Uwagi w związku z zapowiedzianą wystawą zbiorową" (S. Hirszenberg: Notes on a forthcoming exhibition), *Nowy Dziennik*, February 13, 1933, 8.

53. Quoted in Schmidt, *First Buber*, 179, from Buber's essay "Das jüdische Kultur-Problem und der Zionismus" (1905).

54. See Erich Karl Borck, "Aus dem Nachlass von Samuel Hirszenberg," *Ost und West* 12 (1912): 130–36; further images, 137–38; Renata Piątkowska, "Pożeganie z Golusem: Samuel Hirszenberg w Jerosozolimie" (Farewell to Exile: S. Hirszenberg in Jerusalem), in *Jerozolima w kulturze europejskiej* (Jerusalem in European culture), ed. Piotra Paszkiewicza and Tadeusza Zadroznego (Warsaw: Instytut Sztuki Polskiej Akademii Nauk, 1997), 529–37.

Ideologies
of Jewish Folklore

Reshumot – *The Russian Years*

MARK W. KIEL

"A time to gather"—this is the dictate of the hour.
— Chaim Nachman Bialik, 1913

A fter four years of continuously interrupted preparations, the first issue of *Reshumot* (Records), a journal of "Memoirs, Ethnography and the Folklore of the Jews," appeared in Odessa in 1918, during the brief period of Ukrainian independence (March 1917–August 1920). *Reshumot* had the distinction of being the first Hebrew journal of Jewish folklore and, as it turned out, the first successfully sustained journal of its kind to appear in a Jewish language.[1]

Edited by Alter Druyanov, Yehoshua Hone Ravnitsky, and most importantly Chaim Nahman Bialik, *Reshumot* represented a broad (though not necessarily very sophisticated) vision of Jewish folkloristics akin to Max Grunwald's *Mitteilungen zur jüdischen Volkskunde*. Ideologically Hebraist, *Reshumot* was not fanatic in defining its linguistic program. It solicited folklore texts in their original languages and willingly published Yiddish sources. The journal's impact on Zionist readers was considerable, especially in Odessa, where Ahad Ha'am and his circle had disparaged diaspora culture and particularly Yiddish folk culture. Bialik parted ways with Ahad Ha'am as he became increasingly conscious of the crucial role that folklore had played in the formation of his own national consciousness.

The folklore "crusade" of the war years owed much to the field study expedition led by S. Ansky that was launched by the Jewish Historical Ethnographic Society in 1912. But in the immediate postwar years, it was *Reshumot*, rather than the Russian-language journal of the Ethnographic Society, *Evreiskaia starina*, that could best claim the mantle of Ansky's legacy.[2]

Along with basic political amelioration in the wake of the Russian revolution, which included the abolition of Tsarist laws discriminating against Jews, the appearance of *Reshumot* represented new hope for Jewish self-expression in a liberated society. It signaled the resumption of major cultural projects that the war had cut short. Jews in Odessa had been aware of the impressive political and cultural achievements gained by Jews in Warsaw since the German occupation of that city in 1915. In the Ukraine the occupation was briefer than in Poland, but Jewish national expression flourished nonetheless.[3] Even the pogroms that broke out in the Ukraine and the resulting devastation and large-scale popular despair hardly impeded the progress of Jewish cultural activities. On the contrary, the tragic events heightened the significance of the new journal's call to rescue the remnants of Jewish folk culture. The fact that mass murder rather than modernity proved to be the real culprit in the demise of that culture lent an apocalyptic, almost religious zeal to the work of "collecting and preserving" (the slogan of European folkloristics) the last vestiges of traditional life. The secular cultural program, in fact, rendered these fragments into holy relics. The turbulent times and the traditional, sacred phrases used to describe the language of this mission all but erased the fine line between the religious and secular impulses behind these *Rettungsgedänke*.

At the outset, in 1914, the editors had successfully solicited public interest throughout the Pale, and beyond, in what they presented as a national obligation of the highest priority. By means of a well-circulated prospectus, the editors called on the people to "rescue" and "record" Jewish folklore "from out of the mouths of the elders and their offspring."[4] In cadences calculated to stir the hearts of readers intimate with the biblical idiom, the brochure offered slogans drawn from the modern folklore movement in Europe: "Go unto the camps of Israel and search them well; their treasures and archives, their ancient artifacts, written down or drawn, and whatever else may be suitable to the task of collecting Hebrew folklore."[5] The editors' appeal also evoked powerful echoes of the old Russian populist credo of "going to the people."

For those who watched with growing apprehension the accelerating pace of change in Jewish society, the prospectus took its place alongside earlier warnings by Simon Dubnow and S. Ansky, as well as Shaul M. Ginzburg and Pesach Marek (who collected and published a landmark anthology of Yiddish folksongs), that all trace of the vanishing world would be irretrievably lost to Jewish memory unless its preservation and conservation began at once.[6]

Bialik had announced his own detailed program of "ingathering" the literary treasures of Jewish culture, or *kinus*, in 1913. "Folk dialogues," he said, as well as "tales, animal fables, proverbs, anecdotes, witticisms, folksongs etc.: all the best and the finest of this genre should be culled from all fields of literature, from the post-aggadic period to this day, from all classes of people."[7] *Kinus* became as popular a slogan as the parallel Yiddish imperative, "*Zamlt!*" Bialik had already applied the word *kinus* to the material he collected for his *Sefer ha'agadah* (1908). Two years later, in 1910, he presented the outlines of a broad interpretation of culture, including folklore, with the intention of translating everything into Hebrew while preserving its authentic Jewishness. Keeping it Jewish, he recognized, was a task not easily accomplished and with which he wrestled for many years. In addition, he called for the creation of a variety of Jewish publications including a journal of folklore.[8]

As a folklore journal, *Reshumot*, as its editors intended, was more than just an academic publication. Just as Dubnov, in his famous appeals to galvanize would-be Jewish ethnographers and historians in 1891 and 1892, the editors of *Reshumot* aimed at a purpose that transcended dispassionate scholarship.[9] Bialik's commitment to folklore, which began in his youth at the Volozhin Yeshiva, crystallized when he met I. L. Peretz. In Warsaw, the other great city of the Jewish Renaissance, bustling with Jewish life, Bialik was persuaded by Peretz to focus his talents on behalf of the folk.[10] During the years he spent working on the *Sefer ha-agadah* he turned his attention away from his personal literary creations.[11] The romanticism of the national movement, and the very effort to revive Hebrew as a modern language, turned the objects of study and the nation's cultural heritage into a spiritual patrimony.

The *Reshumot* prospectus contained a guide for collectors of folklore, both oral and written, recalling the far more ambitious and professional questionnaire supplied by Ansky to his amateur collectors in 1912.[12] Unlike Dubnov or Ansky, who as diaspora nationalists focused their attention specifically on Eastern Europe, the Zionist *Reshumot* placed equal emphasis on European and Oriental Jewish communities (the *'edot hamizrah*).

Although the immediate response of readers was enthusiastic, the war delayed the journal's scheduled appearance. Major setbacks were caused, first, by a ban on all Yiddish and Hebrew publishing in Russia, followed by continuing shortages of paper and print, and finally by the dispersal of those involved in the journal, in the wake of the revolution. Nevertheless, in 1918, as soon as the opportunity presented itself, the editors managed, in rather short order, to bring out an impressive volume of close to five hundred pages. The second volume appeared abroad, in 1922, but was prepared in Russia during the preceding years.

Thanks to the distinguished committee of editors, their widespread and carefully cultivated contacts, and the reputation of their publishing house, "Moriah," *Reshumot* had little trouble in attracting a noted array of contributors from among the *maskilim*, scholars, journalists, and essayists who had been active in the

Hebrew and Yiddish press. Individual folklore collectors submitted a variety of shorter and longer entries. Some were well known to readers, such as the veteran folklorist Sh. Beilin, the rather isolated, Siberia-based Rabbiner (official rabbi). Beilin, a Yiddishist, often published in Grunwald's journal as well as in *Evreiskaia starina*, *Voskhod*, and other journals.[13] Others were relatively unknown to the Russian and Polish Jewish reading public. While there was a separate section devoted to memoirs, neither folklore nor ethnography appeared under their own rubrics. Whether by design or because of a dearth of material collected in the field, folklore and ethnography were dispersed mainly under the headings of "Language and the Book" and "Customs and Manners." Bialik was conspicuously absent from the array of contributors.

I. Volume One

Much of the first volume was devoted to the memoirs of the modern founding fathers of the Hebraic revival and the Zionist movement in Russia, such as the poet Y. L. Gordon, the literary critic A. Y. Paperna, and the Zionist chronicler S. L. Tsitron.[14] Samuel A. Poznanski, the noted *Wissenschaft* scholar, and rabbi of the liberal Tlomacka Street Synagogue in Warsaw, wrote about pre-Karaite messianism in Persia. Sh. A. Horodetsky wrote about Rabbi Elimelekh of Lizhensk and the Apter Rov, Avrom Yehoshua Heschel.[15] Simha Assaf, who was teaching in Haim Tchernovits's modern yeshiva in Odessa, contributed an article on the role of books and the reverence for them by the "people of the book" through the ages.[16] Bialik was well aware that he was including material on subjects that lay outside the journal's stated purposes, but in the absence of journals specializing in those subjects, he felt it was the responsibility of *Reshumot* to fill that gap.[17]

Other essays dealt with local lore and history, as well as aspects of rabbinic culture. While not specifically directed to the study of folklore, these articles (such as Tsitron's memoir of life in Bialik's alma mater, the Volozhin Yeshiva) were inevitably full of ethnographic data. Shimon Bernfeld wrote an important article about Ladino and the viability of Hebrew as a natural Jewish language of folklore. Noah Prylucki, Yehuda Leib Zlotnick, and A. Z. Idelsohn wrote the principal specifically folkloristic studies. In the highly charged partisan atmosphere of the period, each of these folklorists, along with Bernfeld, shared the pages of the liberal *Reshumot* despite their ideological differences.

SHIMON BERNFELD

Shimon Bernfeld, the Hebrew (and sometimes Yiddish) journalist who promoted the idea of a cultural history of Jewish folk life, wrote about the Hebrew elements in Ladino, or Judezmo, a language with which he had become familiar while serving as chief rabbi of the Sephardic community in Belgrade.[18] An ardent Hebraist, like Bialik, he regarded Yiddish and Ladino (Judezmo) as ephemeral, though—unlike Ahad Ha'am—"legitimate" (that is, spiritually authentic) Jewish languages.[19] For Bernfeld, however, Hebrew remained the "natural" and primary historical language of the Jews. He measured the Jewishness of diaspora folk languages according to the amount of Hebrew words they absorbed as a result of developing religious, cultural, and linguistic needs. Hebrew, he maintained, endowed Judezmo and Yiddish with a sense of living cultural continuity.

More importantly, Bernfeld's focus on a living culture of Hebrew, with its borrowings from literary sources, bolstered the position of the editors that challenged the assumption that folklore was created only in the folk language and only by the folk. This was important to Bialik, Peretz, Sholem Aleichem, and others who wrote their own "folksongs," whether in Hebrew or in Yiddish, in search of a symbiotic relationship between the folk on the one hand and its writers and artists on the other. As was the case in European literature, all the important Hebrew and Yiddish writers refined, polished, and honed folklore into works presentable as literary art, but which they nevertheless defined as *folkstimlekh* (i.e., in the folk style), *folksliteratur*, and *folkslider*—a literature as much by as for the folk.[20] Bialik, who at times disparaged folklore in its raw state, imagined a time when Hebrew folksongs (*shirei 'am*) would spring up spontaneously from the folk. In that eventuality, Bialik felt assured that his Hebrew "folksongs" would serve as their model, just as Yiddish folksongs served as his inspiration.[21]

NOAH PRYLUCKI

If Bernfeld shared the editors' Hebraist ideology, Prylucki made a clear statement of his independent principles by submitting his article "Klezmer Language in Poland" in Yiddish. Although he was quite capable of writing Hebrew, Prylucki left it for the editors to translate his introduction and explanatory notes.[22] By the time of its appearance, he was already Warsaw's elder statesman of Yiddishist politics and a Deputy to the Polish Sejm, representing the Folks-partey, which he founded in 1915. His political work was a natural extension of his scholarly interests and his professional work as a lawyer and people's advocate.

Although Prylucki and the Folks-partey were sometimes accused of being anti-Zionist, they in fact did not officially oppose Zionism or the study of Hebrew so long as these were not fostered at the expense of Yiddish or of Jewish political involvement in Polish affairs. As heirs to Dubnov's political legacy in Poland, Folkists steered a middle course between the religious and secular parties, and between the socialists and Zionists. In return, Folkists won the regard of other parties and of a broad range of people.[23] Prylucki knew Bialik personally, and the two men maintained a high mutual regard for each other.[24]

Ironically, while Prylucki was active on all cultural fronts, practical and literary, the one area where his reputation suffered was folkloristics.[25] His critics, who included Ansky, Ber Borokhov, and Yehuda Leib Kahan, found his work often folkloristically unsubstantiated, of dubious value, and sometimes downright laughable.[26] Of course, like the editors of the journal, Prylucki cared less about rigorous standards than about the mission of fostering national consciousness. Thus, for example, he included in his collections composed and authored songs as genuine folksongs, if they were generally popular. Nevertheless, even his sharpest critics were appreciative of Prylucki's many valuable contributions to the Jewish cultural renaissance, not the least of which was the founding of the first journal of Jewish folklore in Yiddish.[27]

Prylucki's essay in *Reshumot* showed that he had taken his critics' words to heart. His claims that elements of *klezmer* jargon had become common slang and possessed cognates in contiguous languages were more circumspect and carefully annotated. Alter Druyanov supplemented Prylucki's entries with variants drawn from Russian and Lithuanian Yiddish literary sources.

YEHUDA LEIB ZLOTNICK

Of all the articles in the journal, Y. L. Zlotnick's piece on Warsaw-district customs relating to the Jewish life cycle, holidays, and festive foods (with extensive supplementary notes, again provided by Druyanov) may have adhered most scrupulously to contemporary professional standards in the field of folkloristics.[28] At the same time, his motivations were wholly in line with that of the journal. "We sin a great sin against our people," he wrote, "if we lose the memory of any [unrecorded] custom still practiced from our spiritual treasure, especially as it seems that the end of all customs has arrived and they are being erased one by one, because of the conditions of our time."[29] Zlotnick, a liberal-minded rabbi, who signed this piece as "Yehuda Elzet," found it prudent, perhaps, not to publicly admit his participation in a secular Zionist journal; but his identity, and his other numerous aliases, soon became an open secret.[30] Although combining a career in the rabbinate with an interest in folklore was not unusual in Germany, where even Orthodox scholarship was significantly secularized, it was almost unheard of in Eastern Europe. Nevertheless, Zlotnick wrote as a learned rabbi, justifying his work by citing numerous legal sources favoring folk customs. Within the next few years, Zlotnick would become well known as a folklorist and, in 1920, as a founding member of the Religious Zionist "Mizrahi" party in Poland.[31] Among religious Jews in Poland, he was a rare and militant voice of liberal nationalism, addressing himself to both Orthodox Jews and Poles. Like Prylucki, with whom he had worked both in politics and in scholarship, Zlotnick was a friend and ardent admirer of Bialik.[32] But far more than Prylucki, who was an avowed secularist, Zlotnick represented the type of ideal image that Bialik tried to project, directly or indirectly, in some of his writings, particularly *Sefer ha-agadah* and his essay *Halakhah ve-agadah*. To Druyanov's enduring chagrin, Zlotnick was also a Yiddishist among the Hebraists.[33]

Zlotnick's folkloristic interests were related to his religious and political calling. With his unapologetic and warm appreciation of religious folk custom (*minhag*), Zlotnick advocated a history-of-religion approach to the explanation of customs and their historical and regional variants. He rejected both the comparative-cultural and historical approach to Jewish folklore: the former because it was too quick to accept behavioral cognates from other cultures as points of provenance; the latter because it settled for understanding a custom's earliest, original meaning. His sympathetic approach to religious life was virtually ignored by secular East European Jewish folklorists in the interwar period.

A. Z. IDELSOHN

The editors' choice for their volume's premier article reflected the value they attached to the study of the folk culture of the Oriental Jews. "Yemenite Jews: Their Songs and Melodies" by A. Z. Idelsohn was an abridged, less academic version of his study *Gesänge der jemenischen Juden*, published in Germany in 1914 as the first volume of his monumental *Hebräisch-orientalischer Melodienschatz*. The *Gesänge* was a deluxe edition of over 200 songs that Idelsohn had collected from the Yemenite community in Palestine in 1905.[34] The Hebrew edition also included some musical notation.

The German book, partly sponsored by the Imperial Academy of Sciences in Vienna, which also provided Idelsohn with his recording equipment, was a straightforward academic work that gave a formal presentation of his considerable findings and stuck close to the scholarly sources.[35] There he saw the larger purpose of his work as a contribution to the history of synagogue and church music; both, he would argue further in subsequent works, had their origins in Oriental Jewish music.[36]

In Hebrew, however, Idelsohn expressed himself more freely than he would have dared in German, and with good cause. More than some historical curiosity of value only to scholars and musicians, what he presented in *Reshumot* was a lost Jewish treasure whose retrieval, he believed, could fuel the national revival. Jewish folkloristics, which came into its own as it acquired a romantic vision of itself, previously had failed to emulate its European model in one crucial respect. Whereas European folkloristics established its academic standing by providing the evidence of the folk's connection with its mythopoeic past, Jewish folkloristics was unable or unwilling to point out the living relics, the contemporary folk survivals, of the biblical period. Idelsohn's "discovery" of the songs of the immigrant Yemenite community in Palestine placed Jewish folkloristics on a par with European folkloristic research. Talking to these Yemenite Jews, recording their music, and observing them sing, dance, pray, and celebrate their life-cycle events, reveling in the nuance of their Hebrew pronunciation and in their native dress, Idelsohn believed he had unearthed the "true Jews," the missing link to the Biblical past:[37]

> The melody of the Yemenites is most important to us because it was protected from external influences, especially from Aryan influence and thus remains thoroughly Semitic ..., and because we find in it many elements that are related to the melody of the Ashkenazim in Poland, and from this, proof for the antiquity of these two types of melody. ... It is surely known that the Yemenites had no contact with the Ashkenazim throughout the period of the *galut*. We may, therefore, conclude that the common elements in the Ashkenazi and Yemenite melodies have their origins in an older period, which is to say, they are relics of the ancient Hebrew melody before the *ḥurban* [destruction of the Temple], ... which triumphed over foreign influences and remained Judaic treasures in the four corners of the Diaspora. ... These relics are the melodic expression and echo of the Hebrew national soul."[38]

Here was the Jewish primitive, a "naive," culturally unsullied, plain Jewish "folk" that worked with its hands. Unlike such politically self-conscious, constructed identities as the Zionist *ḥalutsim* [pioneer farmers] or the Russian *narodniki* [ideologues of the Russian peasantry], the Yemenites were the "real thing." Through these exotic Jews, whose legendary history harked back to King Solomon, European Zionists could recapture their desert roots, their original folk heritage, and with it, a romantic "native" basis for their European-bred nationalism.[39]

If this was parity with the nations, however, it was a tainted parity. Romanticism either posited or presumed a racial connection to the peasantry, but when Ashkenazi Jews looked into the faces of the dark-skinned Yemenites they saw neither their own reflection nor what they wanted to be. Idelsohn found them "not pretty."[40] The strikingly Western features portrayed in E. M. Lilien's biblical bedouin characters represented the Zionist self-image of choice. Idelsohn's characterization of the Yemenites is highly stereotypical, approaching a crude racial anthropology. And yet, it was out of genuine admiration that Idelsohn wanted to appropriate Yemenite culture for Ashkenazi Zionism. Although Idelsohn wrote that it is a "fact that in some details the Eastern type was preserved in [the Yemenites] in its Semitic purity," he admired the details and the ostensibly "Semitic" purity of their culture, not their race.[41]

Orientalism, a stylistic and academic adjunct of European nationalism, lay at the core of Idelsohn's ambivalent attitude toward the Eastern communities, allowing him to connect with the East while keeping a respectable distance.[42] Rather than "ethnography," which was the discipline that Ashkenazi Jews used in studying themselves, Idelsohn's fieldwork among the Yemenites was "ethnology": that is, as S. D. Goitein candidly observed, "it was the kind of anthropology empires conducted in foreign countries among primitives."[43]

Idelsohn's work on the Yemenites was just the beginning of a great oeuvre that made him the leading Jewish ethnomusicologist of the Zionist movement.[44] He assiduously and painstakingly collected, recorded, transcribed, and formally described the Hebrew music of world Jewry in all the major communities of the East and West and then wove his grand collection into even grander theories of "Jewish music."[45] Like Bernfeld, he believed in a Hebrew folklore even if it was not the spoken tongue. Idelsohn's work heeded Bialik's call to put a seal on the corpus of the past by shaping it into a living legacy, a canon, and a usable past.

II. Volume Two

The second volume of *Reshumot* was prepared and ready to go to press in 1921 when, like all Hebrew publications, it was shut down by the Communist Party. It did not appear until a year later in Tel Aviv. Nevertheless, it shows the directions in which the editors had anticipated taking the journal before they left Russia.[46]

In the new volume, the section entitled "Tefutsot Yisrael" (in the Diaspora)—featured prominently in the first volume—was dropped. This was not the only apparent casualty of the civil war conditions that beset Russia at the time. Material on the mountain Jews of Bukhara, Persian Jews, and other exotic communities that the editors had commissioned had not reached the journal because of the "upheavals."[47] Yet, with the exception of the third volume (which was devoted entirely to the latest wave of pogroms), the first volumes, up until 1930, generally followed the model set in 1918.

The second volume compensated for the omission of some of the more common subjects of Yiddish folklore in the first. The Yiddish poet and children's writer Z. Rozental contributed ninety-three Yiddish folksongs of various lengths and themes that he had collected in Bessarabia and Odessa.[48] This major collection was supplemented by a group of seven songs contributed by one A. D. Yablonski (from Berdichev).[49] A major shortcoming of both collections, a not uncommon problem of Yiddish folksong collections, was the absence of either musical notation or the transcription of words in their regional pronunciations (a standard procedure of *Mitteilungen*). The collectors did, however, note that some of their songs were variants of specimens collected earlier by Ginsberg and Marek, or by Kahan.

Once again, while many of the articles were not directly concerned with ethnography, they provided rich detail in describing Jewish social life and institutions. H. Tshemerinski, better known as Reb Mordkhele, the Yiddish humorist, wrote about "My

Shtetele Motele" (near Pinsk), describing his father's home, the local trades and livelihoods, the social and economic relations with non-Jews, and the typical personalities of the town.[50] Tshemerinski was also a well-known Territorialist and Yiddish philologist. Despite his political differences with the Zionist-Hebraist editors of *Reshumot*, this longtime resident of Odessa was a close friend of Druyanov and assisted Bialik and Ravnitsky in their translation of *Sefer ha-agadah* into Yiddish.[51]

S. Assaf wrote about the position of the rabbi in the Jewish community and on *smikhah* (rabbinic ordination) in "On the History of the Rabbinate in Germany, Poland, and Lithuania."[52] Berdichevsky, under his pen name, Bin-Gorion, collaborated with Druyanov on a conspectus of magic books, and A. Vayler contributed a list of folk abbreviations.[53]

The premier essay of the volume was clearly Druyanov's "The Jewish Folk Joke," an outstanding contribution and a rare departure of Jewish folkloristics into analysis and theory.[54] The preoccupation with *kinus* tended to exclude theory as a "luxury." Druyanov, however, with the help of a vast network of friends and correspondents, had been collecting Jewish jokes since around 1909 and had amassed thousands of specimens from written and oral sources, mainly from Yiddish.[55] Full of self-confidence and considering himself an expert on jokes, Druyanov felt compelled to offer his own understanding of the material, although it was in good measure heavily influenced by Freud's *The Joke and its Relation to the Unconscious* (1905).[56] Druyanov's name is generally overshadowed by Bialik's, but undeservedly so. He was an independent thinker and writer, at times critical of Bialik, who made his own mark in Zionist history as a publicist of broad erudition and as a historian of Hibbat Ziyon.[57] He was also the driving force behind *Reshumot* and, with his collection and reflections on jokes and humor, he secured his position in Jewish folkloristics.[58]

Druyanov had been convalescing in a Dresden sanitarium and

under strict medical orders not to do any heavy reading, when a friend brought him an issue of *Der jüdische Humorist.* "From that time on," he wrote, "I made up my mind to record in my notebook every joke that came my way."[59] What began as a convalescent's amusement soon turned into a serious avocation.

The literature on Jewish jokes was already considerable, but it was generally neither folkloristic nor altruistic. Antisemites denied that Jews had a sense of humor and told "Jew jokes" to ridicule them. Defenders of the Jews used jokes from the storehouse of Jewish lore to demonstrate their humanity without necessarily referring to the material as folklore or folk jokes.[60] Once Jewish jokes achieved the respectable status of folklore, they took their place as part of the legacy that had to be preserved. Druyanov wrote, "I liked this task of collecting, not just because the jokes are amusing but, as I saw from the very first, these folk jokes are a key, like no other, to the secrets of the soul of the people."[61]

Following Freud, Druyanov saw jokes as a primitive manifestation of the creative process. In their selection of words and striving for style, jokes called for an artistry situated on the boundary between the vernacular and literature.[62] Reviewing the philosophical question as to whether humor is aesthetically pleasing or inherently ugly (the position taken by Aristotle and the one towards which halacha inclined), Druyanov—again like Freud and other anthologists of Jewish humor, as well as proponents of Jewish secularism—found, in the first place, that Jewish jokes were very funny but also very revealing; the appreciation of jokes was an aesthetic experience.[63]

That is not to say that Druyanov did not find that a good portion of his jokes were in bad taste or had sexual connotations. On the contrary, these were plentiful and they alone could fill a volume. They were certainly folklore, and Freud himself used them unapologetically. In 1908, the same year that he published his pioneering *Yidishe sprikhverter un redensartn* (Yiddish proverbs and expressions), Ignatz Bernstein had put together a manuscript of

Erotica et Rustica, bawdy sayings, that he circulated privately, much to the disgust of Ahad Ha'am, and that inevitably made its way into numerous popular editions.[64] Not wanting to appear a trafficker in shady goods, however, Druyanov, who had been contemplating a similar limited edition of dirty jokes, decided not to follow through with that project. His task, after all, was in the national interest.[65]

Druyanov's enthusiasm for Jewish jokes was shared by his coeditors. With Bialik's hearty approval, Ravnitsky was busily engaged in collecting jokes at the same time for his own book.[66] Ravnitsky, helped by numerous correspondents, collected exclusively Yiddish jokes and, while he, too, certainly revised them, his claim was to publish them in their originally reported form.[67]

Druyanov, following the model of the *Sefer ha-agadah*, revised his jokes as he translated them into Hebrew. Rather than competing with Ravnitsky's work, however, Druyanov's work complemented it.[68] His *Jokes and Riddles* appeared in 1922, a year before Ravnitsky's *Yiddish Jokes*.[69]

Druyanov also wrote in Yiddish and in 1912 published a collection of several hundred Yiddish sayings (*sprikhverter*) in the Warsaw newspaper *Fraynd*.[70] Druyanov shared Bialik's respect for Yiddish. He staunchly defended its honor against the distinguished Hebraist, Y. H. Taviov, whose research showed evidence of a living Hebrew folklore that must have delighted *Reshumot*'s editors.[71] In 1919 he published the first edition of his impressive collection of some three thousand proverbs and expressions, all in Hebrew and Aramaic, "from the mouth of the folk."[72] But he parted ideological company with the editors in deprecating Yiddish and Yiddish folklore. The editors regarded Yiddish folklore as their genuine legacy and a model for their Hebrew folklore. Nevertheless, they would have agreed with Taviov—just as Druyanov had specifically said—that Hebrew was the Jewish language of intellectual reflection and therefore it produced a higher form of linguistic humor than Yiddish.[73] Moreover, it was the one unifying national language of the Jews.

Applying a sophisticated linguistic analysis of the structure of jokes, Druyanov concluded, contrary to what was popularly assumed (and somewhat in contrast to Freud, who analyzed the rhetorical devices of translatable jokes), that Jewish jokes did not typically rely on subtle language techniques, as such, to get their point across.[74] The jokes of the Tevye variety, with their playful use of Yiddish to mangle Hebrew, were in the minority.[75] Consequently, Jewish jokes were eminently translatable, and many were common to the numerous Yiddish dialects and the European languages Jews spoke. That they were translatable demonstrated that folklore could exist in Hebrew as in other modern European languages without losing their Jewish character. Indeed, "the rootedness [*hit'ezrahut*] of the Jewish joke in Gentile languages," Druyanov mused sociologically, "is like the rootedness of the Jew himself amidst the nations."[76] Because of their nonlinguistic character, Jewish jokes could thus wend their way into other nations' repertoires of nonlinguistic jokes, just as the jokes of other cultures had entered Jewish folklore. "Most of our jokes are aggregates that pass by word of mouth from place to place and no one knows their parentage."[77] Through this socially transforming process, borrowed jokes became authentically Jewish.

Druyanov adopted much from Freud's views on theories of the joke, from Aristotle to Bergson.[78] Druyanov, like Freud, presumed that Jewish jokes were a product of Jewish history. Yet he also differed with Freud's conclusions. In *Jokes and the Unconscious*, Freud stressed the peculiar nature of Jewish jokes, taking the view that Jewish jokes were an entirely Jewish creation and conveyed a unique sense of humor. Druyanov, in contrast, stopped short of drawing such broad national-cultural inferences.[79]

Instead, Druyanov adopted Freud's idea that, like dreams, Jewish jokes served as an escape valve for the subconscious. In disguised form, they allowed the ego's forbidden, subversive wishes to be fulfilled under the cover of a smile. A joke is a moment of self-assertion in the form of an attack on the hypocrisies of convention and authority, antisemitism, and assimilation. In Jewish jokes no subject was spared ridicule—neither rabbis nor religion, nor even God. Despite the rabbinic injunctions against joking, the Talmud itself acknowledged, "There is no generation that does not have its jokers."[80] The secularism of the jokes made them all the more attractive to Jewish folklorists.

Druyanov's article never received the critical response it deserved, either in Zionist and Yiddishist scholarship of the interwar years, when attention was focused elsewhere, or in Soviet scholarship, where it was considered politically off limits.[81] The question of the psychological nature and the psychological analysis of the Jewish joke began to attract attention in the late 1920s when the first of Theodor Reik's famous articles on the subject appeared.[82] This interest gained momentum toward the second half of the twentieth century and has remained a lively topic of discussion, although addressed mainly to contemporary issues.[83] Druyanov, though occasionally acknowledged, hardly figures in any of these discussions. Nevertheless, since the 1920s, numerous collections of jokes appeared. Among them, Druyanov's *Jokes and Riddles* has remained the most popular, as much a classic of Jewish folklore as Bialik and Ravnitsky's *Sefer ha-agadah*.

III. The Significance of Bialik's Departure

Because of its prominence, *Reshumot* was among the first victims of the Communist crackdown. The Party's henchmen in the *Evsektsiia* (Jewish Section) eagerly applied the politics of the Cultural Revolution to Jewish society. Outstripping their Russian comrades when it came to rooting out "clericalism," they amazed Party leaders with their single-minded determination. As a folkloristic journal, *Reshumot* was indeed, as its editors intended, more than just an academic publication. Bialik helped broaden the secular framework to include practically anything and everything from the Jewish past, which a militant Jewish secularism was determined to categorize as obsolete and irrelevant and which the Party found dangerous and counterrevolutionary. Hebrew was declared guilty by association with the old-time religion and with reactionary Zionism. *Reshumot*, a Hebrew journal, associated with many rabbis, avowedly Zionist and Hebraist, had no future in Soviet Russia. As for the fate of the journal, an early forced exit from the Soviet scene proved to be a blessing in disguise, since it allowed both the journal and its editors to survive in Tel Aviv. From that point, its history falls outside the purview of this study.

Given the Communist authorities' delegitimization of the vast corpus of Jewish culture that Bialik had promulgated as indigenous Jewish folklore, Soviet Jewish folkloristics scholars were barred from participating in the work explored further by Louis Ginzberg, Berdichevsky, Bernard Heller, and the YIVO scholars. Forced to ignore the works of scholars abroad, Soviet folkloristics was generally isolated during the Stalin years, although the study of native Russian folk narratives (the *bylini*) and ethnopoetics continued to be a major aspect of Russian folkloristics. The opportunity to engage in similarly high-level Jewish research was already brought to a close in the relatively tolerant 1920s, when Russian studies saw the short-lived flowering of formalist analysis.[84] There was little possibility of a Jewish folk renewal, as the editors of the *Reshumot* envisaged it, once access to its withered sources became restricted and off limits.

When the books in Bialik's luggage were examined by Soviet customs officials prior to embarking from Odessa, one Party watchdog, apparently an admirer, asked the poet if he might have a copy of *Yidishe agodes*, the Yiddish edition of *Sefer ha-agadah*. Bialik obliged, and inscribed it with the old Yiddish folk saying *Vos*

mir zaynen, zaynen mir, ober yidn zaynen mir (We are what we are, but we are Jews).[85] Of course Bialik did not know what lay in store under Stalinism, but he well understood that his departure symbolized the attempt to impose on the Jews a new definition of who they were. The sovietization of Jewish culture had begun. Painfully aware that Russian Jewry was becoming isolated, Bialik left the young *Evsek* with some urgent wisdom.

Notes

1. רשומות: מאסף לדברי זכרונות, לאתנוגרפיה ולפולקלור בישראל. For publication history and summary of articles see M. Glikshteyn, די אינהאַלט פון היסטאָרישע זשורנאַלן און זאַמלביכער (The content of historical journals and edited volumes), *Fun noentn over*, July–December 1938, 279–91. For a generally positive contemporary review, see *Hatequfah* 16 (1922): 511–15. Volume 3 was published in 1923, in Berlin; volumes 4 (1926), 5 (1927), and 6 (1930) were all published in Tel Aviv. Volume 1 was reprinted in Tel Aviv in 1925, volume 2 in 1927.
2. Abraham G. Duker, "*Evreiskaia Starina*: A Bibliography of the Russian-Jewish Historical Periodical," *Hebrew Union College Annual* 89 (1931–32): 525–603.
3. Salo W. Baron, *The Russian Jew under Tsar and Soviets* (New York: Schocken, 1987), 160–62, 182–84, 395–96 n.19; Solomon I. Godelman, *Jewish National Autonomy in Ukraine 1917–1920*, trans. Michael Luchkovich (Chicago: Ukrainian Research and Information Institute, 1968).
4. The prospectus is reproduced in the introduction to the first volume of *Reshumot*, iv–vii; it is also mentioned in Druyanov's letter, in Yiddish, to Ansky (May 21, 1913) inviting him to participate, *Fun noentn over* 3 (1947): 89.
5. *Reshumot* 1 (1918): iv.
6. Shaul M. Ginzburg and Pesach Marek, Эвреискиe народные песни в россии (Yiddish folksongs in Russia) (St. Petersburg: Voskhod, 1901); *Reshumot* 1 (1918): vi; cf. Dov Shtok's introduction to the new series of *Reshumot*, in the aftermath of the second and greater Jewish catastrophe (n.s. 1 [1945]: i–iii).
7. הספר העברי (The Hebrew book), in כל כתבי ביאליק (Bialik's complete works) (Tel Aviv: Dvir, 1962), 215–16.
8. C. N. Bialik, על תעודת הכנסיה התרבותית (On the purpose of literary collec-

tion), in דברים שבעל פה (Utterances) (Tel Aviv: Dvir, 1935), 1:9–14.

9. S. M. Dubnov, *Об изучений историй русских эвреев и учреждений исторического общества* (On the historical study of Russian Jewry and the founding of the [Jewish] Historical Society) (St. Petersburg: Voskhod, 1891); נחפסה ונחקרה: קול קורא לאסף חומר לבנין תולדות ישראל בפולין וברוסיה (Let us search and investigate: A call to collect material to develop a history of the Jews in Poland and Russia) (Odessa: Pardes, 1892).

10. Mark W. Kiel, "Vox Populi Vox Dei: The Centrality of Peretz in Jewish Folkloristics," *Polin* 7 (1992): 89–120.

11. Dan Miron, בואה, לילה: עיונים ביצרות ח״נ ביאלק ומ״י ברדצ׳בסק (Come, night: Studies in Ch. N. Bialik and M. Y. Berdichevsky) (Tel Aviv: Dvir, 1987), 127–29.

12. S. Ansky, דאָס ייִדישע עטנאָגראַפֿישע פּראָגראַם (The Jewish ethnographic program), ed. L. Shternberg (St. Petersburg: Baron Horace Ginzburg–Jewish Ethnographic Expedition, 1914).

13. Beilin submitted a *badkhn*'s blessing over wine (383–84), which he had earlier published in Max Grünwald's *Mitteilungen zur jüdischen Volkskunde*. On Beilin, who, remarkably, continued to publish in the Soviet period and was active until he died in 1942, see Khaim Beyder, ייִדישער פֿאָלקלאָריסטיק: ראַבינער בייַלין און זײַנע דער מעשֹות (Jewish folklore studies: Rabbiner Beilin and his tales), *Tsukunft*, January–March 2000, 31–33.

14. Y. L. Gordon, על נהר כבר (On the River Kvar), 9–96; A. Y. Paperna, זכרונות ושמעות (Memoirs and hearsay), 148–65; S. L. Tsitron, מלחמת הדינסטיות בישיבת וולודין (Dynastic struggle in the Volozhin Yeshiva), 123–35.

15. S. Poznanski, מיסדי כתות בישראל (Founders of sects in Israel), 207–16; S. A. Horodetsky, לקורות החסידות (On the history of Hasidism), 217–52.

16. עם הספר והספר (People of the Book and the book), 292–316.

17. *Reshumot* 1 (1918): ii.

18. היסוד העברי בלשון הספרדית היהודית (The Hebrew component in the Sefardic Jewish language), 255–71. See also Bernfeld's autobiographical sketch in ספר זכרון: לסופרי ישראל החיים אתנו כיום (Book in honor of contemporary Jewish writers), ed. N. Sokolov (Warsaw: He'asif, 1889); cf. the discussion of Bernfeld's importance to the period by Micha Yosef Berdichevsky (under the pseudonym Bin Gorion), מאמרים (Essays) (Tel Aviv: Dvir, 1960): 216–20. On Bernfeld's interest in folk history see his "Eine Kulturgeshichte," *Ost und West* 2 (1902): 751–56.

19. On Bialik's ultimate loyalty to Hebrew over Yiddish see his *The Hebrew Book*, trans. Minna Halkin (Jerusalem: The Bialik Institute, 1951).

20. אגרות חיים נחמן ביאליק (The letters of C. N. Bialik), ed. F. Lachover (Tel Aviv: Dvir, 1938), 2:109. Cf. Eliyohu Shulman, חיים נחמן ביאליק: זײַנע אָריגינעלע

ייִדישע לידער, זײַנע איבערזעצונגען, און זײַן באַציִונג צו דער שפּראַך פֿראַגע (C. N. Bialik:
His original Yiddish songs, translations, and attitude toward the language
question), *Pinkes far der forshung fun der yidisher literatur un prese* 3 (1975):
50–107. On Peretz's crafting his own folklore see Khone Shmeruk, פרצעס
ייִאוש ווידיע: אינטערפרעטאַציע פֿון י. ל. פרצעס בײַ נאַכט אױפֿן אַלטן מאַרק (Peretz's
vision of despair: Interpretation of Y. L. Peretz's *At night on the old market-
place*) (New York: YIVO, 1971), 133–35; Dovid H. Roskes, פרצעס שאַפֿערישע
פֿאַראַט פֿון דער ייִדישער פֿאָלקס מעשה (Peretz's creative betrayal of the Yiddish
folktale), *Proceedings of the World Congress of Jewish Studies*, Division C
(1982): 349–55.

21. F. Lachover, ביאליק: חייו ויצירותיו (Bialik: His life and works) (Tel Aviv: Dvir,
1962), 3:620; Ziva Shamir, הצרצר משורר הגלות: לחקר היסוד העממי ביצרת ח. נ.
ביאליק (The Cricket, poet of the exile: Research on the folk basis of C. N.
Bialik's works) (Tel Aviv: Papyrus, 1986), 13.

22. לשון הכליזמרים בפולניה (Klezmer language in Poland), 272–91; see also
לעקסיקאָן פֿון דער נײַער ייִדיתשער ליטעראַטור (Lexicon of modern Yiddish literature), ed. Shmuel Niger and Jacob Shatzky (New York: Congress for Jewish Culture, 1968–81), 7:217.

23. Mark W. Kiel, "The Ideology of the Folks-partey," *Soviet Jewish Affairs* 5,
no. 2 (1975): 75–89.

24. N. Prylucki, באַרג אַרױף (Uphill) (Warsaw: Nayer farlag, 1917), 69–75.
After Bialik declined Ansky's invitation to join the 1912 expedition—he
thought it would be too strenuous—he did not hesitate to recommend
Prylucki along with Peretz and Dinezon. See letter to Ansky (March 14,
1912), in Lachover, *Letters of Bialik*, 2:134; see also Bialik's letter to Ansky
(November 17, 1912) on the physical difficulties of the expedition, 117.

25. Prylucki wrote extensively on philology, folklore, literary criticism, the-
atre, and politics. For an overview of his work see *Lexicon*, 7:216–23.

26. Borokhov did not mince words: "Prylucki had a good idea: to collect Yiddish ethnographic-geographic proverbs, and for that we owe him our
thanks. Good intentions, however, require sound methods. Ninety percent
of Prylucki's collection is, simply put, garbage, to be thrown out." Ber
Borokhov, שפּראַך־פֿאָרשונג און ליטעראַטור־געשיכטע (Linguistics and history of
literature), ed. N. Mayzl (Tel Aviv: I. L. Peretz Farlag, 1966), 154. At the
same time, commenting on Prylucki's response to a review of his work by
Ansky, Borokhov warned against vituperation in אונדזער יונגער וויסנשאַפט
(Our young science), ibid., 156. See also Y. L. Kahan, שטודיעס וועגן ייִדישער
פֿאָלקסשאַפטונג (Studies on Jewish folk creativity), ed. M. Weinreich (New
York: YIVO, 1952), 46–53.

27. Prylucki's journal, entitled somewhat egotistically (as Borokhov complained) נח פרילוצקיס זאמלביכער פאַר ייִדישן פאָלקלאָר, פילאָלאָגיע און קולטורגעשיכטע
(N. Prylucki's miscellanies for Jewish folklore, philology, and cultural history), appeared in two volumes (Warsaw: Nayer farlag, 1912, 1917).

28. ממנהגי ישראל: קובץ ממנהגים שלא נזכרו או שלא נתבררו עדיין כל צרכם (Jewish customs: Collection of unfamiliar folk customs), 335–77. The article was
dedicated to his mentor, S. Poznanski.

29. Ibid., 338.

30. Elzet was one of the many of the many aliases the author used in his long
career as a folklorist and writer. Zlotnick's article was introduced as having
been written by a rabbi in a "small Polish town" ("Jewish customs," 335);
idem, רשמות לתולדות חיי הספרותיים (Notes on the history of my literary life)
and the appended "selected bibliography" of his works, *Edoth* 2, no. 3–4
(April–July 1947): 247–48. His secular interests led him so far as to write
biographies of such martyred heroes as Socrates, Jesus, and Giordano Bruno.

31. "My Literary Life," 245–55. See *Lexicon*, 1:4–5, s.v. Yehuda Avida.

32. Kiel, "Ideology of the Folks-partey," 89 n. 58. His admiration for Bialik
can be seen in his pamphlet ביאַליקס טרערן, צונויפֿגעזאַמלט אין איין לאָגעל אַרײַן
(Bialik's tears, collected in one vessel), by Yehuda Elzet (Warsaw, 1918).

33. In 1924, Druyanov wrote to Zlotnick (then living in Montreal), lamenting
that he, Zlotnick, wrote in a language that had no future. "Return us,"
Druyanov pleaded, "to those who give their lives for the rebirth of the
Hebrew spirit." Druyanov wrote in a similar vein to S. Beilin. See A.
Litai's introduction to Druyanov's כתבים נבחרים (Selected works) (Tel Aviv:
Brit rishonim, 1943), 1:13. Bialik expressed similar feelings about Peretz
and Sholem Aleichem, *Letters of Bialik*, 1:26.

34. יהודי תימן (Yemenite Jews), 3–66; *Gesänge der Jemenischen Juden* (Leipzig:
Breitkopf & Härtel, 1914).

35. *Gesänge*, 3–4.

36. Ibid. Cf. תולדות הנגינה העברית: מהותה, יסודותיה, והתפתחותה (The history of Jewish melody: Its nature, basis, and development) (Berlin: Dvir, 1924); *Jewish
Music in Its Historical Development* (New York: Holt, 1929).

37. "I remember in 1932," S. D. Goitein wrote, "when the late Professor
Louis Ginsburg … stayed in Jerusalem … I brought him to the Yemenite
'Goral' synagogue. … Visibly moved, he said to me, after the service:
'Now I know what Judaism is'" ("Research among the Yemenites," in
Studies in Jewish Folklore, ed. Frank Talmadge [Cambridge: Association For
Jewish Studies, 1980], 122).

38. Idelsohn, "Yemenite Jews," 25.

39. Goitein, "Research," 121.
40. "Yemenite Jews," 7.
41. Ibid.
42. Edward Said, *Orientalism* (New York: Pantheon, 1978); cf. Paul Mendes-Flohr, "*Fin-de-Siècle* Orientalism: The *Ostjuden* and the aesthetics of Jewish Self-Affirmation," *Studies in Contemporary Jewry* 1 (1984): 96–139. For an important anthropological critique of Said, see James Clifford's review in *The Predicament of Culture: Twentieth Century Ethnography, Literature, and Art* (Cambridge: Harvard University Press, 1988), 255–76.
43. Goitein, "Research," 125. Goitein referred to the "classic" work of Erich Brauer, *Ethnologie der Jemenitischen Juden* (Heidelberg: Winter, 1934), whose more careful description of the Yemenites (51–59) may be compared to Idelsohn's, for an indication of a growing sophistication in methodology. Moisei Berlin's earlier *Очерк этнографий эбреискoгo народонаселения в россий* (Essay on the ethnography of the Jewish population in Russia) (St. Petersburg: Royal Geographic Society, 1884) calls itself an "ethnography" insofar as it describes an indigenous people. Written with great sympathy by a "learned Jew" in the service of the Interior Ministry, it had, however, all the earmarks of the imperial ethnology that tried to explain the uncivilized to the civilized. Berlin used the language of the "other" to defend Jewish dignity and their civil rights. On the peculiar position of the "insider" having to resort to the "science" of the "outsider," see Clifford, *Predicament of Culture*, 275–76.
44. Idelsohn also published the first *Shiron* (popular songbook) in Palestine in 1913 (*Encyclopedia Judaica*, s.v. "Shiron," 8:1224-25).
45. Idelsohn excluded from his collection secular folksongs of a class character which called his theory of unity into question. He also included songs that were in line with his theories despite their questionable folk credentials, such as sacred songs of known authorship. For this he was later vilified by Marxist critics (Moishe Beregovski, צו די אויפגאַבעס פון דער ייִדישער מוזיקאַלישער פּאָלקלאָריסטיק [On the tasks of Jewish musical folkoristics], in פּראָבלעמעס פון פּאָלקלאָריסטיק [Problems in folklore studies], ed., M. Viner [Kharkov-Kiev: Melukhisher natsminfarlag, 1932], 1:104–14). Although from a less partisan, albeit secular, point of view, Y. L. Kahan also had problems not with the idea of religious folks songs as such, but with the specific specimens Idelsohn chose (see *Studies*, 51).
46. *Reshumot* 2 (1922): v–vi.
47. Ibid., v.
48. Five betrothal songs, 34 children's songs, forty love songs, three soldiers'

songs, two on emigration, and 19 others miscellaneous types (שירי עם [Folk-songs], 359–75). Rozental, who was first published by Ravnitsky, eventually collected about three hundred songs. Between the wars he achieved prominence in Romania. In 1940 he was arrested by the Soviets as a Zionist and was imprisoned for fourteen years. See *Lexicon*, 8:340–42.

49. שירי עם (Folksongs), 376–78. I have been unable to identify Yablonski.

50. His article, עירתי מוטלה, 3–124, appeared posthumously. This essay was translated into Yiddish by M. Lipson, who, like Druyanov (see below), collected several volumes of Jewish jokes, which appeared in Yiddish and Hebrew translation (*Lexicon*, 5:197–98).

51. C. N. Bialik and Y. H. Ravnitsky, די יידישע אגדות (Jewish legends) (New York: Sklarsky, 1948), vii. This is a photographic reproduction of the second edition, printed in Berlin in 1922. The first edition was published in Odessa, 1917–19. See also *Dictionary*, 6:108–13.

52. לקורות הרבנות באשכנז פוליניה וליטא (On the history of the Rabbinate in Germany, Poland, and Lithuania), 259–300.

53. M. Y. Bin-Gorion and A. Druyanov, רשימי קונטרסים (Lists of booklets), 437–38; A. Vayler, ראשי תיבות העממים (Popular abbreviations), 457–58. Vayler contributed to the first volume as well. I am not sure if he is the Eliezer Pinhas Vayler mentioned in the *Lexicon* (3: 346–47), who was an Orthodox Jew and later, a member of Agudat Israel.

54. ההלצה היהודית העממית, 303–57.

55. See A. Litai's introduction to Druyanov, *Selected Works*, 1:16 (d); A. Druyanov, ספר הבדיחה והחידוד (The book of jokes and riddles) (Frankfurt a.M.: Omonut, 1922), 7. Moscow and Odessa were wishfully also listed as places of publication.

56. *Book of Jokes*, 7.

57. Litai, "Introduction," 5; A. Druyanov, כתבים לתולדות חיבת ציון ויישוב ארץ ישראל (Writings on the history of Hibbat Zion and the settlement of the Land of Israel), 1–3 (Jerusalem: Vaad Leyishuv Erets Israel, 1919–32).

58. Shtok, "Introduction," ii.

59. *Book of Jokes*, 7.

60. See Druyanov's bibliography, *Book of Jokes*, 10–11; Sig Altman, *The Comic Image of the Jews: Explorations of a Pop Culture Phenomenon* (Teaneck, N.J.: Fairleigh Dickenson University Press, 1971), 121–81. An overlooked early example of a collection of Jewish jokes in defense of the Jew is Judas Ascher's *Der Judenfreund; oder Auserlesene Anekdoten, Schwänke und Einfälle von den kindern Israels*, 3rd ed. (Leipzig: Baumgarer, 1810). The introduction to the 1810 edition refers to yet an earlier brochure of *Anekdoten von*

guten Juden (Dan Ben Amos, "The Myth of Jewish Humor," *Western Folklore* 32, no. 2 [April 1973]: 113).

61. *Book of Jokes*, 7.

62. Ibid., 8.

63. D. H. Monro, "Humor," *The Encyclopedia of Philosophy*, ed. Paul Edwards (New York: Macmillan, 1972), 4:90–93.

64. David Davidovich, אישים והשקפותהם: על חקר הפולקלור היהודית (People and their views: On researching Jewish folklore), *Yed'a 'am* 51/52 (1984): 158–59; see also G. Weltman and M. S. Zuckerman's recent edition of Bernstein's collection, published in paperback, with translations, as *Yiddish Sayings Mama Never Taught You* (Van Nuys, Calif.: Perivale Press, 1975), with approbations on the front cover by I. B. Singer and Henry Miller.

65. Druyanov, "Jewish Folk Joke," 303–4; Litai, "Introduction," 16 (d).

66. Lakhover, *Letters of Bialik*, passim.

67. Y. H. Ravnitsky, ייִדישע וויטסן (Yiddish jokes) (Berlin: Moriah, 1923), vii.

68. Bialik and Ravnitsky, *Jewish Legends*, 1: vii.

69. Druyanov and Ravnitsky consulted each other while working on their respective collections. Of the two projects, Druyanov's was the more ambitious, certainly, as it included both a broader range of sources and analysis. From Ravnitsky's introduction to *Yiddish Jokes*, it appears that it was Druyanov who helped him arrive at a conceptual-historical understanding of the material (*Yiddish Jokes*, vi-vii; cf. Druyanov, "Jewish Folk Joke," 313–14). Like Bialik and Ravnitsky, Druyanov made use of aggadic language and jokes that relied on the exaggerated dialectic of *pilpul*, and halachic language in order to achieve a uniform folk style in Hebrew. Unlike the collaborators of the aggadic collection, however, who at Ravnitsky's insistence translated all the Aramaic into Hebrew, Druyanov attempted to retain the original folk character of the language by preserving contemporary colloquial Aramaisms.

70. Zalman Reyzin, לעקסיקאָן פֿון דער נײַער ייִדישער ליטעראַטור, פּרעסע און פֿילאָלאָגיע (Dictionary of recent Jewish literature, press, and philology) (Vilna: Kletskin, 1926), 1:743–45.

71. Druyanov, "Jewish Folk Joke," 317. On Taviov see Mordkhe Volf Kiel, פֿאָלקלאָר און וועלטלעכקייט: נחום אויסלענדערס גרונטשטריכן פֿון ייִדישער רעאַליזם (Folklore and secularism: Nokhum Oyslender's *Principles of Jewish realism*), *Yivo bleter* n.s. 4 (2003): 266–67.

72. Y. H. Taviov, אוצר המילים והפתגמים (Treasury of proverbs and expressions), 2nd ed. (Jerusalem: Moriah, 1921).

73. "Jewish Folk Joke," 317.

74. Ibid., 317–23. European jokes, Druyanov believed—mistakenly, as it turns out—had been found to rely typically on subtle word play in order to achieve a generally light comic aim, a *calambour*, or a *double entendre*. He called this linguistic process *Midrash lashon* in contrast to Jewish jokes, which generally, although not exclusively, resort to some cognitive play, or *Midrash ha-maḥshavah*, a story or anecdote whose meaning is revealed at the end with a sudden and devastating impact ("Jewish Folk Joke," 306–17; Salcia Landmann, *Der Jüdische Witz* [Olten: Walter Verlag, 1962], 36). Landmann apparently allowed European jokes placed in the mouth of a Jew, and downright antisemitic jokes, to slip into her work. See the serious criticism of her book by Friedrich Torberg, who thinks that it is precisely these defects that account for it being a best seller ("Wai geschrien! oder Salcia Landmann ermordert den jüdischen Witz; Anmerkungen zu einem beunruhigenden Bestseller," *Der Monat* 14, no. 157 (1961): 317–23.

75. "Jewish Folk Joke," 312.

76. Ibid., 311. "It is curious: This folk type of the Jewish joker—mainly a poor joker—rose from our ground, and tied by its navel to our ground, found its literary image and form, more than in our languages, in those languages which are not ours. Here for, example, are Hailk Pikl or Bogrov, or Sender Glatis, or Franzos, or DeCosta and Itzig Yenkeles or Zangwill" (ibid., 314).

77. See the foreword to the *Book of Jokes*, 7; "Jewish Folk Joke," 313–14.

78. Ibid.

79. Ibid., 310–11.

80. *Y. Berakhot* 81, and Druyanov's epigraph, "Jewish Folk Joke," 303.

81. Y. L. Kahan left some important comparative observations, and bibliography, questioning the Jewish origins of the so-called "*Ekht yidishe vitsn*" (genuine Jewish joke) in Ravnitsky's collection. See Kahan, *Studies*, 266–74.

82. T. Reik, "Zur Psychoanalyse des jüdischen Witzes," *Imago* 15 (1929): 63–68.

83. See *Jewish Wry: Essays on Jewish Humor*, ed. Sarah Blacher Cohen (Bloomington: Indiana University Press, 1987), esp. "A Selected List of Jewish Humor," 234–41.

84. Heda Jason, "Precursors of Propp: Formalist Theories of Narrative in Early Russian Ethnopoetics," *PTL: A Journal For Descriptive Poetics and Literature* 2 (1977): 471–516; Felix J. Oinas and Carl Stief, "Folklore," in *Marxism, Communism, and Western Society*, ed. C. D. Kerning (New York: Herder and Herder, 1972), 3:365–72.

85. Y. H. Biletzky, ביאליק ויידיש ח'צ (Bialik and Yiddish) (Tel Aviv: Peretz farlag, 1970), 57.

THE SCIENCE OF JUDAISM AND THE SCIENCE OF MAN

Some Jewish Threads
in the History of Anthropology

HARVEY E. GOLDBERG

My first academic discussions with Ismar Schorsch took place in the mid 1970s, when he was spending a year in Jerusalem. I was then working on editing an unpublished book written by Rabbi Mordecai Ha-Cohen of Libya, who lived from 1856 through the 1920s, on the history and customs of his own community of Tripoli.[1] At the time, this was a novel effort. Much of the work on Jews in Middle Eastern communities in recent times was ethnographic, and most historians dealing with the region focused on the great pre-modern figures. "Is what I am doing part of Jewish history?" I hesitatingly asked Ismar while asking him to read a draft of my introduction to the volume. His answer was a definite and encouraging Yes. Over the years, contact with Ismar has taught me that no matter in what direction my interests may lead, I may very well chance across a

This paper was written during the tenure of a fellowship at the Center of Advanced Judaic Studies, University of Pennsylvania, in the Fall of 2003, and at the Institute of Advanced Studies at the Hebrew University of Jerusalem in the Spring of 2004. It partially reflects research carried out with aid of the Memorial Foundation for Jewish Culture and support from a grant by the Israel Science Foundation (grant no. 907/02). I am indebted to Orit Abuhav, whose search of the archives of the Hebrew University as part of her doctoral research brought to light some of the documents cited herein, and for her comments on an earlier draft of this paper. I also thank Jeffrey Feldman for his comments.

path reconnecting them to the concerns of Jewish history.

During that year, Ismar himself was conducting research on major figures in the development of *Wissenschaft des Judentums*, delving into obscure publications and reading letters that scholars wrote to one another a century and a half before. It seemed remote from my own focus, but from time to time I have consulted his writings on the subject, particularly when pondering the history of my own discipline—anthropology. Of late, I have reread the description of the early coalescence of *Wissenschaft* appearing in his paper "Breakthrough into the Past."[2] Several features of the story told there are worth noting. The initial *Wissenschaft* group was short-lived (five years), and only about forty years later did Leopold Zunz succeed in persuading Heinrich Heine's biographer to pay historical attention to it. The people involved in the small group ended up going in very different directions— some even converting to Christianity—while others forged diverse paths of Jewish life and thought in Central Europe which continue to have reverberations today. What was clearly shared by the individuals in question was the historical setting that pressed them to engage in intense interchange, and the sense of crisis that connected them while facing an uncertain future about what Judaism and being Jewish might mean in the future. I submit that these characteristics, of a situation full of questioning that in some ways comes to be definitive for generations thereafter, may also prove relevant for grasping aspects of the history of anthropology. In particular I suggest, they may throw light on Jewish aspects of that intellectual tradition.

I. Jews and Anthropology: General Background

It has long been known that many leading figures in the development of cultural and social anthropology, which began to take on its modern forms in England, France, and the United States at the turn of the twentieth century, were Jewish. Until recently, this fact appeared to be of passing interest, for their major writings only occasionally remarked upon Judaism, and most were not known to have salient Jewish involvements in their lives. Certainly, connection to Jews and Judaism was not a subject that later entered into classroom lectures or discussions of their contributions. The link between anthropology and "being Jewish" did not seem more worthy of attention than the growing entrance of Jews into many other fields of academic endeavor. But trends beginning in the 1960s, which gave greater prominence to "ethnicity" and also sought to critically assess what factors led to the emergence of a "science of man" that honed its conceptual tools on societies outside Europe, suggested that asking who had been involved in shaping the discipline and what it meant to them in their own social setting was not an uninteresting question.

In 1995 I published an article entitled "The Voice of Jacob."[3] Beginning with a consideration of how anthropology had been linked to the study of the Hebrew Bible, a topic with nineteenth-century beginnings that "went underground" and resurfaced around 1960, it branched out into documenting many instances in which leading anthropologists who were Jewish had at one time or another showed concern with the biblical text, with studying "religion" in a way that was not prejudicial to Judaism, or had concretely engaged in activities that could be identified as Jewish. Some of the instances cited were partially known, and others were "dug up" for the first time; but the main significance of the paper was to point to the breadth of the phenomenon, which suggested that the topic could be profitably mined in greater depth. I was unaware at the time that other researchers were asking similar questions. Simultaneous with my paper and since then, a number of focused studies have delved into these topics, adding considerable thrust to the scattered discussions that existed before.[4] I summarize some of them in a manner that does not do full justice to their contents, but which provides analytic directions enabling my further exploration of the theme and its significance.

The volume of *Jewish Social Studies* in which that paper appeared also included an article by Pierre Birnbaum on the "Impact of the Dreyfus Affair" on French-Jewish sociologists, referring to Emile Durkheim and his school.[5] Two years later, Ivan Strenski published a full-length study on Emile Durkheim and his colleagues and students (many, but not all, of whom were Jewish), placing them in relation to the issues facing French Jewry at the time.[6]

In 1996, Barbara Kirshenblatt-Gimblett published a monograph-long article on the links between Max Weinreich and the anthropologist Edward Sapir and how their common interest in linguistics, and the interweaving of language and culture, was expressed in Weinreich's work at YIVO. The paper added to the growing understanding of the Jewish background, intellectual interests, and activities of Sapir, who, together with his teacher and later colleague, Franz Boas, shaped the modern study of anthropologically oriented linguistics in the United States.[7]

Two researchers in England, one a literary scholar and the second an anthropologist, have produced several volumes that present the rich intellectual and social background of Prague-born Franz Steiner (1909–1952).[8] Steiner was an accomplished poet who developed an interest in anthropology that brought him to study at Oxford, and he briefly taught there until his early death. Steiner was a committed Jew and Zionist and made a strong impression on his colleagues, including Mary Douglas.[9] I suspect that contact with Steiner is part of the background to E. E. Evans-Pritchard's many references to the Hebrew Bible in his *Nuer Religion*.[10]

More recently, George Stocking, the leading historian of the development of anthropology, wrote an article about Sol Tax (1907–1995) of the University of Chicago, who founded the international journal *Current Anthropology*.[11] He shows how, when Tax met Jews on an archeological expedition to Algeria in 1930, he made a connection between his Jewish background and his anthropological and ideological interests.

In 2003, Matti Bunzl provided a chapter on "*Völkerpsychologie* and German-Jewish Emancipation."[12] He showed the clear Jewish agenda of this field that developed in late-nineteenth-century Germany and its direct impact on the cultural anthropology of Franz Boas. This article adds depth to a number of studies that have considered Boas's Jewish background in relation to his intellectual project, some of which will be mentioned shortly.[13] Bunzl's paper can also profitably be read together with a 1997 article by Thomas Hauschild showing how the influence of *Völkerpsychologie* and its practitioners was eliminated from German anthropology at the turn of the twentieth century as racist ideas came to dominate the field there.[14] Most recently, Jeffrey Feldman has critically examined the way the discipline of anthropology has looked at its Jewish "roots and routes" and suggested productive lines for further research.[15]

These studies and others suggest that there may be interesting relationships between attempts to formulate general ("universal") approaches to the study of society and culture on the part of Jewish anthropologists, and the diverse situations in which Jews were found, and which they interpreted for themselves, in the nineteenth and twentieth centuries. Their growing number and depth also lead us to ask about the relevance of these developments to the concerns of Jewish historians. This parallels a discussion by Ezra Mendelsohn asking whether Jewish historians should pay attention to figures who "were Jewish" but whose lives and careers moved them away from active Jewish life and involvements (even to the extent of conversion to Christianity).[16] In considering the question, Mendelsohn shows how such people were often strongly associated with other Jews of similar background and interests, and how their life-trajectories adhered to patterns followed by many. One of the three figures he discusses is Franz Boas. We begin with a discussion of Boas in order to draw out some of the conceptual lines of the existing research on the Jewishness of anthropologists that will guide us in taking the discussion further.

Boas, after migrating to the United States from Germany, was preeminent in shaping academic anthropology in the United States. His studies in physical anthropology (including Jews as subjects) challenged notions of race as being fixed and as determining the histories of human populations. His work was widely appreciated by Jews and Jewish leaders, while he himself viewed his findings as first and foremost a contribution to science, and not to the study of any specific group. His envisioned future for Jews in the United States was assimilation, and he held a similar position regarding African Americans. Mendelssohn identified Boas's assimilative strategy as one kind of response that was common among Jews at the time and was therefore deserving to be seen as a Jewish response. While insisting on the generality of his concerns and projects, Boas agreed to their being put to the service of those with more "particular" commitments. A paper he delivered in Paris in 1937 on issues of race was reprinted by Salo Baron as the lead article in the first volume of *Jewish Social Studies*.[17] He also allowed his name to be attached to an (abortive) initiative to set up an Academy of Sciences in Jerusalem in the late 1930s, as a means for rescuing Jewish and non-Jewish scientists from Europe.[18] Boas's liberal orientation enabled him to adopt an assimilatory outlook while working with others who were committed to preserving Jewish culture and identity in America.

A somewhat different way of exploring Boas's links to Jewish history has been suggested by Ellen Messer in a paper comparing him to the German-born leader of Reform Judaism in America, Kaufmann Kohler.[19] Messer stresses the similar background of the two men, including a liberal upbringing cultivated in Germany and a hoped-for amelioration of their situation in the United States. Both struggled with the dilemmas of trying to understand the role of tradition in social life and formulating an optimal relationship between group belonging and broad human values. The resolutions each person chose were different, but there was much overlap in the cultural resources on which they drew. In a 1907 article that argues for the importance of ritual in Jewish life, Kohler cited nineteenth-century scholars who were formative in the creation of anthropology: E. B. Tylor and W. Robertson Smith.[20] If I may transpose Messer's thesis to a different idiom: in that historic setting with its characteristic tensions, one might imagine Kohler as having a brother (or sister) who became an anthropologist, and Boas as having a brother turning to be a Reform rabbi.

This emphasis on historic milieu in understanding how ethnic-religious backgrounds figured into intellectual endeavors is developed further in Strenski's study of Durkheim. Strenski insists that the way to understand how Jewishness may have entered Durkheimian sociology is *not* by focusing on the content of Judaism, seeking some "essential" formulation of Judaism and trying to find a refraction of it in the content of Durkheim's theories. Instead, he locates Durkheim vis-à-vis the challenges facing Jews in France in his day. He also explores the web of contacts within which Durkheim was enmeshed, including Jews and Gentiles, to see who may have influenced his sociology and been influenced by it. Beyond that, Strenski tunes into various ways in which "Judaism" may have been culturally encoded and talked about. In particular, he focuses on the eminent Indologist, Sylvain Lévi, who was a teacher of two of Durkheim's leading students, Marcel Mauss and Henri Hubert, and who conveyed to them an approach to religion containing many elements which were to be prominent in Durkheim's sociology of religion. Strenski points out that Lévi was a leader within French Jewry and claims that much that Lévi had to say concerning religion in India was a way of talking *about* Judaism.[21] One aspect of this strategy is his insistence that Ancient Judaism and the religions of India were part of the same cultural world, in opposition to the growing emphasis on the separation of Aryans and Semites that appeared in Continental scholarship in the second part of the nineteenth century. Strenski's interpretation assumes that "Jewishness" can be a feature of networks of social interaction and enter into the reworking of cultural materials that interest members of those networks in ways that cannot be determined in advance. This makes it possible to ask not only whether anthropologists who were Jews were part of Jewish history, but also whether the latter should be seen as part of the history of anthropology.

II. The Students of Franz Boas: Differing Jewish Paths

This emerging approach may be applied to material concerning prominent anthropologists who bridge the worlds of Germany, the United States, and France. Working out of the network approach, it is instructive to ask about Boas's students, many of whom were Jewish. The history of anthropology in the United States was a complicated process, but a simplified picture which places Boas as the founding father whose descendants spread out across the academic map of the country would encapsulate a significant aspect of the story. I begin by discussing four of Boas's prominent students: one as a reference point and three others somewhat more extensively. The first is Alfred L. Kroeber (1876–1960), and the others are Robert Lowie (1883–1957), Edward Sapir (1884–1939), and Paul Radin (1883–1959). While Jewish matters were never central in their writings, I suggest that ignoring the Jewish elements in their stories impoverishes the understanding both of the development of anthropology and of modern Jewish history.

Kroeber is sometimes viewed as Boas's successor (even when Boas was still alive) as the central figure in American anthropology. This was expressed in his enduring theoretical interest in the nature of culture, his concern with all branches of anthropology, and his influence over the careers of students and colleagues. Kroeber, like Boas, although born in the United States, was a bearer of German culture on American soil. Like his teacher, he lived for a while on the Upper West Side of Manhattan where people of "cultivated" German background, both Gentiles and Jews, lived side by side and shared much in common. Theodora Kroeber (his second wife) describes his preparatory-school student body as follows: "Four-fifths of his [Dr. Sachs's] pupils were Jewish—the sons of rabbis and of intellectually oriented German-Jewish immigrants—who were more motivated toward learning than were most of the Anglo-Saxon, Dutch, and other ethnic groups of the city."[22] Another indication of this overlapping is that Boas was connected to the New York Society for Ethical Culture, established by Felix Adler, son of a reform Rabbi.[23] Kroeber was not Jewish, but his first wife was named Henrietta Rothschild. Theodora Kroeber sums up the situation in her husband's words: "[As to] the relation of Gentiles and Jews of German extraction ... one knew the difference, but assumed it did not matter. ... [The Jewish families] took it for granted that one did not believe in religion."[24] One has to envision a situation in which, from the point of view of many Jewish families, their Germanness (perhaps, more broadly, their cultivated Europeanness) was the main ingredient of what we now call "ethnicity." It did not entail "conversion from" Judaism but in a sense was the highest expression of that Jewish background, the special texture of which would be dissolved into the more elevated and refined cultural amalgam that immigrants like them could contribute to American society. This was a paradigm that theoretically could be inviting to people of differing backgrounds, but, as often happens in such situations, it turned out be particularly attractive to young intellectually oriented Jews, including those who developed an interest in anthropology.

Somewhat younger than Kroeber were three other students of Boas: Lowie, Sapir, and Radin. They were contemporaries and remained in personal and professional contact over the years.[25] Lowie was the closest to the German-Jewish profile outlined above. He came with his family to the United States at the age of 10. Robert Murphy describes Lowie's family as "alienated from their religious heritage and assimilated with German or German-Austrian culture."[26] He also states, "Behind the forbidding aspect of the Germanic professor was a kind and shy man, totally committed to his discipline and his students, strictly observant of a hierarchy of manners, but equally dedicated to egalitarianism in the realm of thought."[27] Lowie was appointed to the University of California, Berkeley, in 1921, becoming Professor of Anthropology four years later. Several of his books, such as *Primitive Society* (1920) and *The History of Ethnological Theory* (1937), were classics in their generation. Lowie gave testimony to his attachment to Germanic intellectual tradition. In a book that summarizes the professional side of his life, which he finished at the time of his death, he testifies how throughout his life he continued to read for pleasure in German.[28] More remarkably, at the end of World War II, he published two books on Germany and German culture, the second written after carrying out fieldwork in that country.[29]

The first book, *The German People*, states in the preface: "As needs hardly be emphasized, I speak throughout as an anthropologist. Political history does not interest me except as a background for cultural developments." Lowie achieves this separation by discussing Germany up to the year 1914. He includes a section on the Jews, placed in the context of German history and culture. His insistence on the enduring worth of German culture is perhaps epitomized in the dedication:

> To my old friends, ALFRED L. KROEBER and PAUL RADIN,
> who still read their Goethe

As will be seen, the reference to Radin may also provide an opening to what (however Lowie may have viewed it) might be called Jewish dimensions of Lowie's life.

Paul Radin was born in 1883 and came to the United States with his family a year later. Below we will explore possible Jewish sides to Radin's anthropology, but there is little that needs to be "uncovered" about his Jewish beginnings. Radin's father, Adolph Moses (1848–1909), was a rabbi, and the *Encyclopaedia Judaica* contains three entries discussing him, Paul's elder brother Max (1880–1950), and Paul himself.[30] Adolph first moved to upstate New York and was appointed rabbi in Elmira, while also ministering to Jewish inmates in the State Reformatory there. The family eventually moved to Manhattan, where they became friends of the Lowies. Paul must have received a solid Jewish education. During his student days, he, along with Henrietta Szold, worked at translating Louis Ginzberg's *Legends of the Jews* from German into English.[31] I doubt whether he would have been employed to do this based on his knowledge of German alone. Ginzberg was probably acquainted with the whole Radin family. A letter from the 1920s is preserved in which he corresponds with Max, then a Professor of Law at the University of California, Berkeley, referring to the sociological approach to Judaism of Max Weber.[32] Paul's subsequent scholarly undertakings did not directly address matters of Jewish culture and religion, but his writings were highly respected within anthropology.[33] His work based on a single member of Winnebago society moved the study of religion among "aboriginal" peoples to new levels. Cora Du Bois (who was a student of Lowie's) describes his 1920 *Autobiography of a Winnebago Indian* as "one of the first significant life histories of an American Indian viewed as a unique human being."[34] His *Method and Theory of Ethnology* (1933) is today considered a forerunner of the critical anthropology that has emerged over the past two generations.[35]

Cora Du Bois comments that this book should be read

together with Lowie's on the history of ethnology. She similarly states that two books named *Primitive Religions*, one published by Lowie in 1924 and the other by Radin in 1937, should be treated as a pair (see below).[36] Finally, it should be noted that Radin is an exception to the pattern in which the outstanding students of Boas ended up in key academic positions. He entered into conflicts with his teachers and colleagues in a manner that combined intellectual disputes with at times volatile personal relations. He moved a great deal during his career, including time spent in England and Europe. His name shows up in an exchange of letters from 1928 between a New York City supporter of the new Hebrew University and Judah Magnes, chancellor of the university. In them, the idea of securing funds to develop anthropology in the university is raised, with special reference to "a course in Arabic–Jewish sociology." The letter about that course, dated October 18, 1928, mentions Paul Radin, indicating that he might be helpful in raising funds from the Rockefeller Foundation after visiting the University and giving a few lectures there.[37] As in other attempts to insert anthropology into the university's curriculum during its first decades, this came to nought, but the letter directs us to networks of ties that may have carried Jewish vibrations running through the anthropological project.

A few remarks on Edward Sapir are in order. Born in 1884, he immigrated to the United States in 1889. He and Lowie began their graduate studies at Columbia at the same time, while Radin began a few years later. Some now think of Sapir more as a linguist than as an anthropologist because of his influential *Language: An Introduction to the Study of Speech* (1921). That book can profitably be read today, more so, for example, than Lowie's *Primitive Society*. One of its major points is that there are no human "primitive languages," and in other ways it sets out the basics of linguistics as a social science. Sapir taught at the University of Chicago (1925–31) and at Yale (1931–39). His ties to matters Jewish are by now fairly well known as documented in some of the sources already cited. In the discussion below, it is not only his personal engagement with Jewish culture but his interchanges with Lowie and Radin that will enable us to expand our understanding of the processes involved.

III. Letters to Robert Lowie

My discussion of these figures continues with reference to a number of letters written to Lowie by the other two men (one from Radin and several from Sapir) which are preserved at the University of California, Berkeley.[38] This sampling does not pretend to be based on a full examination of correspondence with Lowie but reflects a quick search over several hours in which the letters from Radin and Sapir caught my attention in particular. The friendship and continuing connection among these men is apparent in many of them. Radin addresses Lowie as "Dear Robert" and Sapir mostly writes "Dear Lowie" but changes to "Dear Robert" in the 1930s. The letters from Sapir to Lowie often refer to "Paul" without further explanation, demonstrating the common concern that both men had with regard to Radin at various stages in his zigzag career.[39] This does not mean that relations were always equally smooth among all the three. A letter from Sapir to Lowie indicates how Radin distanced himself from Boas, and Lowie mentions that around 1929 there was strain between him and Radin.[40] In addition, the letters could also serve as a platform for discussions of professional disagreement, which, as will be seen in an example below, should also be viewed on the background of solid personal association. In terms of our general question, we wonder whether a common European-Jewish background may have entered into this enduring triadic friendship, and we begin to consider the question by referring to several Jewish links in Lowie's career.

My initial search of the Lowie correspondence was motivated

by a single question relating to the development of anthropology at the Hebrew University. In one of his memoirs, Raphael Patai mentions that, with the encouragement of Judah Magnes, he wrote to Lowie late in 1946 asking for a discussion of the discipline of anthropology.[41] Patai says that he received a response to this letter. Earlier, he indicates that he sent to Lowie (along with many others) the first (1945) issue of the journal *Edoth* published by the Palestine Institute of Folklore and Ethnology that Patai had cofounded, and received an acknowledgment from him.[42] I was hoping to find some record of this correspondence in the Lowie archive and was not successful, but there is no reason to doubt it took place.

What prompted Magnes and Patai to think of Lowie in the first place? What follows is mostly speculation, except for the fact that Patai, since arriving in Palestine in 1933, had come to be aware of American anthropology and the Boasian school; so Lowie's scholarly reputation must have been known to him.[43] Other reasons with a "Jewish geography" side to them might have been involved as well. Magnes grew up in Oakland, California, and may have been aware of faculty members at nearby Berkeley, where Lowie had become an eminent professor. Max Radin taught at the University of California Law School in Berkeley from 1919 and might have continued the old link between the two families. His name appears in the correspondence mentioned above about the possibility of Paul coming to Jerusalem (see note 37), and he actively supported the Hebrew University, ultimately bequeathing his library to that institution.[44] It is easy to imagine that if Max did not initiate turning to Lowie in the search for an authoritative anthropologist, then he would have reinforced the suggestion if asked.

Why did Lowie take the trouble of replying to Patai's correspondence? Was it strictly professional, so that he might have responded to a request coming from any university in the world because of his view of science as international?[45] Did he feel it as a compliment, given the fact that he was already in his sixties and may have sensed that newer developments in anthropology were passing him by? What did he know about the Hebrew University? If the figure of Magnes was at all familiar to him, he may have been aware that the university's chancellor had studied in Germany at the turn of the twentieth century, or he may have recognized his name from Jewish life in New York (1906–22). To the extent that he had some knowledge of the institution on Mt. Scopus, he might have (correctly) surmised that it was an institution which when it originated was strongly based on academic traditions from Germany and Central Europe. In this instance, as in others, such as Lowie's participation in the Conference on Science, Philosophy, and Religion organized by Louis Finkelstein in the postwar period,[46] Lowie could make an anthropological contribution in a universalistic mode, with the Jewish side of his involvement (if it existed) left in an unspoken state.

What is clear is that Lowie in his contacts with Radin and Sapir had acquaintances and friends with varying degrees of active Jewish interests and affiliations, and he must have known about these. In one letter from Chicago, Sapir reports to Lowie about meeting a person who was connected to a mutual acquaintance in Berkeley, and indicates in parentheses that she is Jewish.[47] At a more substantive level, another letter asks for Lowie's reactions to papers that Sapir sent him, including an unpublished article on "The Jewish State Language."[48] To the best of my knowledge, this article was never published, but it seems reasonable that the renascence of spoken Hebrew in contemporary Palestine and its possible relation to a future Jewish polity engaged Sapir's imagination both as an anthropological linguist and as a Jew. Another letter, from Radin during September 1920, also refers to Zionism. Radin indicates that he is soon to end his Zionist activities and travel to England.[49] It is written in a matter-of-fact manner assuming that Lowie knew to what Radin referred. There is no explanation whether this meant that Radin changed his views on

Zionism (but see the Hebrew University correspondence above), whether he was ceasing active involvement, or some other shift of course. It does suggest that Jews of that background who had very different ideological orientations were moving in the same circles. Likewise, there is every reason to think that Lowie's involvement with Sapir did not change as the latter became more taken up with Jewish culture in the last years of his life. Lowie, for his part, continued to view himself as representing German culture, but it might be asked whether this particular mode of universalizing and de-Judaizing oneself had any resonance in his anthropological work.

IV. Jewish Responses and Anthropological Analysis

Some clues may be found in a long letter to Lowie by Sapir written after the former published his book *Primitive Religion* (1924).[50] There might have been some expectation that just as the earlier *Primitive Society* was considered a masterful summary and integration of what was known at the time, the subsequent volume would do the same for the topic of religion. Sapir, however, in part of the letter, directly expresses to him a different view:

> Your book on "Primitive Religion," which I should have written you about ages ago, has been completely read and with very great enjoyment indeed. It is remarkably lucid, full of interesting details and has many hints that suggestively link primitive religion with other interests. You will, however, I hope, not take it amiss if I say that it falls somewhat short of the standard of "Primitive Society." It is not so much compacted and it betrays, in ways that are probably not altogether clear to you yourself, a lesser inherent sympathy for its subject matter than was shown in the earlier book. The conscious desire to under-

stand religion and to refrain from the rationalist's sly twinkle in contemplating it are evident enough, but I don't think one could honestly say there is much of an emotional participation in the subject. There's curiously much said about such things as association and curiously little about religious ecstasy, the compulsive power of religious symbols, and other of the more irrational aspects of religion. Perhaps I can best articulate my reaction to the book when I say that it seems rather a series of chapters on the methodology of primitive culture that happen to draw largely on "religious" material than a true probe into the religious psychology of primitive religion.

If I were writing such a book (which, needless to say, I do not dream of doing), I should probably have such chapter headings as "The Psychology of Ritual," "Religious Ecstasy," "Prayer," "The Religious Transvaluation of Experience," while such interests as "Association" and "Religion and Art" and "Women in Religion" would seem too external to the theme to deserve prominence as chapter-headings. The sympathetic reader feels, I believe, that you are heading all the time for religion, but somehow never quite get there. At last analysis, of course, it is a matter of temperament. You are so built as to be able to write an admirable study of such things as social structure, historical methodology, analysis of intellectual belief, literary criticism on its culture-historical side, and so on and so on, but, if I do not err, not on any subject that requires a wholehearted participation in an intuitively reached type of behavior. Your book is precisely what I should have supposed it would be, only, if I may be a little Irish, rather more so.

All this does not mean that I do not consider the book exceedingly valuable. Indeed I do! It is a fine piece of work that is as definitely conditioned by your type of personality as a garden is surrounded by a fence. Perhaps you would like a few details on individual chapters. ...

This letter, written with a combination of collegial intimacy and critical intellectual engagement which is probably rare in any setting, suggests that there is something about Lowie's personal style which keeps him from deeply entering the realm of religion.[51] But Sapir takes Lowie "as he is" and does not probe from whence this reluctance may stem. The letter, I submit, assumes that much is tacitly understood between the two individuals, based as likely as not on a shared cultural background in its concrete contemporary setting. Sapir may have ultimately moved in a somewhat different direction with regard to his Jewish past, but he had a clear understanding of Lowie and his historical choices. It is not difficult to imagine that the effort entailed in constructing an assimilative path (over more than one generation),[52] pulling oneself (and one's family) out of a given religious (implying also ethnic) milieu without connecting to any another, might leave people desensitized to matters of religions generally. The Lowie swim away from Jewish currents was also a loss to anthropology.

Turning to Paul Radin, it may also be possible to detect refractions of the religious tradition and group to which he was heir in aspects of his research on religion. In the letter to Lowie cited above, he says that he will soon depart from England and "I do not intend to return to America." In order to help pay for his first year abroad, he is about to "leave for British Columbia to do some fieldwork among the Salish for Sapir." But he continues: "To tell you the truth I am not at all interested in fieldwork, or for that matter, in anthropology any more." These sentiments and plans did not work out in the directions suggested. Radin spent some time at Cambridge University but eventually returned to the United States. He continued to publish in anthropology but earned a reputation, both personally and in his writings, of a someone who was critical and at times sharp in the manner in which he expressed his disagreements. A case in point is his debate with Wilhelm Schmidt of Austria concerning the subject of "high gods" among "primitive" peoples.

Radin's study of one man in Winnebago society, Crashing Thunder, criticized notions of a "primitive mentality." This society produced an individual with a worldview based on reflection and contemplation that included a sophisticated idea of a supreme god. Radin claimed that philosophically oriented individuals articulating a religious world view that included a supreme god idea might appear in any society, along with other members of the society whose religious life was less grounded in cognitive agility.

In this discussion, Radin was addressing the question of "primitive monotheism." There was a claim, first made by the Scottish anthropologist Andrew Lang, that among the world's "simpler" people, as measured by technology (e.g., "hunters and gatherers"), there sometimes existed a notion of a high god who existed above and beyond the more proximate spirits and deities. High gods were sometimes viewed as creators, and more commonly as sources of good, but in other ways did not resemble God of the Hebrew Bible, Christian tradition, and Islam. The identification of such quasi-monotheistic gods among technologically simple people—who presumably were closer to humankind's earliest stages than other groups—was a challenge to evolutionary conceptions that saw societies, in all realms of culture, moving through a series of progressive levels. Radin's position was that monotheism, in terms of widespread and institutionalized beliefs, was indeed unusual in simpler societies, but that any society might engender individuals, or priestly classes, with monotheistic ideas and apperceptions that were not widely shared.

Radin's main foil in discussing this matter was a well-known Austrian Catholic ethnologist, Pater Wilhelm Schmidt. Schmidt had an extensive knowledge of the world's cultures, as well as familiarity with Old Testament and New Testament history. He once was mentioned in many textbooks of anthropology because of his adherence to the theory of primitive monotheism, which he elaborated after Lang's initial formulation. Sometimes it is mentioned that this theory makes sense to a worldview anchored in Genesis which depicts the Fall of Man. Adam was a monotheist, but his descendants degenerate both morally and religiously.

Radin's disagreement with Schmidt had been expressed earlier, but I quote from his *Primitive Religion*: "In spite of [Schmidt's] admittedly great critical powers one is, quite naturally, deeply suspicious of his treatment of the facts wherever they would seem to militate against the dogmas of the church, and that, in the realm of the history of religion, unfortunately is practically everywhere."[53] Lowie was aware of this debate but is much more reserved in discussing it. He refers to criticism of Schmidt's thesis and, without mentioning Radin explicitly, notes that if "Catholic or personal prejudices" are found in his work, "there is no evidence ... that the results have been twisted except through the common foibles of humanity."[54]

In a 1997 article, the German anthropologist Thomas Hauschild pointed to an antisemitic bias in the work of Schmidt and other German anthropologists in the first half of the twentieth century. The theory of primitive monotheism, whatever base it had in ethnographic fact, was also a way of depriving the ancient Hebrews of any special contribution to Western civilization. Even the "simplest primitives" had grasped the basics of the monotheistic idea. For some reason, the idea had remained with the Hebrews while it disappeared among the other peoples of the ancient Near East, but the composers of the Hebrew Bible cannot be credited with having developed it. To quote from Schmidt: "The scriptural narrative referring to the times of primitive revelation really belongs to the oldest period of mankind's evolution," and "it is utterly out of the question that such a picture could have been sketched by the Israelites, could have been excogitated out of nothing, at some later period in their history."[55] The theory was one way of undermining a widespread conception of European civilization as standing on two foundation stones, one Greek and one Hebrew, by grinding away at the latter.[56]

Explicating primitive monotheism was not the only theoretical tactic for excluding Jews that summoned up ethnological knowledge. The eighteenth-century discovery of the relationship between Sanskrit and European languages led, in the nineteenth century, to the exploration of the "Aryan" roots of Europe.[57] While there was substance to this search, it also could play the role of providing Europe with a romantic primordial past that was an alternative to the historical link to the "Semitic" Bible and the ancient Near East. This intellectual maneuver was not lost on contemporary observers. It was remarked upon by Israel Zangwill, who introduced Radin when he delivered the lecture "Monotheism among Primitive Peoples" to the Jewish Historical Society in London in April 1924. Zangwill (author of the 1909 play *The Melting Pot*) notes the contemporary push in the United States to restrict immigration to "Nordics" and that "by a Chauvinistic school of thought in Germany, Jesus is now definitely rejected as a Semitic alien."[58]

Radin must have known about these interpretive projects but did not address them directly in that lecture. In a chapter on "monotheistic tendencies" in a later book, he briefly points out that evolutionary thinking is still commonly applied to the religion of ancient Israel.[59] The substantive correspondence between Schmidt's theory and the implied portrait of man's theological "degeneration" in Genesis is more obvious than what the theory erases through silence. But I don't think it is possible to fully understand Radin's debate with Schmidt without taking into account a sensitivity to the way Judaism was portrayed in scholarship and, by extension, a concern with fair and accurate portrayals of any culture or religion.[60]

V. Enter Claude Lévi-Strauss

It should be possible to continue this discussion by examining other American anthropologists of European-Jewish background and their colleagues who were linked to Lowie, Sapir, and Radin, and by considering how the associative web of their research concerns may have ensnared (or been ensnared by) Jewish experiences. Instead, we conclude this excursus by once again crossing the Atlantic to engage one of the best-known anthropologists of the twentieth century, Claude Lévi-Straus (b. 1908). Lévi-Strauss's *Tristes Tropiques* is one of the prominent literary autobiographies of the mid twentieth century.[61] It is an account of two journeys from Europe to the Americas, and simultaneously a story of personal, intellectual, and professional development as well as of physical survival. The longer journey, in 1934, took the young Parisian savant to São Paolo and subsequently to visits among the Amazonian societies which later figured in his innovative anthropological analyses. The second, in 1941, took place shortly after the armistice that set up the Vichy government, and Lévi-Strauss describes how he just barely booked passage on a ship that took him out of the country; he succeeded in part because it belonged to the company that had taken him on the earlier voyage. This provides an opening, from my perspective, for looking at links between the two passages.

In a chapter entitled (in the English translation) "How I became an Anthropologist," Lévi-Strauss presents his intellectual genealogy. He explains that anthropology (French *l'ethnographie*) "affords me an intellectual satisfaction: it rejoins at one extreme the history of the world, and at the other, the history of myself." On the background of his training in philosophy and Durkheimian sociology, a significant moment and break came when in the 1930s he read Lowie's *Primitive Society*. The cultural forms analyzed there made him "drunk with the open spaces" and "my astonished eye could hardly take in the wealth and the variety of the scene."[62] He delved into the world of Anglo-American anthropology, citing in particular the debt to Lowie, Kroeber, and Boas. To French detractors who claimed that he was unduly influenced by American philosophy, he points out that these scholars, "European by origin, and themselves educated in Europe ... stand for ..., where knowledge is in question, the synthesis for which

Columbus provided the objective opportunity four centuries ago."[63] It appears, however, that the ability to empathize with the project of Lowie, Kroeber, and Boas may not only have been in the realm of modes of knowledge.

Having "met" Lowie through his then-classic book, was there anything else that they came to share? Both were especially interested in the indigenous societies of South America. Lévi-Strauss in part was able to escape in 1941 thanks to an invitation to come to the U. S. to teach at the New School of Social Research, in which relatives of his and Lowie had a hand.[64] Both men placed themselves in a chain of European intellectual culture, with Lowie stressing his German tradition and Lévi-Strauss the French.[65] In each instance, this was done while minimizing (but not totally erasing) Jewish components of their background. Perhaps there was also a convergence in what might be called the emotive tone that informed their work on indigenous societies. Earlier, we mentioned the remarks by Sapir to Lowie that he lacked the capability of "whole-hearted participation" that was required to study religion. A curious inversion of this perspective appears in Lévi-Strauss's discussion of religion among the Bororo. He begins by explaining that his grandfather (with whom he lived during World War I) was the Rabbi of Versailles and that a long corridor led from his home to the synagogue, but young Claude did not develop a connection to the religious life of his forebears. "Even to set foot in that corridor was an awesome experience; it formed an impassable frontier between the profane world and that other world from which was lacking precisely the human warmth which was the indispensable condition to my recognizing it as sacred."[66] This quote is "curious" because many discussions of Lévi-Strauss's œuvre underline the highly "cerebral" emphasis in his approach to culture (note how he writes of "recognizing it as sacred"), and I have occasionally heard those who have met him personally describe his polite but highly distanced and reserved manner.[67] Is there an "elective affinity" between this intellectual/affective disposition and the emotional energies required to strictly supervise the flow of experience from one's intimate background into one's public and professional persona?[68] Lowie in his autobiographical account makes clear his attachment to German culture, never once appending the adjective "Jewish." But with regard to his two books on Germany he notes:

> Some have even gone so far as to accuse me of having written an apology for the Germans; this is absurd, if for no other reason than that the Nazi regime liquidated almost all my European relatives. Although I was not especially close to them, I was certainly not amiably disposed toward a government that sent them to be destroyed in Polish furnaces.[69]

While separated in age by twenty-five years, both Lowie and Lévi-Strauss had to face the horrors of World War II, which were part of the history of the "self" and the "world."

Continuing the account of his attraction to American anthropology, Lévi-Strauss insists that "It is to a historical situation, not an intellectual tradition, to which I am paying homage"[70] He claims that the fieldwork which Boas, Kroeber, and Lowie carried out, shortly after the turn of the twentieth century, took place when the groups they studied were relatively intact in terms of maintaining aspects of their traditional lives, still unknown in terms of serious research, yet soon to be destroyed in brutal interaction with American society. To illustrate the uniqueness of this juncture he tells of one man who escaped the destruction of the California tribes—"un Indien échappé seul, miraculeusement, à l'extermination des tribus californiennes" and ended up as a "college porter in the University of California."[71] The English translation utilizes a somewhat different phrase: "and it happened that one Indian escaped, as if by a miracle, from the holocaust."[72] I assume that Lévi-Strauss knowingly agreed to the use of the word "holocaust" in the English rendition, and even if this is not the case, is it too far-fetched to see this story of survival in California ("history of the world") and his own survival ("history of myself") as intertwined, whether or not the French intellectual made this explicit? His Euro-American predecessors, Boas (who sought a career in the United States because as a Jew he had few prospects in Germany) and Lowie's family, in traveling to America, had consciously decided to move beyond what they perceived as particular Jewish culture, allowing it (from their personal perspectives) quietly to extinguish. Lévi-Strauss himself, who comments that "even for my parents, Judaism was only a memory,"[73] was forced to exit rapidly from Europe to escape being placed in a concentration camp. All of them became intrigued with and committed to documenting and explicating indigenous lifeways which they assumed would soon disappear. If the historical situations in which they were enmeshed unquestionably formed part of Jewish history, is it forced to view the anthropology in which they were engaged as partially comprising one mode of Jewish self-expression running through the twentieth century? Given the paradoxes of modern Europe that both beckoned and rejected Jews, that demanded that they participate in national life as individuals while never completely forgetting their group origins, and that pushed them away from Europe while they remained loyal to its culture, were the seemingly doomed lifeways that had evolved on American soil attractive to them because they were "good to think?"

VI. Final Thoughts

The phrase "good to think" is taken from Lévi-Strauss's study of what was once known as "totemism," understood to consist of links between social groups and animal species that represented them or to which they were connected in other symbolic-religious ways. This formulation was suggested in opposition to the

materialist theory that totem animals took on religious significance because they were "good to eat."[74] It represented a step in
social theory that illuminated how the structures, dilemmas, or
contradictions of social life are transposed into cognitive and symbolic realms and also elevated processes of cognition within social
life to a place of importance they had not enjoyed before.

Both Lowie and Lévi-Strauss were far too intelligent to
"deny" their Jewish backgrounds in any crass way (had they
wanted to), and far too aware of history and social processes to
think that their personal origins could be erased by sleight-of-
hand. But they both seemed to assume that through the use of
powerful and subtle individual intellect they could precisely determine where they stood and in what direction they were moving
vis-à-vis the flow of Jewish history and the life choices of other
Jews. But much as their scholarly and analytic achievements are
inspiring, I find it hard to accept that when Lévi-Strass claims that
"the ethnological vocation is a flight from civilization, from a century in which one doesn't feel at home" and contrasts himself
with Margaret Mead who "felt part of her society and her
time,"[75] that this stance is without any connection to his biography, his family's ethnoreligious trajectory, or the modern history
of Jews in France. Similarly, when Robert Lowie was pressed to
make explicit (above) that he was "not amiably disposed toward a
government that sent [his relatives] to be destroyed," and referred
to the crematoria as "Polish [not German!] furnaces," it is hard to
escape the feeling that there is not some degree of overdetermina-
tion in his passionate attachment to German culture. Such heroic
expressions of individual ability and right to establish or limit cultural affiliation in lonely cognitive splendor are particularly striking
in leading practitioners of a discipline which above all has stressed
social context and linkage. Is it far-fetched to imagine that the
cultural empathy which these ethnological giants held in abeyance
from their own heritage and ethnic milieus were eventually lav-
ished on the societies of the New World whose histories (like that

of the Jews?) appeared to perhaps be nearing their ends?

Viewing the fascination of researchers carrying a European and Jewish background with native American societies and their lifeways, I cannot help being reminded of the remark about *Wissenschaft des Judentums* that its purpose was to "give Judaism a decent burial." Ismar Schorsch and others have shown the inappropriateness of this judgment as a key to understanding the motivation of *Wissenschaft* scholars, but it does represent one understandable response among a range of possible reactions to what appears to be a declining culture to which one has some connection.[76] In juxtaposing this perception to the work of Boasian-derived anthropology, it is important to remember that even though the approach to culture that Boas offered applied in principle to all humankind, the practical definition of the discipline as dealing with "aboriginal" peoples whose cultures had to be "salvaged" through research remained dominant for another half century. Only in the 1930s did the American Anthropological Association first define acculturation as an important subject of study. Subsequent shifts in this direction were the mobilization of anthropologists for intelligence work during World War II and their engagement with issues of "development" in various countries of the Third World in the postwar decades. Still, in an Inaugural Lecture at the newly established chair in social anthropology at the Collège de France in 1960, Lévi-Strauss's definition of the field was mainly in terms of "those 'primitives' whose modest tenacity still offers us a means of assigning to human facts their true dimensions." Aware, "alas, [that] they are all destined for extinction," he declared himself "their pupil; their witness."[77] Did Lévi-Strauss and the European-American anthropologists whose work initially grabbed his attention have a sense that they were giving the cultures of the New World a "decent burial?" And if so, in addition to the theoretical underpinnings that they formulated for the task, did this resonate with the way they had processed their own family and cultural backgrounds? Whatever the answer might be, both anthropologists and those intimate with Jewish culture know that burials are full of opposing meanings. They are orchestrated by those still living, and at times contain the barely visible seeds of an emergent future.

Notes

1. See Mordecaï Ha-Cohen, הגיד מרדכי (Higgid Mordecai: The history of Libya and its Jews, their communities and customs), ed, and annotated by H. Goldberg (Jerusalem: Ben-Zvi Institute, 1978), and its partial translation into English, *The Book of Mordechai: A Study of the Jews of Libya*, trans. and ed. Harvey E. Goldberg (London: Darf, 1993).
2. Ismar Schorsch, "Breakthrough into the Past: The *Verein für Cultur und Wissenschaft der Juden*" in *From Text to Context: The Turn to History in Modern Judaism* (Hanover: University Press of New England for Brandeis University Press, 1994), 205–32.
3. Harvey E. Goldberg, "The Voice of Jacob: Jewish Perspectives on Anthropology and the Study of the Bible," *Jewish Social Studies* n.s. 2 (1995): 36–71.
4. In addition to the studies cited, see my own further exploration of the topic in Harvey E. Goldberg, "Louis Finkelstein's *The Jews*: A Mid-Twentieth Century Presentation of Judaism," in *Key Texts in American Jewish Culture*, ed. Jack Kugelmass (New Brunswick, N.J.: Rutgers University Press, 2003), 199–209; "Modern Jewish Society and Sociology," in *Oxford Handbook of Jewish Studies*, ed. Martin Goodman (Oxford: Oxford University Press, 2002), 975–1001.
5. Pierre Birnbaum, "French Jewish Sociologists between Reason and Faith: The Impact of the Dreyfus Affair," *Jewish Social Studies* n.s. 2 (1995): 1–35. Emile Durkheim, often dubbed one of the "fathers of sociology," was equally important in shaping social anthropology, particularly with regard to the study of ritual.
6. Ivan Strenski, *Durkheim and the Jews of France* (Chicago: University of Chicago Press, 1997).
7. Barbara Kirshenblatt-Gimblett, "Coming of Age in the Thirties: Max Weinreich, Edward Sapir, and Jewish Social Science," *YIVO Annual* 23 (1996): 1–103, esp. 23. See also Regna Darnell, *Edward Sapir: Linguist, Anthropologist, Humanist* (Berkeley and Los Angeles: University of Califor-

nia Press, 1990), 398–406, and Edgar E. Siskin, "The Life and Times of Edward Sapir," *Jewish Social Studies* 48 (1986): 283–92, and references therein, along with the references in Goldberg, "Voice of Jacob."

8. *Franz Baermann Steiner: Selected Writings*, edited and with an introduction by Jeremy Adler and Richard Fardon, 2 vols. (New York: Berghahn Books, 1999), *From Prague Poet to Oxford Anthropologist: Frank Baermann Steiner Celebrated: Essays and Translations*, ed. Jeremy Adler, Richard Fardon, and Carol Tully (Munich: Iudicium, 2003).

9. In the introduction to her influential *Purity and Danger: An Analysis of Concepts of Purity and Taboo* (New York: Praeger, 1966), Mary Douglas indicated that her interest in ritual purity was stimulated by two of her teachers, Steiner and M. Srinivas. Srinivas, a Hindu, became one of the leading anthropologists of India. A memoir of Steiner by Douglas appears in *Steiner: Selected Writings*, and another by Srinivas in Adler, Fardon, and Tully, *From Prague Poet.*

10. E. E. Evans-Pritchard, *Nuer Religion* (Oxford: Oxford University Press, 1956), and see the discussion of this book in Goldberg, "Voice of Jacob."

11. George Stocking, " 'Do Good, Young Man': Sol Tax and the World Mission of Liberal Democratic Anthropology," in *Excluded Ancestors, Inventible Traditions: Essays Toward a More Inclusive History of Anthropology*, ed. Richard Handler, History of Anthropology 9 (Madison: University of Wisconsin Press, 2000), 171–264.

12. In *Worldly Provincialism : German Anthropology in the Age of Empire*, ed. H. Glenn Penny and Matti Bunzl (Ann Arbor: University of Michigan Press, 2003), 47–85.

13. Leonard B. Glick, "Types Distinct from Our Own: Franz Boas on Jewish Identity and Assimilation," *American Anthropologist* 84 (1982): 545–65, esp. 557; Ellen Messer, "Franz Boas and Kaufmann Kohler: Anthropology and Reform Judaism," *Jewish Social Studies* 48 (1986): 127–40; Ezra Mendelsohn, "Should We Take Notice of Berthe Weill? Reflections on the Domain of Jewish History," *Jewish Social Studies* n.s. 1 (1994): 22–39, esp. 32; Gelya Frank, "Jews, Multiculturalism, and Boasian Anthropology," *American Anthropologist* 99 (1997): 731–45; Douglas Cole, *Franz Boas: The Early Years* (Seattle: University of Washington Press, 1999).

14. Thomas Hauschild, "Christians, Jews, and the Other in German Anthropology," *American Anthropologist* 99 (1997): 746–53.

15. Jeffrey Feldman, "The Jewish Roots and Routes of Anthropology," *Anthropological Quarterly* 77 (2004): 107–25.

16. Mendelsohn, "Should We Take Notice." See also Amos Morris-Reich,

"Disciplinary Paradigms and Jewish Assimilation: The Jews as Object of Research in Early Formulations of Social Science" (Ph.D. diss., Hebrew University, 2003).

17. Franz Boas, "Heredity and Environment," *Jewish Social Studies* 1 (1939): 5–14. Max Radin and Edward Sapir (see below) appear as members of the Editorial Committee of the new journal.

18. Raphael Patai, "The Jerusalem Academy," in *Journeyman in Jerusalem: Memories and Letters, 1933–1947* (Salt Lake City: University of Utah Press, 1992), 298–316; Goldberg, "Voice of Jacob."

19. Ellen Messer, "Franz Boas and Kaufmann Kohler."

20. K. Kohler, "The Origin and Function of Ceremonies in Judaism," *Central Conference of American Rabbis Yearbook* 17 (1907): 205–9.

21. Strenski, *Durkheim*, 119.

22. Theodora Kroeber, *Alfred Kroeber: A Personal Configuration* (Berkeley and Los Angeles: University of California Press, 1970), 21.

23. Morris E. Opler, "Franz Boas: Religion and Theory," *American Anthropologist* 69 (1967): 741–44.

24. Kroeber, *Alfred Kroeber*, 25–26.

25. Many examples can be found in Darnell, *Edward Sapir*. See also the introductory comments in *Letters from Edward Sapir to Robert H. Lowie*, ed. Robert H. Lowie (Berkeley, Calif.: mimeo, 1965). This is a collection of letters gathered together by Lowie in typescript before his death, to which he added an introduction and explanatory notes. It was apparently placed in the public domain by his wife, Luella Cole Lowie, in 1965.

26. Robert F. Murphy, *Robert Lowie* (New York: Columbia University Press, 1972), 10.

27. Ibid., 2.

28. *Robert H. Lowie, Ethnologist: A Personal Record* (Berkeley and Los Angeles: University of California Press, 1959), 169.

29. *The German People: A Social Portrait to 1914* (New York: Farrar and Rinehart, 1945); *Toward Understanding Germany* (Chicago: University of Chicago Press, 1954).

30. *Encyclopaedia Judaica* 13: 1497–99.

31. See volume 3 of Louis Ginzberg, *The Legends of the Jews*, 7 vols. (Philadelphia: Jewish Publication Society of America, 1909–38).

32. The letter is in the Ratner Center at JTS, but I have misplaced the reference.

33. Lowie, *Letters from Edward Sapir*, 70 n. 26, describes Radin as "one of the most colorful figures in his generation ... a gay, intelligent, lovable, civi-

lized wanderer in anthropology and adjoining fields. His volume of work is enormous, and there are no field workers better than he."

34. Cora Du Bois, "Paul Radin: An Appreciation," in *Culture and History: Essays in Honor of Paul Radin* (New York: Columbia University Press for Brandeis University, 1960), ix–xvi (see p. xii). See also Stanley Diamond, "Radin," in *Totems and Teachers: Perspectives on the History of Anthropology*, ed. Sydel Silverman (New York: Columbia University Press, 1981), 67–97.

35. Paul Radin, *The Method and Theory of Ethnology: An Essay in Criticism* (New York: McGraw-Hill, 1933), repr. with an introduction by Arthur J. Vidich (New York: Basic Books, 1965). This book bears a dedication to Lowie on his fiftieth birthday, followed by two lines of poetry in German (from Goethe?): *Jugend ist ja dem Alter so nah, durchs Leben verbunden, / Wie ein beweglicher Traum Gestern und Heute verband.*

36. Robert H. Lowie, *Primitive Religion* (New York: Boni and Liveright, 1924); Paul Radin, *Primitive Religion: Its Nature and Origin* (New York: Viking, 1937).

37. See the following letters in the archive of the Hebrew University of Jerusalem, File no. 86: Isidore D. Morrison to Judah L. Magnes, 18 Ocotober 1928; Judah L. Magnes to Arthur Ruppin, November 11, 1928; Arthur Ruppin to Judah L. Magnes, November 12, 1928; Judah L. Magnes to Isidore D. Morrison, November 16, 1928; Judah L. Magnes to Ben M. Selekman, November 16, 1928; and Ben M. Selekman to Isidore D. Morrison, November 21, 1928. The first letter mentions that Paul is the brother of Max Radin, whom Magnes "know[s] very well," and the letter from Ruppin to Magnes mentions the recent visit to Palestine by Maurice Fishberg, a physical anthropologist from New York who worked very closely with Boas on the study of Jewish immigrants. It is worth mentioning that Stocking's study of Sol Tax (note 11) shows Tax's concern with the issue of relations between the Zionist project and the Arab residents of Palestine.

38. Robert Harry Lowie papers, BANC MSS C-B 927, The Bancroft Library, University of California, Berkeley. The letters from Sapir to Lowie were gathered together in a mimeoed booklet, described above (note 25). Lowie's papers contain other extensive correspondence with major figures in anthropology.

39. Relationships among them also are apparent in Darnell, *Edward Sapir*, esp. 70.

40. Sapir to Lowie, March 25, 1926, Bancroft Library; Lowie, *Robert H.*

Lowie, 137.

41. Patai, *Journeyman*, 457.

42. Patai, *Journeyman*, 455. Orit Abuhav (pers. comm.) suggests that Melville Herskovits, another (and younger) student of Boas, may have facilitated the connection between Patai and Lowie, as Patai had a more extensive correspondence with Herskovits; Orit Abuhav, אנתרולוגיה ואנתרופולוגים בישראל: מבט מבפנים על התפתחות האנתרופולוגיה הישראלית "Anthropology and anthropologists in Israel: Internal perspectives on the development of Israeli anthropology) (Ph.D. diss., Hebrew University, 2004).

43. Orit Abuhav, פני אדם: על תרומתם של האתנולוגים אריך בראואר ורפאל פטאי לחקר האתנולוגיה של היהודים (The human countenance: The contribution of the ethnologists Erich Brauer and Raphael Patai to the anthropology of the Jews), *Jerusalem Studies in Jewish Folklore* 22 (2002): 159–77, esp. 174. R. Patai quotes Lowie frequently in מדע האדם: מבוא לאנתרופולוגיה (The science of man: An introduction to anthropology), 2 vols. (Tel Aviv: "Yavneh" for the Palestine Institute of Folklore and Ethnology, 1947/8).

44. *Encyclopaedia Judaica*, 13:1498. Max Radin, in 1946, was a vice president of the Academic Committee for the Hebrew University, affiliated with the American Friends of the Hebrew University. Paul lived in Berkeley for many years, and Cora Du Bois, "Paul Radin," xv–xvi, mentions how acquisitive he was of books, particularly on the topic of comparative religion. Some of these may have made their way to Jerusalem with Max's library. Paul Radin's name is stamped on the copy of Frazer's six-volume translation of Pausanius in the National and University Library there.

45. Murphy, *Robert Lowie*, 31.

46. Fred Beuttler, "For the World at Large: Intergroup Activities at the Jewish Theological Seminary," in *Tradition Renewed: A History of the Jewish Theological Seminary of America*, ed. Jack Wertheimer (New York: Jewish Theological Seminary of America, 1997), 2:667–735; Goldberg, "Finkelstein's *The Jews*." Lowie did participate and present a paper in one of Finkelstein's conferences. See his "Parochialism and Historic Instruction," in *Learning and World Peace: Eighth Symposium of the Conference on Science, Philosophy and Religion*, ed. L. Bryson, R. M. MacIver, and L. Finkelstein (New York: Harper, 1948), 89–98.

47. Lowie, *Letters from Edward Sapir*, 58–59, March 25, 1926.

48. Sapir to Lowie, July 5, 1917, Bancroft Library.

49. Radin to Lowie, September 25, 1920, Bancroft Library.

50. Sapir to Lowie, March 21, 1925, Bancroft Library.

51. Lowie, in his last book, partially acknowledges that level of criticism. In

reference to his *Primitive Religion* he says, "the American super-intelligentsia—Goldenweiser, Radin, Benedict, Sapir—had decreed ... that I was devoid of imagination, hence incapable of dealing with religious consciousness" (*Robert H. Lowie*, 133).

52. Luella C. Lowie added a footnote to one of the last pages of *Robert H. Lowie* mentioning the books from "his grandfather's collection of Goethe, Schiller, Lessing, von Humboldt, Herder, or Wieland" (170). Compare note 65 below, regarding the family heritage of Claude Lévi-Strauss.

53. Radin, *Primitive Religion*, 76.

54. Lowie, *History of Ethnological Theory* (New York: Rinehart, 1937), 192, 193.

55. Wilhelm Schmidt, *Primitive Revelation*, trans. Joseph J. Baierl (St. Louis: B. Herder, 1939), 221.

56. It should be noted that this particular antisemitic slant did not necessarily feed into National Socialist ideology. As a Catholic, Schmidt was an opponent of Nazism. In a posthumously published article on religion, Lowie notes: "It did not take Hitler long to discover that the churches and the clergy are his implacable enemies" ("Religion in Human Life," *American Anthropologist* 65 [1963]: 532–42). In the early 1950s, Schmidt served as president of the International Congress of Anthropological and Ethnological Sciences, and in that capacity sent a circular to the Hebrew University inviting a delegate from Israel to be present at the Congress (Hebrew University Archives, Social Sciences File no. 2276/2277, Poznanski to Schmidt, May 27, 1952).

57. Thomas Trautmann, *Aryans and British India* (Berkeley and Los Angeles: University of California Press, 1997).

58. Israel Zangwill, foreword to *Monotheism among Primitive Peoples*, by Paul Radin (London: George Allen and Unwin, 1924), 11–14, esp. 13. See also Susannah Heschel, "Revolt of the Colonized: Abraham Geiger's *Wissenschaft des Judentums* as a Challenge to Christian Hegemony in the Academy," *New German Critique* 77 (1999): 61–85.

59. Paul Radin, *Primitive Man as Philosopher* (New York: Appleton, 1927), 368–70.

60. Marvin Harris, *The Rise of Anthropological Theory: A History of Theories of Culture* (Walnut Creek, Calif.: Altamira, 2001), 289–92, discusses debates over the place of religion in Schmidt's anthropology but makes no reference to Radin.

61. Claude Lévi-Strauss, *Tristes Tropiques* (Paris: Plon, 1955); trans. John Russel (New York: Athenum, 1964). Except where noted otherwise, page refer-

ences are to the English translation.

62. *Tristes Tropiques*, 62, 63.

63. Ibid., 63.

64. Ibid., 24.

65. This division is obviously over-schematic. See James Boon, "Lévi-Strauss, Wagner, Romanticism: A Reading Back ...," In *Romantic Motives: Essays on Anthropological Sensibility*, ed. George W. Stocking, History of Anthropology, 6 (Madison: University of Wisconsin Press, 1989), 124–68. But even Lévi-Strauss's Jewishness had a strong French side to it. His great-grandfather, Isaac Strauss (1806–1888), had lent his private collection of ritual artifacts to the Exposition Universelle in Paris in 1878, and the collection eventually was incorporated into the Musée de Cluny. See Barbara Kirshenblatt-Gimblett, *Destination Culture: Tourism, Museums and Heritage* (Berkeley and Los Angeles: University of California Press, 1998), 81, and Feldman, "Jewish Roots," 113.

66. Lévi-Strauss, *Tristes Tropiques*, 215. Referring to the continuation of this passage, which leads to a discussion of the etiquette of eating, John Cuddihy offers an interpretation of Lévi-Strauss's work that links ancient religious associations with Jews' moves toward entrance into contemporary European society (*The Ordeal of Civility: Freud, Marx, Lévi-Strauss, and the Jewish Struggle with Modernity* [New York: Basic Books, 1974], 156–60).

67. See, among others, Clifford Geertz, "The Cerebral Savage: On Work of Claude Lévi-Strauss," in *The Interpretation of Cultures: Selected Essays* (New York: Basic Books, 1973), 345–59. Writing from another perspective, Johannes Fabian, *Time and the Other: How Anthropology Makes its Object* (New York: Columbia University Press, 2002), 67, notes how Lévi-Strauss's discussion of fieldwork emphasizes the term "observation" without being joined to "participant" as is characteristic of much ethnographic research. Consider, also, the passion evoked by Lévi-Strauss when he reads Lowie's analyses of South American social structures in the passage quoted in the text at note 63. These reflections coincide with my own personal perceptions during his trip to Jerusalem in 1984–85. Lévi-Strauss provides his own thoughts on that visit in Didier Eribon, *Conversations with Claude Lévi-Strauss*, trans. Paula Wissing (Chicago: University of Chicago Press, 1991), 155–58. In that book, Lévi-Strauss also shares with the reader how he was characterized by Simone de Beauvoir, who decribed his "detached voice" and "deadpan expression" (12). See also Feldman, "Jewish Roots."

68. See both their responses in Goldberg, "Finkelstein's *The Jews*," 204.

69. *Robert H. Lowie*, 144.

70. Lévi-Strauss, *Tristes Tropiques*, 64.
71. Lévi Strauss, *Tristes Tropiques* (French edition), 65; English translation, 64. This probably refers to the Yana speaker to whom the name Ishi was given and who worked with Kroeber for many years. See Theodora Kroeber, *ISHI in Two Worlds: A Biography of the Last Wild Indian in North America* (Berkeley and Los Angeles: University of California Press, 1961). Darnell, *Edward Sapir*, following p. 172, includes a 1915 photograph of Ishi with beside him Radin, Sapir, Lowie, and T. T. Waterman, who was a student of Kroeber's. That summer, Sapir worked on the Yana language with Ishi (Kroeber, *ISHI*, 148).
72. Lévi-Strauss, *Tristes Tropiques*, 64.
73. Eribon, *Conversations*, 156. But this might be a simplification, given that young Claude studied Hebrew in preparation for a Bar Mitzvah, which he mentions in his conversations with Eribon and also referred to in a casual remark during his visit to Jerusalem (in my presence). Feldman, "Jewish Roots," 115, highlights the challenge in understanding what Jewishness means to Lévi-Strauss: "The actual model of Jewishness that emerges from Lévi-Strauss' responses [to Eribon] is difficult to categorize and frustrating to reduce to type."
74. Claude Lévi-Strauss, *Totemism*, trans. Rodney Needham (Boston: Beacon, 1963).
75. Eribon, *Conversations*, 67.
76. Ismar Schorsch, "From Wolfenbüttel to Wissenschaft: The Divergent Paths of Isaak Markus Jost and Leopold Zunz," in *From Text to Context*, 233–54, esp. 236; Heschel, "Revolt of the Colonized."
77. C. Lévi-Strauss, *The Scope of Anthropology*, trans. S. O. Paul and R. Paul (London: Jonathan Cape, 1967), 52–53.

JEWS IN CENTRAL EUROPE

ON CONVERSION AND INTERMARRIAGE

The Evidence of Nineteenth-Century Hungarian Orthodox Rabbinic Writings

DAVID ELLENSON

Upon receiving the Jewish Cultural Achievement Award in Historical Studies from the National Foundation for Jewish Culture in 2003, Ismar Schorsch reflected on his own contributions to modern Jewish historiography and explained what motivated his intellectual commitments:

> What fascinated me about the turn to history in modern Judaism was the introduction of time into a religion predicated on timelessness. The rabbinic axiom that the Torah is indifferent to chronology reflected a pervasive bias against historical thinking. Instead the midrashic imagination created the paradox of a canon without closure. The power of a revealed text spawned an infinity of meanings. Not only did commentary emerge as the quintessential Jewish literary genre, but it also promoted a dialogue across the ages.

He then went on to contrast the approach of the historian to that of the textual exegete: "Historical thinking was bent on getting at the author's intent. The provenance of the text became paramount. Context provided the key to understanding the text."[1]

In identifying the notion of "text and context" as the novel contribution that *Wissenschaft des Judentums* made to modern Jewish consciousness, Ismar Schorsch did more than identify the leit-motif of his own considerable scholarship. He pointed to a historical approach that has guided many of us who have been his students—both in the classroom and through his writings.

In my own case, I was privileged to first meet Ismar Schorsch during the 1970s when I was a graduate student at Columbia University. At that time he did me the great favor of reading the entire manuscript of my doctoral dissertation on Rabbi Esriel Hildeshei-mer of Germany, and his many corrections and insights into that text immeasurably improved the book I eventually wrote on Hildesheimer.[2] The Chancellor subsequently invited me to speak at a symposium held at the Jewish Theological Seminary in 1981 on "Orthodox Rabbinical Responses to Conversion in the Modern Period," thereby sparking what has now been two decades of my abiding interest in this topic. My debt to him has, therefore, been considerable, and has only deepened during these last four years that I have served as President of Hebrew Union College – Jewish Institute of Religion. He serves as a model for me of how one can combine scholarly integrity with communal and institutional commitment, as I myself attempt to confront the considerable ongoing challenges of leading a Jewish seminary in the modern world.

The essay that follows presents and analyzes diverse homiletic and halachic sources that derive from representative and prominent members of the nineteenth-century Hungarian Orthodox rabbinate and their milieu. In writing on the topic of rabbinic views of conversion to Judaism, I consider these texts in light of the political and social conditions as well as the denominational fractiousness that marked that era. These writings are illuminated by their context and in turn may be used to explore the distinct and evolving ways in which these Central European rabbis sought to sustain Jewish communal integrity and religious life over the course of the 1800s. Such an essay takes up a theme Professor Schorsch first assigned me and replicates the historical approach that has always been the hallmark of his work. It will hopefully be an appropriate expression of my gratitude to him.

At the turn of the eighteenth century and during the first years of the nineteenth, the impact of Emancipation and Enlightenment on Jewish religion and society in Hungary, which would eventually be considerable, was as yet felt barely, if at all, and religious observance still overwhelmingly marked the Jewish community. The Reform movement had not yet arisen as a major force on the Central European Jewish scene. Endogamy was still the rule, as significant interaction between Jews and Christians as social equals was still extremely rare. This apparent quiescence is reflected in the sermons and legal opinions written by Orthodox rabbis of the period, as exemplified by a sermon delivered by Rabbi Moses Schreiber (1768–1839) of Pressburg (Bratislava) on Purim in 1795.

Better known as the Hatam Sofer, Rabbi Schreiber is famed historically as the architect of "ultra-Orthodox Judaism." It was he who popularized the mishnaic statement *ḥadash asur min ha-torah* "all innovation is forbidden by the Torah" (*'Orla* 3:9), to condemn even the slightest deviation from received Jewish custom and practice as a major violation of Jewish law. While the Hatam Sofer regularly employed his legal writings and sermons to inveigh against religious and social trends that he found disturbing,[3] he apparently felt no need in these twilight years of the eighteenth century and on into the initial years of the 1800s to express any alarm over conversion or intermarriage. His Purim sermon attests to the calm still surrounding these issues in the Central European Jewish world of the time.

At the outset of his homily, Rabbi Schreiber commented on *Yevamot* 109b, where the Talmud states that proselytes cause "evil" (*ra'*) to befall Israel. Schreiber interpreted this statement as embodying rabbinic objection to the tendency, ascribed to some converts, to observe the commandments in an overly scrupulous manner. Such super-strict adherence to Jewish practices established a standard of Jewish conduct few born Jews could attain. Here the Hatam Sofer clearly drew on select classical Jewish teachings that articulate a positive attitude toward proselytes and their exemplary patterns of conduct.

Schreiber then addressed the traditional rabbinical opposition to conversion for any ulterior motive (*le-shem davar*).[4] According to Jewish tradition, the motives of one who would enter "under the wings of the Divine Presence" should be as selfless as those of the archetypal convert, Ruth. However, that same tradition spoke of the many proselytes welcomed by Mordecai after the evil Haman and the enemies of the Jews had been routed. These converts were seen as coming to Judaism because they now feared the power of the Jews, as described in the final chapter of the book of Esther. The Hatam Sofer—who viewed all the laws of Judaism as eternal—thus felt constrained to explain how Mordecai could ignore the proscription forbidding the acceptance of proselytes motivated to convert for other than purely spiritual reasons.

The Hatam Sofer resolved this dilemma by recourse to the famous talmudic story found in *Shabbat* 31a where a prospective convert says to the great tannaitic sage Hillel, "Convert me on the condition that you teach me all the Torah while I stand on one foot," to which Hillel responded, "That which is hateful to you, do not do to your friend." According to medieval rabbinic commentary, Hillel brought this man into the Jewish fold despite his unreasonable demand because he regarded the gentile as one who had begun a process of instruction in Torah that would ultimately transform him into a selfless adherent of Judaism (*mittokh she-lo li-shmah, ba li-shmah*).

Mordecai, Schreiber argued, had done nothing more than follow Hillel's precedent. While he received into the fold proselytes whose motives could initially be regarded as suspect, Mordecai knew "in his soul that he would study Torah with them so that even though they did not initially come for selfless motives, they ultimately would do so (*she-lo li-shmah, yihyeh li-shmah*). These persons were destined to become righteous proselytes, for they stood "in awe of the Torah and its commandments as well as the One Who commanded it." Rabbi Schreiber proclaimed, "The rivers clap in great joy," because even the descendants of the evil Haman became "righteous proselytes." The entrance of these individuals into the Jewish fold therefore immeasurably enriched "the Jewish world" (*tevel yisra'eli*).[5]

Schreiber's positive attitude toward conversion is also reflected in his legal writings. In an 1810 responsum, he referred to an earlier case confronting a seventeenth-century rabbi. A man came to him with suspicions that his gentile maidservant had replaced his own newborn son, who he feared had died at birth, with her own baby boy. However, the man was uncertain. The man wanted to know whether this child, who he suspected was not his son, should be circumcised by a *mohel* and raised as a Jew. The rabbi, the Hatam Sofer reported, ruled that the child should be circumcised for two reasons. One, the man was not positive that the child was not actually his. If the child was his, then the son should certainly enter into the Covenant of Abraham. Second, even if the child was a gentile, "What do we lose if we enter the son of a gentile under the wings of the *Shekhinah*? Circumcise him!"

The Hatam Sofer, in commenting on the ruling of this rabbi, stated that the rabbi's instruction was incomplete. The child's uncertain halachic status (*safeq yisra'el safeq goy*) could have been completely remedied by having the child immersed in a *miqveh* through the agency of a *bet din* "for the sake of conversion."[6]

In another responsum, the Hatam Sofer was asked whether one ought to recite the blessing for conversion over a minor (*ger qatan*) who is brought by his mother for conversion through the agency of a *bet din*. While *Ketuvot* 11a provides a warrant for this practice, the *Shulḥan Arukh, Yoreh De'ah* 268:7, asserts that such a child has the right to protest and annul his conversion when he matures. The blessing said at the time of his conversion might therefore become, in retrospect, a "blessing in vain," and the rabbi in the case at hand therefore feared that it perhaps ought not to be recited to begin with. The Hatam Sofer acknowledged that a strict reading of the law might well lead to such a conclusion. However, while an *ex post facto* act of renunciation of Judaism was theoretically possible, the Hatam Sofer stated, "We have not heard of such a thing when the mother brings him." The blessing should be recited.[7]

In analyzing the variety and subsequent evolution of Hungarian Orthodox rabbinical attitudes toward conversion, these three texts are significant for several reasons. First and foremost is the fact that Schreiber offered no objection to conversion on either religious or social grounds. Second, he adopted legalistically lenient positions, which testified to his assumption that converted children would be raised in a traditional Jewish community. Indeed, in the second responsum, he not only presumed that the child would be raised as an observant Jew, but he clearly found it unimaginable that a child raised in such an environment would ever wish to repudiate his Jewishness. Schreiber's acceptance in these responsa indicates that while Jewish–gentile contacts did occur, leading to issues related to conversion to Judaism, neither assimilation nor intermarriage was yet a problem that he felt compelled to combat within his community at this point in its history.

By 1817, there were early signs of the emergence of a Reform movement in European Judaism. The Hatam Sofer himself inveighed against Reform in *Ele divrey ha-brit* (1819), and in an oft-quoted responsum written several years later, he stated that if secular law permitted it, "In my opinion it would be advisable to push them [the Reformers] beyond our borders. Our daughters would not be given to their sons, nor our sons to their daughters—they to theirs and ours to ours."[8]

The Hatam Sofer recognized that his position in this responsum was completely theoretical, as the governmental authorities would not grant such power of excommunication to the Orthodox rabbinate. Nevertheless, this responsum attests to a Jewish world in which the Orthodox rabbinate could no longer take the religious traditionalism of the community for granted.

A responsum by Rabbi Akiva Eger (1761–1837) at this time makes plain how this realization shaped rabbinic rulings on conversion. Though he served for most of his career in Prussian Posen, Eger was born in Eisenstadt (then a Hungarian city) and was educated in Hungarian *yeshivot*. A cherished colleague of the Hatam Sofer, the two were so close that Eger's daughter became the Hatam Sofer's second wife after the death of his first wife. Eger was, thus, an intimate of the foremost circles of the Hungarian Orthodox rabbinate. His responsum addresses the question of "an uncircumcised gentile" who had approached a rabbi and asked the rabbi to circumcise and convert him to Judaism.[9]

At the outset of his responsum, Rabbi Eger noted that the rabbi who sent him this query was concerned, first of all, about the illegality of conversion to Judaism, such acts being then forbidden "by the law of the kingdom." Governmental prohibition of conversion to Judaism was quite common in many parts of Central Europe during much of the nineteenth century. Indeed, while the Hungarian government granted equality to Judaism as a state-recognized religion in 1867, it would not recognize the right of a Christian to convert to Judaism until 1895.[10] Eger was sensitive to this reality, and he pronounced, for the record, that all Jews—and especially a rabbi—must of course obey the dictates of the king. Consequently, in those regions where conversion to Judaism was prohibited, the rabbi should surely not officiate at a conversion.

Having addressed this significant practical concern, Eger then went on to address the issue of conversion itself. After all, the prospective convert had told the rabbi that he intended to travel to a locale where conversion to Judaism was legally permitted. Therefore, he did not ask the rabbi in the case to convert him, but only asked that he teach him Bible (*miqra*) and the daily prayers. While this was not against the law, strictly speaking, the rabbi was still wary of giving religious instruction to this would-be Jew; he therefore asked Eger whether he was permitted to teach the prospective convert, bearing in mind that a talmudic rule forbade instructing a gentile in Torah. The rabbi asked Eger whether this rule applied, as well, to a gentile who intended to convert.[11] Eger responded by first citing the dictum of the Maharsha (Rabbi Samuel Eliezer ben Judah Halevi Edels, 1555–1631), who, commenting on the well-known story of Hillel in *Shabbat* 31a, concluded that one need not be concerned about the admonition "One who instructs a gentile in Torah deserves death," as the deed of Hillel indicated that "it is permitted to teach Torah to a gentile who comes for purposes of conversion."

Yet, alhough Eger cited the Maharsha, he sought to limit the application of the ruling advanced by the early modern sage. On the basis of a comment in the Tosafot on *Yevamot* 24b, Eger stated that Hillel knew that this man desired to convert for the sake of heaven. Hillel therefore converted him immediately—prior to offering him instruction. As no contemporary rabbi possessed the wisdom of Hillel, no present-day authority could follow his example. Consequently, the ruling of the Maharsha was irrelevant for modern-day rabbis. Eger therefore refused to grant his questioner permission to offer this potential convert instruction. In so doing, Rabbi Eger effectively banned conversion in almost all cases. The logic of his position meant that no rabbi could any longer instruct a gentile who desired to become a Jew, nor could any rabbi claim sufficient insight to know *a priori*—as Hillel had—the motives of a would-be proselyte.

The Eger responsum thus contrasts in its strict interpretation with the sort of leniency previously allowed by the Hatam Sofer in matters related to conversion and illustrates how the attitudes of one segment of the traditional rabbinate had begun to shift. This strict ruling reflects a social-religious context in which Reform had arisen, where Jewish–gentile social interaction was now beginning to occur with greater frequency, and where the religious behavior of converts, after conversion, could no longer be taken for granted.

However, this was not the only Orthodox rabbinic response to the new situation. Rabbi Eliyahu Guttmacher of Posen reacted in a radically different manner to this transformed reality. An analysis of his writings will reveal this other response.

❧

Eliyahu Guttmacher (1795–1874) was a well-known mid-nineteenth-century Central European rabbi, born in Borek, Posen. As a youth, he studied with Akiva Eger, and throughout his lifetime Guttmacher regarded Eger as his most outstanding teacher. His writings on conversion therefore grant us another insight into the evolving approaches regarding conversion that informed the Orthodox rabbinate in the Central European orbit.

Writing in 1858, he dealt with a case in which a Gentile man in Mezeritsch desired to convert so that he could marry the young orphaned Jewish woman whom he loved. The rabbi who posed the question to R. Guttmacher believed the young man probably would become pious. The prospective *ger* had studied and apparently accepted the Thirteen Principles of Maimonides as the authoritative beliefs of Jewish faith and he had familiarized himself with the *siddur* and the traditional order of Jewish prayer. The rabbi was therefore inclined to carry out the conversion. However, he wanted R. Guttmacher's approval before performing this ritual act.[12]

R. Guttmacher initially noted that while it was Jewishly permissible for the rabbi to accept this young man as a proselyte, the young man should produce a secular legal document stating that it was legally permissible for him to do so before the rabbi could conduct the conversion. Guttmacher was clearly concerned about complying with the regulations of the secular authorities, just as his teacher Rabbi Eger had been. Yet whereas Eger refused to permit instruction in Torah for a gentile who would later undergo the ritual of conversion in a community where this was permitted—and thus presumably halted the entire procedure—Rabbi Guttmacher merely insisted on obtaining a permit from the secular government before allowing the conversion.

Guttmacher then turned his attention to the substantive matter of Jewish law in the matter before him and focused the first part of his discussion on the passage in *Yevamot* 109b concering the "evil" which will befall those who convert gentiles to Judaism. Basing himself on the commentary of the medieval Tosafot on this passage, Guttmacher, quickly limited the scope of this dictum by claiming that it applied only to those who converted gentiles to Judaism precipitously or to those who sought out gentiles in order to solicit their conversion. In his opinion, active proselytizing on the part of Jews was forbidden.

In the case of individual gentiles who sought admission on their own into the Jewish people, however, R. Guttmacher adopted a different attitude—even when this request derived from a yearning for a Jewish mate. Indeed, he claimed that there was greater "accountability" (*ahra'iyut*) for those rabbis who "rebuffed" (*dehiyyah*) such would-be converts than for those rabbis who accepted these persons into the Jewish faith, despite their nonspiritual motives, and even if legitimate doubt remained about the sincerity of their declaration of intent to become completely observant following their conversion. R. Guttmacher stated that the law (*din*) supported this stance because, even if a convert misled the rabbinic court about his intent to observe the commandments, the conversion was still upheld as valid once the appropriate rites of entry were performed under the supervision of a qualified *bet din*.

Furthermore, if the candidate for conversion was worthy and the rabbinic court rejected him, the damage to the Jewish people was potentially catastrophic. R. Guttmacher thus opposed the stance of his teacher, Rabbi Akiva Eger, and justified his own position on the basis of an aggada (*Sanhedrin* 99b) concerning Timna and the Jewish Patriarchs—Abraham, Isaac, and Jacob. According to this legend, Timna approached the Patriarchs and beseeched them to convert her to Judaism. However, they refused her request because they believed her desire was impure: they felt she was motivated to enter Judaism by her love for the Patriarchs alone.

Guttmacher went on to note that as a result of their rejection, Timna was prevented from building a faithful household (*bayit ne'eman*) in Israel. Instead, she married a non-Jew and the Jewish people were ultimately severely punished, for, according to Jewish lore, Timna bore Amalek, the eternal archetype of all enemies and persecutors of the Jewish people.

Guttmacher argued that the Patriarchs would have better served the Jewish people had they adopted the lenient example set by Hillel. Here Guttmacher again differed with his teacher, R. Eger—Eger having refused to grant present-day legitimacy to conversion based on Hillel's precedent. Guttmacher held, rather, that those rabbis who would be stringent in regard to conversion should bear in mind their own burden of culpability (*aḥra'iyut*); for rejecting "a good soul" (*nefesh ṭov*) constituted a graver threat to the Jewish people than the responsibility involved in accepting an individual "who was not worthy" (*eino ra'uy*).

As a result of these considerations, R. Guttmacher ruled that the rabbi should certainly be lenient in this case and accept this gentile man as a convert to Judaism. He stated that it was of little import that he had an orphaned Jewish girl in mind as a future marriage partner. Despite the stricture in *Yoreh De'ah* that decreed that conversion prompted by an "ulterior motive" was not to be allowed, R. Guttmacher did not regard this "ulterior motive" as a decisive ground for rejecting this man's conversion. Rather, he averred, the conversion of this man and his subsequent marriage would constitute the fulfillment of a "great mitzvah" for the Jewish people.

To be sure, nothing in this responsum indicated that R. Guttmacher expected anything less than complete Jewish observance from this potential convert. Nevertheless, R. Guttmacher concluded by stating that he rendered an explicit judgment on this matter precisely because his rabbinic colleagues as well as the Jewish people needed to be aware of the dire consequences that might result from a refusal to accept a potential proselyte. In the contemporary period, there was no reason to fear that converts would cause Israel to stray "from the correct path," because Israel does that without them! "On account of our many sins, lawless violators (*prisim*) now lead our people." Hence, all negative statements about converts no longer apply. Indeed, given the piety of many converts, "Would that we should learn from them" (*halevay*).

Seven years later, Guttmacher adopted a similar position in another case that came before him. Writing in 1865–66, Guttmacher observed that civil governments now commonly permitted civil marriage between Jewish men and non-Jewish women.[13] These couples had no intention of dissolving their bonds, and many of these unions had already produced children. The question that Guttmacher addressed in this responsum was whether such married women could be converted, insofar as they may "desire to enter into the religion of the Jews," and the Jewish "husbands also awaited ... this [act of] kindness (*hesed*)."[14]

In framing his opinion in this way, it is clear that R. Guttmacher was inclined to rule leniently in the particular case before him and accept this young woman into the Jewish fold. Of course, both R. Guttmacher and his rabbinic interrogator knew that there were halachic obstacles to the conversion of such women. Indeed, R. Guttmacher cited these problems at great length. At the same time, he recognized in this responsum—as he had in the previous one—that other precedents could be employed that would permit the conversion and subsequent entry of these women into the Jewish community. He observed that these couples had already fulfilled "their desire," that is, consummated their unions, and as a result, there could no longer be grounds for claiming that their aspiration for conversion was prompted by an ulterior motive. Therefore, Guttmacher concluded that the conversions should be performed for these women. It could even be said that the desire of these women to convert to Judaism "was an act done for the sake of God" (*dvar ha-Shem*).

Advancing an argument that would later be adopted by other modern Orthodox rabbis,[15] R. Guttmacher further contended that such women should be converted to Judaism "in order to save the husband" from violating a Jewish legal prohibition, namely against a Jew having intercourse with a gentile. According to Jewish law, the punishment for a Jewish man having intercourse with a gentile woman was that he would suffer *karet*, excision from heaven. R. Guttmacher felt that the rabbis were duty-bound to prevent such transgressions inasmuch as they had the legal options to do so in these instances. Clearly, the task of the rabbi—insofar as he was able—was to "grant merit" (*le-zakkot*) to Jews.

Finally, R. Guttmacher observed that if each gentile woman married to a Jew converted, then all future children who might issue from these would also be Jews. Any older children, born prior to the conversion of their mothers, should be converted as well. Undoubtedly, Guttmacher was concerned with the unity of the family as well as the status of the non-Jewish spouse and the religious state of his children. These values clearly informed his halachic stance, which was diametrically opposed to that of Rabbi Eger.

In an additional responsum regarding a potential convert and his family, Guttmacher reconfirmed his stance. In this instance, the individual who wished to convert had a Jewish wife who had previously apostatized from Judaism and embraced Christianity. Currently pregnant, this woman already had given birth to a son and daughter fathered by this gentile man. She had stated that she and her children now wanted to return to Judaism, and her husband expressed a desire to convert. However, the rabbi who posed this question to R. Guttmacher stated there was apparently an ulterior motive involved, for the wife's Jewish mother, as well as the wife's Jewish siblings, had stated that they would share the family's apparently considerable wealth with her and with her husband and children on condition that the entire family embraced Judaism. Thus, R. Guttmacher was being asked not only whether to convert this gentile man to Judaism, but also whether it was legitimate to deal with an entire family seemingly prompted by the base motive of financial gain.[16]

R. Guttmacher began by pointing out that the children were already Jewish from the viewpoint of halachah. After all, Judaism technically does not recognize the possibility of "apostasy," that is, conversion to another religion. The classical reasoning for this is based on the rabbinic dictum put forth in *Sanhedrin* 44a, "A Jew, even when he sins, remains a Jew." While the woman in this case clearly had committed a sin by "marrying" her husband and "converting" to Christianity, her "lawlessness" could not remove her status as a Jew. Therefore, her children—in light of the traditional rule that matrilineal descent is determinative of Jewish status—were Jewish.

R. Guttmacher defined the children as *anusim* (compelled ones), a term reserved in halachic literature for forced converts and others who were not allowed to express their Jewishness publicly through no fault of their own. If the rabbinical court did not accept their father as a convert to Judaism, the children could not be rescued from their "gentile state," even though they were—strictly speaking—Jews. If the father were not accepted as a convert, the rabbis would have "pushed the children away with two hands from the community of Israel."[17]

R. Guttmacher contended that the rabbinical court was therefore obligated to rescue the children from that fate by accepting the father as a convert, even if this act was "a bit contrary to the law" (*qeṣat neged ha-din*).[18] The rabbinic dictum, "Do not say to a man, 'Sin so that your friend will gain merit,'" was not legally applicable in this instance. While the *bet din* might be faulted for committing a "minor sin" in accepting such a candidate as a proselyte, the subsequent mitzvah that would flow from this act would offset this "minor transgression." For should the father convert, he would actually fulfill the biblical commandment, "Be fruitful and multiply."

R. Guttmacher then returned to the oft-quoted passage in *Yevamot* 109b condemning those who accept gentile converts to Judaism, and he again dismissed it as legally irrelevant because its terms were limited by special conditions: It was meant to condemn active efforts at outreach, that is, "to mix strangers (*zarim*) among the Jewish people"; and the rule was applicable only if there was no compelling reason to accept the gentile candidate into Judaism. In this case there had been no outreach efforts to convert the Jewish father—he had approached the rabbi of his own accord. Second, "in this instance, there is good cause and reason" (*ta'am u-sevarah*) to perform the conversion. Consequently, Guttmacher reasoned, "it is a commandment to do so."

Finally, the principle "Everything depends on the judgment of the court" provided an additional warrant for performing the conversion. If the rabbinical court decided that such a conversion constituted a "benefit" (*tovah*) for the Jewish people, then it was imperative—there was a "need" (*ṣorekh*)—for the conversion be conducted so that this man and his family could be ushered into the Jewish community.

R. Guttmacher maintained that the court in question had an obligation to "rescue" the woman and her children—as they were Jews—from the "sin" and "negative influence" of living with a non-Jewish husband and father. Therefore, it was "permissible to accept him" as a convert. While the rabbi and the rabbinical court had good cause to be skeptical as to whether the man would be an observant Jew subsequent to his conversion, it could not be known with certainty that he would return to his former ways. Indeed, he might even become an observant Jew. Therefore, for sake of his family and in light of the precedent concerning Timna in *Sanhedrin* 99, R. Guttmacher concluded by maintaining that the conversion of this man would constitute a "benefit" for the Jewish community. The man should be accepted as a proselyte and the family should be welcomed back into the Jewish people. By converting the father, a "blemish" (*pesul*) would be removed from the family.

Rabbi Guttmacher was no less aware than the Hatam Sofer or his teacher R. Eger that Jewish life in mid-nineteenth-century Hungary and Central Europe was marked by changed social-religious circumstances. His responsa reflect his judgment that the optimal policy for the Orthodox rabbinate to adopt regarding conversion in light of these conditions was one of leniency and accommodation. Other colleagues, including strict interpretationists living in Hungary during this period, disagreed. In their view, only a stringent stance on conversion could save the Jewish community from dissolution in an era of religious reform and non-observance. It is to an analysis of their position that this essay now turns.

When, on July 28, 1849, the government of Lajos Kossuth proclaimed Jewish civic emancipation, it was conditioned on the reform of Judaism and the gathering of a rabbinical assembly that would call for the modernization of the community. In short, Jews were required to abandon their particularity as a prerequisite for full emancipation. Many members of the "enlightened-progressive" sectors of the rabbinate applauded this trend toward "Hungarian nationalism." However, the ultra-Orthodox were bitter opponents of all attempts at modernization. A rabbinical assembly in Mihalowitz in 1866 formally forbade all changes in synagogue ritual and architecture and went so far as to prohibit secular education and the study of foreign languages.[19]

The government itself continued to push for Jewish acculturation into Hungarian life, and in December 1867, a bill sponsored by Minister of Education and Religious Affairs Jozsef Eötvös removed whatever disabilities remained against individual Jews by elevating them to the civil and political status enjoyed by individual Christians. While Judaism itself was still not accorded full status as an "accepted religion" by the government, Eötvös intended to promote further Jewish acculturation by calling a Jewish Congress in 1868–69 that would centralize the institutions of the Hungarian Jewish community and allow the influence of progressive Jewish elements to grow. The Orthodox leadership of Hungary actively resisted all such attempts at centralization. They were successful in promoting their own cause, and the legal unity of the Hungarian Jewish community was soon broken. The government permitted the Orthodox to create their own educational and administrative institutions apart from liberal elements in the community. While intermarriage remained at most a marginal phenomenon (by contemporary standards), the rabbinical leadership of the Orthodox community remained keenly aware that "secularist tendencies" had caused the erosion of traditional Judaism even among observant Jews in France and Germany, and they fought tenaciously to resist such outcomes in Hungary. All this provides the backdrop for the response the Orthodox rabbinate would now display toward conversion.[20]

In one responsum, Rabbi Judah Aszod (1794–1866), *Dayan* and *Rosh Yeshivah* of Dunaszerdahely, addressed the question of an abandoned, four-year-old, partially circumcised boy of unknown lineage (*asufi*), whom a Jewish couple wished to adopt as their own. The boy was found in a city where a majority of the citizens were non-Jewish, and the parents wanted to know if a conversion was required.

R. Aszod stated that there was no reason to assume that this boy was Jewish. While he was partially circumcised and there was, therefore, some possibility that he was Jewish, there were stronger grounds to assume that he was not. After all, the boy did not speak any Yiddish. R. Aszod further claimed that if the mother had been Jewish, then she would have left him in a Jewish neighborhood, as Jews are known as *rahmanim bnei rahmanim* (compassionate people who are the children of compassionate people). Yet he was left in a lodging (*akhsanyah*) of gentiles. Finally, in a city where the majority of residents were non-Jewish, R. Aszod ruled that there was no question but that the boy should be considered a non-Jew. He surely required *hattafat dam brit* in order to be converted. Indeed, even if he were a Jew with an improper circumcision, a number of authorities ruled that he would need to be recircumcised (Rashi, Ran, Turei Zahav, and the Tur). R. Aszod held that this boy needed to be immersed and circumcised no less than any other gentile who would seek entry into Judaism and the Jewish people.

Though R. Aszod acknowledged that it was halachically permissible to convert this boy, he ruled that such a conversion not be performed. First, there was no obligation to bring a minor child like this into the Jewish community. Indeed, R. Aszod advised the prospective parents that they should wait until the boy was sufficiently old to seek conversion on his own. He clearly feared that in the world of contemporary Hungarian Jewry, the boy might well be nonobservant. Better for him to remain an unconverted gentile living among Jews than to admit him formally into the community. The era when the Hatam Sofer could approvingly cite a rabbi who wrote, "What do we lose if we enter the son of a gentile under the wings of the *Shekhinah*? Circumcise him," had long since passed. Indeed, R. Aszod believed that the optimal policy for the Jewish couple to pursue would be to send the boy out into the world—to a judge or magistrate—and have the secular authorities assign custody so that neither the individual Jews involved nor the community could be accused of any perfidious act. His perception of the precarious position in the world occupied by Jews despite emancipation, combined with his determination to defend the tradition against the dissolution threatened by changing social and religious norms, led him to issue an opinion that was completely at odds with the position R. Guttmacher had adopted.[21]

Rabbi Akiba Yosef Schlesinger (1837–1922) was born in Pressburg (Bratislava) and grew up to become one of the most extreme spokesmen for ultra-Orthodox Judaism in the modern world.[22] His "Note on the Acceptance of Converts Who Have Increased in Our Time" appended to the second edition of his *Lev ha-'ivri*, first published in 1865, reflected the attitude toward conversion that had now come to dominate the most extreme elements in the Hungarian Orthodox community. Schlesinger complained that his was a lawless era in which every person "does what is right in his eyes" and follows the ways of the gentiles. He criticized, as well, the majority of persons who had internalized a modern notion of "freedom of religion" (*ḥeirut ha-dat*). As a result of these conditions, he claimed, the "number of persons who attach themselves to the House of Jacob has increased." Schlesinger admonished his fellow Jews to carefully obey the strictures of Judaism, "Know, my brothers, the will of God as contained in His Torah and observe His Law."

Schlesinger noted that the Talmud (*Pesachim* 87b) proposed that "God exiled Israel only so that they should add proselytes to the community." However, he countered, the Sages also said, "Proselytes are as troublesome to Israel as a sore" (*Yevamot* 109b). As Rashi, in opposition to other commentators on this passage, commented, "This is because they are not scrupulous in their observance of the commandment, and Israel learns from them." Citing *Yevamot* 24b, he further observed that converts were not to be accepted either in "the days of the messiah, or in the days of David and Solomon," for then one could not be certain whether their motives were selfless.

To be sure, Schlesinger acknowledged that Israel might be redeemed on account of those gentiles whose motives for conversion were pure. He contended that the *Pesachim* passage applied to them. However, the *Yevamot* 109b passage refers to those who converted for ulterior motives—either out of fear of Jewish power or on account of "their lust" for Jewish partners. These people were "the mixed multitude," mentioned in the Exodus 12:38, who attached themselves to Israel during the time of the exodus from Egypt, and from whom have descended those Jews who have oppressed us "in our generation," "those Sadducees and heretics, who are not descended [genuinely] from the Children of Israel." It would have been better had they remained in their gentile state, for these apostates are "worse than idolaters." These are the people of whom the Talmud says (in *Niddah* 13b), "These converts delay the coming of the Messiah." Why should one be surprised that "the heretics" among our people, that is, the Reform, have accepted them? After all, "One species of heretic has found another of his kind." Indeed, Israel would rejoice if those Jews who follow the ways of the gentiles would actually leave the Jewish fold altogether.

R. Schlesinger continued his polemic by pointing out, as had R. Eger, that the seemingly expansive and inclusive precedent involving Hillel in *Shabbat* 31a was actually more restrictive than commonly interpreted. Citing the writings of Isaac Luria, Schlesinger argued that Hillel converted persons during the tannaitic period whose motives were seemingly not selfless because he recognized "the root of their souls," that is, he knew that their intentions were ultimately pure. However, he asserted, "we" today are not the equals of Hillel and are unable to rely on "such esoteric teachings" and insights. Instead, the community must rely solely on "the words of this Torah that are written in our pure *Shulḥan Arukh*, which states that prospective converts should be discouraged from entering the Jewish people." And, as prominent rabbinic authorities commenting on the halacha in *Yoreh De'ah*

268:2 state, "We need to threaten the would-be proselyte. Perhaps in this way, we will separate him from Israel."

Schlesinger concurred: "It seems to me that in our day, everyone needs to do their utmost to discourage them." As we are not oppressed as in previous generations, "we need to do our utmost to be stringent with them. Righteous proselytes alone" are to be accepted, not those who "innovate the religion or perform the commandments according to their [own personal] viewpoint." Converts must accept all the Torah, neither adding to nor subtracting from it. Should they reject even a single law, they are themselves to be rejected (*Bechorot* 30b).

The Talmud (*Yevamot* 109b) therefore says, "Evil after evil befalls those who "jump to increase converts and apostates" (*meshummadim*). Schlesinger concluded his diatribe by saying, "Guard your spirit, and after careful examination," be certain that prospective converts will be "complete (*shalem*) Jews, distinguished [from non-Jews] by name, language, and dress, and by the wearing of ritual fringes, earlocks, and a beard." Only then should converts be accepted into the Jewish people, and not to the community of "the Sadducees, God forbid."

The vehement, if not fanatical, attitude Schlesinger expressed regarding conversion in the modern era cannot be viewed apart from the vitriolic judgment he passed against religious Reform in particular and in terms of his opposition to acculturation in general. The issue of conversions was just one dimension of this larger ideological struggle and was decided on the basis of his uncompromising determination to protect traditional Judaism from all internal and external threats.

The responsa of his older colleague, Maharam Schick (1807–1879), display exactly the same sentiments. Educated in Pressburg under the tutelage of the Hatam Sofer himself, R. Schick served in Hungary throughout his career and was rabbi in Hurst from 1861 until his death. In a responsum written in the 1870s concerning a baby boy born to a Jewish mother and gentile father,

Rabbi Schick acknowledged Jewish law did impose an obligation on a *bet din* to circumcise such a child.[23] After all, the boy was halachically Jewish, as his mother was a Jew. Nevertheless, R. Schick argued that the court was not required to fulfill its mandate in this instance. The rabbinical court had the same right to deny services to this boy born of an intermarried Jewish mother as it would have in the instance of a "Jewish sectarian," such as a Karaite. The mother, as evidenced by her union with a non-Jewish man, was no better than such heretics, and privileges that would normally be accorded a Jew under halachic prescriptions could legitimately be denied her offspring. Indeed, R. Schick believed that the Jewish community should, as a matter of urgent policy, "be distant from them. We have no obligation to attach them in anyway [to our people and our religion]."

R. Schick recognized that his ruling represented a stringent departure from normative Jewish practice—after all, the child's mother was Jewish—and he conceded that many rabbinic colleagues would disagree with his ruling.

Nevertheless, he insisted that his decision against circumcising the child was proper policy for the Orthodox community to adopt, as the erection of "such a fence and border might well establish a boundary that would prevent licentiousness and put a stop to Jewish women marrying gentile men." Citing the stipulation in *Yoreh De'ah* 334:1, "Excommunication is imposed on one who deserves it, even if there is reason to assume that this will cause his defection from the fold," as a warrant for his position, R. Schick maintained that "we are authorized to create a 'fence for the Torah' (*seyag la-torah*) here" and not perform the circumcision.

To be sure, R. Schick concluded his responsum by urging other rabbis to agree to this ruling. For, he observed, in "this licentious generation (*dor paruṣ ha-zeh*) it may well be that "sinners" who marry gentile men and women will not consider the commandment of circumcision to be of import. Such a "fence" might well prove ineffectual. Indeed, such persons might even rejoice in such a prohibition. Therefore, each rabbi must exercise "discretion" (*shiqqul da'at*) before erecting such a "fence."

In an 1875 responsum,[24] R. Schick dealt with the same issue once again and expressed a view identical to the one he had articulated in the first responsum. Here the case involved a widow married to a non-Jewish man in a civil ceremony, despite receiving several warnings not to do so. She was now pregnant by her non-Jewish husband. She already had one son from her first husband (presumably Jewish), and the rabbi who posed the question wanted R. Schick to instruct him as to whether he should refuse to circumcise a new son should one be born to this "shameless woman" (*ha-prisah ha-hi*) as a result of her union with this "uncircumcised man" (*'arel*).

R. Schick noted once again that according to the law, such children should be circumcised. However, he repeated the position reported above and argued that there was reason—perhaps even an obligation—to go against convention "in order to stand in the breach against this evil woman in this licentious generation." Otherwise, others might follow her example and commit this "abomination" (*to'evah*). Schick added, "We should not fear being stringent here, even if this causes her to apostatize." Indeed, she should be expelled from the synagogue and not be allowed to purchase kosher meat. "Anything that can possibly be done to distance her from Judaism" should be done, for she has "no portion or inheritance in our midst. The truth is that such a great act of abomination should arouse the children of Israel to stand in the breach."

Schick went so far as to cite the *Shulḥan Arukh, Even Ha-'ezer* 260:16, which states that a woman who intermarries should be flogged, as she has violated an injunction of the Torah. He urged all Jews to heed the teachings of Ezra, who taught that Jews who intermarry sin against God and disobey His commandments. Employing the same phrase that the Hatam Sofer had used regarding religious Reformers, R. Schick stated, "Your daughters should not be given to their sons, nor your sons to their daughters."

R. Schick did acknowledge, once again, that the law required the *bet din* to circumcise the boy. But he once more stated that the need to establish "a fence around the Torah" trumped the law in this instance. Any community that has the ability to "erect a fence" that would strengthen Judaism is required to do so. On the basis of the warrant provided by *Yoreh Deʿah* 334:1, Schick contended that previous generations had not hesitated to refuse circumcision in such cases, and he asserted that they had excommunicated nonobservant Jews, even if that caused them to abandon the Jewish people. He felt that the rabbis of his generation should follow their example and do no less. And, he said in conclusion, should his generation of pious Jews fail to distance itself "from the dwellings of these evil people, ... we might well begin to follow their ways." The need for erecting and upholding a boundary against the forces and individuals that threatened to undermine traditional Judaism justified strong measures.

The stringency and harsh tone evident in these writings testify to the impact of social reality on these rabbis' religious consciousness and, in turn, on their doctrinal rulings. Their writings bespeak the transformations that marked Hungarian and Central European Jewish life during the course of the nineteenth century. The relaxed attitudes that marked the opinions of the Hatam Sofer on conversion during an era when traditional rabbinic leadership could take the religious observance of the community for granted were no longer deemed appropriate by his successors, at a time when large sectors of the community were nonobservant or were attracted to religious reform. While a rabbi such as Guttmacher advocated a policy of inclusion that would retain as many Jews as possible within the ambit of the community, the consensus that ultimately dominated the Hungarian Orthodox rabbinate on matters of conversion and intermarriage was diametrically opposed to the Guttmacher position. Theirs was a reasoned sectarian posture designed to protect "authentic Judaism" from the forces of dissolution that had already undermined and threatened to erode even further a traditional Jewish way of life and belief.

Notes

1. Acceptance speech, "An Appreciative Memoir," at http://www.jtsa.edu/about/communications/speeches/nfjc.shtml.
2. David Ellenson, *Rabbi Esriel Hildesheimer and the Creation of a Modern Jewish Orthodoxy* (Tuscaloosa: University of Alabama Press, 1990).
3. For example, see Haim Hamiel, החת״ם סופר על ריפורם, על העברית, ועל גורל ישראל בין העמים (The Hatam Sofer on reform, Hebrew, and Israel's lot among the nations), *Sinai* 44, no. 3 (Kislev 5724): 164–66.
4. See *Shulḥan Arukh*, *Yoreh De'ah*, 268:12.
5. Hatam Sofer, דרושים ואגרות (Sermons and letters), Sermon 37.
6. שאלות ותשובות החתם סופר (Responsa of the Hatam Sofer), *Even Ha-'ezer*, no. 125.
7. Ibid., *Yoreh De'ah*, no. 253.
8. Ibid., *Ḥoshen Mishpaṭ*, no. 89.
9. תשובות ר' עקיבא איגר (*Teshuvot* Rabbi Akiva Eger), no. 41.
10. Natanel Katzburg, מלחמתם של יהודי הונגריה למען שויון זכויות דתי בשנות ה90 למאה הת״ט (Hungarian Jewry's war for equal religious rights in the 1890s), *Zion* 22, no. 2–3 (5717): 145.
11. The Talmud proscribes the teaching of Torah to gentiles in *Ḥagiga* 13a and *Sanhedrin* 59a.
12. אדרת אליהו, *Yoreh De'ah*, no. 87.
13. See Katzberg, "Hungarian Jewry's War," passim, mentioning in several places that civil marriage between Jews and non-Jews was legal in Hungary during this period.
14. אדרת אליהו, *Yoreh De'ah*, no. 85.
15. See David Tzvi Hoffmann, מלמד להועיל, *Yoreh De'ah*, no. 83, and *Even ha-'ezer*, no. 8.
16. אדרת אליהו, *Yoreh De'ah*, no. 87.
17. For an identical opinion see Rabbi Zvi Hirsch Kalischer of Thorn, in שאלות ותשובות רבי עזריאל (Responsa), *Yoreh De'ah*, no. 229.
18. See Hoffmann, מלמד להועיל, *Yoreh De'ah*, no. 83, where the same reasoning is applied in an identical case.
19. T. D. Kramer, *From Emancipation to Catastrophe* (Lanham, Md.: University

Press of America, 2000), 4–6.

20. Ibid., 7–12, 27.

21. יהודה ועלה, no. 237.

22. For a superb description of Schlesinger, see Michael Silber, "The Emergence of Ultra-Orthodoxy: The Invention of a Tradition," in *The Uses of Tradition*, ed. Jack Wertheimer (New York: JTS, 1992), 23–84. Silber discusses the text considered here on p. 81.

23. Maharam Schick, שאלות ותשובות (Responsa), no. 14.

24. Ibid., *Yoreh De'ah*, no. 249.

GERMANS OR GERMAN-SPEAKING JEWS?

The Case of the Jews of Moravia, 1848–1938

MARSHA L. ROZENBLIT

I n their memoirs, written after the Holocaust changed every-thing, Jews from Moravia remembered that this province of the Habsburg Monarchy, later part of the "Czech" part of Czechoslovakia, contained three distinct groups: Germans, Czechs, and Jews. Joseph Wechsberg, who grew up in Mährisch Ostrau/Ostrava,[1] for example, remembered that "The Czechs spoke Czech, the Poles spoke Polish, the Germans spoke German, the Jews spoke Czech at the tax-collector's office or in court and German among themselves. It was a fine melting pot in which no one really melted."[2] Before World War I, he noted, "the Czechs had been the have-nots and the Germans the haves. The Jews, many of whom spoke German and sided with Vienna, were the almost-haves."[3] All three groups had their own schools: the Czechs sent their children to Czech schools, the Germans to German schools, and the Jews to Jewish school,[4] in which the lan-guage of instruction, he forgets to remind us, probably because it was too obvious to mention, was German.

Memoirists disagree on whether everyone got along, but whether they emphasize good relations or social distance, they all indicate the existence of three groups. Peter (Eisenberg) Erben, who grew up in Frýdek-Mistek in the 1920s, insisted in his memoirs that until the entry of the Wehrmacht in 1939 the Jews "lived on good terms with the Czech and German inhabitants." Indeed, his family had a fine life and the Jews were well liked by everyone.[5] Likewise, Michel Huttarsch, who had the dubious distinction of suffering under the Nazis as a first-degree *Mischling*, that is, someone with two Jewish grandparents (in his case a Jewish mother), and then suffering as a German when the Czechoslovak government expelled all Germans in 1945–46, recalled in his memoirs that before the 1930s, Germans, Czechs, and Jews lived peacefully together in Moravia. He had close relations both with his mother's Jewish relatives in Brünn/Brno and his father's German family in Wachtl, many of whom were radical German nationalists who later became Nazis.[6] Ruth Elias, on the other hand, emphasized the real separation between Jews and Germans in the German girls' gymnasium she attended in Mährisch Ostrau/Ostrava after she completed her four years in the Jewish elementary school. Moreover, she was horrified when her classmates in another school in Troppau/Opava jumped over the border into Germany to kiss the earth. They were *Volksdeutschen* (ethnic Germans), and she, by implication, was a German-speaking Jewish Czechoslovak.[7]

The Jews of Moravia provide an extremely interesting case study of the degree to which Jews in Central Europe became German when they adopted German language and culture in the nineteenth century. Recent studies of nationalism in general and on nationalism in the Habsburg Monarchy and its successor states in particular have emphasized the constructed nature of national identity and the impact of the political context on its development.[8] What better group to study than the Jews, who chose a German identity but crafted one that suited their desire to remain Jews. Moreover, choosing a German identity and holding fast to it was not an obvious choice in the late Habsburg Monarchy. After all, the Monarchy was not a nation-state, but rather a dynastic state not dominated by any particular nation even if the "nationalities conflict" became the central issue in politics. Exploring the German-Jewish identity that the Jews of Moravia constructed in the Habsburg Monarchy and maintained in interwar Czechoslovakia will shed much light on Jewish identity in modernity and on ethnic and national identity in Central Europe.

That the Jews of Moravia eagerly adopted German and identified as members of the German community is very well known. In 1900, fully 77.4 percent of the Jews of Moravia indicated on the census that they used German as their language of daily speech.[9] Even when the rising Czech nationalist movement put a lot of pressure on Jews to switch to Czech language and culture, the largely bilingual Jews of the province continued to adhere to the German identity that they had adopted as they modernized. They did so even though everyone in Habsburg Austria regarded the language rubric of the census to be an indicator of national allegiance. They did so despite the fact that the Czechs, who formed over two thirds of the population in the Bohemian lands—the provinces of Bohemia and Moravia—were clearly ascendant politically and created a situation in which it was expedient for Jews to indicate Czech language on the census. They did so even though the Jews in nearby Bohemia responded to Czech nationalist pressure and increasingly opted for the Czech rubric on the census at the turn of the century.[10] Moreover, the allegiance of Jews to the German language persisted in interwar Czechoslovakia. Moravian Jews may have been extremely loyal to the new Czechoslavak state, and they revered Thomas Masaryk as they had adored the Emperor Franz Joseph, but they continued to speak German and send their children to German schools.

Some of Moravia's Jews presumably went beyond the issues of language and education and considered themselves Germans. Most Moravian Jews, however, felt more comfortable with an identity as German-Jews or German-speaking Jews. They were part of the German cultural community, which they supported tirelessly. They also formed an integral part of the German political community, certainly before World War I when Moravia was part of the Habsburg Monarchy, although less so in interwar Czechoslovakia, whose Germans resented their place in the new state and then became completely radicalized under the influence of Nazi Germany in the 1930s. But for the most part, Jews always considered themselves part of a separate Jewish group in the province, a Germanized Jewish community distinct from the larger community of Germans. That the Germans themselves increasingly turned to biological, *völkisch*, or racial definitions of Germanness which excluded the Jews from the German *Volk* surely intensified the Jewish sense of separateness, but such separateness derived largely from the persistence of both Jewish ethnicity and the social structures to support it.

The Moravian Jewish sense of forming a distinct Jewish group did not derive so much from antisemitic exclusion on the part of the Germans, who in fact rather needed Jewish numbers to maintain the German community and so, before the 1930s, avoided too much overt antisemitism. On the contrary, Moravian Jews maintained a distinct identity as German-Jews because in many of the small communities in which they lived, located in overwhelmingly Czech-speaking South Moravia, they were the Germans, or rather they formed the majority of the German-speaking community. Moreover, a sense of Jewish separateness was fostered by the persistence of the so-called *politische Judengemeinden* (that is, juridically autonomous Jewish towns, distinct from the Jewish religious communities; to be explained below), and by the persistence of a large network of German-Jewish elementary schools, many of which were the public schools of the *politische Judengemeinden*. Finally, a separate Jewish identity enabled Moravian Jews to avoid the nationality conflict by siding neither with the Germans nor with the Czechs, but by simply declaring themselves to be Jews (albeit German-speaking ones). Such an option was not legally available in the Habsburg Monarchy, which forced everyone to declare their language of daily speech *(Umgangssprache)* on the census, a rubric which everyone unofficially regarded as a measure of national belonging. Thus Jews who declared their language to be German were counted as Germans. In interwar Czechoslovakia, however, the dominant Czechs allowed the Jews to declare themselves members of a Jewish nationality if they so desired, and Moravian Jews especially availed themselves of this option. Indeed, on the censuses of 1921 and 1930, over half of the Jews of Moravia declared themselves to be members of the Jewish nationality, a far higher percentage than was true in Bohemia, where only 14 percent did so.[11] Not all of these Jewish nationalists were Zionists. They simply felt that in Czechoslovakia it was better to be a Jew than a German, especially if their primary identity had always been as Jews who spoke German rather than as Germans who practiced Judaism.

This article demonstrates how Jews in Moravia understood their German identities solely in cultural and political, but not ethnic, terms. After surveying how Moravian Jews came to adopt German language and culture, it will explore how Jews formed a part of the German cultural and political community as a distinct Jewish group. Relying on memoirs and on newspaper accounts, it shows that Jews did in fact gain acceptance into the community of Germans, at least before the Germans became utterly radicalized in the 1930s. The article then examines how the German–Jewish schools, which persisted in Moravia into the twentieth century, created a space in which Jews participated in the German cultural community as Jews, absorbing German culture within a Jewish social universe. The last part of the article looks at interwar Czechoslovakia and how Moravian Jews combined loyalty to the state with a German cultural and Jewish ethnic identity.

I. Becoming German

The connection between the Jews of Moravia and German language and culture goes back to the late eighteenth century when
the Austrian emperor Joseph II, who wanted to modernize, centralize, and Germanize his polyglot realm, issued his famous Edicts
of Toleration. These edicts, issued in different years for different
provinces (1782 for Moravia), removed many of the burdensome
restrictions on Jewish economic life, thus enabling Jews to engage
in more respectable and lucrative forms of commerce and industry
than the peddling, horse and cattle dealing, and other forms of
petty trade to which they had long been relegated. In addition,
the edicts (and subsequent legislation) abolished the juridical
autonomy of the Jewish communities, subjected Jews to military
conscription, and required Jews to keep their commercial books
and contracts in German (rather than Yiddish) and to take family
names. Most important, the edicts opened Christian schools to
Jewish students and required Jews either to send their children to
Christian schools (with German the language of instruction) or,
more realistically, to establish their own German-language Jewish
schools. In Galicia and Hungary—the parts of the Habsburg
Empire in which most of the Jews in fact lived—traditional Jews,
allied with local aristocrats who opposed any orders from Vienna,
subverted Joseph II's edict, and few modern German-Jewish
schools came into existence. In Bohemia and Moravia, on the
other hand, no anti-Habsburg aristocracy existed, and Joseph's
bureaucrats managed to co-opt traditional Jewish elites to establish schools that would provide a German secular education to
Jewish children. Initially, these schools offered no Jewish education at all. Jewish children received a basic German education
here during part of the day, and the boys attended traditional che-
der the rest of the time. Later, the schools offered Jewish subjects—Hebrew, Bible, prayers—alongside German reading,
writing, and arithmetic. Within a few generations, the schools

succeeded in transforming the Yiddish-speaking Jews of Bohemia and Moravia into a completely German-speaking community.[12]

In the late eighteenth and early nineteenth centuries, learning German carried little nationalist baggage. German was simply the language within which the central government of a far-flung empire functioned, the language that served as a lingua franca, the language of economic exchange. It was a useful language to know and, for Yiddish-speaking Jews, an easy language to learn. At that point, apart from the largely German-speaking Habsburg hereditary lands (roughly present-day Austria), most German-speakers in Austria were peasants or urban craftsmen and merchants living in the Bohemian and Moravian borderlands, in Bukovina, and in Hungarian Slovakia and Transylvania; or, they were Habsburg officials, professionals, merchants, and industrialists who adopted the German language in order to pursue certain careers in the government or in the economy. "Germans" then were simply those who spoke German, either because they always had done so or because of their economic or political position. One could easily become "German" simply by learning the German language and adopting German culture. Such a reality neatly dovetailed with Enlightenment notions about the acquisition of *Bildung*, that untranslatable term that includes high culture, but also refinement, moral virtue, and social respectability. Many Habsburg subjects, not only Jews, became "German" as they took advantage of an expanding higher education system, which at that time was entirely in German, and adopted new economic and political roles.[13] German identity was not neutral, of course. It included a sense both of the superiority of German culture as a world-class culture and also of the conviction that the "Germans" of the empire were the *Staatsvolk*, the group on whom the empire rested, the people who deserved to dominate politically, culturally, and economically.

Only in the late nineteenth century did German identity rigidify and come to include an ethnic, *völkisch* dimension. In

Bohemia and Moravia, largely in response to the challenge of the growing Czech national movement but also because the Austrian government after 1879 ruled with the support of Slavs (mostly the Poles) rather than the German Liberals, Germans increasingly saw themselves as a beleaguered, endangered group that had to mobilize to protect its rights and privileges. Germans, especially those in the German borderlands, became increasingly shrill as they fought to protect what they deemed German territory from the incursions of the Czechs or other Slavs. Most Germans eschewed the extreme positions of Georg Schönerer's Pan-German Party, which, alongside its vicious antisemitism and anti-Habsburg animus, espoused a radical German nationalism based on a racial definition of the German *Volk*. Yet increasingly the Germans in the Habsburg Monarchy adopted ethnic and biological definitions of Germanness and assumed that there were rigid boundaries between the Germans and everyone else. They came under the influence of German nationalist activists who wanted everyone to adhere to the more rigid definitions of national belonging that they advocated.[14] These activists still insisted that the Germans were the *Staatsvolk*, but now that term had a more ominous meaning, especially to the Czech and other nationalists who resented not only Habsburg domination, but what they perceived as German nationalist hegemony within the Monarchy.

The Jews of Moravia had learned German and adopted German culture in the first half of the nineteenth century, at a time when the more flexible notions of German identity held sway. To them, learning German was profoundly practical, enabling them to take advantage of the economic opportunities open to them because of the end of anti-Jewish restrictions and the growth of the economy. Moreover, in 1848 and especially in 1867, Jews all over Habsburg Austria deeply appreciated that the German Liberals had granted them emancipation. The Austrian government continued to guarantee Jewish equality even after the Liberals no longer dominated, and thus Habsburg Jews felt enormous loyalty to the central government in Vienna, which they regarded as their best protector from antisemitism. The German identity of Jews in the second half of the nineteenth century was bound inseparably to their Habsburg loyalties.[15] For Jews, German identity was linguistic, cultural, and political, but not ethnic or *völkisch*. They remained Jews in an ethnic sense—that is, as members of the Jewish people, a community of descent bound by a common history and destiny. Interestingly, for Jews, German identity was connected to the persistence of a Jewish social milieu conducted in the German language.

Most of the Jews of Moravia lived in towns and small cities in the Czech-speaking southern part of the province. Like Central European Jews in general, they suffered severe restrictions in the late Middle Ages and early modern period, including repeated expulsions. Most cities, especially the five royal free cities, excluded the Jews. In the late eighteenth century, even after the reforms of Joseph II, onerous restrictions on the number of Jews who could marry guaranteed that no more than 5,400 tolerated families had the right to live in the province. In 1798, Emperor Francis II stipulated that Jews could only reside in fifty-two *Judengemeinden*, Jewish communities, which, although they no longer had traditional Jewish autonomy (that is, the right to live according to Jewish law), nonetheless were juridical entities with the same municipal rights as a village, town, or city, including the one in which they were physically located and which bore the same name. These Jewish communities had access to a special fund, the *Landesmassafond*, established by Joseph II in 1787 from various Jewish taxes to support the needs of poor Jewish communities. The Jewish population in Moravia in the first half of the nineteenth century remained quite small. At the time of the Revolution of 1848, there were approximately 37,000 Jews in the province.[16]

Liberal legislation after 1859 guaranteed to the Jews of Moravia—as elsewhere in the Habsburg Monarchy—the right to reside anywhere. Jews were no longer hemmed in by the marriage restrictions or the requirement that they live in a designated number of Jewish communities. They began to move to cities from which they had long been excluded. Yet unlike in Bohemia or Galicia, in Moravia the old *Judengemeinden* continued to exist as independent political entities. The authorities dissolved some of these communities, mostly ones that were too small to be viable, and merged them into the towns in which they were located. But twenty-seven communities—now called *politische Judengemeinden* (or *Israelitengemeinden*)—continued to exist. These new *Judengemeinden*, which formed a geographically distinct part of towns which bore the same name, took care of municipal services for the people who lived within them and, at first, handled Jewish religious services as well. Jews, of course, no longer had to live in them, and they took advantage of the new freedom of movement to move elsewhere—to the larger town of which they formed a part, to other cities, and also in large measure to Vienna—in search of economic and personal opportunities. Many non-Jews moved into the *Judengemeinden*, which were often poor and run-down, especially after the more prosperous Jews had left. Jews who moved to the cities and towns from which Jews had long been excluded organized Jewish religious communities, *Israelitische Kultusgemeinden*, to satisfy their religious needs. In 1890 the Austrian government mandated that only *Israelitische Kultusgemeinden* could administer Jewish religious affairs. As a result, *Israelitische Kultusgemeinden* formed to take care of Jewish religious matters in the *politische Judengemeinden*, leaving the latter in charge only of city services like tax collection, police and fire protection, and schools. The residents of the *Judengemeinden* elected a separate town government and participated as a unit in elections for the Moravian Diet and Austrian Parliament.[17] The special Moravian Jewish *Landesmassafond* also continued to exist, and its funds went to support both Jewish schools and the increasingly financially strapped *politische Judengemeinden*, whose residents could not afford to pay for the city services they provided.[18]

As a result of the freedoms guaranteed by the liberal legislation of 1859, the 1860s, and the emancipation of 1867, the demographic profile of the Jews of Moravia changed dramatically. Many Jews left the old *politische Judengemeinden* in search of economic opportunities elsewhere. The Jewish communities of Brünn/Brno and Mährisch Ostrau/Ostrava grew rapidly. In 1848 there were only 445 Jews in Brünn/Brno, but by 1869, 4,505 Jews resided in the Moravian capital. The number of Jews continued to grow, so that by 1900 the city contained 8,238 Jews, who formed 7.5 percent of the total population of 109,346. The rate of growth was even higher in Mährisch Ostrau/Ostrava, although it contained less than half as many Jews as the capital. In 1848 no Jews lived in the city, and in 1869 it only contained 267 Jews; but by 1900, 3,272 Jews lived there, forming 11 percent of the total population of 30,116. Jews did not flock to Olmütz/Olomouc, Iglau/Jihlava, and Znaim/Znojmo in the same numbers, presumably because economic opportunities were less pronounced than in Brünn/ Brno, a major center of textile production in which many Jews played a prominent role, or than in Mährisch Ostrau/Ostrava, the Moravian center for coal mining and steel production. At the same time, the number of Jews in the *Judengemeinden* declined precipitously. In 1848, 3,670 Jews had resided in the *Judengemeinde* of Nikolsburg/Mikulov, the leading center of talmudic learning in Moravia. By 1880, that number had declined to 1,139, plus 74 other Jews in the town of Nikolsburg itself. In 1900 only 757 Jews lived in the *Judengemeinde* and 143 in the town of Nikolsburg. Similarly, 1,973 Jews lived in the Boskowitz/Boskovice *Judengemeinde* in 1848, but by 1900 that number had declined to 598, plus 252 Jews in the town of Boskowitz/Boskovice itself. On the other hand, especially in areas with economic opportunities, sometimes the Jews simply moved out of the *Judengemeinde* into the city. In Prossnitz/Prostějov, a center of textile production and later also of the clothing industry, the *Judengemeinde* contained

1,742 Jews in 1848. In 1890 only 797 Jews lived in the *Judenge-meinde*, but 953 resided in the "Christian" town. In 1900 the figures were 566 and 987 respectively. Despite migration, including substantial migration to Vienna, the Jewish population of Moravia as a whole grew modestly from 37,585 in 1848 to 42,644 in 1869, and 44,175 in 1880. It remained stable until 1900 (44,255), after which it declined, numbering 41,255 in 1910, 37,989 in 1921, and 34,632 in 1930.[19]

One of the interesting features of Jewish migration within Moravia in the late nineteenth century is that, with the very important exception of Brünn/Brno and Mährisch Ostrau/ Ostrava, German-speaking Jews did not leave the predominantly Czech-speaking southern part of the province to move to the German-speaking north, or even to other cities which were over-whelmingly German. Economic opportunity obviously figured far more prominently in the process of migration than the desire to live with other Germans. To be sure, the Jews who moved to economically prosperous industrial cities like Brünn/Brno and Mährisch Ostrau/Ostrava did join large and politically dominant German communities. In 1880, for example, the Austrian census determined that 60 percent of the population of the Moravian capital used German as its *Umgangssprache* (its language of daily speech), and in 1900, 64 percent did so. On the other hand, Jews did not migrate in large numbers to other provincial cities domi-nated by German speakers, presumably because those cities did not offer the same economic opportunities as the two largest cities of the province. Thus, although Znaim/Znojmo was almost 90 percent German-speaking, Iglau/Jihlava 85 percent German, and Olmütz/Olomouc 65 percent German, the Jewish communities of those cities rose only marginally and remained very small.[20] Apart from the two largest cities, Jews did not move to the pre-dominantly German-speaking areas of the province. In 1900, the districts with the highest percentage of German-speakers— Hohenstadt, Mährisch Schönberg, Mährisch Trübau, Nikolsburg,

Römerstadt, Sternberg, and Znaim—contained very few Jews, only 3,437, or 8 percent of all the Jews in Moravia.[21] Nikolsburg had once contained the largest Jewish community in Moravia, but Jews abandoned Nikolsburg, a district with 94 percent German-speakers according to the 1910 census, for economic or personal opportunities elsewhere.

Jews may not have moved to predominantly German-speaking districts (apart from the two largest cities), but wherever they lived they felt that they belonged to—or formed a distinct subgroup within—the German cultural and political community. Memoirs written by Moravian Jews certainly indicate a sense of belonging to the German cultural community. Friedrich Bill, an engineer from Brünn/Brno, for example, remembered that "the Jews, with few exceptions, belonged to the German cultural community [*Kulturgemeinschaft*], which they maintained at great financial sacrifice and with total passion."[22] Eric Fischer, a geographer born in 1898 in Vienna, spent many summer vacations as a child with his mother's family in Brünn/Brno. Like so many others, his great-aunt Paula actively supported the German theater, participated in the activities of the women's auxiliary of the German National Liberal Party, at least until it turned to antisemitism, and even afterward remained convinced of the superiority of German culture. It was clear to him then that "Brno was still outwardly a German city," but "living with a Jewish-German-speaking family, one noticed little of the basically Czech character of the larger metropolitan area."[23] Norbert Troller, an architect whose father owned a hat factory in Brünn/Brno, recalled that only a third of the population of his home town were German, but the center of the city, its inhabitants, businesses, and architecture, felt German, and the Germans controlled City Hall. The Jews, he noted, spoke both German and Czech, "but favored German. The growing Jewish middle class eagerly sucked up German culture. Many proudly considered themselves bearers of German culture."[24]

While Arnold Hindls insisted that the Jews of Leipnik/Lipník sent their children to German schools because of economic pressure from the German notables,[25] and Norbert Troller felt that all ambitious people naturally wanted to send their children to schools in the officially privileged language,[26] all other memoirists relate how they attended German schools, or German-Jewish schools, as a matter of course. Ruth Elias, for example, whose father owned a sausage factory, described the festivities that accompanied her first day of school at the (German) Jewish elementary school in Mährisch Ostrau/Ostrava. After four years she wanted to attend a Czech school (this being in Czechoslovakia, after all), but her aunt Irma, who raised her, would not hear of it and sent her to the German Girls Reform-Realgymnasium.[27] Similarly Joseph Wechsberg, born in 1907 to a family of bankers, attended the (German) Jewish public school in Mährisch Ostrau/Ostrava, and then the German gymnasium, where the majority of students were fellow middle-class Jews.[28] Memoirists also emphasize Jewish support for German theater. With the creation of Czechoslovakia in 1918, Wechsberg relates, the German theater in Mährisch Ostrau/Ostrava closed, much to the chagrin of the "older people, who said it was a tragedy they had lost 'their' theater, which had been built during the monarchy with 'their' money.' " They (that is, German-speaking Jews) then proceeded to establish a new theater association, which mounted theatrical productions in the *Deutsches Haus* rather than in the City Theater, which now produced only Czech plays. Wechsberg's mother avidly supported the new association, chaired by a Jewish brewer.[29]

Going to German schools and attending the German theater, however, did not necessarily make Jews German. Wechsberg assumed that Jews formed a separate group in his home town. Describing the Café Palace in the 1920s, for example, he labels it "a citadel of national and religious tolerance ... the only coffeehouse in town that was frequented by Czechs and Germans and Jews."[30] Similarly, Norbert Troller talked about the Czechs, Germans, and Jews who attended the German schools of Brünn/ Brno, where the instruction was "chauvinistically German but patriotically Austrian."[31] Arthur Hanak, born in 1912 in Olmütz/ Olomouc, wrote, "I myself am neither German nor Austrian. I was born in Olomouc/Olmütz. I was raised in German cultural circles. The interests of my family leaned more toward Vienna than to Prague."[32] Ruth Elias described the absolute difference between Germans and Jews most compellingly. Her horror at the behavior of her *volksdeutsch* classmates who kissed the soil of Germany, quoted at the beginning of this article, reflects the fact that she, a German-speaking Jew, felt no kinship with German-speakers who understood their German identity in *völkisch* terms and who venerated Germany.

That the Jews were not Germans was not only a result of the increasing popularity of *völkisch* notions of German identity. Indeed, the continued existence of the *Judengemeinden* and the German-Jewish schools fostered the notion among Czechs, Germans, and Jews alike that the Jews formed a third group, albeit a Germanized one, in Moravian society. It was true that the number of old *Judengemeinden* declined, and many Jews abandoned them for nicer locations, but their persistence served as an institutional reminder that while Jews had joined the German cultural and political community, they continued to inhabit a separate Jewish space. This space, moreover, was not devoted to the needs of the Jewish religion but was one through which Jews could function in the political arena.

Despite its hyperbole, the Jewish press can provide illuminating insight into the degree to which Moravian Jews belonged to the community of Germans. The only Jewish newspaper in the province, the *Jüdische Volksstimme*, a Zionist weekly newspaper published in Brünn/Brno from 1900 to 1934, attacked the Jews of Moravia, especially the wealthy textile manufacturers in the capital, for their complete subservience to German culture and politics. These polemics, of course, are typical of Zionist polemics everywhere against "assimilationists"—that is, Jews they deemed to be traitors to the Jewish nation. The newspaper took for granted that the Jews belonged to the German linguistic and cultural community, and while it urged Jews to learn Czech if they did not already know the language, it did not advocate any change of loyalty from the German to the Czech cultural community. The paper chided Jews for caring more about the *Deutsches Haus*, German reading clubs, and the German School Association than about Judaism and the Jewish community,[33] and it often used very nasty language, labeling such Jews *Teutonogermanen, Judenteutonen,* "servants of Wotan," or "amphibians with Jewish lungs and *völkisch* German gills" (*JVS,** 1.i.01:4, 15.viii.01:6, 1.ix.01:4, 1.v.02:6).[34] It also incessantly warned that such German loyalty led not only to greater Czech hostility, but also to greater German antisemitism. After all, "the precarious situation of Germandom in Moravia has not at all protected the Jews who feel German and vote German from the most horrible insults of the German nationalist press, and all the self-sacrificing devotion of the 'Jewish Germans' of Moravia have not prevented German festivals in Brünn, [whose organizers] do not reject Jewish money, from taking on an antisemitic flavor" (*JVS,* 1.iii.00:2–3). Germans, the paper declared, eagerly took Jewish money to support their institutions, but they utterly hated the Jews and refused to regard them as fellow Germans.

A close reading of the polemics reveals, however, that the opposite was in fact the case. Germans did accept the Jews as part of the German cultural and political community in Moravia. Antisemitism existed among the Germans, to be sure, and many German organizations excluded Jews. More interesting, however, is the fact that many German organizations, especially but not only

---

* Henceforth *Jüdische Volksstimme* is cited via abbreviated date and page(s) in parentheses in the text.

in the towns and cities in which Germans relied on Jewish numbers to create a viable German community, refused to exclude the
Jews,[35] much to the repeated discomfort of the Zionists. Thus for
example, in 1898 the German gymnastics association in Olmütz/
Olomouc, a city of approximately 20,000 in northern Moravia
which was 64 percent German-speaking and 8 percent Jewish,
withdrew from the Moravian-Silesian gymnastics district when
the latter declared itself *judenrein* (*JVS*, 1.xii.00:3, see also
1.ii.02:6).[36] The German School Association, which supported
German schools in areas where Germans formed too small a percentage of the population for state-supported German schools,
famously refused to exclude Jews, and so the antisemites formed a
separate school association.[37]

The *Jüdische Volksstimme* fully expected the Federation of
North Moravians, which it labeled "a known antisemitic Germanization organization," to expel its *Judenteutonen*, and it assumed that
the German School Association only retained its Jewish members
because it needed Jewish money so badly (*JVS*, 1.v.02:6). When
the Federation of North Moravians rejected the "Aryan paragraph," the rule that the organization would not accept Jews as
members, by postponing the decision for five years, the newspaper
seemed rather disappointed and declared that the Germans only
wanted Jewish political support in the upcoming diet elections. It
used the opportunity to lambaste Jews for their loyalty to the gods
of Germandom (*JVS*, 1.vi.02:5–6, 1.vii.02:3). A few years later,
the paper was indignant that the Prossnitz/Prostějov Jewish community provided space in the Talmud Torah school for a public
lecture by this organization (*JVS*, 1.iv.04:6). Similarly, when the
Federation of South Moravians roundly rejected the Aryan paragraph in 1903, the Zionists attributed it to a need for Jewish
money and votes and attacked Jewish members as toadies (*Schma-
rozer*). They assumed the Federation would soon expel the Jews
(*JVS*, 15.vi.03, 15.vi.04:4). The Zionists were annoyed that the
supposedly antisemitic Germans of Mährisch Ostrau/Ostrava

appealed to the Jewish gymnastics association to join them in a German demonstration against Czech gymnasts in late 1902. The Jewish gymnasts, a Zionist group, refused the invitation, but, much to the chagrin of the Zionists, the *Israelitische Kultusgemeinde* and the Jewish Women's Philanthropic Organization marched in solidarity with the Germans (*JVS*, 1.x.02:6). The Zionists simply believed that it was only a matter of time before these German organizations showed their true antisemitic colors (*JVS*, 15.ix.04:1–2).

At the same time, the Zionist paper also revealed the extent to which many non-Jewish Germans withdrew from German organizations, leaving those organizations almost entirely Jewish in membership. Writing from Prossnitz/Prostějov, one Zionist remarked in late 1901, "With the exception of the Federation of North Moravians, all the local [German] organizations consist entirely of Jews, naturally with the exception of two or three token Goyim [*Paradegojs*]" (*JVS*, 1.x.01:3–4). The Jews had become the Germans, the bearers of German culture, in many regions, especially in small towns with Czech majorities, less so in the larger cities. In Leipnik/Lipník, for example, the German Gymnastics Club was "entirely Jewish," the Zionist press claimed, while even it admitted that such was not the case in Brünn/Brno (*JVS*, 15.vi.03:2–3). It was ridiculous, the Zionist newspaper insisted, that Jews were such enthusiastic German nationalists, such "fanatics of Wotan," in Czech towns. There, the paper noted, Germans had become Czech, leaving "Semitic Germans" as the bearers of Germandom (*JVS*, 15.ix.04:1–2). In Prossnitz/Prostějov, the paper noted, there was no German society—just rich, assimilated Jewish snobs who wanted to show off (*JVS*, 20.xi.08:1–2).

II. Jews and German Politics

The Zionists reserved their most heated polemics for the realm of politics. Zionist leaders castigated Jews for supporting the German liberal parties, which, they insisted, were all antisemitic. Jewish political support for the Germans, they warned, had dire consequences. Jewish votes for Germans often led to the victory of German parties in many electoral districts which might otherwise have had a Czech majority. The Czechs, therefore, bitterly resented the Jews and boycotted Jewish businesses, which led to the economic destruction of many shopkeepers and merchants in small towns in the Czech countryside.

Jews in Moravia had, in fact, more political clout than their numbers would suggest, and they did use that clout to support German political parties and to help ensure German liberal dominance in local politics. Until the introduction of universal male suffrage in 1907, the franchise was severely restricted, and voting took place according to a curial system that favored the aristocrats, the wealthy and middle classes, and the cities. Jewish shopkeepers, merchants, and manufacturers voted in the urban curia, in which they were disproportionately represented and which elected more representatives to the Moravian diet and the Austrian parliament than the rural communes. The curial system favored the Germans, and the political *Judengemeinden* further augmented German strength. As independent entities they generally voted for German parties, but if they had been subsumed into the towns in which they were located, their support for the Germans would have been rendered insignificant by the Czech majorities in those towns. Jewish electoral clout was first undercut by the Moravian Compromise of 1905, which divided the Moravian electorate into German and Czech voting cadasters. Beginning in 1906, Germans elected German representatives and Czechs elected Czech representatives to both diet and parliament, and the small number of Jews had no impact at all on either outcome.[38] The introduction of universal suffrage in 1907 rendered Jewish votes in Moravia utterly insignificant. Jews retained disproportionate electoral clout in municipal elections because of the persistence of curial voting until it was abolished by the new Czechoslovak Republic which eliminated altogether the curias, the national cadasters, and the political *Judengemeinden* when it came in after World War I.

In the first years of the twentieth century, when the nationalist conflict in the Bohemian lands had reached fever pitch and the Jews still had electoral clout in Moravia, Zionist spokesmen inveighed against Jewish political support for the Germans, which, they asserted, invariably led to the Czech boycott of Jewish businesses. In late 1900, for example, the *Jüdische Volksstimme* warned the Jews of Prossnitz/Prostějov not to vote for the German candidate in the upcoming (1901) elections in the urban curia of the parliamentary voting district of Olmütz/Olomouc–Prossnitz/Prostějov–Deutsch Brodek even though he was the virtuous and beloved mayor of Olmütz/Olomouc. In 1897, it reminded its readers, the "truly German-minded" Jews of overwhelmingly Czech Prossnitz/Prostějov had voted for a German candidate and the Czechs had taken economic revenge, much to the detriment of the Jews in the city. It would therefore be "madness for the Jews not simply to remain home on election day. It would not be treason [to the German cause] but rather self-protection" (*JVS*, 1.xii.00:3). The Jews of Prossnitz/Prostějov did not take this advice. Indeed, the Zionist paper noted, on election day there were more leaders of the Jewish community at the polls than there were in the synagogue on Yom Kippur (*JVS*, 1.ii.01:3). Although the Czechs won a mandate, they took revenge on the Jews, who presumably voted for the German candidate, by reinvigorating the economic boycott of German and Jewish businesses, the *svůj k svému* (each to his own) movement, which mostly hurt small Jewish merchants (*JVS*, 15.iii.01:6, 1.v.01:6, 15.v.01:6).[39] Certain that Jewish support for German politicians led to Czech antisemitism (see, e.g., *JVS*, 1.iv.02:6, 1.iv.04:2,

1.vii.04:1), the Zionists were equally convinced that the German liberals, who still dominated provincial and parliamentary politics in Moravia, were profoundly antisemitic, even if in mixed areas where they needed Jewish votes they did not publicly engage in antisemitic invective and continued to include Jews on their electoral slates (*JVS*, 15.vii.01:1–2, 15.v.02:2–3, 1.ii.04:2–3). After every election, when Czech nationalists renewed their economic boycott against Jewish merchants in revenge for Jewish electoral support for German candidates, the Zionists felt vindicated (*JVS*, 15.xii.02:6, 15.iii.04:2–3). They also inveighed against Jews for their doglike loyalty to the German liberals, who, the Zionists insisted, hated the Jews and refused to hire them for government jobs (*JVS*, 15.iii.04:2–3, 1.xi.05:4).

In fact, however, while the German liberals themselves increasingly advocated a more biological definition of Germanness than had been the case earlier in the century, and many flirted with antisemitism in order to invigorate German nationalist politics, in Moravia, old-fashioned liberals still dominated in most places. They continued to include the Jews in the political community of Germans and appealed for their votes, perhaps because in fact they needed them to maintain German majorities in many places. For their part, most Jews considered themselves part of the German political community and continued to vote for the German liberal parties (see, e.g., *JVS*, 1.xii.05:2, 15.xii.05:4).[40] Jews even continued to serve in Liberal city government administrations. In Mährisch Ostrau/Ostrava, for example, eleven Jews sat on the city council in 1906 (*JVS*, 1.viii.06:3–4).

The Zionists, however, wanted the Jews to withhold their support from the Germans and to remain neutral in the German–Czech conflict. In the elections for the provincial diet in October 1902, for example, Zionists insisted that it was a "commandment of self-preservation, of political wisdom, and general morality" for Jews, no matter how infatuated with Germanness they might be, to remain neutral in the nationality conflict. Such neutrality was neither anti-German nor pro-Czech, but simply smart. Jewish electoral clout, engineered by Liberals eager to give Germans more power than they deserved, only made the Czechs hate the Jews and made the Germans only pretend to care about the Jews at election time. Jews therefore should not vote (*JVS*, 1.ix.02:4, 15.x.02:1).[41] Several months later, the paper reiterated that supporting the Germans politically was "irrational political madness," indeed suicidal, especially for Jewish storekeepers in the small towns. But the Zionists did not urge the Jews to vote for Czech parties, presumably because the Jews were not Czech. The Zionists simply did not want the Germans to retain an artificial political hegemony with Jewish help, to the unending resentment of the Czechs (*JVS*, 15.vi.03:2–3).

The Moravian Compromise of 1905, and the introduction of universal suffrage in 1907, vastly reduced the significance of the Jews in Moravian elections, a fact that Jews all recognized immediately (*JVS*, 15.ii.06:6, 15.iii.06:2–3). The question nevertheless remained: should they register as Germans in the new national voting system? Despite their policy of neutrality, the Zionists urged those Jews who lived in Czech cities and in small towns in the Czech countryside—a group they estimated at 30 percent of all Moravian Jews—to register as Czechs, but all others to register as Germans (*JVS*, 15.v.06:4). In fact, one gets the impression from Zionist reports that most Jews registered as Germans, except for the Jews in almost entirely Czech towns like Holleschau/Holešov, Ungarisch Hradisch/Hradiště Uherské, Kremsier/Kroměříž, and Prerau/Přerov, who felt Czech pressure to register as Czechs most acutely (*JVS*, 15.x.06:1–2).[42] Zionists assumed that since Germans no longer needed Jewish votes to elect Germans, fewer German Liberal progressives and more antisemitic German nationalists would stand for election, especially since middle class German parties offered a unified voting list (*JVS*, 15.x.06:1–2, 3; 1.xi.06:1–2, 2–3). This assumption led them to lambaste those Jews for their traditional allegiance to the German Liberals, a group of parties which now, no longer reliant on Jewish voters, would become more openly antisemitic. Thus any Jew who still believed "that the Jews of Austria are a part of the German nation" was cravenly hiding his head in the sand, serving the Teutons like dogs (*JVS*, 10.ix.07:3, 1.xi.08:4). In fact, however, Jews continued to form part of the German political community. Because of the retention of the curial system, many nonantisemitic German progressives still won mandates in the Moravian diet and still controlled the city councils of the larger German cities, and Jews continued to vote for those parties. In areas where the German middle class parties united and put forward antisemitic candidates, Jews voted for the German Social Democrats (*JVS*, 15.xi.06:1).

III. German and German-Jewish Schools

Despite their declining political significance, it would appear that the Jews in Moravia continued to support German political parties. They also continued to belong to German organizations and, more importantly, to send their children to German or German-Jewish schools rather than to the Czech schools. Jewish children at both the elementary and secondary school levels almost entirely attended schools in which German was the language of instruction. The government did not publish statistics in such a way as to determine the religion of elementary school children in either German or Czech schools, but the secondary school statistics are very clear. In 1881/82, 784 Jewish boys attended gymnasium in Moravia, 16 percent of the total student body in those elite schools. One hundred percent of them attended institutions in which German was the language of instruction. Similarly, all 447 Jewish boys in *Realschulen* (technically oriented secondary schools) that year attended German schools. In 1890/91, 97 percent of the 705 Jewish boys in gymnasium attended German-language schools, and 99 percent of those in *Realschulen* attended German schools.[43] In the decades that followed, the number of Czech secondary schools grew, but almost all Jews who attended secondary school went to German schools. In Brünn/Brno in 1901, Jews formed 38 percent of the students at the German gymnasiums, 24 percent of the students in the *Realschulen*, and 29 percent of the students in high schools for girls. No Jews in the Moravian capital went to Czech middle schools (*JVS*, 15.iv.03:3).

At the elementary school level, Jews also attended German-language schools, either public schools in the cities or towns in which they lived, or German-Jewish schools. Many of the German-Jewish schools were the local public schools of the political *Judengemeinden*, but some of them were established by the Jewish communities in areas of new Jewish settlement like Mährisch Ostrau/Ostrava. With the exception of the *Judengemeinde* in Trebitsch/Třebíč, which ran both a German and a Czech school, all of the other *Judengemeinden* had only German schools, although most of these schools, unlike many of the German schools of the province, also taught the Czech language. In nearby Bohemia, in the late nineteenth century the Czech-Jewish movement, which sought to convince the Jews to switch their "national" allegiance to Czech, successfully pressured the German-Jewish schools to close, and most did. In Moravia, however, these schools persisted. When the new state of Czechoslovakia eliminated the old political *Judengemeinden*, many of the German-Jewish schools closed their doors, but those established by or taken over by Jewish religious communities continued to flourish, and Jews continued to send their children to them.[44]

These German-Jewish schools varied. Some of them taught a full range of Jewish subjects—Hebrew, Bible, Jewish history, prayers—alongside German reading, writing, and arithmetic. Some of them taught no Jewish subjects but were simply the schools of the local political Jewish communities and contained increasing numbers of non-Jewish students. One would have assumed that many schools followed this model, but in fact, in many cases the non-Jews who should have attended these schools because they lived in these communities simply transferred to the public schools of the local "Christian" town, thus making the schools of the Jewish towns effectively Jewish, or rather German-Jewish. These schools were supervised by the local German Board of Education, and they often received support from the German School Association, which supported German-language schools in the Bohemian lands. Rarely, however, did non-Jewish German children attend these schools.

A study of the school records of the German-Jewish schools in Leipnik/Lipník, Prerau/Přerov, Olmütz/Olomouc, Prossnitz/Prostějov, and Mährisch Ostrau/Ostrava[45] reveals that virtually all the students in these schools were Jewish. In Prossnitz/Prostějov, for example, the four-grade elementary school of the *politische Judengemeinde* offered instruction in German language, Czech language, arithmetic, penmanship, religion, Hebrew, and Bible. In 1884/85, it contained 203 boys and girls, all of them Jewish. There were many Catholic school-age children who lived in the *Judengemeinde*, but all 105 of them in 1885/86 attended schools in the "Christian" town, while 76 children from Prossnitz/Prostějov proper, all Jewish, came to school in the *Judengemeinde*.[46] Not all the Jewish children living in the *Judengemeinde* attended its school, but if they attended a different school, it was always a German one, while the Catholic children went either to German or, increasingly, to Czech schools.[47] With the passage of time, the number of Catholic children living in the *Judengemeinde* grew, but they continued to go to school in "Christian" Prossnitz/Prostějov, and the *Judengemeinde* school remained entirely Jewish. In 1904/5, for example, there were 207 children required to attend grades 1–4 in the *Judengemeinde*, 68 Jews and 139 Catholics. Virtually all the Catholics attended school in the city of Prossnitz/Prostějov. The *Judengemeinde* school contained 4 Catholics, in addition to 50 of its own Jewish children, plus 85 Jewish children from town.[48]

In Mährisch Ostrau/Ostrava, the German-Jewish school was not the local school of a political *Judengemeinde*, but rather a school originally founded by the *Israelitische Kultusgemeinde* in 1863 which became accredited as a "public school" in 1884. Through World War I, the school contained over two hundred students in four classes, and, unlike many of the German-Jewish schools, it persisted into the 1930s, although by that time it offered half of its instruction in the Czech language.[49] This school attracted students from other towns in Moravia, Silesia, and even nearby Galicia, presumably from families that wanted their children to get a German education.[50] The Zionists loved this school because it provided a Jewish atmosphere and some protection from the Czech–German conflict (*JVS*, 1.vii.06:5, 1.viii.06:3–4).

The role of these German-Jewish schools in fostering a sense of a separate German-Jewish identity cannot be exaggerated. Whether they taught Jewish subjects or not, these elementary schools created a space in which Jews joined the German cultural community as Jews. They also reminded everyone that the Jews were a separate group in Moravia, a subgroup of the community of Germans, or rather, a separate community of German-speaking Jews.

IV. In Czechoslovakia

The German identity and German loyalties of the Jews came into sharp relief after the collapse of Austria-Hungary and the creation of Czechoslovakia in late 1918. The new state contained people who identified as members of several different nationalities— Czech, Slovak, German, Magyar, Ruthene—but the dominant Czechs acted as if Czechoslovakia were a Czech nation-state, much to the resentment of the others. The new political leaders, Thomas Masaryk and the Realist Party, unlike many mainstream Czech nationalists, had a history of opposing antisemitism and supporting Zionism. Masaryk, whom most Jews in Czechoslovakia adored just as they had adored the Emperor Franz Joseph, did not think the Jews could be Czech. Wanting to wean Jews away from their traditional German loyalties, especially in politics, Masaryk supported Zionism and the idea that in Czechoslovakia the Jews could belong to the Jewish nation. If they did so, they would no longer count as Germans, thus diluting German numbers. The Constitution of 1920 allowed Jews in the new republic to profess Jewish nationality on the census if they so desired.[51] A very high percentage of Jews in Czechoslovakia availed themselves of this new right, mostly though the pious, traditionalist Jews of Slovakia and sub-Carpathian Ruthenia. In the census of 1921, 54 percent of the 354,342 Jews in Czechoslovakia declared Jewish nationality. In Sub-Carpathian Ruthenia, 87 percent did so, and in Slovakia, 54 percent. In sharp contrast to Bohemia, where only 16 percent of the Jews declared Jewish nationality, 48.5 percent of the Jews of Moravia and 64 percent of the Jews of Silesia professed the Jewish nationality.[52] In 1930, 20 percent of the Jews of Bohemia, but 52 percent of the Jews of Moravia and Silesia (combined), declared Jewish nationality on the census. At the same time, 18 percent declared Czechoslovak and 29 percent German in Moravia/Silesia, while in Bohemia, 46 percent declared Czechoslovak and 31 percent German.[53]

Those Jews who declared their membership in the Jewish nation were not all Zionists. In Moravia, professing membership in the Jewish nation allowed the Jews great freedom to continue their allegiance to German culture without offending the new political masters. They could now assert their loyalty to the Czechoslovak state, continue to speak German, affiliate with the German cultural community, and be Jews by national identity, an identity whose major virtue was that it was neither Czech nor German. They did not feel comfortable becoming Czech, but declaring a German national identity became increasingly problematic in the Czechoslovak Republic. After all, the Germans of

Czechoslovakia did not especially like the new state, resented their place in it, became increasingly racist in their understanding of Germanness, and by the 1930s supported Nazi Germany.[54] Jews therefore could no longer join the German political community, much less the German *Volk*. They were not Germans. They were German-speaking Czechoslovakian Jews. A Jewish national identity allowed them to be Czechoslovakian, German, and Jewish all at the same time. In nearby Bohemia, Jews did not avail themselves of the new Jewish national identity because they had already committed themselves to a greater allegiance to Czech nationalism; but in Moravia, where Jews never allied with the Czechs and where German language and culture persisted, a Jewish national identity worked perfectly. Those Jews who could not bring themselves to register as members of the Jewish nation and continued to register as Germans felt politically isolated.

The actual meaning of German identity for Moravian Jews in the Czechoslovak Republic is hard to ascertain. Jews continued to attend German schools as a matter of course, although most Jews were as bilingual as they had always been. They felt increasing distance from Germans, but not from German language or culture. German identity was no longer bound up with Austrian patriotism, and Jewish loyalty to the state of Czechoslovakia was quite firm, especially as most other states in Central and Eastern Europe descended into authoritarianism and fascism in the 1930s, and Czechoslovakia remained the only functioning democracy in the region.

The tension between their attachments to Vienna and Prague can serve as an interesting symbol of Jewish uncertainty about the meaning of Germanness. Many educated Moravian Jews felt lost in the new Czechoslovakia and moved to Vienna,[55] but some of them returned home, more comfortable in Czechoslovakia than in interwar Austria.[56] Joseph Wechsberg's family "had always considered Vienna, not Prague, our spiritual capital," and before World War I they had visited Vienna regularly, but never Prague.

In 1925, when Wechsberg decided to study law, he had to study in Prague, albeit at the German university, but he only went to Prague to take his exams, spending most of his time in Vienna studying music and going to the opera. Yet he later came to love Prague more than Vienna, which he considered a dying, artificial city by the 1930s. At that point, he felt more at home in Prague, where "everybody was alive and the peculiar border situation— Czechs living next to Germans and Jews—reflected the situation in my home town. I preferred the polemical life in Prague to the decadent elegance of Vienna." Yet, when he lost his job in a law office in Prague, he went back to Vienna, noting "I felt like going home, or at least back." Unfortunately, Vienna in 1935 "wasn't like the old days," so he returned to Prague, where life was not dull and everyone hoped they could avoid the threat of Nazi Germany.[57] Wechsberg's back-and-forth relationship with Vienna and Prague reflects the fact that he felt loyalty and love for Czechoslovakia (and none for the new Austrian Republic), yet he was a Jew of German culture, not a Czech, and therefore not quite at home in golden Slavic Prague.

The Zionists liked the new political realities. They rejoiced that the new state recognized the Jews as a nation, and they hoped that Jews would vote for the newly established Jewish Party in all elections (see, e.g., *JVS*, 26.ii.20:1, 4.iii.20:1, 20.v.25:1, 15.vii.25: 1–2, 4.xi. 25:1). They had no interest, however, in adopting Czech language and culture, and they remained loyal to the German language and culture to which they had long adhered. They inveighed against members of the Czech-Jewish movement, who sought to convince Jews to adopt Czech language and culture, and they especially wanted to retain the German-Jewish schools and to create new ones, because only such schools inculcated Jewish national identity and provided the right kind of Jewish education. The German language in those schools, they insisted, had nothing to do with national feelings but was merely a means of expression (*JVS*, 2.ix.20:5, 6; 20.i.21:1–2; 9.vi.21:1–2; 16.vi.21:

2–3; 23.vi.21:1; 17.vi.25:1; 12.v.27:1). As always, the Zionists felt that a Jewish national identity protected them from both Czech and German antisemitism. Just before the 1921 census, for example, the *Jüdische Volksstimme* advised its readers to register as Jews, because otherwise, if one or another of the nationalities deemed its numbers too low, they would blame the Jews. For Jews to register as Jews would make it absolutely clear that they were indeed neutral in the nationality conflict (*JVS*, 27.i.21:1). Even if Zionists declared their political neutrality, they still formed part of the German cultural community.[58] Like most Jewish communities and Jewish institutions, they continued to function in German. Indeed, when the German Theater Association in Brünn/Brno embarked on a fund-raising campaign in 1924, the Zionist press urged Jews to contribute money but not join the organization. Good Zionists could support German culture, but they should not become members because membership "involved national identification [*Bekenntnis*]" (*JVS*, 31.x.24:4).

V. Conclusion

Jews in Moravia in the nineteenth century and through the 1930s continued to adhere to the kind of German identity that they had adopted in the early nineteenth century. They regarded themselves as members of the German cultural community, and before the nearly total radicalization of the Germans, as members of the German political community. They continued to adhere to older notions of Germanness, which understood Germanness in terms of language, culture, and political conviction, not biological descent or race. They were accepted by other Germans as Germans, at least in terms of the cultural and political community, until the Germans became fully radicalized in the 1930s. Yet they always remained Jews, hence German-Jews, a distinct subset of the community of Germans. Their distinctiveness was not generated by antisemitism, although antisemitic exclusion certainly had some impact. Their distinctiveness derived from their continued commitment to a Jewish identity and from the fact that such identity found support in the very structure of Jewish life in the province. The political Jewish communities and the network of German-Jewish schools surely sought to remind the Jews that they formed part of the German community as a distinct Jewish group. Czechoslovakia may have eliminated the political Jewish communities, and many of the German-Jewish schools closed as a result, but in Czechoslovakia the inability and unwillingness of the Jews to merge fully with the Germans allowed them to continue the old German cultural identity. If they were only Germans in a cultural sense, they could still be very loyal Czechoslovak citizens and Jews at the same time. It is no wonder, then, that they felt grateful to the new state. It should come as no surprise that they responded with fear and dread to the arrival of the Nazis in 1938–39.

Notes

1. The issue of place names is highly contentious in East Central Europe. Most places had more than one name, and the names became a significant issue in the struggle of the national groups for dominance. Wechsberg's home town, for example, was called Mährisch Ostrau by the Habsburg Austrian authorities and by the local Germans, and Ostrava (or Ostrava Moravská) by Czechs and the Czechoslovak authorities after 1918. This article will use all names for all places mentioned so as not to privilege one of the national groups or the contemporary victors. Mährisch Ostrau/Ostrava, today located right near the border of the Czech Republic and Poland, also contained Poles when Wechsberg was growing up.
2. Joseph Wechsberg, *The Vienna I Knew: Memories of a European Childhood* (Garden City, N.Y.: Doubleday, 1979), 148.
3. Ibid., 84.
4. Ibid., 81.
5. Peter Erben, *Auf eigenen Spuren: Aus Mährisch-Ostrau durch Theresienstadt,*

Auschwitz I, Mauthausen, Gusen III über Paris nach Israel: Jüdische Schicksale aus der Tschechoslowakei, ed. Erhard Roy Wiehn (Konstanz: Hartung-Gorre Verlag, 2001), 16, 18. All translations from the German are my own.

6. Michel Huttarsch, *Unter Deutschen, Tschechen und Juden in Mähren: Erin-nerungen 1923–1966* (Darmstadt: Selbstverlag, 1995).

7. Ruth Elias, *Die Hoffnung erhielt mich am Leben: Mein Weg von Theresienstadt und Auschwitz nach Israel* (Munich: Piper, 1988), 34, 39.

8. The literature on nationalism is vast. For good recent overviews, see Rog-ers Brubaker, *Nationalism Reframed: Nationhood and the National Question in the New Europe* (Cambridge: Cambridge University Press, 1996), and Anthony D. Smith, *Nationalism and Modernism: A Critical Survey of Recent Theories of Nations and Nationalism* (London: Routledge, 1998). On the problematic of national identification in East Central Europe, see Pieter M. Judson, introduction to *Constructing Nationalities in East Central Europe*, ed. Pieter M. Judson and Marsha L. Rozenblit (New York: Berghahn, 2005), 1–18.

9. K. u. k. Statistisches Central-Commission, *Österreichische Statistik* (Vienna: K. u. k. Hof- und Staatsdruckerei), 63, no. 3 (1902), 178.

10. On the language issue and the Jews of Bohemia, see Hillel J. Kieval, *The Making of Czech Jewry: National Conflict and Jewish Society in Bohemia, 1870–1918* (New York: Oxford University Press, 1988); Gary B. Cohen, "Jews in German Society: Prague, 1860–1914," *Central European History* 10 (1977): 28–54. Of course, even in Bohemia, most Jews continued to speak German most of the time. On the issue of *Umgangssprache* and nationality in Habsburg Austria, see Emil Brix, *Die Umgangssprachen in Altösterreich zwischen Agitation und Assimilation* (Vienna: Böhlau, 1982). For a wonderful recent study of the very problematic relationship between language and nationality, see Jeremy King, *Budweisers into Czechs and Ger-mans: A Local History of Bohemian Politics, 1848–1948* (Princeton: Prince-ton University Press, 2002).

11. On interwar Czechoslovakia see Franz Friedmann, *Einige Zahlen über die tschechoslovakischen Juden (Ein Beitrag zur Soziologie der Judenheit)* (Prague: J.A. Verb. Barissia, 1933), 23–25; and Ezra Mendelsohn, *The Jews of East Central Europe between the World Wars* (Bloomington: Indiana University Press, 1983), 131–69, esp. 146, 159.

12. Hillel J. Kieval, "Caution's Progress: The Modernization of Jewish Life in Prague, 1780–1830," in *Toward Modernity: The European Jewish Model*, ed. Jacob Katz (New Brunswick, N.J.: Transaction Books, 1989), 71–105, esp. 89–99; Ruth Kestenberg-Gladstein, *Neuere Geschichte der Juden in den böh-*

mischen Ländern, part 1: *Das Zeitalter der Aufklärung, 1780–1830* (Tübingen: Mohr, 1969), 41–65. See also Michael Silber, "The Historical Experience of German Jewry and Its Impact on Haskalah and Reform in Hungary," in Katz, *Toward Modernity*, 107–57, esp. 110–12, and Raphael Mahler, *A History of Modern Jewry, 1780–1815* (New York: Schocken, 1971), 330–41.

13. On the Germans in Habsburg Austria, see Gary B. Cohen, *The Politics of Ethnic Survival: Germans in Prague, 1861–1914* (Princeton: Princeton University Press, 1981); Pieter M. Judson, " 'Whether Race or Conviction Should Be the Standard': National Identity and Liberal Politics in Nineteenth-Century Austria," *Austrian History Yearbook* 22 (1991): 76–95; idem, *Exclusive Revolutionaries: Liberal Politics, Social Experience, and National Identity in the Austrian Empire, 1848–1914* (Ann Arbor: University of Michigan Press, 1996); Peter Urbanitsch, "Die Deutschen in Österreich. Statistisch-deskriptiver Überblick," in *Die Habsburgermonarchie 1848–1918*, ed. Adam Wandruszka and Peter Urbanitsch, vol. 3: *Die Völker des Reiches* (Vienna: Österreichische Akademie der Wissenschaften, 1980), 33–153. On the significance of *Bildung* to German (and German-Jewish) identity see David Sorkin, *The Transformation of German Jewry 1780–1840* (New York: Oxford University Press, 1987).

14. Cohen, *Politics of Ethnic Survival*; Judson, *Exclusive Revolutionaries*; idem, " 'Not Another Square Foot!' German Liberalism and the Rhetoric of National Ownership in Nineteenth-Century Austria," *Austrian History Yearbook* 26 (1995): 83–97; King, *Budweisers into Czechs and Germans*.

15. See Marsha L. Rozenblit, *Reconstructing a National Identity: The Jews of Habsburg Austria during World War I* (New York: Oxford University Press, 2001), 23–25, 28–29, 106–61; Kieval, *Making of Czech Jewry*, 16.

16. On the history of the Jews of Moravia see Theodor Haas, *Die Juden in Mähren: Darstellung der Rechtsgeschichte und Statistik unter besonderer Berücksichtigung des 19. Jahrhunderts* (Brünn: Jüdischer Buch- und Kunstverlag Max Hickl, 1908); *Die Juden und Judengemeinden Mährens in Vergangenheit und Gegenwart*, ed. Hugo Gold (Brünn: Jüdischer Buch- und Kunstverlag, 1929), esp. Max Grünfeld, "Aüsserer Verlauf der Geschichte der Juden in Mähren bis 1890," 8–22. A study of the Jews of Moravia is a scholarly desideratum.

17. Haas, *Juden in Mähren*, 22–28, 38–42.

18. Ibid., 48–50; Hugo Meissner, "Der Mährisch-Jüdische Landesmassafond," in Gold, *Juden und Judengemeinden Mährens*, 67–72.

19. Haas, *Juden in Mähren*, 58–64; *Österreichische Statistik*, 63, no. 1 (1902),

xxxii, lxxxii–lxxxiv, 98–105; Friedmann, *Einige Zahlen,* 6. On the Jewish role in the textile and clothing industry in Prossnitz/Prostějov, see Bernhard Heilig, *Eine mährische Stadt und ihr Ghetto* (Brünn: Zeitschrift des Deutschen Vereines für die Geschichte Mährens und Schlesiens, 1932); idem, *Urkundliches zur Wirtschaftsgeschichte der Juden in Prossnitz* (Brünn: Jüdischer Buch- und Kunstverlag, 1929).

20. *Österreichische Statistik [1880],* 1, no. 2 (1882), 74–75, 80; [*1900*], 63, no. 1 (1902), 98–105.

21. Ibid., 63, no. 1, 98–105.

22. Friedrich Bill, "Kuriose Biographie. Von Franz Josephs und meiner Geburt bis zum Tode Mitteleuropas," unpublished memoir (1954), LBI, p. 8.

23. Eric Fischer, "Memoirs and Reminiscences (1898–1985)," unpublished memoir, LBI, p. 30. In Brünn/Brno, the city center was largely German, but the suburbs were filled with Czech-speaking workers.

24. Norbert Troller, "Meine Erinnerungen: Fruehe Jugend bis zum Tode meines Vaters (1900–1908)," Norbert Troller Collection, LBI, AR 7268, 1/4, p. 6.

25. Arnold Hindls, "Erinnerungen aus meinem Leben," unpublished memoir (1966), LBI, p. 2.

26. Troller, "Erinnerungen," p. 6. Troller incorrectly thinks the government pursued an official Germanization policy. Such was most certainly not the case in the late nineteenth and early twentieth century.

27. Elias, *Hoffnung erhielt mich,* 25, 33.

28. Wechsberg, *The Vienna I Knew,* 79, 81, 201–2.

29. Ibid., 167–68.

30. Ibid., 220.

31. Troller, "Erinnerungen," p. 6.

32. Letter, December 31, 1991, to Albert Lichtblau, then collecting memoirs of Austrian Jews for his volume *Als hätten wir dazugehört: Österreichisch-jüdische Lebensgeschichten aus der Habsburgermonarchie* (Vienna: Böhlau, 1999), attached to an interview with Hanak conducted by Ma'ariv ('Erev Pesach, 1988), unpublished memoir collection, LBI.

33. See, for example, *Jüdische Volksstimme,* 1.xii.00:1, 1.i.01:4. Henceforth *JVS* is cited via abbreviated date and page(s) in parentheses in the text.

34. "Amphibians," incidentally, was the common term used by both German and Czech nationalist activists to insult those who were bilingual, easily mixed in both communities, and moved back and forth between what the nationalists had decided should be rigidly separated communities.

35. In this respect, the situation of the Jews in Moravia resembled that of the

Jews in Prague who were fully integrated into the German cultural community in the Bohemian capital. See Cohen, *Politics of Ethnic Survival*; "Jews in German Society." In the Sudetenland, radical German nationalism flourished, but not in those areas in which the Germans needed Jewish numbers to form a viable community.

36. Population statistics from *Österreichische Statistik*, 63, no. 1 (1902), 98–105.
37. Judson, *Exclusive Revolutionaries*, 230–34.
38. On the Moravian Compromise see T. Mills Kelly, "Last Best Chance or Last Gasp? The Compromise of 1905 and Czech Politics in Moravia," *Austrian History Yearbook* 34 (2003): 279–301; Judson, *Exclusive Revolutionaries*, 262–63. On the role of the *Judengemeinden* in Moravian politics, see articles by Theodor Haas, *JVS*, 1.iii.05:2–3; 15.iv.05:2–3.
39. On the boycott movement see Catherine Albrecht, "The Rhetoric of Economic Nationalism in the Bohemian Boycott Campaigns of the Late Habsburg Monarchy," *Austrian History Yearbook* 32 (2001): 47–67.
40. On the German Liberals see Judson, *Exclusive Revolutionaries*.
41. See also *JVS*, 1.xii.05 (about city council elections in Brünn/Brno).
42. It would be wonderful to know how Jews actually registered—whether as Czechs or as Germans. I hope to locate the German and Czech voting cadasters in the Moravian provincial archives for the larger project on Moravian Jews on which I am working.
43. *Österreichische Statistik*, 3, no. 2 (1883), 36, 44–45; 35, no. 4 (1894), 34–35, 42–43.
44. Haas, *Juden in Mähren*, 52–54. On pressure by the Czech-Jewish movement to force the closing of German-Jewish schools in Bohemia, see Kieval, *Making of Czech Jewry*, 48–55.
45. These records are extant at the archives of the Jewish Museum in Prague (JMP).
46. "Klassenbuch über den Schulbesuch und Fortgang der Schuler … an der viercl. Volksschule zu Prossnitz im Schuljahr 1884/5," JMP, Prostějov, Files 62873, 62749, 62814, 62815; "Schulmatrik der schulpflichtigen und schulbesuchenden Kinder an der vier classigen Volksschule zu Prossnitz im Schuljahre 1885/86," JMP, Prostějov, File 34886b.
47. JMP, Prostějov, File 34886b, 34886c.
48. "Schulmatrik an der vierclassigen Volksschule zu Prossnitz Isr. Gemeinde, 1899/00–1905," JMP, Prostějov, File 64127; "Classenbuch, Volksschule der Isr. Gemeinde, 1904–5," JMP, Prostějov, File 34889.
49. "Israel. Volksschule im M. Ostrau," JMP, Ostrava, File 24996. In the file, there is also a clipping of an article by Ferdinand Kraus on the school from

the *JVS*, 21.iv.32:6.

50. See class lists and statistics in JMP, Ostrava, Files 39103/a, 24957, 24873, 24898d, 24905d, 24883c, 24872b, 24855, 24882.

51. On Jewish attitudes to Czechoslovakia, see, Rozenblit, *Reconstructing a National Identity*, 138–50, 166–68; Kieval, *Making of Czech Jewry*, 183–97; Ezra Mendelsohn, *The Jews of East Central Europe between the World Wars* (Bloomington: Indiana University Press, 1983), 131–69. On Masaryk and the Jews, see Hillel J. Kieval, "Masaryk and Czech Jewry: The Ambiguities of Friendship," in *T. G. Masaryk (1850–1937)*, vol. 1, *Thinker and Politician*, ed. Stanley B. Winters (New York: St. Martin's, 1990), 302–27.

52. Friedmann, *Einige Zahlen*, 23.

53. Ibid., 24–25.

54. Joseph Rothschild, *East Central Europe between the Two World Wars* (Seattle: University of Washington Press, 1974), 73–135; *A History of the Czechoslovak Republic, 1918–1948*, ed. Victor S. Mamatey and Radomír Luža (Princeton: Princeton University Press, 1973); Carol Skolnick Leff, *National Conflict in Czechoslovakia: The Making and Remaking of a State, 1918–1987* (Princeton: Princeton University Press, 1988); and Derek Sayer, *The Coasts of Bohemia: A Czech History* (Princeton: Princeton University Press, 1998).

55. Bertha Landre, "Durch's Sieb der Zeit gefallen: Jedes Menschenleben ist ein Roman," unpublished memoir, LBI, pp. 118–19, 231, 267–68.

56. See, for example, Hindls, "Erinnerungen," pp. 98–100.

57. Wechsberg, *The Vienna I Knew*, 151–71, 238–41, 245, 250–52.

58. The minutes of Jewish communities in Moravia continued to be in German through the late 1930s. See records in JMP.

Revealing and Concealing

Using Memoirs
to Write German-Jewish History

MARION A. KAPLAN

*What I have written strains to be true but nevertheless is not
true enough. Truth is anecdotes, narrative, the snug opaque
quotidian.*

—JOHN UPDIKE, *SELF-CONSCIOUSNESS*

Over the years,[1] both history and memory have had their
critics, most recently post-modernists who have challenged grand narratives and who see memory and history
as mere representations constructed within discursive power relations.[2] This essay will elucidate the arguments raised against
memoirs[3] and will remind us of the important, often crucial,
work that memoirs do for historians.[4] I will argue for their value
in general, how they can and do enrich historical writing. But I
will also stress their importance more specifically, where people
have suffered discrimination or worse—as in Jewish and women's
history.

For social history, "memory is the raw material."[5] In the
1970s, when social historians began to write working class and

*This essay is a revised and expanded version of a talk I delivered at the First Interna-
tional Workshop on Gender in Modern Jewish History: Rethinking Jewish Women's
and Gender History, which took place in Hamburg in 2003.*

*I would like to thank my friends and colleagues Renate Bridenthal, Hasia Diner,
and Atina Grossmann and my daughter, Ruth Kaplan, for their careful reading and
helpful suggestions.*

women's history, they turned toward "memory"—in the form of memoirs or oral histories—to help them write the history of non-elites. Memoirs, also called "ego documents," documents that reveal an individual's self-understanding, fears, and values, provide an entrée into unexplored histories.[6] But memoirs offer more than individual or family stories. In memoirs, authors weave their life stories into their broader cultural or social contexts. Whether in a carefully crafted allusion or an offhand remark, they situate themselves within their societies. Memoirs illustrate not only very private journeys but also a personal sense of the historical moment. They also complicate the texture of more common historical source material such as newspapers or censuses, bringing a qualitative feeling to public records. They surprise us—contradicting, illuminating, and deepening the accepted story.

Memoirs are essential in uncovering the lives of certain marginalized groups. For Jews in Germany, an ostracized minority, they offer the particulars of Jewish public and private life in the kind of vivid detail absent in most other sources: the great variety of religious traditions; the range of places where Jews lived and the myriad ways in which they furnished their living quarters; their complex attitudes toward work and education; their friendships with other Jews and with non-Jews; and their expectations of and behaviors in their families. Without memoirs we would have—as we have had—a very flat picture of Jews, focusing on Jewish elites of wealth and learning. Memoirs give ordinary Jews historical agency.

In addition, memoirs are critical for understanding the Nazi era. Historians have learned from the writings of refugees and survivors who seek to understand what happened, to explain or excuse their own lack of prescience, and to portray life "before" and "during" to their offspring. They often alert us to issues that other sources miss. As witnesses grew older, many of their memoirs took on the character of a legacy. Their authors evinced an urgent need not to forget as they were, indeed, forgetting. Still, the very process of writing may have actually made it possible for some people to remember (if imperfectly) details of fading events and sentiments, even as some may have continued to hide from themselves events too terrible to bring up.

But memoirs of the Nazi era are not just practical correctives or wellsprings of detail. Anna Reading has eloquently argued that when a survivor writes a memoir, it is

> not just a book, it is a life: it symbolically replaces books burnt and cultural and social memories destroyed; it provides a testament in the face of Nazi lies ... creating a memorial. ... It is also a book of death: within each story of a life survived there is the mute reminder of the ... lives untold and abruptly ended.[7]

Further, there is an intrinsic value to giving voice to people who officially had none. If we reject memoirs, we silence Jews again and are left with Nazi government documents and those of a censored and self-censoring Jewish community. These records, too, are one-sided. To use, for example, Gestapo records without reference to the memoirs of those who faced the Gestapo gives a skewed impression, not only leaving out the victims' perspectives but accepting the Gestapo's often inflated view of itself and its derisive view of the Jews it hounded. Jews reacted, analyzed, and resisted, and their memoirs remind us of that.[8] Without their memoirs, we would have—and have had—a one-sided view of the Nazi era: listening to the perpetrators' voices and silencing the victims.

Silence was also a problem for women's history, where challenging the dominant (male) narrative has been a central task. When it was a relatively new field in the 1970s, historians of women, spurred on by and part of the growing feminist movement, sought women as subjects of their own history.[9] Until then, as Virginia Woolf had put it a half century earlier, one could catch only "a glimpse of them in the lives of the great, whisking away into the background, concealing, I sometimes think, a wink, a laugh, perhaps a tear."[10] *Becoming Visible*[11] (the title of one of the first volumes of European women's history in this period) presented major challenges. Women did peek through some economic and demographic statistics (though not others), some political platforms (though not most), some religious, communal, and organizational records (in lesser positions), and some municipal and legal documents (usually as exceptions to male entitlements and privileges). They could also be found in fiction and in prescriptive literature ("how to" books, cookbooks, sermons), being told how to behave.

As historians of women began to document the importance of the private sphere to which women had been relegated—a sphere devalued and trivialized not only by their own societies but by the very disciplines that claimed to analyze those societies—they not only found women in private but noted their pervasive influence in public as well. Further, they sought to uncover women's voices, beliefs, and memories. We were not content to relate women's behaviors but wanted to unearth their worries, sorrows, and triumphs. How did they experience daily life, including such situations as courtship, marriage, childbearing and rearing, work, and faith, not prescriptively but descriptively, from their own experiences, through their own lenses? Women's historians required novel sources, not the public sources that valorized male categories, and thus were among the first to use memoirs for social history.[12]

Historians of German-Jewish women faced issues similar to those of Jewish historians and women's historians with the additional concern of whether such sources existed for a doubly marginalized group. Whereas early modern historians had to make do with the rare and, for many reasons, exceptional memoir, such as Glikl of Hameln's,[13] historians of modern German-Jewish history were far more fortunate. Besides the commonplace sources that occasionally included women, German Jews left a rich bequest in the form of memoirs. Part of the nineteenth-century bourgeois project, which also included diaries and letter-writing, memoirs were private, generally intended for families. Most of these writers had no sense that historians would some day comb through their writings for countless details and insights. Only a tiny number ever held hopes of publication, and an even smaller number succeeded. Most of these memoirs are available to scholars only because the authors' children and grandchildren who no longer read German have donated them to archives.[14] These writings reconstruct individual pasts and simultaneously preserve broader cultural memories for us. Available in several important archives, particularly the Leo Baeck Institute in New York and the Houghton Library at Harvard University, memoirs have provided invaluable resources to scholars of German-Jewish history and have been the most essential and most versatile source for German-Jewish women's history.

Memoirs come closest to revealing Jews and women—and for my purposes, German-Jewish women—as whole persons engaged in private and public life. In elucidating the personally meaningful episodes in a life and how people perceived their own lives, they are often more eloquent than most other sources. In addition, women's memoirs allow historians to gain access to the "thick"[15] details of women's daily lives down to the dinners they cooked and their children's habits of play. These memoirs are often episodic rather than comprehensive, focusing on specific moments, personal minutiae, and "ways of knowing the world and the self that do not divide the heart from the head."[16] In so doing, they help us to interpret their historical and cultural contexts.

Memoirs also provide an unrivaled source for gender analyses: presenting the construction of a gendered self-identity, the power dynamics between men and women, and the relationship between the individual and society in creating, perpetuating, or challenging gender norms and expectations.[17] Indeed, women's memoirs may emphasize relationships more than do men's. While men's memoirs often relate familial and personal stories—in fact some of the examples below come from men—they tend to focus heavily on their educations and career paths, and often on their political observations. Women's memoirs instead center on their grandparents, parents, siblings, husbands, children, and the wider circle of family and friends.[18] Indeed, explaining why I relied heavily (although not exclusively) on women's memoirs in *Between Dignity and Despair*, I wrote that women's memoirs offered an inclusive viewpoint: "Men and children, as well as extended family and friendship networks, were central to women's recollections and hence are visible and active at every turn."[19]

Most significantly, women's memoirs let us hear women's own voices. This is, to be sure, one reason why feminists have traditionally prized women's testimonies. Unlike elite (mostly male) autobiographies, women's memoirs give voice to the experience of a minority, not in the numerical sense of the word but in the experiential sense. They offer readers evidence of women's agency and subjectivity, showing women at work, women appearing before government agents, and women forming their own organizations. They also depict the barriers that men set up against women, depriving them of educations, careers, and legal equality. And, crucially, they reveal how women understood and reacted to these predicaments.

Critics of memoirs contend that these voices can deceive, and they are not entirely wrong. Memory "selects, condenses, and interprets experience"[20] and memoirs often contradict themselves or fluctuate between "then"—when the events occurred—and "now"—when the writer sees the past with the benefit of hindsight and the influence of current ideologies. Moreover, the way memoirs reconstruct the past "is always more coherent" than when it happened.[21] Further, memory and history are distinct despite their links: the "fissure ... between experiencing an event and remembering it ... is unavoidable."[22] In addition, memory and history develop dialectically, influencing each other as they pass into popular accounts.[23] Some critics, engaged in debates about representation, also charge that memoirs are merely constructions, accounts using the narrative conventions of their day. They offer, at best, only a romantic gloss on the past.

Historians who use memoirs, however, know that memoirs do not simply sentimentalize. Although they provide mediated perspectives on "reality," influenced by contemporary mores and expectations, by thoughts of possible readers, by the writer's position in terms of class, politics, religiosity, and so on, they also show debates and ruptures. They outline stereotypes and challenges to those stereotypes. They describe social expectations and how these were negotiated and contravened.

Historians are also aware that memoirs skim over or repress family secrets. "Secrecy about family," writes bell hooks, "about what went on in the domestic household was a bond between us," and Nancy Miller adds that when she wrote about her family she was "flying in the face of the parental injunction not to 'tell' that had haunted [her] adolescence and continued well into [her] adult years ... the shame over family secrets."[24] Hence memoirs cannot give us a direct line to "wie es eigentlich gewesen ist."[25]

Indeed, memoirs often describe an ideal as much as a reality, reporting, for example, the way family life was supposed to be, while repressing or reinterpreting actual experiences. Referring to precisely this kind of idealization in the introduction to *The Making of the Jewish Middle Class*, I wrote that memoirs "do not capture nuances in the role divisions possible even in Imperial Germany. ... Memoirs often describe how family feeling was created and ritualized as much as they convey an accurate state of affairs."[26] Most obviously, the memoirs available to us represent the lives of middle class or upwardly mobile populations, limiting us to that particular group of "successes." Rarely do we read the story of outright failure.[27] Further, the memoirists, or their offspring, who gave the material to a Jewish organization, still had some connection to Judaism, to their Jewish families, or to the

Jewish community. Hence, we rarely find those who had moved far from the religion and community in archives of Jewish history.

Despite these drawbacks, I maintain that memoirs can and do reflect certain collective experiences, social and cultural processes and behaviors, that affected many if not most modern German Jews. They also convey a striking variety of self-understandings within relatively homogeneous groups, such as bourgeois, urban Jews. They do not only add life and the complex texture of the day-to-day. When juxtaposed with other sources, they fill in important gaps and begin to complete and complicate the puzzle. Notably, they have provoked questions about which I had not previously thought, and they have challenged hypotheses I had formulated as a result of other sources. For example, memoirs by Jews (male and female) who proudly proclaim total "assimilation" into German society, intentionally underlining the decline of Jewish belief and behavior and the rise of conversion, sometimes inadvertently tell another story, disclosing continuing Jewish associations and allegiances. In fact, one finds an ongoing tension between the longing to acculturate and the often equally compelling desire to maintain Jewish customs and connections. While we acknowledge their stance, reading critically also shows that the information memoirists provide can contradict their own assertions.

Similar contradictions can be found in German-Jewish women's memoirs. Two examples may suffice, the first having to do with women and work. Bourgeois ideology and social convention required middle class women to be "leisured," that is, not to work for pay or even to be seen working in order to maintain their own and their family's status and reputation. The fear was that if a middle class woman "worked," her husband's or father's businesses would suffer, the daughters would remain unmarriageable, and disgrace would descend upon the family. Statistics seemed to support the ideology, indicating that most Jewish women did not "work." Yet memoirs that submitted to the official ideology offer a multitude of examples of just the opposite: women doing work in the household, work in the pub, work in the front and back rooms of the shop, work typing legal briefs, work ordering stock, work taking in washing or sewing, on and on.

Faced with women's own descriptions of their work, I realized that it would be necessary to rethink the definition of "work." I used the term "unrecognized work," since most of these women clearly "worked" but did not get paid and were, therefore, not included in the official statistics. In fact, until 1907 the German census—as fallible as other human endeavors[28]— called them "helping family members" (*mithelfende Familienangehörige*), a term that allowed the government to ignore or diminish women's (and family members') work and families to save on taxes. But the memoirs spoke loud and clear: women worked far more than the official data acknowledged.

The ways in which women's memoirs unintentionally debunked the term "leisure" provide the second example. Leisure, too, was part of nineteenth-century bourgeois ideology as "the ideal of work was supplemented by the ideal of leisure."[29] For bourgeois men in the *Kaiserreich*, leisure was "time off" or "free, unoccupied time," and "not work." The German term, *Freizeit*, means exactly that—for men. Bourgeois women, too, represented themselves as "leisured," yet their memoirs focus on how anxiously and energetically they strove to create class-appropriate leisure-time activities. Certainly these provided enjoyment, but they also required great exertion.[30] Wives and mothers, aware of the importance of *Bildung* and representation, sought to reflect the status and wealth of their husbands as they carefully choreographed their family's activities. Leisure was work: organizing musical evenings for the wider family, reading fairy tales to the toddlers, planning and carrying out appropriate dinner parties for business associates, arranging summer holidays that would also preserve kin and friendship networks, making the required afternoon "calls" on husbands' business partners' wives, visiting spas in the hope of finding the right marriage partner for a son or daughter. Who did the arranging, cooking, cleaning, shopping, and packing for these occasions? The memoirs caution historians that for women, "leisure" was work.

To scholars who are concerned that memoirs are too subjective and merely reiterate cultural values of the day,[31] I would respond that the above examples show that the opposite can also be the case. The intersection of biography and history, in fact, can set the record straight: popular stereotypes and contemporary representations can meet their comeuppance when confronted by memoirs.

But memoirs provide more than a representation of one individual's subjectivity. Patterns of behavior and emotions emerge when one peruses scores of memoirs. Two such patterns that became noticeable to me may provide examples. The first, a gender analysis of religiosity in the late nineteenth century, leads to the conclusion that women clung to domestic Judaism, to Jewish practice at home, longer than men. The second example illustrates that Jewish men and women experienced gender role reversals during the Nazi era. Neither of these are startling theses. Yet I would not have imagined them had I not been an avid reader of memoirs.

A common assumption regarding religion is that it waned in the nineteenth century.[32] While this may describe a general phenomenon, it is memoirs that call our attention to the very gendered nature of this "waning." Historically, men and women passed on gendered traditions in Judaism: women cultivated a "domestic Judaism," while men "counted" in the public expressions of religion. Families, and particularly women, mediated Judaism on a daily, personal basis since family-based ritual was (and is) an essential part of Jewish practice. As (male) public ritual and Torah study decreased in the nineteenth century, Jews assigned new meaning to religiosity that focused on the home and family. The public and private, however, needed each other. The Sabbath and holidays required both home and synagogue observances. Each had an impact on the other and could reinforce or weaken Jewish life.

In villages and towns, public prayer and private observance tended to reinforce each other. One's loyalty to Judaism as faith and community could be appraised publicly by the stores one patronized or the homes in which one agreed to dine and privately by whether or not one observed the laws of kashruth. For boys in these settings, Judaism meant a close identification with their fathers' rituals, for example in prayer quorums. For the whole family, mothers played a pivotal role in maintaining domestic traditions, with food setting the tone of the household, reflecting its ideology and mentality.[33] Memoirs often cite special Sabbath meals as important markers of identity even when some Jews began to ignore most religious observance. The distinctive Sabbath atmosphere—special foods, special clothing, white tablecloths, candles, and finer tableware—often remembered with nostalgia, was attributed to women's initiative and work.[34] And women took special care arranging for major holidays.[35] Hugo Marx (b. 1892, Heidelberg) believed his mother created their Jewish home: "She demanded ... orthodox ... rituals: a kosher household with separation of tableware and dishes for milk and meat, the strict observance of the Sabbath, from which ... father ... withdrew in order to pander to his passion for smoking."[36]

In cities, where a more competitive lifestyle was thought to require keeping shops open on the Sabbath and where the strict watchfulness of the rural community had been left far behind, many an urban synagogue stood nearly empty except on the High Holidays. With male synagogue attendance in decline, religious behavior privatized. Judaism shifted its focus (though not its theology) to women's domestic practice, particularly the Sabbath, private prayer, and family holidays.[37] Jewish cookbooks can supplement memoirs here, testifying to women's ongoing culinary commitment to Jewish foods—even when ingredients were no longer strictly kosher. The informal transmission of Judaism—affective, private, and personal, including foods, family, and hearth—was in large measure women's domain.

In other words, women shaped the social and cultural milieu in which traditional sentiments were reinforced and also provided memories of their practice to their children. In fact, the memories and the sentiments they evoked may have been more important than men's public practice. Looking back over a lifetime, children seem to have been more emotionally affected by their mothers' behavior as revealed in the home (whether positive or negative) than by their fathers' attendance at synagogue or their own religious instruction. In asserting how "assimilated" he was, Paul Mühsam (b. 1876, Brandenburg) added that Jewish holidays "remained mere names for me." Reporting on the totally *un*religious behavior of his *parents*, he nevertheless remembered that "every Friday evening I saw my mother quietly praying to herself from her prayer book, conscientiously rising up at the prescribed places."[38] Others note that mothers continued to fast long after fathers had stopped this observance.[39] Curt Rosenberg (b. 1876, Berlin), who learned nothing of his religion except his nighttime prayers, noted that his mother taught these to him and he could not fall asleep without them.[40]

Why women maintained their allegiance may be deduced from their roles in religion and society. Memoirs allow us to see that they experienced less dissonance than men between public time and private time, between religious practice and their daily routines. Their private world was more traditional than modern, more easily timed to sacred and seasonal markers.[41] In addition, women could exert some control in the home, whereas Jewish men faced public obstacles to the performance of religious duties. For example, women could control their kitchen: in one memoir, a woman quoted her husband, "What you do in the kitchen is your own business."[42] Even completely secular husbands did not strongly object to women's religiosity, since women in general were deemed the more pious sex.[43]

Yet memoirs also indicate that women did not *successfully* maintain religion. Often they held on longer than their husbands, as the case of Sigmund and Martha Freud indicates,[44] but children's memoirs generally depict a decline in religious practice: with some exceptions, the generation growing up toward the end of the Imperial era showed less involvement with religion in their later lives than had their parents. Thus, privatization preceded marginalization. Women's activities and beliefs did not carry as much respect as those of men. Since men defined status in terms of public observance, both men and women perceived women's home-based observance as less important. Mothers who hoped to imbue children with a religious spirit faced an uphill battle that many of them lost. The philosopher Edith Stein reported that her mother kept Jewish practices, much to the amusement of her children. They negotiated for shorter Seders and she capitulated.[45]

Bettina Kratz-Ritter has suggested that women's inability to pass on religious rituals was connected to men's disinterest in passing on the more formal public and educational aspects of Judaism (usually to their sons). Since men no longer participated regularly in public practice, sons and daughters no longer understood its content and viewed their mothers' rituals as empty.[46] Further, as already noted, since Judaism had always been gendered with both spheres fortifying each other, it was unlikely that the home *alone* could sustain Judaism. When piety became a "feminine" attribute, it was devalued as such.[47]

Women, dubbed "priestesses of the home" by contemporaries, were thus not all-powerful, successfully buttressing religion as men turned away. Rather, as public ritual declined, religion devolved into the home; the home was the *default* position. This is rarely a position of power. Moreover, even the term "priestess" was a term foisted on women by men who conveniently (and hypocritically) blamed them for the demise of religion.[48] Thus, just as the devaluation of religion brought about its feminization, the feminization of religion brought about its devaluation.

However, this process was complicated and contradictory: the feminization of religion also brought about its *heightened valuation* as part of family embourgeoisment. Especially (but not only) in secular families, women combined religious and familial celebrations. They did this with relish, raising their own status and social power in the process. Family—and women's central role in it— and religion reinforced each other and were impossible to disentangle. As the family maintained modern religious practices, religion affirmed family and group connectedness. One woman wrote of the 1880s in Berlin: "Besides the ceremony of Friday nights there was a strict rule of family togetherness."[49] Thus, religion enhanced family and women's role in it just as women promoted religion in combination with family togetherness. The "priestess," then, was neither uniformly powerful nor merely subjected. Memoirs provide this insight that neither newspapers nor prayerbooks nor sermons allow us. Memoirs present a more complex world even as they emphasize that most women held on longer both to religion and to the familial perks that came with it.[50] Statistics bolster this overwhelming impression, showing that women converted and intermarried less than did men.

The story of women and religion found in memoirs shows women as agents of their own lives—but always within boundaries. Rather than valorize women or turn them into powerful giants, my own framework for thinking about women's history rests on work I appropriated not from a feminist source but from a German Jew baptized at birth in 1818:

> People make their own history, but they do not make it as they please; they do not make it under circumstances chosen by themselves; but under circumstances existing already, given and transmitted from the past.[51]

Similarly, when the ever more constricting circumstances of Nazism created fear and turmoil, memoirs allow us to look into the private lives of German Jews. They illustrate a complex situation and open our eyes to the unexpected. Memoirs of men and women uncover the gender role reversals within families that would otherwise have been difficult to discover. Their normal middle class lives and expectations overturned, Jewish women and men embraced new strategies that they would in all likelihood never have entertained in ordinary times. For women, this meant adopting roles as partner, breadwinner, family protector, and defender of the business or practice, tasks that were often strange to them and which they recorded with the apprehension they felt at the time. Increasingly, women found themselves representing or defending their husbands, fathers, or brothers. Many tales have been recorded of women who saved a family member from the arbitrary demands of the state or from the Gestapo. In these cases, it was always assumed that the Nazis would not break gender norms: they might arrest or torture Jewish men but would not harm women. Thus traditional gender expectations afforded Jewish women greater freedom at first, and they regularly mediated between state and family. They were able to manipulate the system slightly, and consequently they took on a more assertive role in the public sphere than ever before. Other women interceded for family members with German emigration or finance officials. In some cases, they not only broke gender barriers but also normal standards of legality. Many memoirs report that Nazi officials had to be bribed and that, despite their original shock at such requirements, women quickly handed them the necessary goods or money.[52]

Women took on even more demanding tasks, some actually assuming responsibility for the entire family's safety. One woman traveled to Palestine to assess the situation there. Her husband, who could not leave, simply told her, "If you decide you would like to live in Palestine, I will like it too." Another woman went to England to negotiate her family's emigration with British officials and medical colleagues.[53] Women also found themselves in threatening situations, in which their bravery benefited from luck. Twenty-year-old Ruth Abraham helped three men: she regularly accompanied her father to the Gestapo for his weekly interrogation; hurried from jail to jail until she found her uncle and then appealed with great trepidation to a judge who released him; and, after the November Pogrom (*"Kristallnacht"*), she managed to free her future father-in-law from Dachau concentration camp by going there in person.[54]

Women behaved in "unwomanly" ways, some putting up a strong front when men became despondent. It is striking that in the testimony of both men and women, women's calm, dry-eyed state in the midst of turmoil is emphasized. Charlotte Stein-Pick recalled her husband's counsel on the day of the pogrom: " 'Just no tears and no scene.' ... But even without this warning I would have controlled myself."[55] Whether this desire to appear calm was a result of middle class upbringing in the face of what they perceived as the Nazi rabble, an attempt by Jews to retain their dignity or their families' equilibrium in the face of persecution, an assertion of Jewish pride in the face of "Aryan" savagery, or a proclamation of female stalwartness to counter the stereotype of female "frailty," it is noted more by women about themselves than by men about themselves. Probably men took this kind of behavior for granted, whereas women, previously allowed and encouraged to be the more "emotional" sex, were particularly conscious of their efforts at self-control.

New roles may have increased familial stress in some cases, since women were "acting like men," but in general both women and men appreciated the importance of the new behavior. After the November Pogrom, women had to run from office to office in order to have their husbands released from concentration camps. Some saw not only to their release but also to the sale of their joint property. Accompanying her husband home after his imprisonment, one wife explained that she had just sold their house and bought tickets to Shanghai for the family. Her husband recalled that anything was fine with him, as long as they could escape.[56]

Even as women took on more responsibilities in public, however, often including new jobs, most traditional gender dynamics with regard to housekeeping, childrearing, and especially cooking, remained the same. And although women pushed for emigration, men (or, ultimately, circumstances) generally made the decisions. That is, husbands decided that the family should flee, or were arrested during the November Pogrom and not released until their wives could provide evidence about their immediate emigration. In sum, while legal decrees, newspapers, Jewish communal records, and emigration and immigration documents, among other sources, provide important information regarding Jewish life in Nazi Germany, memoirs offer a unique perspective, allowing us to investigate the domestic scene, the anxieties, actions, and interactions of Jewish women and men. Moreover, memoirs often provide the only perspective: how would we reconstruct, for example, Lisa Fittko's hazardous trek over a secret route in the Pyrenees leading refugees to the Spanish border?[57]

Such strengths notwithstanding, scholars correctly worry about memory. It is well known that memory is fragile and inaccurate, that eyewitness identification, for example, can be disastrous in court where the utmost level of accuracy is required. But different kinds of memories serve different functions. Memories of childhood customs, family dynamics, foods and meals, yearly vacations, and ritualized events, such as holidays, require far less accuracy and are useful in reconstructing a past. Although some details might not hold up in court, memoirs can still make a claim to a kind of "truth," relying on the writer's memory "as far as I can remember ...." The shifting nature of memory does not disqualify its potential for approaching a verifiable description, nor does the "constructedness of all narratives ... undermine the historical existence of past events."[58] In discussing Andre Breton's comment, "Life is other than what one writes," Susan Rubin Suleiman suggests: "He did not mean that writing is a lie but rather that writing is always one step behind or ahead of or next to the facts of lived experience—all the more so when that experience took place decades ago." Although she agrees with Breton, she adds, "life 'is' not what one writes. But one may never get closer to it than that."[59] Holocaust memoirs elucidate this very point: survivors may get some details wrong, but the overall accounts hold.[60] Commenting on the hazy memories of Jews who tended to date the imposition of the yellow star further back than the actual event, Ruth Klüger writes: "That is because the isolation of Jews was already in full swing before September 1941."[61] They had confused the details but had evoked the spirit of the moment: the date was wrong, the picture right.

It would be a serious mistake to reason that because people who write about their lives may forget, select, exaggerate, become confused, and even lie,[62] a few inaccuracies invalidate everything. Instead, "researchers need to show how memory can be cherished, fostered and preserved without imposing on it a burden of accuracy that it cannot bear."[63] Specifically, historians must assume that memoirs are subjective, that there is always negotiation between remembering and forgetting, that memory may merge with family or communal mythologies, and that when we quote from memoirs we are relying on people's historical consciousness, that is, not just "the facts."[64]

This raises the issue of where we can turn for these "facts." Other forms of historical documentation are also inherently problematic. They too do not hold up to scrutiny for their "objectivity." Statistics, for example, perpetuate the debates of their day (as anyone familiar with the census debates in the United States can surely attest). Joan Scott has ably discredited the idea that "numbers are somehow purer and less susceptible to subjective influences than other sources of information."[65] Similarly, newspapers are notoriously beholden to the prejudices and conventions of their times. Tax records as well report what taxpayers claimed to earn, not always what they did earn. Social historians, however, need to do more than analyze one particular text. Using multiple (constructed) sources, a wide variety of (imperfect) documents, and a multitude of (more-or-less reliable) witnesses, we are trying to write a social history. Memoirs, just like other (flawed) sources,[66] are building blocks that contribute toward a more complete and complex account of an era that social historians are trying to write.

Some critics may consider memoirs that describe economic or leisure-time *activities* as more trustworthy than those, for example, that discuss *thoughts or feelings*. They argue that the latter are not reliable or, worse, that memoirs parrot (consciously or unconsciously) the values and social conventions of the writer's youth or of the era in which they were written; that is, they distort history, especially when written by those who have an axe to grind. This can indeed be the case. It is precisely at this juncture that the historian's responsibility to read and evaluate many sources before coming to any overall conclusions enters. Besides the obvious issues of who is writing, when, where, for whom, and why (the traditional *Quellenkritik*), historians need to be aware of the popular stereotypes to which the memoir writer may be succumbing, as well as of the great variety of experiences and understandings of the writer's contemporaries. With these caveats in mind, however, memoirs can offer insights into what people did on a daily basis and always, at the very least, present what they thought they thought or felt. It is our job as historians to evaluate them in order to see what makes sense, what appears commonplace in its era, and what sticks out as distinctive.

However, although an analysis of how memoirists constructed their thoughts or feelings, represented themselves, or tried to make sense of their lives (paying attention to the language, metaphors, gaps, and highlights used by the writers to frame their experiences) is an interesting project, I am not suggesting that social or women's historians should engage in a literary analysis of each memoir with attention to how narratives are formed or how individuals constructed themselves. This is a worthy project in itself, like that of Stefanie Schüler-Springorum, whose article "Das erfolgreiche Leben des Aron Liebeck" analyzes how one man attempted to turn failure into success by writing his memoir.[67] Nor am I recommending that we use memoirs to write a history of representation, to analyze them for tropes and stereotypes, for the discourse they use, the norms they purport to abide by, endorse, or contest. The project of literary historians, who do insightful, often virtuoso readings, is certainly worthwhile. But the task of social historians is a different one.

While literary historians are engaged in what James Young calls "how [history] is passed down to us," social and women's historians are still trying to untangle "what happened."[68] We must read many texts in search of substantiated, verifiable realities and ask what is typical or what is unusual. We do read for language and notice tropes, but in aggregate. A focus on how narratives are constructed cannot arrive at a social history, a history that high-lights the factual, the possible, and the improbable, a history that paints a landscape, paying attention to the broad overview and the specific landmarks. Peter Gay has reminded us that historians are trained to take texts seriously, to "do their utmost to eliminate as many alternative narrations as possible to settle on the one that to their mind *approaches* the truth most closely" [emphasis added]. They understand that texts are created by social constructions and social myths and they have needed no one "to tell them that the standpoint of individual practitioners, in part unconscious, might impede an objective treatment of the past. They would say so as they happily exposed the partiality of others. But they would treat such traps ... as handicaps to be overcome rather than laws ... to be ... obeyed."[69]

Memoirs reveal and conceal like any source; they are written for a variety of purposes and carry within themselves ideologies and feelings. Sometimes they are clearer than traditional documents, sometimes more opaque. It is our job as historians to analyze them, to find patterns, assess discrepancies, and offer interpretations, even as we notice contradictions and acknowledge varieties. Memoirs can help us approach the lives of our historical subjects—asymptotically, like a curve that comes closer and closer to a line but never quite reaches it.

Crucially, memoirs allow women's historians—and historians of German-Jewish women in particular—to put women's behaviors and subjectivities at the center of their research. Memoirs show women trying to gain more control over the making of their own history, thereby correcting the male-centered bias of previous social history. Revealing heretofore undervalued or misunderstood behaviors and voices as well as fluid and unpredictable relationships between women and men, memoirs have helped uncover women's agency and perspectives, always within circumstances "not of their own choosing" but ones they struggled to shape nonetheless.

Notes

1. Nancy Miller used the Updike epigraph in "Teaching Autobiography" in *Getting Personal: Feminist Occasions and Other Autobiographical Acts* (New York: Routledge, 1991), 121.
2. "Their critics" is a considerable understatement: the past fifty years have seen a vast academic literature, written mostly by literary scholars and critics and, in the past decade, by postmodernists, analyzing autobiography. For two early interventions, see Hans W. Gruhle, "Die Selbstbiographie als Quelle Historischer Erkenntnis," in *Hauptprobleme der Soziologie: Erinnerungsgabe für Max Weber*, ed. Melchior Palyi (Munich: Duncker und Humblot, 1923), 1:157–77, and Roy Pascal, *Design and Truth in Autobiography* (Cambridge: Routledge and Paul, 1960). For a more recent discussion see James Olney, *Memory and Narrative: The Weave of Life-Writing* (Chicago:

University of Chicago Press, 1998). For feminist contributions, see the bibliography of Helen M. Buss, *Repossessing the World: Reading Memoirs by Contemporary Women* (Toronto: Wilfred Laurier University Press, 2002).

3. I do not distinguish between memoirs and autobiographies for the purpose of this paper.

4. The journal *History and Memory*, begun in 1989, contributed to the broad discussion. There are dozens of books on the topic. See, for example and for further bibliography, *Historical Perspectives on Memory*, ed. Anne Ollila (Helsinki: SHS, 1999), particularly Ollila's article, "History as Memory and Memory as History." Also in that volume, see: Natalie Zemon Davis, "Who Owns History?" and Georg Iggers, "The Role of Professional Historical Scholarship in the Creation and Distortion of Memory." See also Dominick LaCapra, *History and Memory after Auschwitz* (Ithaca, N.Y.: Cornell University Press, 1998). For a poststructuralist discussion related to gender and history, see Joan Scott, *Gender and the Politics of History* (New York: Columbia University Press, 1988).

5. Jacques Le Goff, *History and Memory*, trans. Steven Rendall and Elizabeth Claman (New York: Columbia University Press, 1992), xi.

6. The concept of ego-document goes back to the 1950s Dutch Jewish historian Jacques Presser, who used it in his classes and in a history of Dutch Jews during the Nazi occupation (*De Ondergang*) and has been revived more recently by another Dutch historian, Rudolf Dekker. While the latter historians focused on memoirs, diaries, travelogues, and letters—"more or less private writing," according to Dekker—early modern German historians have expanded the concept to include documents, such as judicial, administrative, and economic records, that give a glimpse into an individual's self-understanding, fears, values, etc. Mary Lindemann wrote that egodocuments endowed "ordinary lives with agency, dignity, and texture." ("Sources in Social History," in *Encyclopedia of European Social History* [Detroit: Scribner's, 2001], 1:36, and interview with Rudolf M. Dekker in Andreas Rutz, Stefan Elit, and Stephan Kraft, "Egodocumenten: A Virtual Conversation with Rudolf M. Dekker," in *Zeitenblicke* 1, no. 2 [December 20, 2002], http://www.zeitenblicke.historicum.net/2002/02/dekker/index.html).

See also Winfried Schulze, *Ego-Dokumente: Annäherung an den Menschen in der Geschichte* (Berlin: Akademie, 1996), 28; Andreas Rutz, "Ego-Dokument oder Ich-Konstruktion? Selbstzeugnisse als Quellen zur Erforschung des frühneuzeitlichen Menschen," *Zeitenblicke* 1, no. 2 (December 20, 2002), http://www. zeitenblicke. historicum.net/2002/02/rutz/

index.html.

7. Caroline Heilbrun wrote that weaving was a form of women's speech and women's language in old myths (*Hamlet's Mother and Other Women* [New York: Columbia University Press, 1990], 120). Thanks to Stefanie Zelkind for this reference. Anna Reading, *The Social Inheritance of the Holocaust: Gender, Culture and Memory* (New York: Palgrave Macmillan, 2002), 54.

8. For a debate on the usefulness of Nazi government files vs. interviews and memories of the non-Jewish wives of Jewish men rounded up during the "Factory Action," see Nathan Stoltzfus, "Die Wahrheit jenseits der Akten: Wer nur den NS-Dokumenten vertraut, verkennt den Widerstand der Deutschen. Anmerkungen zum Historikerstreit um die 'Rosenstraße'," *Die Zeit*, October 30, 2003, http://zeus.zeit.de/text/2003/45/Rosenstra_a7e. For Wolf Gruner's response, see: History News Network, Center for History, George Mason University, July 8, 2004, http://hnn.us/readcomment. php?id=23196.

9. Eileen Boris and Nupur Chaudhuri, eds., *Voices of Women Historians: The Personal, The Political, The Professional* (Bloomington: Indiana University Press, 1999).

10. *A Room of One's Own* (New York: Harcourt, Brace, 1929), 47.

11. *Becoming Visible: Women in European History*, ed. Renate Bridenthal and Claudia Koonz (Boston: Houghton Mifflin, 1977; 3rd ed., ed. Renate Bridenthal, Susan Mosher Stuard, and Merry Wiesner, 1998).

12. See, for example, *Life as We Have Known It*, ed. Margaret Llewelyn Davies (London: Hogarth, 1931, repr. New York: Norton, 1975).

13. Robert Liberles, " 'She Sees That Her Merchandise Is Good, and Her Lamp Is Not Extinguished at Nighttime': Glikl's Memoir as Historical Source," *Nashim: A Journal of Jewish Women's Studies and Gender Issues*, 7 (spring 2004): 11–27. See also *Die Hamburger Kauffrau Glikl: Jüdische Existenz in der Frühen Neuzeit*, ed. Monika Richarz (Hamburg: Christians Verlag, 2001).

14. Most of the memoirs were written in German, although some were written in English as the refugees' and survivors' English improved over time.

15. Clifford Geertz, "Thick Description: Toward an Interpretive Theory of Culture," in *The Interpretation of Cultures* (New York: Basic Books, 1973), 6.

16. Buss, *Repossessing*, xxv.

17. *Interpreting Women's Lives: Feminist Theory and Personal Narratives*, ed. Personal Narratives Group (Bloomington: Indiana University Press, 1989), 4–5.

18. Buss, *Repossessing*, 13, notes that men's lives are certainly relational but in ways that men's autobiographies have been unwilling to recognize. See also Nancy Miller, "What Do You Think of My Memoir?" in *But Enough about Me: Why We Read Other People's Lives* (New York: Columbia University Press, 2002), 2.

19. Marion Kaplan, *Between Dignity and Despair: Jewish Life in Nazi Germany* (New York: Oxford University Press, 1998), 7.

20. Hamida Bosmajian, *Metaphors of Evil: Contemporary German Literature and the Shadow of Nazism* (Iowa City: University of Iowa Press, 1979), 23.

21. David Lowenthal, "Nostalgia Tells It Like It Wasn't," in *The Imagined Past: History and Nostalgia*, ed. Christopher Shaw and Malcolm Chase (Manchester: Manchester University Press, 1989), 30.

22. Andreas Huyssen, *Twilight Memories* (London: Routledge, 1995), 3.

23. Le Goff, *History and Memory*, xi. See also Maurice Halbwachs, *On Collective Memory*, trans. L. A. Coser (Chicago: University of Chicago Press, 1992).

24. bell hooks, "Writing Autobiography," in *Feminisms: An Anthology of Literary Theory and Criticism*, ed. Robyn Warhol and Diane Price Herndl (New Brunswick: Rutgers University Press, 1991), 1036; Miller, "My Father's Penis," in *Getting Personal*, 147.

25. "Wie es eigentlich gewesen ist" was the expression used by Leopold von Ranke (1795–1886) in formulating his notion of historical writing and passed down to generation upon generation of historians. For a recent discussion of the "metaphysics" of Rankean thought, see Otto Gerhard Oexle, "Was ist eine historische Quelle?" *Rechtsgeschichte* 4 (2004): 167–70. Thanks to Till van Rahden for recommending this highly suggestive piece to me.

26. For further discussion of the use of memoirs, see the introduction to Marion Kaplan, *The Making of the Jewish Middle Class: Women, Family and Identity in Imperial Germany* (New York: Oxford University Press, 1991).

27. For the rare example of failure, see Isaac Thannhäuser in *Jüdisches Leben in Deutschland: Selbstzeugnisse zur Sozialgeschichte, 1780–1871*, ed. Monika Richarz (Stuttgart: Deutsche Verlags-Anstalt, 1976), 100–114.

28. Of course, statistics too perpetuate the debates of their day. See below at note 65 for Joan Scott's critique.

29. Peter Gay, *Schnitzler's Century: The Making of Middle-Class Culture 1815–1914* (New York: Norton, 2001), 199; quotation from 219.

30. Feminist historians critiqued the notion of "leisure" very early on; see Barbara Corrado Pope, "Leisured Women in the Nineteenth Century," in Bridenthal, Stuard, and Wiesner, *Becoming Visible*, 298–324, and especially

Leonore Davidoff, *The Best Circles: Women and Society in Victorian England* (Totowa, N.J.: Rowman and Littlefield, 1973).

31. Interestingly, at least these critics accept the value of memoirs, if for a different purpose: that is, discourse analysis.

32. By 1850, the core of loyal church people in German cities made up less than 10 percent of nominal parishioners. Protestants maintained high participation in rites of passage—baptism, marriage, and burial—and preserved some home rituals, such as grace or prayers at night (Lucian Hölscher, "Secularization and Urbanization in the Nineteenth Century," in *European Religion in the Age of Great Cities, 1830–1930*, ed. Hugh McLeod [London: Routledge, 1995], 278, 281–82).

33. See Kaplan, *Jewish Middle Class*, chap. 2.

34. Nostalgia need not automatically discredit a memory. Writers may have worked even harder to recall such childhood rituals due to fear of facing a future without them or the regret of already living without them. We have much to learn—details and feelings—from those saddened by what they left behind and from those delighted by what they rejected. For a critique of nostalgia, see Lowenthal, "Nostalgia."

35. Kaplan, *Jewish Middle Class*, 75.

36. Hugo Marx, *Werdegang eines jüdischen Staatsanwalts und Richters in Baden, 1892–1933* (Villingen, Germany: Neckar-Verlag, 1965), 6.

37. Kaplan, *Jewish Middle Class*, chap. 2.

38. This is also an example of memoirs that mention women's ritual practice in the home but do not seem to "count" it, because it was just not seen to be as important as male practice. But it was remembered even in its denigration (Monika Richarz, *Jüdisches Leben in Deutschland: Selbstzeugnisse zur Sozialgeschichte im Kaiserreich*, (Stuttgart: Deutsche Verlags-Anstalt, 1979), 362.

39. Kaplan, *Jewish Middle Class*, 79.

40. Richarz, *Jüdisches Leben ... im Kaiserreich*, 298.

41. Kaplan, *Jewish Middle Class*, 77.

42. Ibid., 79.

43. Similarly in France; see Bonnie Smith, *Ladies of the Leisure Class: The Bourgeoises of Northern France in the Nineteenth Century* (Princeton: Princeton University Press, 1981).

44. Kaplan, *Jewish Middle Class*, 79.

45. Edith Stein, *Aus meinem Leben* (Freiburg: Herder, 1987), 44. Stein became a Carmelite nun but was later murdered by the Nazis as a Jew.

46. Bettina Kratz-Ritter, *Für "fromme Zionstöchter" und "gebildete Frauenzimmer"* (Hildesheim: Olms, 1995), 94.

47. Feminist leaders like Bertha Pappenheim understood this and encouraged women to educate themselves in Judaism (despite, as she noted, the texts' male perspectives), hoping that women's (feminine) piety and (male) knowledge would reinvigorate Judaism (Kratz-Ritter, *"Fromme Zionstöchter,"* 44).

48. Kaplan, *Jewish Middle Class*, 252 n. 2.

49. Ibid., 75.

50. Did all memoirs show this? No. There were women who persuaded their husbands to stop fasting on Yom Kippur (Kaplan, *Jewish Middle Class*, 81) or who bought a Christmas tree for the home (Walter Benjamin, *Berliner Kindheit um Neunzehnhundert* (Frankfurt a. M.: Suhrkamp, 2000), 32, 103.

51. Karl Marx, *18th Brumaire of Louis Napoleon* (1852), trans. Saul K. Padover (New York: McGraw Hill, 1972) from the German edition of 1869, chap. 1, first page.

52. Kaplan, *Between Dignity and Despair*, 129–31.

53. Ibid., 60.

54. Ruth Abraham, memoirs, Leo Baeck Institute (LBI), 2–5. See also her daughter's account of Ruth's story: Reha Sokolow and Al Sokolow, *Defying the Tide: An Account of Authentic Compassion during the Holocaust* (Jerusalem: Devora Publishing, 2003).

55. " 'Nur keine Tränen und keine Szene' … aber auch ohne diese Mahnung hätte ich mich beherrscht" (Stein-Pick, memoirs, LBI, 39).

56. *Sie durften nicht mehr Deutsche sein: Jüdischer Alltag in Selbstzeugnissen, 1933–1938*, ed. Margarete Limberg and Hubert Rübsaat (Frankfurt: Campus, 1990), 325.

57. Lisa Fittko, *Mein Weg über die Pyrenäen, Erinnerungen 1940/41* (Munich: Carl Hanser, 1985).

58. Susan Rubin Suleiman, "Problems of Memory and Factuality in Recent Holocaust Memoirs: Wilkomirski/Wiesel," *Poetics Today* 21 (2000): 548–49.

59. Ibid., 543, 557.

60. Ibid,, 543–59.

61. "Das kommt daher, dass die Ausgrenzung von Juden eben schon vor September 1941 im vollen Gang war" (Ruth Klüger, *Weiter leben* [Göttingen: Wallstein, 1992], 48).

62. Binjamin Wilkomirski's *Fragments: Memories of a Wartime Childhood* (New York: Schocken, 1996), is a different case (Rubin Suleiman, "Problems of Memory").

63. David Cesarani, "Memory, Representation and Education," in *Remembering for the Future: The Holocaust in an Age of Genocide*, ed. Margot Levy (Hampshire: Palgrave, 2001), 3:235.

64. Moreover, I also assume that an examination of "generational transmission" of the entire *Habitus* (in Bourdieu's sense) of bourgeois life, as suggested by Miriam Gebhardt (at the First International Workshop on Gender in Modern Jewish History), would face similar difficulties. Apart from a slew of definitional issues, generational discourses need a warning flag too. Looking back on their elders will provide us with an easy debunking of parents' "Scheinideologien" but will still leave us trying to get to the ways in which the older generations lived their lives. Moreover, generations are gendered too, and to ignore that will find us spinning our wheels. For the problem of identifying what is a generation, see Karl Mannheim, "The Problem of Generations," in *Essays on the Sociology of Knowledge*, ed. Paul Kecskemeti (New York: Oxford University Press, 1952), 276–322, and the very skeptical approach taken by Alan Spitzer, "The Historical Problem of Generations," *American Historical Review* 78 (1973): 1353–85.

65. Joan Scott, "A Statistical Representation of Work," in *Gender and the Politics of History*, 114.

66. Sources themselves, it has been argued, can no longer be defined today. According to Oexle, "What so-called 'sources' are is no longer definable. Historical material is what is used to answer a historical question. The question decides what ... the material used to answer this question can and must be" ("Was ist eine historische Quelle?" 179).

67. Stefanie Schüler-Springorum, " 'Denken, Wirken, Schaffen': Das erfolgreiche Leben des Aron Liebeck," in *Juden, Bürger, Deutsche: Zur Geschichte von Vielfalt und Differenz 1800–1933*, ed. Andreas Gotzmann, Rainer Liedtke, and Till van Rahden (Tübingen: Mohr Siebeck, 2001), 369–93. After my essay was completed, Michael Stanislawski's *Autobiographical Jews: Essays in Jewish Self-Fashioning* was published by the University of Washington Press (Seattle, 2004). He, much like Schüler-Springorum, draws on current literary theory (though he also uses contemporary neurosciences) to question scholars' use of memoirs for information. Through an often brilliant reading of several Jewish autobiographical texts, he concludes that historians must distinguish between the writers' search for their "selfhood" and a factual depiction of their lives and times. Of course, this is the historian's job—to use *all* sources with care.

68. James Young, *At Memory's Edge: After-Images of the Holocaust in Contempo-*

rary Art and Architecture (New Haven: Yale University Press, 2002), 11. Young suggests "making historical inquiry the combined study of both what happened and how it passed down to us." This is an ambitious project.

69. Peter Gay, *Savage Reprisals: Bleak House, Madame Bovary, Buddenbrooks* (New York: Norton, 2002), 153, 155. See also the epilogue, in which he addresses the challenges of postmodernism.

How German and How Jewish Were the German Jews?

Reflections on the Problem of Identity

SHULAMIT VOLKOV

I would like to start by quoting from a letter, written from Berlin by my late father in that eventful spring of 1933. It was addressed to his future wife, my mother, who was by then already back at her parents' home in Tel Aviv. She had left Germany on 16 April, as soon as she was able to secure her newly acquired medical degree, and expected him to join her immediately thereafter. But the young Rudolf Otto Heinsheimer, born in 1908 in the peaceful resort town of Baden-Baden, an assistant in the prestigious law faculty at the University of Berlin, was undergoing a severe personal crisis and had deep misgivings concerning his next steps. He was desperately struggling to put into words what a decision to leave Germany really meant for him. After all, he wrote, it involved freeing himself "from a whole series of things unshakable and unquestionable. ... From this country and your belonging to it, that were till now self-evident; from the language and the culture, that were till now your natural foundations; ... from the never-doubted urban milieu of Central Europe; from the life habits and the lifestyle of an intellectual petit-bourgeois; from the climate and seasons of the temperate zone, etc."[1] Considering her Russian background and her clear-cut sense of Jewish belonging, how was he to explain this "self-evident certainty with which I was a German—even if it were a thousand times an error" to the woman to whom the letter was addressed?[2]

My father was probably not typical of German Jewry. If any-thing, he stood at the cutting edge of assimilation, so to speak, representing complete Germanness within the broader spectrum of German-Jewish identity in his day. While his parents, a physi-cian and the daughter of a well-to-do banker, never converted, they made sure that the local Protestant church properly accepted their three children. It was a procedure preferred by quite a few Jews in their circle. So my father, thoughtful and methodical as ever, duly reported that he planned to leave the church within days, or as soon as he got the formal approval of his parents, "although I could of course do it," he added, "against their wishes too." "But would you like me to join Judaism immediately?" he continues the letter, "... I, who know so little of its religion, its history, its language, its culture, etc. and who cannot have any sense of 'natural belonging' to it at all? And should I also immedi-ately announce my joining the Zionist Organization?" He contin-ues, "Can I? May I? I think not. Since to be a member of such a community is for me more than the simple acquisition of a mem-bership card. I do not wish to be a Jew, or a Zionist, only because external circumstances bring me to it, but only when I am drawn to it, belong to it, from within." And then, perhaps in order to reassure his faraway love, he concludes: "But I believe with cer-tainty now, that it will come to that."[3]

No doubt, my father was acutely aware of the enormous shift required of him. By a sheer act of will, he now had to relinquish one identity and replace it with another. He was not sure he had it in him to go through with all that. It was tearing him apart from within. His self-awareness as a German had previously been unshakable, and by the beginning of May 1933, he was still ready to reaffirm it, despite the fact that his university career had just been brought to an abrupt end under the most humiliating cir-cumstances, and despite the fact that by then his immediate social circle included many fellow-students from Palestine—all adamant Zionists and Jewish nationalists. He was 25 years old at the time.

His purist stance on matters of identity may have had something to do with his youth. He was looking not for a practical solution but for a genuine way out of an inner upheaval. But in that, too, he may have been an exception. Later on, as early as my own memories go, he always stood out among his contemporaries. He was a German-Jew, a "Yekke" as they were often called then, who insisted on speaking only Hebrew, a man who always maintained close ties with non-German emigrants, immersing himself entirely in the life and culture of his new homeland. In these letters, one touches the pain of separation surely shared by many, but otherwise they hardly reflect the identity problem faced by German Jews as a whole.

Most of them would have defined that problem in very different terms. Especially common was their insistence on what came to be known as their hyphenated German-Jewish identity. For a number of generations, the majority of the Jews living in Germany upheld more or less comfortably two parallel identities— German *and* Jewish—and maintained belief in their full, even inherent compatibility. This, indeed, is a story told many times. It begins, like modern German-Jewish history as such, with Moses Mendelssohn. *His* task was to prove that Judaism could function and prosper, together with other religions—and in fact even more naturally than those—within any modern state. Such a state, to be sure, had to observe a clear distinction between church and polity; but that, after all, was precisely the meaning and the basis of its modernity. Under such circumstances, Mendelssohn refused to see the potential for conflict.[4] Others also searched for harmony. So did the anxious and dedicated members of the *Verein für die Cultur und Wissenschaft der Juden* in Berlin of the early 1820s, for instance, combining their newly acquired academic education with a slowly reforming Jewishness; patiently, scientifically— according to their own conception—working to reshape it to fit their new Germanness.[5] This was also the story of Heinrich Heine, a one-time member of the *Verein*, forever vacillating between his Jewish background and his German patriotism, never quite free of the burden imposed by the tension involved, either before or after his conversion.[6] It was the story of the great Jewish reformers, who wished to introduce proper *Sittlichkeit* (respectability) into the synagogue, making it more "civilized" and acceptable to bourgeois taste.[7] It was the story of all those preachers and thinkers who for more than a century tried every avenue for bringing together what they perceived as the two sides of their existence. It was, of course, the story of the founders of the *Centralverein deutscher Staatsbürger jüdischen Glaubens* (the Central Organization of German Citizens of the Jewish Faith) later, during the 1890s, who wished to combine precisely these two components of their lives into the centerpiece of their ideology.[8] It was, perhaps in its most fully crystallized fashion, the story of Hermann Cohen, the neo-Kantian philosopher who—more than anyone else—labored to define the symbiotic relationship between *Deutschtum* and *Judentum*.[9] And it was finally the story of all those who, though perhaps less self-consciously and less elaborately, strove daily to combine their ever more deeply felt German self-consciousness with their still-cherished traditional community. Significantly, in fact, they often did this with a good measure of ease and elegance, with not too much inconvenience and with only occasional and temporary embarrassment. Individual examples to that effect can be endlessly multiplied. It is indeed a well-known saga.

However, this familiar tale is too often told either totally out of context or within restricted and very limited confines. After all, when Moses Mendelssohn was struggling to formulate the compatibility of Judaism with modernity, Germanness was hardly an issue at all. Schiller's and Goethe's quest for a Germany, which they knew not "wo es liegt" (where it lies), was no rhetorical gesture. The Holy Roman Empire, the only truly German political entity at the time, was by then no more than an empty vessel, meaningful perhaps only as the protector of the many small, sometimes tiny, often indeed only virtual political entities within it. At that time, while *patriotism* was normally directed at one or another of the particular German states, *nationalism* was not yet even an option. At the dawn of the modern era, being *more* or *less* German was either seen as a vague matter of marginal significance or as problematic for everyone in the German-speaking milieu of Central Europe, by no means only for Jews.

For centuries, the only aspect of life that had had any meaning for one's personal identity, beyond one's immediate familial ties and local community, was—if anything—religion.[10] Like nationalism later on, religious identity made claims to primacy and exclusivity. As far as Jews were concerned, the relevant dualism was that between Christianity and Judaism, not between *Deutschtum* (Germanness) and *Judentum* (Judaism). Even by the eighteenth century, the slow and hesitant secularization, under the aegis of the Enlightenment, did not suffice to change this state of affairs. Mendelssohn's intellectual friends expected him to convert to Christianity, not to become more "German." Later, even so principled a champion of emancipation as Wilhelm von Humboldt seemed to believe that most Jews would eventually find their way to equality through conversion, and while he did not expect them to accept Christian dogma, he did expect them to embrace Christianity as the religion of a humanist culture.[11] Finally, it was Heinrich Heine, who so aptly coined that familiar saying, making conversion the only reliable *"entrée-billet* to European culture."

Heine may have later had second thoughts, but during much of the pre-1848 period, this was indeed a main entry-gate for Jews who wished to be finally equal to their Christian neighbors—not always entirely satisfactory perhaps, but for quite a few of them apparently unavoidable. The continuing trickle of conversions throughout the nineteenth century serves to underline the persistent importance of religion in the centuries-old "game" of shaping identities. Converting one's children, as we have seen in my father's case, was regarded as proper, even desirable, even while converting oneself was increasingly considered embarrassing or disgraceful. Clearly, the strategy of conversion lost much of its efficacy toward the latter part of the nineteenth century.[12] After all, the novelty of emancipation was in opening the option of belonging without conversion. Indeed, in post-emancipation Germany, during much of the second half of the nineteenth century, the great majority of Jews preferred to uphold their religious belonging, combining it with a new sense of Germanness—a supra-religious category becoming ever more important at the time.

From the outset, Germanness included Germans of the two major Christian confessions, of course, Protestants and Catholics. But as in other European countries, overcoming religious diversity proved a tangled issue for rising nationalism. This was most particularly the case in Germany. Early German nationalism had a distinctly Protestant flavor. Immediately after the fall of Napoleon, it was at the Wartburg near Eisenach that the first nationalist celebration had been staged—a clearly Protestant site with explicitly Protestant connotations. Catholicism, it was assumed, could not be expected to give up its old-style universalistic claims. It took the full force of Romanticism to make the Catholic cathedral in Köln a site of joint German national pride, and only many decades later was it possible to fully integrate Catholics within the German national movement.[13] Catholics did share in the new Germanness of liberals—and some democrats—during the *Vormärz* and in the revolution of 1848. Theirs, however, was always a somewhat different Liberal-Nationalism, and later events, especially during the *Kulturkampf*, served only to demonstrate their fragile position, even within the newly created German nation-state. As late as 1907, the renowned Protestant theologian Adolf Harnack stated, "In numerous and important questions of life and of the common weal, our nation is at the outset divided into two camps, and this state of affairs, starting from the center, works its way into the periphery of our existence, deep into the smallest and most everyday aspects of our lives. Everywhere one confronts confessional prejudices; everywhere one encounters the fence, indeed the wall of confession."[14]

Thus, beyond the circle of north German, often Prussian, Protestants, Germanness was often not an obvious, straightforward anchor of self-identification. As time went by, and with the continuous discrediting of the *Großdeutsche* (great-German) solution to the so-called "German Question," things were not made any easier for Catholics. When Harnack elaborated on the "essence of Christianity," the counterimage for his own, distinctly Protestant identity was not, of course, Judaism, but Catholicism.[15] Confessional issues never stopped undermining the simple notions of German self-identity. It was part and parcel of its ambivalent nature. Jews could take comfort in this situation. At least on the face of it, theirs was not the only identity under fire.

Clearly, Catholics were always seen as a camp *within* a divided nation, while Jews were all too often denied membership in that nation altogether. But such membership was for a long time a rather complex matter. Beginning in the Enlightenment and during the times of monarchical Absolutism, being "German" could only mean one of two things. It could mean sharing with others an equal civil status within one of the particular German states, or it could mean partaking in German *Bildung*, that one defining element of the only national class in Germany at that time—the *Bildungsbürgertum*, the educated bourgeoisie. Citizenship as a major source of self-identification could not play any role in a country still ruled by aristocratic bureaucracies and autocratic rulers. At that time, civil rights were too rare in Germany to be made a criterion of belonging to a nation, a proof of one's *being German*. To be sure, there were always those who insisted that such rights and only such rights ought to be the relevant criteria. Perhaps the most outspoken representative of this position among German Jews was Gabriel Riesser. Riesser, a Jewish attorney from Hamburg, and by 1848 a major activist at the National Assembly in Frankfurt, wrote his "On the Position of the Jews in Germany" in response to a publication by an obscure church official from Heidelberg, Heinrich Eberhardt Paulus, who had called on all Jews in Germany to finally provide "a proof of their German nationality" by converting to Christianity. It is instructive to recall Riesser's reply: "There is only one baptism that leads to unity in the nation: that is the baptism of blood in the battle for freedom of the motherland."[16] And he was as good as his word, especially during the revolution that followed. Note, however: it was finally *blood* that united, in his case too.

In any case, Riesser's arguments notwithstanding, patriotism was clearly not enough. Belonging, at this stage, was above all a cultural matter. It was *Bildung* that defined one's place within that mysterious new entity, "*Deutschtum*," and served as the clearest boundary; although here, too, the line between "in" and "out" was constantly shifting. And indeed, Jewish claims to belonging relied most particularly on their proven dedication to this *Bildung*.[17] The theme of Jewish interest in and commitment to it occupies center stage in what we call "German-Jewish historiography," and its argument runs as follows: *Bildung* was the main route open to Jews who wished to join bourgeois German society. Some historians date their eagerness to pass through this gate to the first half of the eighteenth century, claiming that Jews were already noticeable in literary circles, for instance, even then.[18] Certainly in later years they were prominent in the artistic and scholarly life of Germany and contributed disproportionately to the various spheres of its culture. The tale of Jewish accomplishment in Germany is a familiar one. It was a source of pride for German Jews and often seems to have remained so for present-day historians as well.

However, *Bildung*, too, was a problematic concept on which to construct the Germanness of the Jews. Its immanent ambivalence can easily be shown, since a mechanism of exclusion was doubtless inherent within it. I have elsewhere touched on this mechanism,[19] but here I would like to point out yet another aspect of the fundamental dilemma it must have posed. "Jewish commitment to the humanistic ideal of Bildung," wrote George Mosse, "was based on the correct perception that only through transcending a German past, which the Jews did not share, could Jew meet German on equal ground."[20] But in fact from its inception, and even in its mildest forms, nationalism, embedded in a concept of a shared past, was joined to German *Bildung* in all its forms and variations. It made Jewish participation in the overall project of enlightened education all the more problematic, sometimes even impossible. It burdened their so-called emancipation from the outset.

The first notes of that still-not-quite-apparent dilemma were sounded in Johann David Michaelis's response to Christian Wilhelm von Dohm's *On the Civil Improvement of the Jews* of 1781.[21] Michaelis, a renowned orientalist and philologist, was an expert on Jewish matters, not known for antisemitic views. But here he voiced the early misgivings of all later *völkisch* thinkers. With the full force of his scholarship, Michaelis argued the uniqueness of the Jews as a separate *Volk*. They could never be like other Germans, he claimed, not only because of their loyalty to an old religious code but because this code had formed their character forever. They could never become German enough, not simply because they were of a different stock, but because they possessed a different history, anchored far back in the sun-ridden deserts of the Middle East. No amount of cultural assimilation could erase their foreignness.[22] *Bildung* was, accordingly, simply irrelevant.

This, of course, Michaelis did not say. But it was surely a direct implication of his position. *Bildung* was presumably open to all who would and could embrace it—but while Jews undoubtedly showed themselves fit for the task, it was precisely their inescapably faulty Germanness, now being gradually defined, that prevented their full entry through this route. From the moment a national, *völkisch* definition of that much desired Germanness was introduced into public discourse in Germany, from the moment it found itself merging so comfortably with *Bildung*, Germanness lost its power of inclusivity. This was soon made apparent to the women of the enlightened Berlin salons, for instance, as national-ism prospered in the wake of the French occupation.[23] It was repeatedly made apparent to Heine, Börne, or Felix Men-delssohn-Bartholdy, despite their fame and success. Jews could enter German society and acquire its culture—but in the eyes of some, they could only rarely become fully German in the process.

This dilemma became the mark of their existence. Still, they never gave up. Just as confessional distinctness could be construed as a general, not a particularly Jewish, problem, so, too, could the *völkisch* issue. German, not merely German-*Jewish*, identity was in the process of being constructed through much of the nineteenth century, and always, even when in combat against a foreign invader, defining boundaries seemed a rather confusing task. In the early years of the nineteenth century, feudal notions of authority still enabled princes from the Rhine area to serve not only at the Prussian court, but also at that of the Russian tsars. The king of Saxony was reproached for his loyalty to Napoleon not on national grounds but as a tactical blunder. In some circles, to be sure, it may have already been conceived as a form of treason— but that was long the exception, not the rule.

Later, and even within the more distinctly national camp, boundaries remained unclear. Let us not forget how complex modern identities tend to be—for everyone, not merely for Jews. Eric Hobsbawm emphatically argued this, for instance, in his *Nations and Nationalism*.[24] As for the German case in particular, consider what the historian Jürgen Kocka wrote in an essay pub-lished some two decades ago: "One could be a man from West-phalia and a Catholic, a Socialist and a citizen of the Bundesrepublik, a German and a European, belonging to Western Civilization," he said. "These belongings mix in various ways, a little differently for each one. The resulting requirements of loyalty may cause some tension, but as a rule it is possible to combine them."[25] This, while no doubt true for our time, can also apply slightly altered to much of the nineteenth century. The German national "imagined community" was then far from complete, and the multiplicity of identities was perhaps even more apparent then than now. In 1880, Theodor Mommsen, the renowned historian of ancient Rome, compared Jews to "the Saxons and the men of Pommerania" in an essay entitled "Another Word about Our Judaism," his public reply to Heinrich von Treitschke's aggressively antisemitic article of the previous year.[26] The German nation, he wrote, "relies on the combination and in some sense on the mixing together of various German tribes ... and it will be its end ... if one began to see a stranger in the other." "The entry into a great nation," he added,

> requires a price; the Hanoverians and the men of Hessen or Schleswig-Holstein are ready to pay it, and thus we feel indeed that we give up a piece of ourselves. But we give it up for the sake of our joint fatherland. As the Jews too are not led by any Moses now to the Promised Land...it is therefore their duty to shed—as much as they can without acting against their conscience—their uniqueness and break down decisively the boundaries between themselves and the rest of the German citizens.[27]

This, I believe, is a most instructive quote. To begin with, it clearly defines a Germanness that could include Jews; and, indeed, echoes of this multiethnic definition often resounded among them. This was most emphatically the case for the leading members of the *Centralverein deutscher Staatsbürger jüdischen Glaubens* at the turn of the twentith century. Theirs, they endlessly reiterated, was a German *nationality* and a Jewish *Stammengenossenschaft* (tribal community).[28] Having proven many times over that their *religion* was no hindrance to full participation in the making of German identity, they were now arguing that their sense of particular *ethnic belonging* was likewise no hindrance to its full enjoyment.

This may sound somewhat forced today, no doubt, and the antisemites of the time, to be sure, were convinced neither by Mommsen nor by the *Centralverein*. However, within the mainstream discourse of Imperial Germany, although Jews were not the only significant social element repeatedly attacked as "fellows without a Fatherland," these seemed to be perfectly legitimate arguments.[29] The Jews' chosen and declared *national* identity, they insisted again and again, was German. They were ready for every sacrifice in order to sustain it—quite literally, in fact. Over ten thousand Jewish soldiers were killed on the front during World War I—Germanness confirmed in blood, once again.

But if we return to the Mommsen passage cited above, the difficulties associated with that simple claim will soon reappear. Mommsen's tone was tolerant and friendly, but he too had his demands. Jews, accordingly, "ought to break down decisively the boundaries between themselves and the rest of the German citizens," he wrote. His vision, too, was apparently that of a unitary Germany. Jews were to become like others as completely as possible, though "without acting against their conscience," as he put it. And, in fact, a considerable number of Jews were ready to join this call. It was the line taken by Harry Breßlau, for instance, a colleague of Mommsen's and Treitschke's at the Berlin University. Becoming like others, he pleaded, was merely a matter of time. It would surely all work out in the end.[30] But it did not. On the whole, Jews—their common rhetoric to the contrary notwithstanding—were not ready to accept this presumably easy solution. Perhaps they could not.

To begin with, it is useful to remember that Jews were not only—and surely not *always*—preoccupied with becoming *like* others. The issue of productivization is perhaps the best and the best known case in point. From the start of the controversy over emancipation, the unique occupational profile of the Jews was repeatedly produced as a sign of their un-Germanness. Where was the loyal land-bound peasant among them? Where the happy artisan? Early in the age of emancipation, Jews were normally city-dwellers, petty merchants, moneylenders, and traveling salesmen. Theirs was in no way a reflection of the social structure characteristic of Germany as a whole. This, however, could easily be reformed, ran the common argument. An energetic program of productivization was all that was required. But despite much verbiage, such a program never materialized. During the early stages of industrialization, and later too, as capitalism became more fully developed, it would have been absurd for a group (such as the Jews) with commercial and financial advantages to revert to the precapitalist roles of peasants and artisans. One wanted to move on to bigger and better businesses, into more modern forms of commerce and production, into the larger banking establishments, into more promising financial ventures, and into the professions. One wanted to make it up the social and economic ladder. Productivization could wait, or alternatively it could be applied to Jews who immigrated from the east. Finally, it could be placed at the service of those romantic dreamers who fantasized about Jewish agricultural settlement in Palestine. It was of no real use to German Jews.[31]

Jews had indeed differed in more than religious matters and they remained different, even while changing with modernization. They were modernizing most effectively in social and demographic matters. They embraced modern education with particular alacrity. It is easy to show their prominence in schools, at the universities, in women's education. The less well off among them were also open to change and advancement, and they easily took on new habits and new tastes. After all, the old ones were never really theirs in the first place.[32]

All that may have at first reinforced their Germanness. They were often associated with rapid modernization. The grand department stores in Berlin best symbolized their role, and though this sometimes aroused envy and resentment, it could still be considered essentially "German": it was, after all, German industrialization they participated in, German electrification of the big cities, the growth of the German metropolis, the new biochemistry, the revolutionary physical sciences, and so on. But in fact, Jews were often entirely impervious to the question of how "German" it all made them, being rather more absorbed by the question raised from the opposite perspective: how "Jewish" it all proved them to be.

Throughout the nineteenth century, while Jews were repeatedly examined for their ability and readiness to assimilate, many of them continued to uphold, reform, and reshape the elements of their Jewish identity. This was probably rarer among those German Jews of whom we usually hear—the rich, the famous, and the outstanding in all walks of life. But they too were not quite so indifferent to that side of their existence as later historiography would sometimes have us believe. Much of the cultural activity undertaken by Jews during the nineteenth century was indeed pursued with the conscious intention of preserving and adapting Judaism to the new circumstances dictated by emancipation, on the one hand, and to the general modernizing trends influencing Europe as a whole, on the other. But much of it was no more than the continuing routine of a community life that had never completely lost its vitality and relevance. By the 1870s, the years of religious strife within Judaism were over and indifference became the major threat to Jewish identity. But even then, it should be remembered, 10 to 20 percent of German Jews were still Orthodox, following more or less the letter of Jewish law. They lived along the River Main—in Hessen and lower Franconia, but also in parts of northern Baden and Württemberg, in East Friesland, and also—not surprisingly—in the once-Polish province of Posen. In small towns up and down the country one could still find what Leo Baeck called *Milieufrömmigkeit*, a life bound up by the Jewish calendar, traditional customs, and the repetitive events of a Jewish life cycle. Urban Jews were surely more varied in their attitudes to formal religiosity, ranging from indifference or atheism, to committed Liberal Judaism, or even to the strictest Orthodoxy. But everywhere, old communities managed to uphold some of their traditions. Magnificent new synagogues were built during these years, and in practically all of them Hebrew prayer was still the rule. Even those who joined the congregation only on the High Holidays still used these occasions to signify their persistent sense of belonging.

Socially, too, some symbolic codes of behavior were kept alive. Endogamy was no longer complete, it is true, but there is more than one way of looking at the figures on intermarriage. By the end of the nineteenth century these were noticeably on the rise, but if by 1900 the proportion of Jews in Prussia who took non-Jews as partners in marriage was around 10 percent, that can surely be seen as a kind of achievement. After all, Jews made up only slightly more than 1 percent of the overall population of Germany. By that time their lives were mingled more completely with those of non-Jews than ever before: in schools, in cultural meeting points, even in resort areas. Had they totally given up the idea of endogamy, the intermarriage figures would have been much higher still. Sociability, indeed, is a core concept for measuring the force of Jewish identity. Jews everywhere seem to have preferred Jewish partners, and not only in marriage. The world of business was still essentially segregated, and friendship was kept within Jewish circles, too. Gershom Scholem's comments on the close Jewish circle of his well-to-do, religiously indifferent parents are a case in point,[33] and such assessments recur in many other memoirs. Jews, of course, entertained in the respectable German fashion, discussed German politics, and—perhaps even more— were involved in German cultural affairs. But they did so, more often than not, among themselves. One becomes aware of this only in retrospect. My father surely had many non-Jewish acquaintances during his student years in Berlin, but he mentioned only Robert, Edgar, and Fritz—all three of them Jews from a background similar to his—and we, at least, never heard of anyone else.

Such self-evident preferences no longer relied on old prohibitions concerning kosher food or Sabbath observance. They were more often than not based on new kinds of affinities: on a similar level of modernization and secularism, on common interests and tastes, on shared values. By the late nineteenth and early twentieth centuries, Jews lost much of their old uniqueness, indeed, but became alike in many other ways. By then they had behind them a whole century of participating in the formation of Germanness without giving up their Jewishness. Some of them, in fact, even felt the need to reappropriate for themselves values associated with a neglected Judaism. They sometimes showed a renewed interest in Jewish literature, old and new, and were experimenting in applying the notions of *Volk* and *Nation*—so prevalent in the world around them—to their own case.[34]

And one should never forget: secure contacts among themselves also provided, no doubt, a relaxed haven for Jews in a world that was all too often rife with antisemitism. Had things developed differently, all these trends of reaffirming Judaism, working as forces of *dis*similation, recapitulating the dual nature of their identity might have remained no more than half-forgotten experiments. As it turned out, precisely those remnants of old Judaism and the new "invented" traditions served Jews well in hard times. For those who perished, these might have provided some solace and some meaning at the last moment. For those who survived, they were the initial building blocks on which to construct new lives and new identities elsewhere.

Jews, then, were never so completely German as they themselves wanted to believe, nor were they ever so completely Jewish as their enemies argued. Theirs was a complex identity, like that of so many men and women in the modern world; one that in normal times could be both inspiring and enriching. For a century and a half they labored to make the best of it. But finally the times were no longer normal and, for all the solace their compound identity provided, it turned out to be yet another aspect of their tragedy.

Notes

1. All of the extant letters of my father are in my possession and the ones sent from Berlin between April and July 1933 were originally numbered by him. The quote above is from letter no. 12; translations from the German are mine.
2. Letter no. 15.
3. Ibid.
4. The literature on Moses Mendelssohn is immense. My comments are based on his "Jerusalem, oder über die religiöse Macht und Judentum" (Berlin, 1783), in *Gesammelte schriften*, ed. G. B. Mendelssohn (Leipzig: Brockhaus, 1843–45), 3:255–362. From among the more recent publications on Mendelssohn, see David Sorkin, *Moses Mendelssohn and the Religious Enlightenment* (Berkeley and Los Angeles: University of California Press, 1996).
5. Most illuminating for various aspects of the history of the *Verein* are some of Ismar Schorsch's essays collected in *From Text to Context: The Turn to History in Modern Judaism* (Hanover, N.H.: University Press of New England, 1994), esp. "Breakthrough into the Past: The Verein für Cultur und Wissenschaft der Juden," 205–32.
6. For Heine, too, the bibliography cannot possibly be summarized here. For his links to Judaism see Siegbert S. Prawer, *Heine's Jewish Comedy: A Study of his Portrait of Jews and Judaism* (Oxford: Clarendon, 1983).
7. This aspect of reform was especially stressed by George L. Mosse. See, for example, "Jewish Emancipation: Between *Bildung* and Respectability," in *The Jewish Response to German Culture: From the Enlightenment to the Second World War*, ed. Jehuda Reinharz and Walter Schatzberg (Hanover: University Press of New England, 1985), 1–16.
8. The outstanding historian of the *Centralverein*'s activities is surely Arnold Paucker, whose work is collected in *Deutsche Juden im Kampf um Recht und Freiheit: Studien zu Abwehr, Selbstbehauptung und Widerstand der deutschen*

Juden seit dem Ende des 19. Jahrhunderts (Teetz, Germany: Hentrich and Hentrich, 2003). For the question of identity see also Eva Reichmann, "Der Bewußtseinswandel der deutschen Juden," in *Deutsches Judentum in Krieg und Revolution 1916–1923*, ed. Werner Mosse and Arnold Paucker (Tübingen: Mohr-Siebeck, 1971), 511–612; and from a different perspective, Jehuda Reinharz, *Fatherland or Promised Land: The Dilemma of the German Jew, 1893–1914* (Ann Arbor: University of Michigan Press, 1975). The most recent work on the *Centralverein*, using new archival material, is Avraham Barkai, *"Wehr Dich!": Der Centralverein deutscher Staatsbürger jüdischen Glaubens 1893–1938* (Munich: Beck, 2002).

9. Among the more recent publications, see David N. Myers, "Hermann Cohen and the Problem of History at the Fin de Siècle," in *Resisting History: Historicism and Its Discontents in German-Jewish Thought* (Princeton, N.J.: Princeton University Press, 2003), 35–67, and among the somewhat older pieces, Amos Funkenstein, "Hermann Cohen's Legacy," in *Perceptions of Jewish History* (Berkeley and Los Angeles: University of California Press, 1993), 270–90.

10. Despite a growing body of literature on nationalism, its link with religion is only sporadically treated for the European case. From among the "modern classics" in this field, it was surely Benedict Anderson, in *Imagined Communities: Reflections on the Origin and Spread of Nationalism*, 2nd ed. (London: Verso, 1991), who contributed to this topic most significantly. For some of the modern research see, for instance, *Nation and Religion: Perspectives on Europe and Asia*, ed. Peter van der Veer and Hartmut Lehman (Princeton, N.J.: Princeton University Press, 1999); and *"Gott mit uns": Nation, Religion und Gewalt im 19. u. frühn 20. Jh.*, ed. Gerd Krumeich and Hartmut Lehmann (Göttingen: Vandenhoek and Ruprecht, 2000).

11. This summary of Humboldt's position is based on Michael A. Meyer, "Judaism and Christianity," in *German-Jewish History in Modern Times*, vol. 2: *Emancipation and Acculturation: 1780–1871*, ed. Michael A. Meyer (New York: Columbia University Press, 1997), 170.

12. There are no precise data on conversion. It is, however, estimated that the overall number for the nineteenth century was around 23,000, although numbers were probably higher after 1871 than before. For late nineteenth century attitudes see Alan Levenson, "The Conversionary Impulse in Fin de Siècle Germany," *Leo Baeck Institute Yearbook* (*LBIYB*) 40 (1995): 107–29.

13. See Thomas Nippersey, "Der Kölner Dom als Nationaldenkmal," in *Nachdenken über die deutsche Geschichte* (Munich: Beck, 1986), 156–17. On the

integration of Catholics into the German national movement see Helmut W. Smith, *German Nationalism and Religious Conflict: Culture, Ideology, Politics, 1870–1914* (Princeton, N.J.: Princeton University Press, 1995).

14. Quoted in Smith, *German Nationalism,* 13, from Harnack's "Protestanismus und Katholizismus in Deutschland," *Preußishe Jahrbücher* 127 (1907): 295.

15. On Harnack's series of lectures, given at the University of Leipzig in the winter-semester of 1899/1900 and then published as *Das Wesen des Christentums* (Leipzig: Hinrichs, 1900), in our context, see Uriel Tal, "Theologische Debatte um das 'Wesen des Judentums'," in *Juden in Wilhelminischen Deutschland 1890–1914,* ed. Werner E. Mosse (Tübingen: Mohr, 1976), 599–632.

16. Gabriel Riesser, "Vertheidigung der bürgerlichen Gleichstellung der Juden gegen die Einwürfe des Herrn H. E. G. Paulus" (1831), in *Gesammelte Schriften,* ed. M. Isler (Frankfurt a.M.: Verlag der Riesser-Stiftung, 1867), 2:152.

17. George L. Mosse has argued this point most convincingly. See primarily *German Jews beyond Judaism* (Bloomington: Indiana University Press, 1985).

18. See Azriel Shochat, *Der Ursprung der jüdischen Aufklärung in Deutschland,* translated by Wolfgang Jeremias (Frankfurt: Campus-Verlag, 2000), a book that seems to be attracting renewed attention now (Hebrew original, 1960). See now especially Shmuel Feiner, *The Jewish Enlightenment,* translated by Chaya Naor (Philadelphia: University of Pennsylvania Press, 2003).

19. See Shulamit Volkov, "The Ambivalence of *Bildung*: Jews and Other Germans," in *The German–Jewish Dialogue Reconsidered: A Symposium in Honor of George L. Mosse,* ed. Klaus L. Berghahn (New York: Peter Lang, 1996), 81–98.

20. Mosse, "Jewish Emancipation," 14.

21. Christian Wihelm von Dohm, *Über die bürgerliche Verbesserubg der Juden* (Berlin, 1781).

22. Michaelis's outstanding work was his *Mosaisches Recht,* 6 vols. (Frankfurt a. M., 1770–75, and later, enlarged editions: 1775–80, 1780–93, 1793–1803). On his life and work see Anna-Ruth Löwenbrück, *Judenfeindschaft im Zeitalter der Aufklärung: Eine Studie zur Vorgeschichte des modernen Antisemitismus am Beispiel des Göttinger Theologen und Orientalisten Johann David Michaelis* (Frankfurt a. M.: Peter Lang, 1995).

23. From the literature on the salons, Hannah Arendt, *Rahel Varnhagen: The*

Life of a Jewess (London: East and West Library, 1957), is still the most illuminating. See the complete edition, edited with an interesting introduction by Liliane Weissberg (Baltimore: The Johns Hopkins University Press, 1997). Among later works see especially Deborah Hertz, *Jewish High Society in Old Regime Berlin* (New Haven: Yale University Press, 1988).

24. Eric J. Hobsbawm, *Nations and Nationalism since 1780* (Cambridge: Cambridge University Press, 1990).

25. Jürgen Kocka, *Geschichte und Aufklärung* (Göttingen: Vandenhoeck & Ruprecht, 1989), 151.

26. This exchange as well as a number of additional contributions to the debate are reprinted in *Der Berliner Antisemitimusstreit*, ed. Walter Boehlich (Frankfurt a. M.: Inselverlag, 1965).

27. Ibid., 214, 227.

28. For examples see the quotes in Reichmann, "Der Bewußtseinswandel," passim.

29. On the Socialists, considered at least until the outbreak of the First World War to be "Vaterlose Gesellen," see Vernon L. Lidtke, *The Outlawed Party: Social Democracy in Germany 1878–1890* (Princeton, N.J.: Princeton University Press, 1966).

30. See Harry Breßlau, *Zur Judenfrage: Sendschreiben an Herrn Prof. Dr. Heinrich von Treitschke*, 2nd ed. (Berlin: Duemmler, 1880), repr. in part in Boehlich, *Antisemitismusstreit*, 54–79, 93–98.

31. See Avraham Barkai, "The German Jews at the Start of Industrialisation: Structural Change and Mobility 1835–1860," in *Revolution and Evolution, 1848 in German-Jewish History*, ed. Werner Mosse, Arnold Paucker, and Reinhard Rürup (Tübingen: Mohr, 1971), 123–49; Henry Wasserman, יהודים, בורגנות ו"חברה בורגנית" בעידן לברלי בגרמניה (1840-1880) (Jews, bourgeoisie, and "bourgeois society" in a liberal age in Germany, 1840–1880) (Ph.D. diss., Hebrew University, 1979). For a case study of later years see Shulamit Volkov, "Die jüdische Gemeinde in Altona, 1867–1890," in *Das jüdische Projekt der Moderne* (Munich: Beck, 2001), 97–117.

32. See Shulamit Volkov, "Jüdische Assimilation und Eigenart im Kaiserreich," in *Antisemitismus als kultureller Code*, 2nd ed. (Munich: Beck, 2000), 131–45.

33. See Gershom Scholem, מברלין לירושלים: זכרונות נעורים (From Berlin to Jerusalem: Memories of youth) (Tel Aviv: Am Oved, 1982), 29–34, as well as "On the Social Psychology of the Jews in Germany," in *Jews and Germans from 1862 to 1933: The Problematic Symbiosis*, ed. David Bronsen (Heidelberg: Winter, 1972), 9–32.

34. I have elaborated on this theme in Shulamit Volkov, "Die Erfindung einer
    Tradition: Zur Entstehung des modernen Judentums in Deutschland," in
    Das jüdische Projekt, 118–37.

Jewish Society
and Community
in America and Israel

FROM THE DIARY
OF A YOUNG AMERICAN ZIONIST,
1924–1925

NAOMI W. COHEN

I. Introduction

Simon Greenberg, a distinguished Conservative rabbi of the twentieth century, was born in a small village in the Ukraine in 1901. A few years later, his family emigrated to America. Educated in New York City, he attended public schools and Hebrew school. As a teenager he joined Young Judaea, the youth group of the Zionist Organization of America (ZOA), where he worked as a club leader. His affiliation with Young Judaea sparked a lifelong commitment to Zionism, both as a movement for a Jewish homeland in Palestine and as a significant force within the American Jewish community.

Although Greenberg came from a traditionally observant home, he enrolled in the Conservative rabbinical school of the Jewish Theological Seminary (JTS), class of 1925. The school allowed him to complete his course work in Jerusalem, and, armed with assignments for independent study, he set out for Palestine. Arriving in September 1924, he joined two close friends with whom he spent most of his time. His detailed diary, the first full record by an American Zionist for the academic year of 1924–25 that I have seen, is a faithful account of his activities.

I am grateful to Professor Moshe Greenberg, who gave me access to his father's diary. He and his brother, Dr. Daniel Greeberg, permitted me to publish this account. My thanks for their help go also to Jeremy Cohen, Rahel and Yoel Darom, Hillel Halkin, Jan Kaufman, and Judith Rosen.

More significant, the diary on a deeper level is a commentary on the beliefs and practices of American Zionism during the first years of the Mandate. To be sure, Greenberg, an observant Jew schooled in the Hebrew language and in Jewish studies, was not the typical American Zionist. But like his fellow Zionists generally, he hoped for a Jewish homeland fashioned according to American standards and one to which American Jews could easily relate.

The reader of the diary meets a handsome, energetic young man, popular with his friends and his teachers, who was thrilled by all aspects of his first trip to Palestine. In an impressionistic account, he relates his experiences with exuberance and deep emotion. He felt, he said, like a witness to or participant in a new era of Jewish history. It was an exciting time to be in Palestine, years in which Zionists worldwide concentrated more on building up the land and less on politics. Greenberg described the physical growth of the *yishuv*, the pre-state Jewish settlement in Palestine, and how its social and cultural institutions were rapidly mushrooming. The poet in him was also stirred by the breathtaking beauty of the land.

More than a tourist, Greenberg was a resident of Jerusalem, admittedly temporary but nonetheless a resident. Living like other Jerusalemites without the customary physical conveniences, he tasted the varied cultural riches of the city and he became acquainted with the life of the *yishuv*'s youth. A student as well, he broke new ground; enrolled in the first class of the Hebrew University, he was the first American in the University's Institute of Jewish Studies. Only many years later did the American Conservative and Reform seminaries send their rabbinical students for a year's study in Israel.

Greenberg and his friends made use of every opportunity for exploring the land. Differing from the casual visitor who only skimmed the surface of the high spots as well as the antiquarian who sifted through the ancient ruins, the young men were captivated by both the old and the new. Their rich education in biblical and postbiblical history stood them in good stead, enabling them to visualize the ancient sites alongside the radical alterations of modern man. What they saw made a dramatic and lasting impression. Their reactions were heightened by an almost gut-like affinity for Eretz Yisrael (E.Y.). They "had Palestine in their bones," a phrase used on one occasion by a British prime minister.[1] In the case of these Americans, "Palestine in their bones" meant an ethnic consciousness or an active awareness, fine-tuned by education and daily prayers, of their Jewish national heritage.

Equally impressive were the scores of individuals Greenberg encountered. From all walks of life, whether government officials, yeshiva students, academics, artists, visitors, or *ḥaluṣim* (pioneers), and whether religious or secularist, Zionist or non-Zionist, famous or ordinary—the acquaintances he made testified to a society where the entrenched prewar social order was giving way to a new and as yet fluid social structure. In Jerusalem during the early years of the Mandate, socioeconomic distinctions, public status, and even age differences were relatively unimportant; the basic divider was that of language. Adopted automatically by the "Anglos," particularly those connected to the academic world, the young American was soon made privy to the news and gossip circulating in Jewish Jerusalem. (I identify the prominent people Greenberg encountered, or those who would become famous, in the notes. Others are referred to by initials.) Greenberg also observed the major ethnic groups—the Jews and their subgroups, the Arabs, and the British. Reconstructing his comments, the reader is made well aware of the hardening and long-held tensions between the *yishuv* and the British and between the Jews and the Arabs.

Greenberg visited Palestine when the image of the noble *ḥaluṣ* pervaded American Zionist literature and discourse. As taught by the Zionist youth groups after the Great War, the *ḥaluṣ* was the self-sacrificing pioneer, a devotee of modern Hebrew, intellectual in inclination (in Greenberg's words "a *chalutz* with Spinoza in his back pocket"), who chose a life of manual labor in Palestine, a life of service and creativity, out of sheer dedication to Zionism. Professor Arthur Goren has elaborated on the idyllic image of the *ḥaluṣim*: "The communal settlements they were building were Zionism's most exalted achievement. Not only were they in the forefront of the renewal of national life; they also offered the world a singular example of a democratic, egalitarian and just society-in-the-making."[2] They became the "ultimate" Zionists, Goren added, who, like America itself, were inspired by the prophetic ethic. Albeit with some criticisms, Greenberg shared in the glorification of the *ḥaluṣ*—another recurring subject in the diary—and his visits to the pioneer settlements usually vindicated his idealistic beliefs.

Descriptions of the people he met and the sites he visited reveal Greenberg's philosophy of Zionism. His was a spiritual-cultural Zionism that overlay his affinity for the land itself. He learned it from his teachers at JTS who transmitted in turn what they had learned from their teachers and colleagues, particularly Solomon Schechter. Those men adopted the teachings of Aḥad Ha'am; they believed that a Jewish center in Palestine would inspire Diaspora Jewry in their individual centers to cultural creativity and the use of Hebrew as a living language. Unlike Aḥad Ha'am, however, they held religion to be central to their concept of Jewish culture. That type of Zionism, which questioned the statist aims of Theodor Herzl and affirmed the existence of Judaism in the Diaspora, had characterized the young Conservative movement in the United States since prewar days and suited its American setting well.

The diary picks up and elaborates two specific themes that flowed from Greenberg's philosophy of Zionism: the use of Hebrew and the subject of religion. The young American believed that Hebrew was the means of uniting world Jewry, and he preached the need to develop the language in both Palestine and the Diaspora. Impatient with immigrants to the *yishuv* who held on to their first language, he tried for a short time to discipline himself to the use of Hebrew exclusively in his speaking, reading, and writing. On the subject of religion he was more outspoken. He had little tolerance for Orthodox extremists, anti-Zionists who despite their piety buried themselves in a fossilized tradition and a world of their own. Nor could he empathize with the irreligious or the antireligionists who had rebelled against Orthodoxy but, unfamiliar with Western Conservatism and Reform, continued to regard Orthodoxy as the one authentic Judaism. Both themes, Hebrew and religion, figured in his thoughts on education of the youth.

Greenberg neither negated the Diaspora nor concerned himself with political or statist objectives. He dreamed rather of a Jewish center in Palestine that would provide the cultural and religious inspiration for world Jewry. That center, however, would never replace the one in America. Although he personally toyed with the idea of settling in Palestine, he grew up in the American setting of a "comfortable" Zionism, a time when Palestinianism had replaced political Zionism, and he readily accepted the fact that *'aliyah* had little appeal for Americans. A proud American, he never questioned whether his religio-cultural Zionism conflicted in any way with his loyalty to America.

Indeed, the diary reveals a young man whose values were as much American as they were Zionist. His outlook was shaped by an American academic emphasis on a scientific and critical mindset; he measured people and places by American standards; and his judgments reflected the democratic, internationalist, and pacifist creed of the postwar American liberal. As an American, Greenberg took issue with fellow Jews in Palestine who failed to understand that religious affirmation was the cornerstone of Jewish identification in the United States. What he wanted was a combination, American-style, of tradition with modernity, the creed of Conservative Judaism. Despite his youth, Greenberg was representative of other serious American Zionists who criticized such shortcomings in E.Y.

Admittedly, Greenberg would have preferred a richer American Zionism, one in which a greater emphasis was put on the Hebrew language and Jewish studies instead of philanthropic drives. His stay in Palestine also alerted him to ideological inadequacies in the American Zionist movement—how, for example, it was perceived by many Jews as well as non-Jews as no more than refugeeism. Nonetheless, he was proud of the Americans who settled in E.Y. and of the material gifts from American Jews. Although he was critical at times of American Jewish leaders and of American materialism, he thought that the *yishuv* had much to learn from the United States and its Jews, be it in standards of cleanliness, appropriate organizations for young people, city planning, and, above all, modern forms of worship.

Many of Greenberg's judgments and prejudices were predicated on his rootedness in *Western* civilization. Although his own roots were embedded in Eastern Europe, he sneered at the shtetl Jews in Palestine, as well as those from the Middle East, who clung to their outworn customs and rejected the incursions of modernity into their world. The proper Easterners he found were those like the students or young *ḥaluṣim* from Russia and Poland who had emancipated themselves socially and culturally. The others remained obstacles in the way of creating a modern Jewish homeland. His Western outlook encompassed the Arabs as well. Despite his sympathy for the disease-stricken children or for the peasants exploited by Jewish land speculators, he could not excuse their indolence or ignorance. He admitted that the *yishuv* would have to find the proper (and moral) treatment for the Arabs in its midst, but at least for the time being the Arabs were largely a primitive people seemingly insensitive to progress. Doubtless the average Zionist in America and Western Europe shared those views. Indeed, Greenberg's reactions some eighty years ago are relevant even today, when the major problems facing the state of

Israel are the divide between the ultra-Orthodox and the secularists, the mutual antipathy of the Ashkenazim and the Sefardim, and the incessant Arab–Jewish friction.

The diary suggests that American Jews endeavored early on to shape the developing society in Palestine in the American image. Greenberg's criticisms during the first decade of the Mandate heralded a trend that grew more pronounced over time, especially after the creation of the state in 1948. As American Jews steadily increased their financial aid to the *yishuv* and then to Israel, they developed a proprietary air toward the country. They had the right, many said, to mold the behavior of the Jewish homeland, be it in religion or even in politics and diplomacy. The reasoning was simple: (1) The more American the *yishuv* (or state) was, the better a place it would be, and (2) the more American the *yishuv* (or state) was, the more comfortable American Jews would feel about lending it their support.

Since the focus of this essay is on a young American whose impressions of Palestine enriched his devotion to the Zionist ideal, a good deal of the diary has been omitted. The details of his studies in Jerusalem, his lengthy philosophical musings, and the descriptions of the places he explored have also been cut. In the excerpts from the diary that follow I have occasionally corrected wording as well as errors of spelling, grammar, and punctuation. For the sake of continuity and clarity I have frequently omitted words in sentences and paragraphs without resorting to elliptical marks. In a few instances I have included Greenberg's explanatory notes directly into the text. My own explanations of words or phrases appear in brackets. I provide a synopsis of Greenberg's professional career after his visit to Palestine after the extracts from the diary.

II. From the Diary

LIVING IN JERUSALEM

S̲u̲n̲d̲a̲y̲,̲ O̲c̲t̲o̲b̲e̲r̲ 5̲,̲ 1̲9̲2̲4̲.̲ I left the boat about 8 A.M. and together with the rest of the Jewish group got into one of the three man-power boats which take you to the landing spot in the harbor. Before I knew it, medical exam, revenue inspection, et al. were completed, and an automobile was ready to take us to Jerusalem.

[A glimpse of Tel Aviv.] The city is a busy, booming place, but is not beautiful. There are practically no trees. That is to be expected since there are few natural trees in this part of the world. But what is far more serious in my opinion is that the streets are narrow. Even those beautiful buildings that they do have do not show off well at all because of this lack of space and approach. Sidewalks are narrow, gutters not well paved and also narrow. Then there is a large number of all sorts of stands with petty wares in a number of the open spaces, stands that do not add to the beauty of the place at all. Of course the Hebrew character of the city cannot be doubted from the moment one enters. Children shouting their wares of cakes and candies and Hebrew conversation are met everywhere. But so are a good number of other languages. It is the old story of the amazing babel of tongues throughout the Mediterranean coast cities.

We proceeded with our auto to Jerusalem, first traversing part of the coastal plain of E.Y. dotted with huddled Arab settlements. From the car as one passed the Arab villages one could get an inkling of the lazy life that a village Arab leads. There is absolutely nothing it seems that he has to do. Out in the center of the field, under a canopy very simply constructed to act as a shade against the bright hot sun, groups of men sat playing cards, dominoes, or else smoking their pipes—totally carefree and apparently indifferent to everything about them.

The road leading through the hills to Jerusalem is an exact duplicate of a narrow winding stairway. One makes the sharpest curves near the steepest precipices—really quite a thrilling experience for one who tries it the first time. The hills of Judea seem to be of ripe old age sleeping restfully under the sun's glare. They have no vegetation on them. Only here and there, where terraces [flat-topped sections of earth with vertical sides, often resembling steps] were built and trees planted, do they approach signs of life. Otherwise one sees but rock, rock, rock. The terraces are encouraging in that they give an inkling of what can be done.

The first thing that struck me in Jerusalem were the narrow streets with no or very narrow sidewalks. Wide, clean streets are ever so significant an indication to me of the temper of a city. But Jerusalem is not dirty, it is simply dusty. All the buildings are made of stone, due of course to the scarcity of wood. There are a number of fine structures—the numerous buildings erected by the various governments to house their representatives, the infinite number of structures of religious denominations from all the four corners of the earth, and attractive private homes. But practically none of the buildings have a chance to stand out really due to the lack of a decent approach and background. It is a case of over-concentrated beauty.

MONDAY, OCTOBER 6. Ever so happy and ready, I prayed with more than ordinary feeling and proceeded at once to become part of my new environment. The American School for Archeological Research opened its sessions today. I registered for some 6–8 hours of work—Archeology, History of Palestine and Syria, taught by Dr. [William] Albright, the director of the school; Hebrew orthography with Dr. [Max] Margolis, an exchange professor from Dropsie College; and Spoken Arabic, to be taught by some native Arab.

From school I wandered around a good part of the new city—the section known as Zikhron Moshe. It is well known that streets here have no name. True the natives get around somehow, but for the stranger it is most embarrassing. One has to ask constantly, and it is surprising to find how many people do not know their own city.

In the afternoon we [Greenberg and his two American friends] got a view of the Mosque of Omar. We were not permitted to tread on the "holy ground" just then, and we had to remain satisfied with viewing it from the outskirts of the surrounding court. Not far away was the Wailing Wall, and I got my first glimpse at that too rather hurriedly. There was a small group, predominantly of women, pouring forth their souls at this remains of ancient Jewish glory. Nor could I forget the dingy, dirty Street of David leading up to the Wall. As surely as the Wall is a symbol of ancient Judea's spiritual and national health, thus surely is the Street of David a symbol of the sores still plaguing the people of David. I can't believe that the miserable beggars that lined the alleys on the eve of Yom Kippur, that the feminine-looking "earlocked" yeshivah boys, that the superstitious weeping women, are worthy representatives of the generations that the Temple symbolizes. What's the sense of reading idealism into this uncouth mass? They have no vision. They have no creative energy.

TUESDAY, OCTOBER 7 [THE DAY BEFORE YOM KIPPUR]. I had my final meal before fasting with the C.s and went to pray at the synagogue of which L. is president. It is the "modern" synagogue of Jerusalem, so called because they don't shout at will during the prayers and because decorum is preserved. All of the high officials of the government pray here. The High Commissioner [Sir Herbert Samuel][3] and his son and wife were there as well as Dr. [Judah] Magnes[4] and family. The structure is not very large so that everyone could boast that he sat but a few feet away from His Excellency [H.E.]! It is a fairly impressive scene to see him walk in and out with his bodyguard, and the whole congregation standing to honor him. Norman Bentwich [the British Attorney General] occupied the chair at the right of H.E.

WEDNESDAY, OCTOBER 8, YOM KIPPUR. Spent the whole day in the synagogue, going out for a brief space only to visit Rabbi Kook's minyan,[5] but ten steps to our right where a small group of patriarchs and young yeshivah students were praying. Then to a minyan of Bukharan Jews right across the street from us—these were orderly, and in a rather gaudily decorated room. Jerusalem is full of such groups praying separately. There is no really large and beautiful synagogue. In a way this is better, since too large a group I believe detracts from the intensity and spontaneity of prayer.

It was interesting to watch Magnes, the one time Temple Emanu-El [*the* Reform "cathedral" in New York City] rabbi praying now as the most Orthodox of Jews, remaining in the synagogue practically all the time, prostrating himself at *alenu* and in all ways part of this group. It seems that [the] man is finding his soul in E.Y., or a certain peace that he did not have in America. Bentwich led *shacharit*; H.E. came again for the *neilah* service and remained to the end.

In the evening we went to a dance given by the Menorah, an association of ex-Legionnaires[6] to which we were invited by a former Young Judaean. There I got an idea of how some of the citified Jerusalem youth entertains itself and met some interesting people—among others Sir Gilbert Clayton, for a time Acting High Commissioner.

THURSDAY, OCTOBER 9. The great thing this trip thus far did for me is that it gave concrete backgrounds to ideas I formerly had. For example, I know all the complaints that are directed against the colonists against the Z.O. [Zionist Organization] and the *chalutzim*, etc., but now I have a very concrete picture. Anyone who did not see the Arabs cannot speak with accuracy about them. Not that I discovered a new angle or new solution to the Arab problem, but merely the word Arab has a new, fuller meaning for me now.

Jerusalem is a most interesting city and I can easily see that I would not at all mind spending my life here. It has color, it has intellectual activity. The physical inconveniences such as the kerosene lamp, no running water, etc., one does not mind at all. The houses are far more beautiful inside than one would expect from the outside. The air is wonderfully dry, and the heat is never distressing. The evenings are always cool.

FRIDAY, OCTOBER 10. We must insist upon a rich Hebrew literature because Hebraic culture is the crystallization of the best and most universal elements in Hebrew literature. It is only thus that we can hope ever to give a vitally new expression to the old Hebraic ideals, or even create a new Hebraic culture. Hence my absolute and uncompromising insistence on the preeminent value of knowing and creating even the meanest thing in Hebrew.

SATURDAY, OCTOBER 11. After prayer we went under L.'s guidance to visit the tombs of the members of the Sanhedrin, in the outskirts of the city, in the section called Kidron. There in the rocks of the hills of Jerusalem we saw the hewn graves, 71 in number.

On the way we passed an Arabic wedding procession. The bride was perched high on a camel, loaded with trunks containing her trousseau. Behind her were all her friends of the village clapping their hands and singing songs. Arab dandies on prancing steeds preceded the march. They were all bound for the neighboring village in which the bridegroom lived. An Arab in the procession who spoke Hebrew well told us that the groom had paid 110£ for the bride. Arabs are complaining of the tremendous rise in the price of brides! That may in a way explain the attitude of the Arab to his wife. She is his slave in all things. It is not an uncommon thing to see in the villages an Arab riding on his donkey with his wife walking alongside him, a baby tied to her back and a bundle on her head.

In the evening I succeeded in getting into a mass meeting arranged for Dr. [Chaim] Weizmann.[7] I heard Magnes speak in Hebrew. He took the opportunity to point out that one of Dr. Weizmann's greatest achievements is his discovery that American Jewry is not merely a dollar-mad community but has certain vital spiritual interests. Weizmann rose. He spoke in his usual quiet manner, no oratorical stunts. There was no boisterous enthusiasm during the meeting. Very little applause. The whole appeared like a gathering coming to hear the report of its appointed leader.

SUNDAY, OCTOBER 12. Everyone present [at a wedding of a *ḥaluṣ* and *ḥaluṣah*], except K. and me, was dressed in the typical *chalutz* uniform—blouse, khaki knickers or trousers. Clothes are taken by the *chalutz* to be an index to the man. A dark suit, collar and tie are signs of subjection to the laws of convention and formality, which they bitterly despise. We were very obviously only tolerated.

Their main pastime was the famous *chalutz* dance, the "Horah," a very simple dance in which as many can participate as can join the circle that the size of the room permits. They dance till utter exhaustion, a peculiar ecstasy being generated by the repetition of the same step and melody. *The chasidim of modern times!* It appeared to me that a good deal of the joy and mystic exaltation was based on the sense of despair, of dissatisfaction with the world and life as it is. The *chalutz* movement is based not merely on zeal for the reestablishment of a Jewish people but equally on total disgust with the artificial life that one lives in civilized countries, weariness with all its conventions, lies, and hypocrisies. These young men and women see in E.Y. the opportunity for throwing all of that into the dirt heap and starting anew. Among these youths we have a large number who have ideals of human living, social programs for society, and the courage to try to live those ideals.[8] It is that fact which makes for their uniqueness and greatness.

We wandered over the spot where the University is to be built, stood on the cornerstone laid by Dr. Weizmann, and learned the horah dance on its lawn. There could hardly be a more beautiful spot for a university.

TUESDAY, OCTOBER 14. Visited K., and I expressed opinions that I had often voiced to others. The trick is to try not to be a phonograph always playing the same records. I may be sacrilegious but I think the Lord is undoubtedly far wearier of listening to the same prayers than the pious are in offering them. Nor has He any method of escape. He must listen. And I doubt whether He himself could get our Orthodox friends to change as much as one letter of that which has been said for these past centuries.

THURSDAY, OCTOBER 16. Last evening Y. spent some time talking to me about her own hopes and about her reactions to the British government. Again evidence of the difficult position of the youth educated in this country. Life is as yet not sufficiently rich and varied to make room for them. They want to leave to complete their studies, etc. The whole problem of education here is a very complicated one and far from being solved. As for the British—she works as a clerk in an office and complains of all sorts of petty discriminations between Englishmen and the natives. Her opinion was that Turkish rule was better in that with money one could have done anything, and the Jews were undoubtedly in a stronger social position than they are now. I have always had an almost unbounded love and admiration for the English people and government. She shook my faith a good deal. Also, from her account of the [Arab] riots that took place in Jerusalem three years ago, the question of whether the English are trying to use the policy of "divide and rule" became a very real one to me.

<u>FRIDAY, OCTOBER 18.</u> B. [a new friend of Greenberg's age and a former ḥaluṣ who had come from Poland] talked to me about the youth groups in the country, the Scouts and the Maccabees [a sports group]. He complained of the lack of harmony in the leadership, of the petty personal considerations that work havoc, and of the urgent need for a youth organization. The adults are doing very little to see to it that the work gets the proper support. That there is a crying need for a youth movement here is ever so evident. We need it to give content to the life of the youth. E.Y. youth is subject to and is in part beginning to fall prey to those pitfalls of materialism, self-indulgence, and stupid light-mindedness that the youth of the whole world meets. Very little is being done in an organized way to counteract that.

<u>SATURDAY, OCTOBER 19.</u> B. visited me and we got into a discussion of the religious life of the *chalutzim*. He himself is altogether free yet he has an honest respect for Judaism. What was important is what he told me of the spiritual void that not only he but a good number of his serious minded friends experience. He appreciates the fact that while they overthrew the old, they as yet created no new holidays, and he believes that if the proper individual appeared a reaction would set in among a good many *chalutzim*. He could not understand why it is that the American and English Jews were more religious. I told him of religious thought and life in America, all of which was a complete revelation to him.

<u>SUNDAY, OCTOBER 20, HOSHANAH RABBAH.</u> In one prayer service of *chasidim* I joined the men in a dance that kept up uninterruptedly for twenty minutes. They have the same spirit of ecstasy that the *chalutzim* have in their dances. There is this difference—the *chalutzim* dance around what? —land, language, new social order? A good number merely try to dance away from present dissatisfaction. But the *chasidim* all dance around the Torah. If only they would have the slightest coloring of the modern scientific attitude of mind. Yet it was encouraging to see young *chalutzim* join hands and dance with *chasidim*. Both are bound to exert a mutual influence upon one another.

Week-long Trip on horseback along the southwest coast of Palestine [Led by Professor Albright and beginning on October 22. Since specific dates given in the diary are incorrect, the entire trip is treated here as one segment.]

We visited Artuf, an old but unprogressive Jewish colony. It is in the heart of the country that was the stage of Samson's activities. Its hills mark the boundary between the Shefelah [region at the foot of the Judean hills] and the plains that were occupied by the Philistines. The people of the colony were disappointing. Even a fourteen-year-old youngster raised in the colony did not speak more than a few words of Hebrew.

That first day gave me one of the best lessons I ever had in Jewish history. The rocky dome-shaped hills of Judea proved ultimately too much for the Philistines who were accustomed to fighting with chariots and cavalry. If even to this day it is impossible to march in any other formation but single file—in antiquity it must have been more so.

This was the first time I saw an Arab village at close range. The houses are all made of all kinds of stones piled together and held by mud dried in the sun. They have no windows or chimneys. The smoke of any fire that they make inside comes out through the door or opening. It is only the very large and exceptional village that has anything like a school. The water supply comes from the village well. From the well to the homes the water is transported on the heads of the people. The vast majority of the water carriers are women.

The Arab village is full of all sorts of dirt, eye-diseases, and deformed stunted children. By far the most horrible thing to look at is a child's face literally covered over with flies and the child going on without in the least noticing it. The flies attack especially the diseased eyelashes or sores on face and neck. The whole gives one the impression of the most primitive civilization. To speak of these people as having a united conscious will or attitude is ridiculous. They don't even know when their holy days occur. Villages located near cities are usually notified of a holy day by the discharge of three cannon-balls. That of course does not tell them what the holy day is, and they pay very little attention to it.

Professor Albright said that Arab opposition to Zionism is gradually cooling down because the fear that was inspired in them by certain Zionist speeches as well as by their own agitators had no basis, since the Jews did not come in hordes and drive them from the land. The anti-Jewish boycott, refusing to sell Jews land, was a complete failure, he said, not only because of Arab love of "baksheesh," but also because of a theory held among the rich and the intelligentsia that after the Jews bought up the land, a little revolution will get it all back for them.

We reached Gaza for the night. We visited the few Jews found in town.

There were some 6 or 7 families in all, the remains of a once rather flourishing community of 20 families. The war ruined Gaza to a very large extent; the city that was once the pride of the South is now rapidly declining. Ruins of homes destroyed by the British bombardment of the town were evident wherever we turned.

RUCHAMAH. Ruchamah from the distance looked beautiful. It was the one cultivated and well kept spot in miles and miles of neglected land. It has a rather peculiar history. Bought originally by rich Russian Jews who were ruined by the war, further mismanagement and reverses forced it into the hands of the Anglo-Palestine Bank. The bank not being a land agency hasn't very much use for it and would like to get rid of it, but there is no purchaser. In the meantime, in order not to permit the land to lie waste entirely there are 7 families living there as laborers, paid by the bank and working and watching the soil. However, even in that small group we found a number of individuals who were of a fine type, Mr. and Mrs. B. for example. He is a *chalutz* who left his medical studies for the plow—recently married, living far from friends and relatives, understanding the situation perfectly and carrying on without grumbling. What Ruchamah needs is a *kvutzah* [a collective settlement of *ḥaluṣim* and a word used by Greenberg interchangeably with *kibbutz*], a *chalutz* group to work it on a cooperative basis. I heard my first complaints against Zionist mismanagement in the country—high-salaried officials and a superfluity of officials.

Visited Tekoa, the home of the prophet Amos, then Frank Mountain on which Herod had built a summer home and fortress. The Crusaders too had a fortress there. From there to Bethlehem—then on the main road in a glorious gallop to Jerusalem.

WEDNESDAY, OCTOBER 29. Afternoon at a tea of the American School of Archaeology. Met among others Dr. Klausner,[9] Dr. Magnes, Mrs. Ben-Yehuda.[10] It was quite a representative gathering.

FRIDAY, OCTOBER 31. Afternoon visit with Prof. Margolis to Dr. Klausner. He lives in Talpioth, the beautiful new Jewish section of Jerusalem. Klausner is an interesting man, simple, devoted, learned. Spoke at length about the inner circles connected with the Hebrew University. The details are most interesting, in part very discouraging, really astounding. He considers it unfortunate that men who were far removed from Zionism, essentially Reform Jews, should have come to a position of dictating the policies of the University.[11] [Klausner also criticized] the limited scope of University's programs; the poor response of men invited to teach; the peculiar arrangement for research work only; the funds withheld by the Zionist Organization; the 30 graduates of gymnasia going to Italy to study because the University was not open; the danger of the Hebrew University narrowing itself into an ecclesiastical institution.

SATURDAY, NOVEMBER 1. At ten to Bezalel [Art] School to listen to a lecture on art by [the founder] Prof. Boris Schatz, of course in Hebrew. He spoke on the defects and good points of works the pupils did during vacation and were on display on the walls of rooms.

Some talk about preparations for tomorrow, Balfour Day. Some trouble is expected due to the rumor that Jews are taking over the Mosque of Omar. (The rumor originated in the refusal of the government to permit the repair of the Mosque.) This is the first time in my life that I have the feeling of expecting trouble the next day. Uncomfortable but without fear, since the government has the situation well in hand. Yet, to walk the dark alleys of Jerusalem alone at night would be inadvisable. Arabs started after riots 3 years ago to kill individual Jews. Jews followed by terrible reprisals, with good effects. In colonies on roads, in more than one instance a dead Arab was found on the very spot where the day before a Jew had been found. That plan worked.

Evening—a visit to the Maccabees, the sport club of the Jewish youth of Jerusalem. Gave me a concrete picture of part of the youth activities here. There is *much, very, very much* to be desired. A youth movement here with real plans and men is most imperative.

SUNDAY, NOVEMBER 2 [BALFOUR DAY]. Day passed very quietly in city. Many Arabs closed shops after urgent promptings of agitators, some from honest convictions or at least deeply roused prejudices.

TUESDAY, NOVEMBER 4. To Betar. It is the site of Bar Kochba's last stronghold. Place still called by natives Jewish ruins. Saw Bar Kochba's and later Roman defenses—the mole on the south side hewn out of rock by Bar Kochba and his men. That was probably the side from which the Romans attacked, since the approach from there was most gradual. Prof. Margolis, Dr. Magnes, plus whole American school were there.

THURSDAY, NOVEMBER 6. Meeting of Palestine Oriental Society. Papers read on most recent archeological discoveries and in general on subjects of Palestinian interest.

SATURDAY, NOVEMBER 8. In the evening visited choir of the cultural committee of the Histadrut [national labor federation]. They were learning Mozart's

"Requiem." Choir consists of about forty young men and women who come there out of sheer love of song; the majority are laborers, and among the boys the prevailing dress was the *chalutz* uniform. This business of dress is very important. It is a counteraction to the wealthy European styles. The laborers make it a special point to dress plainly. At public meetings their leaders appear in unpressed trousers, no ties, well-worn shoes. That is very healthy, because there is a danger of having here a repetition of what we have in the U.S.—the stupid attempt of the poor to outdress the rich, sacrificing thereby what little opportunity they do have of getting at the really worthwhile things.

SUNDAY, NOVEMBER 9. To a tea at Hotel Allenby, given in honor of Lipsky.[12] Col. Kisch as chairman.[13] Except for the tea it was a fairly dry meeting. Lipsky spoke in English with an interpreter. He couldn't get into the spirit of a real talk, and the translation was abominable. Of course all of Jewish Society turned out. Ben Zvi was there for the laborers,[14] a glaring contrast in his dress and manner to the Society there gathered.

Thence to a meeting of the council of the Scouts. This organization has a future here if anyone has.

MONDAY, NOVEMBER 10. Miss R. is in the country for five years and continues speaking English as do most Englishmen and Americans. They are good Jews, but not intellectually and spiritually. They still sort of "Help their brethren." I have yet to find among them that stubborn devotion to Hebrew, so necessary at this period of Jewish development in E.Y., that is so prevalent among the Russian, Polish, and German youth that come here.

Mr. C. took me to look through the Jewish Pasteur Institute[15] where he is now doing some research work. The English are trying to build a rival institute, since it seems their theory is that all higher forms of learning must be of English origin, not from the natives.

SATURDAY, NOVEMBER 15. A visit to Gershon Agronsky where we talked of men and happenings.[16] Dr. and Mrs. Gamoran were there.[17]

SUNDAY, NOVEMBER 16 [DAY TRIP TO JERICHO & ENVIRONS]. We headed first for the Dead Sea. Except for some rickety straw shelters built to house the army detachment there stationed, the shore was entirely bare.

Jericho is a dead city in a very live fertile valley. This is the new Jericho. The site of the Jericho which Joshua conquered is still under the ban of his curse [Joshua 6:26]. Only one attempt was made [in ancient times] to rebuild it, and the ruins of that attempt were excavated in 1907–8 and are visible now.

We passed through the main street, and one gets the impression here too of a sleepy place. Men sitting around smoking, playing some Arabic game with dice and checkers, or just lying around and sleeping.

From the new site we proceeded to the Tel of ancient Jericho. We examined all of the excavations there made. The usual supply of pottery was there. If I were an antique collector I would bring home a trunk full of jar handles, bottoms, necks, and shards.

My thoughts vacillated from events that happened here thirty-five centuries ago to what may still happen here a few centuries into the future. One moment I saw Joshua cross the Jordan—the next one I saw Rutenberg harnessing the Jordan's waters.[18] As for the present, the outstanding asset of this whole section is its history. In the world of human memories, the Jewish people was like the Midas of the golden touch. Anything that came into contact with it took on significance and importance for mankind.

MONDAY, NOVEMBER 17. I visited the opening of the Health Week in E.Y. initiated by the Hadassah women's organization and carried through with the cooperation of the government and other institutions. H.E. opened the ceremonies, the afternoon being reserved for the Society folk. Sir Herbert spent some two hours, stopping at every booth and examining everything.

TUESDAY, NOVEMBER 18. A visit to Dr. [Michael] Guttmann [a Hungarian rabbi and Talmudic scholar], who arrived from Breslau last week and is going to deliver lectures on Talmudic subjects at the Hebrew University.

Evening to the opera to see "Aida" [in Hebrew]. A most excellent performance, surpassing all I hoped for. At times one imagines it would be better if some rich Maecenas were to support the opera here. But a good deal of its unique appeal is due to the spirit of self-sacrifice and love of art which was displayed by all concerned—conductor, actors, and audience.

FRIDAY, NOVEMBER 21. Off to see the Tower of David. From there we went to the Western Wall to recite the Friday evening prayers. There were all shades of religious fervor, of the earlocked vociferous *chasid*.

SUNDAY, NOVEMBER 23 [AFTERNOON TRIP TO BETHLEHEM AND HEBRON]. Within a half hour after leaving Jerusalem we were at Rachel's grave. If ever nobility was clothed humbly, the grave of Mother Rachel is such an instance. Surrounding it on three sides is a disheveled Moslem cemetery. Above the grave stands a poverty stricken tomb set up by Sir Moses Montefiore with the typical dome. From Rachel's grave to Bethlehem.

Bethlehem is a Christian city. Of its twelve thousand inhabitants only 300 are Moslems—and no Jews. Being the traditional birthplace of Jesus, and being held by Christians since the Crusades, it is only natural that monasteries and churches should be the chief pride and glory of the city. We visited only the Church of the Nativity built over the spot where Jesus is believed to have been born.

Dr. Gamoran, who was with us, told us that the next point of interest was to be Solomon's pools, not more than a 5–10 minute ride from Bethlehem. Three reservoirs believed to date from the time of Solomon are used by modern Jerusalem for its water supply. One's sense of the continuity of Jewish history is quickened when standing in the presence of these concrete remains of generations long gone that we have inherited. The neighborhood between the pools and Hebron was the country in which the Maccabees did a good deal of their fighting. There probably isn't a foot of soil in Judah which was not fattened by blood of Jews fighting in its defense.

Naturally, the first point of interest [in Hebron] was the Machpelah cave which was purchased by Abraham for four hundred silver coins. We proceeded to Abraham's well. Near it there is now a Turkish sweat bath which still has the bath of stone used by Abraham. Barring all other considerations, I doubt whether Abraham ever used so dirty a place for cleansing purposes. I had thought all along that I had seen the dingiest, darkest, narrowest streets ever built for human habitation. But Hebron's Jewish ghetto convinced me that I had a poor imagination.

The trip for the day was ended by a visit to the Slobodka Yeshivah which is now being transferred to Hebron.[19] We found 22 good-looking young men sitting in a small, poorly ventilated room, literally shouting as they were shaking over their Talmudic treatises. What a pitiful waste of good mental power! There are more of them coming, we were told. They live on 4£ a month given them by the yeshivah. Sights like that may be excellent food for strangers who go to see how "semi-civilized" backward people live. But for one who feels part and parcel of the group, who comes not as a sightseer but as one who would know the condition of his dearest relatives, such things are painful. I know all the spiritual energy stored up in such young men, and feel all the more keenly the terrible crime in spending it in that futile way.

After supper B. brought to my room an interesting chap from Soviet Russia by the name of S. He is a *chalutz* of three years standing and is only about 21–22 years old. Alert, clean-looking, nervously energetic, a former leader of the youth organization of Soviet Russia. He came to talk about the youth here and the need for a youth movement here, and at the same time to find out conditions among the youth of America. He is one of the great number here who have identified themselves completely with the rehabilitation of E.Y. I made some definite proposals for concrete steps we might take to organize something on a small scale. Yet I doubt whether anything will turn out. Feeling as I do that I am only a visitor, I do not feel that I have the right to take the initiative in a work in which I will not be able to carry on. But I'm glad I met another of those youths who are not *parlor idealists* but men who make a determined effort to *live* in terms of their *ideals*.

WEDNESDAY, NOVEMBER 26. A most interesting three hours talking to S. again. There is much talk about the morality among the *chalutz* groups. I asked him about it, and he made these interesting observations. (1) Compared to the moral standards prevailing among the so-called intelligent Jewish youth of Eastern Europe, the *chalutz* is the symbol of purity and abstinence. (2) Considering that there is an outstanding preponderance of men, the fact that there are no commercial prostitutes in the country is significant. The only place that has such is Haifa, due to the sailors that land there. (3) The title Tel Aviv has, the Paris of E.Y., is because you have a middle class there that merely wishes to transfer European standards to E.Y. soil. Hence, they brought European sex standards with them. (4) The sexual experimentation going on in the [*kibbutzim*] is not a sexual promiscuity but merely a conscious attempt to arrive at a more rational relationship between the sexes. (5) Free love tried as a social experiment is rapidly dying out, though there are charlatans who take advantage of the state of flux in which all social institutions find themselves. (6) the reason why the *chalutzim* are so suspected of immorality is this: There is no civil marriage in E.Y. They refuse to go through the Jewish religious ceremony. Hence it all appears bad, though in reality a sexual purity of high order prevails.

From this we passed to another subject. He wants to see in America a movement started among the youth to come here and work. Why doesn't the youth come and encourage the others and contribute its bit? His words met only a shamed face on my part for all he said was true. Only if America's youth come here would we stamp the [American Zionist] movement as a real national movement, not merely as a movement to give refuge to the persecuted.

The Arab question, which pained me more than anything I have thus far heard in connection with Zionist work, represents a moral problem not easily to be solved. Now the land being bought is the rich land in the Emek [Jezreel Valley], which is settled by Arabs living there for centuries under a system of absentee landlordism. They have to be removed before Jews can settle, an obvious dispossession. The Jews buy legally, but the results are not of the very best and tend to rouse the population for causes very easily appreciated.

SUNDAY, NOVEMBER 30. To tea at General [Ronald] Storrs, governor of the Jerusalem district. The general is a really extraordinarily cultured man. We spoke of Jerusalem and he had occasion to say that the only thing the matter with the city is that the *English* had not taken it fifty years ago. Also that next to English, Greek is the greatest language; also that the Jews do not have a sense of responsibility in their buildings, and if not for him, shoddy buildings would have disgraced the landscape; also that the best in Europe is to be traced back exclusively to the Greeks; also that the English having so rich a literature have no need for any other. H. challenged his statement about the Greek origin of all things good, but Storrs preferred to cite Christianity and Greek thought.

MONDAY, DECEMBER 1

[Here Greenberg offers a sharp critique of a speech by the American writer and Zionist Maurice Samuel, who had stated that Jews couldn't mix with other peoples and that they were a thorn in Gentile flesh. Greenberg's rebuttal, which denies the validity of Zionism based solely on antisemitism, is an illuminating passage on his own position.]

Of all the stupid viciously harmful doctrines now preached to spread Zionism and rouse Jewish consciousness, this one stands out most objectionably and painfully. It is not true that the Jew cannot mix. If there is any reason why he does not mix, it is social and spiritual. The Jews did not remain alive because they couldn't mix, but because they did not want to mix and disappear. Now, assuming that the Jew can't mix, it is nothing less than courting bitter race hatred to say in the very next breath that we are a thorn in the side of the Gentiles and should not be tolerated. What will happen to the ever-increasing number of Jews in the world? Where should they go?

Can't [Samuel] visualize a time when men will be able to live together though they differ in their views? Can't he preach Zionism as a doctrine based on the positive desire of a group to live in conditions that would be more suitable for them to work out their own salvation as they see best? If the only way to rouse Jewish consciousness is by the negative way of making them feel an abysmal separation between them and their neighbors, thus encouraging forces of separation and race hatred already too effectively active in the world, then the whole thing is not worthwhile! Why not try to live and preach the doctrine of Jerusalem, of world peace! My, what food such stuff is for a Polish antisemite or an American [Henry] Ford![20]

Thursday there was a clash between Arabs and Jews at Afulah, where Jews were going to plow land formerly occupied by Arab tenant farmers. An Arab was killed and some 15 wounded on both sides. There is no assurance whatever that the Arab was killed by a Jew. Quite the contrary, the shot was at close range, and no weapons were found among the Jews but were found among Arabs. But that is beside the point. The thing that interested me was the account of the efforts made by Jews to satisfy the right claims of all concerned. Not only is the owner paid for his land but the Arab receives an indemnity. In this case all signed documents that they were satisfied with what they received and left in peace. Trouble was started by some Christian Arabs apparently under organized propaganda.

TUESDAY, DECEMBER 2. To Prof. Guttmann's to take my first lesson in Talmud with him. This will perhaps give me the distinction of being the very first student of the Hebrew University to actually start taking courses!!

SUNDAY, DECEMBER 7. In the afternoon we took another trip to Hebron with Adil Effendi. He belongs to the powerful Palestinian Mohammedan family of the Husseini. His cousin is the Mufti, the head of all Mohammedan holy places. Since Adil is L.'s friend, we had the extraordinary experience of actually entering the mosque. After the one ceremony of covering our shoes with special slippers, we entered. The place is most impressive. A circle of Arabs sitting on the floor listening to one of their elders expound the Koran added to the general powerful impression the whole scene made on me.

On our way back we visited the home of a Christian Arab, also a friend of L., in Bethlehem. There we met a group of rich Arabs who had made their money abroad (mostly America) and are now living here on their income, rather disgusted with the lack of activity and entertainment. They showed no special love for the country. Yet, I found a pamphlet on "The Case Against Zionism" on the table. These people know Zionism is bringing into the country exactly what they miss in it—life, movement, activity—but it seems they would prefer to see their child die than to have him cured by a Jewish doctor.

TUESDAY, DECEMBER 9. An official holiday in Jerusalem commemorating [General] Allenby's entrance into the city. The afternoon was spent in REGISTERING FOR COURSES at the HEBREW UNIVERSITY ON MT. SCOPUS.

WEDNESDAY, DECEMBER 10. Visit to the Gamorans. Discussed politics, the usual subject here. Of interest is the fact that the Arabs refused to cooperate in the Health Week work. They were afraid of being accused of being friendly with the Jews. Storrs and his lady can get very few words of commendation from Jerusalem Jews. They cannot and will not forgive him his actions during the riots here [in 1920].[21]

SATURDAY, DECEMBER 13. Prayed at the synagogue of the Karliner *chasidim*. What a motley crowd with their long earlocks, long silk frocks, and white knitted caps under the *talith*. The youngsters dressed exactly like the men. There is no attempt whatsoever made at beautifying the outer form of the service. Each one *yells*, literally speaking at the very top of his voice, the youngsters competing with the elders. Here and there stood a reverent old man, praying in silence, his face and body expressive of the utmost piety and heartfelt supplication. These old gentlemen fan dying embers of spirituality within you. But if they can keep still, why must those others yell?

A football game was going on in Talpioth between a Jewish and English team. Saturday afternoon sports are becoming popular. If the commercial spirit could be kept out of the sports they would be perfectly welcome! Football has taken hold of the whole of the country, some say for the good, some for the bad.

SUNDAY, DECEMBER 14. Perhaps it is sheer selfishness that urges me to remain here. Where else in the world can I feel so completely at one with myself?

MONDAY, DECEMBER 15. The evening spent at a concert of the Musical Society. Thus far Jews are the culturally predominant *group* here, but Hebrew is not yet the predominant culture.

WEDNESDAY, DECEMBER 17. Present at the reception given in honor of Rabbi Kook on his return from America. Thousands of Jews crowded the street where his home and school are situated. The police had a hard time of it. It is far from an easy matter to keep a yeshivah boy or a *chasid* away from his rabbi.

SATURDAY, DECEMBER 20. A most vociferous discussion with Is. on the comparative value of Diaspora Judaism and Judaism in E.Y. It started with my saying that if I were not at bottom a coward, I would go back to the U.S., get fifty young boys and girls with $1000 each, and start a settlement in the Emek. I am absolutely certain that I can find the proper people, who would be willing to come on the very simple proposition, "Come what may, we will live and die in

Eretz Yisrael." A group of this kind from America would be of the utmost value in testing the spiritual vigor of American Jewry, in injecting a new kind of blood into the settlement here, in assuring the Jewish people itself that E.Y. is not merely a refuge for those who cannot go anywhere else, and above all it would give fifty young people a chance to really live a life of creation, struggle, and perhaps achievement. I do not in any way belittle the value of Diaspora Jewry, but I shall live in the Diaspora, if I do, not out of conviction that there is where I would most care to live, but out of sheer lack of courage to break with the connections of a lifetime.

In the evening to an entertainment given by the children of the Jerusalem Gymnasium. I left before the end, being unable to tolerate the lack of order in everything that was done and in the lack of ordinary good behavior on the part of the audience. Perhaps elsewhere I might overlook such things, but here I simply can't. The children looked bright, healthy, and alert. But they are totally lacking in discipline. They're "smart," too darn smart, and very often remain that way all their lives.

SUNDAY, DECEMBER 21. My usual argument with Is., this time on the shamefully insignificant role the Rabbinical Assembly [the organization of American Conservative rabbis] is taking in Zionist affairs—the lack of vision, energy, and initiative that characterizes the graduates of our institution.

MONDAY, DECEMBER 22. In the afternoon the official opening of the Institute of Jewish Studies took place at the University. We got no official invitations; since the capacity of the hall was limited to 100, the notables of the various groups of Jerusalem took precedence. Dr. Magnes told us to come anyhow, and we did. The assembly took place in the lecture hall of the biochemistry department of the University, the only department doing work for some time now. Some 110 people were present. The Moslem National Council did not permit any Arab savant to speak nor did the Arab mayor of Jerusalem accept the invitation to say a few words. They did not want to show the slightest act of cooperation with the Jews. A few learned Arabs had initially accepted the invitations, Dr. Magnes told us later, but were compelled to withdraw their acceptances. Nor did our chief rabbis come. They too, it seems, feared that the Orthodox community here would accuse them of supporting a heretical institute.

Saw Bialik here for the first time,[22] sitting at Magnes's left. It is a commonplace remark to make, but he does not look like a poet but rather like a successful business entrepreneur.

Tuesday, December 23. Talked with Dr. Dinaburg.[23] I took the occasion to point out that in spite of the fact that America is the so-called dollar land, the Hebrew University is drawing heavily on America for funds, for professors, directors, and even students. Those are interesting and significant facts.

In the evening we went to the Magneses. They had arranged a Hanukkah supper for the kiddies and asked some older folks for the evening. We talked much of the future plans for the University. The library building, for which funds are already forthcoming (10,000£ from America) will be the central structure to be started next year.

Sunday, December 28. Morning spent in a trip on horses to Anatot, the birthplace of Jeremiah. A dirty Arab village is still on that spot, from where one can very clearly see the desert of Judea, the Dead Sea, and the mountains of Moab.

In the evening to a Hanukkah gathering at Yellin's.[24] We walked through Meah Shearim and passed a number of so-called synagogues where Jews were celebrating the holiday with song and story. The evening at Yellin's was especially well-spent.

Wednesday, January 7, 1925. For some time now I have been wondering to myself why pious Orthodoxy—earlocked, bearded, kaftaned Orthodoxy— calls forth so little sympathy from me. I know all the greatness of soul, depth of feeling, etc. that our fathers who were thus attired had. Now I think I can state the reason. That sort of dress and the sort of mental and spiritual outlook they represented were admirable enough for the generations perhaps up to the 19th century. But in our own day they symbolize to me the cloak under which ignorance, bigotry, and superstition take refuge. Were I to attack their ignorance or superstitions, my own conscience or some outsider could call me an infidel or blasphemer.

Thursday, January 8. To a meeting of the Palestine Oriental Society where 7 papers were read. A half-hour tea breaks up the reading of the papers and gives one an opportunity to listen to Herbert Samuel, Storrs, Bentwich et al. sipping tea!!

Saturday, January 10. In the afternoon Is. and I were invited to tea at the Bentwiches. When we came there we found the attorney-general with a group of English men and women, just returned from a game of hockey. The Sports Club of Jerusalem paid 10,000£ for a field. Yes, E.Y. is a very poor country! One can't really get very much at these social occasions. Do I know much more about the attorney-general now than I did 3 days ago? Only that he isn't overly attractive in a hockey outfit, that he is a genial chap, and that his wife smokes like a major, as do all English-Jewish society women here.

SUNDAY, JANUARY 11. To tea with His Excellency the High Commissioner and Lady Samuel!! A number of students of the American School were there. Nothing exceptional about the tea or cakes or about anything else, except that it was nice to get a chance to spend some time with the "Lion in his Den."

Prof. Margolis asked us to come to him in the evening, which we did. He is with a relative, a former representative of Habonim [a Zionist youth group] in E.Y. and now attached to the political department of the Zionist Executive.

MONDAY, JANUARY 12. Afternoon saw the Hakoach [football] team beat the English-Palestine army team. Their dexterity is artistic and perfect. I would not, however, encourage these international games here. They cause bad blood. Englishmen may be good sports when they play among themselves. They fall below their "advertised" standard when losing to others.

THURSDAY, JANUARY 15. Magnes, Margolis, Is., and I walked from the University through the fields back to town. Time and again Magnes kept asking us: "Did you ever, anywhere else in the world, feel the significance of the subject matter as much as you do here, when it is delivered in Hebrew before an audience that understands? Did you ever think that the form in which a subject is delivered should influence the content so profoundly?" And the student body, how they sit and drink in every word spoken by the professor. What a thirst there was here for knowledge of a higher and profounder type. And what joy it is for me to be here and feel part of it all.

We spoke of the establishment of the Department of Pedagogy. Again it may be America that will provide the required personnel.

TUESDAY, JANUARY 20. Visited Mozah and the convalescent home being erected there by the Laborers' Organization. The building is an achievement in architecture, and the institution is an excellent example of what cooperative effort can accomplish.

From there we proceeded to Dilb, the first communistic or cooperative colony that I visited. The place is only three years old. The finest structures are devoted to the livestock, the people living in temporary wooden huts and tents. We saw part of them at work (men and women), cleaning the cows, barns, and chicken coops. The bulletin board announced a discussion on the book "The *Kvutzah*" for this Saturday. Six children from 3–5 were under the care of a kindergarten teacher who showed us their schoolroom and work. Unconsciously I asked one of the children where "his" seat was, and was gently reminded that there is no such thing as mine and yours. One closet contains all the clothing of the children, which is the common property of all. The mothers cannot devote themselves to the children because of other work they must do. That sort of communism is most attractive. Dilb does not use "force" in an attempt to foist its ideas on everyone else.

FRIDAY, JANUARY 23. Evening to Dr. Magnes for supper. Spoke of liberalizing "liberal" Judaism and Kaplan's "New Approach to Judaism."[25] Magnes thinks that Kaplan overstressed the place of E.Y. Magnes wants a Diaspora Judaism too, and in that I agree with him heartily. Far from negating the Diaspora, I believe that the reason which ultimately justifies all our efforts here, namely our belief in the spiritual value of our heritage, justifies our preservation of our identity in the Diaspora also. We want this center for other reasons, and not because we believe that Judaism has no place and no future elsewhere. It has. Only the existence of a Jewish E.Y. would make that place and that future so much more secure.

World politics were discussed which recalled Magnes's days as a pacifist. He wants yet to go back to the States to preach the doctrine: "Root yourself deeply in the Jewish past. Then struggle for the realization of the great *human* ideals such as Justice and Peace!!"

THURSDAY, JANUARY 29. In the evening K., whom I met at the Scout administrative committee, came to my room. We are a committee to discuss the relationship between the Scouts here and other Jewish youth organizations. He gave me a detailed account of the various youth movements of Central and Eastern Europe. Even scouting is used by the various governments for their own political motives. It's interesting the way the English manage or try to manage the Arab scouts here.

SATURDAY, JANUARY 31. We walked around the settlement of Kolandiah. There was no distinct Sabbath atmosphere that I could feel. A number of the young folks were around doing odds and ends, as an American farmer on Sunday. One was whitewashing his coop, another bringing water as on every other day. There was no "public" work, i.e., no work on their buildings, but these people are quite removed from the traditional Sabbath. Yet perhaps they will gradually get around to that too. Some brought their parents from the other side. These now have a service on Saturday. The best we can say for E.Y. is that nowhere does one feel the Sabbath as he does here. There is but one danger. If Eastern

European Jews get hold of the situation we may be forced into a narrow ritualistic observance. The Eastern European radical has as yet shown no genius for reinterpreting his religion. He is most capable as a radical objector and rebel to all of it.

WEDNESDAY, FEBRUARY 4. In the evening a visit from a student at Rabbi Kook's yeshivah. He is young, with a very alert mind, and with an ability to express his views. He was himself a good example of the superiority of Kook's school over other yeshivahs. He spoke of the Rambam and of the value of philosophy—things unheard of in other yeshivahs.

SATURDAY, FEBRUARY 7. Walked with Agronsky to the ruins of the city of Jericho. He had some interesting things to tell about the relations with the Arab press, which are better left unrecorded. Afternoon and evening spent on gossiping about practically every man of any prominence in the American Jewish world—from "Pope" [Cyrus] Adler [the president of JTS] to the host of Seminary students. When editor of the Jewish Telegraphic Agency in New York, Agronsky came into contact with all of them. The gossiping fest threw some more light on the nature of the men who are the moving powers of our little world.

SUNDAY, FEBRUARY 8. In Jerusalem with H. She spoke of the Aaronsohn family, one of the most·bitterly hated families in E.Y. (Agronsky spat fire every time the name was mentioned.) H. just worshiped them. The Aaronsohn family is at Zikhron Yaakov. The two outstanding members are dead—Aaron, supposed to have fallen out of a British airplane and Sarah, who shot herself when the Turks imprisoned her during the war as a spy.[26]

TUESDAY, FEBRUARY 10. The morning spent in participating in the grand celebration of [Arbor Day]. The schools marched in full force to Bet Hakerem. There Lady Samuel planted the first tree and about 11 children planted their saplings along the newly-laid out streets of the section. Then all repaired to a fine field situated in the heart of the hills of Judea.

WEDNESDAY, FEBRUARY 11. In the evening to a meeting of the student body of the University. They want to organize. It was a very lively affair and gave me an opportunity to understand better some of those numerous types of students we have in those classes. It gave me an idea why it was so hard for American Zionists to work with the Europeans at the international Zionist conferences. These Europeans have such a peculiar notion of parliamentary procedure. If Young

Judaea in America does nothing more than teach children how to carry on a meeting in proper order, it has justified its existence. Of outstanding interest to me is watching the way the Eastern European mind works—the emphasis on the theory. They want to know exactly what the organization is going to do and the form its activity will take etc., etc., before they create the first elementary machinery which makes any action at all possible. After endless discussion, a committee to formulate a tentative constitution was elected. I shall be one of the members. Hence I'll have an opportunity to see from the inside what will take place.

FRIDAY, FEBRUARY 20. Afternoon to play some baseball with the rest of the Americans. Among the players was Dr. Magnes. He plays a good game and was very clearly proud of it.

SATURDAY, FEBRUARY 21. Long walk with J. through streets and buildings of the old city which I had never before visited. Among other things we visited the French monastery built over the spot where the palace of Pontius Pilate stood and where Jesus was sentenced to the cross. It is the beginning of the Via Dolorosa. Also visited a Hadassah milk station. Two Jewish nurses were in attendance doing the regular work, for milk has to be handed out whether it be Saturday or not. The Orthodox authorities here who shout so loudly at every violation of the Sabbath are doing nothing to meet the needs of the situation. And while I am on the topic of our Orthodox policemen of the Almighty, I may say that while they shake the very foundations of the earth with their cries against a *chalutz* who does not wear *tzitzit*, they haven't as much as whispered a protest against those of their own party who most grossly violate the fundamentals of Judaism in their business practices. The meanest, most dangerous, practice is connected with land transactions, in which petty traders raise prices in a most shameless and heartless way. They even advise Arabs to hold out or they offer them a price they never dreamed of asking. Nor have these people done anything to improve the relations between employer and laborer.

SUNDAY, FEBRUARY 22. To a meeting again of the student body at which the proposed constitution was to be discussed. It started at 8 P.M. and closed past midnight without one clause being adopted. The meeting ended with no outcome because of lack of parliamentary procedure and due to the confounded European habit of having a dozen motions before the house at the same time.

A TOUR OF THE COUNTRY

Bearing letters of introduction from Magnes, Greenberg and his two close friends took a month-long tour of the land. Their itinerary, which was prepared by Magnes, led them along the coast to Haifa, and from there they traveled eastward through the Emek and northward to Lake Kinneret and the Galilee. At several points they veered off course in order to explore the environs of certain places. They covered a few distances by train, by car, and on horseback, but for the most part they hiked. They visited towns and cities, small villages (some run cooperatively), and kibbutzim; all had been founded after 1870, most by Jewish pioneers from Eastern Europe and some by Baron Edmond de Rothschild.[27] (Greenberg loosely used the words "colony" or "settlement" to describe most places.) Meeting friends and acquaintances, as well as some prominent people, at the places they explored, they weren't at a loss for meals or a night's lodging. As in Jerusalem, they experienced the fluidity of social classes.

Throughout their trip they saw the old and the new, archeological remains and Bedouin tribes alongside modern agricultural cultivation and the beginnings of industrialization. Here too Greenberg's likes and dislikes and his special interests, religion—or the vestiges that remained in the settlements—and schools for the children, were most apparent.

The trip was long and arduous, but the young men's interest never flagged. Departing from the usual tourist route, they climbed mountains, forded streams, and tasted the primitive life of Arab and some Jewish villages. While they viewed the remains of ages long past and learned the history of Palestine in ways not provided by books, they were ever conscious of how the yishuv was reclaiming land from the desert and making it fertile. For the first time they saw the New Jew living in communities which had determinedly rejected the petty trade image so long associated with Jews. If the young Americans weren't charmed by the sights and inhabitants of Eretz Yisrael before they started, they were when the tour ended. As Greenberg wrote on his return to Jerusalem, "It is a maddeningly beautiful country."

The following excerpts from Greenberg's very full account are but a sampling of his rich experiences during the tour. The primary focus of those passages is on the yishuv as filtered through the eyes of an American student. Passing judgments based on American standards, Greenberg saw both negative as well as positive aspects of a developing society. In some cases he was asked about American Jewry and its need, if any, of Zionism.

WEDNESDAY, FEBRUARY 25. In Rechovot we visited A. Aharoni, the famous zoologist of E.Y. He is to be connected with the University, with the department of [zoology] and biology. A most remarkable man he is!

When I visited the synagogue in Rechovot with its large collection of the Hebrew classics it occurred to me that in one respect at any rate we idolize the *chalutz* where he really falls behind his ancestors, i.e., in respect to his literary and intellectual activities. After a hard day's work the Jew was accustomed to go back and spend hours over volumes that required far more intellectual power and concentration than do the Hebrew translations of modern world literature. The *chalutz* does not approach his intellectual life with nearly that reverence and deep sincerity which characterized the attitude of our ancestors towards their studies.

From Rechovot we struck across the fields to Gederah. We were told that there was a road leading to the colony. But the Arabs had been plowing their fields, and when they plow, roads mean nothing to them. We passed a few Arab villages and landed in Gederah. It is not a very large or overly prosperous colony. It is, however, among the oldest ones, having been started in 1884. We had dinner in the kitchen where the workers eat. There are some 70 young men here now engaged in tobacco preparation. There is a fine spacious synagogue, a school, and a kindergarten in the colony. But the elderly Jews, as in other settlements, complain about the disuse into which the synagogue has fallen.

From Gederah we walked to Ekron, founded in 1884 by the Baron. A typical Hebrew colony with wide streets, fairly well kept houses, schools, synagogue, etc. The children and young ladies we saw are in the vast majority healthy and attractive looking, distinctly superior to their neighbors. The difference between even the worst Jewish settlement and the neighboring Arab village is the difference between [New York's] Lower East Side and Riverside Drive.

THURSDAY, FEBRUARY 26. We started out for Nes Zionah. The road there was lined with *chalutzim* and *chalutzot* who were laying a stone road in the deep sand. Seeing bright feminine faces breaking large stones to fit them for the road has become a commonplace. On either side of the road were Jewish orange groves, all heavily laden with their ripe fruit. I have been eating oranges endlessly these days. We buy them, large and juicy, 4 for a nickel, and they serve instead of water. A fine new synagogue is now being built with the help of the never-failing Baron.

From Nes Zionah we started for Be'er Yaakov. The whole neighborhood was unusually thickly settled with Bedouin tribes. They pitched their tents on land owned by Arabs who refuse to sell because they know that all land near a Jewish settlement is bound to rise in value. We reached Be'er Yaakov, a small settlement, and got into a conversation with the teacher. He told us the history of the settlement; being somewhat interested in archeology, he had made investigations and came to the conclusion that this place is built on the ruins of a very ancient settlement. In his school (a building of one large room which serves also as synagogue and auditorium) he had a collection of flint tools and old coins found by him or by children in the colony. Among them was a coin of the Hasmonean period, the well-known coin with 3 wheat stalks.

To Rishon Lezion—a beautiful place. We came first to the newly built Yemenite section—it makes a most pleasing impression. The street is wide, the houses white and surrounded by gardens well kept by the industrious Yemenites, and all well supplied with trees and flowers.

The synagogue in the center of the town resounded just then with evening prayers. We went to join in. Only the very old and the very young were present. The same old story. But why one should go there I don't know. These people insist on asking you to pray in the Ashkenazic pronunciation, speak their Yiddish, making no effort to change. E.Y. had no influence on them. They are not part of the new but merely hangovers of the Diaspora.

FRIDAY, FEBRUARY 27. Went to visit the famous wine cellars of Rishon Lezion. We had a good drink of grape juice, their new product which they are now [during Prohibition] shipping in large quantities to America. From there we left for Nachlat Yehudah. The interesting part of this settlement are the "farmerettes," 18 girls doing *everything* a farmer does—the modern Amazons!

The next destination was Mikveh Israel [an agricultural school]. Showed our letter of introduction to the head of the school and were at once supplied with a guide to show us around. It is a beautiful modern school. There are 150 regular students taking the 3-year course and some 70 laborers who train here for a year and then go off to the colonies or their *kvutzot* to carry on their work..

We left for Tel Aviv. In the evening a group of Americans and English gathered. A discussion on Americans in E.Y. ensued, and I aired some ideas. Their one answer is "It is all right for you who are going back; try and live here!" The difficulty with most of them is that they are in Tel Aviv as the appendages of rich pious parents who came to spend their last days here. The girls sit around doing nothing in particular and think the place is dead because they can't attend the shows, operas, lectures, concerts etc. on account of their ignorance of Hebrew. Beyond and above all, some simply could not understand how one can get along with "those Russians."

SATURDAY, FEBRUARY 28. In Tel Aviv: To the services of [a] Rabbi Benjamin, [leader of the] Association of American Jews in Palestine—as perfect a picture of a ghetto service as I've ever seen. He delivered his lecture in Yiddish. With his eyes closed and face turned heavenward he damned the *chalutzim* who play ball on Saturday and do not go to him and his ilk to sanction their marriage relations. He is a powerful demagogue of the worst kind. There are no young men there, all old rich American Jews mostly interested in real estate here, probably doing their share in the outrageous boosting of prices now going on. Whether or not Jews are religious in Tel Aviv, there is no place in the Diaspora where one is quite as conscious of the Sabbath as here. Every store, except two drug stores, was closed.

SUNDAY, MARCH 1. From Tel Aviv to Saronah we passed a large number of sub-urbs of Tel Aviv. The largest and most interesting is the B'nai Brak settlement of Orthodox Jews, among the first instances I saw where Orthodoxy showed it has real creative ability. Leaving Saronah we came to the orange groves of Petach Tikveh, the largest Jewish colony in the country. The settlement itself falls far below Rishon and Rechovot for beauty. However, large cooperative groups of workers are in the colony now, especially those of the religious Mizrachi organization. We ate in the public kitchen and slept in the barracks of one of those groups. The barrack had a rather good collection of Hebrew classics. It is these fellows that are redeeming Orthodoxy in this country.

The one large impression thus far gotten on our tour is the sense of a Jewish *countryside*. Up till now I knew what a Jewish farmer was, or an isolated Jewish settlement. But from Rechovot to Petach Tikveh there is a fairly solid line of Jewish settlements, and as you walk hour after hour among fields and past villages worked and built by Jews you get the feeling of a Jewish country-side!

MONDAY, MARCH 2. On the way to K'far Saba we passed the Yarkon river. The current is exceptionally powerful—the stream being deep and narrow. It is the water power which Rutenberg intends utilizing for supplying electricity to Jaffa–Tel Aviv and the environs. K'far Saba has some forty families. There I saw a Jewish shepherd.

TUESDAY, MARCH 3. From the train station to Chaderah. This is the place once famous for its swamps and malaria, now for its forests and good health. These forests were planted some 35 years ago by a group of young fellows whose sport was to bet on who would bury whom. All of them died from malaria contracted while working in the swamps. But they left behind them the forest and the basis for one of our largest and most beautiful settlements.

WEDNESDAY, MARCH 4. We reached Binyaminah, a PICA settlement which boasts a fine modern creamery and a beautiful flower garden which is to prepare flowers for the perfumery factory now in the process of being built.

THURSDAY, MARCH 5. Left Binyamina for Zikhron Yaakov, the one large colony the Jews have that is situated in the mountains. Our first stop was the Aaronsohn home. It is a little palace, undoubtedly one of the historic spots of the country. From the remains of the collections and works of Aaron, which were reclaimed from Turkish vandalism, one clearly sees that here was a man of the very first class in ability and energy. We had a princely lunch at the Aaronsohns and hiked to Shefeya, where the girls' orphanage of the Joint Distribution Committee is situated.

FRIDAY, MARCH 6. From Shefeya to Atlit by train. There we stopped to see the great salt works of the PICA and the ruins of the fortresses which were the last to be evacuated by the retreating Crusaders. Here as everywhere else the Hebrew language was the "Open Sesame." Our breeches and golf socks label us at once as Americans, and we are viewed somewhat as freaks, for lo and behold "Americans! Speak Hebrew! And are tramping through the country." All are anxious to know about the progress of Zionism in America. I often suspect that a great number are not overjoyed by the news that Zionism in America is deepening, becoming fuller in content and more spiritual. If American Jewry will, in addition to its economic superiority become spiritually superior as well, how will other Jews justify their claim to world leadership of Israel. Now the compensation is "You have wealth but we have spirit." It is the defense mechanism whereby they maintain their self-respect and a component of their attitude towards America and Americans.

Near Atlit there is also a group of 14 young Jews, living as fishermen, the first I saw in my life. In Haifa: In the evening we went to pray at the Biram School, the Haifa "Reali" school [a model high school founded by the educator Dr. Arthur Biram]. We were invited by Dr. Biram to remain for supper and to meet the other Americans who were his guests. The group at supper included two wealthy American visitors with their chauffeur and pupils who boarded at the school. After sitting at a meal with the [rich] fellows, I got a better impression of their importance than I could get out of a dozen newspaper reports about their doings. Mr. L. told me that Prof. Kaplan is coming to E.Y. with Dr. Weizmann for the opening of the University. Another rumor on which we got some information is that Norman Bentwich is leaving his post at the end of 1925, not because he wants to leave the country—he is too good a Zionist for that—but since he was an appointee of the military administration and not the Colonial Office, he cannot advance in rank. If he returns to England he may be in a position, 2 or 3 years hence, to return with more power.[28]

SATURDAY, MARCH 7. Prayers at the Biram School and then to look over the Technikum [original name for the Technion, a university of engineering sciences] and the dormitory for the pupils of the Reali school now under construction. The three structures are among the strongest factors making for the development of the city.

We had lunch at Mrs. Friedlaender's[29] where we spent five hours, a good deal of the time in gossiping about men and events. She has a good deal to say and spoke rather freely to us.

SUNDAY, MARCH 8. Saw Haifa today. Spent some two hours visiting classes in the Reali school, where we found an excellent staff with German thoroughness and strictness. Then to the public school, where the Dalton plan of student self-government is being tried in the upper classes with some success.

Haifa is entering upon a booming period and the dirty, despicable hand of the Polish Jewish land speculator is already beginning to be felt. Of all the heart-breaking phenomena in E.Y. the land speculator gives one more heartache than any other.

MONDAY, MARCH 9. Left Haifa by train. The train passes the great flour mills erected by PICA and what is the largest industrial establishment of the country, the cement factory, also belonging to this organization. Reached Nahalal in the Emek. It is a fine settlement famous more especially for the fact that only 3 years ago it was a swamp. Here too there is a group of girls learning agriculture. From Nahalal we walked for about two and a half hours where within a comparatively small radius are concentrated some 6 Jewish settlements—labor groups and farmers.

We are camping with the Markenhof group, started by a German nucleus but having further different additions. We just completed eating supper, and the *kvutzah*, some 30 men and women, are now sitting around the table and dividing the work among themselves for tomorrow. In the course of the apportionment, problems of agriculture necessitating scientific training arise and the experts of the group are called upon to give their opinions. Hebrew is of course the language constantly used, only now and then a newcomer falls back into German to explain some point too difficult for his newly acquired language to expound.

Purim celebrations have already started throughout the country. Here the group decided to read the Megillah. They wanted it read in the traditional tune. Since none of their own was able to do it, I did it for them.

TUESDAY, MARCH 10. Left the group and made for Balfouriyah. This settlement interested me especially, it being the first American attempt at actual colonization [1922]. The place is very well laid out, the houses are good, there is water (Balfouriyah supplies some of the groups in the neighborhood also). People told us that there are from 6–16 American families of some forty in the settlement.

From there a half hour's walk to K'far Yeladim [an agricultural school, literally the children's village] of the Joint Distribution Committee. It is really a little village by itself with 110 children and their teachers and supervisors. We decided to climb the mountain rising behind the orphanage and challenging Mount Tabor for the highest point in the Emek [probably Givat Hamoreh]. This turned out to be the most strenuous climb I ever made in my life (1690 feet). From the peak we saw the whole of the Emek and much more.

To Merchaviah and from there we walked to Ein Harod, one of the most interesting and the second largest communistic group in the country. One of the members of the group, in addition to being well acquainted with all the details of the theory and practices of the group, knew how to express himself. For some three hours we talked and walked through the whole "commonwealth."

WEDNESDAY, MARCH 11. In the morning we saw the Ein Harod school in action. Then to Beisan [Bet Shean]. The whole section is very well supplied with water. Ein Harod has the spring at which Gideon tested his soldiers. We passed Tel Joseph, the only place in the Emek which has electricity. Through fields of Bedouins, through swampy fields to Beisan. There of course the first thing of interest were the excavations, the site where some steles [then thought to date to the period] of the Tel-el-Amarna tablets[30] were found.

From Beisan to Jesir where a group of 40, men and women, work some PICA land. They have inherited the houses of the Arabs who lived here before the town was bought. The settlement is directly on the Jordan river. Three bridges cross the river here, one dating from the Crusaders' period, one for the railroad built by the Turks, and one completed only this week for traffic. There is just a bit of tension in life here now. Bedouins in great numbers have started to penetrate from across the Jordan, driven to cultivated settlements because of the lack of rain in Transjordan. Their profession here is to steal. Hence two members of the group keep special watch at night.

Tomorrow morning we enter the Galilee.

THURSDAY, MARCH 12. Deganiah A and Deganiah B are beautiful and interesting places. The details of their social order resemble very much those of Ein Harod. Deganiah is situated below sea level and for 8 months a year they have some very strong heat. The children do not mind it in the least; they can stand heat which would cause sunstroke for the older folks of the group. The same with the cows raised on the spot—they take to the heat better than the original ones brought in.

It seems to me that if a New Word is to be spoken in E.Y. it will be spoken not by Tel Aviv, and perhaps not even by Jerusalem and its University. It will come from places like Ein Harod and Deganiah. If one is foolish enough to guess as to the nature of the New Word, he would say that it will be an emphasis on the *Dignity of Labor* and the crime of living on the physical toil of others. They are planning their whole course of life on that basis. The education system expresses it, and there is no dissonance between doctrine and practice, for what the child learns in school, *that* is what his parents live.

FRIDAY, MARCH 13. Entered Tiberias and went to clean up a bit in the *hot* springs. We found the old city dirty, noisome, and hopeless—a disgrace heaped by man on so beautiful a natural location. In the evening to one of the "regular" synagogues. The city as a whole is populated mostly by Sefardic Jews and Ashkenazim who are *chasidim*. There is very little new about it except the children. Hebrew is none too prevalent, the Sefardic Jews having practically identified themselves, at least in exteriors, with their Arab neighbors so that it is hard to tell which is which.

SATURDAY, MARCH 14. We walked to Migdal, a small Jewish settlement on the sea, from where we climbed the hill on which the fortress of Irbid is located. At one time the haunt of brave souls, at others that of highwaymen, it is now a refuge for sheep and a curiosity for those who have enough strength and interest to climb its steep approach.

SUNDAY, MARCH 15. We decided to go to Metullah by auto. Saw all the Jewish settlements between Tiberias and Metullah. The colonies that were started and supported by the Baron's organizations leave the worst impression. His human material was poor, and he or his officials accustomed them to pauperism. Besides, his whole organization does nothing to revive the spirit, or the outlook of the Jewish people, thinking that by merely settling them in a colony they become farmers. It is altogether untrue, for on every turn, in colonies like Rosh Pinah and Petach Tikveh the Jewish small dealer outlook and interest is visible.

We came to Metullah and ate with the *kvutzah* of the young men, all of whom are graduates of Mikveh Israel. Among other things our guide explained to us how to work his gun (which he constantly had at his side). This country, judging even from what it is now, must have been like the U.S. Wild West only 10 or 12 years ago. Practically every *chalutz* has a quality that is an absolute necessity here, and that is unquestioned physical courage and bravery. It is to them that we ought to be thankful for the respect the Arab now has for the Jew in E.Y. And that is no mean thing.

On our way to the Upper Galilee we went to Capernaum, famous in the life of Jesus. He is recorded as having preached in that town and then cursing it for not listening to his words. At present there are the ruins of a splendid synagogue built undoubtedly by the Romans in order to gain the confidence of the masses. Some typical Jewish designs cover many of the rocks—the Star of David, the pomegranate, grapes, candelabra, etc. But also symbols of the rule of Rome—the triumphant march, the eagle, lion, etc., which Jews later defaced. Here there is at present a monastery.

MONDAY, MARCH 16. We passed a *kvutzah* of shepherds, 4 men and 2 women, devoted to the raising of sheep. They live in tents in the middle of nowhere, a two-hour walk from Metullah. There are hills and deep valleys in between, the whole having a very primitive and savage aspect. We talked to some [shepherds] in the evening as they came back from the fields with their flocks. Intelligent and learned fellows who give one the impression that they are living here out of disgust with "civilization," and not out of ignorance of its contents.

The best treat for the boys of a *kvutzah* is a cigarette. They don't often buy their own, and they express great joy when some are offered them. We were always well supplied with boxes of cigarettes.

<u>WEDNESDAY, MARCH 18.</u> At Sufsaf we had our lunch in the house of the sheik of the town. We entered and made ourselves at home during his absence. When he came he at once offered us some of his sour milk and *halavah*, and coffee. Of course we had to partake of his hospitality. He was angry at our eating even our bread. "In my home eat my bread," which is a sort of tissue paper made of flour and water. Sufsaf is visited by sightseers because one of its dwellers had taste enough to choose the arch of one of the old synagogue structures for his door. All of these ruins testify to the large and active Jewish community that once flourished where now there is no sign of a Jew.

From there we traveled to Meron where the grave of R. Simeon bar Yochai is located, the shrine of *chasidim* and mystics. From Meron to Peki'in. Its population is made up of Arab Christians and Moslems, a large number of Druse, and 76 Jews. It is the only Arab village that contains a Jewish community. That community is believed by some to date back to the days of the Second Commonwealth, never having gone into exile. One of their elders told us in remarkably good Hebrew that they call themselves neither Ashkenazim nor *chasidim* nor even Yehudim. They live exactly as do the Arabs, speak and dress like them, etc. They have a synagogue of their own, and now the Office of Education established a Hebrew school there, so that Hebrew is again becoming their spoken language.

<u>THURSDAY, MARCH 19.</u> At Acco we fell into conversation with a Jewish policeman in a coffee house. He showed us through the large government prison there. Then some wandering through the city, which is typically Oriental. Then by car along the shore of the Mediterranean to Haifa, where we bunked at our old place. Our trip is well nigh completed.

<u>FRIDAY, MARCH 20.</u> At 6:30 we left Haifa, passed through the Emek again, this time in a speeding car, and got an idea of what most tourists see. The road led through Nazareth and Shekhem so that I had the opportunity to see these two beautifully located cities.

At 11 A.M. we were back home in Jerusalem again. Found some mail that had accumulated. Among the letters was a cable from Young Judaea, appointing me the official representative at the opening of the University.

JERUSALEM AGAIN

<u>SATURDAY, MARCH 21.</u> In the afternoon to Prof. Margolis and with him to Dr. Magnes. At first we had a long discussion on the lifestyle of the *kvutzah*. Magnes is very enthusiastic, Margolis is extremely skeptical.

In the evening I stepped into the meeting room of the World Union of Jewish Youth to get some copies of their publication in which two of my poems on Jerusalem appeared.

SUNDAY, MARCH 22. The talk of the day is of course on the opening of the University. [What Greenberg described at the end of December was the opening of one division of the University, the Institute of Jewish Studies.] An infinite number of requests for tickets have come in. Tourists beyond number claim admission on the plea that they came on purpose to attend this affair. Among these tourists is of course a goodly number of the learned classes, the wealthy, and those who did devoted service to the cause in various countries. In general it appears that the population of the city has doubled since I left.

Along with this event, the accompanying subject for conversation is "What will the Arabs do?" Every day the papers bring reports of the manifestoes they publish, of the strike planned on the day of Balfour's arrival, of papers appearing in black frames, of prayers in the mosques, *and of threats of disorder.* The last is of course the item that concerns everybody most. That the government is taking special precautions is clearly evident. British and native gendarmerie under British command are evident in all parts of the city. Patrol at night was increased. (An Arab neighbor told Mrs. W. that there is going to be a war on Wednesday because the English vizier is coming and he is giving Palestine to the Jews! That is a sample of what is being preached to the masses.) If there will be anything doing we will be in the heart of it, because we are in the Old City and at the spot where a good deal of the riots last time took place. But one may be sure that this time also, if anything happens, it will not be in the nature of a pogrom but of a clash, for the Jewish young men in the city are not sitting around idly either. Life is rather tense and will be till after the opening exercises are over.[31]

MONDAY, MARCH 23. Additional forces patrolling the city keep coming constantly. The Arabs will probably not attempt any riot action, though here and there they might try to kill one in a dark corner.

TUESDAY, MARCH 24. Today was the last day of the term at this University. Back at home at 11:30 P.M. through deadly quiet, thickly policed streets.

WEDNESDAY, MARCH 25, DAY OF BALFOUR'S ARRIVAL. Walked through the Old City this morning and found practically all the stores of the Arabs closed. Some of the old Jewish merchants too were closed down out of fear. To all intents their general strike was really general, at least in Jerusalem; Arab cabmen, chauffeurs, and even bootblacks were not around. However, no disturbances whatsoever took place. We walked through their most thickly populated sections, spoke Hebrew, but were molested in no way whatsoever. Police were everywhere visible. In general though, the stranger would get the impression that a great holiday was being celebrated. The Jewish quarters were especially in high spirits, so that as a grand total the Arabs accomplished very little in their strike. Yet I wonder as do very many others whether this was an opportune time to raise so great a rumpus with opening exercises. It is an open secret that it is more a political than an academic occasion, a fact which is to be regretted. Two things the opening may accomplish or has accomplished: (1) An amphitheater in a beautiful spot has been erected (2) Interest in what the Jews are doing in E.Y. has been aroused the world over.

FRIDAY, MARCH 27. Spent some time in the morning with Meyer Levin, a young chap of Chicago who is here as a reporter for the *Menorah Journal* to cover the University's opening.[32]

SATURDAY, MARCH 28. Evening I had to go to the Hotel Allenby to meet E. on Scout affairs. I found in the Allenby all of Jerusalem's high society—tuxedos and evening gowns sitting around the lobby waiting for the dance. Jerusalem is full these days with high and mighty ones from the world over. You can't turn around without rubbing shoulders with some "professor" or "Herr Doktor," "Herr this" and "Herr that." The opening of the University has brought them from all the four corners, and not only Jews but hosts of Gentiles—representatives of governments, of academic institutions, societies, etc. I am not used any more to such a dizzying rushing existence.

SUNDAY, MARCH 29. Magnes asked me this morning to take over the editing of the English pamphlet describing the opening and the work of the Institute of Jewish Studies. I found the English translations so poor that I decided to recommend non-publication and reconsidering the advisability of publishing a [new] Hebrew pamphlet. Spent some time at the printer's on the Hebrew pamphlet, then to the Zionist executive offices to wait for Magnes. I was assigned to do a piece of work together with the other boys in connection with the last minute arrangements being made for academic lectures on Thursday and Friday morning. More and more I think that the whole [program of festivities] is not worthwhile. It is a blownup affair. It is speculation in the spiritual realm the same as there is speculation in the economic realm in Tel Aviv.

MONDAY, MARCH 30. Spent the whole day chasing around town trying to locate some of the professors scheduled to deliver talks. Succeeded in seeing the Grand Rabbin [Israel] Levi of France and others at a meeting of visiting professors at which plans for some sort of an international association of the Jewish learned were to be formulated.

In the evening to the gala performance of [the play] "Belshazzar" by the Art Company that only recently returned from Berlin. It was the first performance in Jerusalem. The High Commissioner with Lord Balfour as his guest were present. Of course the front of the theater was just mobbed but mounted police and a host of gendarmes plus a special guard of honor of local Maccabees, boys and girls dressed in white, preserved perfect order. Balfour, Weizmann, and Samuel all appeared at intervals of a few minutes, the crowd giving each an ovation. Spirits were very high within the theater. The boxes were occupied by all the highest in British and Jewish officialdom. The performance itself surpassed all expectations. Rarely is anything seen even on Broadway that attained such artistic perfection.

TUESDAY, MARCH 31. In every Jewish settlement the desire to go to Jerusalem is fever high; group after group of teachers, pupils, and laborers are coming. Jerusalem is a grand boiling pot. Met Professor Klausner who introduced us to [the famous poet] Saul Tschernichowsky who came to Jerusalem as did everyone else.

WEDNESDAY, APRIL 1, THE OPENING OF THE UNIVERSITY. The great day came and passed. Since Solomon dedicated the Temple Jerusalem was probably not in such a holiday mood. Never in all its existence did it witness such a cosmopolitan and distinguished gathering. Never did Jewry receive such recognition from the people of the world.

At 3:00 the procession started. From one side came the High Commissioner and Lady Samuel, preceded by Scouts of Honor and followed by their son and daughter-in-law. From the other side came Lord Balfour with Dr. Weizmann, followed by all of Zionist officialdom and by the government and University representatives. Most of them in their official gowns made a rather impressive sight. A 200-voice choir then sang "From Zion will go forth the Law," and Weizmann introduced Rabbi Kook to deliver the opening prayer. The Rabbi did not know what an opening prayer means. He spoke on and on and in a most undignified way. After him Weizmann delivered a 12-minute talk in Hebrew, then in English—not a great speech but well delivered. He introduced the High Commissioner, who was received with a grand ovation. One could feel he spoke not merely as the governor representing the British Isles but as a Jew. Weizmann then introduced Balfour. As was expected he was greeted most cordially by the audience. He spoke extemporaneously, and I could not but admire the extraordinary energy of that old man who spoke for a half-hour.

When he got through the audience was rather restless; they were not in the mood for listening further. But Bialik was on the program. He rose to speak and made the mistake of thinking that he could overcome the restlessness that had seized the audience. He insisted upon going through all he had prepared in spite of attempts to cut him short. The program was finally over after a closing prayer. The choir sang, the band played "Hallelujah," while the platform paraded back to the University building. The crowd waited until after "Hatik-vah" was played and then poured out. It was a grand spectacle.

THURSDAY, APRIL 2. Today I read the newspaper reports of the whole cere-mony. In the reading the events of yesterday took on greater significance for me than they had when I was standing on Mount Scopus and witnessing the whole thing. The effect on the outside world is of the greatest. Weizmann, who was at first blamed as the cause of the whole scene, is now praised as the magi-cian, the far-sighted one, etc.

FRIDAY, APRIL 3. Papers keep on bringing reports of the echoes of the events throughout the Diaspora. To those of us right on the spot, the significance of the event grows from day to day. April 1, 1925 is already a sort of legendary day, and I can imagine with what pride we shall be able to say that we were for-tunate enough to be spectators on Mount Scopus.

Magnes asked me this morning to make a list of all the congratulatory documents sent from all corners of the globe. Some beautifully inscribed parch-ments came from Jewish communities and academic bodies of all kinds and all countries. Some 240+ messages in all.

SATURDAY, APRIL 4. At 5:00 to E. for tea and for a report on the Scout sessions recently held. To Miss L.'s school to meet the group of students that came from England to witness the opening ceremonies. Actually meeting Jewish students from other countries cannot but lead to greater consolidation of world Jewry. E.Y. will be the meeting ground for world Jewry, the bond that will link the scattered bodies. The bond that is most effective is that of language. We must carry on propaganda to have all conscious national Jews learn Hebrew.

SUNDAY, APRIL 5. Called to help the committee to arrange the affair for tonight when the students of the University will receive officially the some 130 stu-dents that came from England and the Continent.

<u>Tuesday, April 7.</u> In lorries to Sebastiah to see the ruins of Samaria of the days of [Kings] Omri, Ahab, and Herod. The work was done by the Harvard School with money from [the American banker] Jacob Schiff.[33] We intended to climb Mount Gerizim to witness the Passover ceremonies of the Samaritans. This we did not do because we came into town just about ten minutes after some eight people were hurt by stones hurled from the mountain sides by Arabs.

<u>Wednesday, April 8 – Passover Eve.</u> Seder at the home of E. Then for a walk down Jaffa Road, where the parading crowds and the singing gave ample evidence of the holiday spirit.

<u>Friday, April 10.</u> L. came back happy about the results of the interview he arranged between Rabbi [Israel] Levinthal [of New York] and His Excellency. Levinthal came to investigate the advisability of presenting Jeshurun [the "modern" congregation] with a building on the lines of an American Jewish center. He got the opinions of many—which were all favorable—and that of H.E. was almost enthusiastic.[34]

<u>Wednesday, April 15.</u> My last day in Jerusalem. It was a full day, occupied with parting with acquaintances I met everywhere.

<u>Thursday, April 16.</u> Left Jerusalem for Tel Aviv. For the evening K. arranged a meeting with Bialik at Bialik's home. We were very cordially received. His exterior, whose prosaic aspect strikes everyone at first, is not nearly as prosaic when he begins to talk. His whole body comes into action and his face shines with a new light. In answer to K.'s question on the relationship between E.Y. and the Diaspora, he said: "Three times already the Jews spread over the world with a new idea. To Egypt they came with Abraham's God-idea. To Babylon with the Prophets, to Rome with Christianity. The new idea may be the sense of responsibility for the whole of mankind." This was a most fitting close for my stay in E.Y.

III. Epilogue

Greenberg set sail from Haifa on April 17, 1925, and after a few days in Italy and England arrived home on May 13. He returned to Eretz Yisrael on countless occasions, but it was the trip of 1924 that was most strongly embedded in his memory. He settled in

Jerusalem in 1992, and there he died a year later.

Although Greenberg never relinquished his dream of living in E.Y., he fashioned a distinguished career in the United States.[35] Ordained in 1925, he was appointed very shortly thereafter as rabbi at Har Zion, a young congregation in Philadelphia. In a tenure of over forty years, he built the synagogue into the most prestigious Conservative congregation of the city. A skilled and inspiring preacher, he reached out to all age groups with appropriate activities, ranging from kindergarten and nursery school to adult study groups. He quickly gained prominence as an articulate spiritual leader, and he won the lasting respect and affection of his congregants. (He relinquished the pulpit in 1945, but he was called back annually to officiate at the High Holiday services.) In his manifold activities that made Har Zion an example of a synagogue-center, he emphasized ideals that he had voiced during his year in Jerusalem—a religious cultural Zionism and a rich Jewish education. At the same time he actively participated in communal affairs, both general and Jewish. He served as president of the Rabbinical Assembly from 1937 to 1939.

In 1932 Greenberg was appointed lecturer in education at JTS, and thirteen years later he accepted a full-time position on the administrative staff of the chancellor, Dr. Louis Finkelstein. He continued to teach both education and homiletics, but his principal duties were as an administrator. Always a warm and outgoing person, he enjoyed the friendship of both the faculty and the students. He and his wife Betty were gracious hosts, and students found in them and in their home models for their future rabbinic careers. Greenberg cut a distinctive figure in the Columbia – Union Theological Seminary – JTS neighborhood as the rabbi with the excellent posture who strode rapidly to work from his apartment on Riverside Drive and 114th Street. Within the Seminary family he also gained acclaim as the unsurpassed *ḥazzan* of the school's synagogue whose chanting of the prayers was truly inspirational.

Greenberg became involved in virtually all activities of the Seminary that bore on the school and the Conservative movement at large: the cantorial school, intergroup and interfaith programs, Jewish Museum, Camp Ramah, as well as the Rabbinical Assembly and United Synagogue. Two major undertakings in which his role was central were the creation of a branch of the Seminary in Los Angeles (University of Judaism) and the establishment of a Seminary presence in Israel (see below).[36] His work for the various projects included fund-raising, development of lay support groups, and the forging of close ties between the Seminary and individual rabbis and their synagogues. He contributed much thereby to the image of the Seminary as a national Jewish presence both in Jewish and non-Jewish circles.

Of all the Seminary's postwar projects that engaged Greenberg, the one most closely related to his stay in Jerusalem in 1924 was that of Seminary activity in Israel. Even as a student he had looked for a Conservative presence in the *yishuv.* A long-time active member in Zionist organizations since his days in Young Judaea, he became very much involved shortly after the establishment of Israel in Finkelstein's plans to forge a nexus between the Seminary and the new state. Neither he nor the chancellor, both of whom believed in a transcendent spiritual connection between E.Y. and the Diaspora, sought to alter the American orientation of the Seminary or to become involved with Israel's political agenda. Rather, as the historian Eli Lederhendler has explained, they thought of ways by which the Seminary tied to Israel could engage in furthering the development of Judaism. According to both Finkelstein and Greenberg, a Seminary center in Jerusalem would establish the school "as a place of learning in greater proximity to the world of learning in Israel."[37] Both the American and the Israeli side, and indeed the entire world, would be enriched thereby. Ambitious plans including a student center and an exchange of professors were drawn up, and Greenberg as a major negotiator shuttled back and forth between New York and Jerusalem. But progress was delayed during the administrations of Finkelstein and his successor largely because of the Seminary's budgetary concerns and the opposition of the Orthodox in Israel to Conservatism.

Most remarkable but often ignored was Greenberg's relationship with Finkelstein. The two men shared an overriding commitment to the Seminary, and Greenberg, unlike other members of the faculty or administration, was the chancellor's personal consultant, advance man, and general troubleshooter rolled into one. When Finkelstein set out to enter and conquer a yet unexplored field for the Seminary, it was Greenberg who was usually delegated to test the waters—first, to scout out the possibilities of developing a new program, and second, to nurture its first steps along the desired lines. Most important was the deep friendship and mutual loyalty that bound the two men together. Greenberg sat in the first row of the Seminary's synagogue next to Finkelstein and the renowned talmudic scholar Professor Saul Lieberman; he often walked home from services with the chancellor, and he was the only one I ever heard address Dr. Finkelstein as "Louie." During those years, some casual observers expressed wonder at why Greenberg had exchanged a post in Philadelphia in which he had reached the pinnacle of success for that of a subordinate to Dr. Finkelstein. But doubtless he believed that the Seminary under Finkelstein was closer to achieving his, Greenberg's, long-held goals for American Jewry—a vibrant Conservative faith, an attachment to E.Y., and a knowledge of the riches of the Jewish cultural tradition. For Greenberg the idealist and man of faith, that was recompense enough.

While at the Seminary Greenberg also wrote books and essays on education, faith and ethics, and Jewish thought and tradition.[38] His writings, like his job, showed him to be a man who lived by the principles he preached.

Notes

The number of articles and books on the Mandate period in Palestine continues to grow rapidly. An overview of the political setting is provided by Bernard Wasserstein, *The British in Palestine: The Mandatory Government and the Arab–Jewish Conflict, 1917–1929*, 2nd ed. (Cambridge, Mass.: Blackwell, 1991). Economic, social, and cultural conditions are discussed in all sorts of works, from the demographic and statistical to the anecdotal. Old but still valuable for background material are the summaries in ESCO Foundation, *Palestine: A Study of Jewish, Arab, and British Policies*, 2 vols. (New Haven: Yale University Press, 1947) and Howard M. Sachar, *A History of Israel* (New York: Knopf; Philadelphia: Jewish Publication Society, 1976). More relevant to Greenberg's experiences are the biographies and autobiographies of the "Anglo" circle in which he mixed. For example, see those of Judah Magnes, Norman Bentwich, Louis Lipsky, Frederick Kisch, and Max Margolis.

References in the notes are given only for material that cannot be found in encyclopedias and other standard works.

1. In 1930, before he appointed a representative to investigate Arab–Jewish friction in Palestine, Prime Minister Ramsay MacDonald reportedly said to leaders of the Jewish Agency that "No one who had not Palestine in his bones could grasp the whole breadth of the problem" (Naomi W. Cohen, *The Americanization of Zionism, 1897–1948* [Hanover, N.H.: University Press of New England, 2003], 119).
2. Arthur A. Goren, *The Politics and Public Culture of American Jews* (Bloomington: Indiana University Press, 1999), 165–76.
3. Sir Herbert Samuel was the first British High Commissioner for Palestine (1920–25). During the war, his interest in Zionism had developed into plans for the establishment of a Jewish state, and he also participated in negotiations leading to the Balfour Declaration. His tenure as High Commissioner was concerned primarily with replacing the military government of the country with a civil administration. Although criticized for leaning

to the side of Arab nationalism, his policies contributed to social and economic improvements in the *yishuv*.

4. American-born Judah Magnes, who had been ordained at Reform's Hebrew Union College, had been a popular rabbi and communal worker in New York. During the war his popularity waned because of his pacifism and his opposition to political Zionism. When he came on *'aliyah* in 1922, he became active in the establishment of the Hebrew University in Jerusalem and was named its first chancellor in 1925. Although Greenberg was twenty-four years his junior, he and Magnes became close friends.

5. An Orthodox Jewish scholar and expounder of religious nationalism, Rabbi Abraham Isaac Kook was appointed in 1921 to the influential post of Ashkenazi chief rabbi of Palestine. He ran a famous yeshiva in Jerusalem.

6. Veterans of the Jewish Legion who had fought as volunteers with the British during the war.

7. Dr. Chaim Weizmann was president of the World Zionist Organization 1920–31 and 1935–40 and leader of the Jewish Agency after 1929. He emphasized "practical" Zionist activity in postwar Palestine. Long an Anglophile, he had lent his expertise in chemistry to the British war effort. Helped by important contacts in England, he emerged as the leading Zionist diplomat at the outbreak of the war, and he contributed to the Allied endorsement of the Balfour Declaration and the award of the Mandate to England. As the man who represented Zionism to British and other world statesmen, he set up Zionist headquarters in London. In 1948 he became the first president of Israel.

8. It is possible that Greenberg was influenced by the views of American Zionist leader Louis Brandeis. The latter envisioned the *yishuv* as a laboratory-like settlement which would experiment with progressive economic and social forms of living. See Allon Gal, *Brandeis of Boston* (Cambridge: Harvard University Press, 1980), Melvin S. Urofsky, *A Mind of One Piece: Brandeis and American Reform* (New York: Scribner's, 1971); and Evyatar Friesel, התנועה הציונית בארצות־הברית בשנים 1897-1914 (The Zionist movement in the United States, 1897–1914) (Tel Aviv: Ha-Kibbutz Ha-Meuchad, 1970).

9. Dr. Joseph Klausner, a prolific writer and scholar, later taught modern Hebrew literature and the history of the Second Commonwealth at the Hebrew University.

10. Mrs. Ben-Yehuda was the widow of Eliezer Ben-Yehuda, pioneer in the revival of Hebrew as a living language.

11. Klausner doubtless meant the American banker Felix Warburg, a friend of Weizmann and major benefactor of the University during the Mandate period.

12. Louis Lipsky, an American journalist who, under the influence of Theodor Herzl, was a prominent member of the American Zionist movement from its very inception. In 1925, following the withdrawal of the Brandeis group from the ZOA, he was elected president. Greenberg had met him previously in the United States.

13. In 1923 Weizmann appointed Frederick H. Kisch, a former officer in the British army, to an important post on the Zionist Executive Committee in Jerusalem. During 1929–31 Kisch also served in the enlarged Jewish Agency.

14. Itzhak Ben Zvi was a longtime leader of the Labor party who became the second president of Israel in 1952.

15. A biomedical research institute that was established in Paris with branches in other countries.

16. The journalist Gershon Agronsky, later Agron, was active in the American Zionist movement from his youth. Only a few years Greenberg's senior, he was the editor of the Jewish Telegraphic Agency and director of the press office of the Zionist Executive in Jerusalem. In 1932 he became editor-in-chief of the *Palestine Post*, which in 1950 was renamed the *Jerusalem Post*. From 1955 to 1959 he served as mayor of Jerusalem.

17. Emanuel Gamoran, the same age as Greeberg, was a major innovative force in the development of Jewish education in America. He taught at the Friedlaender classes of the JTS, and in 1923 he became director of Reform's Commission of Jewish Education.

18. Pinchas Rutenberg was an electrical engineer who initiated plans for the irrigation and electrification of the Jordan valley and for the entire country. He helped establish the port of Tel Aviv, and under a concession from the British he founded the Palestine Electric Corporation in 1921. For a short while he served as chairman of the Vaad Le'umi (National Council) and on the executive of the Jewish Agency.

19. Supported by Americans, the yeshiva at Hebron was the scene of American casualties during the Arab riots of 1929.

20. The auto king Henry Ford was at that time staging a vicious antisemitic campaign through his newspaper, the *Dearborn Independent*.

21. When the Arabs rioted against the Jews in Jerusalem in 1920, Storrs forbade any action by Jewish self-defense units. British troops were also forbidden to enter the Jewish quarter (Wasserstein, *British in Palestine*, 64–65).

22. An ardent Zionist who was educated in Russia, Chaim Nachman Bialik settled in Palestine in 1924. Recognized by then for his writing that had begun earlier, he became the preeminent figure of modern Hebrew literature.

23. Ben-Zion Dinaburg (later Dinur) was a historian and instructor at a teachers training school. A prolific writer, he went on to teach history at the Hebrew University.

24. Dr. David Yellin, of an old Jerusalemite family, was a prominent educator and public figure in the *yishuv.*

25. Professor Mordecai Kaplan, professor of homiletics at the JTS, was then working out the principles of a new religious denomination, Reconstructionism. See Mel Scult, *Judaism Faces the Twentieth Century: A Biography of Mordecai M. Kaplan* (Detroit: Wayne State University Press, 1993).

26. Aaron Aaronsohn won worldwide fame as an agronomist who developed a new species of wheat. From a prominent family of the first 'aliyah, he aroused bitter resentment by his public activities. Not only did he differ politically from the then-established leaders of the second 'aliyah, but his active role in organizing the pro-British spy ring Nili led his opponents to charge that he thereby left the community vulnerable to Turkish reprisals.

27. The French banker Baron Edmond de Rothschild, philanthropist and major benefactor of agricultural settlement in Palestine, also underwrote industrial projects and cultural institutions in the *yishuv.* His interests in Palestine, which began in the 1880s, were administered first by the Jewish Colonization Association (ICA). Their duties were taken over after the war by the Palestine Jewish Colonization Association (PICA). Opposed at first to Herzl's political Zionism, the Baron believed that quiet, practical work had to precede a Jewish state.

28. Bentwich returned to Palestine in 1931 and later became professor of international relations at the Hebrew University.

29. Lilian Friedlaender was the widow of Professor Israel Friedlaender of the JTS, who was killed in the Ukraine in 1920 while on a postwar relief mission.

30. Written in Akkadian, the Tel-el-Amarna tablets of the second millennium BCE were found in Egypt, 1890–1936. Among other things, they shed light on the pre-biblical civilization of Palestine, The Beth Shean steles are slightly later.

31. The opening of the University was considered the high point of the *yishuv*'s development in the 1920s. Although the Jewish settlers were never totally free of Arab disturbances, the major riots of the decade occurred in

1921 and 1929. The imminent departure of Sir Herbert Samuel in 1925 may also have raised the apprehensiveness of both Arabs and Jews.

32. Levin became famous in later years as a foremost American Jewish novelist. His trip to Palestine in 1925 awakened in him a strong attachment to Jewishness and Palestine.

33. Schiff had endowed a program in Semitics at Harvard as well as a Semitics museum in the 1890s.

34. Judah Magnes and some English-speaking associates had formulated plans in 1923 for an American-style synagogue in Jerusalem. Their particular scheme failed, but the idea was picked up by the United Synagogue, the organization of Conservative synagogues in America, which for some ten years ran a building fund for the modern congregation in Jerusalem, Jeshurun. Rabbi Levinthal came to Palestine to investigate the prospects of the project, and Greenberg's friend L. (Louis Lober), president of Jeshurun, was his escort (Cohen, *Americanization of Zionism*, chapter 4).

35. For this section on Greenberg's professional career I have drawn on *Tradition Renewed* ed. Jack Wertheimer, 2 vols. (New York: JTS Press, 1997), passim; Pamela S. Nadell, *Conservative Judaism in America: A Biographical Dictionary and Sourcebook* (New York: Greenwood, 1988); *Rabbinical Assembly Memorial Book, 5754* (New York: Rabbinical Assembly, 1994); and my own recollections.

36. Deborah Dash Moore, "Another Glowing Chapter: The University of Judaism," in Wertheimer, *Tradition Renewed*, 1:793–819, and Eli Lederhendler, "The Ongoing Dialogue: The Seminary and the Challenge of Israel," ibid., 2:177–270.

37. This entire paragraph is based on Lederhendler, "Ongoing Dialogue"; the quotation comes from p. 211.

38. See for example Greenberg's collection of essays, *Foundations of a Faith* (New York: Burning Bush Press, 1967).

THE SCHECHTERS' SEMINARY

SHULY RUBIN SCHWARTZ

For virtually the entire twentieth century, the Jewish Theological Seminary has enjoyed a reputation as the premier center for *Wissenschaft* Jewish scholarship in America and the fountainhead of the Conservative movement. Both its academic accomplishments and its role in spearheading Conservative Judaism have been well chronicled and acknowledged.[1] Less well known, however, is JTS's devotion to strengthening the Jewish heart and spirit. Yet, ultimately, the preeminence of JTS derived not from its dedication to scholarship and the Conservative movement alone but rather from its devotion to those goals as well as to spiritual growth. These commitments stem directly from the broad vision of Solomon Schechter—president of the newly reorganized Jewish Theological Seminary from 1902 until his death in 1915—and his wife Mathilde. They—both singly and together—intuitively understood that the success of American Judaism would hinge on maintaining the delicate balance between mind and soul. Each worked tirelessly to ensure that JTS would long be a place that both modeled and fostered the synthesis of heart and intellect.

By assuming the presidency of JTS, Solomon Schechter secured its reputation as a center for serious Judaic scholarship because of his renown as a brilliant and devoted scholar and academic. But Schechter also actively worked to enhance JTS's place as the premier institution of higher Jewish *Wissenschaft* scholarship in several ways. He raised the level of rabbinic education by transforming the rabbinical school into a graduate-level school. More important, he recruited promising young scholars, including Louis Ginzberg, Alexander Marx, Israel Friedlaender, and Israel Davidson. These men (except for Friedlander, who died tragically in

1920) enhanced JTS's reputation for decades through their scholarship and teaching. Their contributions to the fields of rabbinics, Hebrew literature, and Jewish history, coupled with the outstanding library that Marx built, furthered secured JTS's position as a center for Jewish scholarship in the United States. Schechter also established Conservative Judaism on a firm footing both through his writings and by founding the lay organization, the United Synagogue of America, in 1913.[2]

But in addition to his scholarly and organizational achievements, Solomon Schechter cared deeply about the Jewish spirit, and he worked to integrate it into the fabric of JTS life as well. His mission was not only to create a foothold for Jewish scholarship in America but also to combat the religious crisis of the age. In his view, to successfully spread what he called "positive Judaism," JTS rabbis needed both immersion in serious Jewish study and experience in a "strictly Jewish home." Because of this, Schechter enforced ritual requirements for admission to rabbinical school that including regular prayer and kashrut and Shabbat observance. He also concerned himself with students' emotional lives and physical well-being. Herman Rubenovitz, a 1908 JTS ordainee, recalled that Schechter "found time to interest himself in the personal problems and needs of each Seminary student."[3]

Schechter shared the commitment to critical scholarship that his Reform counterpart Kaufmann Kohler and his institution, Hebrew Union College, embodied. But Schechter wanted more: he wanted an institution where both Jewish scholarship *and* the Jewish spirit would flourish, thereby modeling a Conservative Judaism devoted to the Jewish mind and soul. Kaufman Kohler himself acknowledged his colleague's success in this area, noting that while Solomon Schechter brought about a revival of Jewish learning in this country, "the chief lesson he preached ... is the lesson so much needed, of great spirituality."[4]

Given Schechter's enormous influence on JTS and the Conservative movement, it is not surprising that, as Mel Scult reminds us, in the first half of the century JTS was often called "Schechter's Seminary" by Orthodox Jewish leaders. In so doing, they were acknowledging intuitively the "centrality of Solomon Schechter to its functioning."[5] Yet, as vital as Solomon Schechter's actions were to the success and growth of the Seminary, JTS was equally transformed by Mathilde Schechter's complementary accomplishments. Mathilde was herself highly educated and devoted to Jewish learning. She shared her husband's vision of advancing Jewish scholarship and revitalizing Judaism in America. But she, too, believed that JTS would succeed only if it answered both the intellectual and spiritual needs of American Jews. And she especially devoted her attention to impressing the importance of the Jewish spirit upon others within the JTS community. Mathilde Schechter's accomplishments are often eclipsed by those of her husband, but it was the successful partnership of both Schechters—working both separately and together to cultivate the mind and the body—that left a lasting imprint on students, on the future of Jewish learning in America, and on Conservative Judaism.

Even at the start of her married life, Mathilde, ten years his junior,[6] dedicated herself to balancing Solomon's intellectual pursuits with other elements—physical, emotional, and spiritual. Mathilde Roth had recognized that by marrying Solomon Schechter, she would lead a life in which Jewish intellectual life would be the core, and she was eager for that life. But, within her home, Mathilde embraced many other aspects of Judaism, which she shared with others by hosting guests in their London home and attempting to set a joyous, friendly tone. The Schechters would regularly open their home to scholars, students, and friends. In Mathilde's recollection, "scholars and literary men came and went as they pleased, and all day long the hall door was never locked."[7]

When the Schechters moved to Cambridge, England, university students interested in Jewish studies would visit the Schechter home for classes and Shabbat afternoon tea. Charles Hoffman, a 1904 JTS ordainee, recalled that "Mrs. Schechter shone as the gracious hostess, cheering and heartening both the young men and sometimes also the young women who repaired there from their several colleges. It became, as it were, a second home for them, where Jewish influences, from which they were largely separated, could be retained."[8] While Solomon would nourish their minds, teaching and studying with his guests, Mathilde would nurture their spirit.

This notable Schechter hospitality continued when the Schechters moved to the United States for Solomon to assume the presidency of JTS. Reprising their successful open house tradition, the Schechters established a setting where students felt both socially and spiritually at ease. As Herman Rubenovitz recalled, on Sabbath and holidays there were always Seminary students and other guests, including distinguished visitors, impoverished scholars, and stranded rabbis. He described the visitors sitting at Solomon's table, but he noted that it was Mathilde who "presided," and she did so with "much grace and such fine tact." As Mathilde later described it, Solomon "brought them and I kept them." Jacob Kohn, a 1907 ordainee, recalled that the Schechter home "was a kind of altar, on which were offered to the spirit of friendship and hospitality, not chiefly material things, but the larger blessings that flow from a noble woman's heart and mind." Students looked up to Mathilde "as if she were a sort of foster-mother to them," sharing their sorrows and joys, telling her their activities and problems, and bringing their brides to meet her.[9]

Mathilde's influence on the Seminary community was apparent in other venues as well. Involved in preparing banquets, student receptions, and other social activities for the JTS community, Mathilde became best known for designing the Seminary's sukkah. She enlisted students to help build it, women to decorate it "with every variety of vegetables and flowers," and children to aid in any and all tasks. The local Seminary community celebrated Sukkot together, and students fondly remembered that the sukkah "could hardly be surpassed in beauty." Mathilde understood how important her involvement in the JTS community was to her husband's success as a religious leader. As one of the students later recalled, Mathilde intuitively knew that "without the women's touch, without her help in the synagogue and the home, Judaism would be sadly deficient and inadequate."[10]

A lover of music, Mathilde also saw congregational singing as a vehicle for increasing worshipers' interest in religious services. To this end, she organized the Society for Ancient Hebrew Melodies and coedited with her friend, the attorney and composer Lewis Isaacs, *Kol Rinah: Hebrew Hymnal for School and Home*. At JTS, Mathilde helped inaugurate services which one colleague recalled as "so inspiring that they served as an example for many congregations throughout the country." As Mathilde later explained, congregational singing was the key to a spiritually uplifting prayer experience because " 'it is not enough that a Chazan or a choir chant the prayers. No one can write our love letters, neither can anyone do our praying or sing our hymns for us.' "[11]

After her husband's death, Mathilde continued her efforts to foster community spirit at JTS. She maintained their open house tradition, and as one student recalled, "There was a catholicity in her entertainment that was dictated by a true benevolence and a rare insight into character."[12] But Mathilde understood that no matter how hospitable she herself was, she would be unable single-handedly to ensure the community-like atmosphere which she believed was necessary for the Seminary and, ultimately, for Conservative Judaism to succeed. It became her mission to develop other avenues to strengthen the sense of community.

First, she galvanized the focused energy and dedication of Conservative Jewish women by launching National Women's League in 1918. It would serve as the women's auxiliary branch of the United Synagogue of America, the lay organization founded by Solomon. Mathilde hoped her organization would

motivate Conservative Jewish women to revive Jewish observance and strengthen the Jewish spirit.[13]

Second, in terms of the Seminary community itself, Mathilde
was convinced that students needed to live in the neighborhood
in order for JTS to promote Jewish living adequately. Mathilde's
original idea was for a "quasi-dormitory and restaurant for students of the Seminary and for other students in the neighborhood." As one of the students recalled, it was "to be an extension
of her own home, permeated by an atmosphere of hospitality,
kindliness, holiness." Mathilde first approached the JTS Board of
Trustees with the idea. Though the board declined to support it,
Cyrus Adler, Solomon Schechter's successor, informed her that
board members individually recognize "its needs and sympathize
with the purposes of it." Trustees Louis Marshall, Sol Strook, and
Jacob Schiff each offered to contribute $250 a year of their own
funds. They agreed to support the project for two years if other
funds were found to carry it out.[14]

Mathilde, secure in her belief that this Student's House would
be essential to the success of the JTS community, convinced the
Women's League to take it on as one of its first projects. Mathilde
took an interest in every aspect of the venture, from the color of
the curtains to the games that were purchased to the food on the
menu. The House had lounges with Victrolas and pianos, including a "breezy reading room and library" and an "airy" dining
room designed to counter homesickness and "feelings of estrange-
ment." Located on 117th Street and Morningside Drive, the
house opened to students in January 1919. That month, the
Women's League held its Executive Council meeting at the
house, and it continued to meet there regularly. By 1920,
Mathilde reported that "scarcely a day passes without clubs meeting and dining there, afternoon and evening." As one of the students recalled, the Student's House became "the home and
cultural center for the student body of the seminary and of the
university." This atmosphere was achieved through Friday night

dinners, student activities, and occasional visits by professors. As another student remarked, "All these occurrences, no less than the more formal and purely intellectual occasions, helped greatly to weld more closely a student body. ... It added to our loyalty to the Seminary." Just as Mathilde had predicted, the Student House enabled the Jewish spirit to flourish alongside the intellect.[15]

Yet, as successful as the Student House was, it was open to all Jewish students in the area. To further strengthen JTS specifically, Mathilde also envisioned establishing a designated residence hall for JTS rabbinical students. She is thought to have been instrumental in convincing Louis Brush to leave a bequest to JTS for just such a facility. According to Hanna Marx, Schechter pleaded with Brush to provide funds for a residence hall after she learned that a gifted Seminary student had undergone minor surgery because he had been overworked and undernourished. When Brush died in 1917, he left JTS $1.4 million for a dormitory, reportedly the single largest gift to a Jewish institution at the time.[16]

Through the Women's League, Mathilde also initiated projects designed to intensify Jewish living beyond JTS. Mathilde understood that the religious spirit she was creating at JTS could not be replicated in the larger Jewish community without certain essential tools. She saw it as the mission of the Women's League to develop guidebooks, anthologies, and stories for women to use in promoting Jewish observance in the home. She oversaw the preparation of Sabbath kiddush cards; a collection of inspirational legends based on Louis Ginzberg's *Legends of the Jews* entitled *Friday Night Stories*; and several pamphlets on Jewish life, including *Shabuoth* by Charles I. Hoffman and Elias L. Solomon and *Passover* by Mordecai M. Kaplan.[17]

The Women's League also looked to the future, hoping to educate Jewish girls so that they would be better prepared than their mothers to establish Jewish homes. To that end, the organization approved an ambitious plan for a summer camp for girls as a way to model Jewish living. The Women's League endorsed an existing camp, the Camp for Girls at Sylvan Lake, in return for assurances that the camp would be conducted in accordance with Jewish law and that the counselors would be recommended by the League. Pleased with the partnership for the first year, the Women's League withdrew its support after a disappointing season in 1921. Though it would be almost thirty years before the Conservative movement would successfully establish its own educational summer camp, Ramah, the Women's League had recognized early on that the summer months could be valuable in educating youth for Jewish living.[18]

Even after her death in 1924, Mathilde was not forgotten within the Seminary and the Conservative movement. For one thing, through her legendary open houses and the JTS sukkah, she had directly inspired rabbinical students' wives to follow her example in their own communities. One such woman was Mignon Rubenovitz. Though she had earned a B.S. in psychology in 1911 from Columbia University's Teachers College, Mignon turned her focus after her 1915 marriage to Herman Rubenovitz "to serve Zionism, the synagogue and Hebraic culture." When her husband assumed the pulpit of Temple Mishkan Tefila in Boston, Massachusetts, Mignon consciously emulated Mathilde Schechter, whom she described as the perfect helpmate. Mignon hosted guests for Sabbath dinner and opened her home for congregational and Hadassah meetings and study groups. She also agitated for increased communal observance of Jewish holidays, and she, too, devoted her efforts to building a memorable community sukkah to heighten awareness of the festival. She strung cranberries, string beans, peppers, and eggplants to decorate a synagogue sukkah. "At 6:30 a.m. with our parishioners still in bed, the Rabbi and the Rebbitzen could have been seen walking down Elm Hill Avenue and Warren Street, a goodly mile, each carrying a heavily loaded suitcase" filled with necessary items, such as wine, cookies, and silver serving bowls. Mignon noted with satisfaction that as a result of these efforts, the knowledge and joy of the festival grew.[19]

Though Cyrus Adler succeeded Solomon Schechter, it was Louis and Adele Ginzberg who took on the role that the Schechters had played in the Seminary community itself. The Ginzbergs became known as "Mr. and Mrs. Seminary." As the foremost scholar on the faculty, Louis Ginzberg ensured the institution's continued scholarly renown. Adele enhanced its spirit. She hosted open houses on Sabbath and holidays and invited each member of the Seminary's senior rabbinical school class for Sabbath lunch. She also inherited the Seminary sukkah project from Mathilde and oversaw it for decades. Adele raised funds, shopped, and supervised its decoration with fresh fruits, vegetables, and greenery. Under her direction, the sukkah developed a reputation throughout New York City for its beauty. Louis Finkelstein, who took over from Adler as president of the Seminary in 1940, annually expressed his gratitude to Adele for her leadership role in decorating it so magnificently, noting that seeing it so adorned was "among the high points of my life during the whole year." Adele acknowledged the role that Mathilde had played in ensuring her own success, recalling that when she arrived in 1909 as a newlywed, Mathilde behaved "like a mother to me ... and through her shining example, I learned a great deal."[20]

When Adele, or "Mama G." as she was affectionately known, was widowed in 1953, she, like her mentor, Mathilde, continued to oversee the sukkah project and open her home to the Seminary community. She also invited rabbinical students for Sabbath meals until shortly before her death in 1980.[21]

Successful as these efforts to promote community spirit at JTS were, they failed to reach female students in a sustained way. As the leadership of the Women's League increasingly recognized, the institution could not meet the spiritual needs of its female students because it did not provide housing for them. The Teachers Institute, founded by Solomon Schechter in 1909 to prepare future Jewish educators, remained for decades the only school open to women. It quickly developed a reputation as the premier institution for advanced Jewish education for women, but, because there was no housing for female students, women were effectively denied the opportunity to benefit directly from the community spirit cultivated in the Student's House, professors' homes, and Shabbat services.[22]

To resolve this problem, the Women's League announced that, beginning in 1956, it would refocus its fund-raising efforts. Rather than supporting JTS as a whole, as it had done for decades through its annual Torah Fund campaign, the Women's League would now earmark its fund for a new residence hall for female Teachers Institute students. In responding to this decision, Chancellor Finkelstein acknowledged the direct connection between such efforts and the work of Mathilde Schechter earlier in the century. He also recognized its significance as a crucial way for JTS to manifest its concern for the well-being of female students:

> I cannot but be deeply moved by the generosity of the National Women's League. ... A residence hall so that all of them, coming from different parts of the United States, may be housed near the Seminary, and be taken care of by us, follows the highest traditions of the National Women's League. I very well remember the first Student House of the Seminary established by Mathilde Schechter about 40 years ago. How much it meant to all of us students to have that Student House.[23]

Within a few months, the Women's League began to refer to this fundraising campaign as the Mathilde Schechter Dormitory for Women Project, and proponents routinely noted the appropriateness of this designation. As one of its chairmen explained, "it is only fitting that a Dormitory for Women, as an adjunct of the Jewish Theological Seminary of America, be named for the illustrious woman who conceived the idea, our own Mathilde

Schechter." The chairwoman further elaborated the significance of such a residence hall in providing women with a "dignified home-away-from-home." Adele Ginzberg noted that such a project extended Mathilde's "zest for the well-being of the Seminary students," for it was the "deep root" of "the seed that she had planted fifty years ago."[24]

After decades of fundraising, the Mathilde Schechter Residence Hall finally opened in 1976. However, given the needs of JTS and the increasing popularity of coeducational residence halls on university campuses in the 1970s, the Mathilde Schechter Residence Hall opened as a coeducational undergraduate residence hall. At its dedication, Chancellor Gerson D. Cohen heralded its founding as "an auspicious beginning to the new era in Seminary history."[25]

When Cohen assumed the chancellorship in 1972, he understood that he, too, needed to find appropriate venues to ensure the Seminary's excellence, both academically and spiritually in his era. He saw the Mathilde Schechter Residence Hall as part of this larger effort, but this alone would be insufficient to meet the needs of Seminary students. Cohen recognized the necessity of creating a social structure that would operate alongside the academic core of the institution. To this end, Cohen created the Office of Student Life and for the "first time ... clearly designate[d] student personnel work as a separate entity." The original proposal for such an office was submitted by Joseph Brodie and Neil Gillman, then the deans of the School of Judaica and the Rabbinical School respectively, because they recognized that "the effort to create a sense of community throughout the school has succeeded much better on the academic level than on the social level." An office dedicated to student life would help ensure that a sense of community would be maintained amidst the quest for academic excellence. The Office would be responsible for working with groups such as the student-faculty committee and for personal and religious counseling. It would also coordinate student-wives programs, retreats, *ongei shabbat*, Shabbat programming, and the student newspaper. While approved initially for rabbinical school students, Cohen envisioned that its purview would soon expand to "include attention to the spiritual needs of the students in the other schools of the Seminary."[26]

The Office began functioning in the 1975–76 academic year under Brodie's direction, and the highlight of its first year was the Purim *Se'udah*, an event that brought together students and a few faculty members for joyous celebration. During this period, Deans Gillman and Brodie together with their wives—Sarah Gillman and Deborah Brodie—regularly entertained students and their spouses in their homes on Shabbat. Other members of the faculty also opened their homes to students, perpetuating the Schechters' original vision of combining learning and living—the mind and the heart—to sustain a vital Jewish life.[27]

Within a year, the Office of Student Life also took over the supervision of resident advisers and faculty at the Mathilde Schechter Residence Hall. It trained them to deepen the morals and mores of the students even as the students furthered their scholarly learning in class. Within two years, the then Women's League campaign chairman Evelyn Henkind reported the success of the residence hall in creating "opportunities for students to enjoy a fine experience in Jewish living." By 1980, Chancellor Cohen noted that the Mathilde Schechter Residence Hall and Goldsmith Hall, a newly acquired facility for married students, have together "regenerated the sense of community among our students and faculty.'" As Evelyn Auerbach, Henkind's successor, put it, the residence hall had "brought Campus Life to Broadway & 122nd Street, allowing our students to live Jewishly 24 hours a day. Women hold and participate in Shabbat Services; extracurricular student activities abound; and Jewish student life flourishes."[28]

In the early 1980s, the Office of Student Life expanded to encompass a "Va'ad Gemilut Hasadim" which coordinated a wide array of community outreach activities, including staffing home-less shelters and soup kitchens, organizing clothing and blood drives, and spearheading an annual Tzedakah campaign. Through this initiative, JTS provided cocurricular opportunities for action that complemented the Jewish values that students learned in class.[29]

This commitment to supporting a broad approach to education and student life continues under the leadership of the current chancellor, Ismar Schorsch. In addition to providing several kinds of daily and holiday religious services for the community as a whole, the Office of Student Life also sponsors community barbe-cues and Shabbat dinners and facilitates student programming and arts festivals. Resident directors and Jewish life directors in each residence hall concern themselves with the emotional well-being of residents as well as with the students' religious and spiritual development. The Office of Student Life also added a separate Counseling Center to meet students' individual needs. Several JTS schools sponsor annual retreats for their students in order to foster a deeper sense of community. Rabbis in Residence work with students in the professional schools to foster religious forma-tion and growth. The Va'ad Gemilut Hasadim has expanded its community outreach and social action programs on both a global and a local level to include mobilizing in response to national and international emergencies as well as providing opportunities for JTS students to read weekly with local elementary-school stu-dents.[30]

This attention to education in its broadest sense continues the efforts and dreams of Solomon and Mathilde Schechter. Both then and now, Seminary leaders understood that outstanding faculty and first-rate learning are in and of themselves incapable of single-handedly fulfilling JTS's mission. For that, the institution must enliven the heart and spirit as well as the intellect.

The essence of JTS and, ultimately, of the Conservative movement that it serves derives then, not from Schechter's Seminary but from the Schechters' Seminary. Solomon and Mathilde together modeled the essential elements of Judaism for twentieth-century America, and their partnership enlivened both JTS and the Conservative movement during the twentieth century. As JTS addresses the challenges of the twenty-first century, it can gain both inspiration and direction from the lives and lessons of both Solomon and Mathilde.

Notes

1. See, for example the essays in the two-volume *Tradition Renewed: A History of the Jewish Theological Seminary of America*, ed. Jack Wertheimer (New York: Jewish Theological Seminary, 1997).
2. Mel Scult, "Schechter's Seminary," in Wertheimer, *Tradition Renewed* 1:45, 61–63, 76–77, 88; Shuly Rubin Schwartz, "The Schechter Faculty: The Seminary and *Wissenschaft des Judentums* in America," ibid. 1:295–319.
3. Robert S. Liberles, "*Wissenschaft des Judentums* Comes to America: A Chapter in Migration History, 1890–1935," ibid. 1:338–39; Solomon Schechter, "Rabbi as Personal Example," in *Seminary Addresses and Other Papers* (New York: Burning Bush Press, 1960), 126–29; Scult, "Schechter's Seminary," 60; Herman H. Rubenovitz, "The Architect of Conservative Judaism—Solomon Schechter: As I Knew Him," sermon lecture, 1963–64, mimeograph, JTS library, 5–6.
4. Schechter, "His Majesty's Opposition," in *Seminary Addresses*, 241–42; Kaufman Kohler, "Solomon Schechter: Memorial Address, delivered 18 Dec. 1915," *Jewish Theological Seminary Student's Annual* 3 (1916): 116.
5. Scult, "Schechter's Seminary," 45.
6. She was born in 1857 in Guttentag, Silesia; he in 1847 in Foscani, Rumania.
7. Paula Ollendorf, "Mathilde Schechter," *Outlook* 5 (December 1934): 7; Alexander Marx, "The Life of Mathilde Schechter," *United Synagogue Recorder*, January 1925, 10–11; Mel Scult, "The Baale Boste Reconsidered: The Life of Mathilde Roth Schechter (M.R.S.)," *Modern Judaism* 7 (February 1987): 1–27; Mathilde Roth Schechter, memoir, undated, Solomon Schechter papers, Jewish Theological Seminary of America, New York, N.Y. [JTSA]; Deborah B. Karp, "Mathilde Schechter Comes to America," *Outlook* 72 (Summer 2002): 30.

8. Charles I. Hoffman, "Mrs. Schechter as Helpmeet," *United Synagogue Recorder*, October 1924, 7.

9. Rubenovitz, "Architect," 6; Mignon L. and Herman H. Rubenovitz, *The Waking Heart* (Cambridge, Mass.: Nathaniel Dame, 1967), 19, 268–69; [Althea Silverman], "Woman's Field," *United Synagogue Recorder*, October 1924, 26; Jacob Kohn, "The Beauty of Mrs. Schechter's Character," ibid., 6; Bertha Badt-Strauss, " 'Aunt Mathilde': Mathilde Schechter, Friend of Youth," *Outlook* 23 (December 1952): 4–5; Mrs. Jacob S. (Fanny) Minkin, "Mrs. Solomon Schechter: An Anniversary Appreciation," *Outlook* 2 (December 1931): 2.

10. "Mrs. Schechter's Funeral," *New York Times*, August 29, 1924, arch. 101-21, Mathilde Schechter papers, JTSA; Mathilde Schechter, interview with Mrs. Morris (Althea) Silverman, in "Woman's Field," *United Synagogue Recorder*, April 1923, 17; Hoffman, "Helpmeet," 7; Hanna Marx, "Mathilde S. [*sic*] Schechter," *Outlook* 9 (December 1938): 5.

11. "Hebrew Choral Society Planned," *Boston Globe*, February 10, 1905, 21, in "ephemera M.S.-Newsclips" folder, box 20, "Schechter, Mathilde, Correspondence," arch. 101-20, Schechter papers; *Kol Rinah: Hebrew Hymnal for School and Home*, ed. Lewis M. Isaacs and Mathilde S. [*sic*] Schechter (New York: Bloch, 1910); Marx, "Mathilde S.," 5; Mathilde Schechter, interview, *United Synagogue Recorder*, April 1923, 17.

12. Kohn, "Beauty," 6.

13. Mathilde Schechter, "A Task for Jewish Women," January 21, 1918, repr. in *Outlook* 2 (April 1932): 1.

14. [Althea Silverman], "Women's Field," *United Synagogue Recorder*, April 1927, 25; Louis M. Levitsky, "Five Years at the Students' House," *United Synagogue Recorder*, January 1925, 8; Cyrus Adler to Mathilde Schechter, May 20, 1918, arch. 101-20, Mathilde Schechter papers, JTSA.

15. [Althea Silverman], "Women's Field," *United Synagogue Recorder*, April 1927, 25; Jenna Weissman Joselit, "By Design: Building the Campus of the Jewish Theological Seminary," in Wertheimer, *Tradition Renewed*, 1: 276–77; Executive Council of Women's League, minutes, January 29, 1919, "Executive and Board minutes," Women's League Archives, New York [WLA]; Mathilde Schechter, "Address," *Seventh and Eight Reports of the United Syangogue of America and the Women's League Annual Reports* (New York, [1920]), 105; Hoffman, "Helpmeet," 7; Levitsky, "Five Years," 9.

16. Mathilde Schechter to Louis Marshall, December 30, 1915, transcribed in Mel Scult, "Mrs. Mathilde Roth Schechter: Her Life and Letters," unpub. ms., pp. 110-11, 82 n. 77. I am grateful to Mel Scult for sharing this manu-

script with me. Louis Marshall to Mathilde Schechter, January 6, 1916, arch. 101-20, Mathilde Schechter papers, JTSA; Marx, "An Appreciation," 5; Kohn, "Beauty," 6; Joselit, "By Design," 279–80.

17. *They Dared To Dream: A History of National Women's League* (New York: National Women's League of the United Synagogue of America, 1967), 11. *Friday Night Stories* (New York: Women's League of the United Synagogue of America, 1919) was adapted by Sulamith Ish-Kishor from Louis Ginzberg's *Legends of the Jews*; Schechter, "Address," 108; "A Valorous Woman" (editorial), *Outlook* 2 (September 1930): 2; Minkin, "Mrs. Solomon Schechter," 2; Mrs. Moses Hyamson, "Mrs. Samuel Spiegel: An Appreciation," *Outlook* 15 (December 1944): 3.

18. Executive Council of Women's League, minutes, May 1, 1919, May 17, 1920, December 20, 1920, December 19, 1921, "Executive and Board minutes," WLA.

19. "Biography"; "Biographical data folder"; *Jewish Advocate* (Boston), August 15, 1957; Jen S. Margolis, "Mignon L. Rubenovitz 75 Years Young," unidentified newspaper clipping, box 14, Herman H. and Mignon L. Rubenovitz papers, JTSA; Israel J. Kazis, eulogy for Mignon Rubenovitz, delivered November 29, 1968, reprinted in *Temple Topics*, December 1968; Dorothy Crandall, "Jewish Homes Hum in Preparation for Passover," unidentified newspaper clipping, Mishkan Tefila Archives, Chestnut Hill, Mass.; Miriam Feinberg, phone conversation with author, February 8, 2000; Mignon L. Rubenovitz, *Altars of My Fathers* (Boston: Jewish Museum, Temple Mishkan Tefila, 1954), 8; Rubenovitz, *Waking Heart*, 19, 26, 98, 104, 172, 232, 244, 263, 265–71, 275, 284; Bobbie Richards, phone conversation with author, February 8, 2000; "Mignon Rubenovitz … Remembered," "Mignon Rubenovitz" folder, rg 10, Hadassah Archives, New York, N.Y.; Mignon L. Rubenovitz, "Museum Within a Temple," *Jewish Advocate* (Boston), December 11, 1958, 7.

20. Eli Ginzberg, *Keeper of the Law* (Philadelphia: Jewish Publication Society, 1966), 243–46; idem, "The Seminary Family: A View From My Parents' Home," in *Perspectives on Jews and Judaism in Honor of Wolfe Kelman*, ed. Arthur A. Chiel (New York: Rabbinical Assembly, 1978), 117–26; "Presentation of Mathilde Schechter Award," *Women's League Biennial Convention Proceedings* (1980), 75–76; "Irrepressible, Unforgettable 'Mama G,'" *Outlook* 51 (Fall 1980): 4, 20–21; Ira Eisenstein, *Reconstructionist Judaism: An Autobiography* (New York: Reconstructionist Press, 1986), 84–85; Louis Finkelstein to Adele Ginzberg, October 19, 1945, RG 1c-47-49, JTS records, JTSA; "Quotable Quotes," *Scope*, February 1964, 2.

21. Eli Ginzberg, interview with author, October 25, 1994, New York, N.Y.; Israel Shenker, "Adele Ginzberg, at 90, Says, 'So What?' " *New York Times*, May 16, 1976; Adele Ginzberg; "Publicity and Public Relations" folder, file 5a, WLA; "Presentation of Mathilde Schechter Award," 74–75.

22. David Kaufman, "Jewish Education as Civilization: A History of the Teachers Institute," in Wertheimer, *Tradition Renewed*, 1: 578–84.

23. National Women's League of the United Synagogue of America, *Biennial Convention Proceedings, Nov. 11–14, 1956*, 28.

24. Helen Sussman, "Our Dormitory Project," *Outlook* 27 (May 1957): 4; Jessica Alexander, "A Living Monument to Our Founder," *Outlook* 28 (September 1957): 6; eadem, "Mathilde Schechter Dormitory," in National Women's League of the United Synagogue of America, *Biennial Convention Reports of National Activities and of the Branches, Nov. 16–20, 1958*, 30; Adele Ginzberg, *Outlook* 28 (December 1957): cover.

25. Syd Rossman Goldstein, "The National Women's Patrons Society," Women's League for Conservative Judaism, *Biennial Convention Handbook, Nov. 14–18, 1976*, 40; Baila R. Shargel, "The Texture of Seminary Life during the Finkelstein Era," in Wertheimer, *Tradition Renewed*, 1:562 n. 102.

26. Neil Gillman and Joseph Brodie to Gerson D. Cohen, memorandum, November 5, 1974; Gerson D. Cohen to Joseph Brodie, June 13, 1975, personal files of Joseph Brodie.

27. Joseph Brodie, conversation with author, February 23, 2005.

28. Brodie, conversation; Evelyn Henkind, "Reports of Our National Activity Chairmen: Torah Fund-Residence Halls," Women's League for Conservative Judaism, *Biennial Convention Handbook, Nov. 12–16, 1978*, 31; Paula E. Hyman, "The Unfinished Symphony: The Gerson Cohen Years," in Wertheimer, *Tradition Renewed*, 1: 248; Evelyn Auerbach, "Torah Fund-Residence Halls," Women's League for Conservative Judaism, *Biennial Convention Handbook, Nov. 16–20, 1980*, 31.

29. "Va'ad Gemilut Hasadim: Helping out for Heaven's Sake and Office of Student Life," n.d.; "Va'ad Gemilut Hasadim: Center for Community Outreach," n.d.

30. Ibid.; www.JTSA.edu.

American Jews, American Capitalism, and the Politics of History

ELI LEDERHENDLER

Our necessities have been mistaken for our propensities.
— EDGAR ALLAN POE

It was Ismar Schorsch who drew my attention to the early modern economic arguments for toleration of the Jews and to modern ideological debates concerning the Jews and capitalism; in whose seminars I was sensitized to the relationship between the work of modern Jewish historians and the great social projects of emancipation and integration in which they and their communities were engaged; and who, above all, afforded me a living example of the intellectual excitement of Jewish history as a calling. These are lessons that I have not forgotten. The following is written with abiding gratitude to my teacher.

One observation that stands out in the general estimation of Jewish Americans is that they proved to themselves and others that the American dream was more than a myth.[1] Within a generation of their arrival as immigrants, many Jews had entered the American middle class; within two generations they had leapt to the level of America's oldest elites, in terms of income and higher educational achievement.

Back in 1909, when the single most important factor determining immigrant workers' income level was duration of residence in the United States, Russian-born Jewish workers performed economically more or less as one might expect. Just over 57 percent of them had been living in America for five years or more, and they were, thus, a bit more than midway between the newly arrived and the more established immigrant groups; they were likewise situated slightly over the midpoint of the industrial wage scale rather than at the bottom or the top.[2] Thereafter, however, Jews outpaced most other ethnoreligious groups in economic mobility. As early as 1930, fully 71 percent of the sons of Russian Jewish immigrants in Boston entered the job market as white-collar workers. In 1951, 12 percent of the Jewish households in New York City (where most Jewish immigrants lived) had annual incomes over $10,000, as compared with only 5 percent of non-Jewish households.[3] A 1970 study found that "Jews, regardless of ethnic ancestry, attain higher levels of education, occupation and income than all other subgroups."[4] By 1990, Jews were found to have a per capita income almost twice as high as the national mean.[5] Such attainments, solidified and broadened over a period of decades, have permitted Jews to enjoy an enhanced public image and higher-profile involvements at all levels of politics and government on the threshold of the twenty-first century. All this suggests that Jews have performed extremely well within the American system.

Yet, as the conservative economist and social thinker Milton Friedman once put it, "Two propositions can be readily demonstrated: first, that the Jews owe an enormous debt to free enterprise and competitive capitalism; second, for at least the past century the Jews have been consistently opposed to capitalism and have done much on an ideological level to undermine it."[6]

The assessment that Jews, despite their particularly strong orientation toward individual achievement, have also maintained a singular profile as the nation's most consistently left-leaning and liberal ethnic group is widely shared. It has become a mainstay of social and historical writing on American Jewish history, especially with regard to the twentieth century. It is a perennial topic that continues to generate new scholarship and discussion, and, fittingly, the *American Jewish Historical Quarterly* dedicated its special issue for America's bicentennial to a discussion of this subject.[7]

Notwithstanding the uninterrupted presence and periodic resurgence of conservative political trends within the Jewish community, the liberal posture, for the most part, is today still considered more "habitual" among many Jews and their leaders, while conservative positions possess an oppositional or "dissident" character.[8] American Jews' liberal or left-leaning bias is a point upheld among liberals as a badge of honor, just as it is decried among conservatives as a defect, but it is rarely in dispute. Can it really be that these reluctant capitalists have been among the most successful examples of socioeconomic mobility in America?

"Liberal" is a label which may fit historically with the emergence of a free enterprise and free market system,[9] but in the American political lexicon, especially since the mid twentieth century, liberalism has come to convey something well beyond the assurance of constitutional liberties, governmental checks and balances, the protection of property, and the inviolability of contracts. Its sense is closer to notions of egalitarianism in general and redistributive economic justice in particular, and it is in that sense that American Jews' liberalism appears out of step with their economic prowess.[10] With their disproportionate support not only for civil liberties but also for social policies that favor disadvantaged sectors and minority groups, Jews stand out as ideological "malcontents" in the world of free enterprise, of the "bottom line," of self-interest, and of conceptualizations of politics as essentially pragmatic arrangements—an extension of the nation's "business." This ostensibly marks Jewish Americans as notable exceptions to their class and, arguably, to the national consensus and thus becomes an ethnic marker or social boundary that constructs Jewish identity.[11]

"Identity" is, indeed, the paradigmatic issue that has engaged the attention of most American Jewish historians, revealing much about their constructions of Jewish society, their conceptions of America, their perspective on the normative status of the middle class, and the low priority that they have placed on economic and political analysis. Although a few among them have engaged in crosscultural comparisons that highlight the historical specificity of the American Jewish experience, these constitute the exceptions rather than the rule.[12] This essay is an attempt to engage some of these issues, using as background the discourse on Jewish ethnicity as it has been related to American politics and economics. In particular, I am interested in the construction placed on the apparent exceptionalism of Jews in American society, an exceptionalism formed by their dual character as a group with a high profile both in economic mobility and among American liberal constituencies.

There are two regnant approaches in this regard. One is to claim that the Jews' political culture and economic status are mutually reinforcing (and thus "rational"), because of a congruence of values or a confluence of interests.[13] Thus it may be argued that Jews are liberal out of conviction, but also that their basic interests are vested in a liberal, open society which has best assured their own economic and social integration.[14] There are, in fact, some socioeconomic indicators that indirectly bear this out, insofar as the consolidation of white-collar, professional, and upper middle class status among the Jewish population coincided with liberalizing trends in the American economy and social policy from the mid 1930s to the 1970s.[15] There are, in addition, suggestive data from public opinion research that shows that social and political elites and "opinion makers"—groups whose socioeconomic status resembles that of the Jews—are more apt than the general American public to interpret or to resolve the tensions between capitalism and liberal democracy mainly in a liberal direction.[16] That, in turn, implies that liberalism need not conflict with elite status—indeed, that the two may be perceived to be linked.

The other approach is to argue that the Jews' political culture and their significant economic success are fundamentally at odds with one another, in the context of American sociopolitical norms, and thus "irrational," but nevertheless attributable to different aspects of Jewish heritage, or different aspects of ethnic loyalty. "Why," asked the political scientist Kenneth Wald, "should Jews, by objective standards one of the highest-status groups in the United States, maintain such a firm commitment to liberal political values ... that seems, contrary to all common sense, to *increase* with economic achievement?" He, along with several other scholars, argues that Jews may remain liberal, not because their integration into American society was won through liberalism, but *despite* their successful integration, as they attempt to hold onto a sense of their own religio-ethnic distinctiveness.[17]

In dealing with these issues, social theorists and historians of both of these schools of thought have tended to focus on issues of culture—that is, the heritage brought by Jewish immigrants from their old countries—employing a language of continuity of values or historical development between Old World Judaism and New World Jewish realities to explain Jewish exceptionalism in the American context. Heritage is thus made to bear a dual explanatory function, with Jewish success in America seen as an effect of the Jews' pre-immigration history, while social and political values at variance with American ideology are *also* viewed as functions of Jewish identity. There is, in both approaches, a fascination with Jewish origins, a quasi-axiomatic assumption that ethnic *identity*, amidst American social and economic conditions, is what is fundamentally at stake, and a concern for Jewish group identity in the future.

Examples of the heritage argument abound with respect to the linkage between Jews and the left, or liberalism.[18] Almost as conspicuous have been the concomitant claims about the linkage between Jewish heritage and economic success in America, especially in literature published in the second half of the twentieth century, when Jewish poverty and anti-Jewish discrimination lost the salience they had possessed up through the 1930s. A number of brief examples should suffice.

The eminent economist and economic historian Simon Kuznets, for example, writing in Louis Finkelstein's postwar compendium *The Jews: Their History, Culture, and Religion*, referred *en passant* to "the *well known middle-class virtues* of the Jews" [emphasis added], which, he argued, when free to develop over a long period, "can produce a level of wealth-holding that is ... above average."[19] These heritage values, in turn, are said to have reinforced Jewish integration in American society. One of America's premier social scientists, Robert Park, writing in 1950, intoned the dictum that the "energy" and "drive for achievement" demonstrated by Americans Jews were "quintessentially American."[20] Similarly, the economic historian Nathan Reich wrote in a 1950 essay on the role of the Jews in the American economy that "American reality put a high premium on geographical and mental mobility, entrepreneurial ability, ambition, resourcefulness—all qualities which Jews possess in large measure."[21]

Later in that same decade, the sociologist Nathan Glazer argued that what he termed "Jewish Puritanism" (a nod to Max Weber's Calvinists)[22] could be traced back as far as late antiquity, a mentality that included such stock elements as a "strong emphasis on learning and study ... Jewish habits of foresight, care, moderation." These "middle class habits," in tandem with the Jews' economic experience since the Middle Ages, meant that, Jewish immigrants from Eastern Europe, though impoverished, "*carried with them the values conducive to middle-class success*" [emphasis added].[23]

This discourse continued in subsequent decades as well. The sociologist Robin M. Williams, Jr., writing in Charles Stember's *Jews in the Mind of America* in the mid 1960s, agreed with the common wisdom that "all along, historic 'Jewish' values have fitted relatively well with non-Jewish 'American' ones." He paired work ethic together with liberal politics in an omnibus assertion that, in

America, "Jews and gentiles alike have prized personal achievement and success, active striving and ambition, religious freedom and cultural pluralism, humanitarianism, voluntarism, material prosperity, democracy, individual freedom and responsibility."[24]

Similarly, Milton Konvitz, the prominent expert in labor relations, in an address on "Judaism and the Pursuit of Happiness," meshed Judaic values with American ones, particularly as related to the union of matter and spirit that he found at the heart of Judaism. "The ideal of Judaism," he told his audience, "is a kingdom of heaven on this earth in which every man will live under his own vine and his own fig tree, enjoying God's bounty, free from want and fear, in a social order based on justice, freedom and righteousness." Judaism, he claimed, thus combined a healthy acceptance of "the vital needs of the whole human being" with what he termed an "asceticism … of affirmation … that serves the self in its quest for fulfillment," rather than a renunciation of the body and its needs.[25] The connections between a dialectical self-denial, salvation, and this-worldliness are, of course, intended to remind us of Weber's proto-capitalist ethics.

Almost routinely, then, the sociologist Milton Gordon, in his now-classic work on assimilation, reiterated the idea that the cultural history of the Jews explains their rapid economic rise: "Jews arrived in America with middle-class values of thrift, sobriety, ambition, desire for education, ability to postpone immediate gratifications for the sake of long-range goals, and aversion to violence already internalized."[26] A doctoral dissertation in sociology at the University of Pennsylvania in 1976 followed suit with, "Perhaps in no other area did things American and things Jewish so overlap as in the economic. Through economic activity, Jews most easily integrated into American society, not by forsaking their own ideals, but by stressing their Jewish qualities."[27] In the 1980s, Thomas Sowell's study of American ethnicity claimed, yet again, that "the internal values and traditions of the Jews were almost tailor-made for success in the American economy." Jews possessed not only "specific skills," but also "a way of life adapted to centuries of urban life and commercial and industrial activity. ... In short, the Jews had the social patterns and values of the middle class, even when they lived in slums."[28] And in a recent essay on "Jewish overrepresentation," David A. Hollinger reiterates that "In order ... to survive and prosper, Jews developed to a higher degree than other European descent groups the distinctive set of skills on which the modernization process most depended: calculation, language fluency, recordkeeping, close attention to detail, a facility for abstraction, and the mobility and flexibility required" to make the most of modern conditions.[29]

Indeed, no less an authority than the historian Aryeh (Arthur) Goren, speaking in 1979, confirmed this trend of thought at a public lecture in Philadelphia. In a statement that may be seen as a definitive text on this topic, and worth quoting at length, he pondered, "Why the ardor with which so many Jewish immigrants embraced the American dream of material success?"

> The inner life the Jews had lived for generations ... prepared them for the American experience. In their self-contained traditional communities they had molded a social order which compared to that of other groups was remarkably open. The Jewish economy had required it. ... The hazards inherent in commerce and the endemic political and economic instability hardly allowed the formation of fixed classes. ... Contingency in life—the very notion of living in exile with its perpetual threat of catastrophe—was part of the warp and woof of the religious culture. Survival required flexibility in the face of the unpredictable and pluck in the face of misfortune. The Jewish immigrants on coming to America, therefore, accepted change more readily than others. ... In this sense, the Jews had been conditioned for generations for the competitive, volatile social economy they came to. In a word, Jewish life armed even the impoverished with middle class values.[30]

The burden of Goren's argument is that to the extent that Jewish integration in American society has succeeded, it has done so because Jews were "eased" into American mental habits by historical and cultural preconditioning. The Jews' own cultural baggage prompted them to embrace the American ethic; therefore, no overbearing, let alone coercive, Americanization program was required for this to be accomplished. In-group, ethnocultural loyalty and acculturation to the wider society blurred into a single psychosocial phenomenon, making it difficult, on the one hand, to distinguish Jews from other Americans, while making it ostensibly easier to distinguish Jews *from other immigrants*, on the other. Exceptional among their fellow immigrants, Jews were marked by the rapidity of their social ascent (overcoming obstacles of social and economic discrimination), and this in turn gave them their distinctive profile.

It bears noting that the America construed here is itself represented by a variety of paradigmatic outlooks, identities, and cultures, so that the question of where the Jews fit in is assessed primarily in cultural terms: they are one among a variety of American ethnicities. Social class, for example, does not figure prominently in this construction. Goren remains faithful here to his overriding concern with the discourse of identity pluralism in American society, a field in which he is a leading authority. It is indicative of Goren's approach that in introducing his own collection of essays on Jewish ethnic politics, *The Politics and Public Culture of American Jews*, Goren opens with a discussion of identity, using as his point of departure Israel Friedlaender's 1907 lecture, "The Problem of Judaism in America," which deals with assimilation and the issues of Jewish continuity amid conditions of freedom.[31]

The tendency to conflate class with ethnicity (middle class status or "values" with Jewishness itself) is not only a feature of works that deal with American Jewish immigration, but also appears in social research about later generations. A notable example is Calvin Goldscheider's "cohesion" hypothesis, which argues that contemporary Jewish ethnicity inheres in the frequent encounters and associations shared by Jewish, self-employed businesspeople and professionals, by virtue of their disproportionate presence in those particular social strata:

> As occupational levels increase, new forms of occupational concentration have developed at high socio-economic levels. ... The "new" occupational concentration has not resulted in stratification convergences between Jews and non-Jews. ... If for no other cultural or structural reason, the commonality of class and status among Jews, of occupational concentration and educational achievement at high levels, would result in social bonds, economic networks and common life-styles and interests.[32]

Similar class status or occupational preference—understood as social propinquity—here becomes the definitional ethnic attribute, taking precedence over any other ethnocultural or religious characteristic.

Despite the apparent ubiquity of this trend of thought, it neither represents the entirety of discourse on Jews, class, and capitalism—as will be evident when we compare it with alternative constructions proposed by both Jewish and non-Jewish scholars and observers—nor does it entirely accomplish its explanatory goal; for, once we factor in the Jews' exceptional political liberalism as a complicating (and perhaps contradictory) datum, the value-confluence theory appears to require qualification.

The problem becomes clearer if we consider that most *non-Jewish* Americans manage to uphold free-enterprise, free-market ideas without joining them up with an affinity for social-egalitarian liberalism. However true it may be that classic libertarian economic ideas mesh with democratic institutions, such institutions are not a sufficient foundation for social-egalitarian ideologies.

Jewish hyperliberalism, therefore, is not a Friedmanesque social-philosophical or moral concomitant of the American capitalist ethic; it cannot be said to have been preconditioned by generations of middle class values or historical experience; and its sources cannot credibly be said to lie in a confluence of Jewish values and American ones. At the very least, we are required to take a closer look at the linearity of the culture/heritage hypothesis as deployed to explain value-continuity between impoverished but "middle class" Russian Jews (some of whom were socialists) and affluent middle class American Jews (of whom many are still left of the American political center).

It is sobering to recall that it was once possible to inscribe, in a book sympathetic to Jews, such lines as, "The reason for the Jewish preponderance in the cloth industry is not far to seek. Tailoring is a sedentary pursuit and therefore has an appeal to the Jew who is unfit for the heaviest kind of manual labor."[33] Treating the Jewish experience under American capitalist conditions as an artifact of the Jews' pre-immigration life, culture, or values can sometimes verge perilously close to such long-discredited essentialist arguments. In its cruder versions, the thesis of direct continuity between Old World and New World Jewish experience, insofar as Jews allegedly transferred protocapitalist and peculiarly Jewish economic values from one world to the other, is somewhat reminiscent of the old Sombart hypothesis about the Jewish predilection for modern capitalism.[34] Even in its more sophisticated and historically nuanced versions (such as Goren's), however, the value-transfer thesis still privileges a discourse of identity ("character" or "culture") over other factors.

Heritage factors did play a significant role in Jewish attitudes toward economic life, although not necessarily in the manner described by proponents of the "middle-class values" thesis. A reading of 19th-century *haskalah* literature, for example, shows that the *maskilim*, who strove to promote modern economic and social values in Jewish society, decried the hobbling effect of time-honored Judaic values—such as blind faith in providential assistance—on Jewish economic progress.[35]

Jews' economic and political behavior, however, rather than constituting a realm determined mainly by internal Jewish traditions, predilections, predispositions, or mentalities, is in fact that realm in which the Jews' *environment*, not their heritage, almost always plays a more dominant role. Jewish economic and political behavior, therefore, derives most often from considerations of *adaptation, opportunity,* and *the terms of their encounters with non-Jews*—all of which tend to have very specific ramifications in different countries and time periods.

Thus, there is no primordial Jewish approach to capitalism (whether positive or negative) because Jews, in their economic capacities, are creatures of their habitat. Jews become capitalists in capitalist societies; they are poor and economically backward in societies that are themselves poor and underdeveloped. This much is apparent from a comparison of social and economic conditions among the masses of Russian Jews at the end of the nineteenth century and the greatly ameliorated conditions obtaining among their counterparts in America within two decades of their immigration.

It is essential, moreover, to distinguish the Jews' experience of capitalism in America from their European experience. In Europe, historically, Jews occupied a peculiar economic "place" or were assigned a special "function," mediating between town and village, by virtue of which they were deemed useful and tolerated (but also hated). In America, Jews did not form such a caste but rather one wing of a new kind of class, built on the rubble of premodern, ascriptive, and fixed hierarchical relations. Even as they clustered in certain niches of the economic system, such behavior was never a precondition for toleration in America.

These niches were also porous (shared with other subgroups); temporary (characteristic of one generation, two at the most); and for the most part never stigmatized.[36]

Rather than posit an attachment to heritage as the basis for political and economic behavior, I would argue that Jews' behavior in American economic and political life is explainable to a large extent by the ways in which Jews encountered the American system. They encountered it as members of a religious minority and as foreigners who needed to adapt to a new environment— that is, their premigration cultural and social lives were *discontinuous* with American reality. The question then becomes: Could the dynamics of Jewish socioeconomic and cultural adjustment to America have produced among Jews an ethos of collective social responsibility as well as its ostensible opposite, a spirit of self-reliant, entrepreneurial individualism?

Their resettlement in a country far removed from their mother culture, their overwhelmingly urban concentration, and their gravitation to occupational and consumer enclaves that afforded them some social coherence as a group formed a context in which Jews became Americans within mostly Jewish social networks. That they might display a combination of individual achievement–oriented skills and at the same time form an affinity for communally conscious, albeit novel, social-political ideals, running somewhat counter to what other middle or upper class Americans viewed as the norm, is not an unreasonable supposition.[37]

In short, the peculiar duality of Jewish Americans in terms of their economic and political behavior might be traced to their encounter with America. In contending with American capitalism, both as disciples and as reformers, Jews had to reinvent, not clone, themselves. The effects of habitat—rather than heritage alone—could be the primary key to understanding Jewish exceptionalism.

Alternative approaches embodying such a perspective fall into two main categories: (a) those which view immigration more as an "uprooting" than a "transplanting," and therefore delimit the determinative power of heritage factors, and (b) those which are inclined to look at empirical conditions in the United States (such as opportunity structures, labor recruitment, and mediating institutions) as having largely determined immigrant adaptation patterns, and as reshaping even such heritage factors as may be carried over from one society to another.[38]

Consider, to begin with, the perspective shed on the subject by the impressions of Hutchins Hapgood, a sympathetic contemporary observer of the immigrant scene, who commented on the changeover to American ways required in order to make the typical Russian Jew into a "proper" American capitalist:

Some of them ... rose by small degrees to the position of great financial operators. But they became so only by growing to feel very intimately the spirit of American enterprise which enables a man to carry on the boldest operation in a calm spirit. To this boldness the son of the orthodox parents of our Ghetto has not yet attained. Coming from the cramped "quarter," with still a tinge of the patriarchal Jew in his blood, not yet thoroughly at home in the atmosphere of the American "plunger," he is a little hesitant, though very keen, in business affairs. The conservatism instilled in him by the pious old "greenhorn," his father, is a limitation to his American "nerve." He likes to deal in ponderable goods, to be able to touch and handle his wares, to have them before his eyes. In the next generation, when in business matters also he will be an instinctive American, he will become as big a financial speculator as any of them.[39]

Hapgood's stereotypical portrait was a polemical response to fellow journalist Jacob Riis's unflattering, and itself tendentious, depiction of "Jewtown's" single-minded materialism and pathologically extreme self-denial: "Thrift is the watchword of Jewtown, as of its people the world over ... at once its strength and its fatal weakness, its cardinal virtue and its foul disgrace," to which Riis added that, compared with German immigrants, Jews displayed a low level of economic self-motivation.[40]

It is difficult to take either Riis's jaundice or Hapgood's apologetics completely at face value. It is harder, however, to similarly dismiss the Chicago sociologist Louis Wirth as a mere purveyor of stereotypes and shibboleths. Wirth, whose work reflected the "assimilationist" school of American urban sociology, wrote a fairly judicious, if rather overgeneralized, think piece in 1943 about the significance of traditional Jewish learning as a tool for ethnic and cultural survival. In the essay he distinguished between education as the transmission of patterns of communication uniquely employed within a group and the secular, instrumental nature of modern public and professional education. His analysis is of prime relevance to the present discussion because of the disjuncture that he saw between the core value–maintenance systems of Judaism and modern, urban life.[41]

While suggesting that modern Jews' disproportionate recourse to public and higher professional education might owe something (among other factors) to a transvaluation of the old Judaic educational routines, Wirth was careful to delineate the survivalist rationale of the latter from the assimilationist effect of the former. He concluded that Jews were highly adaptable to attractive cultural environments; that they had retained a sense of a core culture of their own (with a considerable assist from the antisemites); but that Jewish values—education, in the traditional, culture-bonding sense, in particular—were operating under a distinct handicap in the American, urban, capitalist setting and had had to be considerably adjusted.[42] Insofar as Jewish learning, viewed as a technique for reinforcing a positive cultural self-awareness in a hostile world and for maintaining links of in-group communication and solidarity over a global dispersion, also had economic benefits, Wirth said, this was a singularly premodern, collateral by-product:

The frequent interchange of communication among the distant Jewish settlements ... did more than merely preserve the cohesion of a religious and ethnic community; it furnished the bases of the peculiar economic and intellectual advantage which the Jews enjoyed in comparison with their indigenous neighbors. This constant traffic of men, of goods, and of ideas provided the source of the continuous renewal of the culture and prevented it from lapsing into the parochialism and stagnation characteristic of the Dark Ages in Europe.[43]

He reflected on the impact that modernization, migration, urbanization, and exposure to Western cultures had had in terms of disabling the primary mechanisms of Jewish social and cultural insularity. Jews in American cities were in the rather enviable position (given the context of the early 1940s) of facing assimilation as their major challenge; but Wirth speculated as to "how much of the anomalous status of the Jews today"—caught as they were between discrimination and assimilation, progress and anxiety—was due to the long-term effects on the Jews of their participation in the industrial revolution and the capitalist economy.[44]

Wirth's views on the deleterious impact of modernization and capitalism on the coherence and stability of Jewish group life echoed similar views expressed the previous year by Salo W. Baron, the preeminent Jewish historian in America. Baron evaluated the advent of capitalism very positively as far as it had had a beneficial impact on the status of Jews as individuals in European society; but he held that the benefits accruing to the Jews in the wake of capitalism ("population increase, better geographic distribution, new economic opportunity, higher standard of life, political equality and complete intellectual freedom"),[45] had to be weighed against significant losses: "In fact," Baron argued,

it was capitalism, operating from its inception in the direction of political emancipation and cultural assimilation ... [and] the new emphasis upon individualism [that] seriously undermined the Jewish group life. ... The ensuing disorganization of Jewish communal life often undermined the Jewishness of even those members who still paid it formal allegiance. ... Much as the Jew as an individual may have benefited by ... capitalism, he undoubtedly lost a great deal *qua* Jew. ... The combined forces of individualism, materialism, rationalism and secularism have placed so many question marks upon the future destinies of Jewry as to outweigh [capitalism's] benefits.[46]

Wirth essentially agreed with this argument. His coupling of the capitalist spirit with developments that were at odds with traditional Jewish values was, therefore, neither singular nor remarkable in itself. It is his underlying methodological paradigm, however, that can help us to place his analysis into a particular historical context—and thereby to sharpen our contextual understanding of why later constructions appear so very different.[47]

Wirth's point of departure, as a sociologist, was the interaction between majority and minority, and his attention was always drawn to the dynamics that either favored the integration of minority group members within the majority society or, alternatively, inhibited such integration. Thus, discrimination against Jews in higher education or employment, he argued, might have an identity-reinforcing effect insofar as Jews, finding obstacles in their path to integration, might be thrown back onto their sense of belonging to a particular (disfavored) group. At the same time, job discrimination and college quotas were themselves said to be rooted in a spiral of Jewish efforts at integration: "The disproportionate crowding of the Jews into the professions ... gave rise to a reaction expressing itself in Jewish quotas. ... [But] the quota system in higher educational and professional institutions has mainly resulted in intensifying the individual struggle for admission and advancement."[48]

In this paradigm, Jews always appear in the subordinate role of a minority group, primarily acted upon rather than defining their social relations. It is highly indicative that Wirth concluded his essay on "Education for Survival" by attempting to draw inferences from the Jewish case that might be applicable to African Americans. Despite the wide disparities between them, in terms of the different types of group they respectively constituted as well as in terms of their respective histories, Wirth was bound to make the connection between these two "classic" American minorities, traveling along roads that might converge as they pursued "the goal of a happier adjustment to the world in which they must live."[49] The paradigmatic focus on ever-shifting but mainly assimilatory social relations disallows the use of "identity" or "culture" as analytical categories unto themselves; rather, these are functions deployed by groups while they seek integration into a larger social order.

By comparison, the ethnic diversity paradigm that underlies Arthur Goren's argument, for example, and other standard works on American ethnicity from the 1970s,[50] derives from a period in which American Jews by and large no longer thought of themselves as a subordinate "minority" (still less, a minority comparable to the way that African Americans are still considered a "minority"). The older anxiety of status had given way to an anxiety of "identity," precisely because socioeconomic integration had been so very successful. The diversity perspective rejects the binary, hierarchical, majority–minority situation and therefore, in place of social or class-bound determinants of mobility, looks at ethnic culture and ethnoreligious values as factors in their own right, capable of interacting on an "equal" basis with the culture and values that immigrant groups encounter in their new homes.

In the years since the end of the 1970s, newer scholarship has further complicated or qualified the transfer-of-values hypothesis, lending added support to the environmental hypothesis. Perhaps the most noteworthy innovation in the field of American Jewish historiography has been the advent of feminist historians and their application of gendered analyses to immigrant and ethnic history.

Of particular relevance in the present context is Susan Glenn's monograph on East European Jewish immigrant women, *Daughters of the Shtetl*. Though she draws our attention to certain continuities between East European life and immigrant life in New York, her major contribution regarding the transfer or adaptation of values lies in her observation that generational and gendered divisions of labor in the Jewish family economy underwent an important realignment as a direct result of Americanization: whereas married women in Jewish communities of Eastern Europe often undertook some role in sales or other business activity (a market stall or other family business, such as tavernkeeping), in the New World the direct participation of married Jewish women in either production or sales fell sharply. By contrast, their adolescent daughters were far more likely to join the labor force in America, thus taking upon themselves family economic responsibilities that were once their mothers'.[51]

Glenn argues that part of this shift might be traced to Jewish husbands' reluctance to expose their wives to mixed-sex workplaces like factories—an attitude related to Old World religious values. She suggests that the same inhibition was not operative in the case of unmarried daughters, whose sexuality was not fully recognized in Jewish religious tradition.[52] With this nod to the prolonged power of traditional values, however, Glenn goes on to argue that the most important factor in the new constellation of work and gender roles in the immigrant family was their acceptance of the American middle class ideal of the male breadwinner. An employed wife was a reproach (in terms of social status) to any man; an employed daughter, on the other hand, was merely a recognition of necessity, given the limited possibilities of maintaining a family on only one income.[53]

The questions that may be inferred from Glenn's work are: *whose* middle class values are being internalized or transmitted here, and *which* middle class values are we dealing with? Older studies had referred to Jews' "industry and temperance" (Hapgood) or to their culturally-bred readiness to take financial risk and loss in their stride (Goren). Here, however, we are dealing with a middle class virtue of a different sort—a new definition of men's and women's worthiness—that was not an effective aspect of East European Jewish social realities or traditions.[54] Its Western, bourgeois message rapidly changed the Jewish immigrant family economy. The notion of a common, transmissible seedbed of Jewish "middle class values," construed as an undifferentiated ethic and defined largely along Weberian lines, does not help us to account for the enactment of such basic changes. Middle class values, like most other values, are culture-bound.

The same is true, argues the historian Hadassa Kosak, of working class values and political culture. Where Glenn asks us to qualify the linear approach when dealing with the transmission of gender-related, cultural practices, Kosak (following the sociologist Ann Swidler's theoretical critique of Weber) takes a more radical route: she bids us view culture itself as inherently plastic, multivariant, and a source of "tools" to be applied to ever-changing life situations, rather than a prescriptive guide that can predict behaviors.[55] Thus, the act of migration may have prompted Jewish workers to fall back on some of their own values to orient themselves; but the new situation dramatically altered the interplay between the normative and the deviant, between old and new, prompting them to create a "new vocabulary" of social protest, mutuality, and universal rights:

> The new political culture was forged in shopfloor struggles, consumer boycotts, rent strikes, street demonstrations and parades ... [which] transformed the social ethos of the old world community from one which had been severely con-

strained by the political restrictions of the Russian Empire and by a communal power structure marked by rigid traditionalism into something very different. ... Culture and ethnicity were transformed from an insular tradition into an armory for purposes of political contestation and as a tool for appropriating political power. ... At the historical moment when the old social and political arrangements of the traditional community had disappeared and the new power structures had not yet taken root, this process endowed hitherto marginal groups [such as workers and women] with new power and authority.[56]

Cultural divergence was established in Kosak's and Glenn's research by comparing "old country" ways with acquired "New World" norms. A close comparison of a different, and highly suggestive, sort is offered by an English economic historian, Andrew Godley, in his recent work *Jewish Immigrant Entrepreneurship in New York and London 1880–1914*.[57] Godley asks why, if immigrant Jews in London and New York shared the same cultural background, were their respective patterns of entrepreneurship so markedly different? While American immigrant Jews moved rapidly and in large percentages from employee to self-employed and employer status, the same was not true of Jews in similar (or better) circumstances in London. Godley finds no economic factor to provide a reasonable explanation. As he observes, in London profits from entrepreneurship were fairly high, and Jewish immigrant entrepreneurship increased to 13.1 percent in 1900–1906, rising again to 18 percent in 1907–14. Yet, in New York, Jewish immigrants became entrepreneurs earlier and at a much higher rate—increasing from 18 percent in 1880 to 34.3 percent in 1905—*despite a falling rate of profit* over that period.[58] Godley hypothesizes a new environmental cultural factor that might explain this difference in economic behavior: "Certainly," he deduces, "they were not responding to financial signals alone." How might immigrant Jews have been influenced by prevailing cultural norms in

England and in America?

Godley argues that Jews assimilated aspects of the local culture of class and status and that this significantly altered the supply of entrepreneurs in the two communities. "In Britain ... Jewish immigrants may have become increasingly reluctant to leave paid employment and so required higher profits for any given level of entrepreneurship." Underlying such behavior was the availability in Britain of a higher-status alternative to blue-collar work that was respectable enough in status terms and more secure than the risks of self-employment—the "journeyman" or highly skilled craftsman—a category that Godley finds very common among veteran Jewish immigrants in London.[59]

In the United States, as in England, self-employment was deemed preferable to wage labor as a route to respectability and financial security. In America, however, rather different values applied. Immigrant Jews in New York picked up on the self-employed model as part of what "being American" was all about:

> British, and especially English, culture, by contrast, stood for the elevation of a time-honoured reliability of custom and law, for the importance of yeoman stock, and the dignity of the worker. While the Victorian gentry invented an earlier rural mythology, British workers ... were sentimental about pre-industrial autonomy, skill and craft.[60]

Godley concludes, therefore, that, "cultural assimilation had an important influence in Jewish immigrant occupational status."[61] His findings, moreover, appear to confirm earlier comparative research done by Selma Berrol, an American scholar, who sought to establish the relative importance of mediating social institutions in determining Jewish economic mobility. Berrol also showed, using different data, that from 1880 to 1914 the occupational profile of London immigrant Jews did not change. "Most of the Russian and Polish Jews were still wage earners, the rest were

selling in the streets and in stores, and the smallest proportion
were employers." It was not until 1930 that London Jewry was
characterized by modest prosperity, while the pace of mobility in
New York was markedly more rapid.[62] The difference in timing,
she argues, was due to different opportunities, linked in the first
instance to the size of the immigrant population and, crucially, the
size of the veteran, more affluent German-American Jewish community: "In New York, the bourgeois German Jewish community was larger and thus able to provide more factory jobs for
immigrant workers and entry level white collar positions for their
children [who] had easier access to commercial training [in public
schools and] were prepared to use these opportunities to enter
fields such as accounting, sales, and insurance at an earlier date
than their coreligionists in London."[63]

Significantly, Berrol also comes back to an argument based on
divergent cultural and social values in the two immigrant environments—values, she points out (as does Godley), which have persisted to some degree over the century since the immigrant
period: "The more rigid class structure inherent in English society
... a society that thought you should know your proper station
and remain there" influenced Jewish immigrant mobility patterns.
By contrast, the second-generation children of immigrants in
New York were not so handicapped. The greater entrepreneurial
opportunities afforded to their parents made it possible for them to
turn to higher education in the municipal colleges, which
"seemed to say, forget your working class origins and aim for
middle class professions."[64]

The environmental (or "habitat") argument employed by Berrol
and Godley bears a number of ramifications for our discussion.
Not only does it illuminate questions of historical experience,
comparing the divergent paths taken in different countries by Jews

from the same cultural origins; it also illuminates the historiographical issue that is at stake: namely, why is it that most American Jewish scholars have been intent on explaining Jewish economic and political behavior through ostensible continuities between pre-immigration culture and post-immigration ethnicity? The contrast between this and the altogether different approach taken by contemporary Anglo-Jewish historians to the interplay of heritage, ethnicity, and class shows that historiography, like history, is very much culture-specific and environmentally shaped. It is in their estimation of the centrality of class status to the Jewish narrative that recent Anglo-Jewish historians most clearly demonstrate their Englishness and offer a mirror image of the American Jewish historiography of post-immigration ethnicity and identity.[65]

Younger Anglo-Jewish historians, in particular, present a picture of immigrants being constrained and levered into "Englishness" by an overbearing Jewish communal and philanthropic bureaucracy. For them there was no easy segue from old-country "middle class" values to the social and cultural conventions of their new home, but rather a rude introduction to the pecking order of the British class system, brokered (or enforced) by their Jewish benefactors, who used class privilege and economic pressure to promote a forced-pace course of anglicization.[66]

Even though "uptown" paternalism and elite-sponsored acculturation campaigns are also well-known themes in the American historiography of the mass immigration period, the somewhat hackneyed terms of the cultural conflict between "uptown" and "downtown" have long been subordinated to wider questions of immigrant integration, and in any case are generally not presented in terms of coercive power or "social control."[67]

This historiographical difference is evidently rooted, to some extent, in the difference in historical experience itself. In the English case, the Jewish community grew from some 60,000 in 1880 to about 300,000 in 1914—a five-to-one ratio of growth (some of which may be attributed to natural increase, and some to the considerable presence of transmigrants en route to America or South Africa, who did not get the chance to develop strong communal roots in the country).[68] In the American case, by contrast, the newcomers outnumbered the established community ten to one, creating a megacommunity that numbered some 3.3 million in 1918, and their lives soon took on a social dynamic of their own.[69]

Given this difference in historical experience, one can readily account for the greater weight assigned by Anglo-Jewish historians to the role of the established Jewish community in immigrant integration; but does this adequately explain the combative, aggrieved tone that Anglo-Jewish historians achieve in writing on this subject?

In selecting the Jewish communal establishment and its class-bound ideology as the open wound in the discourse on Anglo-Jewish identity, the new historians of British Jewry remind us that the legacy of the nineteenth-century campaign to win emancipation and the subsequent desire to celebrate that status has been a strong and lasting one. That legacy is considered an obstacle to critical self-study and therefore to be eschewed, but more than that: it inspires contemporary shame and requires an active effort to dismantle and disown it.

In this connection we also need to consider the accusatory style deployed against previous generations of Anglo-Jewish historians. Contemporary historians argue that the sins of the old Jewish establishment did not end in the mass immigration era itself but continued to influence the historical (mis)representation of English Jewry in later years, which, until the advent of the 1980s, is said to have been "mired in self-effacement and apologetics." Its narrative was primarily one of progress from toleration to emancipation to integration, and it came to be seen as rather dismissive (read "snobbish"—read "class") in virtually ignoring the less illustrious, everyday lives of the East European immigrant cohort, its radicals, pacifists, women, and the poor.[70] The structure of the historical narrative was such as to invite conformity to the model of Anglo-Jewry that had achieved emancipation and thus closed the historical circle left open since the expulsion from medieval England.

Despite efforts to combat these staid and now obsolete points of view with a new, multicultural and class-conscious historiography, David Cesarani has charged, there was a lingering tendency to fall prey to a "careless usage" of the notion of "community," conjuring up a "false impression of homogeneity, shared values, and accepted sources of authority for a social collectivity in which none of these things actually obtained." Even relatively sophisticated works, he asserts, showed a "reluctance to consider class allegiances in juxtaposition with ... 'communal unity'."[71]

The younger historians' campaign against the Jewish establishment and its historical self-image of social advancement, in favor of a competing, underdog narrative, is put forward as an argument against the Jews' exclusion from Britain's new multicultural historiography, one that is pitted solidly against the more conservative "British heritage" tradition (read "white," "Christian," English, and Thatcherist)[72] and all its tradition-bound assumptions. The class perspective and intra-ethnic Kulturkampf led by the younger historians is a bid for inclusion in a left-leaning academic discourse about the "real" history of Britain[73]—a history, it should be noted, in which Jews participate actively by virtue of their immigration and their labor, which invokes a far more acceptable (perhaps even heroic) heritage than that of supplicants seeking emancipation.

This critical historiographical trend is not entirely accepted— and not merely among apologists for the "old regime." There are those who criticize the modus operandi of British Jewish philanthropists but would still query the monochromatic depiction of the Anglo-Jewish establishment as the "villains of the piece," and who note the "irony that in comparative studies of race relations in Britain the notion of Jews as sponsors is held up as a useful example in the discussion of how immigrants can be assisted to become accepted by society."[74]

More pertinent to our discussion, however, is Lloyd Gartner's dissent from the growing influence of "class" over "ethnicity" in the newer Anglo-Jewish labor history. The American-born scholar is widely credited with opening a new era of Anglo-Jewish historiography with his pioneering 1960 study of East European Jewish immigrants in England. Yet, he felt constrained to remind his younger colleagues, "Worker is not some indivisible ... ontological category. Culture, upbringing, and much else determine what sort of worker a man or woman will be. Being a Jew is one of those determinants." He went on to argue that, "To claim, as some appear to do, that the Anglo-Jewish community diverted the immigrants from proletarian class consciousness, ascribes far too much power to the men who ran the community."[75] Clearly, Gartner was bringing his American Jewish perspective to bear, not just in seeking to reduce the image of an all-powerful Jewish upper class to more moderate proportions—in line, perhaps, with its American "uptown" counterpart—but also in privileging cultural and ethnic background and values over class-based issues.[76]

American scholars of Jewish immigration, as already noted, have largely replaced an older anxiety of status (which still animates Anglo-Jewish history) with a survival anxiety, constantly probing the effects of Americanization on the coherence and viability of the Jews' culture, religion, and way of life.[77] Even when they ostensibly address issues of status—as the new gender studies certainly appear to do—they often merge this with issues of "identity."[78]

If a rationale of group self-definition is the holy grail of American Jewish historiography, it makes sense to see this (at least in part) as reflecting the absence of a defining moment for American Jewry as a national community, akin to the English emancipation, and the consequent structuring of its metanarrative on successive cycles of immigration and integration, each lasting several generations, and each producing its own (successively larger) social elites. Thus, American Jews and their historians continue to develop a more open-ended and dynamic relation with the rest of American society and American history. To be bound to a narrative of class and status conflicts would be to go against the logic of this fluid, mobile experience; yet the quest for identity markers ought not to predetermine a one-sided preference for heritage-transfer theories.

Cultural stability and religious coherence were not the Jews' strong suits in late nineteenth century Europe, even Eastern Europe, and we must expect that transcontinental migration put a premium on further adjustment and adaptation. This proved to be true in the realm of religion, which is always the area of the most pronounced cultural conservatism; how much more so might this apply to other spheres of life (the economic and the political, for example)? There is reason, as more recent scholars have argued, to be skeptical about the notion that Jewish culture and values were readily or linearly transplanted from Eastern Europe to the American context—the disparity in basic conditions of life being so vast and the social and cultural dislocation occasioned by immigration being so significant.[79] And there is sufficient reason to view the values-consistency or cultural-transfer theory as an expression of the anxiety of identity that exists at the core of post-war American Jewish life.

How, then, might we better go about accounting for Jewish economic and political exceptionalism in American society?

I suggest that motivation for change, rather than habitual or culturally transferred values, offers the best avenue for exploring these issues. If we take a leaf from the Anglo-Jewish historians' notebook and look at status rather than culture, we may find ourselves closer to the roots of Jewish exceptionalism. We need to put ourselves back in the era before World War II in order to recall the status anxiety that plagued American Jews, and to then see both capitalist achievement and political liberalism as alternative (perhaps even complementary) strategies of acculturation.

America offered equality of opportunity, in principle as well as in practice, for many; but its social order erected barriers to that equality, for many others. In adopting the American ethos of self-reliance and capitalist enterprise, Jews were responding to what seemed most attractive and most attainable in the American dream, in comparison with their Old-World condition. In adopting the American passion for justice, Jews were responding to what was still missing, or not working, in the American dream. When we recall that Jewishness was a social handicap, not a cultural asset of particular worth in American terms, we begin to come to grips with the powerful motives that drove Jews to fight their way up and out, toward grasping that dream. They were not reenacting or transplanting the culture of their ancestors. It was change, not continuity, that allowed them to live more comfortably as Americans.

Could not such motivation for change be found in most if not all of America's immigrant and minority groups? The answer here would surely be affirmative, because immigration itself indicates a desire for change. Why, then, the disparities between Jews and other Americans, particularly after the initial years of immigration, if motives and social environments have been similar?

That, in a nutshell, was the question that Thomas Kessner asked in his comparative study of Italian and Jewish immigrant mobility in New York. Kessner was careful to hedge his hypothesis about relative Jewish success, placing great emphasis on structural and objective socioeconomic factors—such as rates of return migration, entry-level positions in the industrial economy, urban background, and particular industrial skills—while reserving the option to cite cultural values as an added element of explanation (though he argues that this came into play mostly with regard to the second generation, not the immigrants themselves).[80] It is significant in this regard that even Kessner, when resorting to a more speculative use of the ethnicity/values argument, does not tie the disparity between the two groups to one specific cultural "imprint" but rather cites the relative unwillingness among Italian immigrant families to "trade in their ties with the past."[81]

The Jews, then, were endowed with a rather distinctive freedom to *choose* to adapt, so that they were simply faster in their Americanization than others. The discontinuity between Old World and New World was embraced, not resisted. Other groups arrived in America and experienced culture shock, but they were aided by the stabilizing props of an officially constituted church parish, authoritative clergy, parochial schools, a patriarchal family structure, and a relatively high degree of two-way traffic between old home and new. Jews had to do without most if not all of these. Their motivation for change was matched by far fewer inhibiting social restraints.

The American scholar Daniel Boorstin once observed that most of the characteristics of American culture are at variance with those embedded in traditional Jewish culture. The recognition that pre-immigration Jewish culture and the values of American culture were quite different and ought to be kept conceptually distinct does not preempt in any way the exploration and development of an authentic Jewish identity in America. Rather, as Boorstin proposed, it is the existence of just that tension, rather than an ostensible mutuality, between the Jews and America, that creates the potential for a fruitful encounter. "To overlook the distinctions in favor of the supposed similarities or identities of the Jewish and the American experiences," therefore, would be a profound error: "This is ... not to say that American Jews are any less Americans because they are Jews, but that if they would accept their double inheritance they must also accept the burden of an inner tension."[82]

Notes

1. The epigraph is quoted by Daniel J. Boorstin, "A Dialogue of Two Histories: 'Jewish Contributions to America' in a New Light," *Commentary*,
October 1949, 311. The source is Poe's review of *The Poets and Poetry of
America* by Rufus W. Griswold, published in the *Boston Miscellany*, November 1842. It may be found in *Edgar Allan Poe, Essays and Reviews*, compiled
and annotated by G. R. Thompson (New York: Literary Classics of
America/Viking Press; Cambridge: Cambridge University Press, 1984),
1:549.
2. Russian "Hebrews" employed in manufacturing in 1909, some 57 percent
of whom had lived in the United States five years or more, earned an average weekly wage of $12.71, a bit less than Finns. Jewish immigrants who
had come from countries other than Russia (these would include Romania, Hungary, and Austria, for example), almost three-quarters of whom
had been living in America five years or more, and thus were better established than the "Russians," were earning commensurately more than the
Russian Jews.

    At the time, Irish immigrant workers, over 90 percent of whom were
resident in the country five years or more, were earning $13.01. German
workers, 86 percent of whom were five or more years in America, earned
a bit more: $13.63; while Swedes and Norwegians (with 87.4 and 79.3
percent in the five years or more category, respectively) were earning top
dollar: $15.36 for Swedes and $15.28 for Norwegians. The average weekly
wage for native-born American mining and manufacturing workers, all of
whom spoke English and 98.2 percent of whom were literate, was $14.37
per week.

    At the lower end of the wage scale stood Slovaks, 60 percent of whom
were in the five years or more category, but who earned less than Jews
($11.95), as did Poles (54 percent veteran residents, with earnings averaging
$11.06) and south Italians (47.8 percent veteran residents, with a weekly
wage of only $9.61). See U.S. Immigration Commission, *Report* (Washing-
ton, D.C.: Government Printing Office, 1911), 1: 367, 474, 439, 352, as
compiled and presented in Robert Higgs, *The Transformation of the American
Economy, 1865–1914: An Essay in Interpretation* (New York: Wiley, 1971),
116–18 (table 5.2). Cf. Arcadius Kahan, "Economic Opportunities and
Some Pilgrims' Progress," in *Essays in Jewish Social and Economic History*, ed.
Roger Weiss (Chicago: University of Chicago Press, 1986), 113, who
notes that the weekly wage for the majority of East European Jews in New

York City twenty years earlier (1890) was $10.13 for males and $5.80 for females.

3. For the Boston data, see Stephen Thernstrom, *The Other Bostonians: Poverty and Progress in the American Metropolis, 1880–1970* (Cambridge: Harvard University Press, 1973), 151, also cited in Arthur A. Goren, "Freedom and Its Limitations: The Jewish Immigrant Experience," *The Annual Sol Feinstone Lecture* (Philadelphia: Gratz College, 1979), 6. For the New York City data, see Nathan Glazer, "The American Jew and the Attainment of Middle-Class Rank: Some Trends and Explanations," in *The Jews: Social Patterns of an American Group*, ed. Marshall Sklare (New York: Free Press, 1958), 141. For data on Jews in other American cities in the 1930s, see *Jewish Population Studies*, Jewish Social Studies Publications 3, ed. Sophia M. Robison with Joshua Starr (New York: Conference on Jewish Relations, 1943), and cf. Nathan Goldberg, *Occupational Patterns of American Jewry* (New York: Jewish Teachers Seminary and Peoples' University Press, 1947).

4. Seymour Martin Lipset, "The Political Profile of American Jewry," in *Terms of Survival: The Jewish World Since 1945*, ed. Robert Wistrich (London: Routledge, 1995), 150.

5. William Darity Jr., David K. Guilkey, and William Winfrey, "Explaining Differences in Economic Performance among Racial and Ethnic Groups in the USA," *American Journal of Economics and Sociology* 55 (1996): 413; cf. Barry Chiswick, "The Earnings and Human Capital of American Jews," *Journal of Human Resources* 18 (1983): 313, 321–24.

6. Milton Friedman, "Capitalism and the Jews: Confronting a Paradox," *Encounter*, June 1984, 74.

7. Vol. 66, no. 2 (December 1976).

8. On Jewish political conservatism, see Arthur A. Goren, "The Conservative Politics of the Orthodox Press," in *The Politics and Public Culture of American Jews* (Bloomington: Indiana University Press, 1999), 100–109; Stephen D. Isaacs, *Jews and American Politics* (Garden City, N.Y.: Doubleday, 1974); Jonathan D. Sarna, "American Jewish Political Conservatism in Historical Perspective," *American Jewish History* 87 (1999): 113–22; and Murray Friedman, "Opening the Discussion of American Jewish Conservatism," *American Jewish History* 87 (1999)" 101–12.

Interesting light is shed on the in-group "consensus-building" character of Jewish liberalism and the correspondingly noninstitutionalized and oppositional aspect of Jewish conservatism by a series of studies by Laurence A. Kotler-Berkowitz comparing political convictions among Jewish organizational leaders and the lay Jewish public: "The Politics of American Jews: Cohesion, Division, and Representation at the Institutional Level," *Jewish Political Studies Review* 12 (2000): 21–54; "Political Diversification and Division in the American Jewish Community: The Effect on Consensus Building and Jewish Advocacy," *Journal of Jewish Communal Service* 71 (1995): 266–74; "Ethnic Cohesion and Division Among American Jews: The Role of Mass-level and Organizational Politics," *Ethnic and Racial Studies* 20 (1997): 797–829. Cf. Jonathan D. Sarna's illuminating essay on Jewish continuity and discontinuity, in which this conservative-leaning scholar extols the virtues of communal dissidence and multiform cultural and religious expression as against knee-jerk communal consensus: אתגרים מבניים להמשכיות היהודית (Structural challenges to Jewish continuity), *Gesher,* summer 1994, 31–35.

9. Milton Freidman, *Capitalism and Freedom* (Chicago: University of Chicago Press, 1956); cf. Louis Hartz, *The Liberal Tradition in America* (New York; Harcourt, Brace, 1955); Herbert McClosky and John Zaller, *The American Ethos: Public Attitudes toward Capitalism and Democracy* (Cambridge: Harvard University Press, 1984), chaps. 1–2; Michael Novak, *The Spirit of Democratic Capitalism* (New York: American Enterprise Institute/Simon and Schuster, 1982).

10. For a useful discussion of the terms of American liberalism and its reception among American Jews, see Henry L. Feingold, "From Equality to Liberty: The Changing Political Culture of American Jews," in *The Americanization of the Jews*, ed. Robert M. Seltzer and Norman J. Cohen (New York: New York University Press, 1995), 97–118; cf. Lipset, "Political Profile," 151–64; Steven M. Cohen, *The Dimensions of Jewish Liberalism* (New York: American Jewish Committee, 1989).

11. Ben Halpern, in an essay from the early 1970s, recalled that Jewish liberalism was less a mark of successful Americanization, in the institutional sense of political integration, and more a mark of abiding group distinction (יהדות ואמריקאיות) [Jewishness and Americanism], in נדודי עמים והגירה בתולדות ישראל ובתולדות העמים [Migratory nations and immigration in Jewish and world history], הרצאות בכנס העיון בהסטוריה [Historical Studies Seminar Papers] [Jerusalem: Israel Historical Society, 1973], 296–97).

12. For some crosscultural studies, see Paula E. Hyman, *Gender and Assimilation in Modern Jewish History: The Roles and Representation of Women* (Seattle: University of Washington Press, 1995); Selma Berrol, *East Side/East End: Eastern European Jews in London and New York, 1870–1920* (Westport, Conn.: Praeger, 1994); Nancy Green, "The Modern Jewish Diaspora: East

European Jews in London, Paris, and New York," in *Comparing Jewish Societies*, ed. Todd Endelman (Ann Arbor: University of Michigan Press, 1997).

13. See, e.g., Lawrence H. Fuchs, *The Political Behavior of American Jews* (Glencoe, Ill.: Free Press, 1956); Michael Walzer, "Liberalism and the Jews: Historical Affinities," *Studies in Contemporary Jewry* 11 (1995): 3–10. Cf. Charles S. Liebman and Steven M. Cohen, who stress that Jews' liberalism is a function of their class embeddedness ("American Jewish Liberalism: Unraveling the Strands," *Public Opinion Quarterly* 61 (1997): 405–30; and cf. Edward C. Banfield and James Q. Wilson, "Public-Regardingness as a Value Premise in Voting Behavior," *American Political Science Review* 58 (1964): 876–87.

14. This last position is upheld most recently by Marc Dollinger, *Quest for Inclusion: Jews and Liberalism in Modern America* (Princeton: Princeton University Press, 2000). Cf. Leonard Fein, *Where Are We? The Inner Life of America's Jews* (New York: Harper and Row, 1988), esp. chaps. 11–12. A somewhat different thesis, articulated by Benjamin Ginsburg, has it that Jewish liberalism in America is but a modern example of the Jews' historical "fatal embrace of the state," to which Jews were driven by the antisemitic pressure of the old-line social elite and corporate business elements in the late nineteenth and early twentieth centuries. The liberal "embrace" of the state served Jews as a means to advance to a more favorable social position, under the aegis of the government. Ultimately, this argument regards Jewish political behavior as rooted in a Jewish political tradition, though it is a negative, reactive tradition (Benjamin Ginsburg, *The Fatal Embrace of the State* [Chicago: University of Chicago Press, 1993], esp. chaps. 1–3).

15. Jennifer L. Hochschild reports that between the mid 1930s and the mid 1970s—a period that corresponds historically to American Jews' definitive entry into the middle and upper middle class—there was a redistribution of income that favored the middle and upper middle classes, mainly at the expense of those in the top 20 percent, measured by income. Thus, in 1935–36, the highest 20 percent received 51.7 percent of aggregate income earned in the United States, but in 1977 held only a 43.8 percent share. Those in the next lower 20 percent increased their relative share of the wealth from 20.9 percent in 1935–36 to 24.7 percent in 1977. In the next lower 20 percent, there was also an increase, from 14.1 percent to 16.9 percent. Policies favoring economic redistribution appear to have had a role in strengthening those middle and upper middle brackets.

Citing other research, Hochschild also reminds us that from the 1940s to the late 1970s, under social policies that must be defined as "liberal," there occurred "an increase in the educational attainment of the population, a reduction in the differential between white and non-white family incomes, an increase in governmental transfer payments, an increase in the share of national income received by labor through wages and other compensation, and a decline in the share of national income received by capital in the form of corporate profits and interest." Although Hochschild argues that equality did not "trickle down" to those in the lowest 40 percent bracket, for our purposes here the data appear to indicate that liberal policies (such as those favored by Jewish voters) and a better deal for the salaried middle and upper middle classes (in which the Jews were solidly situated) went hand in hand. See Jennifer L. Hochschild, *What's Fair? American Beliefs about Distributive Justice* (Cambridge: Harvard University Press, 1981), 3–4.

16. McClosky and Zaller, *American Ethos*, 9–16. The "elites" in question are defined as, "citizens who join political organizations, work for the adoption of legislation and other public policies, or participate in the campaigns for the election of candidates. [The category] would include judges, lawmakers, local officials, newspaper editors, party activists, and leaders of civic organizations ... [as well as] leaders in the fields of education, business, labor, law enforcement, civil rights, political and social reform, fraternal organizations. ... The American elite, in sum, is a highly open and permeable body of people active in roles that influence public opinion and shape public affairs" (13). Jewish Americans fit many of these categories.

Among the data in the McClosky and Zaller study that are suggestive are their findings that "influentials" are more apt than the general public to agree with the statement "It doesn't matter to me what church a man belongs to, or whether or not he belongs to a church at all," as well as more apt to say that "the United States was meant to be 'a country made up of many races, religions, and nationalities'" and express vehement disagreement with the proposition that America was meant to be "a Christian nation" (see table 2-1, p. 24). The "influentials" are half as likely as the general public to agree that "religion can still answer most of today's problems," and almost half of the "influentials" say that they are "not at all" or "not very religious" (table 2-3, p. 26). The "influentials" are three times more likely than the general public to oppose prayer in public schools (table 2-5, p. 31) and rate tolerance for all religions as "extremely important" to a considerably higher degree than even those in the general public whose sophistication is rated "high" (table 2-6, p. 32).

17. Kenneth D. Wald, *Religion and Politics in the United States* (Bombay: Popular Prakashan/Congressional Quarterly, 1992), 96: "Because of a strong collective memory of persecution, it has been claimed, Jews tend to think of themselves not as part of the established elite, but rather as a group on the margin of society, defensive and vulnerable. ... Hence, Jews make common cause with other subordinate groups in clear defiance of their immediate economic interests." Cf. Michael Alexander, *Jazz Age Jews* (Princeton: Princeton University Press, 2001).

18. See n. 13 above, as well as Gerald Sorin, *The Prophetic Minority: American Jewish Immigrant Radicals, 1880–1920* (Bloomington: Indiana University Press, 1985). Adam M. Weisberger, *The Jewish Ethic and the Spirit of Socialism* (Frankfurt: Peter Lang, 1997) offers a comparative look at Jews in Imperial Germany.

19. Simon Kuznets, "Economic Structure and Life of the Jews," in *The Jews: Their History, Culture, and Religion*, ed. Louis Finkelstein, 2nd ed. (Philadelphia: Jewish Publication Society, 1966), 2:1622.

20. Robert A. Park, *Race and Culture* (Glencoe, Ill.: Free Press, 1950), 354–55.

21. Nathan Reich, "The Role of the Jews in the American Economy," *YIVO Annual of Jewish Social Science* 5 (1950): 201.

22. Weber himself, of course, did not view the Jews as economic Calvinists *avant la lettre*, but rather defined Jewish "rationalism" as traditionalist and conservative in orientation and social effect (see Gary Abraham, "Max Weber on 'Jewish Rationalism' and the Jewish Question," *Politics, Culture and Society* 1 [1988]: 358–91; cf. Edna Bonacich, "Middlemen Minorities and Advanced Capitalism," *Ethnic Groups* 2 [1980]: 213–14).

23. Glazer, "Attainment of Middle-Class Rank," 143–44. Glazer's view here will strike the reader as somewhat contradictory to another statement he wrote, at about the same time, regarding Jews, modernism, capitalism, and religion (in his *American Judaism* [Chicago: University of Chicago Press, 1957], 10):

> [Significant numbers of people] no longer live for salvation, no matter how defined, but for life on this earth, in this world, interpreted in purely non-religious terms. There are Jewish thinkers fond of pointing to the fact that Judaism has always emphasized this life rather than the life beyond the grave, as if to suggest that this puts Judaism in a better position than Christianity in the modern world. But in so doing they deceive themselves. Judaism governed all the minutiae of life, not to enhance it in the way in which

contemporary men wish to enhance it, but to fulfill the word of God. ... Judaism is as badly off [in conditions of secular modernity] as any other religion.

24. Robin M. Williams, Jr., "Changes in Value Orientation," in Charles Herbert Stember et al., *Jews in the Mind of America* (New York: American Jewish Committee/Basic Books, 1966), 345.

25. Milton R. Konvitz, "Judaism and the Pursuit of Happiness," *The Menorah Journal* 49 (Autumn–Winter, 1962): 127–28 (originally delivered as the Horace M. Kallen Lecture at the New School for Social Research).

26. Milton M. Gordon, *Assimilation in American Life: The Role of Race, Religion, and National Origins* (New York: Oxford University Press, 1964), 186–87.

27. Richard Lee Benkin, "Social and Cultural Development of Jewish Life in Eastern Europe and Specification of American Jewishness" (Ph.D. diss., University of Pennsylvania, 1976), 224.

28. Thomas Sowell, *Ethnic America: A History* (New York: Basic Books, 1981), 93–94.

29. David A. Hollinger, "Rich, Powerful, and Smart," *Jewish Quarterly Review* 94 (2004): 598.

30. Goren, "Freedom and Its Limitations," 7–9.

31. Goren, *Politics and Public Culture*, 1–3.

32. Calvin Goldscheider, "Modernization, Ethnicity and the Post-war Jewish World," in *Terms of Survival: The Jewish World Since 1945*, ed. Robert Wistrich (London: Routledge, 1995), 134–35; idem, "Self-Employment and Jewish Continuity," *Studies in Contemporary Jewry* 2 (1986): 205–7; cf. Calvin Goldscheider and Alan S. Zuckerman, *The Transformation of the Jews* (Chicago: University of Chicago Press, 1984), 183–84.

33. George Cohen, *The Jews in the Making of America*, Knights of Columbus "Racial Contributions to America" (Boston: Stratford 1924), 123.

34. See, for example, Gerald Krefetz, *The Jews and Money, The Myths and the Reality* (New Haven: Ticknor and Fields, 1982), and Joel Kotkin, *Tribes: How Race, Religion, and Identity Determine Success in the New Global Economy* (New York: Random House, 1992), 6–7, 41–51. On the Sombart controversy, see Lujo Brentano, *Der Wirtschaftende Mensch in der Geschichte* (Leipzig: Meiner 1923), chap. 11 (esp. 429–51); Salo W. Baron, "Modern Capitalism and Jewish Fate," *The Menorah Journal* 30, Summer 1942, repr. in his *History and Jewish Historians: Essays and Addresses* (Philadelphia: Jewish Publication Society, 1964), 47–49.

35. Mordechai Levin, ערכי חברה וכלכלה באידיאולוגיה של תקופת ההשכלה (Social and economic values in the ideology of the Haskalah) (Jerusalem: Mosad

Bialik, 1975), 16–18, 120–21.

36. For useful remarks on the effects of ethnic clustering and Jewish economic progress, see Kahan, "Economic Opportunities," 105–7; Ira Katznelson, "Between Separation and Disappearance: Jews on the Margins of American Liberalism," in *Paths of Emancipation: Jews, States, and Citizenship*, ed. Pierre Birnbaum and Ira Katznelson (Princeton: Princeton University Press, 1995), 190–205.

37. This line of thought is carefully argued by Ira Katznelson in "Between Separation and Disappearance." Edna Bonacich has argued that traditional middlemen minorities, upon encountering a modern capitalist society, may still prove particularly effective in the new system precisely because of in-group networks. Their adaptation to the new system and group awareness go hand in hand. See Edna Bonacich, "A Theory of Middlemen Minorities," *American Sociological Review* 38 (1973): 583–94. For a spirited discussion that links liberalism to the persistence of ethnic and community consciousness, see Will Kymlicka, *Liberalism, Community and Culture* (Oxford: Clarendon, 1989).

38. Apart from the literature to be discussed below, see esp. Kahan, "Economic Opportunities"; Sigmund Diamond, "The Recruitment and Integration of an Immigrant Labor Force: Some Problems of the American Experience," in *Migratory nations and immigration*, 125–49; Stephen Steinberg, *The Ethnic Myth: Race, Ethnicity, and Class in America* (Boston: Beacon, 1981).

39. Hutchins Hapgood, *The Spirit of the Ghetto* (New York: Funk and Wagnalls, 1902, repr. Cambridge: Harvard University Press, 1967), 29–31.

40. See Jacob Riis, *How the Other Half Lives: Studies among the Tenements of New York* (1901, repr. New York: Dover, 1971), 86; and see his comment:
    > Were the question raised who makes the most of life ... who resists most stubbornly [life's] leveling tendency—knows how to drag even the barracks upward a part of the way at least toward the ideal plane of the home—the palm must be unhesitatingly awarded the Teuton. The Italian and the poor Jew rise only by compulsion. (22)

41. Louis Wirth, "Education for Survival: The Jews," *American Journal of Sociology* 48 (1943): 682–91.

42. Ibid., 690.

43. Ibid., 683.

44. Ibid., 687–88, 690–91.

45. Baron, "Modern Capitalism," 53.

46. Ibid., 53, 54, 56.

47. I acknowledge here my debt to my colleague and former student, Dr. Amos Morris-Reich, who sensitized me to the crucial role of disciplinary paradigms in the social sciences in formulating the ways in which Jewish assimilation is approached. מִכֹּל תַּלְמִידֵי הִשְׂכַּלְתִּי. See his doctoral thesis, "Disciplinary Paradigms and Jewish Assimilation: The Jews as Object of Research in Early Formulations of Social Science" (Ph.D. diss., Hebrew University, 2004).

48. Wirth, "Education for Survival," 690.

49. Ibid., 691.

50. See, e.g., Herbert Gutman's programmatic essay "Work, Culture, and Society in Industrializing America, 1815–1919," *American Historical Review* 78 (1973): 531–88. Gutman discusses the importance of enduring cultural legacies among successive immigrant groups who shaped and reshaped the contours of the American working class.

51. Susan A. Glenn, *Daughters of the Shtetl: Life and Labor in the Immigrant Generation* (Ithaca: Cornell University Press, 1990), chaps. 1–2.

52. Ibid., 69–70, 81–82.

53. Ibid.

54. While it is true that Russian *maskilim* in the latter part of the nineteenth century began to champion the "protection" (as they put it) of women from the drudgeries of the world of work and of moneymaking, and to promote the idea of women as spiritual and emotional companion rather than practical helpmate, the crucial point would seem to be that these were ideas imported from Western culture, not indigenous to the Jewish milieu. See Levin, "Social and Economic Values," 151–53; cf. Michael Stanislawski, *For Whom Do I Toil? Judah Leib Gordon and the Crisis of Russian Jewry* (New York: Oxford University Press, 1988), 28, 125–28.

55. Hadassa Kosak, *Cultures of Opposition: Jewish Immigrant Workers, New York City, 1881–1905* (Albany: State University of New York Press, 2000), 4–9; cf. Ann Swidler, "Culture in Action: Symbols and Strategies," *American Sociological Review* 51 (1986): 273–86; eadem, "Cultural Power and Social Movements," in *Social Movements and Culture*, ed. Hank Johnston and Bert Klandermans (Minneapolis: University of Minnesota Press, 1995), 25–39.

56. Kosak, *Cultures of Opposition*, 4, 9, 160.

57. Andrew Godley, *Jewish Immigrant Entrepreneurship in New York and London 1880–1914* (New York: Palgrave, 2001).

58. Ibid., 106–7.

59. Godley's data are based on Jewish marriage records. He uses such informa-

tion as the use of English in signing marriage registers and the immigrant or native-born status of the brides in order to gauge roughly the exposure of immigrant Jewish journeymen to cultural assimilation. There is more than a small degree of inference involved here, but the argument is not without merit. See ibid., chap. 3.

60. Ibid., 128.

61. Ibid., 123.

62. Berrol, *East Side/East End*, 130–31.

63. Ibid., 137–38.

64. Ibid., 145–46. For a similar discussion of the role of New York's City College, and of mediating institutions in general, in Jewish immigrant mobility in America, see Sherry Gorelick, "Social Control, Social Mobility, and the Eastern European Jews: An Analysis of Public Education in New York City, 1880–1924" (Ph.D. diss., Columbia University, 1975).

65. I would like to thank the Hebrew and Jewish Studies Department of University College London for inviting me to teach a comparative course on Jewish urban histories during the fall term of 2003, which afforded me the opportunity to further acquaint myself with the recent trends in British Jewish historiography.

66. See, e.g., David Feldman, *Englishmen and Jews: Social Relations and Political Culture, 1840–1914* (New Haven: Yale University Press, 1994); Michael Rozin, *The Rich and the Poor: Jewish Philanthropy and Social Control in Nineteenth-Century London* (Brighton: Sussex Academic Press, 1999); Bill Williams, *The Making of Manchester Jewry, 1740–1875* (Manchester: Manchester University Press; New York: Holmes and Meier, 1976).

67. For example, Moses Rischin's classic work of the early 1960s, *The Promised City: New York's Jews 1870–1914* (New York: Harper and Row, 1962), already sought to nuance the so-called "Germans versus Russians" dichotomy. Further work on the matter was done by Zosa Szajkowski, "The Yahudi and the Immigrant: A Reappraisal," *American Jewish Historical Quarterly* 63 (1973): 13–44. Arthur Goren's seminal work, *New York Jews and the Quest for Community: The Kehillah Experiment, 1908–1922* (New York: Columbia University Press, 1970), almost begs to be seen as a work about "social control" but instead takes up issues of ethnic democracy and ethnic pluralism.

There are a few notable exceptions. One is Gary Edward Polster, *Inside Looking Out: The Cleveland Jewish Orphan Asylum, 1868–1924* (Kent, OH: Kent State University Press, 1990). Significantly, it deals with dependent wards of the Jewish community, rather than with the immigrant community at large. Another exception to the rule is Gorelick, "Social Control, Social Mobility, and the Eastern European Jews," which makes explicit use of the term "social control." There is, however, a "smoking gun" in Gorelick's case, which makes clear that she has deployed an ideological reading of Jewish immigrant fortunes that is much closer to the younger Anglo-Jewish historians. The dedication to Gorelick's father, at the beginning of the thesis, explicitly endorses a class-conscious approach to social history.

68. Lloyd Gartner estimated that Jewish immigrants to Britain totalled only some 120,000 in this period (to which we must add their children). In 1911, he notes, there were 106,082 "Russians and Poles" in England and Wales. See Lloyd P. Gartner, *The Jewish Immigrant in England, 1870–1914* (London: Allen and Unwin, 1960), 30, 49.

69. See *American Jewish Year Book* 21 (1919–20): 601.

70. *The Making of Modern Anglo-Jewry*, ed. David Cesarani (Oxford: Blackwell, 1990), 10; Tony Kushner, "Heritage and Ethnicity: An Introduction," in *The Jewish Heritage in British History: Englishness and Jewishness*, ed. Tony Kushner (London: Frank Cass, 1992), 13–14, 20; idem, "The End of the 'Anglo-Jewish Progress Show': Representations of the Jewish East End, 1887–1987," ibid., 78–105; David Cesarani, "Dual Heritage or Duel of Heritages? Englishness and Jewishness in the Heritage Industry," ibid., 29–41.

71. Cesarani, *Making of Modern Anglo-Jewry*, introduction, 4–5. The older impulses were not yet dead, Cesarani complained:

> In 1987, there was a good deal of interest in the possibility, ultimately unfulfilled, that the [new] Jewish Museum might be housed in Cromwell House—clearly a throwback to an earlier tradition. When Manchester Jewry organized a celebration of its bicentenary in 1988, the major event took place in the grounds of Chatsworth House—home of the Duke of Devonshire[. But, other than the duke's support of Israel,] there was no reason for the choice of location other than the desire to identify with rural, aristocratic English heritage in its classic form. (Cesarani, "Dual Heritage," 38)

72. Thatcher is mentioned disparagingly on the first page of Tony Kushner's introduction to *The Jewish Heritage in British History*, and again on the fourth page. Bear in mind that the previous Chief Rabbi, Lord Immanuel Jakobovits, was Thatcher's favorite spiritual guru. Seymour Martin Lipset reminds us, further, that Thatcher chose to represent "the most Jewish district in Britain, Finchley" (north London) ("A Unique People in an

Exceptional Country," in *American Pluralism and the Jewish Community*, ed. S. M. Lipset [New Brunswick, N.J.: Transacton, 1990)], 5).

73. The programmatic bid for inclusion is most clearly voiced in Tony Kushner's introductory essay in *The Jewish Heritage in British History*.

74. Harold Pollins, *Economic History of the Jews in England* (London: Associated University Presses for the Littman Library of Jewish Civilization; Rutherford, N.J.: Fairleigh Dickenson University Press, 1982), 141.

Similarly, the social scientist Edwin C. Black has felt compelled to defend the Jewish Board of Guardians, the quintessential expression of Anglo-Jewish upper-class philanthropy, against the new historiography, though he (along with the others) uses the term "social control" (*The Social Politics of Anglo-Jewry, 1880–1920* (Oxford: Blackwell, 1988), 102–3:

> The board could justly claim that it had helped to create a general public impression of Jews as purposeful, responsible, industrious, even moral. However demeaning conditions of assistance might have been, the Jewish Board of Guardians proved an effective institution in the tasks it had undertaken. Those in need found assistance, small traders and businessmen and apprentices were provided with opportunities. The board, by any broad scale of evaluation, succeeded.

75. Lloyd P. Gartner, "Eastern European Jewish Immigrants in England: A Quarter-Century's View," paper delivered on July 11, 1985 to the Jewish Historical Society of England, and published in *Jewish Historical Studies: Transactions of the Jewish Historical Society of England* 29 (1982–86): 303–4.

76. For a further discussion of ethnicity and class, in the Anglo-Jewish immigrant context, see David Feldman, "There Was an Englishman an Irishman and a Jew ... Immigrants and Minorities in Britain," *Historical Journal* 26 (1983): 183–96; cf. Anne J. Kershen, "Trade Unionism amongst the Jewish Tailoring Workers of London and Leeds, 1872–1915," in Cesarani, *Making of Modern Anglo-Jewry*, 34–52.

77. See, as a recent example, the comprehensive five-volume collective history, *The Jewish People in America*, ed. Henry L. Feingold (Baltimore: The Johns Hopkins University Press, 1992).

78. The inseparability of culture, class, and gender is a point argued by Paula E. Hyman, for example, in her essay, "Culture and Gender: Women in the Immigrant Jewish Community," in *The Legacy of Jewish Migration: 1881 and Its Impact*, ed. David Berger, Social Science Monographs (New York:

Columbia University Press and Brooklyn College Press, 1983), 157–67. Diane Ashton similarly meshes class and gender in *Rebecca Gratz: Women and Judaism in Antebellum America* (Detroit: Wayne State University Press, 1998). Cf. the opinion of the British scholar Lara Marks, who notes that American historians play down class or confuse class with gender and ethnicity ("Carers and Servers of the Jewish Community: The Marginalized Heritage of Jewish Women in Britain," in Kushner, *Jewish Heritage*, 108.

79. See Deborah Dash Moore's comments on the radical changes engendered by immigration, in "The Construction of Community: Jewish Migration and Ethnicity in the United States," in *The Jews of North America*, ed. Moses Rischin (Detroit: Wayne State University Press, 1987), 108, 111.

Further light on this issue is shed by comparative studies about Catholic ethnic groups, such as the study done by the ethnicity scholars Andrew M. Greeley and William C. McCready, who attempt to measure the one-to-one transferability and endurance of mother-culture values to contemporary America and find very ambiguous results:

If one begins ... with the assumption that virtually all differences that do in fact exist among ... [American] ethnic groups ... can be explained in terms of the cultural heritages whence they, or more likely their parents or grandparents came, then our search has been something less than a complete success. The majority of differences are in fact of the sort that could be predicted by ... the literature [on social values in] the ... countries of origin, but a substantial minority of the differences are exactly opposite to [these] predictions. ("The Transmission of Cultural Heritages: The Case of the Irish and Italians," in *Ethnicity: Theory and Experience*, ed. Nathan Glazer and Daniel P. Moynihan [Cambridge: Harvard University Press, 1975], 227)

80. Thomas Kessner, *The Golden Door: Italian and Jewish Immigrant Mobility in New York City 1880–1915* (New York: Oxford University Press, 1977); idem, "The Selective Filter of Ethnicity: A Half Century of Immigrant Mobility," in Berger, *The Legacy of Jewish Migration*, 169–85.

81. Kessner, "Selective Filter," 176.

82. Boorstin, "Dialogue of Two Histories," 311–16.

A JEWISH MONK?

A Legal and Ideological Analysis of the Origins of the "Who Is a Jew" Controversy in Israel

MICHAEL STANISLAWSKI

Tout commence en mystique et finit en politique.
— CHARLES PÉGUY

On July 30, 1998, Oswald Rufeisen died in the Stella Maris monastery on Mount Carmel. Three days later, he was laid to rest in the Catholic cemetery in Haifa, accompanied by prayers in Latin and Aramaic. His sole surviving relative, his brother, Aryeh of Bustan Ha–galil, said kaddish, as other mourners read from the New Testament, Isaiah, and the poetry of Hayyim Nahman Bialik.

This rather syncretic funeral made the news in Israel since Oswald Rufeisen was of course also known as Brother Daniel, the Jewish-born Carmelite friar[1] who was the plaintiff in the first and in many ways most famous "Who Is a Jew?" case to reach the Israeli Supreme Court—a case, or rather *cause célèbre*, with immense political, legal, and ideological ramifications that con-

An earlier draft of this essay was presented at the Tel Aviv University Seminar on Legal History, and I thank Prof. Assaf Likhovsky for that invitation and his and his colleagues' and students' helpful comments. Similarly, while serving as Attorney General of the State of Israel, Israel Supreme Court Justice Elyakim Rubinstein took time out from his extraordinarily busy schedule to read this essay and correct some errors. All that remain, are, of course mine alone.

tinue in many crucial ways to this moment. Reams of pages have been written about this case, from all religious and political points of view, either denouncing or, more usually, supporting the ultimate 1962 Israeli Supreme Court decision that rejected Rufeisen's claim that he was a Jew and thus had the right to immediate citizenship under the Law of Return.

Quite surprisingly, however, the vast literature on this case and on the "Who Is a Jew" controversy in general contains very little detached scholarly analysis of the Brother Daniel case from a legal, historical, or ideational perspective. Apart from its sparse, if elegant, treatment in Amnon Rubinstein's classic textbook on Israeli constitutional law[2] and the problematic polemical treatment in Avner Shaki's two-volume *Who Is a Jew in the State of Israel*,[3] I have been unable to locate any serious study of the arguments, claims, and assumptions of either the prosecutors or the judges in this fundamental episode in the history of the Jewish State. Moreover, most of the commentaries on this case, judicial or journalistic, present a factually imprecise and often distorted account of Brother Daniel's life and the chronology of his case; indeed even the justices of the Israel Supreme Court themselves erred in significant ways in recounting the facts of Rufeisen's life and his road from a small Galician village to the Carmelite monastery on Mount Carmel.

What I should like to essay here is a necessarily brief and truncated analysis of the arguments and assumptions made on all sides of the Brother Daniel case. To do so, however, I must begin with a short methodological discussion and then all too quickly summarize three background issues: Rufeisen's life story; a far less well known "Who Is a Jew" case that preceded and presaged the Brother Daniel decision in crucial ways; and finally, the political and legal context in which that decision occurred in the Israel of the late 1950s and early 1960s.

❧

First, a methodological excursion: I approach this subject as a historian, rather than as a theorist of jurisprudence contemplating the possibility of a truly "objective" mode of legal decision-making. Without taking a firm stand on the technicalities of the century-old dispute, both in America and on the Continent, between legal formalists and realists, or the more recent debates between the followers of sociological jurisprudence and critical legal studies, I proceed from the conviction that judges' decisions—like any texts—can be parsed for their ideological underpinnings and exegetical assumptions, as well as their manipulations of "facts" and "history," so long as the analyst is cognizant of, and responsible to, the specific discursive context in which these decisions were written. Already in 1921, Benjamin Cardozo, in *The Nature of the Judicial Process*, criticized lawyers and judges who take refuge in the excuse that the language of craftsmen is unintelligible to those untutored in the craft;[4] and his disciple Richard Posner has recently (and repeatedly) expanded on this alert, mounting a steady attack against the manifold ways in which lawyers, judges, and legal scholars claim exclusive guildlike jurisdiction over their turf, rejecting necessary forays from scholars in other disciplines, not to speak of the public.[5] At the same time, it is crucial to note that the task of the historian, in analyzing such texts, is not simply to point out the factual or interpretive "errors" in these decisions—an enterprise beset by its own epistemological complexities, to say the least—but to attempt, far more subtly, both to interrogate the myriad and highly complex ways in which judges' decisions are informed and conditioned, often unconsciously or only semiconsciously, by their personal, ideological, and judisprudential preconceptions, and to comprehend, as Cardozo put it, that "there are times, to speak somewhat paradoxically, when nothing less than a subjective measure will satisfy objective standards. Some relations in life impose a duty to act in accordance with the customary morality and nothing more."[6]

This general principle becomes all the more complex when it

intersects with perceptions of national interest—or, more broadly, with nationalist ideology—and hence a few words are necessary here about the complex relationship between nationalism, nationalist perceptions of history and identity, and the professional assessment of these matters. Almost from the dawn of modern nationalism, keen observers have noted that every nationalist enterprise—like all revolutionary movements and possibly all political or religious movements of any persuasion—has had to invent largely counterfactual histories of its origins and growth; these "foundation myths" always assert the inevitability and antiquity of their self-evident truths and do not admit too much complexity and contradiction in their teleological narratives. Already in the mid nineteenth century, Ernest Renan quipped that a nation is a group of people united by a mistaken view about the past; about such "inventions of tradition" and "invented communities" there is now a formidable literature, which I have learned much from but also dissent from in important ways, some of them relevant to this study. Briefly put, although it is highly important to understand that nationalist movements—all nationalist movements, Zionism included—are creations of a specific moment in European and world history; share a consistent pattern of development and growth; and reconstruct (or distort) the history of their group as ineffably and inevitably leading to the emergence and success of their nationalist enterprise—recognizing all that, it does not follow, as the regnant theory holds, that "nationalisms create nations, not vice versa." To be sure, the meaning of the terms "nation" and "people" have changed radically over the course of the last two centuries, precisely as the result of the rise and influence of nationalist movements. But as theorists of "ethno-nationalism" such as Anthony Smith have argued, contra the prevailing notion, this does not mean that terms such as "nation" or Volk" had no ethnic valence in previous centuries, meanings in some ways similar to, and connected with, their later nationalist meanings, albeit in highly complex and

hardly straightfordwardly linear ways.[7] And beyond the termino-
logical morass there lies a sociological and ideational reality—or
rather, realities—that are vastly undervalued by the school of
thought whose bible is Benedict Anderson's *Imagined Communities: Reflections on the Origin and Spread of Nationalism*—recently
and tellingly translated into Hebrew[8]—and whose warring high
priests have been Ernest Gellner and Eric Hobsbawm. Indeed,
although the case of the Jews has not yet received the sophisticated theoretical treatment it merits in this regard, suffice it here
to say, very telegraphically, that long before 1789, Jews conceived
of themselves and were conceived by others both as what we now
call a "people" and as a "religion"—a theoretical dichotomy
introduced, or at least popularized, by the Enlightenment's ontological distinction between the realms of the private and the public, the church and the state, the appropriate purviews of Caesar
and of God. Hence, pre-eighteenth-century notions of Jewish
peoplehood were very different in their essence and implications
from later retrojections, whether nationalist or anti-nationalist.
Symptomatically and symbolically, when modern Jewish nationalism was invented in the late nineteenth century, a new term had
to be coined in Hebrew to convey the notions of nationalism and
nationality—*le'umiyut*, from one of the Biblical synonyms for
nation, *le'om*, as opposed to the far more common *'am*, as in *'am
yisra'el*, the perennial "people of Israel." In modern Hebrew,
there is a clear if often unconscious distinction between the adjec-
tives *le'umi*, meaning "national," and *'amami*, meaning "popular."
Until recently, Israeli passports and other legal documents distinguished between Jews and non-Jews on the basis of their *le'om*,
not their *'am*. But equally significantly, both *le'om* and *'am* are
ancient words, used continuously through the millennia to convey something akin to, if different from, their post-1789 meanings. Modern Jewish nationalism, one might conclude, did not
invent the Jewish nation, but neither did the pre-nationalist
notion of nationhood coincide with its later meaning.[9]

This is a crucial analytic starting point for any study of the history of Zionist conceptions of Jewishness, including those propounded—or often, merely assumed but not articulated—by judges of the Israeli Supreme Court. Their decisions have often invoked both "facts" about Jewish history and assumptions about the very nature of Jewishness and Zionism that are extremely tendentious, if not simply "wrong," according to the canons of modern historicism. In the case of *Rufeisen*,[10] these preconceptions were particularly instrumental not only to the ultimate result, but to the very essence of the debate from its very start, as we shall see.

To understand the story, one must review the bare facts about Brother Daniel's life.[11] Oswald Rufeisen was born to a Jewish mother and father in Żywiec, Poland, on January 29, 1922. In 1934 he joined the Akiva Zionist movement and was active in its ranks throughout the 1930s. On September 1, 1939, he fled from the Nazis into what would soon become Soviet-occupied territory, making his way to Vilna, where he joined a *hakhsharah* collective known as Kibbutz Akiva, in which he and his brother lived from December 1939 until the Axis invasion of the Soviet Union, at which point they escaped further east. For the next year and a half, Oswald Rufeisen posed as a *Volksdeutch*, using his native German and Polish language skills to serve in various capacities as an assistant and translator to the Gestapo and S.S., in the process saving many Jews from certain death. In August 1942 his Jewishness was unmasked by a fellow Jew, and he sought refuge in the convent of the Order of the Sisters of Resurrection in the Belorussian town of Mir, famous throughout the Jewish world for its renowned yeshiva, which had recently been removed to Shanghai. In the Mir convent, Rufeisen discovered Christianity on his own, and three weeks after arriving there, on his father's birthday, he asked the Mother Superior to baptize him into the Roman Catholic faith, which she rather reluctantly agreed to do. After spending over a year in the convent, Rufeisen joined a Partisan unit, with which he fought in the forests of Byelorussia until the end of the war. Then, in June 1945, he returned to Poland and entered a Carmelite monastery, choosing this order since he knew that its headquarters were in Palestine, to which, as a Zionist, he still hoped to move. For the next seven years he studied to become a priest and was ordained in June 1952. Throughout this Jacob-like fourteen years, he maintained his heart's desire to move to the newly established State of Israel, and in the summer of 1959 finally received permission to do so both from his order and from the Polish government; in line with its standard procedures, the latter insisted that he renounce his Polish citizenship and nationality upon leaving the country, leaving him stateless.

Arriving at the port of Haifa clad in his brown monk's cassock on which hung a large cross, Brother Daniel announced to the immigration officer that he was applying for *'aliyah* under the Law of Return, since he was a Jew. The immigration official, espying the cassock-cum-crucifix-clad applicant before him, rejected Rufeisen's claim that he was a Jew and liable for immediate citizenship under the Law of Return. Hardly surprised by this result, Brother Daniel was committed to receiving public and legal sanction for his deeply held belief that he was indeed a Jew—a Jew by nationality and a Catholic by religion; this was, he claimed, totally in line with the basic Zionist redefinition of Jewishness as a nationality like all other nationalities, entirely independent of religious commitment. As a tonsured friar, however, he was not free to engage in public actions without approval from his order, and hence he applied to his superior at the Stella Maris monastery in Haifa, which he joined immediately upon his arrival in the country, for permission to take his case to the Supreme Court of Israel. Six months later he received a cable from Rome hesitantly permitting him to press his appeal, but without any financial assistance. A Carmelite nun in Haifa contacted Giorgio La Pira, the Catholic pro-Israel mayor of Florence, who supplied four thousand dollars for lawyers' costs; another eight thousand was provided by Joseph Stiassny, the superior of the Ratisbonne monastery in Jerusalem, himself a Catholic son of Jewish parents. Rufeisen had great difficulty finding lawyers willing and able to represent him, until two attorneys affiliated with the Mapam party agreed to argue his case against the Ministry of Interior.

To understand the arguments that ensued, it is helpful first to take a brief look at another case that occurred—as if the historian had planned it this way—at the very moment of Israel's birth.[12] In early 1948, a Jew named Willy and his twenty-five-year-old son, known in subsequent records only as Aleph, applied for an exit permit from Palestine. They had both immigrated to Palestine from Vienna after the *Anschluss*, and after the death of Willy's non-Jewish wife. Upon their arrival in Palestine, no one paid any heed to the fact that Aleph's mother was not Jewish; this was no time to quibble about such matters, and in any event at his birth Aleph had been registered as a Jew in the birth records of the Viennese Jewish community. After the war, however, neither father nor son wanted to remain in Palestine, and at this fateful moment between the UN partition resolution and the establishment of the State, they applied to leave the country and return to Austria. It turned out that they had never given up their Austrian citizenship and had managed to obtain new passports from the Austrian embassy in London, as well as one-way visas back to Vienna, along with the requisite Italian transit papers. Their plans were stymied, however, by the newly established military conscription bureau of Jewish Palestine, the Misrad Sherut Ha'am, which refused to issue an exit permit to Aleph on the grounds that he was obliged to present himself for military service to the soon-to-be-created Jewish State. Aleph objected that he had no intention of serving in any Jewish army; he then quit his job and went into hiding. Several months later, in late May 1948, he was located by the police and was brought to trial for draft-dodging.

In military district court, the defendant contended that since his mother was a Catholic he was not Jewish; that he was not raised as a Jew and never considered himself to be a Jew; that he had no interest in any Jewish national aspirations or in the creation of the State of Israel; and indeed that he rejected any nationalist causes whatsoever, because of his cosmopolitan point of view. In any event, he was not a Jew, either in the national or religious sense of the term, and thus was not liable for conscription into what was now the Israel Defence Force. Instead, he requested permission to leave the country for good, never to return.

The three-judge panel rejected all of Aleph's claims, finding, inter alia, that:

> The accused is a Jew according to Jewish law (*yehudi lefi dat moshe*). He is registered as a Jew in the birth records of the Jewish community of Vienna, and immigrated as a Jew to the land of Israel, where he joined the Jewish community (*knesset yisra'el*). He may not remove himself from his people by a verbal declaration that he does not feel himself to be a Jew. In no country and no nation can one remove oneself from the nation and avoid the civil obligations incumbent on every individual, unless the laws of the state permit this explicitly. According to Hebrew law (*ḥoq 'ivri*) which is in effect until this day no Jew is able to leave his nation. Even a convert remains a Jew.
>
> The accused relies on his Austrian passport and claims that he is not subject to the authority of the Jewish state. This claim is also rejected: the question before this court is not that of an Austrian citizen who came to Israel as a tourist, but of a Jew who left the Diaspora and immigrated to the Land of Israel to settle here. Such a Jew was subject first and foremost to the laws of the Jewish *yishuv* in Palestine and now to the laws of State of Israel, and its laws take precedence over any others."[13]

On this basis, Aleph was convicted and sentenced to hard

labor. He appealed this verdict, and the military appellate court reduced the sentence to six months' imprisonment and expulsion from Israel. He appealed this decision to the supreme military court, which sustained the lower court's verdict but rescinded the order of expulsion. In the event, Aleph served four months of his sentence until he was released for good behavior. He and his father then reapplied for exit visas, which were granted to them after long deliberations, and they left Israel in mid 1949, planning never to return.

A year later, Aleph applied to the Israeli consulate in Vienna for permission to return to Israel as an Israeli resident living abroad. In the space for "religion" on this request he filled in "Austrian Jew" and in the accompanying letter he expressed regret for his earlier actions, explaining that in Vienna he had joined a left-wing Zionist party, had become a believing socialist Zionist, and now wanted to return to Israel to join a kibbutz and work the land, living the ideal life of a Jew, as he put it—*hayim re'uyim leven yisra'el.*[14]

Unfortunately, available records do not tell us what subsequently happened to Aleph: we know of his case only from an inquiry sent to the major Israeli judicial journal, *Ha-Praklit*, in the early 1950s. As was obvious to the eminent jurist who deliberated on this case, the military tribunal had proclaimed that the definition of a Jew for the eminently secular purpose of military conscription ought to be adjudicated, in a Jewish state, by traditional Jewish law, even as they misrepresented that traditional law. Either the eminent judges of both the lower and the higher military courts had no true knowledge of halacha on such an elementary point as matrilinear descent, or they were in fact attempting to adjudicate the matter in accord with something akin to but not synomous with traditional Jewish law—what they referred to as either *dat Moshe* or *hoq 'ivri*, as if to underscore a putatively exclusively biblical, Palestinian, and Hebraic essence of such a legal system.

What is obvious is that the military judges reached their decision about Aleph not on the basis of any formal analysis, either of halacha or of its ostensibly secular counterpart *mishpaṭ 'ivri*, or out of a careful analysis of the legal status of persons of mixed origins under Mandatory Law. Rather, like countless judges in all legal systems before and since, they reached their decision on the basis of their own ideological and political commitments and then invoked a counterfactual rule of law in order to support such a decision. In the jargon of the profession, this was an early Israeli example of "sociological jurisprudence" rather than legal formalism. In accord with basic secular Zionist ideology, which redefined the Jews as a nation rather than a religious community, sharpened by the military and existential realities of the nascent Jewish state, the judges were convinced that Aleph was a member of the Jewish nation: he had to flee from the Nazis because he was a Jew, had been rescued as an immigrant to Zion because he was a Jew, had belonged to the *knesset yisra'el* because he was a Jew, and now was trying to shirk the most significant duty incumbent on a Jew by proclaiming that he was not a Jew! Although never the subject of great public discussion and controversy, and not to my knowledge cited as a precedent in any subsequent debate over "Who Is a Jew," this fascinating case adumbrated all of the complex and often conflicting issues—legal, historical, jurisprudential, emotional, ideological—that would emerge into the open with the Brother Daniel debate and would henceforth dominate, define, and obscure discussions of "Who Is a Jew" to this day. Most important for our purposes, this case alerts us to the fact that the highly problematic intertwining of religious and secular rhetoric in Zionist thought and policies before 1948 would now, in an independent state committed to Western principles of law, justice, and statecraft, lead to unanticipated and possibly irresoluble conceptual, legal, and constitutional dilemmas; most importantly, from the very moment of the birth of the State of Israel in 1948, ideological and practical considerations would override and almost always obliterate formal legal decision-making in the jurisprudence of "Who Is a Jew" cases.

And indeed, at the very time when Brother Daniel was applying for his exit visa from Poland, the young Jewish state was embroiled in a complex political and ideological—though not yet juridical—battle over the definition of who is a Jew, caused in part by the influx of a substantial number of non- or semi-Jewish spouses and children of Jews from Eastern Europe. The problem here was not yet the definition of Jewishness under the Law of Return, which had been passed unanimously by the Knesset in 1950 with a conscious avoidance of a definition of the word "Jew," but the application of a different, and far less significant, law: the "Statute on Registration of Residents" (*Pekudat mirsham ha-toshavim*), issued first in 1949, which ordered that all residents of Israel be registered by the state authorities according to several criteria, including "religion" (*dat*) and "nationality" (*le'om*). As is always noted in discussions of this matter, the Israeli government repeatedly insisted on such data to be inscribed on identity cards not primarily for informational purposes but for security reasons, that is, in order to distinguish easily between Jews and Arabs. In any event, given the unexpected but substantial number of immigrants to Israel from Eastern Europe who were married to non-Jews and had children either before their arrival in Israel or after, the Ministry of the Interior was faced with an interesting dilemma: What was the "nationality" of such spouses and especially of their children? In order to cope with such cases, on March 3, 1958, the Minister of the Interior, Yisrael Bar-Yehuda, of the Ahdut Haavoda party, then affiliated with Mapam, issued a directive—drafted, it seems by none other than Attorney General Haim Cohn, soon to be one of the Supreme Court justices in the Brother Daniel case—that stated that in the rubric of nationality "anyone who in all candor declares himself to be a Jew will be so registered, with no further proof required," and if parents declare their child to be a Jew, their declaration will be considered as "the legal declaration of the child himself." Moreover, the minister continued, "the registration official can take no notice of the fact that according to Jewish law (*lefi din Torah*) (when one of the parents is not a Jew) the status of the child follows the mother."[15]

Two days later, the Minister of Religious Affairs, Zerah War-haftig of the National Religious Party, announced his opposition to this registration procedure, and a cabinet crisis ensued. After fiery Knesset debates and intense negotiations, the Cabinet thought it had reached a compromise position, amending Bar-Yehuda's directive to stipulate that anyone declaring himself or his child to be a Jew would be so registered, on the condition that they not adhere to any other religion. This Government directive would later prove to be crucial to the disposition of the Brother Daniel case, but it did not satisfy the National Religious Party, which then informed Prime Minister Ben-Gurion that it could not remain in the coalition government. After frantic negotiations and further Knesset debates, a No Confidence motion supported by Herut and all other opposition parties as well as the National Religous Party was called in the Knesset, which the government survived, since the Prime Minister announced that he had convened a special Cabinet committee consisting of himself, the Minister of Justice, and the Minister of the Interior to examine the whole question.

In one of the most fascinating and understudied chapters of Israeli history, this committee made the unprecedented decision to refer the matter not to Israeli jurists but to Jewish scholars—*ḥakhmei yisra'el*—both in Israel and abroad. On October 27, 1958, the prime minister wrote a letter to fifty such scholars explaining the government's predicament and its belief that the Cabinet's solution was correct, but that it had agreed to consider "statements of opinion by Jewish scholars in Israel and abroad on this subject," and to formulate registration rules

> in keeping with the accepted tradition among all circles of Jewry, orthodox and non-orthodox of all trends, and in keeping

with the special conditions of Israel, as a sovereign Jewish state in which freedom of conscience and religion is guaranteed, and as a center for the ingathering of exiles.

It is absolutely clear from this letter than Ben-Gurion assumed that his reading of Jewish history and Israeli reality would sway his correspondents; that given the enormity and complexity of the "ingathering of the exiles," "every effort must be taken to strengthen the factors that foster cooperation and unity, and to root out as far as possible everything that makes for separation and alienation." Further, the prime minister insisted that

> the Jewish community in Israel does not resemble a Jewish community in the Diaspora. We in this country are not a minority subject to the pressure of a foreign culture, and there is no need here to fear the assimilation of Jews among non-Jews which takes place in many prosperous and free countries. On the contrary, here there are, to a slight extent, possibilities and tendencies making for the assimilation of non-Jews among the Jewish people, especially in the case of families coming from mixed marriages who settle in Israel. While mixed marriages abroad are one of the decisive factors making for complete assimilation and the abandonment of Jewry, mixed marriages among those who come here, especially from Eastern Europe, result in practice in the complete merging with the Jewish people.[16]

Unfortunately for the prime minister, the list of authorities to whom this letter was sent was vastly skewed to obtain a result contrary to that desired by Ben-Gurion and his secularist colleagues: fully half of the authorities were ordained and practicing Orthodox rabbis, often affiliated with the militantly non-Zionist Agudat Yisrael; the handful of non-Orthodox rabbis included such halachic traditionalists as Saul Lieberman, Louis Finkelstein, and

Abraham Joshua Heschel and only one prominent American Reform rabbi, Solomon Freehof. The academic experts in Jewish law and history in Israel, Europe, and America were predominantly also of a traditionalist religious bent; and even the Hebrew writers who were on Ben-Gurion's list, including S. Y. Agnon and Haim Hazaz, disagreed with him. Suffice it to say that of the forty-five experts who responded substantively to the prime minister's letter, forty-two rejected the Cabinet's decision and insisted that Israel act in accordance with traditional Jewish matrilineal law, even in regard to the legally trivial registration issue. As a result of this rebuff, Ben-Gurion abandoned his plans, and the Cabinet directive of March 1958 effectively remained in force.

It was at this moment that Oswald Rufeisen first appealed the rejection of his claim to Jewishness to the Minister of the Interior. Bar-Yehuda responded that while he personally would accept Brother Daniel's claim to be a Jew, he was bound as a minister to comply with the decision of the Government, namely the Cabinet restatement of his directive, excluding those belonging to another faith from the category of Jewishness. Soon thereafter, the elections to the Fourth Knesset on November 3, 1959, which resulted in an impressive Mapai victory, led to a Cabinet reshuffle, in which the Ministry of the Interior was handed to H. M. Schapira of the National Religious Party. According to Rufeisen's later recollections, Schapira held long talks with him and promised him immediate citizenship if he would drop the case, but Rufeisen was determined to establish a legal precedent.[17]

Unbeknownst to Rufeisen, soon thereafer, on January 1, 1960, Schapira issued a new directive on registration of the population, which further advanced the point of his view of his party, stipulating not only that "in regard to the registration of religion and nationality in the national population registry (now known as *Mirsham ha-ukhlosin*) the following will be registered as a Jew: a) anyone born to a Jewish mother and not a member of any other religion"; but also "b) anyone converted to Judaism according to traditional Jewish law (*mi she-nitgayer kehalakhah*)."[18] Remarkably, however, this directive was kept secret as an internal procedural guide within the Ministry of the Interior and apparently was neither made known to or approved by the Government or the Knesset. Indeed, in the course of the *Rufeisen* Supreme Court deliberations, two of the justices made reference to the 1958 cabinet decision on this point but failed to mention the 1960 regulations, apparently unaware of their existence!

Now, finally, the Rufeisen case was appealed to the Supreme Court, sitting as the High Court of Justice.[19] Upon this appeal, an interim order—technically called an order *nisi*—was issued against the Ministry of the Interior to show cause why Rufeisen should not receive an immigration certificate and a certificate of identity, under the Law of Return. Rufeisen's attorneys contended that the concept of nationality (*le'om*) is not synonymous with the concept of religion (*dat*) and one who is a Jew by nationality—that is, by a subjective feeling of belonging to the Jewish nation—is not required to be a Jew by religion; and that the term "Jew" in the Law of Return refers to Jewishness by nationality. To argue otherwise, they contended, would be to make Israel into a theocratic state. Second, that according to Jewish law—halacha—a convert born to a Jewish mother remains a Jew even after his conversion, as stated in the well-known talmudic dictum *yisra'el af-'al-pi she-ḥaṭa yisra'el hu* (*Sanhedrin* 44a). Third, that the Government decision on which the Minister of the Interior based his decision, defining a Jew as someone born to a Jewish mother and not belonging to another religion, was without legal justification and hence did not have legal force; and finally, that the Ministry's refusal to grant him the status of an *'oleh* and as a Jew was based on arbitrary considerations having nothing to do with the legal issue at hand and hence was itself illegal and prejudicial to the rights of the petitioner.

The Ministry of the Interior was represented by Zvi Bar-Niv, the State Attorney, who refuted the petitioner's claim that according to halacha a convert is fully regarded as a Jew after his conversion, claiming that he is only regarded as a semi-Jew (*mikzat yisra'el*) and is in fact held to be a non-Jew for purposes of inheritance, interest, and counting in a minyan. Thus, Jewishness is a status, in the legal meaning of that term, and hence both indivisible and incommensurate with belonging to another religion. "Jewishness is not a club based on feelings," he explained, and being a Jew "connotes not belonging to another religion. The attribute of a Jew is a common culture, whether you observe it or not."[20] Moreover, he added, what Brother Daniel had been and what he had done before his conversion was irrelevant: the legal issue was whether Rufeisen should be considered a Jew under the Law of Return, which he plainly was not.

Recognizing the importance of this case, for the first time in the history of Israel the Supreme Court sat as a panel of five, as opposed to the usual three, justices—Moshe Silberg, Moshe Landau, Zvi Berenson, Haim Cohn, and Eliahu Manni. This was an interesting group of jurists, combining highly diverse backgrounds, ideological commitments, and attitudes to law and specifically to the place of Jewish law in the Israeli legal system.[21] The most conservative was Moshe Silberg, a *musar*-yeshiva-trained Lithuanian who studied law at Marburg and Freiberg and was the only practicing Orthodox Jew on the Brother Daniel panel. A well-known *talmid ḥakham*, he was not affiliated with any Orthodox political party but was very vocal in his determination that Israeli law be formulated as a synthesis between Mishpat Ivri and Progressive secular jurisprudence; his appointment to the Supreme Court was opposed by the Mapam party as a whole and by Y. Bar-Yehuda in particular, for clearly ideological reasons.

At the other end of the ideological spectrum was Haim Cohn, the former Attorney General and onetime Minister of Justice, closely affiliated with Ben-Gurion since the establishment of the state. Arguably the most controversial, complex, and creative jurist in Israeli history, Cohn was born in Lubeck to the Ultra-orthodox

Carlebach family and arrived in Palestine in the late 1930s to study in the yeshiva of Rav Kook. Soon he abandoned his religious background and beliefs with great force and publicity and became a thoroughgoing secularist, and in due course the most important proponent of the separation of church and state in Israel and its leading civil libertarian. At the same time, he not only retained his expertise in traditional Jewish law but was committed to the applicability of *mishpaṭ 'ivri* in the articulation of secular Israeli law; to him, however, the conclusions of such an ostensibly "Hebraic law" did not have to follow the dictates of halacha but could be construed as the authentic voice of the Jewish legal tradition, which ought to be consulted, at the very least, in the determination of secular Israeli law. As a result, he and Silberg became archrivals on the Court, vying with each other as the Court's supreme authority on rabbinic sources.

Closest to Cohn in background and general outlook was Moshe Landau, a scion of an upper middle class German Jewish family from Danzig, educated in England and renowned in Jerusalem society as a gifted pianist imbued with love of High German culture. A judge in lower courts since 1940, he was a noted advocate of judicial restraint and the nonpoliticization of the judicial system. On the latter point he was often joined by Justice Zvi Berenson, born in Palestine and educated as well in England, who was closely aligned with the Labor Party, serving as chief of staff to Labor Minister Golda Meir before being elevated to the Court. Like so many American Supreme Court justices who surprised their political mentors by displaying independence after their appointment, Berenson often opposed the Labor party's positions while on the bench and was a severe critic of the corruption of the Israeli political system.

Finally, newest to the Court was Eliyahu Manni, born in Hebron in 1907 to a distinguished Iraqi family, raised to the Supreme Court (only a short time before the Brother Daniel appeal was filed) substantially due to the political pressure on the government to appoint a Sephardic Jew, despite his own aversion to being appointed due to his ethnic origin, or what could anachronistically be termed for reasons of affirmative action. For whatever reason, Justice Manni did not contribute any separate opinion to the *Rufeisen* decision, merely concurring with the majority.

The other four judges undoubtedly had an extraordinarily difficult task before them, given the emotional resonances of this case. First, of course, Brother Daniel was not only a Jew-turned-Catholic but both a friar and a priest. Had he been merely an ordinary convert to Christianity, his case would hardly have received such publicity and such psychological and hence political importance. Though clearly legally irrelevant, the fact that he was a priest and a monk, clad before the court and the public in cassock and cross, invariably meant that alongside him in many ways it was the Catholic Church itself, or more precisely, the history of the Church's relations with the Jews, that was summoned to trial in this case.

Moreover, the timing of this appeal was crucial to its disposition: it was first argued before the Court on March 14, 1962—precisely during the period in which the same justices were considering the appeal of the death sentence of Adolph Eichmann. (The Eichmann trial was concluded in December 1961, but the appeal of his death sentence was decided by the Supreme Court only on May 29, 1962, and two days later Eichmann was executed.) It was inevitable, then, that the *Rufeisen* case would be played out against the backdrop of the Eichmann case with its unprecedented detailing before the Israeli public of the history of antisemitism and the particulars of the mass murder of the Jews. To be sure, Oswald Rufeisen was himself not only a survivor of the Holocaust but a recognized armed resister against the Nazis; but his very decision, in the midst of the Holocaust, to convert to Catholicism for purely religious as opposed to utilitarian reasons, and moreover in the wake of the Holocaust to become a Catholic priest, was simply indigestible to an Israeli body politic reeling with the putative lessons of the Eichmann case for the formation of an Israeli Jewish identity. Symbolically and psychologically, then, Brother Daniel seemed to challenge and perhaps even to subvert any clear formulation of the boundaries not only between Jewishness as a nationality and Jewishness as a religion, but equally importantly between Jew and Gentile, between the oppressors of the Jewish people and their protectors, between the fate of the Jews under Nazism and in the long centuries of dispersion, between the Catholic Church personified by this friar in cassock and cross, and Christendom as a whole.

Thus, for virtually everyone involved, both within the courtroom and outside of it, from the start this case was mired in extraordinarily potent ideological and symbolic contradictions that threatened entirely to overwhelm what was, in purely formal and technical legal terms, two rather straightforward questions: What was the meaning of the term "Jew" in the 1950 Law of Return—did that term include a Jew by birth who had converted to Christianity but considered himself to be a Jew by nationality? and secondly, Was the Minister of the Interior correct in refusing such an immigration status and registration of Rufeisen as a Jew by nationality in the Population Register and hence in his identity papers?

Indeed, eight years later, the same five justices would sit on the panel deciding the next famous "Who Is a Jew" case—the Shalit appeal, regarding the registration of children born to a non-Jewish mother as Jews by nationality—and three of them, Berenson, Manni, and Cohn, would constitute the majority in finding against the Minister of the Interior on technical legal grounds, despite the intense emotional and political controversies swirling around that case.[22] Yet, in *Rufeisen*, only Justice Berenson insisted on keeping the deliberations focused sharply on the essential legal issues, trying to determine the meaning of the word "Jew" in the Law of Return and arguing importantly that the Minister of the Interior erred significantly in relying on the 1958 Government directive—and even he could not restrain himself from including some legally irrelevant and highly problematic historical and ideological excursions in his decision.

Moreover, as we have already seen, despite the fact that all parties involved insisted that the Law of Return and the Registration law were secular ordinances totally independent of traditional halacha, both Brother Daniel's lawyers and the State Attorney raised the issue of the halachic status of the petitioner in their arguments and thus diverted attention away from the central legal issues involved. With the halachic door opened, not only Justices Silberg and Cohn but also Justice Landau deliberated at great length over the highly complex issue of the standing of a convert in traditional Jewish law, even as all three agreed in the end that a convert did remain a Jew for all essential legal purposes—a position then debated and disputed by countless other experts in halacha outside the Court, most of whom did not understand or would never accept the irrelevance of either finding to the *Rufeisen* case. Indeed, neither Justice Silberg nor Justice Landau, who voted with the majority to deny Brother Daniel's claim, nor Justice Cohn, the lone dissenter finding in favor of Brother Daniel, believed that the halachic status of a convert had any bearing in the disposition of this case.

Equally important and technically equally immaterial, but highly crucial to the outcome of the case, was the view of the justices of the history of the relationship between the Catholic Church and the Jews through the millennia. Most vocal on this score was Justice Silberg, who declared at the very beginning of his decision that sympathy with Brother Daniel as a survivor and as one who regards himself as a Jew "must not serve as a pretext for desecration of the name of God and of the concept 'Jew' (*asur la she-tishamesh ilah le-ḥilul hashem veha-tokhen shel hamusag yehudi*)." (I must note parenthically that the Supreme Court's official English translation of this decision, issued by the Ministry of Justice, crucially omits the term *ḥilul hashem* and mistranslates this sentence as "to mislead us and to justify our profaning the concept of 'Jew' both in name and in meaning."[23]

Silberg continued:

> What Brother Daniel is asking us to do is to erase the historical and holy [not "sanctified"] significance of the word "Jew" and to deny all the spiritual values for which our people gave their lives in different periods of our long dispersion. To grant his request would dim the lustre and darken the glory of the martyrs who sanctified the Holy Name in the Middle Ages beyond recognition; our history would lose its unbroken continuity and our people begin numbering its days from the emancipation which followed the French Revolution. A sacrifice such as this no one is entitled to ask of us, even one so meritorious as the petitioner before this Court.[24]

Toward the end of the decision he returned to this theme:

> It is not my purpose here to preach religious orthodoxy [*datiut*—not "religion (in general)" as translated] nor to present any particular point of view as to the most desirable course for the future development of the Jewish people .... But there is one thing that is shared by all Jews who live in Israel save a mere handful—and that is that we do not cut ourselves off from our historic past nor deny our ancestral heritage. ... Whether he is religious, nonreligious, or anti-religous, the Jew living in Israel is bound, willingly or unwillingly, by an umbilical cord to historic Judaism from which he draws his language and its idiom, whose festivals are his own to celebrate and whose great thinkers and spiritual heroes—including those burned in Spain and killed in 1096—nourish his national pride.[25]

Seemingly aware at this point of the possible inappropriateness of blaming Brother Daniel for the martyrs of the First Crusade and Spain, particularly since Brother Daniel's own parents had themselves been killed for beings Jews only twenty years earlier, Silberg tried to mute his historical reckoning with the Roman church:

> In order to avoid all mistake or misunderstanding, let me say this: we have no quarrel here with the Catholic Church, and far be it from us to identify the modern Church of John XXIII with that of the medieval Papacy. Most certainly we do not seek to hold Daniel, the convert, responsible for the sins of Nicholas or of Pablo Christiani, apostates of the thirteenth century[26]

—thus, of course, rhetorically doing precisely that.

In response, Haim Cohn's summation of the relationship between the Catholic Church and the Jews was hardly less emotionally driven:

> It is true that the history of our people throughout its dispersion is soaked with the innocent blood of thousands and tens of thousands of martyrs who were racked and tortured, slain and burnt by the Catholic Church and its retinues for their fidelity to the God of Israel. Even the recent outrages of the Nazi holocaust cannot erase the memory of earlier ones, the martyrdom of the Jewish people under the Roman empire and in the course of the Crusades, the Inquisition and the European pogroms.[27]

Continuing with a history lesson that would receive a failing grade from me—that is, it is "objectively" false, ignoring the fundamental Augustinian position on the Jews which made possible Jewish survival in Catholic lands—but, more importantly, that reflected, and I dare say still reflects, much popular Jewish thought on the matter, Justice Cohn went on:

The war of the Church against the Jews was total war, and if it could not compass their spiritual annihilation, it meant to destroy them physically. The fact that the Church was intent as it were upon the glory of the Divinity has made no difference to the Jews throughout the ages and given them no comfort.[28]

Indeed, for Haim Cohn, the lesson of this history was clear, even if it totally contradicted the dictate of history as preached by his colleague Moshe Silberg:

It is difficult not to recall those Jews who, loyal to their ancestral faith, donned the outward garb of the Christian religion [*sic*] so that they might continue to dwell in the lands beloved to them and harvest the fruit of their toils. How loudly they cried: "We are Christians, open up the gates." But had they revealed their true selves, their devotion to the religion of Israel, all gates would have been closed before them.

Times have changed and the wheel has turned full circle. There comes now to the State of Israel a man who regards Israel as his homeland and craves to find fulfillment within its borders, but his religion is Christian. Shall we therefore close the gates? Does the turning wheel of history indeed demand that we deal out measure for measure? Should the State of Israel, "based on freedom, justice, and peace as envisaged by the prophets of Israel," act toward its inhabitants and those who return as did the evil rulers of Catholic kingdoms in the past?[29]

Justice Cohn's answer was clearly No, but this was based in large measure on his own ideological predilections, as he explained:

If I have correctly understood my learned colleague Justice Silber, he is of the opinion that the historic continuity of the Jewish people from those terrible times to the present can never permit us to regard anyone as a Jew who has entered into the covenant of the Catholic Church and joined one of its orders. Although the Church has both in theory and in practice ceased to be our mortal enemy, it can no more deny its past than we can deny ours, and a Jewish Catholic will forever remain a contradiction in terms.

I myself do not postulate an "historical continuity" such as this. If history is continuous and uninterrupted from the start, this does not mean that it does not change, progress, and evolve. On the contrary, changes of times and ideas, evolutions of concepts and cultural values, and continuous improvement of ways of life and of law—all of these are in the very nature of the process of history. ...

Never has there been such a revolutionary event in the history of the Jewish people, scattered and dispersed among the nations, as the establishment of the State of Israel. ... This revolution is not merely of a political character, it renders imperative a revision of the values which we have imbibed in our long exile.[30]

Here, clearly, Justice Cohn revealed the true basis of his decision, and indeed the decisions of his colleagues, save perhaps Justice Berenson, to whom we shall return: not a decision based on an objective legal evaluation of the meaning of the word "Jew" in the Law of Return, but a subjective and overt ideological deliberation on the meaning of nationality and of Zionism. Thus only at the end of his decision did Justice Cohn come to the actual legal issues at play here, finding that in the absence of a clear definition of the term "Jew" in the Law of Return, no definition could later be deemed authoritative without legislative clarification, and that the Minister of Interior is required by law to accept a subjective definition of Jewishness as of all other information given to a Registration official.

Haim Cohn's ideologically driven decision to accept Brother Daniel as a Jew by nationality was paralleled by Justices Silberg and Landau's ideologically driven decisions not to accept Brother

Daniel as a Jew of any kind. To buttress these decisions, they—
along with the State Attorney—cited the words of prominent
scholars in the history of Zionism, ostensibly to prove the irrecon-
cilability of being a Jew by nationality and a Catholic by religion.
Following the lead of the State Attorney, Justices Landau and Silberg then proceeded to cite from a letter Theodore Herzl wrote
in September 1897 explaining to a Christian that he could not
join the Zionist movement; from several of Ahad Ha'am's essays
on the meaning of Jewish nationalism; from Arthur Ruppin's *The
Jewish Struggle for Survival*; from Yehezkel Kaufmann's *Golah ve-
Nehar* (Exile and foreignness) from Raphael Mahler's *Jewish History: Recent Times*; and from Yakov Lestchinsky's *The Jewish Dispersal*. Unfortunately, this is not the place to analyze all of these
citations, except to note that none are, as the lawyers say, on
point—none provide any guidance on the question they are summoned to enlighten, that is, whether anyone can consider himself
a Jew by nationality and a Christian by religion. All are, moreover, fraught with fundamental errors of omission, commission,
and decontextualization. The citation of Herzl's letter by the State
Attorney and the two justices is particularly intriguing, since it is,
in fact, highly misleading historically. First, there were many
Christians who belonged to and even served in important leadership roles in the Zionist movement; suffice it here to note the case
of Colonel Henry Patterson, in many ways Vladimir Jabotinsky's
closest and most responsible comrade-in-arms, who was an official
member of the Keren Ha-yesod's first delegation to the United
States in 1921 and served in other leadership roles in the Zionist
movement both before and after Jabotinsky's departure from the
World Zionist Organization. Second, there were many Zionist
thinkers who in fact argued quite clearly that non-Jews could and
should be members of the Zionist movement—Max Nordau
stands out quite blatantly as the most vociferous "father of Zionism" in this regard, and not only because his own non-Jewish wife
and daughter were indeed committed and active Zionists. Third,

Ahad Ha'am himself in no measure believed what Justice Landau—and in his more nuanced opinion, Justice Berenson—had him represent.

To be sure, Supreme Court justices, whether in Israel or the United States or anywhere else, are not professional historians, nor perhaps should we even expect them to hew to the facts when writing their opinions, as several recent experts in jurisprudential theory have argued. As usual, it is Richard Posner who has argued, in many of his books, that there is a tremendous amount of sheer hypocrisy in judicial opinion-writing, and the public should know and accept the fact that judges are just lawyers trying to give some reasonable ground for their opinions.[31]

Indeed, in *Rufeisen* Justice Berenson himself argued cogently that

> Counsel for both parties have each found support for their views in the opinions and utterances of national and spiritual leaders, historians, and scholars of repute. Speaking for myself, I do not think that these authorities can be of much assistance. Every opinion and utterance may be valid and pertinent in its own period and place, but as times and circumstance change, notions and ideas change as well.[32]

But what in fact was happening in these decisions was analytically even more fascinating: the justices were reading into these texts meanings and conclusions which were, upon any clinical examination, absent in the originals. Without entering here into the minefields of the notions of original intent or postmodernist literary theory, it is blatantly clear that all the justices in the *Rufeisen* case were following in the footsteps of the judges in the Aleph case with which I began and those of countless judges in all legal systems before and since: they reached their decisions on the basis of their own ideological and political commitments, and then invoked counterfactual rules of law and historical precedents in order to support such essentially politicized decisions. As I have already noted, one of the many ironies here is that two of these judges—Landau and Berenson—were among the most outspoken opponents of the politicization of justice and of the court system in Israel; whether they, or their colleagues Cohn, Silberg, and Manni, truly believed that the decisions they reached in this highly charged case were apolitical and based on a detached reading of the law cannot be ascertained from the sources at our disposal.

Finally, a few final words about the overarching question of the separation of church and state raised, wisely or not, by Rufeisen's attorneys: if the term "Jew" in the Law of Return was construed to refer to a Jew by religion, this would make Israel into a theocratic state. Justice Silberg dispensed with this notion summarily:

> This argument is completely unfounded and I reject it utterly. Israel is not a theocratic state because, as the present case demonstrates, the life of its citizens is regulated by law and not by religion.[33]

Justice Cohn only responded to this point obliquely, in noting that

> the traditional religious tests—both positive and negative—for determining who is a Jew are irrelevant in construing the Law of Return. Religious law does not apply in Israel, save in matters of marriage and divorce, and the boundaries and frontier which divide the law, which is binding on everyone, from religion, which is not, are the boundaries and frontiers upon which the rule of law in the State and the basic rights of its citizens depend.[34]

Later in his career, both on the bench and especially off, Haim

Cohn would himself argue most eloquently and frequently that the very application of religious law to issues of personal status, State support for religious institutions, and other admixtures of halacha and Israeli secular law was indeed violative of the separation of church and state crucial to a modern democracy. He would later campaign to have most if not all such laws rescinded, charging indeed that the threat of theocracy was very much potent in Israel. But Haim Cohn's road from Agudat Yisrael Orthodoxy to Ben-Gurion-style authoritarianism to ACLU-like civil libertarianism was not yet complete in 1962.

Finally, Justice Landau noted on this point:

> It is I think superfluous to repeat and emphasize what has already been stressed by Justice Silberg, that the question now before the court has no connection whatsoever with the question of the separation of Religion and State in regard to the constitutional structure of the latter. One need only mention in this connection the words of Herzl already cited ["we shall confine our priests to the synagogue in the same way as we shall confine our regular army to its barracks"].[35]

This was a remarkable argument in the mouth of an eminent jurist such as Moshe Landau: the extent to which religious accomodations and considerations in Israeli law constituted an infringement of the appropriate separation of church and state is dismissed not by an evaluation of actual laws and practices or constitutional theories about such a crucial issue but by a citation of a programmatic statement by Theodore Herzl in 1896. If Israeli law and practice in 1962 had in fact been based on the views of Theodore Herzl in *The Jewish State*, virtually the entire legal and state mechanism would have had to be dismantled; and of course in the real Israel of 1962, the rabbis were hardly kept in their synagogues nor was the army confined to its barracks.

In the end, then, even more than the use and abuse of History in the *Rufeisen* decision, the extraordinary absence of any sustained judicial pondering about the meaning of the separation of state and religion in a democracy, and the justices's conviction that the case before them raised no such issues, may have been the most long-lived and influential legacy of the Brother Daniel case on the Israeli polity.

Notes

1. Almost all commentators on this case refer to Brother Daniel as a monk, although, as the *Catholic Encyclopedia* (New York: Universal Knowledge Foundation, 1913, cited from http://www.newadvent.org/cathen) puts it, "the word monk is not itself a term commonly used in the official language of the Church," and certainly not for the mendicant Carmelite order, whose friars do not live a life of contemplative isolation. As we shall see, the judges of the Israeli Supreme Court erred not only in calling Brother Daniel a "monk," but in not distinguishing between his joining the order and being ordained as a priest.
2. Amnon Rubinstein, המישפט הקונסטיטוציוני של מדינת ישראל (Constitutional law in the State of Israel) (Jerusalem: Schocken, 1996), passim.
3. Avner Shaki, מיהוא יהודי בדיני מדינת ישראל (Who is a Jew in the State of Israel) (Jerusalem: Yad Hahamishah, 1977), passim.
4. Benjamin Cardozo, *The Nature of the Judicial Process* (New Haven: Yale University Press, 1921).
5. Richard Posner, *Overcoming Law* (Cambridge: Harvard University Press, 1995).
6. Cardozo, *Nature*, 109.
7. Anthony D. Smith, *National Identity* (Reno: University of Nevada Press, 1991).
8. קהיליות מדומיינות: הגיגים על מקורות הלאומיות ועל התפשטותה (Tel Aviv: The Open University, 1999).
9. All this follows from the somewhat longer theoretical analysis of this problem in my *Zionism and the Fin de Siècle* (Berkeley and Los Angeles: University of California Press, 2001).
10. Israel Supreme Court, *Oswald Rufeisen vs. The Minister of the Interior*, 62/72. I shall use the official English translation of this decision, except where there are errors in that translation, which I shall note.

11. See Nechama Tec, *In the Lion's Den* (New York: Oxford University Press, 1990), and Dieter Corbach, *Daniel: Der Mann aus der Loewengrube* (Cologne: Scriba, 1993).
12. This case is summarized in Eliezer Globus, שאלות ותשובות בדיני אישיות והמעמד האישי (Questions and answers regarding laws of personal status), *Ha-Praqlit* 10 (1954): 225–44.
13. Ibid., 226.
14. Ibid.
15. See Rubinstein, *Constitutional Law*, 109–52.
16. See translation in Oscar Kraines, *The Impossible Dilemma: Who Is a Jew in the State of Israel?* (New York: Bloch, 1976), 5–7.
17. See Tec, *Lion's Den*, 222ff.
18. Rubinstein, *Constitutional Law*, 109–52.
19. *Rufeisen*.
20. Ibid., 2435.
21. These brief biographical sketches are culled from Elyakim Rubinstein, שופטי ארץ לראשיתו ולדמותו של בית־המשפט העליון בישרול (State justices: On the beginning and character of the Israeli Supreme Court) (Jerusalem: Schocken, 1980), and Pnina Lahav, *Judgment in Jerusalem: Chief Justice Agranat and the Zionist Century* (Berekely and Los Angeles: University of California Press, 1997).
22. H.C. 1601-4/90 *Shalit et al. v. Peres et al.*, 44(3) P.D. 353.
23. *Rufeisen*, 2432.
24. Ibid.
25. *Rufeisen*, 2438.
26. Ibid.
27. Ibid., 2441.
28. Ibid.
29. Again, note the deliberately deceptive translation: "Some Catholic kingdoms of the past"?
30. *Rufeisen*, 2441–42.
31. Posner, *Overcoming Law*, passim.
32. *Rufeisen*, 2451.
33. Ibid, 2439.
34. Ibid, 2440.
35. Ibid., 2448.

THE POSTWAR SUBURBAN SYNAGOGUE IN HISTORICAL CONTEXT

JACK WERTHEIMER

I smar Schorsch has dedicated much of his historical scholarship to analyzing how modern Jewish scholars, particularly in Central Europe, searched for a usable past as they reimagined Jewish life in their own time; as chancellor of the Jewish Theological Seminary, he has engaged in a similar creative task, investing considerable energy in rethinking and revitalizing contemporary Jewish life. In his latter capacity, he has especially focused on the American synagogue, returning time and again to its historical centrality as the "bedrock institution of the total Jewish community,"[1] whose reinvigoration is critical to any program of Jewish renewal.

His chief preoccupation in this regard has been the enhancement of worship services. Addressing a convention of the United Synagogue of America (as it was then called) in 1989, he presciently and controversially urged synagogues to sponsor a multiplicity of services in order to "acknowledge and address the diversity of Jews who frequent our synagogues."[2] Subsequently, the model of concurrent *minyanim* gathered under the roof of a single synagogue has been adopted by all the movements of American Judaism and has even been trademarked under the name "Synaplex." In that same address, Ismar Schorsch argued for a reexamination of synagogue choreography and spatial arrangements, "so heavily dependent on the frontal orientation of the sanctuary."[3] This theme too is now a staple of the synagogue revitalization movement, which aims to create a more intimate setting for prayer and attends to the atmospherics of religious services in order to build a congregation of worshipers. As chancellor, he has advocated on behalf of Jews who "seek the intimacy of informal services, the challenge of textual study, the support of a religious community" and has urged synagogues to address the Jews who yearn not for "edification, but participation."[4] And he has celebrated the transformation of once rigidly formal synagogues into dynamic prayer communities: "Rapidly disappearing are the use of an organ and a highly formal service conducted by clergy in robes. ... A chorus of voices is critical of the once exclusive attention to form, calling for more intimacy and participation."[5] With these programmatic addresses, Ismar Schorsch has used his position at the helm of JTS as a bully pulpit to support and reenergize Jewish worship, joining a cadre of activists intent on renewing synagogue life.

The current phase of synagogue revitalization dates to the 1970s, when *havurah* activists and feminists alike critiqued the synagogues in which they had been raised. Infused with the *havurah* sensibility, rabbis and lay activists worked to replace formal decorum, which cast congregants as spectators; a rigid aesthetic sensibility, which excluded so much of the rich variety of Jewish life; and an indifference to the needs of individuals to express their personal prayers during religious services, which had come to be dominated by the priestlike officiation of rabbis and cantors, rather than congregational participants. Feminist critics, for their part, insisted on equal opportunities for women in all spheres of the synagogue, especially in the sanctuary. Even as these causes have come to dominate discussions of synagogue life, congregations have continued to experiment, adopting new forms of music and innovative ways of teaching Torah within the synagogue, while also reappropriating traditional methods of involving congregants in leading aspects of the religious service. By the turn of the twenty-first century, foundations and Federations had joined in efforts to boost synagogue renewal, convinced that new funding and leadership could enhance public worship and enlarge the pool of American Jews who will engage with a synagogue. It is not difficult to discern in the programs of today's synagogue renewal movement echoes of themes set forth in the speeches of Ismar Schorsch ten or fifteen years earlier.

The specific target of synagogue revitalization efforts has been a particular type of congregation that emerged after World War II—the suburban synagogue. For critics, much of what ails the contemporary synagogue can be traced to the enduring yet baneful influence of the postwar synagogue—its forbidding coldness, unyielding formality, lack of attunement to newcomers, smug self-satisfaction, and obduracy. Understandably, as the object lesson for what must change, the postwar synagogue has come to take on mythic significance in the imagination of zealous reformers. Critics, after all, require a clear target, unobstructed by complicating nuance. But from a more distanced historical perspective, the suburban postwar synagogue is a more complex—and surprising—institution.

The saga of the post–World War II synagogue has been told frequently as a tale of stunning growth and expansion, coupled with dismal results. On the one hand, new synagogues mushroomed across the landscape; on the other, Jews "seldom came to them and even more seldom identified with what was going on inside."[6] Whereas contemporaries celebrated "the flourishing state of the American Jewish community's religious bodies," later observers claimed that "the 1950s revival was more show than substance, that 'what was revived was not so much religious belief as belief in the value of religion.' "[7] "In sum," wrote another analyst of the mid-century synagogue, "the [synagogue] model for the 1950s was nonreligious religion."[8]

If nothing else, the story of the mid-century synagogue certainly is one of explosive numerical growth. In the fifteen years or so following World War II, synagogues were established in record numbers. In 1957, the Synagogue Council of America estimated a "grand total of 4200 congregations,"[9] more than double the number of estimated congregations fifty years earlier,[10] and about a thousand more than in the pre-War period.[11] The Reform movement's congregational arm grew from 290 temples in 1937 to 698 in 1970; in the same period, the Conservative movement's United Synagogue organization increased from 250 member congregations to 832 affiliates.[12] During a two-year period in the mid 1950s, in fact, 131 new congregations joined the United Synagogue and 50 affiliated with the Union of American Hebrew Congregations.[13]

This frenetic growth was fueled primarily by Jewish geographic mobility. Like their fellow Americans, Jews were on the move in the postwar era. Huge numbers abandoned urban neighborhoods, moving from the Bronx and Brooklyn in New York City to Queens and then Long Island or Westchester, from Newark to the Oranges in New Jersey, from Baltimore to the near suburb of Pikesville, from urban Roxbury in Boston to suburban Chestnut Hill and Newton, from Philadelphia and Chicago to their greener suburbs.[14] Growing numbers made their way to warmer regions of the country and settled in the beckoning "Golden Cities" of Los Angeles and Miami.[15]

In these new settings, the children and grandchildren of East European immigrants found themselves in an unfamiliar environment: no longer anchored in the Jewish, largely immigrant, neighborhoods that had nurtured them, they eagerly sought a new central address for Jewish activities on the lonely suburban frontier. As one prototypical synagogue brochure of the time put it, "The community needs a place for our children and we adults need some place to carry on our social lives. What better place can there be than our synagogue?"[16] Here in a nutshell were the dual expectations set by suburban Jews for their postwar synagogue. First, they sought an opportunity for social interaction with fellow Jews because, as one new suburbanite put it, "My real close friends, my after-dark friends, are mostly Jewish; my day-time friends are Gentile."[17] They wanted a place to socialize after work near their suburban homes. And second, they needed a proper center for their children to be socialized and educated as Jews. The following excerpts from a contemporary synagogue fundraising brochure tellingly sought to capitalize on this need:

> Are not all our dreams and hopes centered around our children? Do not wait until the moment when they will come home to us saying: It is your fault that I did not make the right friends. It is your fault that I have to spend time in places that you don't like. It is your fault that my adolescent years were guided by the wrong people. It is your fault that my love and loyalty can be shaken by the slightest wind. Let's not wait for this moment—too much is at stake. Join in a sincere effort to build a Community Center where our children will meet the right friends in dignity, be guided by the right leaders and grow up to be good Americans and Jews.[18]

One would hardly know from this fundraising spiel that religion was to play any role in such an institution, let alone that what was being promoted was a synagogue.

The priorities clearly lay elsewhere. As Lawrence Hoffman has noted astutely, synagogue "floor plans tell the tale": Suburban congregations typically built "huge school wings, but small sanctuaries."[19] Moveable partitions enabled congregations to carve out meeting room spaces and classrooms. Their primary users were children enrolled in religious school programs prior to their bar and bat mitzvah. In contrast to the early decades of the twentieth century, when Jewish schooling was often housed in communal institutions or separate educational settings, the synagogue now assumed the predominant responsibility for Jewish education. It was estimated in the late 1950s that the congregational school accounted for almost four-fifths of the students receiving a Jewish education.[20] Supplementary schools began to absorb a high percentage of synagogue budgets, a necessary investment in light of the new realities of congregational membership, namely that most people who joined synagogues did so in order to secure a Jewish education for their children.[21] In one suburban community studied intensively in this period by Marshall Sklare, "most Jews wait[ed] until their children reach[ed] school age" before joining a synagogue. Whereas "a mere 19 per cent of families in which all the children are under school age belong to a synagogue," Sklare reported, "the affiliation rate triples to 56 per cent in the early-school phase and spurts to 87 per cent when there is a child in the peak years of religious education."[22] Little wonder that congregations increasingly assumed a pediatric mission.

Simultaneously, synagogues also sought to involve adults in a range of activities. Men virtually monopolized synagogue governance in this period, particularly the realms of financial decision-making and board leadership. Women involved themselves far more as volunteers in the helping domains of the synagogue and as participants in educational programs.[23] "Synagogues, like churches," Hoffman observes, developed "a shopping list of programs for suburbanites avoiding loneliness or seeking social services like welcome wagons and book clubs. Religious schools for the children and sisterhoods for the mothers soon dominated the landscape."[24]

Surging enrollments in congregational schools and active social programming accounted for spectacular increases in synagogue membership. Although hard numbers were difficult to come by, it was estimated in the late 1950s that some 60 percent of American Jews affiliated with a synagogue and another 20 percent turned to the synagogue for specific "sacramental events in life," suggesting that "the synagogue was a matter of real concern to perhaps 4,000,000 American Jews."[25] (Surveys of local Jewish communities served as the basis for these estimates.)[26] The laments of over-extended rabbis further illustrate just how uncontrolled the membership boom had become. As one rabbi ruefully observed of his once "small congregation," "I reckoned without due consideration to the likelihood that my quiet suburban community would grow and grow and grow. It has reached such proportions that I can hardly serve all my congregants adequately. ... The congregation has grown too large—and there seems nothing that I can do about it."[27]

Even if the 60 percent figure is inflated, synagogue membership in the postwar era dwarfed rates prevalent earlier in the century. According to one estimate, fewer than a quarter of Jewish families were members of congregations in 1919; seven years later, the 1926 Census of Religious Bodies counted only one synagogue per 1309 Jews. Substantial evidence indicates even lower rates of affiliation during the Great Depression, when membership at religious congregations declined; according to the historian Jonathan Sarna, "synagogues and Jewish educational institutions suffered particularly from the economic downturn."[28] As late as 1951, Herbert Parzen estimated synagogue affiliation as hovering around 40 percent, with no more than 10 percent engaged year-round, rather than solely on the High Holidays.[29] In short, membership in synagogues during the late 1950s and early 1960s represented a high water mark compared to previous decades—and also compared to the late twentieth century.

Attendance at religious services, by contrast, failed to keep pace with membership growth. A survey conducted by the National Opinion Research Center in 1945 found that only 24 percent of Jews claimed to attend religious services at least once a month, compared to 81 percent of Catholics and 62 percent of Protestants; a mere nine percent of Jews claimed to attend once a week.[30] According to a Gallup survey conducted a decade later, the figure for once-a-week synagogue attendance rose to 18 percent, but research in local communities cast doubt on this inflated figure.[31] By 1970, the National Jewish Population Study found only 8 percent of Jewish household heads claiming to attend religious services fifty times a year or more, whereas 55 percent said they attended fewer than four times a year.[32] It is precisely the disparity between growing membership figures and the sparse attendance at worship services that evoked such scornful criticism of the mid-century synagogue even during its period of explosive growth.

The formal and stiff nature of those religious services in most congregations did not help matters. "Uniformity came to characterize American decorum," writes the anthropologist Riv-Ellen Prell. "Reform Jews, and the most acculturated and suburbanized Conservative Jews, ... thought decorum should govern how people prayed and who legislated the tone, volume, and pace of prayer. These more acculturated communities encompassed all of religious life into an aesthetic of uniformity and order."[33]

To one extent or another, synagogues across the denominational spectrum, with the exception of the Hasidic and Haredi sectors of the Orthodox community, insisted on decorous services and formality. Virtually all mid-century congregations placed a substantial social and spatial distance between congregants and synagogue officiants, such as rabbis and cantors. Across the denominational spectrum, rabbis were expected to deliver formal sermons on the Sabbath and holidays. Formal attire was de rigueur: officiants in most Conservative and Reform congregations wore black robes, and a few modern Orthodox synagogues required religious functionaries to don top hats or cutaways. Congregations of all denominations insisted on decorous services supervised by ushers. And only rarely were women permitted to serve as prayer leaders at religious services or even be present on the pulpit, even as women came to play a far more central role as volunteers in realms outside the sanctuary. Finally, virtually all congregations in this period continued to employ an Ashkenazic pronunciation of the Hebrew prayers.[34]

Still, there were important denominational variations. Reform congregations were typified by a "common aesthetic," as Lawrence Hoffman has put it: the services were primarily in English, congregants participated little if at all as prayer leaders; all prayer was recited in unison; everything was read, rather than sung or chanted; and singing was the preserve of the (mainly Gentile) choir. (Few temples even employed a cantor).[35] The ideal Reform religious service included "an inspirational sermon, organ music, and [a] choir"; [these] contributed to ... the esthetic beauty, and a certain grandeur that marked the service."[36] Late Friday night services were the weekly centerpiece of worship services, and only small minorities of members attended with any regularity.

Conservative synagogues generally employed a cantor and included congregational singing; prayers were primarily in Hebrew, albeit with some selections read in English. Of all the religious services, the so-called "late Friday evening services" tended to conform most to American (i.e. Protestant) concepts of decorum.

> This service was scheduled at an untraditional hour, after dinner on Friday evening, rather than at dusk. This was meant to facilitate attendance by a generation that could hope neither to take off early from work on Friday nor to stay home on Saturday. The service was directed to the broad membership, not just those who equated prayer with "davening." The rabbi gave a formal sermon, rather than a *devar torah*, applying Jewish insights to political, social, or cultural issues of the day. The service, lasting about an hour, featured a combination of cantorial settings and English unison or responsive readings.[37]

Some Conservative synagogues incorporated organ or piano music into the Friday evening service, and on other occasions too. Religious services on most other occasions tended to hew closely to the traditional Hebrew liturgy; and only gradually in this period was the annual Torah cycle replaced in some synagogues with the shorter triennial portions—that is, the entire Torah was read over a three-year cycle. Insofar as there was innovation, it consisted of English translations and newly composed English meditations added to the services. Still, many congregations continued to employ Orthodox prayerbooks and Torah commentaries.[38]

Orthodox services hewed closely to the traditional liturgy, contained little English, and retained the *nusaḥ ha-tefillah*, the hallowed melodies for chanting the prayers. In this era, a recently arrived wave of Holocaust-era refugees established a range of new synagogues, some Hasidic, others conforming to what has become known as a Haredi or *yeshiveshe* approach—both types striving to transplant European ways of praying onto American soil. In the Modern Orthodox sector, which at this time was dominant, rabbis delivered a formal sermon and synagogues made an effort to enforce decorum. It was not unusual in Modern Orthodox synagogues for some prayers to be read in English. In the immediate postwar era, Modern Orthodox synagogues contained a significant population of nonobservant members who attended irregularly, even as recent immigrants from Europe and Israel brought in more traditional members. Especially outside of the New York area, some Modern Orthodox and Traditional synagogues provided for mixed seating of men and women[39] and scheduled late Friday evening services to accommodate members who chose not to leave work early during the winter months when the Sabbath begins in the late afternoon on Fridays.[40]

Contemporary observers were hardly oblivious of weaknesses and contradictions in synagogue life. The periodicals of the time, in fact, contain a surprising amount of self-reflection and criticism leveled by rabbis, cantors, and lay leaders at their own institutions, and also much anguished worry that they were missing an opportunity to engage the burgeoning population of new synagogue members. Mordecai Kaplan, for one, portrayed "Jewish spiritual life in this country [as] only skin deep. Jewish life is social rather than spiritual. ... One half of Jewish identity is the product of Gentile exclusiveness and the other half is the product of Jewish association."[41] Others fretted over the sterility of contemporary religious services. "The modern temple suffers from a severe cold," observed Rabbi Abraham Joshua Heschel in the 1950s. "The services are prim, the voice is dry, the temple is clean and tidy. ... No one will cry; the words are stillborn." Harold Schulweis, a prominent West Coast rabbi, understood these remarks to be "directed against the metallic services, against the lugubrious tones of the ritual master of ceremonies intoning the Siddur [prayer book] pagination."[42]

Still others expressed deep frustration with the failings of congregational schools. By the early 1960s, less than a decade after most suburban congregations had been founded, school reformers bitingly critiqued the supplementary school: an article on "The Crisis in the Congregational School" by Max Routtenberg, a Conservative rabbi, was emblematic of the shift in mood. Writing in 1963, Routtenberg lamented the alienation of young people from synagogue services and their indifference to the siddur and chumash: "They are ill-at-ease in the synagogue, unfamiliar with the service, find the prayers irrelevant and boring, and Judaism as a whole a meaningless collection of rites and rituals."[43] Euphoria over synagogue school growth quickly waned and was replaced by self-criticism, perhaps none harsher than an assessment issued in 1958 by the American Association for Jewish Education, which concluded: "Jewish education in America is a mile wide and an inch deep."[44] Given that Jewish education in this period was mainly synagogue-based, this was a severe indictment of congregational supplementary schooling.

To understand the obstacles preventing reform, we would do well to examine the range of preoccupations that drew attention from synagogue leaders during the 1950s. What was foremost on their minds as they scrutinized the postwar synagogue? And how did they invest their energies?

The primary concern of the synagogue sector during most of the 1950s and even beyond was to cope with the explosive growth in synagogue membership—and find ways to help over-taxed personnel and facilities keep up with demands. According to one estimate at the time, an additional three thousand rabbis and educators were needed to meet current needs.[45] If anything, educational personnel were in even greater demand than rabbis. As the president of the American Association for Jewish Education lamented in 1956, "Many communities have spent ... millions of dollars to erect up-to-date school buildings. ... But what benefits can be derived from these splendid structures if there isn't an adequate supply of qualified teachers to fill these modern classrooms? Nearly every Jewish community ... is almost stymied in trying to solve these problems."[46] Moreover, synagogue professionals were acutely conscious of the need to train a cadre of lay leaders because so few of the new suburbanites knew how to run a synagogue in their new environment.[47] As they scrambled to meet these pressing immediate needs, synagogue leaders did not have the luxury of focusing on the deeper questions of engagement.

Moreover, congregations sought to address qualitative issues, for they were suddenly confronted in the postwar era by a vast population of Jews with little experience with synagogue life. Writing of the "new suburbanites of the 50's," Harry Gersh marveled at the novelty of the situation: even though "the average metropolitan Jew is not a synagogue member, ... move this average Jew to Suburbia and the chances are he'll join up."[48] Gersh quoted a rabbi who averred that "most of my new congregation are new to synagogue experience. In the city it takes an effort to become a member. You have to make a decision, go find a synagogue, walk in, and join. Usually, no one helps you, even at the last stage. So it's easier not to join. But out here it's the path of least resistance to join."[49] (Gersh also conceded that in all the joining, "there is little mention of those who come to the synagogue because this is the place where Torah lives. But they are the minority in Suburbia, as they are everywhere."[50]) These first-time synagogue members were engaged in a new suburban experiment in which synagogue participation played a central role. Needless to say, it would take them time to sort out how they wished to participate.

The emerging suburban life was rich with new possibilities. In his study of suburban Judaism, Rabbi Albert Gordon noted the remarkable transformation of Jewish life taking place before his eyes. He quoted the president of the Levittown Jewish Center expressing amazement at the growth of his congregation: "Do you realize that 90% of these people haven't been in a synagogue since they were Bar Mitzvah? And look at them now, working like beavers. I guess it's just that there's a lot we don't know, and we want to know—we're hungry for Jewish learning and Jewish life."[51] Indeed, this hunger prompted a range of experimental programs to teach Judaism to families lacking in Judaic knowledge. It also spurred new efforts to engage young people through synagogue programming. Writing about a congregation founded in the postwar years, Morris Freedman captured the spirit of experimentation:

> Almost the chief impression I carried away with me was to its air of improvisation and its great fluidity. Educational and youth directors seem to come and go; organization and content of class and group work do not always conform to the spit-and-polish standards the national organizations are trying to set. But perhaps this is just what the ... public is buying right now—grandeur in the externals, undemanding informality and trial

and error in substance. ... It is clear ... that the patterns for the future have by no means been fixed; and that what will finally emerge may show only the thinnest connection with what we see today. At any rate, a close and sober look now may offer an opportunity for those deeply concerned to help shape those patterns before the mold hardens.[52]

Whereas later critics viewed the suburban synagogue of that era as hopelessly fixed and unresponsive, contemporary observers at midcentury were struck by the improvisational quality of what was unfolding around them.

Congregations of the time experimented in a number of areas, not the least with the worship service itself. Rabbi Alvan D. Rubin, a Reform rabbi, observed in 1958: "The suburban synagogue has responded fastest in terms of the needs of Jews returning to Judaism. The services in the suburbs are neither classical Orthodox, classical Conservatism nor classical Reform. All have undergone compromises of all sorts in the suburban synagogue's drive for members."[53] Driving this self-reform, in Rubin's view, was competition: given the plethora of options in suburbia, congregations had to keep up; far more than their urban counterparts, they were surrounded by a range of newly established congregations more than eager to siphon off their membership.

Moreover, the new suburban congregations were developing a new style of prayer service, one that particularly took hold in Conservative and Orthodox congregations and only much later in Reform temples. In 1952, Max Routtenberg correctly noted the shift under way in worship services from what he called "davener-centered congregations" of the traditional stripe, in which the individual Jew was guided through his/her own prayers, and "cantor-centered" synagogues, common in the first half of the century across the spectrum, that placed the spotlight on the so-called "star cantor"and transformed congregants into spectators, to "congregation-centered" synagogues—that is, "our best efforts ...

[are] concentrated on making the congregational service as spiritually rewarding as possible," through "congregational chanting."[54] This new model would continue to evolve over the next half century. In the meantime, suburban congregations altered other aspects of their worship services, with Conservative and Reform synagogues introducing the Bat Mitzvah service, and in the case of the latter, also reappropriating the Bar Mitzvah; congregations also began to experiment with Israeli-accented Hebrew[55] and created special services to mark American holidays and honor particular segments of the congregational body—such as Sisterhood Shabbat.

Suburban congregations also engaged in a massive expansion of Jewish adult education thanks to help they received from denominational organizations and educational institutions. Orthodox schools such as Ner Israel in Baltimore and Yeshiva University invested in new adult curricula. Yeshiva, in fact, developed an arm in the 1950s to "stimulate Jewish adult studies by assisting congregations in the organization, development, and effective administration of Synagogue Adult Institutes; to provide guidance ... in the evaluation of courses; to provide ... teaching materials ... and maintain uniform standards." The Conservative movement founded the National Academy for Adult Jewish Study, which set standards for adult education and offered certificates. It also sent prominent rabbis on speaking tours to lecture in congregations across the land. And the Union of American Hebrew Congregations (UAHC) established a new department of adult education and published a series of books to serve as texts for such study.[56] It too sent rabbis to address congregations through a program called the "Jewish Cavalcade."[57] A variety of motives may have drawn members to attend these classes—to keep busy, to have an evening's diversion, to make up for an inadequate Jewish education. One contemporary observer even attributed the flourishing of synagogue Bible classes to conformism: suburban Jews could now keep up with their Christian neighbors who studied Bible in their churches.[58] Though all this is speculative, the scope and ambitiousness of these adult education efforts were unprecedented.

Congregations also received substantial advice from the three major congregational bodies of Reform, Conservative, and modern Orthodox Judaism on management techniques. Each organization developed an arm to offer practical guidance to affiliated congregations on matters such as governance and office administration, financial record-keeping, membership recruitment, and lay/professional relations. The UAHC and the United Synagogue surveyed congregations and shared data to help synagogues learn from one another. For example, the United Synagogues issued a report in 1950 based on a survey of attendance at affiliated congregations;[59] the UAHC published over a dozen reports on its own "synagogue research" and survey of temple schools.[60] They also issued sophisticated guides for affiliates that drew on corporate and church management literature current at the time.[61]

Both the national organizations and local congregations also grappled with the questions of identity and boundaries. As many hundreds of new congregations joined each of the religious movements, questions arose about standards for admission to movement organizations: What precisely does it mean to be a Conservative or Reform or Orthodox congregation? Are there any expectations of congregations that come with affiliation? The Conservative movement tackled this issue over a sustained period of the 1950s before ratifying "Standards for Synagogue Practices" in 1957. This policy required member congregations of the United Synagogue to maintain the dietary laws of Kashrut in their kitchens and to observe the Sabbath in an appropriate fashion, and in time addressed ethical issues, leading to the censure of congregations that sponsored bingo games to raise funds.[62] Orthodox organizations, by contrast, literally drew the boundary on the question of *meḥitsah*—the separation of males and females in the synagogue sanctuary. Leaders of the Orthodox Union barnstormed the country to rally support in Orthodox congregations for the retention of separate seating, and

Orthodox rabbis testified at court trials of congregations that had split over a decision to eliminate the *meḥitsah*.[63]

In the Reform movement, controversy swirled around the advisability of creating a set of standards. The issue was joined when Rabbi Maurice Eisendrath, president of the UAHC, issued a call in 1958 for the formulation of a code in order to remedy what he described as the "anarchic state of affairs" obtaining in Reform temples:

> Hats on, hats off; rabbis robed; rabbis unrobed, *avec* Atorah, *sans* Atorah; one day of Rosh ha-Shannah and two days likewise; Ashkenazic pronunciation and Sephardi likewise; kosher kitchens in Reform social halls—all this and ham and bacon too; Bar Mitzvah encouraged, Bar Mitzvah barred; confirmation at thirteen, at fourteen, at fifteen, at sixteen; on Shavuos, on the Sunday or Friday before—or after; social action stressed; social action suppressed. Some may call this the free development of the religious idea, ... but I too call it anarchy and utter chaos. Such anarchy ... bewilders, distresses, discourages the new congregants who, without seeking the authoritarianism of orthodoxy, nonetheless would like to know not only what the Lord, but what Reform Judaism, requires of them ... a guide, a standard, even that much abused word "code" —is needed.[64]

Other Reform rabbis resisted Eisendrath, arguing against the temptation to impose discipline and to create "a code or a guide of conduct."[65] Still, the UAHC explored the feasibility of devising a code.

Finally, as synagogues attracted ever-increasing populations to their membership rolls, rabbis engaged in a struggle to have a greater say in communal matters. A recurring refrain in discussions by rabbis at the time was to insist on getting their proper due from a communal—that is, federation—establishment that bypassed the rabbinate. The flashpoint in this period was the Jewish Community Center, which received federation dollars while synagogues were left to fend for themselves. But the deeper question was one of leadership: rabbis insisted that they and their synagogues deserved a greater voice in the running of Jewish life.[66]

Given this broad range of concerns, synagogue leaders understandably did not launch an all-out campaign to improve the worship service and overall ambience of the suburban synagogue in the two decades after World War II. But that hardly means they were oblivious to the problem: all they had to do was count the number of members who attended services with any regularity. And quite a few did. Indeed, the disparity between soaring membership figures and actual attendance rates was a stock motif of contemporary discussions of the synagogue.[67]

Yet even if they had the time and energy to address this challenge, contemporary synagogues were hampered by a particular conception of synagogue decorum that had to be vanquished before a serious effort at worship revitalization could be mounted. To focus specifically on the question of liturgical music, it is uncanny how similarly cantors in each of the three movements of American Judaism defined the proper role of such music: Hugo Weisgall, of the Cantors Institute at the Jewish Theological Seminary, issued a plea for synagogues to employ "a competent musician" to oversee the prayer service; he also defined "the presentation of good musical services ... as an educational venture, which might not always elicit popular approval. Should the musical taste of the congregation be below par, strenuous efforts should be made to raise the level of taste and appreciation."[68] Writing on synagogue music in the Orthodox synagogue, Arnold Rothstein insisted that the "ritual service should be decorous." Rothstein was convinced that "the Orthodox synagogue is reaching its nadir in deterioration," expressing "hope that the period of cabaret-opera-concert-like synagogue will soon be over."[69] A similar theme was echoed by a Reform colleague.[70] Across the denominational spectrum, in short, music and the nature of religious services were dominated by a particular set of formal aesthetic values. Only when these norms were modified during the last quarter of the twentieth century could synagogues seriously reconsider their prayer services.

A fair-minded appraisal of the postwar suburban synagogue must acknowledge both the rigidity of synagogue decorum, and also the dynamism and experimentation in other aspects of congregational life. The range of innovations we have surveyed hardly conforms to the stereotypical portrait of the suburban synagogue common in later accounts—any more than does the claim of the Levittown Jewish Center's president that people were eager to learn. Nor does the fixed stereotype of the mid-century synagogue take into account the slow but clear evolution in women's roles, first involving bat mitzvah girls and then adult women in the religious service. And more generally, the stereotype ignores the sheer energy and spirit of voluntarism that characterized the postwar synagogue boom—and the expansion of programming. From his comparative perspective, the historian James Hudnut-Beumler captures the spirit of the times animating synagogues and churches alike:

> Suburbanization resulted in homogeneous communities that, far from being the sterile wastelands their worst critics feared, became the locus of incredible vitality.
>
> These were times and places when and where everything was possible; veritable utopias in which death, cancer and poverty appeared to have been banished. A typical suburban church or synagogue could go years without a funeral or memorial service. On the other hand, the joyful, life-affirming rituals of baptism, first communion, confirmation, bar mitzvah and now bas mitzvah were frequently celebrated in the local houses of

worship. Moreover, ... the prospects for the future were bright: ecclesiastical budgets were ever on the rise, never in descent or tied to the declining incomes of aging and retiring members; building programs were underway (the family proud of their new split-level home would soon be attending a church equally new and worthy of pride); and the typical suburban church or synagogue had exactly what most prospective members were looking for in a religious home—people exactly like themselves.[71]

True, as Hudnut-Beumler observes, there was an insular, naive, and perhaps even self-satisfied quality to these congregations, but perhaps that was an understandable consequence of the rapid upward mobility and unexpected success attained by the new suburbanites who had grown up during the hard years of the Great Depression.

No sooner had the baby-boomer children raised in suburban congregations come of age, than they subjected their synagogues to severe criticism—bemoaning their cold impersonal atmosphere, their rigid division between functionaries and members who were expected to behave like a passive audience, their failure to provide for women's equality, their oligarchic structure of governance. Emerging in the late 1960s and early 1970s, this critique was part of the prevailing onslaught of the times against all establishments. And yet again what is remarkable is how rapidly—not how slowly—congregations responded to the criticism. Take for example, the question of women's participation. A survey conducted in 1978 concerning congregational policies regarding women's participation found that almost all Reform congregations permitted women to chant the service, as did slightly less than half of the Conservative synagogues in the national sample.[72] Women were called to the Torah in nearly all Reform temples[73] and again in roughly half of the Conservative synagogues. Women delivered sermons in almost all Reform temples, in more that three quarters of Conservative congregations, and in 7 percent of Orthodox ones. Most Reform congregations and two thirds of Conservative ones called upon women to open the ark and chant kiddush and havdala. All of this was put in place in the postwar era, and especially in the decade or so after the emergence of the so-called second wave of feminism in the late 1960s, by synagogues that continue to be depicted as static and immovable!

Congregations also innovated in other areas in the late 1960s and 1970s. In addition to being subjected to a feminist critique, the postwar synagogue was also lambasted by the new Havurah movement. A new generation insisted on greater lay participation and engagement, less "hierarchy," more involvement of women and the active presence of children. Havurah members insisted on a dramatic change in synagogue aesthetics and decorum.[74] In response to that criticism, synagogues across the land established their own Havurot in order to create settings for more intimate congregating among their members.[75] It was also a time when Reform and Conservative congregations in far larger numbers replaced the Ashkenazic pronunciation of Hebrew with an Israeli accent. And it was a time when synagogue functionaries, especially rabbis, experimented with less formal ways of behaving in their official roles.

Contrary, then, to the stereotypical presentation of the suburban congregation as impervious to change, synagogue life in the decades after World War II was in a constant state of remaking. Even before the upheavals of the 1960s, the suburban synagogue was anything but a static institution; nor were its leaders oblivious to its shortcomings. It would take a new aesthetic to replace the decorum of midcentury and new models drawn from church reformers to address the most intransigent problem of synagogue life: the difficulty modern Jews encounter when they engage in public prayer.[76] But that is an on-going challenge unlikely to be resolved any time soon.

Notes

1. Ismar Schorsch, "The Centrality of the Synagogue," in *Polarities in Balance* (NewYork: Jewish Theological Seminary, 2004), 1:98.
2. Ismar Schorsch, "A Synagogue is Not a Temple," *Conservative Judaism* (winter 1990–91), 66.
3. Ibid., 67.
4. Ismar Schorsch, "The Modern Rabbinate: Then and Now," in *Polarities in Balance*, 1:130.
5. Ismar Schorsch, "The State of Conservative Judaism at the Turn of the Millennium," address delivered on January 19, 2000, and published in *Polarities in Balance*, 1:85.
6. Samuel C. Heilman, *Portrait of American Jews: The Last Half of the 20th Century* (Seattle: University of Washington Press, 1995), 31.
7. Stephen Whitfield, cited by Jonathan Sarna, *American Judaism: A New History* (New Haven: Yale University Press, 2004), 277.
8. Lawrence A. Hoffman, "From Common Cold to Uncommon Healing," *CCAR Journal: A Reform Jewish Quarterly* 41 (spring 1994), 10.
9. Arthur Hertzberg, "Communal Affairs," *American Jewish Year Book* 59 (1958): 114.
10. Nathan Glazer, *American Judaism* (Chicago: University of Chicago Press, 1957), 12.
11. Wolfe Kelman, "The Synagogue in America," in *The Future of the Jewish Community in America*, ed. David Sidorsky, (New York: Basic Books, 1973), 157.
12. Ibid.
13. Jack Wertheimer, "Recent Trends in American Judaism," *American Jewish Year Book* 89 (1989), 65.
14. For some particularly evocative accounts of how this transplantation process affected synagogue life, see Morris Freedman, "New Jewish Community in Formation: A Conservative Center Catering to Present-Day Needs," *Commentary*, January 1955, 36–47; Lucy Dawidowicz, "Middle-Class Judaism: A Case Study," *Commentary*, June 1960, 492–503; " Paula E. Hyman, "From City to Suburb: Temple Mishkan Tefila in Boston," in *The American Synagogue: A Sanctuary Transformed*, ed. Jack Wertheimer (New York: Cambridge University Press, 1988), 185–205.
15. This process is detailed by Deborah Dash Moore, *To the Golden Cities: Pursuing the American Jewish Dream in Miami and L.A.* (New York: The Free Press, 1994).

16. Albert I. Gordon, *Jews in Suburbia* (Boston: Beacon, 1959), 98.

17. Quoted in Herbert J. Gans, "Park Forest: Birth of a Jewish Community," in *Commentary on the American Scene: Portraits of Jewish Life in America*, ed. Elliot E. Cohen. (New York: Knopf, 1953), 217.

18. Quoted by Gordon, *Jews in Suburbia*, 105–6.

19. Hoffman, "From Common Cold," 10.

20. Hertzberg, "Communal Affairs," 114.

21. On these developments, see my essay "Jewish Education in the United States: Recent Trends and Issues," *American Jewish Year Book* 99 (1999): 10–16.

22. Marshall Sklare and Joseph Greenblum, *Jewish Identity on the Suburban Frontier: A Study of Group Survival in the Open Society*, 2nd ed. (Chicago: University of Chicago Press, 1979), 181. (1st ed., 1967.)

23. In his survey of Jewish suburbia, Albert Gordon concluded that "the women of suburbia are the enthusiastic 'students' in both day and evening classes," but they "complain that they cannot get their husbands to attend formal classes" (*Jews in Suburbia*, 124–25).

24. Hoffman, "From Common Cold," 10. The disproportionate presence of women in the suburban synagogue was noted by a contemporary rabbi who worried, "Have we in suburbia been spending too much time with the women in our temple? How will Judaism be affected if we continue to tailor it to fit the needs of our female congregants; when it revolves around the anxieties of women; when we as leaders, find ourselves catering to the needs of a specific half of our congregation? Is religion in the suburbs becoming too effeminate?" (Alvan D. Rubin, "The Suburban Community," *CCAR Yearbook* 68 [1958]: 177).

25. Hertzberg, "Communal Affairs," 115. In the midwestern suburban community they named Lakeville, Sklare and Greenblum found that 83 percent were "past or present members" of synagogues, a figure that rose to 93 percent when families with children over age 18 were counted (*Jewish Identity*, 97).

26. Albert Gordon surveyed some seventy-eight local communities and correlated overall Jewish population estimates with membership figures supplied by synagogues, but his tables reflect wide fluctuations. In Burbank and Whittier, California, fewer than 35 percent affiliated, whereas in Swampscott, Massachusetts, 86 percent of the Jews were synagogue members (*Jews in Suburbia*, 248–49).

27. Ibid., 95–96. This rabbi's honest self-appraisal stands in marked contrast to the mythologizing in which many of his colleagues engaged when they

aimed to convince themselves and their congregants that their exceptional talents largely accounted for congregational growth.

28. *American Judaism*, 356–57.

29. Herbert Parzen, "Religion," *American Jewish Year Book* 52 (1951): 86–87. Parzen concluded that "synagogue attendance remained the primary problem confronting the religious leadership" (87).

30. Marshall Sklare, "The Ethnic Church and the Desire for Survival," in *The Ghetto and Beyond: Essays on Jewish Life in America*, ed. Peter I. Rose (New York: Random House, 1969), 110.

31. Hertzberg, "Communal Affairs," 118.

32. Fred Masarik and Alvin Chenkin, *Jewish Identity: Facts for Planning, National Jewish Population Study* (New York: Council of Jewish Federations, December 1974), 4. In all likelihood, women attended at a higher rate, but they generally would not have been counted as "household heads."

33. Riv-Ellen Prell, *Prayer and Community: The Havurah in American Judaism* (Detroit: Wayne State University Press, 1989), 62.

34. A worthwhile study of this period would examine when and how Israeli pronunciation of Hebrew was introduced in various types of synagogues. To the present day, the large majority of Orthodox synagogues continue to employ the Ashkenazic pronunciation, although visitors from Israel tend to read with their own accents.

35. For an ethnographic portrait of such a congregation dating as late as the 1970s, see Frida Kerner Furman, *Beyond Yiddishkeit: The Struggle for a Jewish Identity in a Reform Synagogue* (Albany: SUNY Press, 1987).

36. Jeffrey A. Summit, *The Lord's Song In A Strange Land: Music and Identity in Contemporary Jewish Worship* (New York: Oxford University Press, 2000), 63.

37. Michael Panitz, "Completing a Century: The Rabbinical Assembly since 1970," in *A Century of Commitment: One Hundred Years of the Rabbinical Assembly*, ed. Robert E. Fierstien (New York: The Rabbinical Assembly, 2000), 124–25.

38. For a more extensive discussion of changing ritual patterns in Conservative synagogues during this period, see my essay "The Conservative Synagogue," in Wertheimer, *American Synagogue*, 123–32.

39. Lawrence H. Schiffman, "When Women and Men Sat Together in American Orthodox Synagogues," *Moment*, December 1989, 40ff.

40. On the existence of Orthodox congregations in this period that had significant populations of nonobservant members, see Jeffrey S. Gurock, "From

Fluidity to Rigidity: The Religious Worlds of Conservative and Orthodox Jews in Twentieth Century America," *The David W. Belin Lecture in American Jewish Affairs*, no. 7 (University of Michigan, 1998), 27–37. See also a contemporaneous account: Charles S. Liebman, "Orthodoxy in American Jewish Life," *American Jewish Year Book* 66 (1965); see esp. pp. 30–38 on what Liebman labeled the "residual Orthodox" and the "non-observant Orthodox."

41. Jacob Neusner, "Religion," *American Jewish Year Book* 61 (1960): 57.

42. Heschel is quoted and explained in Harold W. Schulweis, "Restructuring the Synagogue," *Conservative Judaism* (summer 1973), 13.

43. Published in Max J. Routtenberg, "The Crisis in the Congregational School," *Decades of Decision* (New York: Block, 1973), 37.

44. Alexander Dushkin and Uriah Z. Engleman, *Jewish Education in the United States: Report of the Commission for the Study of Jewish Education in the United States* (New York: AAJE, 1958), p. 126.

45. Freda Imrey, "Religions," *American Jewish Year Book* 64 (1963): 146.

46. Quoted in Susan L. Rosenblum Shevitz, "Communal Responses to the Teacher Shortage in the North American Supplementary School," *Studies in Jewish Education* 3 (1988): 26.

47. This matter is directly confronted by Abraham A. Fleischman in "The Urban Jews Goes Suburban," *The Reconstructionist*, March 6, 1953, 24.

48. Harry Gersh, "The New Suburbanites of the 50's: Jewish Division," *Commentary*, March 1954, 218.

49. Ibid., 219. Similar themes are evoked in an article written by a rabbi; see Judah Cahn, "The Suburbanite," *The Reconstructionist*, April 5, 1957, 7–11.

50. Gersh, "New Suburbanites," 221.

51. Gordon, *Jews in Suburbia*, 101.

52. Morris Freedman, "New Jewish Community," 47.

53. Rubin, "Suburban Community," 177.

54. Max J. Routtenberg, "Evolving Patterns of Synagogue Ritual," in *Decades of Decision*, 18–19. This analysis appeared originally in *The Torch*, a publication of the Federation of Jewish Men's Clubs (Conservative), winter 1952.

55. The efforts of suburban congregations to rally American Jews for pro-Israel and Soviet Union rallies, and their general role in nurturing allegiance to Jewish peoplehood, is a subject worthy of separate study.

56. These new efforts are surveyed in the articles on "Religion" in the *American Jewish Year Book* for 1951 (52:92); and 1960 (61:56–59). For an extended discussion by Conservative rabbis of the growing adult education

movement in their congregations, see "New Trends in Adult Jewish Education," *Proceedings of the Rabbinical Assembly* 18 (1954), 201–28.

57. The Jewish Cavalcade was begun already in 1948. See Robert Gordis, "Religion," *American Jewish Year Book* 51 (1950): 147.

58. Julian L. Greifer, "Suburbia and Jewish Conformity," *The Reconstructionist*, March 6, 1959, 15.

59. This report was unveiled at a convention of the United Synagogue in 1950. See *United Synagogue of America: Proceedings of the Biennial Convention, Nov. 15–19, 1950* (New York, 1950).

60. Max Feder, *Synagogue Research* (New York: Commission on Synagogue Administration and National Association of Temple Administration of the UAHC, 1957–66) (these appeared as six reports). See also Alan D. Bennet, *Educational Research Survey*, nos. 1–5. (New York: Union of American Hebrew Congregations and the National Association of Temple Education, 1957–61).

61. See, for example, Irving I. Katz and Myron E. Schoen, *Successful Synagogue Administration: A Practical Guide for Synagogue Leaders*. (New York: Union of American Hebrew Congregations, 1963). For an offbeat attempt to address synagogue matters in a humorous fashion, see the collected columns of Jacob D. Schwarz, the head of the department of Synagogue Activities of the UAHC: *The Life and Letters of Montgomery Prunejuice* (New York: UAHC, 1957).

62. For the standards see the *Proceedings of the Biennial Convention of the United Synagogue* (1957), 49–52; on the debate over the permissibility of fundraising through bingo, see the *Proceedings* (1963), 7–28.

63. For some discussion of action taken by these organizations, see Arthur Hertzberg, "Religion," *American Jewish Year Book* 59 (1958): 119; Marc H. Tannenbaum, "Religion," *American Jewish Year Book* 60 (1959), 60. See also Samuel Belkin, "The Rabbi and the Community," *Jewish Life*, February 1956, 25, and an editorial entitled "Victory for Synagogue Sanctity," *Jewish Life*, June 1959, 3–5, for two efforts, replete with military imagery, to rally the Orthodox troops to wage battle against mixed seating.

64. Eisendrath's remarks appear in "The Form and Substance of Reform Judaism," *CCAR Journal* 21 (April 1958): 12.

65. Levi A. Olan, "Some Directions for Reform Judaism," *CCAR Journal* 20 (January 1958): 21–22.

66. For a sampling of the many references to this theme, see Ralph Segalman, "The Synagogue, The Center, the Federation and Survival," *The Reconstructionist*, April 19, 1957, 13–21; a symposium on the relationship

between the synagogue and the JCC in *The Reconstructionist*, January 11, 1958, 7–19; and a symposium in *Conservative Judaism* 16 (winter–spring 1962), 1–50.

67. See, for example, the debate between Rabbis Stuart E. Rosenberg and Bernard Segal, "Religious Revival in America—Fact or Fancy," *United Synagogue Review* (winter 1961), 15–17.

68. Hugo Weisgall, *Proceedings of the Rabbinical Assembly* (1953), 251.

69. Arnold Rothstein, "Synagogue Music in Our Day," *Jewish Life*, June–July 1951, 50–56.

70. Isidore Freed, "The Music of the Synagogue," *CCAR Journal* 17 (April 1957): 38–42.

71. James Hudnut-Beumler, *Looking for God in the Suburbs: The Religion of the American Dream and its Critics, 1945–1965.* (New Brunswick, N.J.: Rutgers University Press, 1984), 7.

72. These data are reported by Sylvia Barack Fishman, *A Breath of Life: Feminism in the American Jewish Community* (New York: The Free Press, 1993), 153.

73. By comparison, a survey of temples conducted in 1950 found that only 30 percent of such congregations called women to the Torah (Morris N. Kertzer, "Religion," *American Jewish Year Book* 53 (1952): 155.

74. This is the overarching theme of Riv-Ellen Prell's *Prayer and Community*.

75. The manifesto for "the havuraization of the synagogue" was written by Rabbi Harold Schulweis, "Restructuring the Synagogue," see esp. p. 19. These developments are even more remarkable considering that the malcontents were no longer within suburban synagogues but tended to be concentrated in urban centers. Their views would come to influence congregants of suburban synagogues and thereby pressure those congregations to respond. One suspects, as well, that congregations were hyper-attuned to the critics because the latter were homegrown: they were their own children. In this way, too, the suburban synagogue remained true to its pediatric emphasis, albeit, in this case, heeding its now grown offspring.

76. Writing at midcentury, Lou H. Silberman observed:

> For him who rejects prayer no verbal or visual embellishment will make worship acceptable. He who holds prayer to be 'self-encounter' will not be able to utilize in any fruitful manner the prayer of him who encounters the living God beyond the confines of his own mind. ... We have turned aside so long that we have forgotten how to join ourselves together as a community. We do not remember what is taking place; that the community is as a "living

person" encountering God; and that this encounter is a total encounter, covering the whole scope of life. ("The Reestablishment of Worship," *CCAR Journal* 3 [October 1953], 13–18)

Fifty years later, American Jews grapple with the same difficulties when they encounter public prayer.

Corporal Punishment in Judicial Rulings

A Reassessment of Educational Policy in the State of Israel

SHMUEL GLICK

I. Introduction

Corporal punishment of children by parents and teachers, its role in children's education, and the boundaries of what is permitted and forbidden for the parent and the educator is a subject that has engaged and will continue to engage the attention of philosophers, ethicists, pedagogues, and jurists of different cultures and religions.

Within that general framework, from an interdisciplinary pedagogic-social-legal perspective, this article deals with the development of corporal punishment as reflected in the interaction between court rulings, the measures instituted by the educational establishment, and the attitudes of the public at large. There is an abundant literature on the history of corporal punishment, both in the cultures of other nations[1] and in Jewish culture.[2] And yet, in the wake of recent rulings of the Israeli Supreme Court,[3] and in view of the increase of violence in Israeli society, the topic is still a source of ferment, and the proliferation of articles pub-

I wish to thank Dr. Menahem Monnickendam, Dr. Yehiel Pickholz, and Mr. David Kerschen for their important comments, and Dr. Tehilla Altschuler, who read the legal section of the article and gave her professional comments.

lished during the last decade indicates that the last word on the subject has not yet been said.[4]

I will attempt to show that the developments in this issue within the educational establishment were not the product of hearings overseen by pedagogic planners in the educational establishment, nor were they the upshot of public debate and discussion. And, although recent Knesset proceedings have provided some general legislative guidance by ratifying international norms for the protection of children, this has not been the primary factor in bringing about legal change. Rather, recent changes in this matter have been the result of court cases instituted against teachers which have resulted in civil and criminal indictments and convictions. Ultimately, the subject of corporal punishment was considered by the Israeli Supreme Court, which determined the appropriate law governing education. The following discussion comprises an examination of the argumentation employed in Supreme Court judgments from 1953 to the present and the ramifications of its rulings for the education system in the State of Israel.

The judgments dealing with educational matters are a highly valuable and reliable resource for researchers into the history of contemporary Jewish education, providing a prism through which the researcher can deduce "from the general to the specific" in an attempt to fathom the social and value-based changes in the educational field. The judgments of the Israeli courts (and particularly of the Supreme Court) mirror the realities and the social changes in Israeli society since the State's establishment. This point was eloquently explicated by the Supreme Court President, Justice Aharon Barak, in his description of the essence of the judicial function:

> All judicial activity is based on values. The judge gives expression to the values of the State. ... He reflects the values of its system ... and not his own values; he gives expression to the

fundamental tenets of the system, and not to his own personal views.[5]

In the early 1950s, Education Ministry guidelines forbade corporal punishment in schools. Nevertheless, the Supreme Court upheld the age-old "educational philosophy" that allowed parents and teachers to inflict certain corporal punishments within the required measure of reasonableness. And yet, at the end of the 1990s the Supreme Court handed down rulings that expressed "a different philosophy," unequivocally forbidding parents and teachers to resort to corporal punishment for disciplinary purposes in children's education—a social, value-laden issue which is broadly disputed in Israeli society.[6]

In its recent rulings, the Supreme Court has decided not to wait for the subject to be resolved through public discussion or decisive legislative action that would reflect the current values of Israeli society. Instead, it ruled according to the educational philosophy that it considered appropriate and desirable for the State of Israel. It was the Supreme Court that enunciated changes in educational policy and required the Education Ministry to implement these changes.

Following the most recent Supreme Court decision,[7] the education establishment decided to make the transition from its policy of declared passivity to an activist policy, and it was no longer satisfied with the circular issued by the Director General of the Education Ministry,[8] which proscribes the use of corporal punishment by teachers.

In the year 2000, basing itself on the Supreme Court's ruling, a number of legal surveys, and psychological studies, the Director General's office in the Education Ministry circulated a letter among school principals unambiguously stating that teachers have no authority to inflict corporal punishment.[9] Over the last few years, teachers convicted of inflicting corporal punishment (and even in some cases where there was no conviction) were also tried by disciplinary courts for civil servants,[10] which punished them with the full severity of the law, imposing additional sanctions, including dismissal.[11]

For a full understanding of the changes in the attitudes on this subject in the course of fifty-six years of statehood, we must first present a brief review of the historical background of corporal punishment as reflected in traditional Jewish sources.

II. The History of Corporal Punishment as a Means of Inculcating Discipline

Corporal punishment as a tool of child-rearing is an ancient practice.[12] In ancient times, childhood was perceived as inherently unruly, an evil to be uprooted, "for man's nature is evil from his youth" (Gen. 8:21). Both parents and educators were required to be strict with children, to ensure that they did not remain rebellious when reaching adulthood. Legitimacy was conferred on corporal punishment and on the strict, even severe, treatment of children, even where, in certain extreme cases, this meant legitimizing the child's execution.[13] From the biblical perspective expressed in the verse "If a man have a stubborn and rebellious son ... when they have chastised him" (Deut. 21:18–21), the child's punishment was regarded as both natural and necessary, intended for his own good.[14] Scripture couches these ideas in casuistic form, and they receive further approbation in the Wisdom literature, such as Proverbs and Ben Sira, which deal with matters of guidance and offer sage counsel: "He who spares his rod hates his son" (Prov. 13:21);[15] the formulation in Ben Sira is even sharper: "Afflict thy son and make his yoke heavy—lest he entangle you in his evil" (Ben Sira 21:13). According to Ben Sira, education must prepare the child for the complete, moral life, and the path to that goal entails the harnessing of instincts, even if not the eschewal of worldly pleasures. To achieve this, the parent and the educator must employ the requisite measures, namely "chastisement," and in the biblical context, "chastisement" usually refers to corporal punishment.[16]

The biblical perspective that regards physical punishment as a legitimate and effective means for education of children also finds its expression in talmudic literature.[17] Toward the end of the Second Temple period, when public enactments ordered "the appointment of teachers of children in every city and every province,"[18] the biblical permit regarding corporal punishment was broadened to include teachers of children (*melamdei tinoqot*), who were regarded as an extension of the father's authority. The Sages demanded that the teacher avail himself of the method judiciously and proportionately, intelligently and having consideration for its educational effectiveness. According to the Tosefta: "The father who strikes his son, and the Rabbi who chastens his pupil, and both of them if they struck and injured—are exempt, but if they injured in excess of what was appropriate for them—they are liable."[19] In other words: if the *bet din* deems that the father or the teacher deviated from what was reasonably effective, that is, if "they injured in excess of what was appropriate for them," then neither the father nor the teacher can take refuge in the defense of "He who spares his rod hates his son."

Spanking was not an end in itself, but at most an educational tool, and being no more than a tool, its degree of reasonable effectiveness determined the potential liability of the person utilizing it. Already in the first generation of the Babylonian Amoraim (third century), we find that Rav instructed his pupil R. Shmuel b. Shilat, who was a teacher, regarding the bounds of efficiency of corporal punishment: "When you hit a child, do so only with the strap of a sandal (which is not painful); he who reads, will read [by himself] and he who does not read, should be in the company of his friend [and that way will learn to read].[20] In other words, even where smacking is permitted to the degree necessary, it must be limited and not painful. The examples cited in the talmudic literature attest to the Sages' disapproval of teachers who were excessively cruel to their students, all of whom were condemned,[21] reprimanded, and even dismissed from their positions. However, none of this prevented those teachers who lacked other disciplinary measures from continuing to utilize the cane, the whip, and the strap.[22] The general, harsh view that "he who spares the rod hates his son" was endorsed by teachers as a matter of course.[23] This was the general trend of rabbinic literature over the generations,[24] and particularly in books of ethics and education, in both the Oriental and Western communities.[25]

At the same time it must be stressed that in rabbinic literature, the question of corporal punishment for a child or pupil was primarily an educational one and not a halachic-legal one. When a teacher went too far and caused substantial bodily injury, the halachic question arose as to whether the spanker was liable for the payment of damages. However, the paucity of discussion in codes of Jewish law and the responsa literature indicates that corporal punishment was not primarily a halachic-legal question, but rather an educational issue.

The second half of the nineteenth century heralded a number of significant developments in Western society with respect to the family and parent–child relationships. Modernization of society included an openness to new educational ideologies. The cumulative effect of these developments was to undermine the hegemony of traditional Jewish authorities in determining the proper pedagogical methods in Jewish education as well.[26] The monolithic, one-dimensional attitude that had characterized the attitude of Rabbinic sources to corporal punishment began to change, and new voices were heard, expressing reservations about cruel physical punishment, or corporal punishment for adolescents. The new voices included Rabbis such as R. Eliezer Pappo (Salistra [Bulgaria], d. 1824);[27] R. Samson b. Raphael Hirsch (Germany, 1808–1888);[28] R. Yechiel Weinberg (Russia, Germany, Switzerland, 1885–1938);[29] and R. Abraham Isaac Hacohen Kook

(Greiva [Latvia], Jerusalem, 1865–1935).[30] At the same time, other traditional voices could still be heard, such as R. Eliyahu Dessler, one of the leaders of the last generation's Mussar movement, teacher and rebbe of thousands of ultra-Orthodox Yeshiva students, who harshly criticized the modern trends that rejected corporal punishment in education.[31] Summing up his own article "Battered Children in Ancient Times," Meir Bar Ilan wrote:

> In ancient times, spanking a child as part of his education was regarded as a desirable and acceptable practice, being prevalent throughout the world and not just among the Jewish people. In this framework the boy and the girl were exposed to violent behavior of their parents, which was often the result of both 'justified' educational motivations and pathological factors. ... If the ancient sources do not provide adequate proof that violence towards children was permitted, then evidence is supplied by later sources of the Middle Ages, which also indicate the same phenomenon.[32] All of the sources reinforce the conclusion that Jewish children, like other children, were spanked by their parents, even though this fact as such is not necessarily an indicator of the quality of "childhood" in its broader context of parental love and care, a phenomenon which must be viewed in an overall context, including additional characteristics and variables.[33]

In our view, these comments are an accurate description of attitudes that prevailed in Jewish society up to and including the twentieth century.[34] Controlled forms of corporal punishment were a legal and legitimate tool for parents and teachers in the process of educating children. Even if there were those who decried the practice, both parents and teachers regarded "moderate physical punishment" as an efficient method of educating and did not recoil from resorting to it when necessary.

The Rulings of the Courts: Defining Punitive Policy in the Schools from the Establishment of the State to the Early 1990s

In traditional society, the ethical-cultural basis of the attitude toward children derived from two basic values: "Honor" and "fear": "A person shall fear his father and mother"; "The fear of your rabbi [teacher] [should] resemble the fear of Heaven." The child was commanded not only to honor and respect his parents and teachers, but also to fear them. Fear of this kind means obedience—inculcated by the fear of disobedience that carries punishment in its wake, even corporal punishment. This was the generally accepted educational-cultural atmosphere of Israel—the land of the ingathering of exiles and cultures. Most Israelis over the age of fifty—both Oriental and Western—grew up in this atmosphere.

As a standing policy, corporal punishment in schools was already prohibited in the guidelines of the Education Department of the National Committee prior to the establishment of the State,[35] and following the establishment of the State, various formulations of the same prohibition were included in the Director-General's circulars disseminated by the Ministry of Education.[36] Even so, over the years these guidelines did not generate any change in actual practice. Anecdotal reports indicate that teachers in the education system, and especially in development towns, continued using corporal punishment as a last resort against disruptive pupils. As long as the punishment was moderate, within the bounds of reasonableness, and constituted an appropriate response to the pupil's objectionable act, without causing the child bodily harm, it was considered a legitimate punishment—a necessary evil.[37]

The Supreme Court addressed this educational issue for the first time five years after the establishment of the State,[38] in its adjudication of Criminal Appeal (Cr.A. 7/53) *Dalal Rassi v. Attor-*

ney-General, and Counter-Appeal, *Attorney-General v. Dalal Rassi,*[39] in a case that did not involve the public education system. Justices Shneour Zalman Cheshin, Moshe Landau, and Simcha Assaf presided. Let us begin with a description of the case: A Catholic nun served as a supervisor and housemother of the Voespia orphanage in Nazareth. In 1952 she was indicted in the Haifa District Court for two acts of assault[40] and for causing bodily injury to two students[41] who were in her charge. Following are the details of the three acts of assault, as described in the judgment:

1. In 1951 she punished the child Samia Giris who ran away from the institute and subsequently returned to it, by slapping her face and pushing her head into the wall, throwing her on the ground, hitting her with her hand, kicking her [in the] back and pulling her hair;

2. In 1952 the accused suspected Afafa J'deon C'lil of having torn her dress; she slapped her face and pushed her head into the wall ...;

3. Geris Ibrahim, a child, testified that one day she had been in the classroom, playing with a reed, and managed to emit sounds from it. When the accused heard the sounds, she slapped her cheek twice, after which she took a needle from one of the other girls and pricked the child's lower lip a number of times, causing her to bleed. The District Court convicted the nun of these offenses, and sentenced her to payment of a fine of 150 lirot, or three months' imprisonment.[42] The nun's attorney appealed both the conviction and the severity of the sentence. His central claim was that the supervisor had punished the girls in the same way that parents punish their children, and that as such there was no cause for her indictment in the first place. The State Attorney appealed the leniency of the punishment.

The central question dealt with in the judgment was whether, and to what extent, a teacher, school principal, or supervisor of a children's institution is permitted to resort to physical punishment as a disciplinary measure. In its judgment, the Supreme Court established the norm that would serve the educational and legal systems for a period of over forty years.

The Court endeavored to avoid conducting the trial from a purely pedagogic perspective, and consequently it was not required to decide "which system of education and punishment the educator should choose." Its sole aim was to decide the question from the perspective of criminal law, that is, which acts would be regarded as criminal offenses. But regardless of its intention, the Court was willy-nilly forced to rule on a major pedagogical question—what constituted permitted and forbidden behavior in educational punishment[43]—and the question of what constitutes "required reasonability," a deviation from which would have implications in the field of criminal law.

Let us examine the justices' arguments in the ruling, which undoubtedly mirrored accepted values of Israeli society during the 1950s: a social melting pot of immigrants from both Oriental and Western countries, many of whom had received a traditional upbringing, in which corporal punishment was legitimate. Justice Cheshin wrote as follows:

> It could be said that when giving his child to be educated a father empowers the educator[44] to guide the child along the right path, utilizing all the measures at the pedagogue's disposal, including the whip and strap. It might further be argued that the father delegates to the educator his power to discipline and to inflict corporal punishment upon the child, but the question would then be what is the source of the father's legal power and authority ... from where does he derive the legal authority to hurt his child ...?
>
> There is no specific legislation on the matter, and we can only rely on what the public has accepted as a matter of tradition, from one man to another, from father to son, from one

generation to the next; in other words accepted practice which has the force of law; and where there is no such practice, there is reliance on the English Common Law.

In this case, with no other choice, Justice Cheshin relied on English Common Law as expressed in the judgment of Sir Alexander Cockburn, Lord Chief Justice of England[45] in 1860 in *R. v. Hopley*, 175 E.R. 1204, p. 1206, which held that when a parent brings his son to a teacher in school he transfers to him all of his parental authority to the extent that it is required for the child's best interests. Thus, according to English law:

> A parent or a schoolmaster ... may for the purpose of correcting what is evil in the child inflict moderate and reasonable corporal punishment, always, however, with this condition, that it is moderate and reasonable. If it be administrated for the gratification of passion or of rage, or if it be immoderate and excessive in its nature or degree, or if it be protracted beyond the child's powers of endurance, or with an instrument unfitted for the purpose and calculated to produce danger to the life or limb; in all such cases the punishment is excessive, the violence is unlawful, and if evil consequences to life and limb ensue, then the person inflicting it is answerable to the law.[46]

Justice Cockburn's judgment was followed by a number of additional rulings in England, supporting its contention that parents are entitled to inflict corporal punishment on their children in order to educate them and inculcate discipline. Over the years it became established English law that the "reasonability" of the punishment would be determined by the totality of the circumstances in the case at hand, considering the child's age, physical state, and mental maturity, as well as the duration of the corporal punishment and the reasons for its infliction.

Justice Rabbi Simha Assaf concurred with Justice Cheshin's ruling, citing sources from Jewish law, which in essence buttressed the permission given to parents and teachers to resort to moderate corporal punishment provided that it was for a reasonable purpose and the use of physical force did not exceed the bounds of reasonable moderation. Justice Assaf concluded his ruling with a quotation from a work known as *Ma`arechet Abraham*, written by Rabbi Abraham ben Model from Ottingen, who was a teacher in The Hague:[47] " 'And I have a secret gift that I give to teachers, that they must be careful not to slap on the head or the face or out of anger ... for this is liable to cause a loss and is remote from any benefit.' Apparently, the appellant did not receive this gift and hence she behaved the way she did."

In this judgment, Justice Cheshin and his fellow justices Assaf and Landau dismissed the appellant's appeal in view of the fact that the corporal punishment administered in this case was deemed extreme and unreasonable. However, the Court endorsed the view of the English law that held that parents *are* entitled to resort to bodily punishment of their children for purposes of their moral edification,[48] and that when sending their children to school, the parents delegate this right to the teachers and the principals. It was stressed, however, that this ruling did not provide a license for parents and teachers to use this punitive tool excessively, to the extent of abusing the child; should they overstep the boundaries of what is permitted and reasonable, it would be considered a criminal offense,[49]

As stated, this ruling reflected the values of Israeli society during the 1950s, when this kind of punishment was viewed as a permitted form of violence.[50] The ruling conferred on teachers a status comparable to that of parents with respect to corporal punishment. The Court ruled that the status of the parents is *in loco parentis*; in other words, the teachers, when functioning in their capacity as teachers, step into the parents' shoes. In its adoption of this doctrine, the Court provided the teachers with a legal authorization for using reasonable, moderate corporal punishment against pupils.[51]

This decision influenced the Israeli education system for almost forty-five years in its forgiving treatment of teachers who struck their students. As stated, from the outset, the declared policy of the Education Ministry was that corporal punishment was forbidden. Nevertheless, teachers continued to use it as a punitive tool, and concomitantly, the education establishment continued declaring its opposition in principle to corporal punishment. But the reality was that the establishment had reconciled itself to the situation, even granting it legitimacy by its policy of turning a blind eye.

The policy of "turning a blind eye," or tacit consent, is evidenced by a collection of data that was found in the "Stanner Index" in the offices of the Ministry of Education's legal counsel.[52] The Stanner Index comprises a few hundred card entries dealing with convictions, accusations, and judgments relating to employees of the education system, from the late 1950s and the 1960s, compiled by Ms. Ruth Stanner, who held that office until 1972. In the index we found complaints lodged against teachers who had employed harsh disciplinary measures against their pupils causing them injury, documentation of disciplinary offenses and ethical offenses, and more. From the file we excerpted twenty cards with the handwritten entries of Ms. Stanner, from 1959–63, all attesting to the general attitude of the education establishment toward complaints about physical abuse of pupils by their teachers, in both the Jewish and Arab sectors.

The cards contain detailed documentation of cases involving twenty teachers from public schools, in both the State and State-Religious streams, six of them from Arab schools, who had brutally beaten their pupils. Among the descriptions, we read about a student being beaten until he fainted; a student who sustained serious head injuries after having disrupted the class; a student who was caned, causing him bodily harm; a student who was slapped on the face and hit on her back, and others.

In most instances, the cards indicated that the cases were

closed for lack of public interest, meaning the end of proceedings against the violent teacher. Only in four cases were the teachers indicted, convicted, fined, and given a suspended jail sentence.

The cases mentioned above, and the consequences of their handling in the framework of the Education Ministry's legal office and outside it, attest to the lenient educational policy that was the norm in the Ministry of Education, despite its declared policy, reiterated every few years in the Director-General's circulars, prohibiting any use of corporal punishment. For as long as the offense did not reach the level of assault causing substantial bodily harm, under §250 of the Penal Code, the case would be closed for lack of public interest;[53] no criminal measures were adopted, nor were any disciplinary measures taken against the teacher who had administered corporal punishment. The repeated directives of the Ministry of Education regarding the prohibition of physical punishment attest to the Ministry's ineptitude in inculcating its policies among teachers, primarily in towns far from the center of the country.[54]

From conversations with many teachers who taught during those years, the picture that emerges is one of frequent beatings of pupils, especially in schools in the outlying development towns, in which the population was primarily of Oriental origin; in schools belonging to the nonpublic but officially recognized ultra-Orthodox "independent" stream; and in public schools in the Arab sector. In all of these schools, moderate corporal punishment was viewed as a necessary evil.

Even in the exceptional cases in which the teachers went too far, and the parents complained to the school principal, matters were normally settled internally, inside the school. The cases brought to the attention and handling of the Education Ministry's legal advisor were apparently the extreme ones, in which the punitive measures involved obvious bodily injury.

In 1976, the State Attorney's office attempted to modify the *Rassi* ruling (Cr.A. 7/53) in its response to the appeal of a primary school teacher, who had witnessed an eighth-grade pupil disturbing a teacher and being impertinent to him.[55] The appellant mentioned the matter to the student, and after classes that day scolded him again. The pupil replied that it was none of his business, prompting the appellant to slap him across the face. The District Court convicted the teacher of assault and imposed a fine of IL 500. The teacher appealed, claiming that under the circumstances he was entitled to use a reasonable amount of force, and that under the *Rassi* ruling the Court should accept his claim that the slap had not deviated from the permitted, reasonable use of force and that therefore he should be acquitted.

However, the Supreme Court dismissed his appeal and saw no reason for reopening the *Rassi* ruling. The case at hand differed from the case that provided the original precedent. In order for physical punishment not to be regarded as an unlawful act, the Court had to be convinced that the measure adopted by the teacher was reasonably necessary, that the teacher did not exceed what was warranted for the achievement of the desired goal, and that he had no other alternative form of action. Under the circumstances, the Court's view was that appellant had exceeded the bounds of what was reasonably necessary.

The Court maintained this policy until the beginning of the 1990s. In Cr.F. 4595/91 *State of Israel v. Moshe Gradin*, heard by Judge Caspi of the Tel-Aviv Magistrates Court, the principal and the guidance counselor of the school were both accused of slapping a minor. The judge accepted the principal's version of the events and acquitted the teacher. In an *obiter dictum*, Judge Caspi noted:

> The acts complained of were not severe. Even though a generation has passed since the Supreme Court ruling on this matter, just as we learned from Rav who was the first and most prominent of the Talmudic Sages[56] and from Maimonides,[57] when society still administered bodily punishments, today too, one

cannot yet contend that punitive, physical responses are absolutely forbidden to educators, and all the more so to parents ... it is all a question of proportion on the one hand, and of adjusting the response to the student's unacceptable behavior, on the other hand.

THE CHANGE IN THE JUDICIAL POLICY AND ITS EFFECT ON THE EDUCATION ESTABLISHMENT

Two legislative factors supplied formal grounds for the metamorphosis in the Supreme Court's policy regarding corporal punishment, a process that began in the mid 1990s. The first was Israel's ratification of the Convention on the Rights of the Child, on 4 August 1991, which provides in §19 (1):

> Parties shall take all appropriate legislative, administrative, social and educational measures to protect the child from all forms of physical or mental violence, injury or abuse, neglect or negligent treatment, maltreatment or exploitation, including sexual abuse, while in the care of parent(s), legal guardian(s) or any other person who has the care of the child.[58]

The second factor was the enactment of Basic Law: Human Dignity and Liberty[59] in 1992. §2 of this Basic Law provides: There shall be no violation of the life, body or dignity of any person as such.

The ratification of the Convention and the enactment of the Basic Law: Human Dignity and Liberty signified the beginning of the reversal of the Court's rulings, beginning with the denial of permission for moderate corporal punishment by teachers and thereafter by denial of permission for corporal punishment by parents. It must, however, be stressed that these legislative proceedings were not necessarily the dominant factors underlying the change in the court rulings, but only the formal reflection of what was in essence a far more pervasive development in Israeli society. I refer to the phenomenon of "judicial activism" which has characterized the approach recently adopted by the Israeli Supreme Court (originally, a uniquely American phenomenon which then spread to other Western countries and began to surface in Israel during the last decade of the twentieth century).[60] Actually, the process began in the mid 1980s with the removal of limitations on "standing" and "justiciability"[61] and continued with the Court's increasing utilization of the test of "reasonableness."[62]

According to this approach, the Supreme Court's role is not just to reflect the existing values of Israeli society in its rulings; it must also guide society towards desirable cultural values that have yet to receive explicit legislative approbation. Notably, this approach has become the occasion of deep controversy among jurists, academics and intellectuals, and spiritual leaders.

The Israeli judiciary's increased involvement in the administration of educational matters was ostensibly the product of constitutional and legal developments in a number of Western countries with respect to human rights in general and in relation to the rights of children in particular, which the Court sought to entrench in Israeli society. The Court's intervention, however, was also the product of legislative inaction:[63] given the religious and social diversity of Israeli society, it was difficult for the Knesset to make a clear, unequivocal statement on matters relating to overarching social values. at large.

The first Supreme Court ruling on the question of corporal punishment in the schools, following the aforementioned human rights legislation, was on 30 August 1994 in Cr.A. 4405/94 *State of Israel v. Marbat Abd Alagni*,[64] presided over by Justices Aharon Barak (then Deputy President of the Court), Mishael Cheshin, and Dalia Dorner. While their judgment did not explicitly reverse the *Rassi* (Cr.A. 7/53) ruling,[65] it effectively emptied it of all content.

The following is a brief description of the case: A teacher in the French-language school in Jaffa wanted to ascertain whether her pupils had obtained their parents' signatures on returned examination papers. One second-grade pupil had failed to get his parents' signature. The teacher pulled his ear so violently that part of the earlobe was removed. The teacher claimed that pulling the pupil's ear was not the product of any desire to abuse or humiliate the child, being intended merely as a warning or deterrent action. The teacher was convicted for assault against a minor, causing severe bodily damage (under §368 of the Penal Law, 5737-1977). She was given an eight–month sentence, consisting of two months of community service and a suspended term in prison. The State appealed against the sentence's leniency, emphasizing the damage caused to the minor, the prohibition of corporal punishment, and the unacceptable norms that had taken root in the school. The State further emphasized the legislative trend toward severity in cases of child abuse. In the State's opinion, the punishment imposed on the teacher was not commensurate with appropriate sentencing standards.

Justice Barak wrote as follows (with the concurrence of Justice M. Cheshin—incidentally, Justice S. Z. Cheshin's son):[66]

> The respondent's behavior was grave. She severely injured the body and the soul of a minor for whom she was educationally responsible. Physical violence against a child is forbidden. Lashings, beating, and ear pulling have no place in the school. The classroom is a place of education and not an arena for violence. The pupil's body and soul are not unprotected. His dignity as a human being is violated if his teachers inflict physical violence on him. ... The principal of the school in which the respondent taught testified that: "We have a practice, though rarely used, of pulling a pupil's ear in order to remind him of something." One of the teachers of the school stated that "hitting the hand lightly with a ruler is permitted. The intention is not to hurt." These forms of conduct must be uprooted. Pulling an ear is not a per-

missible means of jogging the pupil's memory. Hitting with a ruler is not a permissible method of warning.

Corporal punishment had previously been permitted as long as it did not exceed reasonable bounds, as stated in the ruling of Justice S. Z Cheshin (the father). A generation passed, and when his son Mishael Cheshin took his father's seat, he ruled that "these forms of conduct must be uprooted."

From the early 1950s and for a period of forty-five years, permission to use corporal punishment for educational purposes was binding case law, but the Supreme Court replaced it in principle and in practice, in its capacity as the Supreme Court of Criminal Appeals, in Cr.A. 5224/97, *State of Israel v. Rachel Sdeh Ur.*[67] This case was adjudicated by the panel of Justices Theodor Or, Dalia Dorner, and Yitzhak Englard on 20 July 1998 (26 Tammuz 5758). An indictment was filed in Haifa District Court against a kindergarten teacher, accusing her of assaulting and abusing a minor. The kindergarten teacher admitted that she had used force against disruptive pupils, but she claimed that it was moderate force, such as a pat on the shoulder, the bottom, the child's hand, and the like. The District Court granted her an absolute acquittal for the offenses of abuse and assault. In explaining its reasons for the acquittal, the Court contended that the kindergarten teacher's acts did not constitute a criminal offense, because the acts of hitting minors were not "unlawful": the force exercised was restricted and it was exercised for educational purposes.

The State appealed the acquittal and the Supreme Court overturned the respondent's acquittal on the assault charge. In the course of the proceedings, the respondent attempted to rely on §24 of the Torts Ordinance, which provides:

In an action brought in respect of any assault, it shall be a defense ... that the defendant was the parent, guardian, or schoolmaster of the plaintiff or a person whose relationship to the plaintiff was similar to that of a parent, guardian or school-master, and administered to the plaintiff only such chastisement as was reasonably necessary for the purpose of correction.

Addressing this claim, Justice Dorner wrote:

> Based on this interpretative approach, and in reliance upon this provision it emerges that an act committed "as was reasonably necessary for the purpose of [the child's] correction" is not an "unlawful act." However, the "reasonable necessity" is deter-mined by the attitude taken by Israeli society regarding the desirable and legitimate educational methods. Quite naturally, these attitudes will change over time due to social-cultural developments. Thus, what seemed legitimate in the past might no longer be considered legitimate in the present.
>
> Indeed, in the first case that considered the question of cor-poral punishment in the educational establishment—Cr.A. 7/53 *Rassi v Attorney General*—it was held that corporal punishment inflicted by teachers and principals is permitted. But forty-five years have passed since that judgment was given and the out-look reflected in it, allowing the use of violent measures for educational purposes, is no longer commensurate with our accepted social mores.
>
> An educational philosophy that endorses the use of force for educational purposes does not conform to our social norms, and all the more so, in respect of small children ... as a rule, corporate punishment cannot be considered a legitimate mea-sure to be applied by teachers, kindergarten teachers or other educators ...
>
> The use of violence by educators against pupils contradicts the views of Israeli society regarding education, its goals and the means to be used for their achievement, and as such cannot be considered reasonable.

This judgment revoked the permission conferred upon teach-ers by virtue of their status *in loco parentis* as established in the *Rassi* ruling, and it severed the legal connection between the parent and the teacher by its determination that: "The use of violence by educationalists against pupils contradicts the views of Israeli society regarding education, its goals and the means to be used for their achievement."[68]

In ASM 1682/02, *Sarachan Abd el Waab v. State of Israel*, Justice Dorit Beinish added a further gloss to these comments:[69]

> The teacher is occasionally required to deal with difficult situations, even with outright insubordination on the pupils' part, at a time when they [the teachers] are bound by the rules of order and discipline. The educator's power is not in his arm but in his wisdom, his personality and his professional training, all of which assist him in confronting difficulties. It is forbidden for him to exploit his standing and authority in order to hurt his students and it is prohibited for him to discharge his duty by violent, hurtful means. He must never reach a state of violence, either as a matter of course or even as a result of losing his temper. Education with violence engenders additional violence and frustrates our attempts to maintain a society that respects the rights of people, their dignity and their bodily integrity.

In 1953, when discussing corporal punishment, Justice S. Z. Cheshin was wary of stepping outside the legal realm into the realm of pedagogy, writing: "It is not for us to decide which educational system the educator and pedagogue should choose."[70] The comments of Justice Beinish, on the other hand, most definitely belong to the realm of pedagogic statements that might be quoted by leading educators. In pursuit of its activist policy, the Supreme Court of 1998 was not satisfied with important value-laden pronouncements that could contribute to public discourse and reduction of the violence threshold at the hands of parents and teachers. Justice Beinish's statement, thus, extended the previous limits of legal discourse and prescribed an educational philosophy, determining that even an educator or parent[71] who slapped a child should be regarded as a criminal. This was an educational pronouncement that the lower court had purposely avoided.

CHANGES IN THE COURT'S POSITION ON PARENTAL CORPORAL PUNISHMENT

As stated, until 1997 the use of moderate corporal punishment by teachers was tacitly considered "kosher" from a legal perspective, though *a priori* undesirable. But the schools, perhaps reflecting prevailing social norms, reconciled themselves *post facto* to this kind of punishment as a necessary evil, when other options failed.

The situation differed, however, with respect to moderate corporal punishment by parents. Parents are considered to possess a natural, intrinsic right to raise and educate their children as they deem fit, and this right was entrenched in Israeli law.[72] As such, corporal punishment by parents was accepted *a priori* as a legitimate educational act, as expressed in the adage: "The hand that embraces is occasionally the hand which slaps," provided that the minor does not sustain any substantial[73] or severe injury[74] as a result, and provided that the parent does not abuse his child.[75]

In this context, we find that at the beginning of the 1990s, Judge Strashnov discussed the question of when physical punishment exceeds the boundaries of an appropriate educational response, becoming violence and abuse for its own sake (Cr.F. 570/91 [T.A.] *State of Israel v. Assulin*).[76] This case dealt with a father accused of assaulting his son. Judge Strashnov wrote as follows:

> Occasionally it may be quite difficult to distinguish between the resort to force as an educational measure, which is legally permitted, and acts of violence and abuse, *which are absolutely forbidden.* ... It is difficult to establish clear guidelines and rules,

applicable to all persons, and it must be done in a proportionate manner with appropriate discretion. Slapping across the face or hitting the child's bottom as accepted educational measures, are not comparable to the use of fists or hard objects for purposes of hitting, both of which must be unequivocally prohibited. An isolated, rare use of force against an impertinent young child is not the same as systematic, daily beating, intended to humiliate and degrade, and which is totally unrelated to educational measures. ... In sum, it may be determined that when a parent uses corporal punishment on his child, intended for his education and inculcation of discipline and restraint, administered in proportionate measure, calmly and with common sense, it is not reprehensible from an educational perspective, nor is it forbidden from a legal perspective.

Judge Strashnov's ruling (1 December 1992) conforms to the trend in the educational tradition that was accepted by the larger portion of Israeli society with respect to educational punishment by parents.

Between the years 1991 and 1994 there were a number of instances in which parents were indicted for hitting their children, and the judges tended to be strict with parents who exceeded the bounds of reasonability and when the phenomenon of beating was endemic, becoming the norm.[77] Episodic, one-time punishment, however, administered with appropriate reasonableness, was still considered legitimate. For example, in 1994 in Cr.F. 211/93 *State of Israel v. Chachamov*, adjudicated by Judge Ostrobesky-Cohen in the Tel-Aviv District Court, a father was convicted for using violence against his daughters. Judge Ostrobersky-Cohen distinguished between one-time physical punishment and violence as an educational philosophy, which she sharply condemned. Among the arguments presented in her judgment she wrote:

I am aware that the use of a reasonable measure of force may be viewed as a suitable punitive response in appropriate cases, and that the parent is entitled to resort to this educational measure for as long as it is not just one more episode of protracted violence against the minor. ... I am unable to accept the physical and mental violence by parents of the kind that was evidenced in this case as a means of education, whether as a punishment or as a deterrent. ... Corporal punishment, and spanking children may be cathartic for parents in venting their anger and frustrations, but they teach the child nothing except humiliation, insult and anger. ... It is incumbent upon the Court to confront this mistaken world view and root it out, once and for all.

The first substantive change in the case law regarding corporal punishment by parents was in the ruling handed down by Judge Saviona Rotlevi, in Cr.F. 64/96 *State of Israel v. Anon*,[78] in which a husband was accused of regularly spanking his small children and inflicting other physical punishments. Attorney for the accused contended that even if the factual elements of the case were proven, the actions committed by the accused would not constitute an offense, since "reasonable" corporal punishment of his children did not transgress any legal norm, given that case law permitted corporal punishment of children by a parent when it was intended for education or restraint and was proportionate and reasonable.

Judge Rotlevi addressed this claim in her judgment (15 September 1997), adducing educational and psychological arguments to explain why the ruling established by Justice S. Z. Cheshin in *Rassi* was no longer applicable. She wrote the following:

As mentioned, the *Rassi* ruling was handed down on 31.7.1953; we now find ourselves 44 years after the ruling was given. And in the interim, all of the underpinnings supporting Justice Cheshin's judgment have been removed.

The primary legal foundation of the *Rassi* ruling—the referral to British Common Law—was cancelled by the enactment of the

Foundations of the Law Act, 5740-1980, which repealed Article 46 of the King's Order in Council. Today there are no grounds for reliance on a rule derived from English Law.[79]

Indeed, the message from the Supreme Court today contradicts the *Rassi* ruling and determines that physical or mental violence against minors is not a permitted measure.[80]

It was Justice Beinish who put the final nail in the coffin of the *Rassi* ruling that implicitly permitted corporal punishment of children by parents. Her ruling in Cr.A. 4596/98 related to a mother who for a period of two years had consistently spanked her children—aged 7–8 and 5–6—on their bottoms, slapped their faces, hit them with a slipper, thrown shoes at them, and occasionally even struck them with a vacuum cleaner; once she even punched her son (the younger child) in the face, knocking out one of his teeth. The file was initially adjudicated in the Tel-Aviv District Court (Judge Rotlevi),[81] who convicted the mother for assault and abuse of her children. In her statements to the police, the mother claimed that she had normally spanked her children on their behinds, and slapped them across the face as an educational measure, and "as a means of deterrence."

The mother was convicted for abuse of a minor, an offense under §368 C of the Penal Code, 5737-1977, and for assault. Supreme Court Justice Beinish dismissed her appeal, and following a lengthy comparative survey of the legitimacy of corporal punishment of children by their parents in different legal systems,[82] she made the following determination, in §29 of her judgment:

> It is absolutely forbidden for parents to physically punish or humiliate their children and trample their dignity as a system of education. It is a residue of a social-educational outlook that has become obsolete. The child is not his parent's property; he cannot serve as a punching bag, which the parent can hit at will, even if believing in good faith that he is discharging his obliga-

tion and right to educate his child. The child is dependent upon his parent, and needs his love, protection and tender touch. Punishment that causes pain and humiliation does not contribute to the child's character or education; it infringes on his rights as a human being. It damages his body, his feelings, his dignity and his proper development. It distances us from our aspirations to be a society free of violence. Therefore, the use by parents of corporal punishment ... is forbidden today in our society.[83]

Thus we see how the case law underwent a transition over the years. During the early years following the establishment of the State, physical punishment of children was permitted as long as it remained within the bounds of reasonableness. Forty-five years later, in the wake of social-cultural developments in the interim, the original case-law ruling was no longer applicable. The import of this ruling today is that a parent who abuses his child may potentially be regarded as a criminal. Justice Beinish gave the following reasons for her ruling (§30):

> One must also take into account that we live in a society in which violence is spreading like a plague; "minor" violence, if permitted, is likely to degenerate into very serious violence. We must not endanger the physical and emotional integrity of a minor by administering any corporal punishment at all. The yardstick must be clear and unequivocal, and the message is that corporal punishment is not permitted.

To a certain degree, Justice Beinish's judgment triggered public discussion of the matter on its merits. Notably, until the year 2000, in the civil realm (torts), assault of a minor by a parent or teacher was not included in the tort of assault that constituted grounds for a damages suit for injury caused by the assault. On 16 December 1999, M. K. Anat Maor introduced a draft bill proposing to repeal §24 (7) of the Torts Ordinance. Under this section, a parent who had used physical punishment was protected from criminal conviction (the source of the section is in the English version of the Ordinance from 1944). It had provided as follows:

> In an action brought in respect of any assault, it shall be a defense ... that the defendant was the parent, guardian, or schoolmaster of the plaintiff or a person whose relationship to the plaintiff was similar to that of a parent, guardian or schoolmaster, and administered to the plaintiff only such chastisement as was reasonably necessary for the purpose of correction.[84]

The draft bill was accepted, and published in S.H. 1742, 5760, p. 213, on 25 June 2000. What it means is that from the year 2000 onward, where a parent or teacher is convicted of beating a child—which is now a criminal offense—they are also exposed to a civil claim for monetary compensation for the injuries they caused. On the other hand, M. K. Avraham Ravitz (United Torah Judaism) did not sit idly by, and he proposed a law that would circumvent the High Court of Justice. On 6 June 2000 he introduced draft bill no. P/1468, titled "He who Spares the Rod, Hates His Child" (Permission to Administer Corporal Punishment), 5760-2000, intended to permit physical punishment of children by their parents for "educational purposes." In his explanatory note, Ravitz added: "A child is not his parents' property, but they have a moral obligation of the first degree to educate him. And if, within the framework of his education, it becomes necessary to punish him physically with spanking that does not injure him, and is therefore not in the category of violence, it will not be regarded as the abuse of a helpless person, and the parents will be permitted to use this measure in an educational and proportionate manner."

On 19 July 2000, the bill was submitted for deliberation in the Knesset plenum and it received the support of the ultra-Orthodox factions, while Members from the Left opposed it.[85] Ultimately, the proposal was not brought to a vote, and it emerged that Ravitz had reached an agreement with the attorney-general to the effect that parents would not be indicted for having spanked their children with the requisite reasonableness. It turns out, therefore, that the practice of moderate spanking on the bottom is not yet extinct and still commands support.

III. Conclusion

The Supreme Court has made its position clear on corporal punishment, and its recent rulings have certainly contributed at least partially to the curtailing of parental and teacher violence against children. It is not possible to determine whether these changes stem from fear of the law or the internalization of new values within a new generation of parents and teachers. In our view, the last word on the entire matter has yet to be spoken. There is some evidence that the views of the Israeli public regarding physical punishment have apparently not changed very much.[86] On the other hand, and quite significantly, the substance of public discourse on the matter has changed. In public opinion surveys, fewer people are prepared to admit openly that under certain circumstances they support educational spanking, that is, supervised corporal punishment.[87]

Despite these findings, it is necessary to generate constructive dialogue which is prepared to strike a balance between the Law, parental-teacher authority, and the ever-present value of a child's dignity and rights. Only then can we move a step closer towards a less violent world and achieve Tikun Olam for schools and society.

Notes

ABBREVIATIONS

C.A.	Civil Appeal	P.M.	*Pisqei Dinim Mehozi'im* (Judg-ments of the District Court)
C.F.	Civil File		
Cr.A.	Criminal Appeal	Savir	*Data Base of Supreme Court Legal Abstracts*, ed. Noah Savir
Cr.F.	Criminal File		
D.C.	Circular of the Director Gen-eral, Ministry of Education	S.H.	*Sefer ha-ḥuqqim* (Book of legisla-tion)
Dinim	Data Base of Israeli Court Judg-ments	S.S.A.	State Service Appeal
		S.T.	Special Supreme Court Tribunal
P.D.	*Pisqei din* (Decisions of the Supreme Court of the State of Israel)	Tak-El	*Takdin*, http://www.takdinet. co.il/ (Supreme Court of the State of Israel)

1. For the hundreds of articles written on this subject in other countries, see the internet site http://www.corpun.com.index.htm.
2. See the recent comprehensive article by B. Shmueli, ענישה גופנית של ילדים בידי הוריהם על פי המשפט העברי: גישות מסורתיות וזרמים מודרנים (Corporal pun-ishment of children by their parents in Jewish law: Traditional approaches and modern trends), *Plilim* (Tel-Aviv University Law Faculty) 10 (2001): 366–446.
3. Cr.A. 5224/97 *State of Israel v. Rachel Sdeh-Or*, 52 (3) P.D. 374; Cr.A. 4596/ 98 *Anon.v. Anon*, 54 (1) P.D. 145.
4. Between the years 1886 and 2003, more than thirty articles were published in Hebrew periodicals on the subject of corporal punishment by parents and teachers (twelve of them in the last four years), as well as dozens of publications and excellent-quality articles published in the press in Israel, and on various Internet sites.
5. See Word of the Chief Justice of the Supreme Court, at Supreme Court Internet site, http://62.90.71.124/heb/elyon/chief.htm.; See also A. Barak, (The judge in a democratic society), (Haifa: Haifa University, 2004), 399: "A judge is not allowed to impose his own personal values on the society in which he judges. To do so would be to act unlawfully, Any exercise of judicial discretion has consideration for the values accepted by the society and reflects the basic conceptions of the society."
6. See Evelyn Gordon, "The Supreme Court: In Loco Parentis," *Azure* 10 (winter 5761-2001): 88 nn. 27, 28.
7. Cr.A. 4596/88 *Anon. v. Anon*.

8. Circulars of the Director General of the Ministry of Education do not constitute legislative acts (see C.F. (Haifa) 1229/94, *Fatiah Amar et al. v. Principal of Terra Sancta School, Akko, et al.* (P.N. 98 (2), p.1065-1067). Rather, they are a system of procedures that determine the boundaries of authority and responsibility for providers of educational services, on the one hand, and the rights and duties of teachers, students, and their parents on the other hand. The legal force of the Director-General's Circulars and notifications derive from Regulation 2 of the State Education Regulations (Supervisory Procedures, 5710-1950, Art.1, Supervision By the Minister (Amendment 5733-1973)—where it stipulates: "Pedagogical guidance and pedagogical supervision of all educational institutions will be performed by way of the Director-General."

9. See letter of Director-General of the Ministry of Education, 19 March 2000, "Judgment concerning denial of authority for corporal punishment," Appendix A.

10. This court functions in accordance with the State Service (Discipline) Law, 5723-1963.

11. See recently: S.T. 208/00 and appeal against judgment, S.S.A. 1682/02, *Farchan Abd al Wahb v. State of Israel*, before Justice D. Beinish, Tak-El 2002 (2) 1300; S.T. 126/02 and S.S.A. 10501/02, *Smaya Shahin v. State Service Commissioner*, before Justice D. Beinish, Tak-El 2003 (2) 1394.

12. See Mordechai Frishtik, (Physical punishment of children as an educational measure in Jewish history), *Dor LeDor* 5 (5752-1992): 109–34.

13. Regarding the violent character of childhood in ancient times, in the Jewish people and in other nations (who practiced beating or even killing children, and not only did the societal leaders not decry the phenomenon, but occasionally they would encourage it), including an extensive bibliography, see M. Bar Ilan, *The Battered Child in Ancient Times*, http://faculty.biu.ac.il/-barilm/benali.html

14. Regarding the Rebellious Son, see J. Fleishman, "Studies on the Legal Status of Children in the Bible and Ancient East," Ph.D. diss., Bar Ilan University, Ramat Gan, 5749-1989; Elizabeth Bellefontaine, "Deuteronomy 21:18–21: Reviewing the Case of the Rebellious Son," *Journal for the Study of the Old Testament* 13 (1979): 13–31; Don C. Benjamin, *Deuteronomy and City Life: A Form Criticism of Texts with the Word City* (Lanham, Md.: University Press of America, 1983), 211–21.

15. For possible interpretations of this verse, see Shmueli, "Corporal Punishment." See also N. Gutel, חושך שבטו שונא בנו ? הכאת ילדים: 'בין הלכה' ל'הלכה למעשה' לדרכה של מדיניות היהודית-הלכתית (He who spares the rod, hates his

child? Spanking children: Between *halakhah* and *halakhah le-ma'aseh*—The formulation of a halachic-educational policy), *Bisdeh Hemed* 2–3 (5760-2000): 119–39:

> Recently there have been attempts to give a different alternative interpretation to the verse, as though it said: the "rod" does not mean a rod to beat with, but the rod of censure, as implied by the conclusion of the same verse "but he that loveth him chasteneth him betimes," and as such, then Judaism has long internalized the negation of spanking. They took the apologetic track ... and even referred to their conclusion as "the simple meaning of Scripture[!], in their biased attitude, they ignored the general tendency of exegetes, who quite naturally refrained from explaining matters that were clear to the extent of being the literal meaning of the verses.

> I fully endorse this attitude. This apologetic approach was also adopted by Judge Saviona Rotlevi in her argumentation in Cr.F. 64/96 Dinim (District Court) 26 (7) §73–77. She cited from the words of Maimonides in his Book of Commandments (*Sefer HaMitzvot)*, Commandment 300, "Not to exceed the maximum for one liable to whipping, as it is written 'he shall not exceed; lest, if he should exceed' (Deut. 25:3)," but the citation is quite out of context. And, when citing the Maimonides comments in *Hilchot Talmud Torah* 2:2, and other sources which are not consistent with her own worldview, her response is: "These opinions belong to an early period, in which the governing social norms and mores were entirely different from those which we accept today, and we cannot seek guidance from them, especially in view of the purpose section of Basic Law: Human Dignity and Liberty" (ibid., §79). She further states that, "In my view reliance on ancient halakhic sources to justify corporal punishment at the end of the twentieth century is illegitimate, for these sources are the product of a period that preceded the philosophical development of human rights (§80). Of this kind of argumentation it was already said: "and one may not mix two different kinds of seed" (Resp. R Neturnai Geon - ed. R. Brody (Ofek) Y.D. s. 262. See also: Shmueli, "Corporal Punishment," 381, who presents the various interpretations of this verse as a hierarchy of priorities: "The method of the rod, even if we interpret it as hitting, is not illegitimate, but there is a preferred method, which is that of the person who chastens specifically by means of words."

16. Ben Sira's view on educational methods is also expressed in the following verses: "Hast thou children? instruct them, and bow down their neck from their youth" (7:24). "Hast thou daughters? have a care of their body, and

shew not thyself cheerful toward them. Children should not be spoilt or given pleasure to, for ultimately they will embitter the father's life: do not play with him, lest he aggrieve you, and finally—will knock your teeth out" (29:9–10).

17. See Bar Ilan, *Battered Child;* Gutel, "He who Spares the Rod."

18. On the dispute between the scholars over the significance of these regulations, see Shmuel Glick, החינוך בראי החוק והלכה (Education in light of Israeli law and halachic literature) (Jerusalem: , 5760), 1:34–47.

19. *T. Bava Qamma*, 9:11, ed. Saul Lieberman (New York: JTS, 2001), p. 44.

20. *Bava Batra* 21a.

21. On the teacher who hits his students, as grounds for dismissal, see Glick, *Education*, 2:505–15.

22. Regarding the place of the stick and rod as tools of punishment that were used by teachers in the fourteenth century, see ibid., 515 and notes.

23. See Responsa הלכות קטנות ('Small' laws) (Cracow, 1897), 1:125: "Regarding the teachers who hit their students ... it is appropriate to convene courts for that purpose, but the world carries on as though nothing had happened."

24. See for example in Mishneh Torah of Maimonides, *Hilchot Talmud Torah,* 2:2: "Children are to be sent to school at the age of six or seven years. ... The teacher may chastise his pupils to inspire them with awe. But he must not do so in a cruel manner or in a vindictive spirit. Accordingly, he must not strike them with whips or sticks, but only use a small strap."

25. See ברענטשפיגל (Burnt mirror), a book of ethical instruction written in Yiddish, for women and the masses, of R. Moshe Heinich of Jerusalem (d. Prague, 1633), מקורות לתולדות החינוך בישראל (A sourcebook for the history of Jewish education [from the beginning of the Middle Ages to the period of the Haskalah]), ed. S. Assaf and Shmuel Glick (New York and Jerusalem: JTS, 2002), 1:48:

    How to educate children along the correct path − "and he should warn him with a rod, so that he is fearful, and should smack him occasionally, so that he learns what the rod is for ... when the small children do not behave properly, he should threaten them, and [he] should not punish them until his anger has subsided, and in the morning, when they are still in bed he should remind them of their misconduct and hit them with a stick on their exposed skin so that they remember it for a long period.

    And in the book מינקת רבקה (Rebecca's nursemaid), by Rivka, daughter of R. Meir Me-Tiktin (Prague, 1705), part 5 (*Sourcebook* 1:555): "No righteous woman will save the rod from her child, for as King Solomon said, 'teach him with a stick and you will save his soul from death.'" For additional sources in ethical literature that encourage parents to spank their children when they are young, see also מראה מוסר (Mirror of ethics), by R. Yehuda Zeligman, Ulma, Ginzburg (d. 1617) (*Sourcebook,* 1:225); and יש נוחלים: צוואת ר' אברהם הורוביץ ("Those who inherit": The ethical will of Rabbi Abraham Horowitz) (Prague, 1550–1615) (*Sourcebook* 1:632); המאור מנורת (Candlestick of light), R. Israel Al-Nakawa, (Spain, 14th c.), *Sourcebook* 2:88.

26. See the article by Shalom Yaakov Abramovitz (Mendel Mocher Seforim) regarding the need to spank children on the behind and to humble them in the presence of their friends, משפט שלום (Judgment of peace) (Vilna, 1860), 77–86. In one of the notes the author writes: "Esteemed Reader, this noble article is not the product of my own thoughts, for I took it from the Russian language and adorned it in the holy garments, in the honor of our language and for general edification."

27. In his book פלא יועץ (Wonderful advisor) (Constantinople, 1824), on *Ahavat banim, Sourcebook,* 2:569: "But the father should be careful not to be cruel to his son and not to hit him cruelly in anger, and he should do so calmly and with mercy, hit him on his legs, and not on a place where it could leave a scar, for example between the eyes"; on *haka'ah* (*Sourcebook,* 2:571):

> and even for hitting young children, it is not permitted to any person, except for a father to his children and a Rav to his students, and a guardian for those in his care, and even for a rabbi to his students ... and I remember one God-fearing person who was a guardian for children, and on his deathbed he ordered that a proclamation be made in the synagogue, in which he requested forgiveness from all of the children whom he had unlawfully smacked, because even for his small children and his pupils, he never had permission to smack them unlawfully if they had done nothing to deserve it.

28. In his book על יסודות נחינוך (Concerning principles of education) (Tel Aviv: Netzach, 1958), 2:65: "We would be the last ones to recommend physical punishment ... and this applies especially to the parents' home. If the child becomes accustomed to being motivated by his parents' criticism exclusively when he feels it on his skin, and listens to orders only because of his fear of being spanked, his moral intuitions are blunted and this inevitably leads to a disrespect toward the remarks of the teacher."

29. שו״ת שרידי אש (Responsa "remnants of fire") (Jerusalem: Mosad Harav Kook, 2003), vol. 2 siman 49, in the matter of hitting an adolescent youth: "And his excellency was correct in saying that not only spanking, but any manner of physical coercion is liable to be counterproductive, leading to precisely the opposite of what was desired. And the modern pedagogues have already proven that compulsion, or enforced compliance, causes the youth to become stubborn when he becomes an adult."

30. In his commentary on the *Aggadot* of the Talmud, *Ein Iyah* (Jerusalem: Ha-Machon al shem ha-Rav Zevi Yehuda ha-Kohen Kook, 1987), 31:

> And until recent times, the scholars of pedagogy did not understand this, and their style of education was only by way of the rod, until our times in which numerous studies have convinced them of the truths that were already taught to us by the Sages, of blessed memory, "Resh Lakish said, 'Even more than one hundred lashes' "—the intention is that even during a chance educational hour (which was not planned—when the teacher is angered by the pupil's unexpected acts), when he [the student] committed a grave misdemeanor and crime, for which 100 lashes would be appropriate, being the harshest level of corporal punishment for such acts, according to common educational practices,—the intellectual chastisement [with words and not with physical punishment] should be preferred, because the mental spark in man illuminates the darkest recesses of those who pursue errant paths.

31. See מכתב מאליהו (Epistle from Elijah), 11th ed. (Jerusalem: Ha-Va'ad le-hafazat kitvei ha-Gr"a Dessler, 1980), 3:360. Responding to one of his students in 1949, he writes:

> They (the researchers) believe that the child must be educated to be independent, and this is a great error. It is not independence that requires development, but subservience ... and my cousin R. Zissel told me that he even saw it written in one of the Holy books that [even] if the son is obedient, a pretext should be found in order to at least spank him slightly. ... These modern researchers look for ways in which to undermine the fundamentals, which even the non-Jews know, and which originate in God's Torah and the Prophets, and they invented theories which uproot the basic foundations, leading to the education of *insolent Hitlerites, and impertinence abounds.* [emphasis added]

I was amazed that the editors failed to omit this extreme expression from editions of the book. To be sure, when one reads the letter (written in

1949) without omissions it is clear that the author's intention was that education to independence means education to egotism, "myself and no one else," and according to the author, in extreme cases this could even lead to murder and hence his use of the term "insolent Hitlerites." Nevertheless, the use of such extreme and vicious language in relation to the researchers (regardless of their identity) in the post-Holocaust generation is intolerably extreme.

32. Regarding punishment of children in later periods, see Y. Oron, עונש גופני בחינוך הילדים (Corporal punishment in children's education), *Or Hamizrach* 24 (1975): 123.

33. See n. 13 above.

34. In 1979, Sweden became the first state to adopt a law that prohibited the use of corporal punishment by parents.

35. Directives to schools regarding discipline and punitive measures (5707-1957), 3.

36. See D.C. 24/4 (25 December 1963); 25/2 (1 October 1964); D.C. 39/2 (October 1978). Regime and Practice in Schools, §2.4; D.C. September 1991, it is forbidden for teachers to use physical punishment; D.C. 16 (July 1994): Corporal and Verbal Punishment are not consistent with the goals of education; D.C. (March 1997): Unacceptable Responses in High School Education (Mandatory Provisions): corporal punishments, verbal violence . . . .

37. See examples cited below from the "Stanner Index" regarding cases in which teachers were convicted.

38. It will be mentioned that since the first presiding of the Supreme Court on 16 September 1948, in its capacity as the High Court of Justice it has handed down nine judgments that touch upon educational matters, but this is the first one to deal with a fundamental pedagogic-educational question.

39. 7 P.D. 799.

40. Under §250 of the Penal Ordinance, 1936.

41. Under §241 (a) of that Ordinance.

42. Furthermore, she was obligated to pay an additional fine for the commission of other offences, unrelated to this discussion.

43. See §4 of Justice Cheshin's opinion: "In other words: we are not required to determine the educational method that the educator and the pedagogue should adopt when teaching.... instead we are required to clarify to ourselves which of the methods is permitted under criminal law: Which act will be deemed a criminal offence and which act lacks any element of

criminality."

44. Regarding the Anglo-Saxon doctrine of delegation of parental authority to teachers on the one hand, and its parallels in Jewish Law, on the other hand, see S. Nachmias, ‏ענישה גופנית במוסדות החינוך במבחן משפטי‎ (Corporal punishment in educational institutions from a legal perspective), *Ha-praklit* 34 (1986): 234–39.

45. In *Hopley*, a schoolmaster had beaten a fourteen-year-old boy so severely that the boy died of exhaustion from loss of blood. The schoolmaster had written the father and proposed beating the boy "to subdue his obstinacy by chastising him severely ... if necessary, again and again." The father had agreed. The schoolmaster was convicted of manslaughter for using excessive force and imprisoned for four years.

46. See 7 (2) P.D. p. 794. In 1986, §47 of the Education Act in England statutorily revoked the authority of parents and educators to inflict physical punishment in public schools and in State schools. In 1998 corporal punishment was similarly prohibited in private schools. However, the issue has not disappeared from the public agenda in England. See recently Mike Baker, "The Trouble with Discipline", BBC News Online, London 8 October 2004, http://news.bbc.co.uk/1/hi/education/3727448.stm.

47. Fürth, 1769.

48. See also S. Z. Cheshin's ruling in C.A. 319/54 *D.G. v.H.G.* 11 (1) P.D, p. 273, where he said: "Irrespective of our own views, and those of Ms. C regarding the educational value of corporal punishment, there is as yet no unanimity among educators—and certainly not among parents—that its benefits are outweighed by its defects. And, in the absence of any excesses, there is no law forbidding parents from inflicting corporal punishment on their children.

49. See Penal Law, §368 C. Abuse of a Minor or Helpless Person: "If a person commits an act of physical, mental or sexual abuse on a minor or helpless person, then he is liable to seven years imprisonment; if the abuser is the person responsible for the minor or helpless person, then he is liable to nine years imprisonment."

50. See Y. Carp, "Corporal Punishment: The Legal Aspect," in *A Collection of Articles from the Extended Management Conference* (Jerusalem: Israel National Council for the Welfare of the Child, 1992), 4–9.

51. Already back in the 1950s, a legal distinction could be made between the parents' authority to punish their children and the authority of the teachers. See comments of Prof. S. Nachmias, in notes to the Draft Proposal No. 2098, 1 Shevat 5762 (5 January 1992), which originated in the doc-

trine that the teacher was *in loco parentis*. This doctrine first emerged in the thirteenth century"

> when it was customary for parents to choose a private tutor and the delegation of parental authority to the teachers was a voluntary, free, and direct act of the parents; if they were not satisfied they could summarily dismiss him at any time. This is not the case in the modern reality, because in the fifties the parents did not choose private teachers, nor were they able to dismiss the teachers of the school, which was an authority reserved exclusively for the Educational Authorities. Consequently, there was no justification for the endorsement of this doctrine. Furthermore, what is permitted for parents is not necessarily permitted for teachers. The teachers are professionally trained and naturally, a different attitude is adopted towards people with pedagogic and psychological training. Nor can any conclusions be drawn from the forgiving attitude adopted by the public towards parents regarding reasonable corporal punishment, with respect to a teacher adopting the same measures.

52. In the course of writing *Education in Light of Israeli Law and Halakhic Literature*, in 1997–98 we conducted a survey in the Legal Advisor's office of the Ministry of Education, checking all the files in which judgments on educational matters had been given between the years 1948 and 1997. By chance, we came upon an old index, comprising hundreds of cards, gathering dust in the office of the legal advisor of the Ministry of Education and Culture in Jerusalem.

53. The Penal Ordinance was altered in 1977, becoming the Penal Law.

54. See p. 2 in the Stanner Index, which attests to various cases in which teachers were convicted and the majority of which were not even prosecuted.

55. Cr.A. 412/76 *Navil Ribni v. State of Israel*, 11 SAVIR, (9).

56. See at n. 20 above.

57. See הלכות תלמוד תורה (The laws of Talmud Torah) 2:2, "But he must not do so in a cruel manner or in a vindictive spirit. Accordingly, he must not strike them with whips or sticks, but only use a small strap."

58. However, §19 of the Convention stipulates that corporal punishment of children must be prohibited in the laws of all countries that ratify the Convention. However, the ratification of the Convention does not give it the force of local law, and it is subject to the interpretative analysis of the Supreme Court.

59. S.H. 5752, p. 150.

60. According to some, it was during the second half of the 1980s. For the development of judicial activism and the factors that led to it, and the ensuing debate on it, see E. Gordon, אקטיביזם שיפוטי והדיון שאיננו (Is it legitimate to criticize the Supreme Court?" *Azure* 3 (1998): 44–77.

61. "The Right of Standing," in other words, the right of a particular party to petition the High Court of Justice. When the Supreme Court was first established, this right was restricted to litigants with a direct personal interest in the matter. The result was that in numerous cases the public had no right to petition the High Court of Justice. "Justiciability" means the determination of whether a particular question admits of judicial resolution. Here too, the term was initially given an extremely narrow construction, and broad realms of government policy were considered as being outside the purview of judicial consideration.

62. The conversion of "reasonableness" into an all-powerful criterion in assessing the legality of legislative and executive acts. Whereas in the past the Court would ask whether the governmental act was consistent with the language of the law, since the 1980s the Court has begun to invalidate, as a matter of course, decisions which it considered to be "unreasonable in the extreme," the claim being that something which is extremely unreasonable, must *ipso facto* be illegal. Over the last decade use of this criterion has become the norm.

63. Indeed, between the years 1992 and 1994, the Knesset committees, the subcommittee of the Constitution, Law and Justice Committee, and the Knesset Plenum all deliberated the draft proposal for the Amendment of §49 (5) of the Penal Law, which included an explicit defense for the exercise of reasonable force in corporal punishment. At the same time, it rejected a proposed amendment that explicitly exempted parents from criminal liability for reasonable physical punishment of their children (see Gordon, "In Loco Parentis" at nn. 59–67). However, these proceedings did not deal with establishment of a sweeping prohibition of corporal punishment. M. K. Yael Dayan was the only one who argued for an unequivocal prohibition of any physical punishment of children by parents. Her view represented neither the view of the majority in the committee, nor even the minority view, being solely her own view.

64. Cr.A. 4405/94, *State of Israel v. Algani*, 48 (5) P.D. p. 191.

65. See n. 37 above.

66. Ibid., p. 191.

67. 52 (3) P.D. 374.

68. Ibid, §9.

69. 61 Dinim (Elyon) 537.
70. See n. 41 above.
71. See also Gordon, "In Loco Parentis," 66.
72. Legal Capacity and Guardianship Law, §15; Penal Law, §323, which imposes criminal liability on a parent who fails to discharge his duty.
73. The intent is an injury that leaves marks on the child's body, or mental abuse causing significant changes expressed in behavioral deterioration.
74. The intent is serious physical injury, such as bone fractures, burns, injury to internal organs, or severe mental abuse, such as severe rejection, or psychological injury that is the result of the bodily injury.
75. Section 368 C of the Penal Law does not define the term "abuse" and determines the following: "Abuse of minor or helpless person: If a person commits an act of physical, mental or sexual abuse of a minor or helpless person, then is liable for seven years imprisonment; if the abuser is the person responsible for the minor or helpless person then he is liable for nine years imprisonment." The result is that in all indictments of parents under §368 C of the Penal Law, the matter was one of interpretation and judicial discretion.
76. P.M. (District Court, Tel Aviv) 5752 (1) p. 431. See also A. Strashnov, ילדים ונוער בראי המשפט (Children and youth in light of the judicial system) (Tel Aviv: Lishkat Orchei ha-Din, 2000).
77. See Cr.F. 4227/93 (not published) in the Tel-Aviv Magistrates Court. Judge Caspi convicted a father of assault after it was proved that he had slapped his son on a number of occasions, pulled his neck, and forcibly dragged him on the stairs, while the child was screaming. In his verdict the judge stated that today "the possibility and the license for parental corporal punishment has been considerably narrowed."
78. See n. 15 above. In the argumentation of her judgment, the honorable judge incorporated valuable supplementary sources from both halachic and psychological literature.
79. On the current position of English Law, see n. 44 above.
80. See n. 63 above.
81. See page 629 above.
82. The English system, authorizing parents to use corporal punishment on their children; the "reasonability" system, practiced in various states in the United States for determination of the degree of corporal punishment permitted for a parent to inflict on his child; and the system that denies all parental authority for corporal punishment of children and upholds the child's right to dignity, bodily integrity, and mental health, practiced inter

alia in a few states in the United States, and which has received legislative expression in Sweden, Finland, Denmark, Norway, and Austria.

83. Cr.A. 4596/98 *Anon v. State of Israel.*

84. The source of this section is in the 1944 English version of the Ordinance. What it means is that today, where a parent and teacher are convicted of beating their children—which is now a criminal offence—they are also exposed to a civil claim for monetary compensation for the injuries they caused.

85. See *Knesset Proceedings* 37 (2000): 1071–73.

86. See Limor Gal, זה לא פליק זו הכאה (It's not a "flick," it's a beating), *Ha-arets* (29 November 2004). According to a survey conducted by Dr. Yitzchak Levav, a research consultant of the Mental Health Services Department in the Ministry of Health, he reports, broad sections of the Israeli populations do not accept the ruling of the Supreme Court that corporal punishment of children is forbidden. The survey was conducted two years ago and published two months ago in the *Israel Journal of Psychiatry.* See also Orly Fuchs-Shabtai and Shulamit Blank, הורים טובים מדי (Good parents) (Or Yehudah: Kineret, 2004). Judge Beinish's ruling provoked the ire of the authors, a trained pyschologist and a psychiatrist respectively. Based on recent research, they contend against Judge Beinish's logic.

87. Comments of Dr. Y. Kadman in Gal, "Not a 'Flick.' "

INDEX

INDEX

Page references given in *italics* indicate illustrations or their captions. Artworks and major works discussed in the text can be found under the artist/author. Schorsch titles can be found under the author.

Index

Index

Index

Index

Index

Index

Index

Index

Index

Index

Schorsch, Ismar, publications of, 3–4; on anti-semitism, 4–8; on Jewish historiography, 8–13; in *Leo Baeck Institute Year Book*, 8–9, 13; on *Wissenschaft*, 13–16; TITLES: "Art as Social History", 20–21, 76, 220–21; "Breakthrough into the Past", 284; "Emancipation and the Crisis of Religious Authority", 16–18; *From Text to Context*, xiv, 13–16, 91, 220; "Ideology and History in the Age of Emancipation", 9–13; *Jewish Reactions to German Anti-Semitism*, 5–8; "The Philosophy of History of Nachman Krochmal", 8; "Scholarship in the Service of Reform", 15–16

Schreiber, Moses. *See* Hatam Sofer

Schudmaka, Anszela, 244

Schüler-Springorum, Stefanie, 402, 409n67

Schulweis, Harold, 588, 604n75

Scott, Joan, 400

Scouts, 447, 451, 461, 475, 477

Scouts of Honor, 476

Scult, Mel, 488–89

Sdeh-Ur, Rachel, State of Israel v., 624–26

Sebastiah (Israel), 478

Secession exhibition (Munich; 1896), 232

secularism/secularization: fundamentalism and, 129nn52–53; German-Jewish identity and, 415, 426; of German Orthodox scholarship, 264; Hirszenberg and, 248–49; Hungarian Orthodox opposition to, 337–38; Jewish jokes and, 273; modernity vs. postmodernity, 113–14, 129nn52–53; of rabbinic education, 16–18; *Rufeisen* case and, 563–64; ultra-Orthodoxy vs., in Israel, 441

Sefer ha-agadah, 259, 264, 271, 273, 274

Sefer ha-Mitzvot (Maimonides), 636n15. *See Wissenschaft des Judentums*

Sefer ha-roqeah, 149

Sefer hasidim, 136–37, 146, 148–49

Sefer shir ha-shirim (Sulkes), 138

Sefer toledot Ya'qov Yosef, 171

segulot (magic spells), 176

self-annihilation, doctrine of, 167

self-determination, 119

Sephardic Jewry, 88–89, 261; Ashkenazic Jewry vs., 441; in Eretz Israel, 471; German Jewry and, 18–19; historical prejudice favoring, 14; Schorsch scholarship on, 18–19; in 16th-century Italy, 147

sermons: in American synagogues, 586; in early Hasidic courts, 163, 166–67, 172, 174–75, 183

Serov, Valentin, 241

sexual customs, 454

Shabbatai Zvi, 248

Shabuoth (Hoffman and Solomon), 493

Shaki, Avner, 548

Shalit et al. v. Peres et al., 566

Shatzky, Jacob, 51

Shefeya (Israel), 468

Shekhem (Israel), 473

Shema', 134, 139–40

Shever posh'im (pamphlet), 170, 172–73, 175, 177–78, 180, 181–82

Shmeruk, Chone, 134–35

Shmuel b. Shilat, 610

Shneur Zalman of Liady, 152

Shoah. *See* Holocaust, the

Shohet, Azriel, 98

Shtetl (Hoffman), 54

Shulhan Arukh: Even Ha-'ezer 260:16, 343; women's vernacular prayer and, 152; *Yoreh De'ah* 268:2, 340–41; *Yoreh De'ah* 268:7, 325, 331; *Yoreh De'ah* 334:1, 342, 344

Shulhan 'arukh harav (Shneur Zalman), 152

siddur, 135, 150, 153, 329, 588

Silberg, Moshe: on Catholic-Jewish relations, 567–69, 570; Cohn vs., 564; on religion/state separation, 574–75; *Rufeisen* case and, 563, 567–69, 570, 571–72, 574–75

Silberman, Lou H., 604–5n76

Silesia, 372, 373

Simeon ben Yochai, 473

Singer, Bernard, 52–53

Singer, Isaac Bashevis, 61–62

Sklare, Marshall, 583, 600n25

Skolnik, Jonathan S., 251n18

Slobodka Yeshivah (Hebron), 453

Slovakia, 373

Slovenia, 108

smikhah (rabbinic ordination), 269

Smith, Anthony, 550

Smith, W. Robertson, 289

sociability, 205, 206, 425

social history: historical documentation of, 400–401, 409n66; literary history vs., 402, 409n67; memory as raw material of, 383–84, 401

social realism, 238

Society for Ancient Hebrew Melodies, 491

sociology, 289–90, 304, 310n5

Sofer, Moses. *See* Hatam Sofer

Solomon, Elias L., 493

Solomon, Simeon, 220

Index

Index

Index